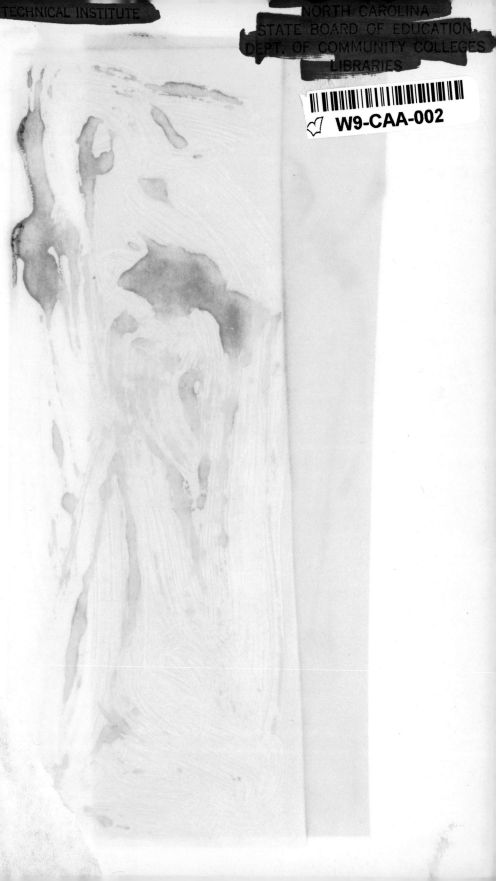

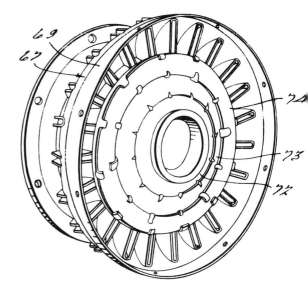

CHILTON BOOK COMPANY

the gas turbine engine

DESIGN
DEVELOPMENT
APPLICATIONS

JAN P. NORBYE

RADNOR, PENNSYLVANIA

Copyright © 1975 by Jan P. Norbye

First Edition   *All rights reserved*

Published in Radnor, Pa., by Chilton Book Company
and simultaneously in Don Mills, Ontario, Canada
by Thomas Nelson & Sons, Ltd.

Designed by Cypher Associates, Inc.

Manufactured in the United States of America

Library of Congress Cataloging in Publication Data

Norbye, Jan P
    The gas turbine engine.

    Bibliography: p.
    Includes index.
    1. Automotive gas turbines.   2. Automobiles, Gas-
turbine.   I. Title.
TL227.N67   1975   629.2'503   75-6733
ISBN 0-8019-5753-2

Preface

THIS IS A BOOK about the automotive gas turbine engine, its tremendous promise, and its march of progress. It has also been necessary to deal at some length with aircraft engines, industrial gas turbines, marine and railroad installations in order to place the motor truck and passenger car gas turbine engines in proper perspective.

During the fact-gathering phase of compiling this work, I have had the benefit of free access to the collections of the New York Public Library, and the Detroit Public Library. I have received valuable assistance from the Society of Automotive Engineers and the Engineering Societies' Library in New York. My colleagues Jim Dunne and Karl Ludvigsen contributed their assistance in research work and in providing illustrations. L. Scott Bailey, publisher of Automobile Quarterly, made material from the magazine's files available for this book.

A special word of gratitude is due to the many leading gas turbine engineers who gave me personal interviews, sometimes in several sessions. Their first-hand information was of major importance in many ways, from guiding my editorial approach to filling in unpublished details of their own work. My sincere thanks to: Charles A. Amann and Alfred H. Bell III of the General Motors Research Laboratories; Jean-Albert Gregoire of Automobiles Tracta; George J. Huebner, Jr. of Chrysler Corporation; Arthur F. McLean of the Ford Motor Company; Noel Penny of Noel Penny Turbines, Ltd.; Giovanni Savonuzzi of Fiat, S.p.A.; George M. Thur of the Environmental Protection Agency; Peter Walzer of Volkswagenwerk AG; and Sam Williams of Williams Research Corporation.

Many officers of companies in the gas turbine industry have been extremely helpful in searching for information and illustrations on my behalf, and I want to thank them all for their efforts: William M. Adams of the

General Motors Public Relations Staff in Detroit; Al Bloemker, Director of Public Relations at the Indianapolis Motor Speedway; David Boole, International Public Relations Coordinator of British Leyland Motor Corp. Ltd. in London; A. J. Budrys of Young & Rubicam Inc. in Chicago; Peter Bush, Director of Public Relations and Advertising at the Boeing Company in Seattle; R. H. Butcher, Press Officer of Rolls-Royce (1971) Ltd. in Bristol; Harry Conner, Public Relations Manager of the International Harvester Company in New York; Charles W. Craig, Public Relations Officer with Chrysler Corporation in Detroit; R. J. Crones, Manager of the Technical Publications Department, Kenworth Motor Truck Company in Seattle; Ken Cruickshank of GEC Turbine Generators, Ltd. in Manchester; Michael W. R. Davis, head of Ford Motor Company Research and Engineering information service in Dearborn, Michigan; W. Demine, Sales administrator of United Aircraft of Canada, Ltd. of Longueuil, Quebec; John J. Dierbeck, Jr., Public Relations Manager for Agricultural/Industrial Equipment, International Harvester Co. in Chicago; William C. Dredge, Vice President of Public Relations for the STP Corporation in Fort Lauderdale; J. Dufour of Turbomeca, S.A. in Paris; Heinz Egger, Public Relations Director of Motoren und Turbinen Union in Munich; Blanche Van Elewyck of Renault, Inc. in Englewood Cliffs, New Jersey; Melvin H. Erickson, Manager, Plants and Programs, of Teledyne CAE in Toledo, Ohio; Eric Falk, Manager of Group External Relations, General Electric in Cincinnati; Eric G. Fielding, of Vickers, Limited in London; Gordon M. Fletcher, Manager of Marketing and Information Services, AiResearch Manufacturing Co. in Phoenix, Arizona; James P. Foley, Manager of Public Relations, Howmet Corporation in Greenwich, Connecticut; Y. P. Francois of Turbomeca in Paris; Fritz Haber, Vice President of Avco Lycoming Division in Stratford, CT; Keith B. Hopkins, Director of Public Relations, British Leyland Motor Corporation, Ltd. in London; A. Jacobsen, Sales Engineering, United Aircraft of Canada Ltd. in Longueuil, Quebec; David C. Jolivette, Vice President of Public Relations, Williams Research Corporation in Walled Lake, Michigan; Koshin Kimura, Chief, Public Relations Section, Toyota Motor Co. Ltd. in Toyota City, Aichi; Hirotaro Kumada, Manager, Public Relations Department, Nissan Motor Co. Ltd. in Tokyo; Rudi Maletz, Press Department, Volkswagenwerk AG in Wolfsburg; J. Bruce McWilliams, Director of Product Planning, British Leyland Motors Inc. in Leonia, N.J.; Norman F. Miller, Manager, Marine-Industrial Engine Marketing, Avco Corporation, Lycoming Division in Stratford, CT; Dennis D. Mog, Product Program Manager, Corning Glass Works in Corning, New York; Walter M. Murphy, Public Relations Director, Ford Motor Company in Dearborn, Mich; Melvin R. Mutcher, Public Relations Manager, Ford Motor Company in New York: Donald G. O'Brien, Public Relations Manager,

Detroit Diesel Allison Division of General Motors Corp. in Detroit; H. P. Pletscher, of the Brown, Boveri Corporation in North Brunswick, New Jersey; Paul M. Preuss, Technical and Product Information, Ford Motor Company in Dearborn, Michigan; Michel Rolland, Relations Exterieures, Regie National des Usines Renault at Boulogne-Billancourt; Maria Rubiolo, Director of Public Relations, Fiat S.p.A. in Torino; J. E. Sallee, Industrial Division Marketing, Caterpillar Tractor Company in Peoria, Illinois; Lawrence J. Sera, Communications Specialist, Solar Division of International Harvester Co. in San Diego, Calif.; William P. Stempien, Product Development Public Relations, Chrysler Corporation in Detroit; Dirk Henning Strassl, Presse-Abteilung der Daimler-Benz AG in Stuttgart-Unterturkheim; Harry Turton, General Motors Public Relations Staff in New York; Gordon A. Wilkins, Manager, Sales Publications Department, Rolls-Royce (1971) Ltd. in Bristol; Herbert W. Williamson, Manager of VW Public Relations, Volkswagen of America, Inc. in Englewood Cliffs, New Jersey; William T. Winters, General Motors Public Relations Staff in New York.

In addition, I want to thank the companies that answered my requests with information by supplying a great deal of documentation without indicating the name of the individual responsible for assisting me: The Norton Company in Worcester, Mass., and The Societe Nationale des Chemins de Fer Francais in Paris.

For the reader who is interested in going beyond the scope of this book, I would suggest that he consult the bibliography included here.

Jan P. Norbye
New York, April 1974

Contents

Introduction

When the Rover turbine car was first demonstrated in 1950, the public was already well aware of the revolution that was taking place in military aircraft engines, and experts predicted a similar revolution in civilian aviation. Against this background, the turbine car was immediately hailed as the car of the future, although the technical press cautioned that it would take at least five years to get a turbine car into production. Now we are in 1974, and we know that the earliest possible date for turbine car production is 1982–83.

Turbine truck production plans have been announced and called off several times by both Ford and General Motors, and the turbine truck program may go through several more on-again off-again cycles before trucks developed for gas turbine propulsion will be in regular production.

Why hasn't the road vehicle followed the airplane in switching from piston engines to gas turbines? One of the prime reasons, according to D. E. Barbeau of Continental Aviation and Engineering Corporation, is that the gas turbine offered a means of significantly advancing the state of the art in aircraft design. "Regions of the flight envelope not previously attainable with piston engines became possible," said Mr. Barbeau, adding, "As a result, impetus was provided to expend a great deal of effort in the development of the aircraft gas turbine."

Use of gas turbines in road vehicles does not offer advantages of the same order. Another and more obvious reason is the inertia of the automotive industry, partly due to the enormous number of units produced in a year, and partly due to the colossal investments in plant and machinery to build piston engines. These factors play a big part in the cost picture. The cost of new plants and plant conversion costs must be covered in the turbine sales price, spread out over a certain number of units built within a certain time.

That part of the cost picture is easy to understand. But when it comes to calculating the manufacturing costs of the individual components, there is much misunderstanding. Some doubt and misrepresentation have been broadcast deliberately by opponents of the gas turbine, and some unfavorable points have been magnified out of all proportion by men who claim an unbiased outlook but who subconsciously fear innovation and seek to preserve the status quo.

Some of the misunderstanding is genuine, for there is by no means any general agreement on the number and types of components in an automotive turbine or on how they should be arranged in relation (1) to each other and (2) to the vehicle and its power transmission system. The facts relating to the cost picture will be examined in detail in a separate chapter devoted entirely to that subject.

Whether or not the gas turbine will become "The" car engine of the future depends on a large number of factors—technical, economical, political, and psychological. The number of alternative power systems is so great that it's unlikely we'll ever see one single type of prime mover replace the venerable gasoline-fuel reciprocating piston engine in all applications.

It's far more likely that different types of future road vehicles will have power systems that are basically different in operating cycles, fuel sources, and power output characteristics. The gas turbine is a likely candidate for a number of applications, from earth-moving equipment to sports cars. It derives much of its strength in the crystal ball scenery from its low emissions levels.

The gas turbine is basically a low-emission engine because of its continuous combustion and excess air consumption. Federally sponsored contracts for gas turbine research have been granted to a number of companies and establishments on the strength of its clean-air potential.

A large part of the effort is dedicated to emission control research, but an equal emphasis is being placed on fuel economy. There can be no doubt that the need for the latter is more pressing. The fact is that the gas turbine has never been notable for its fuel economy, except to say that the development potential was tremendous. That's a turbine supporter's euphemism for "excessive fuel consumption." In all fairness, it must be admitted that misrepresentation has not always been one-sided. Nonetheless, there is already a large bank of evidence to support the contention that the gas turbine can achieve lower specific fuel consumption than the current passenger-car piston engine. This evidence is presented in the chapter dealing with the EPA (Environmental Protection Agency) contracts and the programs associated with the EPA gas turbine projects.

In comparison with the above, all other attractions of the gas turbine for road vehicle use may seem relatively minor. However, there is a long list of them, and they will count heavily in the automobile industry executives' next round of deliberations regarding mass production of gas turbine powered cars.

One of the principal advantages the gas turbine offers for motor vehicle installation is its favorable power-to-weight ratio. Modern passenger car gas turbines develop in the range of 0.3 to 0.6 hp per pound engine weight. This applies to the heaviest (and most favored) type of construction: the free-shaft regenerative gas turbine. For an engine weight of 250 pounds (including accessories) you can get a net output of 75 to 150 hp. That is two to three times more power than is commonly realized in production-model passenger-car piston engines.

The importance of a high power-to-weight ratio for passenger car engines is rarely overestimated. It translates directly into improved fuel economy, primarily because engine weight is reduced and that means less weight to be transported. Secondarily, it means that the vehicle can be lightened, for when the power plant weighs less, the engine mounting system, the supporting frame and/or body structure, springs and suspension members can also be lightened.

It also translates into faster acceleration, since acceleration rates are inversely proportional to weight (all other factors being equal). Reduced vehicle weight means easier working conditions for the brakes (and a possibility of going to lighter brake system components).

The gas turbine is a wholly rotary type of engine, and all rotating parts are fully balanced. Consequently, the turbine's operation is extremely smooth and vibrationless over the whole speed and power range. In order to appreciate the importance of this point, it's enough to reflect for a moment on the enormous expenditures the automobile industry has undertaken in the past 15–18 years in trying to make conventional cars quieter.

Superbly devised mounting systems for rocking V8s, and exquisitely insulated rear axle suspension systems have lowered the noise, harshness and vibration levels to the point where the most offensive properties of conventional types of mechanical components have been disguised or masked so that the overall result is tolerable to today's sophisticated, shrewd, and demanding customer.

A whole science has sprung up to protect the existing specification of the typical American passenger car. Adoption of the gas turbine would enable the engineers to eliminate large amounts of sound deadening materials and insulating materials from the car body, and achieve a considerable weight saving. This refers more specifically to vibration than to noise, for the turbine's noise radiation characteristics involve frequencies entirely different from those dealt with in cars powered by piston engines. A noise problem of sorts can be said to exist.

The gas turbine needs no cooling system. More correctly, it is air-cooled. The simple cycle gas turbine gets some cooling from the excess air flowing through its interior. The regenerative cycle gas turbine gets the same cooling effect from excess air flow, plus the cooling action of the heat exchangers. The closest thing to a radiator on the Chrysler turbine, for instance, is a small cooling tube for the lubricating oil.

Lubrication requirements for a gas turbine are minimal. There are a few relatively lightly loaded bearings, and they deal exclusively with rotary motion. There is no blowby of combustion products into the oil supply. So there is practically no oil consumption and no oil changes should be required. In jet-plane engines the oil is usually changed every 3000 hours or so; in a car this would correspond to about 100,000 miles.

The turbine thrives on cold ambient air, and offers easier cold starting than any other known type of prime mover at sub-zero temperatures. The resistance of a gas turbine to spinning up to starting speed does not change much with a drop in ambient temperature. In contrast, reciprocating engines have everything stacked against them for cold starting with so many lubricated surfaces to get moving against each other in opposition to sliding friction. The turbine also stands in contrast to the diesel, which depends heavily upon cranking speed to build up ignition temperature. Gas turbine proponents say that the cold starting advantage *alone* could mean a substantial reduction in urban air pollution on extremely cold days by eliminating aborted starts. And turbines need no "choke" or other cold mixture enrichments.

One of the features of the gas turbine that has helped assure its place in aviation is the fact that engine failure usually occurs as a gradual deterioration rather than sudden cessation of operation. In the air this quality can make all the difference between a loss-of-life accident and a controlled landing. In road-vehicle operation, the difference is less dramatic but nonetheless must count as a strong point in favor of the turbine.

Noel Penny of Penny Turbines, Ltd., said in a talk given in 1964:

Generally, unsatisfactory turbine performance arises from the accumulation of atmospheric solids in the compressor components, formation of combustion products in the heat exchanger, and progressive erosion of the turbine nozzles and blades. This deterioration shows up as an increase in operating temperature for the same power output or with the safeguards built into our designs, as reduced power for the maximum permitted operating temperature.

The turbine promises extreme life expectancy. Sam Williams, of Williams Research Corp., has indicated that a million miles between overhauls is possible. Whether it is practicable in a passenger car is another matter, for the average car in America only completes about 150,000 miles in its lifetime.

In addition, experience shows that the turbine can function to specification level with a reduced maintenance schedule. There is no such thing as a tune-up for a gas turbine. It has no spark timing to adjust and no spark plugs to clean or replace. The turbine has no carburetor to adjust, and the fuel injection system is simple compared to that used on piston engines. As for mechanical wear, it does not affect turbine emissions to any significant extent as the combustion process is not affected by bearing or turbine wear. At an early date in the history of the automotive gas turbine—in fact a full 10 years prior to the enactment of environmental protection legislation in the U.S., that outstanding engineer and original thinker on technical matters, Sam Heron, pronounced:

Deterioration in the accuracy of the fuel delivery system and high-temperature erosion of the combustion chamber seem to me to be the only sources of emission deterioration, and these cannot be as significant as valve, piston-ring and cylinder, carburetor or mechanical fuel-injection wear in a piston engine.

Theory is one thing, and practice another. Have Sam Heron's views been upheld by actual field testing? On the whole, that question must be answered with a strong affirmative. Whenever the discussion turns to actual experience, we must look to Chrysler for the answer. No other company has built anything like the same number of turbine vehicles or accumulated anywhere near the same amount of mileage. Chrysler built 50 cars in 1963–64, and they had run up 1.3 million test miles when the program was halted for evaluation.

The conclusions are best explained by the head of the program, George J. Huebner, Jr.:

During the course of the program, we had our first opportunity to observe and to judge the behavior of turbine engines under actual customer driving conditions. For over two years our turbine cars were driven in cities and on highways, in the deserts and the mountains as well as below sea level.

Power output of each individual engine as built remained consistently close to its original value, and even normal deterioration of power with usage ceased to bother us after the discovery of a highly efficient engine cleaner. In a piston engine, deterioration is corrected by a tune-up which, although not especially difficult, is costly and time-consuming. In our turbine the lost power is recovered almost instantly by using a harmless compound which is simply introduced into the engine intake. It then removes accumulated deposits while on its way to the exhaust.

However, there were a few parts that gave us 'fits' because we could not readily duplicate field deterioration in the laboratory and consequently could not immediately pinpoint and solve the problem. Regular inspections indicated that some engines had been subjected to temperatures very much higher than those normally allowed by the fuel control. Yet, a check of that component revealed no deficiency. It was finally noticed, however, that some drivers would initiate the automatic starting cycle with the ignition key and then very quickly shift the gear selector from the start position before the engine had reached idle speed, thus by-passing the automatic start system. In a piston engine this is roughly analogous to over-choking resulting in scuffed pistons, piston rings, and cylinder bores. In a turbine the process is different, but the damage is still there, and we end up with scored regenerators and burned turbine blades. Once discovered, the trouble was an easy matter to cure, simply by modifying the automatic start system so that the driver could not over-ride and thus misuse it.

Almost everyone who has had personal experience with turbine cars holds them in high esteem and rates them as superior to piston-powered automobiles. I would not make a statement of such sweeping magnitude and implication. I have been a professional test driver for over 20 years, and I have driven the turbine cars of Rover, Chrysler, Volkswagen and Williams Research Corporation. I have seen demonstration runs with the Renault speed-record turbine car and the GM Turbo-Cruiser bus. Each year I test-drive hundreds of other types of experimental cars, prototypes, and production cars. It is my considered opinion, however, that the turbine has a higher potential for car and truck use than any other type of power plant within my experience. I believe in the future of the turbine car.

Most experts feel that the turbine truck will come first. As I will explain in a later chapter, truck operation is far less demanding an operational versatility in the turbine. Turbine trains, boats, and industrial installations are already commonplace. And, of all possible gas turbine applications, the passenger car is the most challenging. So it seems logical to assume that trucks and buses will come next.

Let me close these introductory remarks with a prediction by a thoughtful man with unusual insight into the subject matter, Noel Penny:

Following the gas turbine for trucks and trains, smaller engines will come on to the market for cars. These will be engines far superior in every way to those in use today. They will be much simpler, be easier and cheaper to make and need fewer raw materials. They will be smaller and lighter for a given power. They will burn cheaper and more varied fuels, and burn less fuel for a given power. They will be sealed at the factory and thereafter need practically no maintenance for hundreds of thousands of miles. Most important of all, they will be quiet and their clean exhaust will dramatically reduce atmospheric pollution and make our cities once again fit to live in. Nevertheless the switch from piston to turbine cannot be made overnight; it will be a very long and sometimes painful process. But it is about to start.

SECTION I

DESIGN

1

Principles of
Operation

IN COMMON WITH all other power systems, the gas turbine is an energy conversion machine. It converts the energy stored in the fuel it burns into kinetic energy available at its output shaft (or, in the case of jet engines, into thrust). The gas turbine is a combustion engine. All combustion engines are heat machines. The four factors needed to run a mechanical heat machine are air, fuel, compression, and ignition. Doing work inside such an engine is a basic process which consists of converting heat energy into motion. This is possible because gases expand when heated.

The gas turbine is a form of *internal-combustion engine.* It is more closely akin, in its operating cycle, to other internal-combustion engines such as the Otto, Diesel [1] and Wankel [2] engines, than to external-combustion engines. And yet the gas turbine seemingly has certain features in common with external-combustion engines that are not shared with other internal-combustion engines.

In external-combustion engines (Rankine [3] cycle and Stirling [4] types) the fuel does not participate in the expansion phase—the power-producing portion of the operating cycle. Instead, there is a working fluid that is alternately heated and cooled to provide the expansion that is necessary to produce power.

The gas turbine's operation is patterned on the Brayton cycle, while the reciprocating piston type of internal combustion engine operates on the Otto cycle. The Otto cycle is named after its inventor, Nikolaus August Otto (1832–1891), founder and leader of the Gasmotorenfabrik Deutz outside of Cologne, West Germany. The Otto cycle patent dates from 1877. The Brayton cycle is named after its originator, George Brayton (1830–1892) an

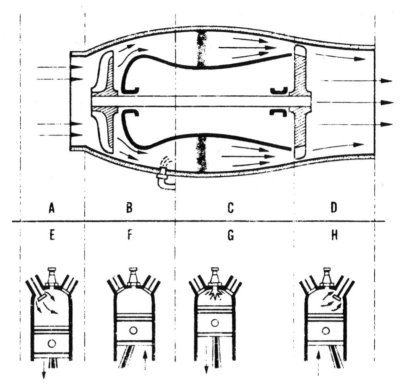

Cycle comparison between four-stroke piston engine and gas turbine engine.

English engineer living in Boston, Mass. His basic gas engine patent dates from 1872.

To grasp the Brayton cycle, it is useful to compare it with the Otto cycle or four-stroke cycle. In a four-stroke engine, only one in four operations produces power; the others are used for preparation and clean-up. One stroke is the movement of the piston from its top position to its bottom position, or vice versa. It's called a four-stroke engine because four strokes complete the operating cycle. One cylinder demands two complete crankshaft revolutions to go through the four strokes. The four strokes are named for their functions: intake, compression, combustion, and exhaust.

The intake stroke is a *down* stroke. The intake valve is open, and fresh mixture is drawn into the cylinder by the vacuum created by the downward motion of the piston. The compression stroke is an *up*-stroke. Both valves are closed, and the upward motion of the piston squeezes the mixture into a small space on top of the cylinder (combustion chamber). The ratio between the volume of the free space above the piston when it is at bottom dead center and that of the free space above it at top dead center is called the *compression ratio*. When the piston is at top dead center, only the combustion chamber is free. At bottom dead center, the free space is made up of the combustion chamber plus the entire cylinder displacement.

A high compression ratio tends to raise the engine's thermal efficiency because when the same amount of fresh mixture is compressed into a smaller space, the combustion will be quicker and more of the fuel's heat value will be available when it can be utilized. Also, the higher pressures, by themselves, cause more of the energy to appear in useable form. The combustion stroke is the working stroke that produces the power. It is often called *power stroke*.

The power stroke is a *down* stroke. Both valves are closed during the power stroke. The compressed gases are ignited by a spark plug, and the expansion forces created by the burning of the air/fuel mixture drive the piston downward under high pressure. The pressure on the piston during the power stroke is a determining factor in producing power. The pressure is in turn directly related to the weight of the air drawn into the cylinder.

The exhaust stroke is an up-stroke, following the power stroke. The motion of the piston pushes the burned gases out of the cylinder through the open exhaust valve. At the end of the exhaust stroke, the cylinder is empty of burned gases and ready for another intake of fresh mixture. The cycle is repeated. The crankshaft makes two revolutions while one cylinder completes the cycle.

The Brayton cycle is a two-stroke cycle, which means that there is a power stroke for each crankshaft revolution—instead of every second revolution, as in one cylinder of a four-stroke cycle engine. The modern two-stroke cycle as commonly used in motorcycle engines, small industrial engines, and marine engines of all sizes was patented by Carl Benz (1844–1929) in 1877. The Brayton cycle belongs in a category of its own. In the Benz two-stroke cycle, the compression is started in the crankcase and completed in the upper end of the cylinder. The Brayton engine has a separate compression cylinder worked by a slave piston. Connecting rods from the slave piston and the power piston are attached to an oscillating beam anchored on an eccentric bearing. The beam is in the horizontal plane when both pistons are in the middle of their strokes. As the power piston goes down, the slave piston goes up. The connecting rod from the slave piston is attached closer to the bearing, which gives the slave cylinder a shorter stroke. The power piston connecting rod is anchored to one end of the beam. At the other end is another connecting rod that turns a crank which forms part of the output shaft. (See diagram, p. 11.)

Fresh air is admitted into the slave cylinder by an automatically operated valve, which closes at the start of an up-stroke. Compression begins. Full compression opens a pressure valve, which admits the compressed air to a pressure pipe leading to an accumulator located at the bottom of the engine. The pressurized accumulator is equipped with a safety valve to guard against over-pressure. The pressure pipe is T-shaped, with one of the T-bars connected to the slave cylinder and the other connected to the power cylinder. There are two valves at the power cylinder end—first the blocking valve that controls gas flow from the pressure pipe, next the mechanically operated intake valve for the power cylinder. The intake valve opens when the piston is at top dead center, and the pre-compressed air rushes in.

A pump metes out fuel to a felt layer located below the valve. The air must penetrate this layer, and this causes formation of a combustible mixture. A continuously burning flame in the cylinder ignites the incoming charge. The intake valve closes before the power piston has reached the halfway point on its expansion stroke. At bottom dead center, cylinder pressure has fallen to atmospheric level, and as the up-stroke begins, the exhaust valve opens to let the consumed gases escape. The exhaust stroke in the power cylinder coincides with the intake stroke in the slave cylinder, and the slave cylinder's compression stroke coincides with the power piston's expansion stroke. That explains the need for the pressure accumulator. It is the only way to maintain pressure from the slave cylinder to the power cylinder.

In the Benz-type two-stroke cycle engine, there are no valves, as the piston opens and closes intake and exhaust ports. It has no slave cylinders, as the crankcase is pressurized. It has timed spark ignition instead of the Brayton's continuous flame. The air/fuel mixture is created either by a carburetor or by fuel injection.

Why do we say the gas turbine's operating cycle is patterned on that of the Brayton engine? It is because the compression action takes place outside the combustion chamber, and combustion is continuous. In the gas turbine, compression takes place in the compressor, and the combustion takes place in the combustor. Expansion starts in the combustor and continues through the turbine wheel(s). The cylinders have been replaced by other mechanical elements, and the reciprocating motion by purely rotary motion, but the cycle is basically the same.

The same events take place in a gas turbine that take place in a four-stroke cycle reciprocating piston internal combustion engine. The difference is that in the piston engine the events all take place in the same place (the cylinder) but are spaced out in time. In the gas turbine, the events are spaced out geographically, which permits continuous action in all areas.

Before we get further into the internal processes in the gas turbine, it is important to establish what kind of hardware we are dealing with. I am indebted to Noel Penny for this definition of a gas turbine:

The basic gas turbine can be simply considered as a fan driven by a windmill. The fan provides compressed air for the windmill and extra energy is added by a heat source. The exhaust from the windmill is expanded through a nozzle to give thrust, the whole contraption being called a jet engine. In the case of an automotive gas turbine, however, the energy in the exhaust is converted into mechanical power by introducing a second windmill, entirely separate from the first and this is connected through gears to the driving wheels of the car.

To translate this fundamental description into technical language is a small step. The fan is the compressor, the first windmill, which drives it, is the compressor turbine, while the second windmill is the power turbine—and so as with the first gas turbine, our present day designs are based on a simple cycle still involving only one compressor, one turbine driving the compressor and one turbine driving the wheels.

Of course, a turbine wheel rotates very much faster than a windmill. The whirlwind of high-temperature gases released in the gas turbine can make the power wheel rotate at speeds of 50,000 revolutions per minute. Because of the very high rotational speeds, the vehicular gas turbine requires special reduction gearing. But, as will be shown later, the torque curve of the two-shaft gas turbine is eminently suitable for vehicle propulsion.

The second windmill (power wheel) may not be part of *all* automotive turbine engines, but it is part of the typical design at the present stage. Gas turbines with two "windmills" are called free-shaft or two-shaft turbines. To explain this turbine's operation let's look at it from the four-stroke point of view:

INTAKE

Ambient air enters the compressor after normal filtration. The gas turbine is not throttled, and there is no carburetor, since the fuel is injected—directly and continuously—into the combustor.

COMPRESSION

Compression takes place in the compressor, which is a fan that pumps air into smaller space than it occupied before. This is a continuous process, so the gas turbine has no compression ratio in the geometrical sense that a piston engine does. Instead, the gas turbine has a *pressure ratio*.

EXPANSION

The air/fuel mixture burns in the combustor, into which the compressed air is ducted. The combustor can have different shapes, but the elements are always the same: fuel is injected into a stream of compressed air and ignited. The burning mixture expands. This expansion provides power to turn the

HEAT EXCHANGER

STARTER

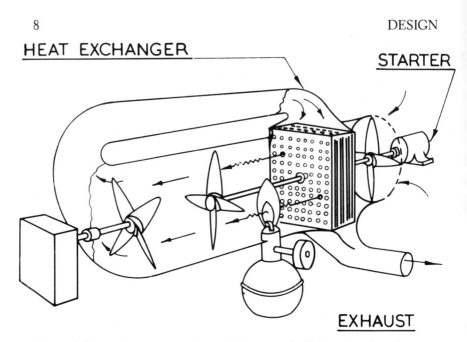

EXHAUST

The two-shaft gas turbine engine can be regarded as two windmills driven by a fan. The engine shown includes a heat exchanger.

turbine wheels. The expanding gases are ducted from the combustor through a diffuser to the primary turbine. The force of the expanding gas flow makes the turbine wheel spin. The turbine is fixed to a shaft—the same shaft that carries the compressor. The gas flow goes on to drive a secondary turbine wheel, which has no mechanical connection with the primary turbine. The only coupling is aerodynamic. The secondary turbine wheel drives the output shaft.

Exhaust

The exhaust gases from the secondary turbine still have a lot of heat energy left in them, and to release these gases into the atmosphere would constitute a serious waste. The exhaust gases are therefore led through a heat exchanger, where most of their heat is transferred to the compressed air entering the engine. The heat exchanger is also called a regenerator. It is a circular disc of porous material enclosed in a pressurized housing. It has a hot side and a cold side. The exhaust flows through the hot side, and the incoming air flows through the cold side. The disc rotates, and that's what produces the heat transfer. When the disc sector from the hot side rolls over into the cool side, some of the exhaust heat will flow into the incoming air.

The exhaust gas from the heat exchanger is ducted out the tailpipe at low pressure and relatively low temperature.

This description relates to the *open-cycle* turbine. It's called an open cycle because it takes fresh air from the atmosphere and exhausts the spent gases into the atmosphere. All automotive gas turbines belong in the open-cycle category.

The closed-cycle turbine operates with a gas other than air (for instance, hydrogen or carbon dioxide), and the entire exhaust volume is cooled and recirculated to the compressor. Closed-cycle gas turbines are mainly used in large stationary plants with a nuclear reactor or a coal burner as a heat source. Automotive application of closed-cycle turbines is feasible but has drawbacks in that it would require both a gas heater and a gas cooler, which would add weight, bulk and cost to the power unit.

Because the gas turbine processes occur in stages, an analysis of what goes on within the engine must be deduced from temperature and pressure measurements taken at various points throughout the system. All such studies

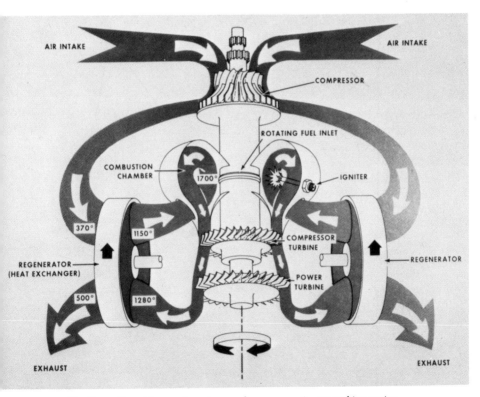

Gas flow path and temperatures in a modern regenerative gas turbine engine.

show that the gas turbine's thermodynamic cycle of compression-expansion is similar to that of the ordinary piston engine. The big difference is this: in the piston engine, heat is added to the gas at a constant volume (that is, all at once, when the piston is near the top of the cylinder), whereas in the gas turbine, heat is added to the gas at a constant pressure, or continuously.

Discussion of the turbines thermodynamic cycle brings us to the point where we must broach a new concept: entropy. Entropy is a theoretical measure of energy pertaining to that portion of heat which cannot be transformed into mechanical work in a thermodynamic machine. In practice, it means that the higher the entropy of the gas in a turbine, the lower its capacity for producing useful work.

This touches directly on one of the key factors in gas turbine efficiency: the higher the temperature of the burning gas, the greater will be the proportion of useful energy to the useless energy it possesses. Converting this energy into mechanical work requires an expansion of the gas from a high-pressure, low-volume condition to a low-pressure, high-volume condition.

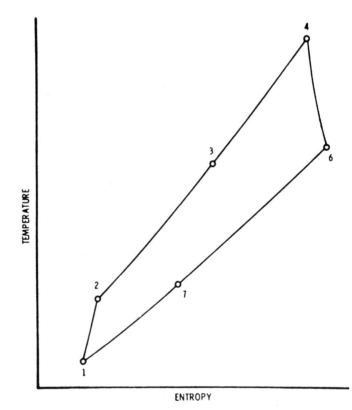

Temperature and entropy of the Brayton cycle.

The entropy chart (p. 10) illustrates the importance of high temperature in gaining high efficiency. This chart also reveals the quantitative difference in temperature between the exhaust gas and the air leaving the compressor. The exhaust is about three times hotter.

The turbine engineer's biggest entropy problem is to heat the compressed air to exhaust gas temperature before it enters the combustor. If an infinite transfer area were available, 100 percent of the exhaust heat could be used to heat up the compressed air. Using a heat exchanger of practical dimen-

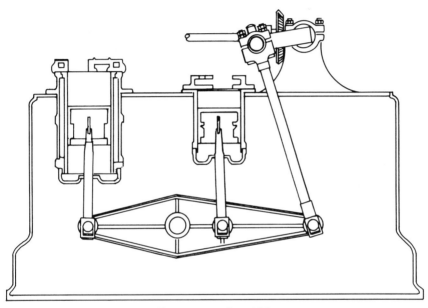

Brayton engine from 1872.

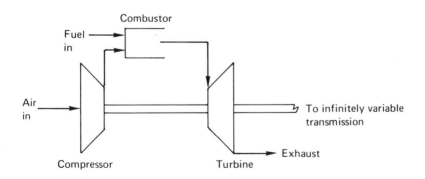

Single Shaft–Simple Cycle

Diagram of a simple-cycle gas turbine.

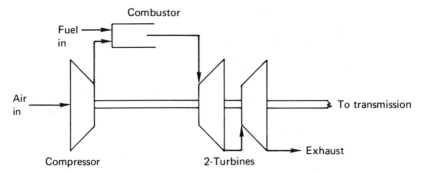

Two Shaft–Simple Cycle

Diagram of a two-shaft simple-cycle gas turbine engine.

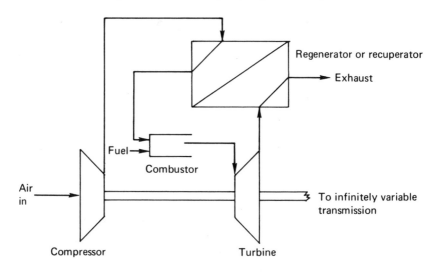

Single Shaft–Heat Recovery Cycle

Diagram of a single-shaft heat-recovery-cycle gas turbine engine.

sions for vehicle installation, between 80 and 90 percent of the exhaust gas heat can be transferred to the compressed air.

Supposing that the flame temperature is fixed at a given point, the value of the heat regeneration becomes evident. If this heat could not be regenerated from exhaust gases, it would have to be produced by burning fuel. Thus, the heat exchangers are prime factors in controlling fuel economy. By the same token, the exhaust gas, after passing through the heat exchanger, has lost 80–90 percent of the difference between its original temperature and

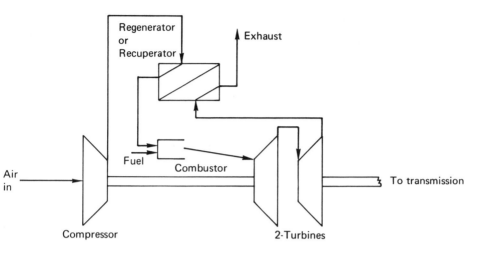

Two Shaft–Heat Recovery Cycle

Diagram of a two-shaft heat-recovery-cycle gas turbine engine.

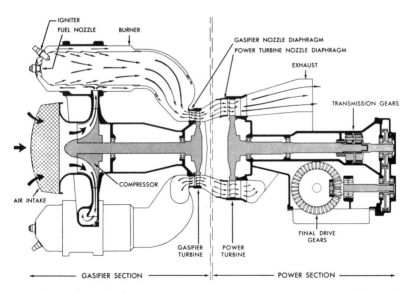

Sectioned view of a two-shaft non-regenerative automotive gas turbine engine, including reduction gear and transaxle.

13

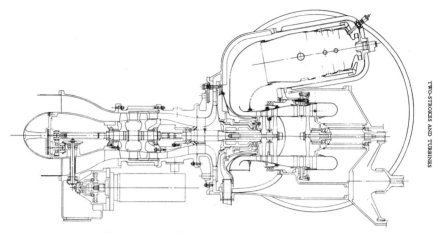

Sectioned view of a two-shaft recuperative gas turbine.

the compressed air temperature. The exhaust gas from a regenerative gas turbine will not be a hazard to the environment on the basis of its temperature.

It is important to realize in connection with the entropy chart that heat added prior to compression is detrimental rather than beneficial, because air expands when heated, and as a result there is a loss in compressor efficiency and capacity in hot weather. This presents a problem, and again I must quote Noel Penny:

"Due to the fall off in power with rising ambient temperature it used to be said that gas turbines should only be sold to Eskimos and not to Arabs. We now overcome this problem by designing for Arabs and trying to sell to Eskimos."

The general measure of gas turbine efficiency is specific fuel consumption (grams [or pounds] per horsepower-hour). Specific fuel consumption is determined by the efficiency of the individual components (such as compressor, combustor, and turbines), the maximum turbine operating temperature, the pressure ratio, and the thermal ratio of the heat exchangers. The higher the maximum turbine operating temperature, the higher will be the pressure ratio which gives optimum efficiency.

At this point it is pertinent to discuss the gas turbine's torque curve. With the typical twin-shaft arrangement, the gas turbine produces maximum torque at stall speed (0 rpm). Torque diminishes in almost linear proportion with increasing output shaft speed. Stall torque ratio is a convenient parameter for evaluation of the turbine's output characteristics. This stall torque ratio is defined as the ratio of torque at 0 power turbine rpm to the torque at

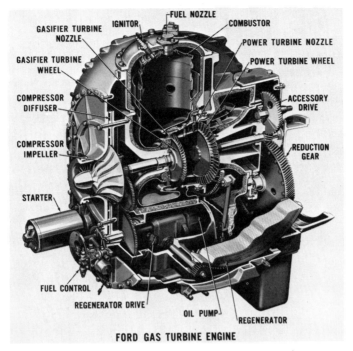

FORD GAS TURBINE ENGINE

Cutaway view through a two-shaft regenerative automotive gas turbine engine.

whatever rpm gives maximum power turbine efficiency (for the same turbine pressure ratio).

In a car, the turbine's torque is greatest at breakaway from a standing position and falls off as the car speed increases, where it is least necessary. This contrasts sharply with the piston engine's torque characteristic which gradually builds from zero at the start to a maximum in the mid-speed range. The free-shaft (power) turbine is, in effect, a built-in torque converter.

However, the maximum torque is only available if the gasifier section (i.e. the primary turbine and the compressor shaft) is running at maximum speed. This means that in starting the car from standstill, the compressor shaft must first be sped up from idle to full speed. This is the cause of a complaint known as acceleration lag, which will be discussed in detail in a later chapter.

The important thing to note at the moment is that the turbine's stall torque is twice as great as the torque available at the rated speed. This means that it is impossible to stall the engine under any load condition. Any increase in torque requirement merely causes the power turbine to slow down, while the gasifier section continues unhindered. And a drop in power turbine rpm immediately results in an increase in torque—an ideal situation.

This brief review of the gas turbine's principles of operation will serve to set the stage for a detailed examination of the various components.

FOOTNOTES

[1] Rudolf Diesel (1868–1913), German inventor, took out his basic patent for the compression-ignition engine in 1892.

[2] Felix Wankel (1902 to date), German inventor, engaged in rotary engine research since the mid-1920s, creator of the first Wankel engine in 1957.

[3] W. J. Macquorn Rankine, (1820–1872) Scottish railway engineer, later professor of engineering at the University of Glasgow.

[4] Robert Stirling (1790–1878) Scottish clergyman, inventor of a regenerator incorporating a hot-air engine in 1816.

2

The Compressor

THE FUNCTION of the compressor in a gas turbine engine is to supply compressed air as efficiently as possible, and to respond with minimum delay to changes in demand for compressed air. Driving the compressor absorbs a great amount of power. About two-thirds of the gross turbine output is expended in driving the compressor, leaving only about one-third for external work. It has been calculated that the compressor drive requires about 100 hp per pound of air delivered per second.

There are two types of compressors in common use on gas turbines—the centrifugal or radial-flow type, and the axial-flow type.

RADIAL-FLOW COMPRESSORS

The radial-flow compressor resembles a centrifugal water pump. The axial-flow compressor, on the other hand, resembles a multi-blade fan with a large hub and short, thin fan blades. Most automotive gas turbines have radial-flow compressors. This type has been chosen for a number of reasons:

1. It is more durable.
2. It is less prone to damage by foreign matter.
3. It is cheaper to manufacture.
4. It has lower maintenance requirements.
5. It makes for a shorter and more convenient package.
6. It has lower inertia, which improves engine response.
7. It is less sensitive to fouling.

But the radial-flow compressor is not without its own set of drawbacks. The centrifugal compressor has a larger diameter than an equivalent one of axial type. Centrifugal compressors usually become less efficient as the size is

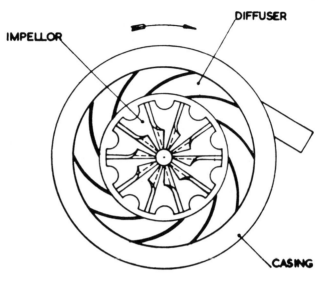

IMPELLOR

DIFFUSER

CASING

CENTRIFUGAL COMPRESSOR

Diagram of a basic centrifugal compressor.

reduced. They also tend to lose efficiency when the pressure ratio is increased. Pressure ratios for a single-stage centrifugal compressor rarely exceed 4 or 4½ : 1. Recent aerodynamic advances have extended the capacity of small single-stage centrifugal compressors to pressure ratios of 10 or 12 to one, with steel or titanium alloy compressor wheels.

Last but not least, the velocity of the discharged air is higher than the peripheral velocity of the compressor wheel, and this sets a practical limit for the compressor wheel diameter and/or its rotational speed, since discharge air velocity should be kept at subsonic levels. Supersonic air waves give rise to compressibility phenomena that cause a loss of efficiency.

In the centrifugal compressor the air flows more or less axially into the compressor wheel and is deflected into a meridional plane by the curvature of the compressor wheel blades nearest the blade root. This section of the compressor is called the inducer. The leading edges of the compressor blades are shaped to accommodate the air flow in its new direction. The air flow exits radially from the compressor housing and its discharge velocity is determined by the velocity of the intake air and the tangential blade velocity. High blade tip speed can lead to supersonic discharge velocities. If this occurs, the supersonic air flow must be diffused to a far lower velocity before

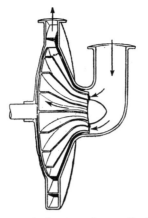

Schematic showing the function of a centrifugal compressor.

it can safely be passed to the heat exchangers or into the combustor. To take care of this problem, the space following the compressor discharge area is surrounded by a vaneless space in which the supersonic wake spends itself as the air flow spirals outward. Surrounding this vaneless space is an annular array of stator blades or channels. This device is known as a diffuser and forms the subject of our next chapter.

Axial-Flow Compressors

In the axial-flow compressor, the air is deflected from a straight radial path into a corkscrewing motion by the rotation of the compressor wheels. The discharge velocity is dependent on the intake velocity and the blade ro-

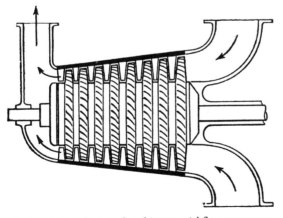

Sectioned view of a typical multi-stage axial-flow compressor.

Two-stage centrifugal compressor (left end of shaft) driven by a two-stage axial-flow turbine.

tational velocity. Centrifugal compressors may have one or more stages but the axial type is invariably a multi-stage unit.

The flow path is more direct in axial-flow compressors than in centrifugal compressors, but at each stage the air must be accelerated in the direction of rotation and then diverted by stator blades to the desired angle of attack for the next stage. Pressure ratio per stage is usually kept low (about 1.5 : 1), necessitating a high number of stages.

The axial compressor is used mainly in large aircraft turbines because it is significantly more efficient than the centrifugal type in large size engines. It is also suitable for higher pressure ratios, due to the use of multi-stage compressors. Such axial-flow compressors can give pressure ratios 2–3 times higher than a radial-flow compressor.

However, in smaller size engines, its efficiency is inferior to that of the centrifugal type. This is mainly due to the high percentage of blade-tip leakage in the small axial-flow compressor. The axial compressor would also suffer in an automotive application from its narrow working band between surge and loss of efficiency, which makes part-load operation difficult. The following text deals primarily with centrifugal compressors as used in automotive gas turbines.

EFFICIENCY

Compressor efficiency is expressed in percentages which are related to the energy which would be put into the air or taken out of it when compressing it or expanding it adiabatically. Adiabatic compression or expansion involves compressing or expanding without subtraction or addition of heat. Compres-

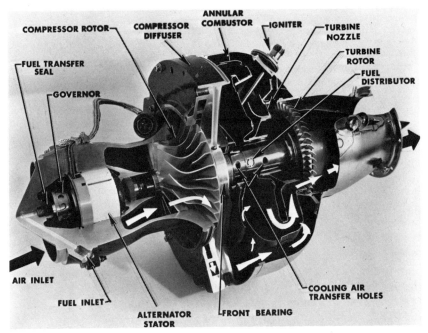

COMPRESSOR ROTOR — COMPRESSOR DIFFUSER — ANNULAR COMBUSTOR — IGNITER — TURBINE NOZZLE — TURBINE ROTOR — FUEL DISTRIBUTOR — FUEL TRANSFER SEAL — GOVERNOR — AIR INLET — FUEL INLET — ALTERNATOR STATOR — FRONT BEARING — COOLING AIR TRANSFER HOLES

Cutaway view of a small turbojet engine with a single-stage centrifugal compressor.

sor authorities usually prefer the more exact "polytropic efficiency" which takes account of friction which does not appear as heat and of heat loss by convection and radiation from the compressor housing. Looking only at a compressor's adiabatic efficiency can be misleading in specific cases, but for general purposes it is quite an adequate measure.

Charles Amann of the General Motors Research Laboratories comes to my support here. He stated in 1973: "The power absorbed by the compressor is manifested as a change in the energy content of the through-flowing air. The through-flow rate is so high that the process approaches the adiabatic condition—that is, one free from heat exchange with the surroundings."

Now we can go on to a theoretical example of what the numbers indicate. Let us say that an input of X amount of energy is required to compress one pound of air with a 4 : 1 pressure ratio at 100 percent efficiency. But if the compressor is only 70 percent efficient, it will require more energy to obtain the same result. How much more? Divide X by 0.70, and the answer is 1.428 X or an extra 42.8 percent of energy input.

George J. Huebner, Jr., director of research at Chrysler Corporation, and regarded as the father of the Chrysler gas turbine car, said in 1960:

At the inception of our automotive gas turbine work, we were aware that the use of radial compressors was mandatory because of their simplicity. We also knew that efficient radial compressors did not exist in automotive sizes and pressure ratios, and no one could give us more than just a hint of the problems to be encountered in the development of such small units. Therefore, in the course of a careful program of compressor and diffuser component development, we had to extrapolate, and in some cases develop our own theory. Years were spent in the search for the optimum proportion between aerodynamic performance, simplicity, and reliability. Our efforts have been rewarded with considerable success and we have achieved a compressor efficiency of over 80 percent—an efficiency which, we believe, will be further increased to 82 percent within a short development period.

Similar advances in compressor efficiency were reported by General Motors: the measured efficiency went from 68 percent in GT 300 of 1953 to 75 percent in GT 304 of 1955. The GT 305 of 1958 reached 78 percent, which was raised to 80 percent in the GT 309 of 1964.

Efficiency is only one of a triumvirate of conflicting requirements in a compressor. The other two are compressor wheel inertia and pressure. We'll discuss the inertia problems first. In an automotive gas turbine, power must be available immediately when the demand signal is given to the engine. This requires the compressor shaft to speed up, and therefore its inertia should be as low as possible to reduce the time lag. How can inertia be reduced? Only by reducing compressor wheel diameter, primary turbine diameter, or placing restrictions on the pressure ratio.

Noel Penny says the compressor design that gives the highest efficiency cannot be used, because it involves higher inertia. Compressor design must be a compromise between the need for minimal inertia and the need for efficiency. The most efficient design would use sweep-back on the blade tips, so as to work better together with the diffuser. But such a design would not give a good enough response. One way to assist compressor efficiency is to fit a vaned stator at the compressor intake, giving the incoming air a pre-swirling action. The pre-swirl vanes could be provided with variable geometry, which could prove highly valuable in terms of response.

Variable diffuser vanes would also make possible part-load operation at higher rotational speeds with higher efficiency than can be obtained with a fixed-geometry compressor. The drawback with variable inlet guide vanes is that they reduce the overall compressor efficiency by about 4 percentage points with a pressure ratio of 4 : 1. The loss is higher with a higher pressure ratio and lower with a lower pressure ratio.

By the use of variable pre-swirl vanes, the engine's idling speed is increased without any change in pressure ratio, and the speed difference between idling and maximum power is reduced. That in turn translates into a reduced acceleration lag. Variable inlet guide vanes can also be a valuable tool for controlling surge. Surge is a random or cyclical rise or fall in gasifier shaft speed. It is the opposite of stable operation.

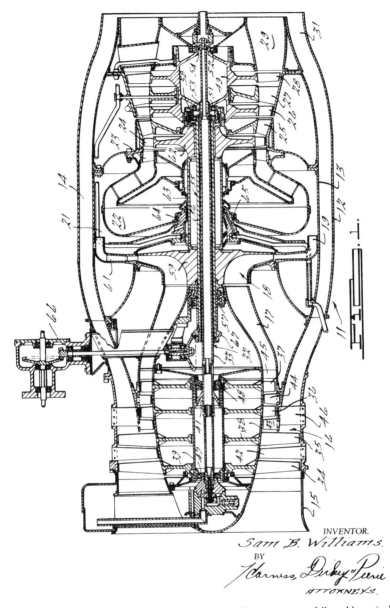

INVENTOR.
Sam B. Williams

BY

Harness, Dickey & Pierce

ATTORNEYS.

Sectioned view of gas turbine engine with a two-stage axial-flow compressor followed by a single centrifugal compressor stage.

23

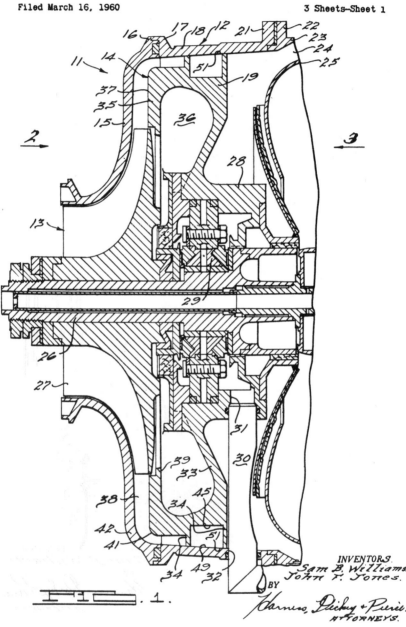

FIG. 1.

INVENTORS.
Sam B. Williams
John T. Jones.
BY
Harness, Dickey & Pierce.
ATTORNEYS.

Compressor assembly including diffuser vanes.

24

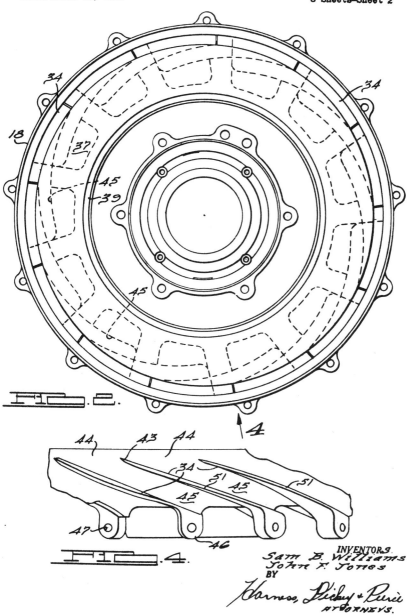

Patented design for diffuser vanes.

25

Surge is caused by aerodynamic phenomena in the compressor. Besides creating a speed control nuisance, surge causes a drop in turbine inlet temperature (which in turn means higher fuel consumption). Potentially, continued operation under surge conditions can prove destructive. But the fact remains that the most efficient compressor operation is reached just at the surge limit.

This, according to General Motors, leads to a conflict between the desire to operate near the choke limit to avoid surge and the need to operate near the surge limit to capitalize on the efficiency capability of the compressor. Abandoning the radial blade configuration in favor of one in which the rotor blades are curved backward, opposite the direction of rotation, offers the possibility of moving the maximum efficiency contour farther away from the surge limit. This desirable characteristic comes at the cost of a reduction in slip coefficient. Other factors remaining fixed, the result is an increase in compressor wheel diameter and higher stress levels.

According to Ford Motor Company:

Determination of incipient surge can be obtained by strain gaging the blading of the compressor wheel at the nodal points of the vanes and observing the vibratory modes, while running through the complete compressor map. Incipient surge will excite the vanes, which then provide data for plotting of a second surge line of the compressor. Engine matching must then be made with sufficient margin from the incipient surge-line characteristic. While this procedure may sound straightforward, it is complicated by the problem of extracting the signal from the strain gages.

Most gas turbine engines utilize bleed to reduce the possibility of compressor surge during acceleration. On automotive turbine engines this air is ducted into a cast manifold, containing a butterfly valve for control. The air flow from this valve passes through a silencer, which lowers the noise level by about 8 decibels.

The shape and size of the compressor blades are extremely important for aerodynamic control of the air flow through the compressor. If flow separation occurs along the blade and shroud surfaces, it will result in a pressure loss. Boundary layer growth in a decelerating flow field will also result in flow separation and high mixing losses.

Local shock losses can occur if the air flow accelerates to supersonic velocities. If separation occurs in the inducer section of the compressor, it can lead to inducer stall. Besides causing a pressure loss, inducer stall creates noise and can become a source of mechanical vibration.

Looking for the cause of all these disturbances we find that at any given rotational speed, the centrifugal compressor has a maximum air flow capacity. When the engine wants more air than the compressor can supply, the compressor is said to be "choked." In such situations, sonic velocity has been reached in one of the flow-restriction areas—either at the leading edge of the blades or at entrance to the diffuser passages.

The pressure ratio is the ratio of initial pressure to final pressure. Intake pressure is atmospheric (14.7 pounds per square inch). A pressure ratio of 4 : 1 means that the compressor discharges at 58.8 psi.

In a turbine engine unit without a regenerator, the most efficient pressure ratio at full load depends mainly on compressor and turbine efficiencies, turbine inlet temperature and compressor inlet (atmospheric) temperature, with higher turbine inlet temperatures requiring a higher pressure ratio.

In a turbine engine equipped with a regenerator, the most effective pressure ratio will be much lower than when a regenerative heat exchanger is not used. Low pressure ratios tend to give high thermal efficiency with high-efficiency regenerators, but there are other factors favoring use of a high full-load pressure ratio.

To obtain improved part-load performance in gas turbine engines, it is desirable for the pressure ratio of the compressor and the maximum cycle temperature to be kept as high as possible when the power output is reduced. Pressure ratio requirements play a key role in determining compressor wheel size.

A pressure ratio of 4 : 1 in a single-stage centrifugal compressor requires an impeller tip speed of the order of 1300–1400 feet per second. With a 6-inch diameter impeller running at those tip speeds, the shaft would have to spin at a rate of 50,000 to 54,000 rpm.

The compressor operates at reasonably low temperatures, but is subject to very high rotational speeds and extreme aerodynamic loads. Consequently, compressor wheel and housing materials must be carefully selected. For instance, Chrysler went to a steel casting for the inducer section of its compressor in 1963, to cope with the stresses. In addition, it was judged necessary to fit a steel shroud over this portion of the blades because the inlet section had been subject to fatigue problems. Both added to the inertia, and were eliminated on the fifth-generation turbine of 1965. Ford used a cast C355-T61 aluminum compressor wheel on its Type 705 truck turbine, and experienced disintegration until a new triaxial stress analysis procedure had been perfected, and a modified compressor wheel was produced.

The diffuser associated with the centrifugal compressor plays an extremely important role in determining overall turbine efficiency. In a non-regenerative turbine, the diffuser stage follows immediately after the compressor discharge, leading the compressed air to the combustion chamber. In a regenerative turbine engine, the diffuser is separated from the compressor and placed between the heat exchanger and the combustion chamber entry. The diffuser's task is to control the compressed air flow and assure its proper distribution. The diffuser should be kept to minimum size while maintaining high air-consumption capacity.

3

The Combustor

THE COMBUSTOR is the part of the turbine where the fuel is added, the air/fuel mixture is ignited, and expansion begins. The primary function of the combustor is to release the chemical energy stored in the fuel. The most efficient combustion is desirable at all turbine inlet temperatures for reasons of fuel economy and emission control. Combustor efficiency may be defined as the ratio of the actual temperature rise to the theoretical temperature rise.

There are two basically different types of combustor, the barrel type and the toroidal type. The former is by far the more common in automotive turbines. The barrel type combustor is shaped like a cylinder, and is usually placed so as to extend radially (or at a slight angle) from the compressor shaft, with a closed dome at the outer end.

As a rule, an automotive gas turbine has one combustor, but two-combustor units have been built (by General Motors, Fiat, and Boeing). Aircraft turbines with barrel-type combustors invariably have multiple combustors (6, 9. 10 or 12) and they are placed side by side in an axial flow pattern.

Turbine engines with toroidal combustors exist for a number of different applications, including automotive. The toroidal combustor forms a ring or torus, located coaxially with the compressor shaft. The characteristics of both types will be discussed in detail later on.

The barrel-type combustor family can be sub-divided into categories according to air flow. First, the *straight-through* type. This model is practically restricted to aircraft engines with multiple combustors. The air flows in the straightest possible path into and the burnt gases out of the combustor. The *elbow* type uses an angular-flow entry port, feeding the primary air into the primary zone from outside the combustor.

In the *reverse flow* type, the primary air is delivered inside the combustor, flows to the dome, and is reversed. This type of combustor has become prevalent in automotive gas turbines. It offers the best compromise between the requirements of compactness, cost, accessibility, and ease of replacement. With this design, a strong toroidal vortex is created along the combustor axis, which causes the air to flow upstream toward the fuel nozzle, out across the combustor dome, and then downstream between the primary holes.

For efficient operation, the combustor must fulfil a number of conditions:

1. LOW PRESSURE LOSS

The expansion process that starts with combustion will lead to a pressure drop across the combustor. The gas flow patterns required to sustain combustion contribute to this pressure drop. And reduced pressure at the primary turbine inlet involves a thermodynamic loss. This loss must be minimized.

2. STABILIZED COMBUSTION

The flame must be stabilized to assure complete combustion and guard against lean blow-out. Because the average gas flow velocity in the combustor substantially exceeds the flame front velocity, it becomes necessary to generate recirculation patterns to keep the flame going.

3. CONTROLLED PRIMARY TURBINE INLET TEMPERATURE

The combustion temperature must be reduced to below turbine material tolerance levels with a high degree of uniformity to prevent hot streaks which could damage the turbine blades. This can be done with properly controlled mixing of dilution air into the combustion products from the primary zone.

4. PROPER SKIN TEMPERATURE DISTRIBUTION

The combustor skin must be adequately cooled to assure long life. This can be accomplished by feeding in a thin film of cooling air.

5. FAST IGNITION

The ignition system must provide reliable starting during all conditions, and the combustor design must allow inflammation within seconds of initial fuel delivery to the primary zone.

6. LOW EXHAUST EMISSIONS

Pollutants in the turbine exhaust are formed in the combustor, and the combustor must be designed to eliminate or minimize harmful emissions.

THE COMBUSTION PROCESS

Experience from the piston engine tells us that internal combustion engines work best at or near stoichiometric air/fuel ratios. The stoichiometric air/fuel ratio is defined as the theoretically correct proportion of air to fuel in the combustible mixture for complete oxidation of the fuel, or about 14.925 parts air to one part fuel. That represents an air/fuel ratio fractionally short of 15 : 1.

It's inherent in the principle of gas turbine operation that the turbine must consume vast amounts of excess air. The specific air consumption of a gas turbine is in the order of four to ten times that of a reciprocating engine, depending on the operating efficiency. The surplus air cannot participate in the combustion process, so ways must be found to pass it through the engine without giving it an opportunity to "blow out" the burning flame in the combustor. The condition that exists if excess air does enter the combustor and puts the flame out, is known as *lean blow-out*.

The key to the gas turbine combustion process lies in burning part of the air with fuel at approximately stoichiometric fuel/air ratio and then diluting the combustion products with the remainder of the air without quenching the reaction and thus wasting fuel by incomplete combustion. The gas speed through the combustor is probably about 50 feet per second or 15.24 meters per second in the primary zone where stoichiometric mixture is being burnt. This 50 feet per second is far in excess of the speed with which flame will spread through quiescent mixture (known as the laminar flame speed). There are indications that the laminar flame speed of turbine fuels is of the order of 1.3 feet per second or 400 mm per second.

The minimum air/fuel ratio used in gas turbines is about 55.5 : 1, but it can go as high as 400 : 1. If the fuel were uniformly mixed with the air, the mixture would not be combustible. The air must be separated, so that only enough air needed to assure continuous combustion is mixed with the fuel. The air that participates in the formation of the combustible mixture is known as "primary" air. The excess air introduced downstream from the primary combustion zone is known as "dilution" air.

After combustion, the hot gases leave the primary zone and move to the secondary zone, where they are cooled by mixing with air entering through the secondary air holes. The combustor temperature spread can be varied by changing the configuration of the hole pattern. Combustors equipped with means to vary the number of inlet air openings, their size and position, are known as variable-geometry combustors. The goal of variable geometry is to change the proportion of air going to the primary zone and air going to the dilution zone. A non-variable geometry combustor can only assure constant flame temperature under one specific operating condition.

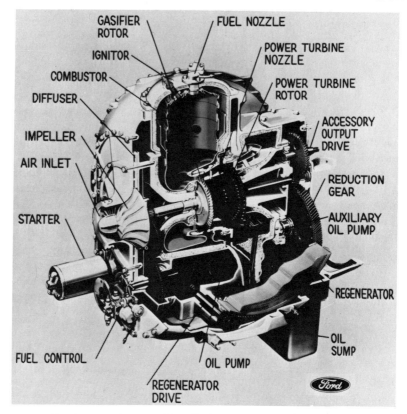

Barrel-type combustor used in a Ford automotive gas turbine engine.

BARREL-TYPE COMBUSTORS

The typical barrel-type combustor can be described as consisting of three zones, although the boundaries between them are not distinct. The primary zone is the section near the dome, closest to the fuel injector nozzle. This is where the main combustion reaction occurs. The adjacent area is a stabilization zone, which often overlaps with the primary zone. Here, some chemical reaction continues, with strong recirculation of combustion products and additional air. The wide range of input rates required for flexible engine operation causes broad shifting of the ceiling for the stabilization zone. The last (lowest) section is the dilution zone, where the remaining excess air is mixed into the barrel, lowering the temperature of the exhaust gases to a level acceptable to the turbine.

The temperature of the gas discharged from the combustor should ideally

Jan. 31, 1961   S. B. WILLIAMS ET AL   2,969,644
DRIVE MEANS FOR A REGENERATOR IN A
REEXPANSION GAS TURBINE ENGINE
Original Filed Oct. 24, 1955   7 Sheets–Sheet 7

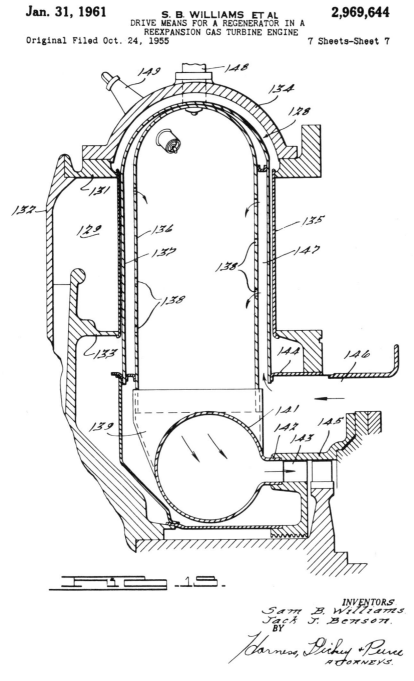

INVENTORS
Sam B. Williams
Jack J. Benson.
BY
Harness, Dickey & Pierce
ATTORNEYS.

Barrel-type combustor design by Williams Research Corp.

33

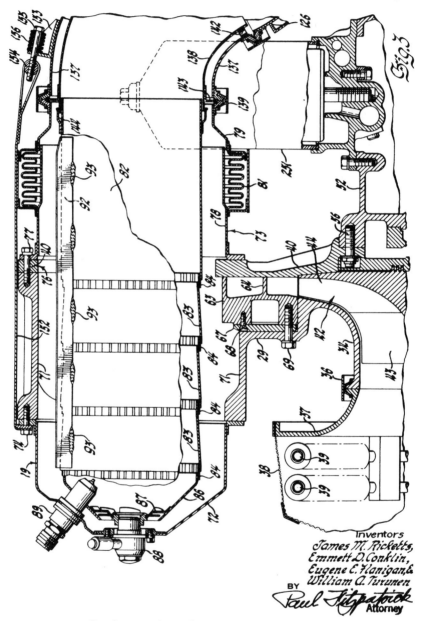

Barrel-type combustor design by General Motors Corp.

34

Oct. 5, 1965

B. T. HOWES ETAL

3,209,536

RE-EXPANSION TYPE GAS TURBINE ENGINE WITH
INTERCOOLER FAN DRIVEN BY THE LOW
PRESSURE TURBINE

Filed April 4, 1960

13 Sheets—Sheet 10

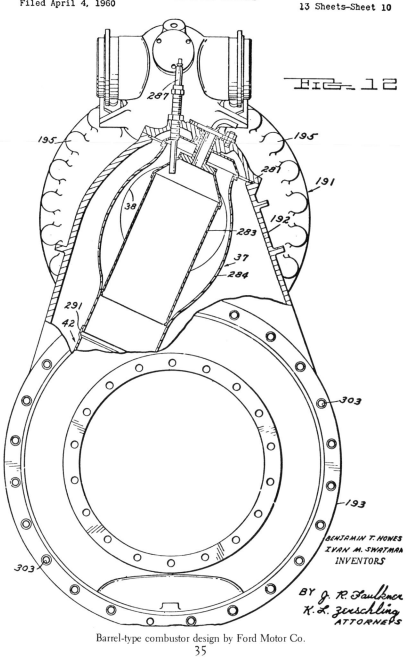

FIG. 12

BENJAMIN T. HOWES
IVAN M. SWATMAN
INVENTORS

BY J. R. Faulkner
K. L. Zerschling
ATTORNEYS

Barrel-type combustor design by Ford Motor Co.

35

be entirely uniform. A local hot streak in the gas stream can cause distortion of the nozzle ring for the primary turbine.

In his work on Rover gas turbines, Noel Penny experienced temperature variations of 212–248° F (100–120° C) in the early units. Penny explained his special efforts in attending to the direction and velocity of the air flow entering the combustor, the position of the primary air holes relative to the airflow towards them, the spray pattern of the injection nozzle, and the positioning, shape, size, and number of dilution air holes, and claimed to have reduced the temperature variations to within 122° F (50° C).

Pressure losses associated with combustors have been in the neighborhood of 5% of cycle pressure for aircraft practice. However, in regenerative engines of relatively low pressure ratio there is a premium on pressure loss from any source. For instance, Chrysler's combustor configuration has been designed for the minimum interaction between the liner and surrounding environment consistent with compactness. Sensitivity of the combustor performance to manufacturing tolerances and asymctrics in the environmental flow are thus virtually eliminated. These conditions also minimize pressure losses due to aerodynamic irregularities in the combustor surroundings. The losses are due mainly to the flow characteristics of the liner itself. A design point loss of 1½ to 2% of maximum cycle pressure is being used with satisfactory performance.

The efficiency of a combustor varies considerably with geometry, fuel type, and ambient conditions. However, experience with the Chrysler combustor has shown efficiencies in excess of 98% for all types of steady-state operation.

Control of the combustor skin temperatures can most effectively be assured by use of an adherent cooling film. Chrysler developed an annular gap arrangement, with variable gap width and axial spacing to regulate the admission of cooling air. These cooling gaps provide a circumferentially uniform temperature and a sufficiently low axial gradient so that thermal stress is minimized. Rover gas turbines used a louvered form of air film admission, which gave rise to higher thermal stresses, but proved fully workable in practice. Noel Penny claims the stresses were minimized by telescoping of the louvers.

Toroidal Combustors

While the barrel-type combustor is shaped like a cylinder, the toroidal combustor is shaped like a ring or a doughnut. The toroidal combustor works in the same way as the barrel-type combustor, with a primary zone, a stabilizing zone and a dilution zone, but the boundaries of the zones are less easily defined.

While the zones in a barrel-type combustor are stacked one above the other in the cylinder, the different zones in the toroidal combustor take the form of smaller rings or toroids within the big one. There are no sectional boundaries. Instead, the zones can be identified by their locations relative to the shaft (close to center, far from center, forwards meaning towards the compressor, and backwards meaning towards the primary turbine).

The compressor discharge air is separated into primary and secondary quantities. The toroidal combustor is mounted coaxially with the compressor shaft and located between the compressor and the primary turbine. The fuel is fed in through the shaft, and injected by slinger-type nozzles carried on the shaft and revolving with it. Ignition is provided by an igniter located in front of the secondary air ports so as to shoot a flame through the ports and ignite the combustible mixture in the primary reaction zone.

Toroidal combustors are usually of the annular reverse flow type, which means that the primary air enters the combustor via a back door—from the rear. A curved plate that forms the back of the combustor has a central clearance opening working as the primary air inlet port. The primary air is admitted to the area nearest the fuel slinger ports at relatively low velocity. Thus we find that the primary zone is close to the shaft, near the inner circumference of the combustor.

The turbine casing in back of the combustor is separated from it by an open space containing a ring of diffuser vanes. These guide vanes set up a swirling motion in the primary air flowing to the central combustor inlet port. The swirl takes the direction of shaft rotation. Secondary air is introduced at selected points along the forward portion of the combustor, and mixed with hot combustion gases. The secondary combustor inlet ports are spaced out along the outer circumference, extending radially around the combustor. The compressed air from these ports is ducted to the forward side of the combustor.

The front plates on the combustor overlap so as to form an annular channel of inclined cross-sectional shape that guides the compressed air from the radial inlet ports to an intermediate area, radially outside the primary zone, but inside of the outlet section, which is located near the outer circumference.

A set of vanes disposed in the annular channel between the overlapping plates is inclined at 15°–35° so as to impart a whirling motion to the air flow. This air mixes with the combustion products from the primary zone, and stabilizes the combustion process. Dilution air is added in the outlet section. Dilution air enters through the secondary inlet ports, which are U-shaped, with trailing edges that direct part of the air flow to the dilution zone.

The exhaust ports are tangential outlets in the combustor wall, sized and spaced so as to exert a certain control over the exhaust gas temperature and

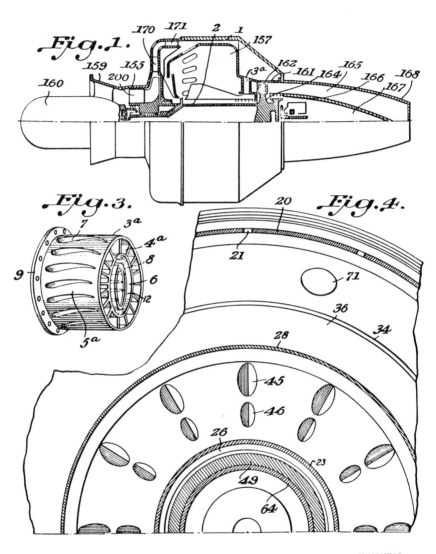

Fig. 1.

Fig. 3.

Fig. 4.

INVENTOR.
Joseph Szydlowski,

Toroidal combustor design by Turbomeca.

Fig.5.

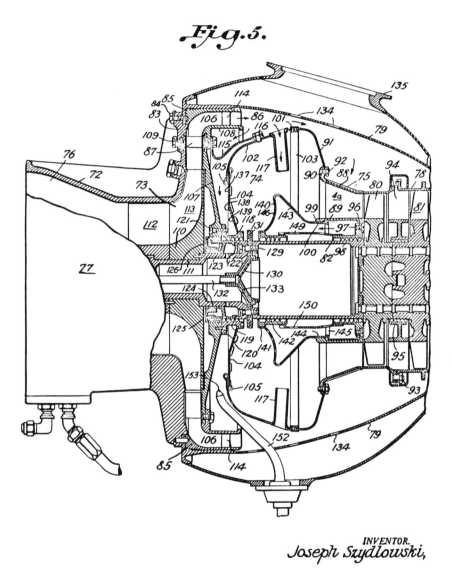

INVENTOR.

Joseph Szydlowski,

Detail of toroidal combustor showing fuel feed through gasifier shaft.

39

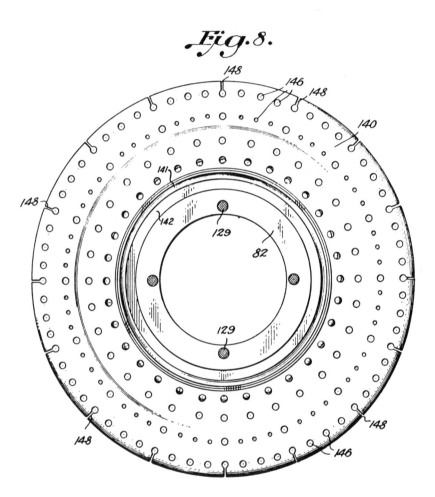

Detail of combustor shell construction for Turbomeca toroidal combustor.

40

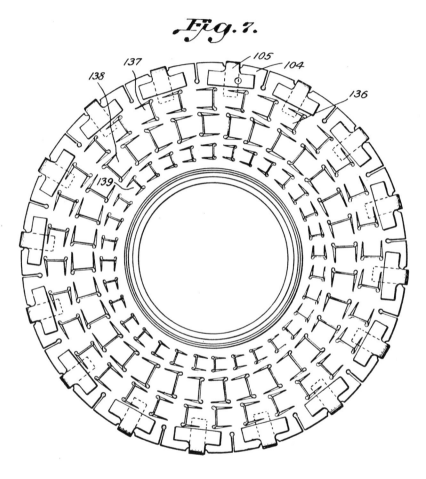

Fig. 7.

INVENTOR.
Joseph Szydlowski,

Detail of toroidal combustor shell construction.

41

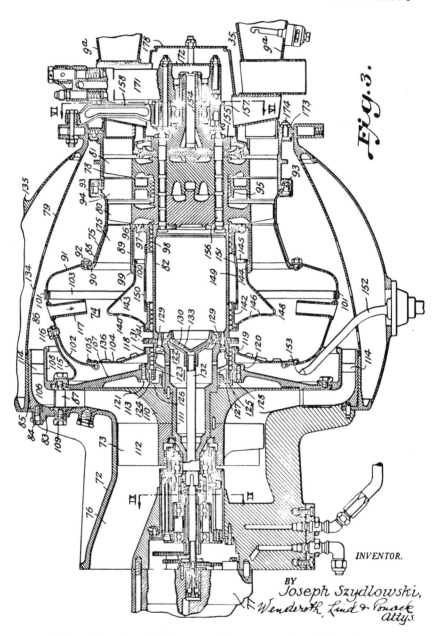

Fig.3.

INVENTOR.

BY Joseph Szydlowski,
Wenderoth, Lind & Ponack
Attys.

Sectioned view through Turbomeca turbojet engine with toroidal combustor.

42

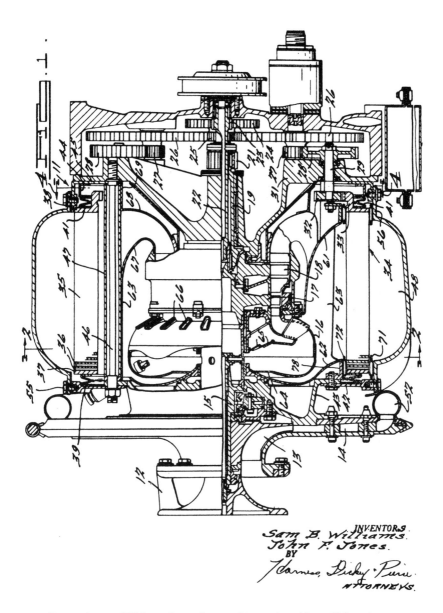

INVENTORS.
Sam B. Williams.
John F. Jones.
BY

ATTORNEYS.

Sectioned view of Williams Research gas turbine engine with toroidal combustor.

43

Jan. 31, 1961   S. B. WILLIAMS ET AL   2,969,644
DRIVE MEANS FOR A REGENERATOR IN A
REEXPANSION GAS TURBINE ENGINE
Original Filed Oct. 24, 1955   7 Sheets–Sheet 3

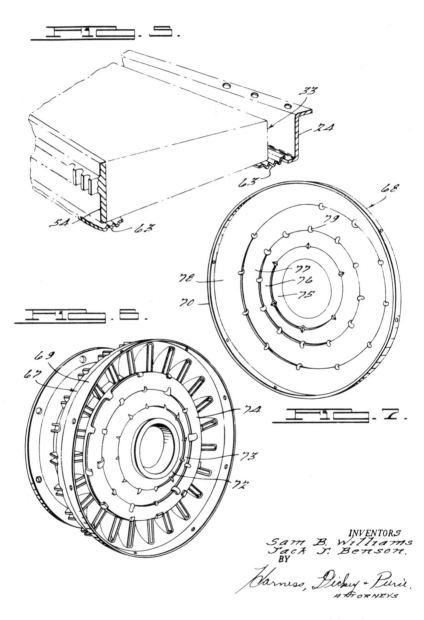

INVENTORS
Sam B. Williams
Jack J. Benson.
BY
Harness, Dickey + Pierce.
ATTORNEYS

Details of combustor shell construction for Williams Research toroidal combustor.

44

maximize its uniformity throughout. The exhaust ports lead directly to the nozzle for the primary turbine.

The advantages claimed for the toroidal combustor and axial fuel delivery system are improved mixture uniformity, lower fuel consumption, reduced exhaust gas odors, and more complete combustion. The toroidal combustor also minimizes the effect of temperature variations during operation, which might otherwise cause uneven burning or uneven temperature distribution in the different areas of the combustor. The parts are simple and inexpensive to manufacture, require little or no maintenance, and are consistent with compact construction.

On the minus side, the toroidal combustor places the hottest parts near the center of the entire gas turbine engine, in close proximity to bearings requiring lubrication, for instance. From a service viewpoint, accessibility to ignition and fuel control systems is compromised. Toroidal combustors are used by Turbomeca aircraft turbines (based on Szydlowski patents dating back to 1949), Lycoming industrial turbines, Williams Research turbojets and turboshaft engines, Waukesha industrial turbines (under Williams license), and some Volkswagen experimental automotive turbines (under Williams license).

COMBUSTOR MATERIALS

The combustor must be made of materials that can resist flame temperatures of 4,000° F (2204° C) without melting. The material should also have high cyclic oxidation resistance and high stress-rupture strength. It should offer good carburization resistance, good weldability, light weight and low cost.

Looking back on 25 years of combustor development, George J. Huebner of Chrysler Corporation said:

Combustors have been developed with an eye to simplicity and reliability. Typical aircraft gas turbine practice was originally adopted, but innovations of our own were quickly introduced. Our studies of combustion and temperature distribution have resulted in the development of combustors which approach complete burning, last a long time, are light in weight, and can be manufactured from relatively low-cost materials.

Chrysler was successful in developing families of low cost, low alloy content materials which are highly satisfactory for the purposes for which intended.

A six percent aluminum-iron alloy, which is coded as CRM-4 (Chrysler Research Material number 4), was used for much of the internal sheet metal in the engine. The strength required of most of these parts is not extreme, and the hot strength of CRM-4 makes it a satisfactory low cost substitute for the far more expensive chrome nickel stainless steels used in aircraft turbines, such as Inconel or Nimonic.

General Motors has long been using a combustor made as a simple cast-stainless-steel cylinder.

LOW-EMISSION COMBUSTORS

Quite early during the debates and senate hearings that preceded the formulation and enactment of the bill that became the Clean Air Act of 1966, the gas turbine was mentioned as a "pollution solution"—a low-emission automotive power plant. The 1970 Amendment to the Clean Air Act set limits for three categories of pollutants—unburned hydrocarbons, carbon monoxide, and oxides of nitrogen. A timetable was proposed, enacted, and modified, so that in today's situation, it looks like this:

All numbers represent grams per mile.

	HC	CO	NO_x
1976	1.5	15.0	3.1
1977	0.41	3.4	2.0

The original 1976 requirement for NO_x emissions was a maximum of 0.4 grams per mile.

How does the automotive gas turbine stack up against the standards? We have data from a simulated test at GM and a full-scale test by the EPA (Environmental Protection Agency) on a Williams Research 80-hp turbine installed in a 1971 AMC Hornet. General Motors engineers computed mass emissions by its simulation program for a 4500-pound passenger car powered by a scaled-down 160-hp version of the GT-309 gas turbine. The Williams turbine has a toroidal combustor and the GT-309 a barrel-type combustor. Here are the results:

	HC	CO	NO_x
GM (GT-309)	0.2	1.1	3.1
Williams	0.44	4.5	2.15

It's immaterial whether or not the GM simulation was optimistic—the figures from the Williams turbine car (which was not optimized for low emissions) prove that the potential for ultra-low emission levels is real.

Before we can discuss emission control methods used in the gas turbine, it is necessary to review briefly the various pollutants and the processes by which they are created. It applies to all types of chemical energy conversion that the process may not be 100 percent complete. That leaves by-products. Some are harmless, while others not only steal efficiency, but usually constitute impurities (toxic waste matter). In an internal combustion engine, the chemical energy conversion process is combustion. And even with stoichiometric air/fuel ratios, the combustion is never 100 percent complete.

Harmless combustion by-products are carbon dioxide and water vapor—both natural constituents of the atmosphere. The major source of hydrocarbon emissions is air/fuel mixture that has not participated in the combustion process. Incomplete combustion occurs in piston engines because the very thin layer of gaseous mixture which makes contact with the relatively cool metal surfaces of the combustion chamber does not reach the temperature that's needed for reaction, and therefore does not burn.

Carbon monoxide formation occurs when there is insufficient oxygen in the air/fuel mixture to allow full combustion. Complete combustion works in the interest of both high efficiency and low HC and CO emission levels. As far as HC and CO are concerned, the most efficient engine is also the cleanest engine.

But the picture is not complete without taking oxides of nitrogen into account. NO_x formation is not a result of incomplete combustion. NO_x concentrations are caused by a chemical transformation which occurs when oxygen and nitrogen are brought together in a very high-temperature environment. The hotter the combustion flame, the higher the NO_x level. In a piston engine, NO_x levels tend to go up when HC and CO emissions come down, and vice versa. The turbine has important advantages here, due to the difference between the Brayton cycle and the Otto cycle.

In a gas turbine, combustion is continuous, instead of intermittent, so that the chamber walls never cool off. Also, contact between the plane and the chamber walls is less intimate. This eliminates the gas quenching that occurs in piston engines and prevents the completion of the process. In the gas turbine, combustion is more complete, with fewer unburned hydrocarbons. The fuel is different, too. Instead of gasoline, the turbine can run on a variety of liquid fuels, such as JP4 or JP5 jet fuel, pure kerosene, diesel fuel, or low-octane gasoline.

Gas turbines also use large amounts of excess air and thus dilute the combustion products to low concentrations. The excess air also assures an ample supply of oxygen to prevent carbon monoxide formation. But NO_x levels tend to be high, because combustion temperatures can reach 4000° F (2204° C), while NO_x formation becomes a problem at 2100–2400° F (1150–1315° C). Below 1875° F (1025° C) HC and CO levels will be too high. However, the gas turbine is more amenable to NO_x control by combustor design modifications.

What goes on inside the combustor? Fuel is injected in atomized form into a turbulent airstream. Fuel droplets begin to evaporate immediately following injection. How do they burn? The process is described as an exothermic chemical reaction between the fuel vapor and the oxygen, as fuel vapor diffuses from the droplet surface to the flame front, while oxygen is diffused from the surrounding air to the flame front. The resulting combustion products are diffused from the flame to the surrounding air. The chemical reaction occurs practically instantaneously, and the combustion rate is determined by the physical process of vaporization of the liquid droplets.

Each droplet is consumed in a finite time X. But half of the droplet is consumed in ⅓X. And it takes ⅔X to consume the remaining half of the droplet. This occurs because while the combustion products from the first half of the droplet diffuse and mix into the surrounding air, their temperature is lowered and the effective air/fuel ratio becomes leaner. The air/fuel ratio is effectively leaner because of the presence of exhaust products which are not required for reaction. And the combustion process is slower with a lean mixture than with a rich mixture.

Droplet size, as emanating from a gas turbine injector nozzle, ranges from less than one micron to 100 microns in diameter. One micron is equal to one-millionth of a meter, or 0.00004 inches. If all droplets could be held below 40–50 microns, the combustion process would be more uniform, and NO_x formation would be reduced. As droplet size is reduced, the time of exposure to high temperatures is reduced. The need to reduce droplet size is manifestly fundamental and very great. With large droplet size, the only way to restrict NO_x formation is to use extremely lean air/fuel ratios.

The additional air in the primary zone will then mix with the combustion products and dilute them further, which considerably lowers their temperature. But operating a turbine with extremely lean mixture in the primary zone still does not drastically reduce NO_x formation. Even if all droplets could be brought down to less than one micron in size, to simulate a vapor, the NO_x emissions are *not* reduced to exceptionally low values.

The reason for that is that with direct fuel injection, the vapor and the air are not homogeneously pre-mixed to the overall air/fuel ratio prior to combustion. The result is that the combustion process remains a diffusion flame, with the rich mixture elements burning first and the lean mixture elements afterwards, in an environment where temperature is dropping.

A brief study of the basics of the gas turbine combustion process is enough to indicate that the following measures are essential to complete emission control:

1. Pre-mixing of air and fuel.
2. Close control of air/fuel ratios.
3. Close control of combustor inlet temperature.
4. Flame stabilization.
5. Dilution and flame quenching.

1. PRE-MIXING OF AIR AND FUEL

Full vaporization of the fuel cannot be achieved without atomization of the fuel droplets. Vaporization is the next step after atomization. It generally consists of a thermally controlled kinetic process of molecules leaving the droplet surface and diffusing into the surrounding air. At low inlet temperatures, the rate of vaporization is determined by diffusion. At high temperatures, the vaporization rate depends on the rate of heat transfer from the air to the liquid.

Evaporation time is a critical factor, because the evaporation process must be completed before the mixture is admitted to the primary reaction zone if mixture homogeneity is to be accomplished. The smaller the droplets, the shorter the evaporation time. Droplets of up to 15 micron diameter evaporate in about one millisecond. Droplets of 25 microns diameter take perhaps 3 milliseconds to evaporate. The curve gets steeper as droplet diameter is increased, so that it takes 5 milliseconds for a 50-micron droplet and 10 milliseconds for a 100-micron droplet. A 200-micron droplet needs almost 70 milliseconds to evaporate.

Atomization greatly increases the surface-to-volume ratio of the fuel, which increases the heat transfer to the droplets, thereby greatly increasing the rate of vaporization. By injecting atomized fuel into a separate premixing zone, mixing and vaporization can take place simultaneously. This approach for obtaining a homogeneous pre-mixed charge requires that the preparation of the air/fuel mixture must be physically separated from the primary combustion zone. If it is not, combustion will spread to the droplet spray that has yet to mix with the air flow. The result will be high NO_x formation and a risk of destroying combustor parts not designed to withstand combustion flame temperatures.

2. CLOSE CONTROL OF AIR/FUEL RATIOS

This question is intimately connected with the matter of combustor inlet temperatures, but we shall try to deal with each separately at first.

Regardless of thermal interplay conditions, the air/fuel ratio has a direct effect on post-flame oxygen and nitrogen concentrations. It is true that NO concentrations can be significantly reduced by going to leaner air/fuel ratios if the same inlet air temperature is maintained.

Conventional gas turbine engine combustors operate with nearly stoichiometric air/fuel ratios in the primary zone. Fuel droplet combustion processes approach stoichiometric conditions.

The most desirable air/fuel ratio is something that varies according to conditions. The two considerations in determining the desired air/fuel ratio are a variable combustor inlet temperature and a desire for constant flame temperature. Note that oxygen concentrations, however, are directly dependent on air/fuel ratio.

Fuel flow depends on load, as signaled to the injection system by the accelerator position. The turbine is unthrottled, so that air admission is limited by compressor speed and air flow velocity only. That means there will be enormous variations in overall air/fuel ratios depending on driving conditions. During startup, the air/fuel ratio is about 35. After warmup, the air/fuel ratio at idle speed settles at around 265.

During acceleration, the air/fuel ratio drops to 56, but when maintaining a steady speed of 75 percent (of engine rated speed capacity) the air/fuel ratio is about 110. The ratio drops to 88 at full speed. During deceleration, the ratio rises to between 330 and 400, depending on duration. What makes the air/fuel ratio in the combustor so important? In plain terms, the air/fuel ratio would not matter much if it were not for its influence on flame temperature.

Lean air/fuel ratios lead to lower combustion temperature, which gives an exponential reduction in the rate of nitric oxide formation. With lower flame temperatures, it takes more time for NO_x formation to reach a given level. Conversely, the amount of NO_x generated in a given amount of time is diminished.

Very lean mixtures are evidently highly desirable from an emission-control viewpoint. But there are problems in getting a lean mixture to burn. Burning even a pre-mixed, lean mixture will be more difficult and require greater combustor volume than burning a stoichiometric mixture. There is a limit to lean-mixture flammability.

A homogeneous air/fuel mixture is considered flammable if it is capable of sustaining flame propagation without any external ignition source. The flammability limit refers to the borderline fuel concentration in the mixture necessary for flame propagation. A flammable mixture must be able to release sufficient heat to compensate for the heat loss to the unburned mixture, and still maintain high enough flame temperature to make sure that the rate of chemical reaction will sustain the required heat release. This means that combustor inlet temperature can have an important effect on the lean limit of flammability (flameout due to excessively lean mixture).

It is also possible to reduce NO_x formation by operating on a rich mixture, but this is a poor approach from a fuel-economy viewpoint, and has other drawbacks as well. With a rich air/fuel mixture, the flame temperature is reduced, because there is not enough oxygen to assure complete combustion. As a result, not all of the heat value contained in the fuel is available for increasing gas temperature. This also leads to high HC and CO emissions.

Combustion products from a richer-than-stoichiometric air/fuel mixture would have to be cooled before being diluted. Any attempt to dispense with the intercooling would result in an intolerable temperature rise in the after-burner section—intolerable because it would lead to large quantities of NO_x being formed. The rich-mixture approach would also require pre-mixing to avoid combustion at stoichiometric air/fuel ratios, as that would cause serious NO_x formation. In addition, there would be a problem of inadequate heat transfer from the rich-mixture combustion products prior to the admission of dilution air. To combat this problem, the combustor body would have to be longer than a practical gas turbine package might allow.

3.   CLOSE CONTROL OF COMBUSTOR INLET TEMPERATURE

It is easier to achieve low NO_x emissions at *higher combustor inlet temperatures*. There are two reasons for this:
1. The combustor lean-mixture blow-out limit is improved with higher inlet temperatures.
2. Fuel vaporization prior to the primary reaction zone is aided by higher combustor inlet temperature.

Yet there is great danger in excessively high inlet temperature because NO_x formation—at a constant air/fuel ratio—will increase exponentially as combustor inlet temperature is increased. That happens because the flame temperature is governed by two key factors: combustor inlet temperature and air/fuel ratio. It is because lean mixtures and full fuel evaporation are desirable that it becomes practical to operate with higher inlet temperatures. For instance, in one GM experiment, combustor inlet temperature was raised from 100 degrees F (37.8° C) to 1,000° F (538° C). This lowered the NO_x emissions by 75 percent. This also proves the value of the heat exchangers for emission control.

4.   FLAME STABILIZATION

Just as NO_x emissions can be lowered by reducing residence time in the primary zone, they can also be reduced by burning a steady flame. That's why stabilization is so important. Flame temperatures can only be controlled by stabilizing the combustion process. It becomes desirable to get the primary zone combustion products out of the primary zone as quickly as possible, and let them recirculate in a stabilization zone until the fuel has been completely consumed.

If the flame temperature can be held below 3,000 degrees F (1650° C) the amount of NO_x formed in the primary zone is negligible, according to Ford, on condition that all combustion takes place uniformly at the same air/fuel ratio.

NO_x formation tends to increase with primary zone residence time while CO and HC are reduced when residence time is extended. But residence time is less important than the primary zone temperature. At a fixed residence time, NO_x formation is relatively independent of all operating parameters except primary zone temperature.

In general, NO_x formation is a slower process than the combustion reactions. The rate of NO formation falls to near zero in the stabilization zone, and the reaction is quenched in the dilution zone. The oxidation of NO to NO_2 occurs so slowly that the exhaust gas contains mostly pure NO which then reacts with the atmosphere and is converted to NO_2 in open air.

Stabilization poses an awkward problem because the combustor inlet velocity is usually 200 to 400 ft/sec. This is higher than turbulent flame speed by at least an order of magnitude. To stabilize a flame at such high velocity, the air/fuel mixture must be within the flammability limits and the air flow must recirculate so as to supply hot combustion products with chemically active species to mix with the incoming charge.

The combustor has a stability range. The stability range can be widened by an increase in inlet temperature. It can also be widened by a rise in pressure.

Combustion pressure and oxygen concentration have a secondary effect on the rate of NO_x formation. The effect of pressure is more important at lean air/fuel ratios than is the case with rich mixtures. Low combustion pressure is desirable for low NO_x content regardless of air/fuel ratio.

It is generally agreed that large combustor volume will be necessary to control the flame temperature in the primary reaction zone. This has drawbacks for both package size and production cost. A high-volume combustor will require more space, which can complicate engine design and installation. The high-volume combustor uses more sheet metal, which translates directly into a cost penalty.

5. DILUTION AND FLAME QUENCHING

Dilution air has considerable influence on NO_x formation, as it quenches the flame and arrests the process. However, there is a risk as reducing the temperature in the dilution zone too much can cause increased emissions of CO and HC.

At the conclusion of the combustion process, it is desirable for the combustion products to revert to their original constituents, nitrogen and oxygen. This should take place in the dilution zone but unfortunately it is a very slow process. The residence time in the dilution zone is too short to allow this reverse process to be completed. To increase residence time is not practical, since it would involve several orders of magnitude for significant results to be obtained.

The matter of emission control is not settled when an experimental combustor undergoes its first successful test. The first question that comes up is repeatability. Can the same unit go through the same test again, with similar or identical results? A number of tests are necessary to prove full repeatability.

The federal driving cycle test conditions include a cold-start requirement, which means that the combustor must be tested for emission performance during ignition and initial warmup period. Emission performance during transient operating conditions must also be tested and proved satisfactory. Then the combustor has to prove its marginal stability limits (due to lean blowout). This is a basic operational requirement that may have been jeopardized during emission control testing and modifications. Other operational requirements are rapid response and exact control of the combustor's variable geometry during changes in operating conditions.

Before the combustor is cleared, it must also prove its emission performance sustainability during 100,000 miles, and the effect of manufacturing variability on emission performance must be minimized. Specific examples of low NO_x combustors developed by leading turbine manufacturers and EPA contractors will be discussed in the chapters dealing with the contributions of each company.

4

The Turbine

THE TURBINE WHEEL, as explained before, is based on the principle of a windmill. It is made to rotate by the air flow directed against it. The turbine has the advantage of not operating in the open atmosphere like a windmill, but inside a housing, with closely controlled gas flow in and out. From the combustor, the exhaust gases are ducted to the primary or first-stage turbine through a collector and a set of nozzle vanes.

The collector can be volute in shape (vortex chamber) or take the form of a plenum chamber. The purpose of this transitional collector is to provide uniform entry conditions to the turbine. Most designs use vortex chambers that set up a swirling flow which reduces the amount of gas flow deflection that remains for the nozzle vanes to produce. The nozzle vanes work as a stator member for the turbine, redirecting the gas flow so as to impinge most effectively on the turbine blades.

There are many advantages to using variable geometry for the nozzle vanes. The first is improved response time. Acceleration in a turbine engine with a fixed-geometry stator leading to the first-stage turbine is accomplished by increasing the turbine inlet temperature (through an increased fuel flow rate).

The increase in power is proportional to the increase in turbine inlet temperature. A device that can open the nozzle vanes under wide-open-throttle acceleration to a point beyond what is feasible with fixed stator geometry can increase the available temperature rise. The non-variable stator is condemned to be a compromise. The variable stator will adjust itself to the requirements of the situation. With variable-angle nozzles, the turbine can be made to produce higher output power at mid-range shaft speed.

The Rover Company has been a leading exponent of variable nozzle

vanes for the first-stage turbine. Their design was a simple mechanical
device with two positions—minimum and maximum—without any intermediate stops. Chrysler pioneered variable nozzle vanes for the second-stage
(power) turbine, and this device, its specifications and characteristics will be
dealt with in a later chapter.

The turbine works by changing the tangential component of gas velocity.
Power output is determined by the product of the torque produced by this
change and the turbine blade velocity.

Since the turbine is gas-driven, the internal aerodynamics of the entire
power unit assumes priority in all studies, design and development work.
Increased understanding of these aerodynamics has led to a gain in efficiency over the years. And higher efficiency means improved fuel economy, reduced engine "package" space requirement, and reduced exhaust
volumetric flow rates.

There are two types of turbines: axial-flow and radial-flow. The axial-flow
type is predominant at present and exclusively used in the aircraft field and
other fields involving high power output. Some have a high number of
stages and closely resemble the reaction-type (Parsons) steam turbine used in
large electric generating stations.

The radial-flow type closely resembles a centrifugal compressor but with
the gas flowing centripetally rather than centrifugally. It is essentially similar
to the Francis type of water turbine used in most large hydroelectric plants.

Most automotive gas turbine engines have axial-flow power (second-stage)
turbines, and the axial-flow type is generally preferred also for the compressor (first-stage) turbine. But radial-flow turbines have found their way into
automotive applications. For instance, Ford used a radial in-flow turbine for
the high-pressure section of its Model 704 gas turbine, and Rover chose the
radial in-flow turbine for the first stage in its free-shaft turbines. The radial-
flow turbine is able to handle higher pressure per stage more efficiently. But
its flow characteristics are much more speed-sensitive than the flow characteristics in an axial-flow turbine.

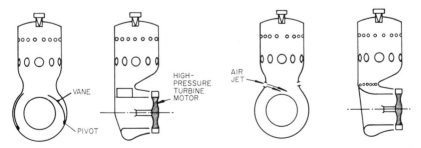

Vane guide (left) or air jet (right) directs combustion gases from radial flow to axial flow, with
swirl, to the first-stage turbine nozzle ring.

Williams Research gas turbine assembly, with turbine wheels in the foreground.

Sam Williams displays a turbine wheel produced as a one-piece investment casting.

The axial-flow turbine works with higher stress levels at the blade roots but lends itself more easily to use in combination with variable-geometry nozzles. The radial-flow turbine is easier to cool, but more sensitive to clearances. Axial-flow turbines permit shorter and simpler ducting, both in and out. Axial-flow turbines generally have lower inertia. For a given output, the axial-flow turbine can work at lower blade speed, which permits a reduction in turbine diameter.

Axial-flow turbines are able to work with higher tangential components of gas velocity, which is a key element in gas turbine operation. The reason is that radial in-flow turbines generally require radial blades, and that means the tangential component cannot exceed blade peripheral speed to any significant degree.

Turning the gas flow from a radial flow path to an axial flow path requires a considerable increase in the turbine wheel's axial dimension. On the other hand, the axial-flow portion of the radial turbine is located at a short radius, which gives a significant reduction in turbine wheel inertia. It has been proved that axial-flow turbines can work with tangential components up to twice the blade speed.

Since the typical modern passenger car turbine engine is a regenerative free-shaft power plant, the following discussion of turbine design, characteristics, and performance will pertain to this type of unit, unless otherwise specified. The operating conditions being more severe for the first-stage turbine than for the second-stage turbine, the discussion is concentrated on the primary (compressor shaft) turbine wheel. It is assumed that both are of the axial-flow type.

Why is the primary turbine always driving the compressor shaft, and the secondary turbine the free shaft (output shaft)? George J. Huebner Jr. of Chrysler gives a very clear explanation:

The power turbine must operate over a wide range of speeds from stall to maximum as required by the vehicle speed. This results in a wide range of flow angles leaving the stage, especially when compared to the compressor turbine.
It is far preferable to have the relatively consistent output of the compressor turbine fed into an interstage passage and second stage nozzles, and the widely varying output of the power stage fed into an exhaust diffuser, than vice versa. The reason, of course, is that the efficiency of a stage depends on the character of the entering flow. Since the compressor turbine handles the major share of the combined turbine output, the loss in efficiency resulting from a poor inlet flow would be unacceptable. It is possible, on the other hand, to design the power turbine so that the velocity energy remaining in the stage discharge is considerably smaller than in the discharge from the compressor turbine. When the discharge flow is then led through an exhaust diffuser and a portion of this velocity energy recovered as static pressure, the effect of the discharge on the efficiency of the engine can be minimized when the power turbine is the final stage.

The engineer's choice of blade peripheral speed and turbine rotational speed will determine the wheel diameter. But the calculations do not stop there. The calculated turbine wheel diameter may turn out to involve very high inertia, in which case the engineer may go back and modify his initial choice of rotational and peripheral speeds.

Low inertia is particularly important for the first-stage turbine, which drives the compressor shaft. Since they are mounted on the same shaft, inertia is no less important for the turbine than for the compressor. Low inertia means quick response. High inertia means slow response. Inertia is measured as polar moment of inertia. That expression may require some explanation. The inertia we are measuring involves a twisting force or moment around a center or pole. Therefore, polar moment. The inertia force is a resistance to any change in the status quo, which shows up as a reluctance to rotate if at standstill, a reluctance to stop revolving, and a reluctance to change the rotational speed up or down when revolving.

A high combined polar moment of inertia of the compressor and turbine means that a large amount of energy is absorbed during acceleration. This energy storage will in turn reduce the rates of acceleration. The polar moment of inertia of a solid disc is proportional to the product of its density, its thickness, and the fourth power of its diameter.

The importance of density explains why low-density materials, such as aluminum alloys, are favored for use in turbine wheels. The problem is that the temperature stability requirements of the turbine wheel necessitate the use of materials having three times the density of aluminum.

The importance of thickness indicates that the ideal axial-flow turbine wheel should resemble a thin wafer. The problem is that as thickness is cut back, it becomes necessary to add more blades, and there's a limit to how many blades can be added. But the major factor is still diameter. An increase in turbine wheel diameter from 5.5 inches to 6.5 inches would raise the polar moment of inertia from a value of 100 to a value of 172.

Since a small diameter inevitably means low peripheral blade velocity at a given shaft speed, it should be combined with high peak tangential velocity, and a wide range of tangential velocity from the blade root end to the periphery. Restricting the diameter of the turbine wheels makes it necessary to use a large number of blades, to avoid exceeding the limits on each individual blade.

The gas flow produces a torque on the turbine wheel, which is developed as a mean net effective pressure on the blade surfaces. This leads to the conclusion that for a given gas pressure, the turbine wheel must have a certain minimum blade area in order to guard against overstress. Blade area can be increased by (1) adding more blades, (2) widening the blades, and (3) increasing the turbine wheel diameter. Again, there are limits to how far you can go in any direction and still retain an efficient turbine of practical size and shape.

The number of blades is limited by the gas flow passage area requirements. In addition, the blade profile and trailing edge thickness can cause blocking of the passages even if the passage area has been calculated to be adequate. Trailing edge thickness is made as thin as possible consistent with thermal stress considerations and manufacturing tolerances.

The turbine works in an environment of high stress and strain loads, which can cause turbine wheel failure. The stresses can be divided into four different categories.

1. Thermal stress.
2. Centrifugal stress.
3. Vibration stress.
4. Gas bending stress.

A turbine wheel that can give reliable and efficient performance over, say 3,000 hours, represents a highly refined combination of skilled engineering design and choice of material.

High-temperature gas enters the turbine through the nozzle vanes at high velocity. The temperature depends on combustor characteristics. The velocity depends on the transition from combustor to turbine (collector and nozzle) as well as the annulus area of the turbine wheel.

The axial velocity component at the nozzle vanes is determined by the air flow mass and the turbine annulus area, while the tangential component is entirely dependent on the geometry of the collector (vortex chamber or plenum chamber).

There is a practical limit on gas velocity. High velocities tend to produce lower reaction which translates into lower turbine efficiency. This again points up the design compromise that is inherent in the dimensions of every turbine wheel: the turbine with the smallest diameter and the shortest blades, which has the lowest inertia, demands the highest gas velocity. High exit velocity from the turbine will cause high losses in the transition and exhaust ducts.

Some efficiency can be regained with high velocity gas flow by allowing higher turbine rotational speeds, but this is not generally regarded as a good solution in automotive turbines, as it will involve higher transmission losses.

Thermal stresses in the turbine wheel are largely dependent on turbine inlet temperature. They are induced by temperature gradients in the turbine blades, predominantly during transient conditions of high compressor speed and high load.

Such conditions exist right after starting, for instance, when the working parts are cool and the turbine wheel temperature gradient, as the high-temperature gas flows through the turbine, reaches its steepest climb. Thermal stress failure tends to show up as low-cycle fatigue cracking on the edges of the turbine blades—both the leading and trailing edges showing similar susceptibility to such failure. To guard against thermal stress failure, the turbine engineer can (a) select a material that will not fail under the existing conditions, or (b) provide a method of cooling the turbine blade.

Turbine blade cooling is usually considered too costly for automotive gas turbines, and most turbine manufacturers have chosen to explore new materials. Both methods will be fully discussed in later chapters.

Then there is another phenomenon, known as turbine wheel creep. It is a term used to describe conditions in which the wheel, or part of it, becomes plastic and deforms, most frequently in terms of elongation. A thermal overload on a local part can cause deformation beyond the elastic limit of the material.

Centrifugal stress generally results indirectly from high rotational speeds, and more precisely from centrifugal force leads that can be identified as direct tension in the turbine wheel due to extreme peripheral speeds. At a fixed rotational speed, the centrifugal stress in the rotor blades tends to vary directly with the annulus area. In other words, the size of the annulus area will largely be determined by the stress limits in the turbine blade roots. In addition, non-planar components of the centrifugal force can give rise to bending loads and shear stresses on the turbine wheel.

These factors can be controlled by turbine wheel design, materials, and fabrication. The smaller the turbine wheel, the lower the peripheral speed of the blades. The blades are airfoil designs, mostly patterned on a parabolic mean line, with a minimum of after-throat curvature. Blade section incidence is usually set at -3 to -5 degrees for the first-stage turbine in order to reduce airfoil drag.

Vibratory stress is usually induced by fluctuations in load, such as pressure pulsations in the gas flow. The turbine blades are exposed to a variety of external excitations which induce stress fluctuations within the blades. Stress levels are determined by the amplitude of the load fluctuations and the hysteresis damping in the turbine blade material. Research by Ford Motor Co. indicates that most turbine wheel vibratory stress failures occur under resonance conditions, which is a condition defined as the coincidence of the frequency of load fluctuations with the natural frequency of the blade.

Gas bending stress is due to static pressure differences within the turbine stage, and changes in gas flow momentum. The tangential velocity change in the gas flow through the turbine wheel is limited by the allowable margin of friction losses (gas-to-skin friction) in the following interstage passage. These factors in turn limit the amount of swirl that can be allowed in the gas flow exiting from the first-stage turbine wheel.

The interstage between the primary and secondary turbines has the task of redirecting the gas flow so as to impart maximum efficiency to the second-stage (power turbine). Its exact configuration is almost entirely dependent on the design and characteristics of the other components.

The inlet to the transitional ducting is located at a small radius (close to the shaft center) because of the inertia requirements of the first-stage turbine. The outlet is located at the periphery—or close to it—because of the stall torque requirements of the second-stage (power) turbine. The interstage configuration is further influenced by the designer's choice of variable or nonvariable nozzles for the second-stage turbine. On some turbines this interstage section includes a bleed–off valve. Its purpose is to permit the engine to idle at lower compressor speed.

Bleeding off gas between the first-stage and second-stage turbines reduces the power and the fuel flow rate when the load is braked, i.e. the vehicle is standing still because it is held back by the brakes. At the same time, there is still torque being applied to the second-stage turbine, and that's wasted. It only serves to put back pressure on the first-stage turbine.

Such a bleed–off valve takes the form of a ring of radial openings in the outer shroud of the interstage ducting. The openings are covered by a band of flat cross-sectional shape, which can be lifted off to open the holes and let the gas escape. Opening the bleedoff valve will reduce the back pressure on the first-stage turbine, and thereby permit the primary turbine inlet temperature to be reduced for the same compressor shaft speed. This means that the fuel flow rate can be cut back, since less fuel is needed to reach a lower temperature. The result is a fuel saving at idle.

The second-stage turbine has no mechanical connection with the first stage turbine. It is carried on the "free shaft" which is also the output shaft. It is driven by the exhaust gas from the first-stage turbine, but its requirements are quite different. Its gas velocity, rotational speed, and stress levels are less narrowly defined than is the case for the primary turbine.

The gas generator section (comprised of the compressor and the first-stage turbine) may be operating at speeds of 40,000 to 80,000 rpm for 75 to 90 percent of the time, while the power turbine has to work at speeds from zero to maximum (0 to perhaps 72,000 rpm).

While the rotational speed of the power turbine is highly variable, its flow area and mass flow are not. The power turbine has more diversified tasks than the first-stage turbine, since it is charged with the torque-producing duties as required at the output shaft. Consequently, the power turbine operates sometimes with very high efficiency and sometimes with very low efficiency, while the first-stage turbine always operates close to its peak efficiency.

The free turbine has to function as a torque converter, which will reduce its efficiency, since the maximum torque conversion ratio is about 2.5 : 1. If the power turbine has an efficiency of 85 percent at design speed, its efficiency under those conditions will be 42.5 percent.

Some interplay or tradeoff here is possible, because the power unit should

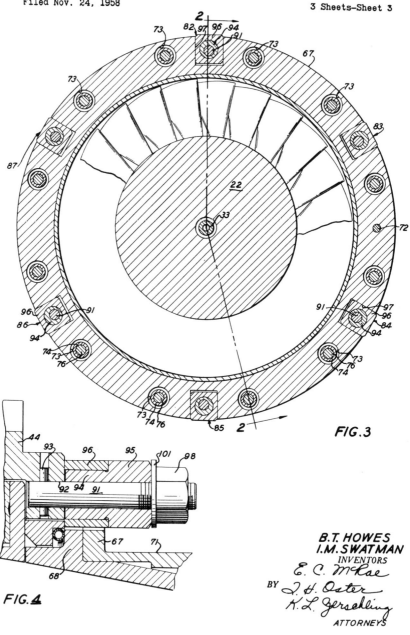

FIG.3

FIG.4

B.T. HOWES
I.M. SWATMAN
INVENTORS
E. C. McRae
BY J. H. Oster
K. L. Gerselling
ATTORNEYS

Detail of turbine wheel construction patented by Ford Motor Co.

62

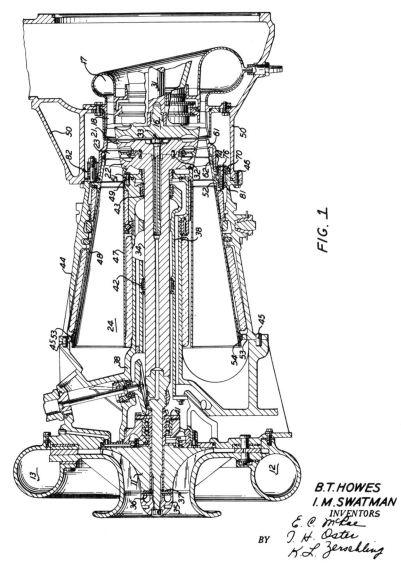

FIG. 1

B.T.HOWES
I.M.SWATMAN
INVENTORS
E. C. McKee
BY   J. H. Oster
K. L. Zerschling

ATTORNEYS

Turbine assembly on Ford automotive gas turbine engine.

63

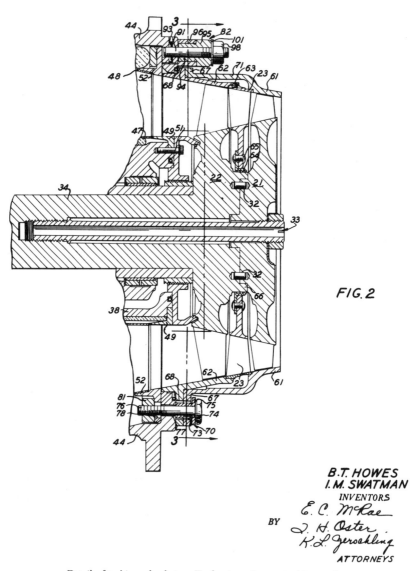

FIG. 2

B.T. HOWES
I. M. SWATMAN
INVENTORS
E. C. McRae
BY   *J. H. Oster*
K. L. Zeroehling
ATTORNEYS

Detail of turbine wheels in a Ford automotive gas turbine engine.

64

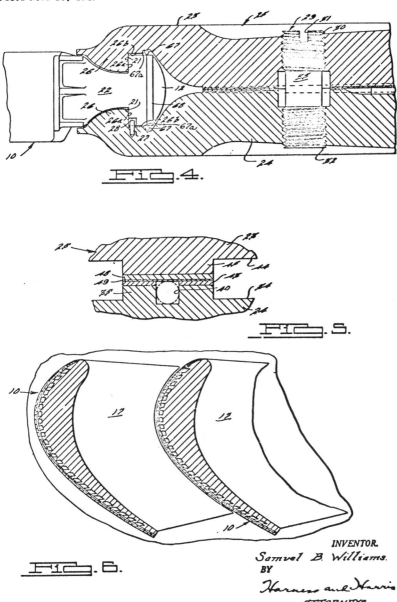

Detail of Sam Williams' patent for turbine blade cooling.

be judged on its total efficiency, i.e. the first-stage efficiency and the second-stage efficiency combined. The first-stage turbine must be credited with a certain exit kinetic energy which can be recovered in the second-stage turbine. In some applications, it may be preferable to take out less energy in the first-stage turbine and maintain higher exit kinetic energy.

In the second-stage turbine, it is desirable to maximize efficiency and minimize exit kinetic energy. The principal reason for that is the desire to obtain the lowest specific fuel consumption. But a contributing reason is the need for a low absolute exit velocity (for environmental reasons). This requires a large turbine exit annulus area, which tends to increase centrifugal stress on the turbine blades and therefore could compromise reliability and longevity in the power turbine wheel. Charles A. Amann of the General Motors Research Laboratories has suggested that incorporation of an annual diffuser *behind* the power turbine would afford an opportunity for partial recovery of the kinetic energy that would otherwise be lost. This diffuser would have the effect of depressing the static depression behind the second-stage turbine wheel by increasing the enthalpy head available to it.

Turbine Materials

The five most essential requirements for turbine wheel materials are (1) low thermal expansion, (2) high thermal conductivity, (3) high modulus, (4) high strength, and (5) good chemical stability. Before we can discuss the specific materials used, it is necessary to briefly review turbine wheel manufacturing methods and their evolution from the beginnings of the gas turbine industry to the present state of the art.

In the early days of gas turbines, turbine blades were fully machined from individual forgings. This was a slow and costly process, and extremely close tolerances were needed to assure uniformity. That in turn led to inspection methods that approached a laboratory examination. Most turbines of this period had blades fastened to the turbine wheel hub by a device known as the fir-tree root. The root of each blade was formed with a fir-tree profile—a form of splines that effectively located the blade root radially and resisted centrifugal force. The blades were inserted axially and secured by peening on each side.

The blades had to be grouped in weight classes with minute ranges, and after assembly, the turbine wheel had to be dynamically balanced. Balancing adjustments were accomplished by removing some blades and substituting others.

Several other methods of fixing the blades to the turbine wheel hub were tried, however. Some used a bulb-root—an unsplined insert of more or less circular cross section. Some makers welded the blades to the hub. Others fixed the blades by shear pins inserted through holes drilled diagonally

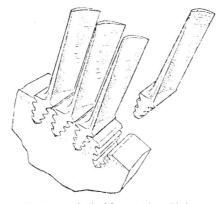

Fir-tree method of fixing turbine blades.

through the blade root and hub, and brazed after assembly. But the fir-tree method has become the typical design for large-scale aircraft turbine blade roots, and is still the most common on other types of gas turbines of a certain size.

For smaller turbines, the industry gradually developed ways to cast aerodynamic surfaces to accurate shapes without any need for finish machining. As this technology progressed, the turbine manufacturers acquired the ability to cast the turbine wheel in one single piece.

Similar methods of fabrication and assembly were used for the turbine nozzle. But there are important differences in the nozzle application, for it is a starter member and the vanes are therefore free of centrifugal loads.

It was found that the individual vanes did not have to be machined from forged parts. Rolls Royce was a pioneer in precision-casting the vanes. They were still cast individually at first, then fitted in helical slots on the inner nozzle ring and secured by side clamp rings. The slots in the outer nozzle ring served only as guides, so as to permit the vanes from freedom of thermal expansion in the radial direction.

When one-piece cast turbine wheels appeared, the industry also went to single-piece integral castings for the entire nozzle assembly. Of course, this is only possible with fixed nozzle geometry.

The maximum cycle temperature in the gasoline-fuel piston engine is higher than the melting point for all the materials that make up the combustion chamber surface, including the ceramic of the spark plug. But the action is not continuous—the chamber is cooled between each firing by a fresh charge.

The gas turbine, in contrast, runs continuously at maximum cycle temperature and many of its working parts operate at levels near the maximum cycle temperature without relief. In addition, the turbine blades are highly stressed, and since the strength of metal drops off rapidly as its temperature is increased, there is a limit to the temperature the turbine wheel can withstand.

The loss of strength with higher temperature is accompanied by an even faster loss of resistance to reaction with oxygen and other elements in the hot gases. But the worst threat is a phenomenon known as thermal shock—a result of sudden and rapid temperature changes. Thermal shock is most likely to occur in parts of non-uniform thickness that do not heat or cool evenly. The turbine wheel is clearly a candidate for thermal shock.

The turbine blades receive the full impact of the expanding gases from the combustor. That seems serious enough in itself, but when you consider that turbine efficiency goes up when temperature rises, you get the idea of how important turbine materials are to the future of the automotive gas turbine.

Sam Williams of Williams Research Corp. told me in 1971 that adding 100° F (37.8° C) to the turbine inlet temperature would add 10 percent of the horsepower output of the engine. Other experts give similar estimates— some even indicating higher power gains. A little arithmetic shows you that if you get 80 hp from a certain engine with a turbine inlet temperature of 1450° F (788° C) you can raise power output to 128 hp if you can find turbine materials that can withstand an inlet temperature of 2050° F (1121° C).

Beyond the high temperatures, turbine wheels must prove capable of withstanding the stress imposed by external and internal debris. By external debris is meant foreign matter that enters the compressor from the atmosphere. It is more prevalent in aircraft turbines than in ground vehicles due to the differences in filtration. Aircraft engines are unfiltered and risk problems with stones and other debris on the runway, and with birds in the air. The filtration necessary for a road vehicle turbine would effectively limit the particle size of external debris.

Internal debris has two sources. The first is combustion deposits which may break away with the gas stream. Such deposits consist mostly of carbon, which usually disintegrates on impact with the engine's working parts. The second source is more serious. Internal parts, moving or stationary, may suffer partial or total failure, and release debris resembling shrapnel into the very heart of the turbine. This can cause serious impact damage.

Resistance to creep is another important factor in the choice of materials for aircraft turbines. Creep is defined as plasticity in the turbine wheel as a result of overheating combined with high centrifugal forces. The creep phenomenon is not expected to cause serious problems in automotive gas turbines, because the turbine wheels have shorter blades and smaller dimensions overall.

In the early days of gas turbines, it was discovered that ordinary grades of steel were not able to function reliably for turbine wheels. Over the years, various exotic alloys have been developed, so that metallic turbine blades still dominate, but most experts believe we are on the threshold of the ceramic age in turbine materials.

Turbine blades made of complex alloys containing high percentages of chromium and nickel, with smaller percentages of more exotic metals such as silicon, tungsten, and molybdenum, have proved capable of sustaining turbine inlet temperatures of 1832° F (1000° C). Early favorites were Nimonic 75, Nimonic 80A and Nimonic 90, all nickel-based alloys developed by the Mond Nickel Company, Ltd. since 1939. Each new number represented an important step of progress in terms of creep resistance.

Nowadays, most automotive gas turbines use turbine wheels made of Inconel 713 or variations on its nickel-based formula. Inconel 713C, was introduced in 1956 by the International Nickel Co. and has largely been replaced by Inconel 738, a vacuum-cast precipitation-hardened nickel-base alloy introduced in 1968. It offers higher tensile and yield strength properties than Inconcel 713C, and offers the extra sulfidation resistance formerly obtained only in higher-chromium content alloys.

The delicate balance of Inconel 738 is nominally (shown in percentages):

Nickel	60.0%
Chromium	16.0%
Cobalt	8.5%
Aluminum	3.4%
Titanium	3.4%
Tungsten	2.6%
Molybdenum	1.75%
Tantalum	1.75%
Cadmium	0.9%
Lesser constituents	1.7%
TOTAL:	100.0%

One notable exception to the use of Inconel 713 or 738 is Chrysler's use of its own alloys. Ever since the late 1940s, Chrysler has undertaken most of its metallurgical research in-house. By 1957 Chrysler had a new alloy known as CRM-3 (Chrysler Research Metal number 3) that enabled an experimental turbine to run 150 hours non-stop with a turbine inlet temperature of 2300° F (1260° C).

Early in the program Chrysler realized large quantities of cobalt could not be used if the turbine engines were to be mass-produced. The world supply of cobalt would not be sufficient to meet the requirements of automobile production. Accordingly, Chrysler set out with an ambitious goal: to develop a low-cost, low strategic alloy content material for turbine blades which would have the hot strength, stress rupture, and creep characteristics of a much used and well-known cobalt-base alloy. This was done, and two such metals were tested in Chrysler turbines. One had a stress-to-rupture value of 30,000 psi at 1500° F (815.5° C) for 100 hours, and the other had a value of 27,000 psi under the same conditions.

Out of the 50 Chrysler cars built in 1963 and equipped with A-831 turbines, 47 were operated with first-stage turbine wheels integrally cast from CRM-6D. The other three cars had turbine wheels made from an expensive, aircraft type, high temperature wheel alloy. They were of the same general design as the Chrysler alloy wheels and although they did not fail, their operation was not completely satisfactory in this design because they caused other engine problems which were not present with the Chrysler material. In addition to these materials tests the opportunity was taken to test progressive design modifications and to explore various turbine wheel fabrication techniques.

Huebner told a group of engineers in 1963—at an early stage in the test program:

"In order to be conservative on power turbine disk and blade life, we found it necessary to choose a design which is heavier than we would have liked, equal to about 140 lb. equivalent car weight in direct drive. As more vehicle experience with this engine is acquired, and the vibrational sources which affect life are more accurately identified, it may be possible to reduce this figure."

Later, Chrysler developed a new and different, but still low cost, version of CRM-6D which proved satisfactory for the first-stage nozzle, which reaches metal temperatures in excess of 1800° F (982° C) under acceleration conditions. A further modification of CRM-6D has proved successful for the variable nozzle interstage vanes.

According to George J. Huebner, Jr., CRM-6D is a high strength, high temperature, low cost turbine wheel alloy. The patent granted for this alloy shows that the material is principally iron and that the alloying elements used are readily available domestically. Chrysler reached its objective of getting equal strength at far lower cost, but the CRM-6D alloys still do not allow higher turbine inlet temperatures than Inconel-713C.

Where can metallurgists go from here? According to Noel Penny, chromium is limited to 1976° F (1080° C). Niobium, a very rare grey metal with a melting point of 3542° F (1950° C) can be used as a basis for alloys that will endure turbine inlet temperatures of 2192° F (1200° C). Entering the world of ceramics, far higher temperatures become realistic for turbine operation, although glass ceramics can only run with turbine inlet temperatures up to 2012° F (1100° C).

This applies particularly to glass ceramics containing lithium alumina sili-

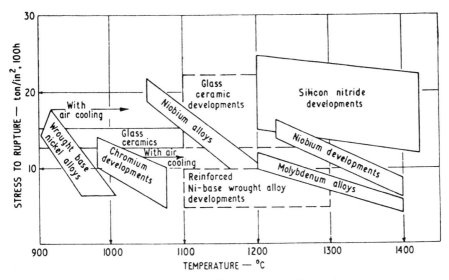

Noel Penny paints this map of turbine material characteristics.

cates. Tests show that the temperature tolerance can be raised by reducing the lithium content and replacing it with magnesium. The resulting material would be called a magnesium alumino silicate glass ceramic with a softening point of 2372° F (1300° C) maximum.

Molybdenum and metal silicates may reach 2400–2500° F (1300–1400° C) but are still both experimental and controversial in nature. According to John V. Hansen of the Norton Co.,

"Superalloys and coatings have reached the upper limits of their effective operating temperatures. Ceramics are the only known materials with all the necessary characteristics of high-temperature strength, corrosion resistance, machineability, and economics to meet the requirements of many future systems."

Ceramics may hold the key to the future, but there are serious problems associated with their use in gas turbines. For one thing, ceramics are brittle. Metal alloys are ductile, and metallic turbine wheels, for instance, usually yield around the points of stress concentration. Ceramics are not so forgiving. The probability of failure also increases with the size of each specific ceramic component, and there are great difficulties associated with the establishment of an acceptable mechanical interface between a ceramic part and a metallic part.

This consideration serves to point up the advisability of combining the ceramic turbine wheel with a ceramic nozzle assembly, ceramic combustor and ceramic ducting, if possible.

Ceramics fabrication techniques are still somewhat lacking in view of turbine requirements. Ceramics machineability is generally poor, and the goal is to avoid machining of ceramic parts, but that poses extra demands on the finish obtained in the forming process. Three different techniques are in use at the moment: (1) reaction bonding, (2) hot-pressing, and (3) vapor deposition. In reaction bonding, fine particles are consolidated and converted to a new bonding through a reaction process with gas.

In hot-pressing, the fine particles are consolidated by a process that combines temperature and pressure application. In vapor deposition, a heated substrate receives solid matter in vaporized form, resulting from the decomposition of a gas or the interaction of gaseous phases.

After many experiments involving ceramics based on oxide, carbide, nitride, and boride, it became clear that silicon carbide and silicon nitride

Flame test of experimental silicon nitride turbine blade at General Electric research and development center.

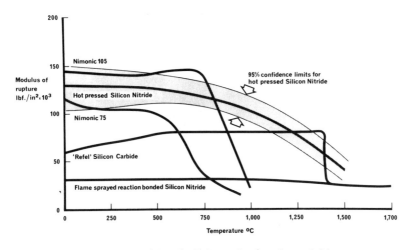

Variation of strength with temperature for various materials

Turbine material characteristics as mapped by Joseph Lucas, Ltd.

were outstanding. The reaction-bonding process was developed first. This method produces silicon nitride by molding, slip-casting, or flame-spraying powdered silicon, and then reacting it with nitrogen.

Hot-pressed silicon nitride is produced by first reacting silicon powder with nitrogen to form silicon nitride powder. This powder is then mixed with certain additives and hot-pressed to the desired shape in graphite dies. Self-bonded silicon carbide is formed by mixing powdered silicon carbide with graphite, suitable plasticizers, and binding agents. The result is an extrudable clay, which can be shaped by injection molding, extrusion, or pressing. Hot-pressed silicon nitride was developed by the Joseph Lucas Group research center in Warwickshire, and the Norton Company holds the U.S. license for the process.

Silicon nitride and silicon carbide exceed all other known materials in tolerance of high turbine inlet temperatures. Although as turbine materials they must be considered as being in their infancy, experience indicates that they can successfully operate in an environment exceeding 2600° F (1450° C). John V. Hansen of the Norton Company has said that his sights are now set on the 3000° F (1650° C) mark.

Tests have shown that silicon carbide and silicon nitride can survive thermal shocks exceeding 100 cycles to 1868° F (1020° C) while tapered discs of alumina crack when subjected to thermal shock in excess of 932° F (500° C).

Both silicon carbide and silicon nitride have extremely high strength, with a value of about 50,000 psi modulus of rupture at 2400° F (1315° C). Above 2500° F (1400° C) the strength of self-bonded silicon carbide falls sharply because its 8–10 percent content of free silicon will melt. Going higher still, it will retain moderate strength up to 3100° F (1700° C).

Hot-pressed silicon nitride (containing 1 percent magnesium oxide) will begin to lose strength at 1832° F (1000° C). This fact is assumed to be caused by the presence of magnesium silicate vitreous phases during the heat rise. Hot-pressed silicon nitride shows higher strength throughout the working temperature range than either hot-pressed or self-bonded silicon carbide. And its potential for improvement is far greater, as indicated by new reactive hot-pressing techniques now being applied at the laboratory level.

Silicon carbide, however, has higher bending strength than silicon nitride. Silicon carbide can resist a bending force of 80,000 psi at 2,500° F (1400° C) while the bending strength of silicon nitride—at the same temperature—is limited to 55,000 psi. Hot-pressed silicon nitride has much higher oxidation resistance than silicon nitride formed by reaction bending, which gives lower density.

In addition to its high-temperature strength and stability, hot-pressed silicon nitride has excellent wear properties and can be fabricated into complex shapes with a minimum of machining or finishing. At the same time, critical improvements in the machineability of intricate ceramic parts have been made possible by recent developments in cutting and shaping tools (diamond tips and diamond wheels).

Turbine Blade Cooling

The heat which is transmitted to the turbine blades from the hot gases will be absorbed and conducted through the wheel to the other rotating parts. This heat flux represents a loss to the cycle and to the mechanical efficacy of the design, as the gases tend to give up heat to mechanical parts where it is both a waste and a problem in terms of clearances and bearing functions. Uncooled blades are exposed to a higher risk of erosion and warpage or other forms of deterioration which will necessitate eventual turbine wheel replacement.

The search for a means of turbine blade cooling began while the gas turbine was still in its infancy. The search may cease if ceramic parts can fulfill their promises, but the question remains topical as long as metal turbine wheels are used. One of the first patents for turbine blade cooling was taken out by Frank Whittle in 1939. In the prior art, according to Whittle, there were proposals for inducing a cooling air flow over the blades by fitting centrifuging vanes on the turbine wheel itself, but he wrote them off as impractical.

Instead, Whittle proposed the use of auxiliary blades, integral with the

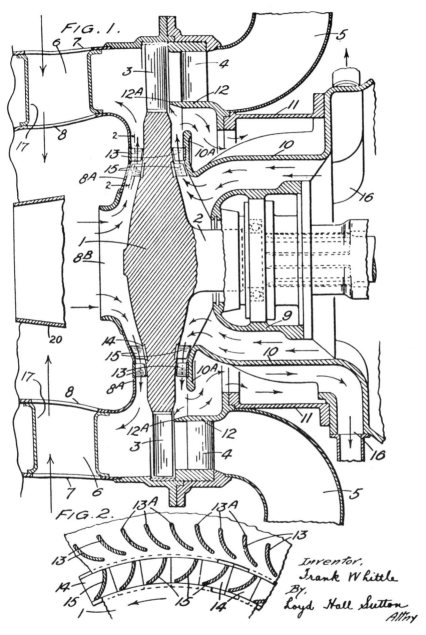

General view of Frank Whittle's method of turbine blade cooling.

turbine wheel, to set up a radially outward flow of air over the turbine wheel surface, and complementary fixed vanes mounted on the turbine casing to receive the air and convert its swirl velocity to radial velocity prior to diffusion over the turbine blades.

Another type of turbine blade construction employs a vane portion having an integral cavity for cooling air. As an alternative, the blade could be provided with two or more passages through its structure. With such devices, cooling air would be discharged from the tip of the blades into the exhaust gases, where it would cool them. This type of internal air circulation would require low pressure, but might need a fairly large pump, which is impractical.

A patent taken out by Sam Williams provides for utilization of the heat from the turbine blades by imparting a velocity head to the cooling air (due to thermal expansion of the air mass). This velocity head may be used to impart a jet effect or reaction boost to the rotating machinery to increase its speed. This effect can be obtained by careful attention to the angle of discharge from the passages. Williams' patent uses turbine blades traversed by a large number of minute passages. This will cut down the amount of cooling air that will have to be supplied, and reduce the pressure required.

With minute passages, the cooling air will have a more intimate scrubbing action on the passage walls, causing a sharper rise in cooling air temperature. This will produce a sharp buildup in pressure velocity, but the cooling air flow will still have lower velocity than the exhaust gases. As a result there will be an extractor effect on the coolant discharge passages on the trailing edge of the blades. This means that a separate pump for pushing cooling air through the turbine blades can be eliminated.

The cooling air may be introduced into the exhaust gas flow without giving rise to turbulence, while the heat loss is eliminated. The exhaust gas temperature will be higher because the cooling air will have a smaller heat difference from the exhaust gases in the turbine mainstream. That means more heat will be passed to the heat exchanger instead of being dispersed throughout the mechanical parts. The heat loss will be recovered and turned into positive work.

I have mentioned before that the cost of cooling systems for the turbine blades tends to be prohibitive. In early-development aircraft turbine wheels the passages were drilled. This is slow, expensive, and opens the door to fatigue failure in the turbine blades. Williams recommends casting by the lost-wax method, in which the passages would be filled with wax, which can then easily be flushed out when the wheel has been cast. By this method, cooled turbine wheels can be made at moderate cost.

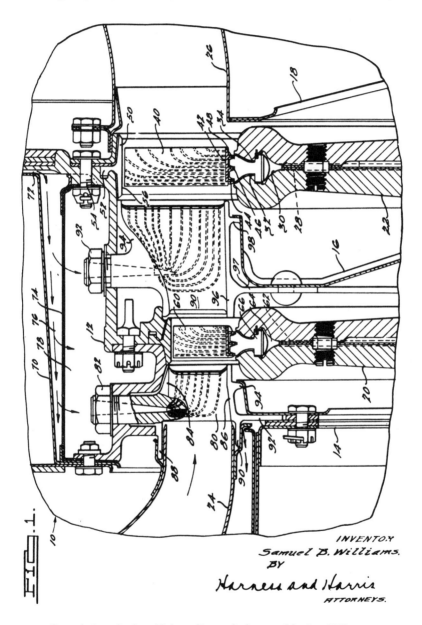

INVENTOR
Samuel B. Williams.
BY

Harness and Harris
ATTORNEYS.

General view of turbine blade cooling method patented by Sam Williams.

77

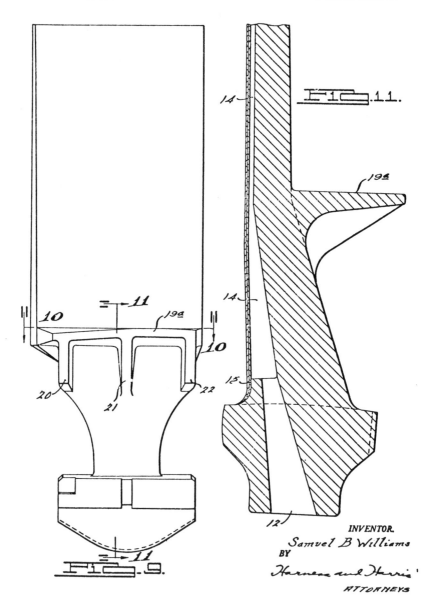

Detail of Williams' air-cooled turbine blade.

701,503   COMPLETE SPECIFICATION
8 SHEETS   This drawing is a reproduction of
the Original on a reduced scale.
SHEETS I & 3

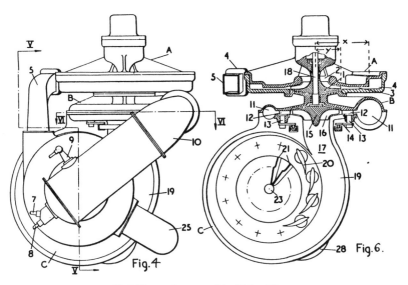

Variable nozzle patented by Richard Barr.

VARIABLE-GEOMETRY NOZZLES

Variable nozzles have been used on both first-stage and second-stage turbines. The purpose and effect of variable geometry is quite different depending on which of the two turbines it is used for. First, let us consider the mechanism itself.

One of the first means of making the turbine stator nozzle blades angle continuously variable was patented in England in 1949 by Richard Barr of Centrax Power Units. In Barr's design, the vanes were mounted on stub pins carrying short levers. The free ends of the levers had pins that engaged in radial slots in an annulus that carries the nozzle vanes. The annulus was supported on rollers for free rotation. It had internal teeth engaged by a pinion carried on a short shaft which also carried a lever. By angular movement of the lever, the pinion and annulus were turned, which then adjusted the angle of the vanes, and thereby the throat area of the nozzle passages they defined.

Another design for a variable nozzle was invented by Willi Henny of

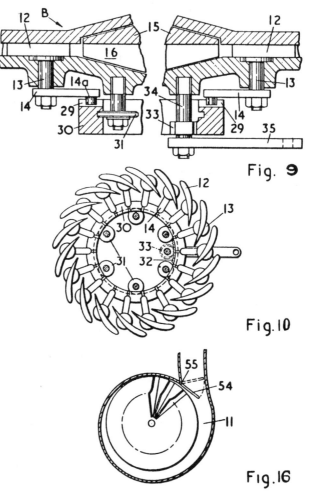

Fig. 9

Fig. 10

Fig. 16

Detail design features of Richard Barr's variable nozzle.

Chrysler and patented in 1960. The Chrysler nozzle assembly differs in detail design but not in principle. Each nozzle blade is attached to the inner end of a pivot shaft. The CR2A had 23 nozzle blades. The shafts extend radially from the blades and are supported in annular bushings secured within the outer shroud. The outer end of each shaft extends beyond the outer shroud and carries a short pivot arm. The tip of the pivot arm rests between two notches on a ring that surrounds the entire nozzle assembly. The ring is carried on bearings that allow it enough freedom of motion to give the pivot arms a full range of angular movement.

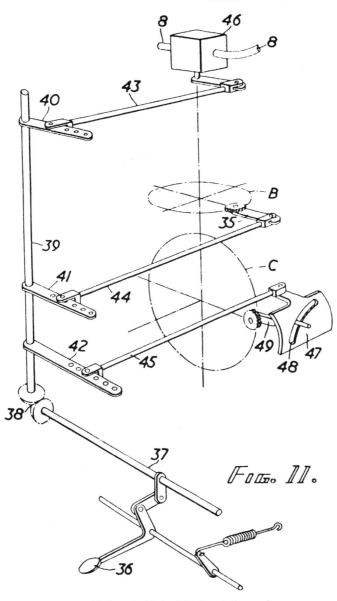

Fig. 11.

Control linkage for Richard Barr's variable nozzle.

81

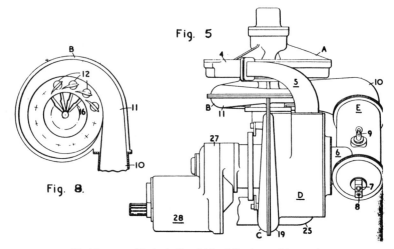

Turbine assembly including Richard Barr's variable nozzle.

The position of the ring is controlled by an automatic control unit that senses engine speed and vehicle road speed. The control unit includes a power cylinder with a piston, and the piston rod is connected to a bracket on the ring. When the piston moves in, the mechanical linkage tilts the nozzle vanes one way, and when the piston moves out, the vanes are tilted the opposite way.

Quite early in its turbine program, Rover designed a simple two-position nozzle (inspired by Richard Barr's invention) for installation on the first-stage radial in-flow turbine. The theory behind the Rover design was to run at high idle speeds with minimum mass flow, and to open up the nozzles when fuel flow was increased.

This gives extra power for acceleration. To understand the process, let's look back to what happens in the piston engine. A modern piston engine coupled to an automatic transmission will respond to the driver's stepping on the accelerator in about 0.3 second. That's the delay associated with taking up any slack in the throttle linkage, delivering an enriched mixture to the cylinders, and firing it.

The process in the gas turbine with non-variable geometry is quite different, and inevitably slower. The turbine responds to accelerator pedal action by injecting more fuel into the combustor, which produces higher turbine inlet temperature. That leads to excess torque on the first-stage turbine, which brings about an acceleration of the gasifier (compressor) shaft.

Fully open nozzles will give the highest torque and best acceleration. Closing the nozzles will reduce the torque and cause the gasifier shaft to slow down (the automatic control device would only close the nozzles when

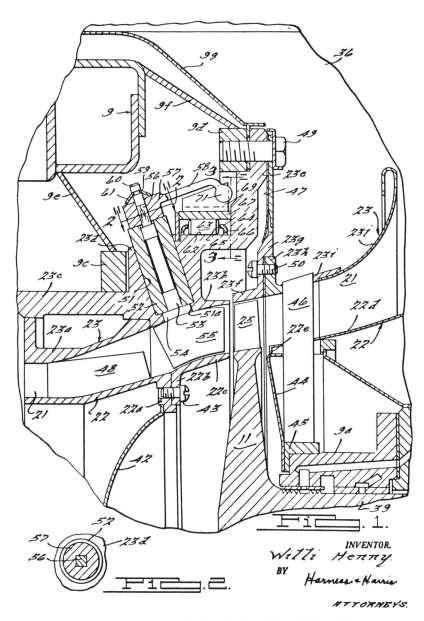

FIG. 1.

FIG. 2.

INVENTOR.
Willi Henny.
BY
Harness + Harris
ATTORNEYS.

Willi Henny's patent was the basis for Chrysler's variable nozzle.

83

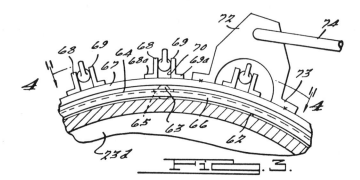

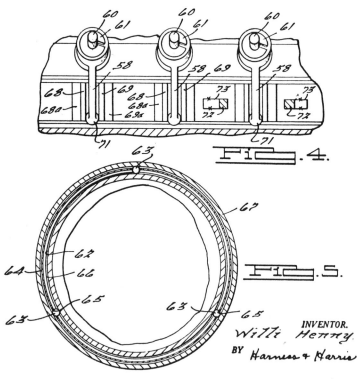

Details of Henny's design for a variable nozzle.

84

the accelerator pedal was released, of course). Closing the nozzles had no braking effect—it just turned down the output of positive power. But it allowed a higher idling speed for the gasifier shaft, meaning it would more quickly reach peak output speed when the accelerator pedal was depressed.

In the Chrysler turbine, by way of contrast, it is the second-stage (free shaft) turbine that has variable nozzles. This is perhaps the most successful application of variable-geometry nozzle concepts to actual use. George J. Huebner Jr. regards it as comparable in importance with the use of regenerators.

Chrysler uses a transonic gas flow first-stage turbine with nonvariable nozzle geometry to drive the compressor. Variable nozzle geometry for the second-stage turbine allows turbine inlet temperature to be sustained near optimum value at part load. This increases the thermodynamic cycle efficiency and thereby improves the fuel economy over the operating range of the engine. It also speeds up turbine response to accelerator pedal action.

While Rover's variable-nozzle was strictly a two-position device, Chrysler's design provides continuous and automatic variation in the angle of the second stage (free-shaft) turbine nozzle blades. It is controlled by compressor shaft rpm and vehicle road speed, so that the gas flow is directed to the turbine wheel at an optimum angle of attack over the entire operating range. Wide open position is used for idling, which permits a lower first-stage turbine idle speed and cuts fuel flow at a given regenerator temperature limit so as to cut fuel flow to the absolute minimum consistent with stable operation and readiness for acceleration.

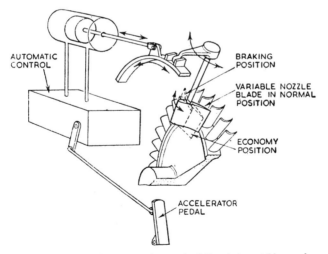

Schematic showing function and control of Chrysler's variable nozzle.

Chrysler's variable-geometry nozzle assembly, and its installation in the main housing.

Closing the nozzles will rapidly increase the pressure drop across the first-stage turbine. This will increase compressor shaft speed and therefore make more power available to the power turbine. That's what's behind its improved acceleration capability.

How big was the improvement? The first-generation Chrysler turbine had an acceleration lag of 7 seconds from idle to maximum gasifier speed. Variable nozzles were installed on the second-generation turbine, and the lag was cut to 3 seconds. Subsequent improvements in component efficiency have further reduced the acceleration lag to 1.5 seconds in the fourth-generation turbine (1963) and 1.2 seconds in the sixth-generation turbine (1966).

The most significant modification in this connection was the adoption of a faster-acting variable-nozzle actuator, which makes the blades snap into their acceleration position much faster than on earlier designs. The action was speeded up by a factor of three, which cuts the adjustment time in going from fully closed nozzles to fully open position by two-thirds.

Reversing the nozzles makes it possible to obtain greater engine braking, which is defined as engine-assisted retardation when the accelerator pedal is released. The driver is accustomed to it and counts on it, not only at high speeds but in all driving situations, and especially when maneuvering in heavy traffic.

This braking effort is natural to a reciprocating engine because friction and pumping work for idle throttle setting are appreciable. With a gas turbine, however, friction is negligible, and a turbine with nozzles fixed in the power position cannot absorb work. When the accelerator pedal is released, these nozzles open to a point where the change in tangential velocity through the wheel is negative. This turbine then acts as a compressor (though not a very efficient one) and absorbs energy from the vehicle, thus reducing its speed.

For maximum braking effort, the nozzle discharge flow should remain "attached" to the blades, whereas the wheel discharge should be separated from the suction side since this results in the largest negative torque. These requirements are not easily reconciled with those of the power output conditions, especially in the nozzles which may be opened by as much as 100 degrees. A blade leading edge which is tolerant of a wide inlet flow angle range is obviously desirable.

Braking torque is highest at high power turbine speeds (high vehicle road speed), but a small reverse torque can actually be obtained even with the power turbine at stall. The variable nozzle therefore offers better control of the cycle temperature and creep torque at idle.

Using the second-stage turbine as a "compressor" to retard the whole power train has two side effects on the free turbine: (1) its flow restriction is increased, which reduces the expansion ratio in the first-stage turbine and raises the inlet temperature that the turbine needs to run, and (2) work is being put back into the gas stream at the power turbine.

Both of these effects drive the temperature upward, and that imposes a limit on nozzle angle setting and the degree of braking attainable. There is no doubt that variable nozzle geometry offers very substantial advantages of particular value in a passenger car. But no advantages are obtained without being accompanied by drawbacks.

The disadvantages associated with variable nozzle vanes are, above all, added cost and complexity. Huebner maintains that this drawback is not as great as one might at first anticipate, but he also admits that the variable nozzle involves some compromises on gas flow path, since the blade shrouds require spherical surfaces. Some loss of efficiency may result, because the nozzle blades require clearance at both root and tip, and that produces leakage paths.

Finally, the mechanism adds a certain amount of weight to the turbine engine, but that is relatively insignificant in proportion to the weight of the entire unit. Since the nozzles are not rotating members, the small amount of extra weight they cause is not critical.

Other applications of the variable-geometry nozzle are rare. General Motors shuns its use, although it has been included in many experimental GM turbines. Williams Research Corp. and Volkswagenwerk reject it on principle, while Ford has no clear policy with regard to variable nozzle geometry. However, it seems that Ford is moving closer to the Chrysler position.

Ford uses a variable nozzle for the second-stage turbine on the 3600 series turbine. It is a self-contained unit consisting of 25 moveable vanes, each vane having a spur gear sector and a ring gear to control the angle variations. The nozzle gear provides over 100 degrees of rotation. The vanes are precision investment castings, each having a shaft as an integral part of the airfoil section.

POWER TRANSFER SYSTEM

The power transfer system is the GM method of obtaining the same advantages—and more—than Chrysler derives from the variable second-stage turbine nozzle. The primary function of the power transfer system is to improve the part-load fuel economy of the engine, and one of its secondary functions is to provide a means of engine braking.

Its principles are based on observation of certain features inherent in the Brayton cycle and in the free-shaft type of gas turbine engine. Normally, turbine inlet temperature falls off as power output diminishes. Since thermal efficiency is a function of the peak cycle temperature at any operating condition, the part-load fuel consumption can be reduced if the cycle temperature can be raised.

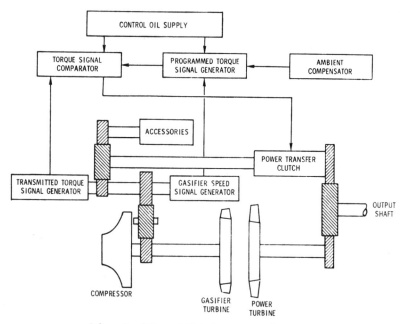

Schematic of General Motor's power transfer system.

Several methods of raising the cycle temperature were explored during the preliminary design phase of the GT 309 turbine unit, including variable nozzle geometry, but all other candidates were discarded in favor of the power transfer system. Basically, the power transfer system is a hydrome-chanical device for transferring controlled amounts of power between the second-stage turbine shaft and the first-stage turbine shaft. A separate shaft is added to the engine, running parallel with the compressor shaft and power turbine (free) shaft, and connected to both via simple, mechanical gearing.

The system, however, contains several clever features that combine to endow the resulting power unit with the desired characteristics. First, the power transfer shaft is broken by a clutch. Secondly, a torque sensor is inter-posed in the gearing between the power transfer shaft and the compressor shaft. Thirdly, the output shaft does not run straight from the free turbine but from a connecting gear in the link between the power transfer shaft and the free turbine shaft. To explain how this setup works in practice, it is most logical to start with the clutch that divides the power transfer shaft.

One set of plates is driven from the compressor (gasifier) shaft, and the other set of plates from the free turbine. The clutch is hydraulically actu-ated, which is why GM characterizes the system as "hydro-mechanical."

The clutch torque can be regulated by means of the hydraulic pressure. The gear ratios are chosen so that the power turbine-driven plates turn slower than the gasifier-driven plates during all normal engine operating conditions. Application of a slight amount of pressure to the hydraulic clutch cylinder results in a torque reaction between the clutch elements turning at different speeds. The torque on the faster-turning, gasifier tur-

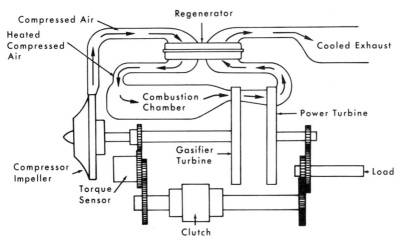

Gas flow path through a turbine engine equipped with power transfer.

bine-connected elements acts to slow this component. The gasifier governor, however, increases the fuel flow to maintain constant speed. The result is an increase in turbine inlet temperature, as well as a slight increase in engine output. By operating the engine at the maximum allowable temperature limit throughout its speed-power range, significant reductions in fuel consumption can be realized.

It also proved entirely practical to use these same components to transfer power in the opposite direction. First of all, this provides a means of developing engine braking by having the output shaft drive the compressor. Secondly, the power turbine can be coupled to the gasifier turbine whenever the power turbine speed exceeds a safe limit, to provide positive overspeed protection. In addition, the power transfer system provides a means of operating the GT-309 as a single shaft engine, with its attendant advantages in certain applications. Finally, when a control system for power transfer was designed, it became evident that the problem of handling variations in gasifier turbine-driven accessory loads could be overcome, and that full rated engine output could be either delivered entirely to the output shaft or divided between the output and accessory shafts without affecting turbine inlet temperature.

Several minor modifications were introduced during the testing and evaluation period of the GT-309. The gears connecting the power transfer shaft to the gasifier shaft (and which also serve for the accessory drive) were beefed up to handle higher torque—which reaches maximum during braking. When the engine is used for braking, the clutch is locked up and no slip occurs. During normal power transfer operation, the clutch is lightly loaded and slipping moderately. Since only a small part of the total output is routed through the clutch, and the slip ratio averages less than 15 percent, General Motors regards the power loss represented by the clutch slip as negligible.

The mechanical design of the clutch is based on experience gained with wet-plate clutches in automatic transmissions. A constant flow of oil is passed through the clutch plates to dissipate the heat that is generated during slipping operation. Ideally, the power transfer system should be able to sense and maintain the desired turbine inlet temperature by regulating the load on the clutch. The GM engineers felt that temperature sensing devices had not yet reached a level of durability or response that would justify their use in the power transfer system. Consequently, they chose to use speed and torque sensors, which were highly developed.

A pitot-type pickup is used to measure the dynamic head of the oil circulating within a vaned annulus formed as an integral part of the accessory drive reduction gear. A heat-sensitive bi-metallic strip positions the pitot head in the annulus to correct for changes in oil density due to temperature.

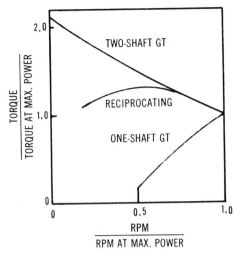

Torque curve comparison between single-shaft and two-shaft gas turbine engines.

This provides a measure of dynamic pressure as a function of the gasifier shaft speed.

The second control signal is also generated at the same point, as the accessory drive can deliver a signal proportional to the torque transmitted from the gasifier shaft through the accessory drive gears. The first accessory reduction gear and second reduction pinion are mounted on the same shaft. These gears have helix angles chosen to make the axial gear thrust forces generated additive. The combined thrust is transmitted through a ball thrust bearing to a hydrostatically located piston and spool valve assembly. The spool valve regulates the piston pressure so as to always balance the thrust put into it. Since this thrust is proportional to the transmitted torque, the piston pressure is a measure of torque.

These signals (speed and torque) are matched up by means of a spool valve comparator which then regulates the flow of oil to the clutch cylinder, increasing or reducing its pressure to maintain the scheduled torque load on the gasifier shaft.

The turbines and compressor are balanced so that a certain amount of power transfer is required even at full power. Under braking operation, the power transfer works in the reverse direction. With the fuel shut off, the turbine output falls off to a very low level, and the compressor becomes a dynamic braking device. The compressor is ideal for this purpose, since the energy expended in driving it is dissipated directly as heat added to the air it discharges. General Motors claimed that the continuous braking capacity of the GT 309 was greater than its rated output power.

To use the engine braking capability, the driver simply lifts his foot off the accelerator in the normal fashion. This gives a signal to the governor to shut off the fuel supply, and the first-stage turbine slows down until the opposing plates in the power transfer clutch are revolving at the same rate.

At this point, clutch torque is zero. As the first-stage turbine continues to slow down, the torque becomes negative, and a negative-torque signal is sent to the control system. It responds by applying full pressure to both hydraulic clutch cylinders so that the clutch is locked and no slip can occur. The result is a direct, mechanical connection between the output shaft and the gasifier shaft (as in a single-shaft turbine). Fuel supply will recommence when road speed falls to a point where the turbine goes to its idle speed setting, or, alternatively, whenever the driver again depresses the accelerator pedal. The power transfer system also provides protection against power turbine overspeeding, by locking the clutch whenever the power turbine overruns the first-stage turbine.

5

The Single Shaft Turbine

THE FREE-SHAFT gas turbine gives full independence between the power section driving the output shaft and the gas generator section driving the compressor. It has been claimed that this type of engine makes it possible to eliminate clutch and gearbox. This is a vague truism, which will not quite stand up in practice, due to fuel economy and performance considerations. Even the free-shaft turbine will need a gearbox to be successful in a passenger car installation. But it's also true that the car could run with a fixed gear ratio.

The free-shaft turbine provides a built-in torque converter effect that gives increasing torque with diminishing rpm, and a stall torque—when the vehicle is at standstill—between two and three times the full-load torque. This torque is not produced, however, unless the gasifier is turning at rated speed. The two gas-coupled turbines act in essentially the same way as the elements of a hydraulic torque converter. The only limitation on engine response to load changes is the rate at which the gas generator section can change speed.

A finite time is required to accelerate the gasifier from idle speed to the point where sufficient torque is developed to provide satisfactory vehicle acceleration. That means there is an acceleration delay. As will be explained later, this acceleration lag is mostly dependent on inertia; in the primary turbine, in the compressor, and in the accessory drive.

The separation of the compressor load from the power turbine destroys the vehicle's dynamic braking ability. There are several methods by which some braking ability can be restored (Chrysler's variable nozzle and GM's power transfer system), but both involve additional hardware and higher cost. This can also be achieved by using a single-shaft turbine.

That is a type of turbine engine in which the first-stage and second-stage turbines are combined mechanically into a single unit to form a high-speed fixed-shaft configuration. This means that the compressor shaft and the output shaft will both run at turbine speed. This changes the torque characteristics of the power unit drastically. Instead of the high stall torque of the free-shaft turbine, the fixed-shaft configuration gives low torque at low rpm, peak torque at peak rpm. This happens because the ability of the single-shaft turbine to produce torque is dependent on the ability of the compressor to deliver air, and the compressor air flow in turn depends on its rotational speed.

Due to the necessity of running the turbine at high speed at all times, the single-shaft turbine inevitably has high specific fuel consumption. If the pressure ratio can be brought high enough to achieve reasonable fuel economy, the resulting expansion ratio will exceed the capacity of a single axial-flow turbine stage, and consequently force the adoption of a two-stage turbine (but still fixed to the same single shaft).

A single, radial in-flow turbine might have the capacity to handle the entire expansion process, but that would involve higher inertia and slower response. To counteract the response problem, it might be possible to increase idle speed, but that again brings a penalty in fuel economy. Other possibilities lie in the use of such devices as variable geometry in the compressor inlet guide vanes, compressor diffuser vanes, and turbine stator member nozzle vanes.

Further, the single-shaft (fixed shaft) automotive gas turbine is associated with difficult and complex transmission problems. The useful speed range for the gas turbine is about 2.5 to one, compared with about 10 to one for the piston engine. In addition, the torque change through the single-shaft gas turbine's speed range is abrupt. Most turbine experts agree that the use of a single-shaft turbine will require an infinitely-variable (stepless) transmission.

No such transmission is yet commercially available for the torque outputs and speed ranges required for automotive applications. Stepless drive is restricted to low-power, low-torque use, as in machine tools, snowmobiles, etc.

United Aircraft of Canada made a feasibility study on single-shaft turbines, and consulted the Borg-Warner research laboratories regarding the transmission. Borg-Warner's experts suggested an eight-speed transmission coupled to a controlled-speed slipping clutch.

The eight-speed automatic transmission consists of a four-speed automatic gearbox preceded by a two-stage planetary splitter that in effect doubles the number of ratios attainable from the gearbox itself. The controlled slipping clutch will transmit constant torque to the wheels at reduced engine speeds, without multiplication. Its advantage is that the stall speed can be adjusted

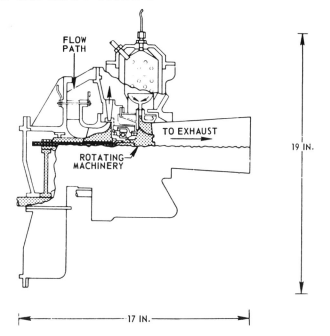

FLOW PATH

TO EXHAUST

ROTATING MACHINERY

19 IN.

17 IN.

United Aircraft's 1972 proposal for a single-shaft automotive gas turbine engine.

in the design process so that the engine can be completely idle or be completely engaged within a fairly narrow range. In addition, when the clutch is locked up, power is transmitted with a higher efficiency than that associated with a torque-converter.

General Motors has also made similar studies, and Charles A. Amann of the GM Research Laboratories made up a list of other possibilities, ranging from a hydraulic torque converter, an aerodynamic torque converter, hydrostatic drive, hydro-mechanical drive, or continuously variable belt drive to electric power transmission. In conclusion, Mr. Amann said: "It is not clear which, if any, of these transmissions will meet the requirements of performance, durability, and cost."

Why—in view of these problems—are we still interested in the single-shaft turbine? The single-shaft turbine is the simplest form of gas turbine, and has obvious advantages in small size, lower weight, and reduced cost compared with the free-shaft gas turbine. It can also be argued that there is a loss involved in each turbine, since neither operates at 100 percent efficiency. By eliminating one turbine, there should be a gain in efficiency.

From an emission-control viewpoint, the single-shaft turbine theoretically offers the same advantages as the free-shaft turbine, which has prompted governmental interest in the simple, low-cost concept.

The United Aircraft of Canada study of single-shaft turbines was sponsored by the National Air Pollution Control Administration of the Department of Health, Education and Welfare. The contract was awarded to this company because United Aircraft of Canada Ltd. had carried out a series of research programs aimed at providing advanced components for small gas turbines for aircraft since 1961. Much of the technology gained in these programs promises to be of value for small automotive gas turbines, as much of the research effort has been concerned with centrifugal compressors and radial-in-flow turbines of advanced design—such as would be needed in a single-shaft unit. United Aircraft has also had significant activity in sophisticated analytical stress calculation and mechanical design innovations.

The single-shaft United Aircraft of Canada engine was conceived as a mathematical model, and the study led to some interesting conclusions. It was a simple cycle unit with a single-stage centrifugal compressor giving a 12 to one pressure ratio, with variable-geometry inlet guide vanes. Turbine engines without heat exchangers are called simple-cycle units, while those equipped with heat exchangers are either recuperative-cycle or regenerative-cycle units. The combustor was a single barrel type unit, and the exhaust gases expanded through a single-stage radial in-flow turbine.

The output shaft power take-off was at the front end, ahead of the compressor, at the cold side. A reduction gear of 10 to one was provided, which later calculations showed would be inadequate for shaft speeds of 135,000 rpm. The calculations showed it would probably take a two-stage reduction gear set to bring output shaft speeds down to the 3600—10,000 rpm range.

In physical dimensions, the engine was very small—17 inches long, 19 inches high, 14 inches wide, and would weigh only about 120 pounds without accessories (160 pounds with accessories).

The performance calculations were based on actual tests performed by United Aircraft of Canada Ltd. and must be assumed to be realistic. The compressor air flow was calculated to be 1.06 pounds per second with a compressor efficiency of 98 percent. The turbine, it was calculated, would withstand inlet temperatures up to 1950° F (1066° C) and give 88.3 percent efficiency. Inlet losses were estimated at .9 percent, exhaust losses at 6.3 percent, parasitic losses at 3.8 percent, and reduction gearing losses at 4.2 percent.

With a fuel flow of 76.2 pounds per hour it was calculated the engine would deliver 150 hp and return a specific fuel consumption of 0.51 pounds per hp-hour. The calculations included installation in a six-passenger 4,000-pound standard U.S. automobile.

The single-shaft turbine would give the car a top speed of 105 mph and enable it to climb a 5-percent gradient at 83 mph. Acceleration from standstill to 60 mph was calculated to take 10.2 seconds, 25–70 mph acceleration to be accomplished in 12.0 seconds.

United Aircraft of Canada Ltd. concluded that the project was feasible and deserved full-scale demonstration (which has not been carried out). The report said that the single-shaft turbine engine would meet government goals in terms of acceleration, fuel economy, and emission levels.

The production costs were claimed to be competitive with those of reciprocating engines modified to meet the same emission standards, and operating costs were claimed to be competitive with present experience, as defined by the U.S. Department of Transportation.

Another single-shaft automotive gas turbine was designed by AiResearch Manufacturing Co. (a division of The Garrett Corporation) under contract with the Environmental Protection Agency.

It was another mathematical study program that did not reach the prototype stage. The vehicle selected for the turbine engine installation was again a six-passenger 4,000-pound U.S. automobile. But the AiResearch engineers chose an infinitely variable transmission system in contrast with United Aircraft of Canada's multi-speed gearbox with slipping clutches.

There were fundamental differences in the AiResearch approach from that taken by United Aircraft of Canada. First, the AiResearch engineers decided to include a heat exchanger (the United Aircraft engine was a simple-cycle unit). Secondly, the AiResearch specifications included water injection at the compressor inlet. An advanced form of recuperative heat exchanger was chosen for the AiResearch design. Its other key design features were variable inlet guide vanes, single-stage centrifugal compressor, barrel-type combustor, and a single-stage radial in-flow turbine.

The entire package including transmission, it was calculated, would weigh 695 pounds and require an installation space of 18 cubic feet. The power plant would be 38.9 inches long, 24.8 inches high, and 31.5 inches wide. The compressor would have a pressure ratio of 6.4 to one and would operate with 89 percent efficiency. Maximum shaft speed would be limited to 88,000 rpm. Combustor efficiency was presumed to be 99 percent, giving turbine inlet temperatures of 1900° C) while turbine efficiency was calculated at 88 percent. The recuperator is estimated to be 85 percent efficient. Power output was calculated at 125 hp, and specific fuel consumption at 0.41 pounds per hp-hour.

Power output is extracted from the compressor end of the shaft (the cool side). A two-stage reduction gear reduces rotational speed to a level acceptable to the infinitely variable transmission. A conventional hydraulic torque converter is coupled to a forward/reverse gearbox whose output shaft is connected to the drive line. An on/off clutch is disengaged during starting to facilitate oil pressure buildup.

The stepless transmission system chosen for this single-shaft turbine was of the toric drive type (related to the patented Hayes and Perbury transmissions). It is a form of friction drive with a toroidal gap between the driving disc and the driven disc. Into this gap are inserted rollers mounted on short shafts.

The rollers are preloaded against the friction surfaces of both discs. The shafts that carry the rollers are attached to movable brackets that allow the shafts to swing about 30 degrees each way from a neutral position normal to the transmission axis. Swinging the shafts changes the contact surface between the rollers and discs. This is where the change in gear ratio occurs. If the rollers contact the driving disc at a small radius, they will contact the driven disc at a correspondingly large radius. This provides a down-gearing, reducing the speed of the driven disc and raising its torque. Swinging the roller shafts so as to contact the driving disc at a large radius will provide an upgearing. Since the roller shafts do not move in notches or steps, gear ratios can be changed smoothly, and an infinite number of gear ratios is available ranging from about 1 to 3 one way to 3 to 1 the other way.

There are many unanswered questions regarding this type of transmission for use in connection with a high-powered turbine engine. They include the friction losses, the wear rate on the friction surfaces, the reliability and longevity, the serviceability and repairability. As far as the turbine car application is concerned, the toric drive is strictly in the experimental stage. For that matter, the single-shaft turbine has yet to demonstrate its capability in a real automobile.

6

Heat Exchangers

THE PURPOSE OF a heat exchanger is to transfer heat from one part of a gas flow to another. In a gas turbine, it transfers heat from the exhaust gas to the compressed air prior to its entry into the combustor, or ahead of the heat source. This heat would otherwise be lost. The amount of heat available in the exhaust gas depends primarily on speed and load. High loads mean hot exhaust.

A passenger car engine, whether it is the piston type or a gas turbine, spends most of its time under part load, while aircraft turbines generally run at steady speed and under high load conditions. Turbojet engines usually have multi-stage compressors with pressure ratios in the 10–12 to one range. Thus, there is no need for heat exchangers on aircraft turbines, but they can make an enormous difference in the fuel economy of an automotive turbine.

As we have seen in the chapters on combustors and turbines, increasing turbine inlet temperature will increase both work ratio and thermal efficiency. Adding a heat exchanger does not change the work ratio, but will raise the engine's thermal efficiency. At very low power, the heat exchanger can feed back up to 80 percent of the total heat required from the combustion process, leaving the fuel to supply only the remaining 20 percent of the total heat.

How much fuel does the heat exchanger save? Dr. Bruno Eckert of Daimler-Benz AG has shown that for a heat exchanger efficiency of 90 percent, the minimum specific fuel consumption is about .34 pounds per hp-hour in an engine running with 1900° F (1038° C) turbine inlet temperature and a 5.5 pressure ratio. If turbine inlet temperature is raised to 2500° F (1371° C) and the pressure ratio to a value of 7, the minimum specific fuel consumption falls to .28 pounds per hp-hour, with the same heat exchanger.

Without a heat exchanger, the turbine could not get below .45 pounds per hp-hour even if the pressure ratio was raised to a value of 16 or below .4 pounds per hp-hour if the pressure was raised to a value of 18.

A 100% efficient heat exchanger would transfer the entire temperature difference between the turbine exhaust and the compressor delivery to the compressed air, with the result that the temperature of the gas finally exhausted to the atmosphere would be the same as that of the compressor delivery temperature. This, however, is impossible to achieve without an infinitely large heat exchanger.

It is generally accepted that an active heat transfer surface of about 1200 square feet is needed for a typical 150 hp automotive gas turbine. Maximum heat recovery for an automotive gas turbine ranges around 90–92 percent. To make this possible, the heat exchanger needs high volume. The use of heat exchangers leads to a considerable change in package size for the gas turbine engine. The heat-exchanger-equipped turbine unit will be 2–3 times larger than a turbine without heat exchangers.

RECUPERATION VS. REGENERATION

There are two basic types of heat exchangers. One type is the static recuperator, the other is a revolving regenerator. In the recuperator, cold incoming air and hot exhaust gases are brought in close proximity while being separated by a thin membrane of high-conductivity metal. The heat-exchange principle of the recuperator is the same as in a normal automobile radiator, with the difference that the radiator uses water instead of exhaust gas as the hot flow element.

The regenerator is a heat sink of large surface area, usually shaped like a thick disc. It is carried on a shaft and revolves. The material is porous, so that the gases can flow through the disc itself. The compressed air is ducted through the disc ahead of the center, while the exhaust gas is ducted through it behind the center. This creates a hot sector and a cold sector. While one sector of the disc takes up heat from the exhaust gas, the other gives up its heat to the cold air coming in. As the disc revolves, the process becomes continuous.

The basic difference is that the recuperator relies on a process of conduction through a wall separating the hot and cold gases, while the regenerator works by exposing a heat storage element to the two gases in an alternating cycle. The recuperator has steady flow, while the regenerator has periodic flow.

Two types of gas flow patterns have been used. These are the drum type and the disc type. In the drum type, the exhaust gases from the turbine flow radially outward through the core in the hot sector, while the cool air flows radially inward through the cold sector of the core. In the disc type of

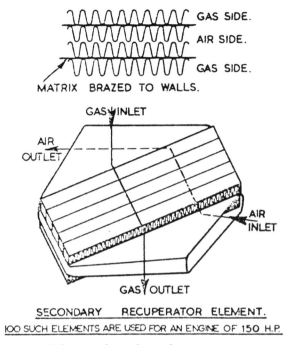

GAS SIDE.

AIR SIDE.

GAS SIDE.

MATRIX BRAZED TO WALLS.

GAS INLET

AIR OUTLET

AIR INLET

GAS OUTLET

SECONDARY RECUPERATOR ELEMENT.

100 SUCH ELEMENTS ARE USED FOR AN ENGINE OF 150 H.P.

Schematic of secondary-surface recuperator.

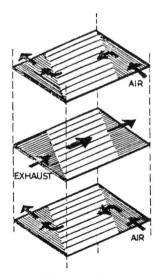

AIR

EXHAUST

AIR

Schematic of the contra-flow recuperator.

101

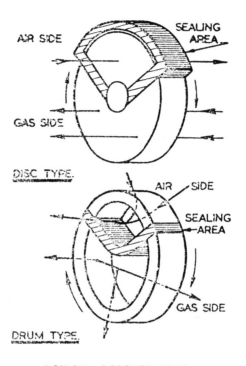

AIR SIDE

SEALING AREA

GAS SIDE

DISC TYPE.

AIR SIDE

SEALING AREA

GAS SIDE

DRUM TYPE.

ROTARY REGENERATORS.

Comparison of drum-type and disc-type rotary regenerators.

regenerator, the cool air flows axially through the revolving core in the cold sector, while the turbine exhaust gas flows in the opposite direction through the hot sector.

In both types, the core is uniform throughout, and what part of it constitutes a hot or cold sector depends entirely on its location relative to the flow paths of exhaust gas and compressed air at a given time. During the core's rotation, its entire web of passages function alternately to let the exhaust gas through while absorbing its heat energy, and to let the air through while giving up its heat to it.

The main advantage of the regenerator over the recuperator is that it saves space. Micro-passages can be used more readily in the regenerator, although both types stand on a theoretically equal footing with regard to the amount of space required for the core. As the volume taken up by a heat exchanger core increases almost in linear proportion to the size of its passages, the regenerator offers a very real space saving for vehicle installations. The regenerator also has an advantage in its self-cleaning characteristic. Static recuperators tend to clog (especially if fuel of poor quality is used) with sooty deposits.

The regenerator is inherently self-cleaning because of the reversal of flow and the cyclic fluctuation of the core temperature during each cycle, thereby reducing the risk of fouling by combustion deposits. While the regenerator is basically more difficult to seal, due to the necessity to provide constant rotation, the regenerator is generally much less sensitive to air leakage through the walls and joints of the core because, throughout the cycle, most of the working surface has no pressure differential across it. For these reasons, practically all current automotive gas turbines use the revolving disc-type regenerator.

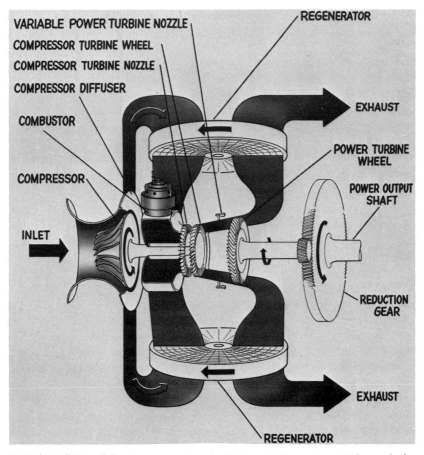

Typical installation of disc-type regenerators on a Ford gas turbine engine. Air flow path also shown.

RECUPERATOR DEVELOPMENT

Recuperative units were tried by several companies in the earlier stages of development. Rover built a series of turbines equipped with primary-surface contra-flow recuperators, and Austin chose a secondary-surface crossflow core. In the U.S., Ford built some of its first turbines with a secondary-surface contra-flow recuperator.

In a crossflow unit the hot and cold streams flow in alternate layers in paths crossing at right angles (90 degrees). In the contraflow unit the two streams also flow in alternate layers, but this time in opposing directions, along paths that do not cross but meet head-on (180 degrees). In the crossflow unit there are corners that will be permanently hot or permanently cold, setting up a temperature distribution pattern that establishes thermal stresses which may lead to structural failure. In the contraflow unit, freedom from such stresses is assured.

The contra-flow recuperator has high efficiency but poses fabrication problems, and tends to be very bulky and heavy. The ducting also gets complicated. The ducting required for crossflow recuperators is simpler, but their efficiency is inherently lower, and that in turn pushes the weight and size up.

For two units of equal efficiency, one contraflow and one crossflow, the former would be about 20 percent smaller and lighter, if the efficiency is 60 percent. To obtain 80 percent efficiency, the crossflow unit would grow so large that the equivalent contraflow unit would be half its size and weight.

REGENERATOR DEVELOPMENT

Chrysler's first gas turbine used a recuperative heat exchanger, but the engineers realized very early in their experience with this unit that this method was simply not good enough for use in a car. As a result, Chrysler went to a regenerator for the second-generation turbine, and has used regenerators exclusively since then. General Motors and Ford followed Chrysler's lead. By 1966, even Rover was convinced of the superiority of regenerators. Relative newcomers such as Williams Research Corp. and Volkswagenwerk never explored the recuperator at all but went straight to regenerators.

In view of the preponderance of regenerative heat exchangers in the later development history of automotive gas turbines, the following discussion will deal with regenerators as applied to free-shaft turbine engines, unless otherwise specified.

As Noel Penny has pointed out:

The regenerator has near-ideal heat transfer utilization of its matrix but yet presents three major mechanical design problems:

1. Isolating gas and air streams at high and low temperatures using static sealing against a rotating disc.
2. Driving the disc at low speed in an engine which is essentially a very high speed device.
3. Supporting a low speed hot mass which is acted on by a rather complex system of forces.

In theory, the regeneration has no effect on net gas turbine power output. In practice, however, the regenerator will cause a slight reduction in output for a given mass air flow and compressor pressure ratio. This is due to the pressure drop in the air flow through the regenerator, which will effectively reduce the pressure ratio, and consequently the gross output of the turbine.

The revolving regenerator is also associated with the threat of leakage of the compressed air to the turbine exhaust. Some types actually transfer a certain amount of air from the cool sector to the hot sector. These two factors reduce the mass air flow to the turbine, and thereby lead to a slight power loss.

Some heat will be stored in the regenerator, and this fact may require special control devices in an automotive turbine installation where changes in load can be both rapid and frequent. At first, the whole regenerator will be cold. As it warms up, it will continue to store heat until it reaches a balance point between exhaust gas temperature and compressed air temperature. Until this balance point is reached, the air/fuel ratio will become progressively leaner.

What happens when power is shut off? The fuel supply is cut back, turbine inlet temperature drops, and compressor shaft speed falls off. But the heat stored in the regenerator will result in higher-than-needed pre-heating of the air entering the combustor. This will result in the production of unwanted power until a new equilibrium is established at idle speed.

REGENERATOR PERFORMANCE

The overall regenerator geometry is determined by the performance characteristics desired of the heat exchanger. Material considerations will be discussed in a following chapter. A large number of factors have to be taken into account before the disc diameter and disc thickness, the area split between hot and cool sectors, the throughway ratio (which is defined as the combined area of the gas flow passages relative to the total face area of the regenerator core), and rotational speed can be determined. Such modifying factors include stresses and deflections in the regenerator, the seal geometry, the core blockage, and the methods of mounting and driving the regenerator.

The effect of rotational speed on regenerator performance is considerable. Effectiveness declines as speed is reduced. This indicated that the regenerator should run at high speed, but that will increase the carryover leakage and the wear rate of the regenerator seals. The regenerator speed must be a compromise between efficiency on one hand and leakage and wear on the other. Regenerators in automotive gas turbines usually rotate at between 20 and 50 rpm at peak compressor shaft speed.

Ideally, the regenerator should have high efficiency and a low pressure drop ratio. The problem is that these goals are in conflict with regard to establishing regenerator geometry. The thermodynamic performance criteria used in evaluating heat exchangers are heat transfer, pressure loss, and leakage. Heat transfer is measured as heat exchange efficiency which is defined as the ratio of heat energy actually transferred to the heat energy transfer potential.

When the fourth-generation Chrysler turbine was being developed, the engineers felt they had reached a satisfactory compromise when effectiveness ranged from 90 percent at idle to 85 percent under full load, with pressure drop ratios of 2.1 percent at idle and 4.5 percent under full load. In comparison the Ford 3600 series turbine was designed (ten years later) for 90 percent efficiency at idle and 88 percent under full load, with a pressure drop ratio of 2.0 percent at idle and 4.7 percent under full load. The example shows how far ahead of its competition Chrysler actually was in terms of heat exchanger technology.

Pressure loss is measured as pressure drop ratio, based on the difference in pressure from the regenerator inlet side to the regenerator discharge side. Actually there are two such ratios—one for the hot sector and one for the cool sector. The pressure drop ratio is the sum of these loss ratios.

Why does there have to be a pressure loss? All heat transfer passages impose a pressure loss on the fluid that flows through them, and in the Brayton cycle, that constitutes a thermodynamic loss. The heat transfer capacity of a surface must be weighed against its friction characteristics. For surfaces employing any given passage shape, both heat transfer capacity and pressure drop ratio increase as the unit passage size is reduced (the hydraulic radius is reduced).

Extremely thin walls are necessary to accommodate a large mass flow with low pressure losses, and it is essential that these thin walls possess adequate mechanical strength and low porosity.

The factors that determine efficiency and pressure loss ratio are the shape of the passages, the Reynolds number, the passage flow length in relation to the hydraulic diameter, gas flow rate in relation to the core heat capacity rate (utilization factor), and the axial conductance in relation to the gas heat capacity rate. The Reynolds number is a dimensionless measure of gas flow characteristics determined by its velocity, fluid density, and fluid coefficient of viscosity.

A typical automotive gas turbine will have regenerator cores with a passage flow length to hydraulic diameter ratio of about 100. That means the passages are like very thin tubes, about 100 times longer than they are wide. A typical utilization factor of .25 or 25 percent means that the gas flow rate is one quarter the magnitude of the core heat capacity rate. A typical conductance factor of 0.012 or 1.2 percent means that the heat capacity rate is almost 100 times greater than the axial conductance in the core structure.

Leakage is measured as a percentage of total gas flow. The leakage does not occur as in a pneumatic tire, for instance—from the compressed air chamber to the atmosphere. It occurs internally inside the regenerator casing. The air in the cool sector is pressurized, while the exhaust gases are fully expanded and simply being pushed out by the pressure of the turbine's continued discharge. That means the cool air seeks to escape into the exhaust gas. The leakage path leads from the cool sector to the hot sector.

The passages are sealed off from each other, but as there are significant temperature differences between the sectors that have to be sealed off from each other, the seals must be designed to accommodate thermal expansion and contraction. The details of the sealing systems will be described in a later chapter.

Leakage of fresh air into the exhaust gas means that this air flow by-passes the turbines after compression work has been invested in it, and that means a direct energy loss to the engine cycle. In addition, there is a certain amount of carryover leakage, as a result of incoming air being trapped in the core passages and carried around to the hot sector.

George J. Huebner Jr. has reported that Chrysler's first regenerators suffered leakage losses exceeding 8 percent of total air flow, but a few years later this had been reduced to below 3 percent.

The regenerator drive arrangement also plays a part in determining its operation under changing conditions and over longer periods.

There are two types of disc mountings. With a center mount, the disc is attached at the inner disc diameter (hub). An outside diameter mounting system uses three or more rollers to carry the disc at its periphery. Most turbine constructors prefer the center (hub) mount, because it tends to be less expensive.

Disc drive systems also fall into two categories. One category uses hub drive, the other peripheral drive. Hub drive usually takes the form of splines on the regenerator disc shaft which fit into the center of the disc. This requires a resilient spring between the metal spline and glass-ceramic hub to take up the thermal expansion of the metal and permit axial movement of the disc without putting an excessive load on the disc hub.

Peripheral drives usually have a metal ring gear attached to the outside diameter of the disc. Most large-diameter discs use peripheral drive. A pinion engages the ring gear and makes the disc revolve.

REGENERATOR SEALS

The basic sealing problem with regenerative heat exchangers stems mainly from the fact that the regenerator core rotates while the duct work is stationary. While changes in rotational speed have no effect on seal leakage, the wear rate of the seals must be expected to increase at higher speeds. The sealing problem is critical because of the high pressure obtaining in the cool sector of the regenerator, the compressed air will try to escape through the gaps between the core faces and the duct work. Stopping this leakage path is the primary duty of the regenerator seals.

The sealing problem is aggravated by the fact that the core must be allowed to float during operation and to take the thrust from the gas pressure on the hot side against the cold side seal with uniform load across the seal surface. Moreover, the seals should ideally be made of a material that does not require lubrication and has the ability to operate over a wide temperature range.

Sealing systems can be divided into two basic types. One type uses a bellows to act as a moveable sealing diaphragm. The second type uses a flat leaf-type diaphragm to form a seal. Both types rely on a flat metal substrate with a spray-coated wear pad rubbing against the core surface.

In a typical bellows-type sealing system, each of the sealing members is kidney-shaped and forms a bellows of looped, continuous shape. The bellows is positioned to separate the pressurized sector from the exhaust sector, and is expandable in a direction parallel to the air flow. The following description of a bellows-type sealing system is based on a patent taken out by Sam Williams, who chose a disc-type regenerator for this design. The details therefore apply to the specific core and are not valid for a drum-type matrix without substantial redesign.

The bellows is made up of a pair of elastic sheets secured at their outer edges to one of the elements to be sealed. It is preferable to fasten the bellows to the stationary duct rather than to the revolving disc. The bellows includes a pair of flexible flat shoes on opposite sides. These shoes are adapted to provide rubbing and sealing contact with the regenerator disc. The shoes are narrower in section than the bellows, so that the elastic sheets can be joined after the shoes have been attached to them, so as to permit them to envelop the shoes.

The bellows seal members on one side of the disc are arranged to seal that one face of the disc against the two ducts—one feeding compressed air to the core, and the other receiving exhaust gas from the core. On the other side is a mirror-image arrangement, with seal members joining the disc face to (1) the duct that feeds pre-heated compressed air to the combustor, and (2) the duct that delivers exhaust gas from the free turbine to the core.

The bellows is pressurized by air or gas conducted through it. This pressurization spreads the seal shoes apart and provides the necessary force to keep the shoes pressed against the sealing interfaces. By this arrangement, any distortion or axial movement of the disc due to thermal differentials will be prevented from causing leakage in the compressed air sector.

The entire bellows seal assembly is quite thin, so that it is capable of transverse bending for the purpose of conforming to interface irregularities. The pressure in the bellows should be higher than the pressure of the gases being sealed. There are two ways of arranging this. A pressure regulating valve can be installed to maintain bellows pressure at the desired level. In that case, the pressurizing fluid can be taken from an outside source, and could also work as a coolant to prevent overheating of the seal material. Another method will use pressurized air delivered from the compressor. A pressure increase above the mainstream pressure can be obtained by ram effect in leading the seal pressurizing air through a set of ram pipes or tubes located next to the compressor diffuser.

The sealing system used for sealing the exhaust gas ducts relative to the disc is generally simpler in construction, because the sealing problem is far less critical with fully expanded exhaust gas than with air pressurized at 58.8–66 psi.

Annular low-pressure seals engage the end surfaces of the disc and seal the exhaust sector. The sealing used on the exhaust gas ducts comprises a flexible sheet metal band secured to a section of the casing, with its opposite face coming in rubbing contact with the regenerator disc. The pressure drop across the heat exchanger on the gas side is sufficient to provide leakproof loading on the seal against the disc.

In comparison with the flat leaf type of seal, the bellows design is simpler and more straightforward, but suffers from an inherent flaw. A bellows is always stiffer in the corners than in other areas, and this puts a restriction on its versatility. It would be helpful if the corners could be eliminated, but bellows designs without corners usually have lower thermal efficiency than conventional designs.

Bellows seals used on regenerators are of the closed-loop type with sharp turns at the intersection of the disc periphery with the crossarm. These stiff corners transmit a load to the seal face that may be 10 times higher than along the rest of the seal surfaces.

This tends to cause excessive seal wear, high disc drive friction, and high disc wear, and can lead to disc failure. As a result, the bellows-type of seal has been discarded by many turbine constructors. Most advanced regenerator designs use flat leaf-type diaphragm seals.

The flat leaf diaphragm type of seal was developed by General Motors for a drum-type heat exchanger, and is based on a patent taken out in 1962 by

William C. Bubniak and others. It was first used in conjunction with a drum-type regenerator, and the following description would not be applicable to disc-type cores without considerable rearrangement due to the different flow paths.

The diaphragm divides the interior of the regenerator casing into first and second chambers. The drum revolves and passes through the diaphragm in the course of its rotation. The diaphragm includes two complete seal grids— a primary seal and a secondary seal.

The task of the main seal structure is to minimize leakage through the primary seal from the high-pressure side to the low-pressure side. The secondary seal grid encloses the primary seal giving a double-wall effect. Each seal structure includes a frame that encircles the regenerator core.

The seals are mounted in the diaphragm, with freedom to move relative to the surfaces to be sealed. The seals bear against the core where it passes through the diaphragm at spaced points on one side of the diameter of the core. The outer rim seal is bolted to the inside of the regenerator cover plate. The inner rim seals are bolted to an arcuate plate extending between the core edges ahead of the bulkhead and bolted to the primary seal blocks. This plate provides a wall between the two regenerator drums and prevents compressed air from flowing through the space between the drums.

The floating mounting for the regenerator matrix provides for matrix expansion relative to the casing. The seals are also anchored to a floating mounting which provides for thermal expansion or distortion.

The diaphragm assembly has a main plate that extends across the entire regenerator. This main plate is bolted to a cover plate, which has a heavy web on its inner surface—facing the main plate. Inner seal bars are bolted to the top and bottom edges of the main plate. The ends of the seal bars are fitted with end caps, located by dowels and free to slide on the dowels. Each inner seal bar carries a hollow block or box with its rear wall open. Outer seal bars are bolted to the hollow block, and define the upper and lower edges of the diaphragm. The diaphragm assembly is attached to the front cover plate, the exhaust ducts, and a rear plate. The main plate, the inner seal bars, the blocks, the outer seal bars, and end caps form a rigid bulkhead.

The primary seal assembly consists of a frame mounted with clearance for radial and lateral movement. Inside the frame are side bars or shoes made integrally with edge members or legs. The inner and outer seal faces are provided by separate sets of bars or shoes, connected with each other via the edge members. The inner seal shoe is mounted in slots on the edge members so that it has freedom to slide and thereby expand relative to the outer seal shoe. It is secured against inward radial displacement by keys inserted in keyways on the shoe itself. The edge seals are spring-loaded against the core.

Rim or bypass seals engaging the core edges are provided to minimize gas leakage past those edges and force the entire fluid mass through the core. Each rim seal is made up of two arcs: a forward arc ahead of the primary seal, and a rearward arc mounted in back of the primary seal.

Sealing segments are mounted in grooves extending across the faces of the bars, and secured by screws. These segments are of graphite or a similar material having good resistance to heat damage and low sliding friction. They are spaced with very slight clearance from the core, but may slide so as to engage its edge portions.

An outer seal segment is mounted in a groove in the inner surface of the edge member, and bears against the outer edge of the core. The core's inner edge is engaged by a graphite rubbing block mounted with freedom to slide against the inner edge. The primary seal assembly is located in relation to the core by four rollers—two on each side surface.

It is kept in proper alignment by the force exerted by eight small coil springs carried in pockets on the outer seal bar. The springs bear against the outer surface of the seal shoe and are retained by threaded plugs which provide an abutment for the springs. The springs also serve, jointly with the rollers, to support the core when the engine is not in operation. This keeps the weight of the core from bearing against the secondary seal.

When the engine is in operation, the pressure drop across the core exerts a force on it in a rearward direction, and a larger force, caused by the pressure drop through the turbine, acting on the core's cross-sectional area also exerts a force on it in the same direction, so that the core is carried by the four rollers when the engine is in operation. The coil springs then merely serve to aid in locating the primary seal accurately.

The primary seal assembly has a floating mounting on needle bearings which permit rocking motion in the seal assembly. It also has freedom to move radially in relation to the drum because of slots provided for that purpose in the end cap and the end wall of the block that carries the outer seal.

Because of the floating mounting of the main seal and the manner in which it is guided, tolerances between the graphite seal blocks and the inner and outer sides of the core can be kept extremely close. The expansible mounting of the inner shoe prevents bowing of the seal frame, which also aids in maintaining close clearances.

The secondary seal is inserted between the primary seal assembly and the seal bar assembly by a rectangular frame made of two thin sheets of flexible material such as shim stock. The shim stock extends beyond the frame into a narrow sawcut around the entire periphery of the primary seal frame and similar sawcuts in the inner seal bar, the hollow block, the outer seal bar, and the end caps. These are the elements that enclose the primary seal assembly.

The sawcuts are deep enough to allow some clearance for radial movement of the primary seal relative to the seal bar assembly, while the flexibility of the shim stock will allow some rocking motion in the primary seal. The sawcuts are wide enough to allow free movement of the shim stock. A contact seal is maintained despite this freedom, because the pressure on one side of the shim stock is considerably higher than on the other side.

Heat Exchanger Materials

The heat exchanger has certain material requirements, such as high thermal shock resistance, low coefficient of thermal expansion, low heat conductivity, low density, and high specific heat.

With turbine inlet temperatures in the 1700–1900° F (927–1038° C) range, heat exchanger inlet temperatures will vary from 1200° F (650° C) to 1400° F (760° C) at full load. Heat exchanger inlet temperatures at idle and part load may be as low as 800° F (427° C) and, surprisingly, as high as 1650° F (900° C).

All the earliest heat exchangers were made of metal, usually stainless steel, though more sophisticated alloys were developed as technology progressed. Dr. John Weaving of Austin preferred mild steel and expressed surprise at how well it was able to stand up to exhaust gas temperatures, citing a limit just short of 1100° F (600° C).

One much-favored alloy was Yorcainic, whose principal constituents were copper (91 percent) and aluminum, with small measures of nickel, iron, and manganese. It proved capable of withstanding continuous gas flow temperatures up to 1200° F (650° C).

The thin alloy foil of metallic heat exchangers poses many problems. It can cause ignition and sustain combustion, and under such conditions, will melt when the temperature reaches the alloy's melting point. This can be triggered by hot incandescent particles on the foil, or by wet fuel droplets reaching the duct area just prior to the core entry.

As was the case with turbine materials, ceramics came in as a possible replacement. Ceramic heat exchangers will not burn. And if temperature does reach the melting point of the ceramic, while the result will be glazing on the surface and softening (melting) inside, the unit will continue to operate without causing damage to other engine parts. This indicates that ceramics have particular advantages for application in rotary regenerators. These advantages loom larger and larger as one realizes how many problem phenomena are associated with disc-type regenerators.

For instance, thermal expansion in a metallic disc causes the disc to bulge in a pattern approaching a spherical shape due to the temperature difference across it. In contrast, ceramic discs have far lower thermal expansion coefficients, so that the disc will tend to retain its original shape regardless of the temperature difference across it. This makes the sealing problem easier to solve in connection with ceramic regenerators.

A glass-ceramic disc offers a low thermal expansion coefficient with only slight crowning, so that it is relatively easy to seal at all points in its temperature range. Ceramics also have lower thermal conductivity, which minimizes the effect of heat transfer through the disc material.

High heat transfer would reduce the temperature difference between the disc itself and the air flowing through it, thereby reducing the regenerator efficiency. That represents a conduction loss, which is most severe at low flow rates (i.e. under part load conditions, with low power output).

The low thermal conductivity of the glass-ceramic material gives a part-load efficiency 5–6 percent higher than at full load, while metal discs work with a part-load efficiency 2–3 percent lower than at full load. However, metal discs have a higher full-load effectiveness due to their thinner walls. Metals walls can be 0.051–0.076 mm (0.002 to 0.003 in) while the glass-ceramic walls require a thickness of 0.102–0.127 mm (0.004 to 0.005 in).

The cost picture is of paramount importance for mass-production applications, and the ceramic disc has very low cost indeed. It may seem paradoxical that the development of materials with higher heat resistance should coincide with a switch to cheaper materials, but that's what has happened. The ceramic core may cost as little as 20–25 percent of the price of a recuperator of similar capacity and effectiveness. In addition, glass and ceramics are far lighter than metals, with about one-fifth the density of steel.

The switch to ceramics came about because Corning Glass Works started a development program on rotary regenerators in 1952. The initial design goals called for a disc with a minimum diameter of 18 inches and a thickness of 3 inches. No less—preferably more—than 60 percent of the area should be open. A limit of 2 percent was set on transverse leakage, and the material had to withstand a pressure ratio of 4 to one.

The first test disc was made of Pyrex tubing, a material that has become common for cooking utensils. But it was not easy to combine the tubes into a regenerator disc and seal them. Attempts at fusion sealing results in distortion at high temperatures. Using a silicone resin as a sealing agent was tried, and after many experiments Corning arrived at a silicon-aluminum mixture that could seal the tubes successfully and survive a rapid recycling test from nearly 1400° F (760° C) to below 200° F (93.3° C).

While the Pyrex experiments continued, Corning tried glass tubes as a regenerator core material. The first core with glass tubes, sealed with the patented silicon-aluminum compound, was tested in 1956. It failed because the bonding agent did not have adequate heat resistance for the regenerator environment. This approach was then abandoned.

Instead, Corning turned to glass-ceramic combinations, and made several discoveries that held promise for heat exchangers. But the direction of further progress was not yet clear. The early work centered on tubes. Then an attempt was made to form sheets from ceramic materials. This approach was given support by the fact that Corning had been successful in forming capacitor ribbon glass and thin glass sheets separated by glass rods. From 1957 onwards, the development work was focused on ceramic sheet, and before long the first glass-ceramic structures had been created.

This structure consisted of making triangular passages by interweaving flat and corrugated sheets. This led to problems with compressed air separating them and opening the passages. A rim was therefore added to provide greater strength——but not a metal rim. Corning built rims consisting of several layers of sintered material——mostly a mixture of high-silica glass. New core materials in turn led to new rim materials and bonding cements. After a period of evaluation, further work was concentrated on glass-ceramic for both core and rim.

This research work led to a new glass-ceramic that was given the trade name Cercor. The new material was announced as a laboratory development in 1958, and its first commercial version became available in 1962.

The regenerator disc construction principles followed closely along the lines of those of earlier types made with other glass-ceramics, with alternate flat and corrugated strips wound around a central hub into the same cross-sectional form as a coil of corrugated cardboard. Instead of being contained by a rim, the disc is cemented into a surrounding base of the same Cercor

13-inch diameter Cercor regenerator discs applied to a Williams Research Corp. gas turbine engine.

Cercor regenerator disc for installation on Ford 707 gas turbine engine.

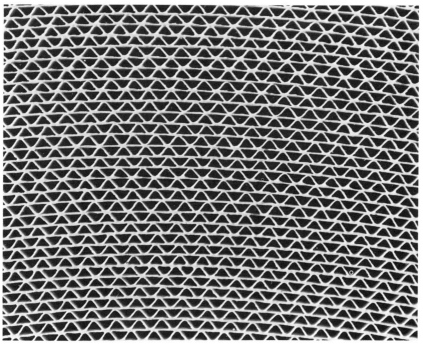

Cellular structure of Cercor regenerator disc.

115

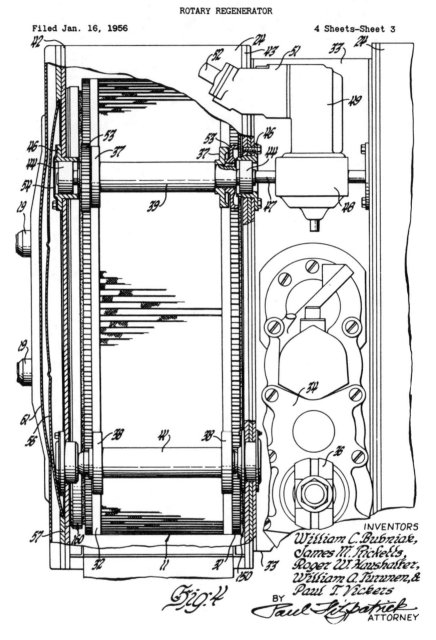

INVENTORS
William C. Bubniak,
James M. Ricketts
Roger W. Hawshalter,
William Q. Turwnen, &
Paul T. Vickers
BY
Paul Fitzpatrick
ATTORNEY

Detail of General Motors regenerator rim-drive system.

116

material, so that the complete disc has the same physical and chemical properties throughout. Size and shape of the cell passages can be varied according to need. The structure is extremely light, with a specific gravity of 1.6 (compared with 2.7 for aluminum and 7.8 for steel).

All Cercor regenerator discs are provided with wear pads to separate them from the casing and provide a low-friction, hard wearing ceramic-to-metal interface. The characteristics of the wear pads on the cold side of the regenerator are not critical, and they are usually made of graphite or carbon. But on the hot side, they must provide low friction and a low wear rate in a high-temperature environment, and normal self-lubricating seal materials cannot survive in those conditions.

Most recent seal systems use wear pads made of plasma-sprayed nickel oxide/calcium fluoride. The nickel oxide content is usually about 80 percent. Such combinations have a friction coefficient as low as 0.25 to 0.35, and a wear rate of 12.7–25.4 micron (0.0005 to 0.001 inch) per 100 hours.

The Cercor regenerator disc is not immune to failure, however. The most common defect in large-diameter discs is fatigue failure, which shows up as segmental cracks near the disc periphery. Radial cracks are a rarer phenomenon, generally due to thermal shock resulting from rapid cycling between low temperatures and extremely high ones. At the present stage of development in glass-ceramic technology, it is often difficult to distinguish between failures resulting from material imperfections and failures that are due to design errors.

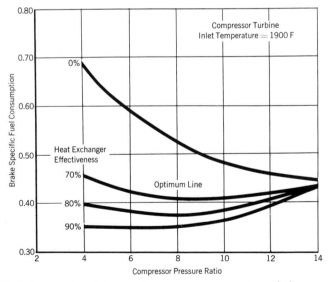

Effect of regenerator efficiency and compressor pressure ratio on fuel economy.

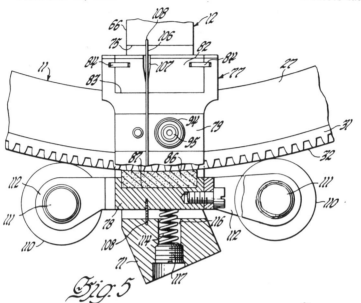

Fig. 5

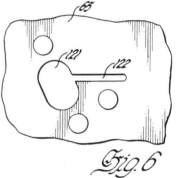

Fig. 6

INVENTORS
William C. Bubniak,
James M. Ricketts,
Roger W. Haushalter,
William C. Turunen, &
Paul T. Vickers
BY
Paul Fitzpatrick
ATTORNEY

General Motors rim-drive design for rotary regenerators.

118

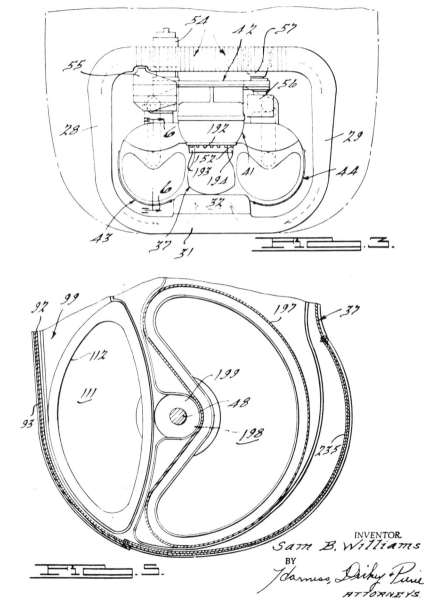

Bellows-type regenerator seal system patented by Sam Williams.

119

Jan. 31, 1961 S. B. WILLIAMS ET AL **2,969,644**

DRIVE MEANS FOR A REGENERATOR IN A REEXPANSION GAS TURBINE ENGINE

Original Filed Oct. 24, 1955 7 Sheets-Sheet 2

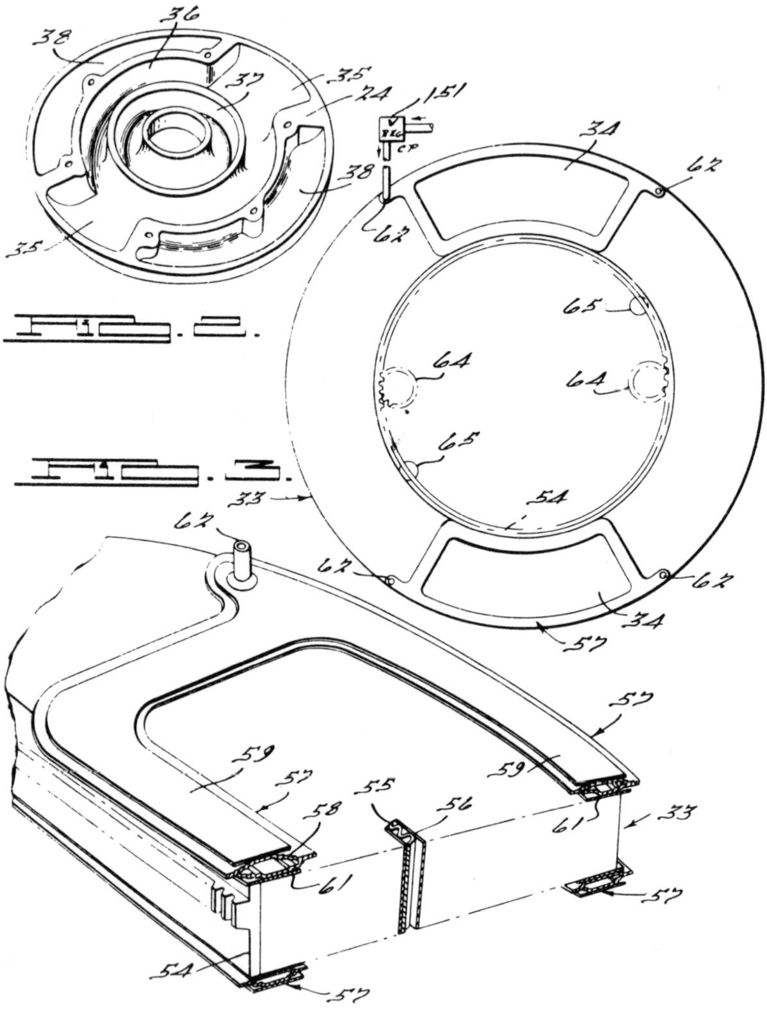

INVENTORS
Sam B. Williams
Jack J. Benson
BY
Harness, Dickey + Pierce.
ATTORNEYS.

Outer seal members for Williams bellows-type regenerator seal system.

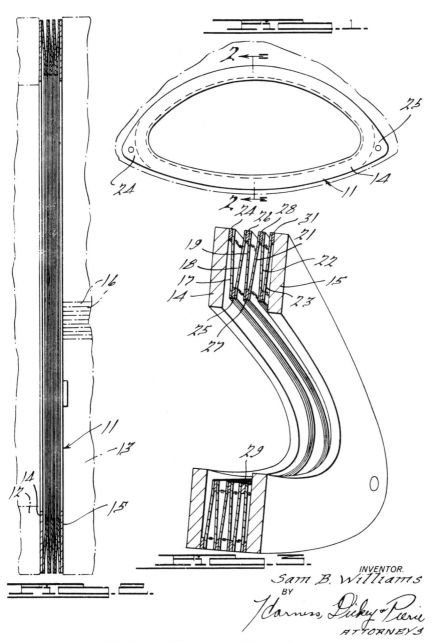

INVENTOR.
Sam B. Williams
BY
Harness, Dickey & Pierce
ATTORNEYS

Details of the bellows in the Williams seal system.

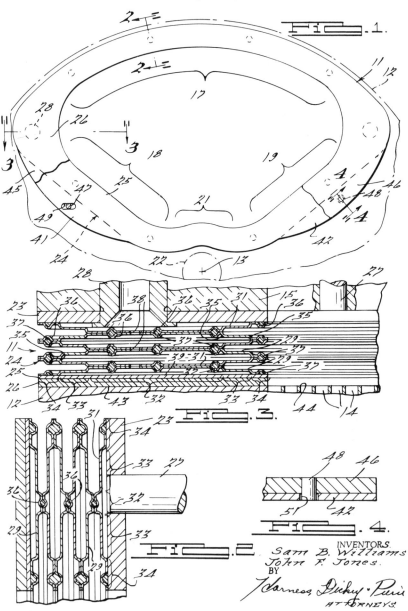

INVENTORS.
Sam B. Williams
John F. Jones.
BY

Harness, Dickey · Pierce
ATTORNEYS.

Detail of seal joints in the Williams regenerator seal system.

122

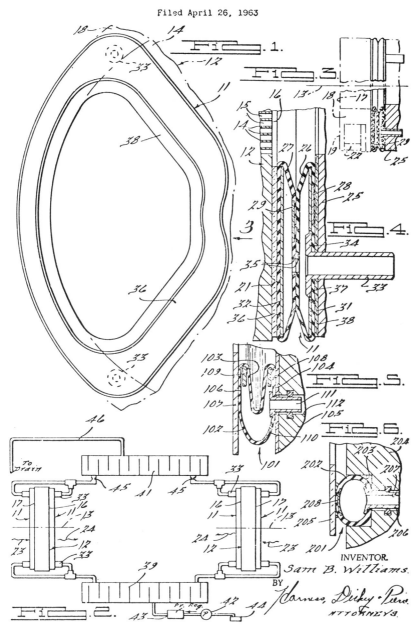

INVENTOR.

Sam B. Williams.

BY

Harness, Dickey & Pierce

ATTORNEYS

Detail of seal grid in Williams regenerator seal system.

123

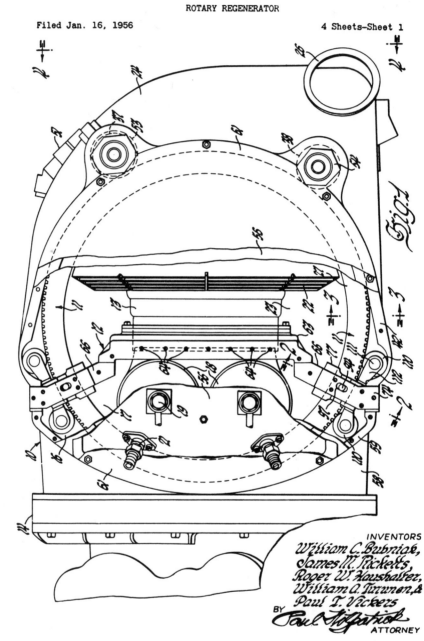

INVENTORS
William C. Bubniak,
James M. Ricketts,
Roger W. Haushalter,
William O. Turunen, &
Paul T. Vickers
BY
Paul Fitzpatrick
ATTORNEY

General view of diaphragm seal used for GM's rotary regenerator.

124

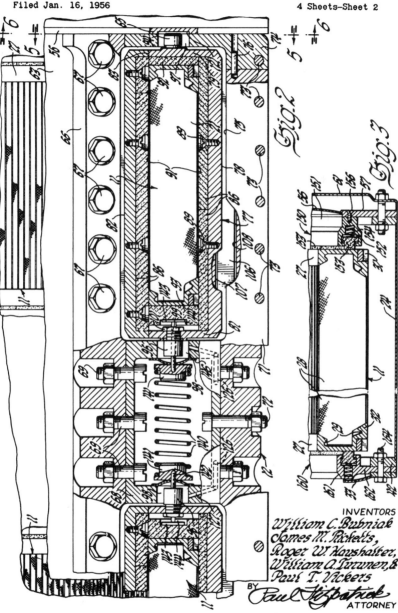

INVENTORS

William C. Bubniak,
James M. Ricketts,
Roger W. Haushalter,
William A. Turunen, &
Paul T. Vickers

BY

Paul Fitzpatrick

ATTORNEY

Detail of General Motors' diaphragm-type regenerator seal.

125

7

The Turbine
Housing

THE HOUSING STRUCTURE for a gas turbine is every bit as important as the cylinder block for a piston engine. Both carry the essential shafts; gasifier section shaft and output shaft in the turbine engine—crankshaft and camshaft in a V8.

Both the turbine housing and cylinder block must provide bearing bases for these shafts. Both must provide bolting and support flanges for other basic components, such as the cylinder heads on a V8 and the regenerator casings on the turbine. Both must provide mounting platforms for accessories such as electric generators and hydraulic and mechanical pumps.

But the turbine housing has duties that go far beyond those of the cylinder block. The piston engine has separate attachments such as intake and exhaust manifolds to direct air and gas flow paths into and out of the cylinders. In the gas turbine, the housing itself must provide guidance for and control over the air and gas flow paths through the power unit. That is necessary because of the nature of the Brayton cycle as opposed to that of the Otto cycle. All the events that make the piston engine run take place in the upper ends of the cylinders, and it is a simple matter to duct gas flow in and out of a number of small, clearly defined areas. But the events that make the gas turbine run are spaced out geographically throughout the power unit, and the gases must be led from one area to another, always with full control over gas pressure and velocity.

Those requirements lead to a series of others, due to the pressure and temperature differences in the air and gas flow. As a result, the housing must have adequate strength to contain the high-pressure gas flow without risk of distortions that might cause misalignment of the working components. The housing must be made of materials that are able to withstand the

Cast iron housing for Williams WR-26 gas turbine engine.

high-temperature gases with sufficient stability and rigidity to avoid transfer of thermal expansion forces to the working components.

It must conform to package size limitations imposed by the vehicle installation. It should be made of low-cost materials, and be simple to manufacture, with a minimum of labor involved in machining and assembly. There are two basic types of housing: (1) the one-piece casting, and (2) the fabricated built-up structure.

Both types are invariably double-wall structures, with an inner shell that has as its principal duty the formation of a passage for the motive gases, and an outer shell that serves to contain the total machinery (except for ancillary equipment).

Cooling must be provided for the inner housing walls to control thermal distortion and limit temperatures to a level consistent with material properties. This can be accomplished by using compressor discharge air to cool the double walls in the front section and the central bulkhead.

The bulkhead is the most difficult part to cool, because it is exposed to temperatures of 1400–1600° F (760–870° C) on both sides. Ford has devised a way to duct a certain amount of compressor discharge air so as to cause it to flow between the bulkhead walls on its way to the combustor plenum area.

The outside surface of the inner housing can be insulated with ceramic fiber insulation to reduce heat transfer from the hot gas stream to the outer shell. Such an arrangement is used on the Ford 3600 series, for instance. This results in relatively low skin temperatures and low heat conduction from the engine to its immediate environment.

The fabricated type of housing is usually built up as a box structure with four double wall sections. The wall sections usually extend around the top and bottom corners so that separate base and cover parts can be eliminated (though a number of designs use separate base and cover pieces for various reasons, such as service accessibility, ease of fabrication, etc.)

In built-up housings, each part is a sheet metal stamping. Such stampings have light weight and low cost. Each wall section is made up of two stampings, substantially identical, with open sides facing each other. The edges are arranged with abutments for overlapping, so that they can be brazed together. In a typical fabricated housing, the four walls can be described according to function:

1. The main housing stampings.
2. The compressed air duct stampings.
3. The heated air duct stampings.
4. The exhaust duct stampings.

The main housing stampings form chambers above and below the regenerators, and collect the exhaust gases that have passed through the cores. They contain exhaust headers that conduct the gases out of the housing. The rear wall portions of this pair of stampings are provided with openings having detachable covers of arcuate shape.

Removal of these covers permits access to the regenerator cores and their seals, making it possible to replace the seals without disturbing the engine structure or the alignment of the working parts. The compressed air duct stampings may include an aluminum casting positioned around the compressor wheel. Its forward end is usually formed as a radial portion ending in a cylindrical section that forms the air intake for the compressor.

The heated air duct stampings have wings disposed in the spaces between the regenerators and receive the heated air from them, ducting it to the combustor. The exhaust duct stampings enclose the exhaust gas diffuser and duct the exhaust gas from the second-stage turbine discharge ports to the hot sector of the heat exchangers.

The wall sections are assembled, usually by brazing, to form an integral unit. However, at least one of the connections is provided with a joint that permits relative movement between sections. This joint is preferably positioned across the gap between sections with high differences in operating

June 18, 1957 G. J. HUEBNER, JR., ET AL 2,795,928

ARRANGEMENT OF COMPONENT ELEMENTS OF A GAS TURBINE POWER PLANT

Filed Oct. 29, 1953 6 Sheets-Sheet 4

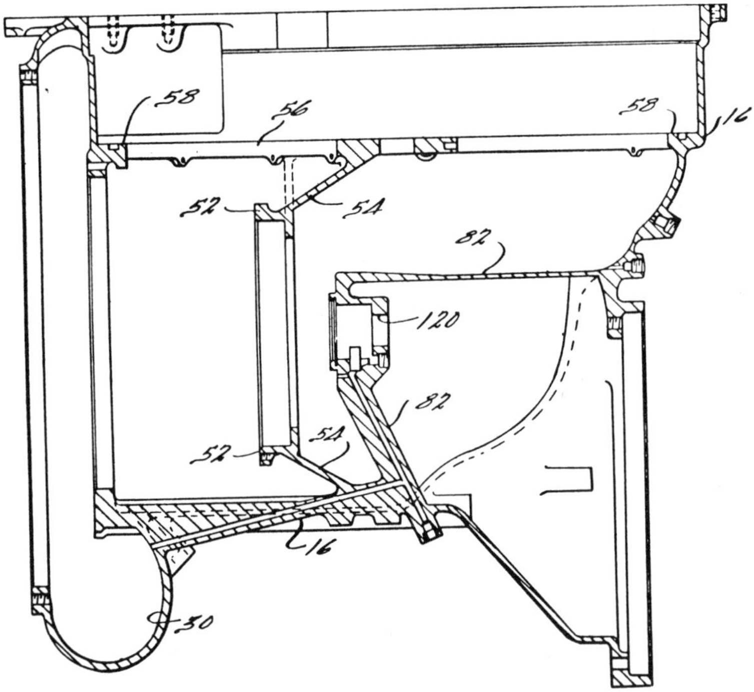

FIG. 4.

INVENTORS
George J. Huebner
Samuel B. Williams
David M. Borden

By Harness and Harris
ATTORNEYS

Housing structure patented by Chrysler.

Aug. 31, 1965
J. J. BENSON
3,203,181
GAS TURBINE
Filed Oct. 18, 1962
6 Sheets-Sheet 1

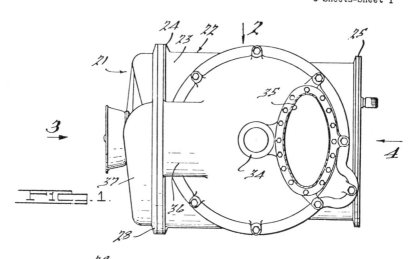

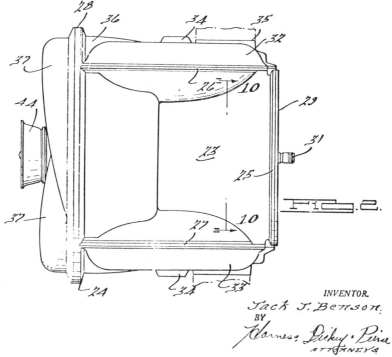

INVENTOR.

Jack J. Benson.

BY

Harness, Dickey & Pierce

ATTORNEYS

Gas turbine housing patented by Jack J. Benson of Williams Research Corp.

130

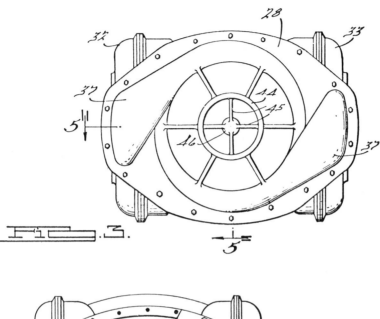

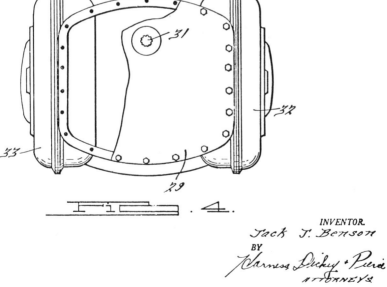

INVENTOR.

Jack J. Benson

BY

Harness Dickey & Pierce

ATTORNEYS

Gas turbine housing patented by Jack J. Benson of Williams Research Corp.

131

temperature. The joint also provides a fluid-tight seal between the sections. This connection helps reduce stress loads which may build up as a result of differential expansion and contraction during changing thermal conditions within the operating range.

The connections between the support members and the inner shell can be made with conical engagement in annular bearing surfaces under resilient tension. This will permit thermal expansion differentials between the inner and outer shells.

The cast housing is a single piece to start with. It is formed by well known foundry techniques, using moulds and cores giving close tolerances and high precision. Most advanced turbines now use the one-piece casting type of turbine housing because of its lower cost for volume production.

The complex shapes involved with internal ducts are more easily achieved with a casting than with a fabricated structure. It assures higher precision and superior uniformity. The most common casting material is nodular iron which has high specific weight but possesses the stability and strength required.

In a typical cast housing, a vertical bulkhead is mounted across the center of the housing to separate the high-pressure gases ahead of the turbine from the low-pressure gases leaving the turbine. The edges of the bulkhead provide sealing abutments for the regenerator cross-arm seals. The housing is essentially a double-wall construction, with compressor discharge air flowing between the two walls in the forward end.

The inner shell provides a base for the combustor and turbine inlet plenum, and also forms a sealing abutment for the front half of the first-stage turbine. The front flange constitutes a mounting base for the gasifier assembly.

Single-piece cast housings usually have integral duct work to and from regenerators to the extent to which it is practical, with the remaining duct work forming part of the regenerator casings.

8

The Fuel System

THE GAS FUEL turbine fuel system differs considerably from the fuel injection system used in gasoline-driven piston-type automobile engines. These cars have low-pressure, port-type, indirect injection. The nozzles inject not into the combustion chamber but into the induction manifold or intake port area. Injection can be timed or continuous. The pump can be mechanical or electrical. Speed control is assured, not by fuel flow but by throttling the air intake duct or manifold (on the same principle used in carburetors).

Finally the fuel itself is not the same. The fuel-injected piston engine runs on gasoline, usually with a high octane rating. The gas turbine is a multi-fuel engine which can burn unleaded gasoline, diesel fuel, and kerosene. The most common aircraft turbine fuels are JP-4 and JP-5 ("JP" stands for jet propellant). JP-4 is a kerosene/gasoline mixture with a high percentage of low-octane gasoline. JP-5 is also a kerosene/gasoline mixture, but with lower gasoline content.

While the gas turbine has this multi-fuel capability in theory, it is not always feasible in practice to change fuels from one type to another in a specific power plant. The fuel system is adjusted for one type of fuel, and a change in fuel type, unless accompanied by readjustment of the fuel system, can result in failure to start.

For road vehicle use, gasoline or JP-4 have many advantages over heavier fuels in respect to low freezing point, ease of handling, rapid settling and consequent easy removal of dirt, ease of starting, and so forth, in addition to giving better combustion.

The typical gas turbine has direct fuel injection, which means that the fuel is injected into the combustor, and is atomized there into finely divided particles. Under the pressure of emission control efforts, combustors with external pre-mixing devices are under development, and, in these, the injector nozzle is aimed into the pre-mixing zone. Details of such devices will be described in a later chapter.

The engine speed is controlled by fuel metering, as the gas turbine is an unthrottled type of engine consuming vast amounts of excess air.

Because there are two basically different types of combustors—barrel-type and toroidal—there are two basically different types of fuel systems. With barrel-type combustors, the injector nozzle is mounted near the top of the barrel. It injects continuously or intermittently (according to injector nozzle characteristics) under high pressure. With toroidal combustors, fuel is supplied through a tube in the gasifier shaft at low pressure and injected—continuously or intermittently, depending on conditions—by centrifugal force.

Fuel metering in a gas turbine for road vehicle installation may involve fewer and lesser problems than in aircraft turbines. The road vehicle turbine does not have the aircraft version's highly sophisticated altitude compensator system, for instance. Nor does it require the dual high-pressure fuel pumps used on aircraft turbines as a safety precaution against failure in one pump. But with respect to clean fuel, the road vehicle turbine's requirements are just as stringent. Efficient filtration is essential to assure reliability and durability in the fuel metering system with its delicate parts, minute clearances and restricted passages. Since the parts in the fuel system for a 150-hp passenger car turbine are smaller than in a 15,000-hp aircraft turbine, the use of multiple filters of progressively finer mesh is of extreme importance.

The fuel metering system must be capable of assuring reliable combustion over a wide range of ambient temperatures. It must regulate fuel supply so that maximum acceleration rates can be achieved without overheating and surge conditions. The system must respond to changes in fuel demand so as to provide variable-speed capability over the entire speed range, from full speed to idle, which is usually a 2-2.5 to one range.

Fuel pumps can be mechanical, hydro-mechanical, or electric. The 2S 140 Rover used a successful hydromechanical fuel system, which was dropped in favor of a more advanced electric system for the 2S 150. The mechanism of the fuel pump can use any of a myriad of principles that provide a pumping action. Most high-pressure pumps are of the piston type (as are common in diesel engines). These are mechanically operated, as are the newer rotary pumps that are beginning to come into use. Electrical pumps are usually of the diaphragm type.

Fuel pump materials have to be carefully selected due to the very poor film strength of many fuels. For the same reason, the operational parts that work under high mechanical loads must be hydraulically balanced.

Some of the first turbojet engines used mechanical Dowty Live-Line or Dowty Gear Pumps as fuel pumps, but they were not satisfactory for fuels with little or no lubricant properties, such as paraffin or gasoline. As a result, new Dowty fuel pumps were developed specifically for turbojet engines.

The Dowty fuel pump was designed with particular protection to aircraft safety, so that damage caused by overloading, by running dry, or by dirt ingress would not cause pump seizure. Such conditions will, of course, cause a drop in performance, but the pump will keep running and enable the engine to sustain operation.

The fuel pump is supplied from the main tank via a low-pressure filter. The pump is regulated by two different devices: (1) the accelerator linkage, and (2) the governor. The accelerator linkage controls a flow restriction valve in the pump body, which opens fully when the accelerator pedal is fully depressed, and closes fully when the accelerator pedal is released.

An adjustable by-pass valve assures a minimum flow of fuel to the high-pressure side of the pump to allow the engine to idle when the flow restriction valve is closed. The output from the pump is delivered at high pressure to the injector nozzle.

The governor is usually of the centrifugal type, and works as an overspeed device which cuts off fuel supply above a certain compressor speed. Overspeed is most likely to occur as a result of a sudden removal of load from the turbine. That will cause the rotational speed of the turbine to rise rapidly, and the centrifugal force acting on the turbine wheel may reach the point where the blades will disintegrate.

A centrifugal governor is often made integral with the compressor shaft, since this reduces the space requirement as well as eliminating the need for a geared connection. As an alternative, the output line from the pump can be led to a fluid-type governor with a counterweight valve to regulate the flow.

Fuel enters the governor housing which is secured to the forward end of the compressor shaft and rotates with it through a port to a central conduit. A second port is controlled by a counter-weight valve, which opens and closes the path for fuel flow to the central conduit. The counterweight valve position depends on the rotational speed of the shaft, as a result of centrifugal force acting upon it.

Three different types of nozzle designed to provide an atomizing spray are used in gas turbines: (1) the simple nozzle, (2) the duplex nozzle, and (3) the excess fuel nozzle.

The simple nozzle uses a single orifice with a swirling path. Due to this swirl, the fuel leaves the nozzle in a spray formation resembling a conical sheet, which then breaks up into droplets.

Flow rate and pressure drop in a fuel nozzle are closely interdependent. The flow rate will rise or fall proportionally with the square root of the pressure drop.

If the nozzle has a pressure drop of 300 psi with a maximum fuel flow of 660 pounds per hour, it will show a pressure drop of only 3 psi when the fuel flow is cut back to 66 pounds per hour. Such enormous variations in pressure drop are detrimental to control of fuel spray formation, which in turn makes it more difficult to control the combustion process and the emission levels.

This type of nozzle is not acceptable for direct injection, but can be used in combination with pre-mixing chambers that are physically separated from the primary combustion zone, so that they work only in an environment where the spray formation is less critical.

The duplex nozzle incorporates two fuel feed systems—a primary flow and a secondary flow. The primary system is designed for the low-volume end of the fuel flow range, and supplies all of the fuel at minimum flow rates. As turbine rpm and fuel flow increase, the secondary system goes into effect. The pressure to the secondary system is closely controlled, so that it goes into action gradually, from the middle of the fuel flow range, until it supplies almost all the fuel at maximum flow.

The excess fuel nozzle has a single fuel feed system with a simple nozzle designed for the maximum flow rate. That means the nozzle will be receiving excess fuel through most of its operational range and practically all of its operational time. The excess fuel is recirculated to the supply tank through a separate return line.

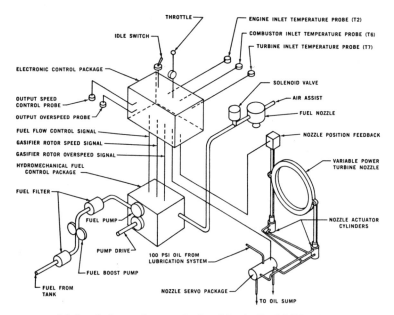

Modern fuel control system developed for the Ford 3600 series.

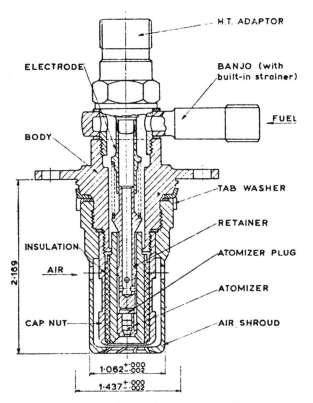

Lucas fuel nozzle as used by Austin gas turbines.

All three types have the same basic disadvantage in common, in that very small openings are required to provide the proper spray formation. Small openings have the drawback that they are susceptible to blockage through dirt ingress and carbon deposit formation. Filtration is not the whole answer, since the fine mesh filters that would be necessary to keep out all particles of orifice size or larger, would run a high risk of clogging. In some areas they may even become a repository for biological growths.

One solution that works very well is the air-atomizing nozzle. In this system, compressed air is introduced into the nozzle to assure a spray of finely atomized droplets over the entire flow range. Air-atomizing nozzles can work with larger openings, and are therefore less vulnerable to clogging. However, the air-atomizing nozzle usually requires an auxiliary air pump for supplying the atomizing air at low compressor speeds, and in some designs, over the full speed range.

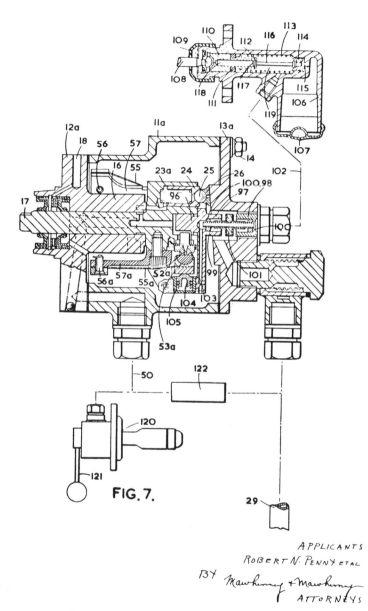

FIG. 7.

APPLICANTS
ROBERT N. PENNY ETAL
BY Mawhinney + Mawhinney
ATTORNEYS

Fuel control system developed by Noel Penny at Rover.

138

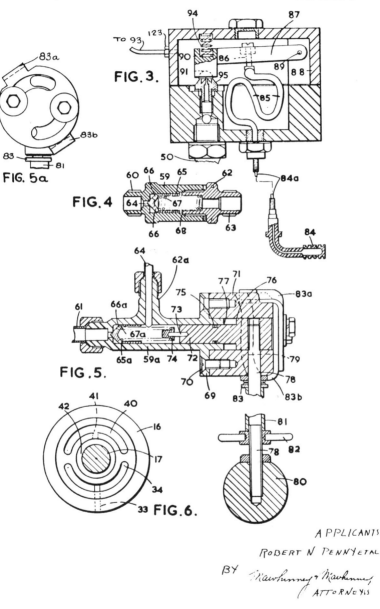

FIG.3.

FIG. 5a.

FIG.4

FIG.5.

FIG.6.

APPLICANTS
ROBERT N PENNY ET AL
BY Mawhinney & Mawhinney
ATTORNEYS

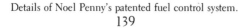

Details of Noel Penny's patented fuel control system.
139

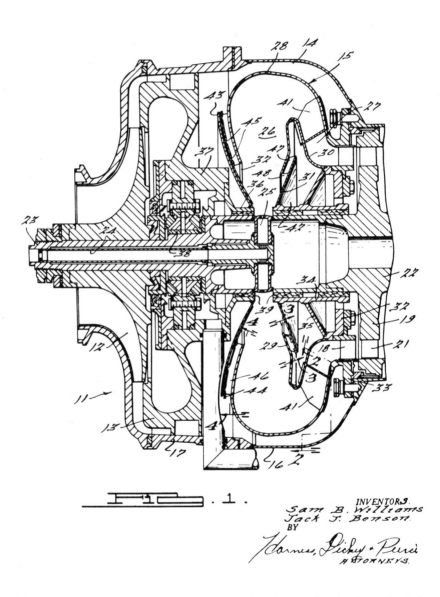

FIG. 1.

INVENTORS.
Sam B. Williams
Jack J. Benson
BY

Harness, Dickey & Pierce
ATTORNEYS.

Williams gas turbine with low-pressure fuel delivery through a hole drilled in the gasifier shaft.

140

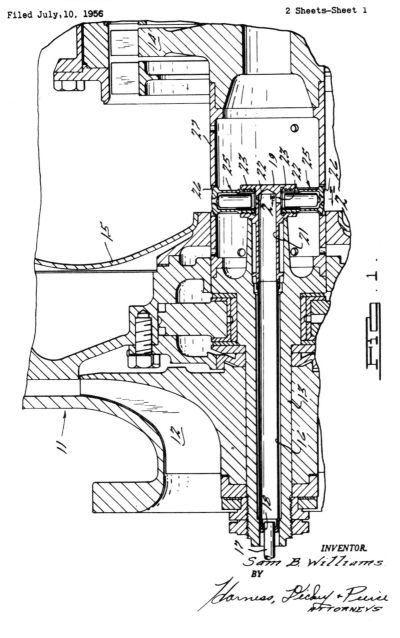

FIG. 1.

INVENTOR.
Sam B. Williams
BY

Harness, Dickey & Pierce
ATTORNEYS

Williams fuel supply conduit and nozzle.

Chrysler turbines use an air-atomizing nozzle because of its generally superior ability to break up all grades of fuel.

Another proposal, which has now largely been abandoned, is the vaporizer. The basic vaporizer is a hot tube with a simple fuel nozzle. The tube temperature is raised by directing a portion of the combustion air so it will flow through it. This results in evaporation of the fuel particles and creates a very rich air/fuel mixture. The tube discharges this rich mixture directly into the primary reaction zone where it is mixed with additional air.

Lycoming used a vaporizing system on an industrial turbine in which liquid fuel was introduced into the burner via tubes immersed in the combustion flame. This approach was given up because the heat balance was extremely critical. The temperature had to be held within a narrow range—high enough to permit all the fuel to vaporize within the tube, but not so high that the tube ends would overheat and burn.

The risk of overheating is present with all types of fuel injection nozzles, so most designs are provided with some form of shielding. Primary zone temperatures can reach 4200° F (2315° C) which creates special reliability problems for all elements present in the primary zone, from igniters and injection nozzles to the combustor sheet metal itself.

Turbines with toroidal combustors and fuel feed through the turbine shaft (Turbomeca and Williams Research) have nozzles mounted on the turbine shaft and rotating with the shaft. The turbine shaft has a central tube which functions as the main fuel line from the governor to the nozzle. The pressure need only be high enough to insure axial flow through the line.

At the rear end of the fuel line, the shaft is drilled with a number of radial passages, evenly spaced out. These passages contain the injector nozzles. Each nozzle is shaped like a dual-bore cylinder and has a float inside its inner cavity. The float is like a loose-fitting piston—free to move back and forth in the cylinder bore (which means radially in and out in relation to the center of the turbine shaft).

The cylinder cavity has a wide bore on the outer half, and a narrow bore on the inner half. The float fits snugly in the inner bore, but does not fill the wide, outer bore. The cylinder has a formation of pockets around the circumference of the inner cavity near the middle, like a belt. The outer end of the cylinder has a small annular central orifice. The float carries a cupola that meets with the tapered orifice walls and closes the orifice.

To understand how it works, let us suppose that the turbine is running at high speed, but that no fuel has yet been delivered to the injector nozzles. The centrifugal force acting on the floats will drive them to their outer limit, so that the cupola closes the nozzle orifice. Fuel reaching the end of the central tube in the shaft will be propelled radially outward by the same force, and enter the inner cylinder chamber through multiple ports in the cylinder bottom. The fuel continues to the outer end of the cylinder due to

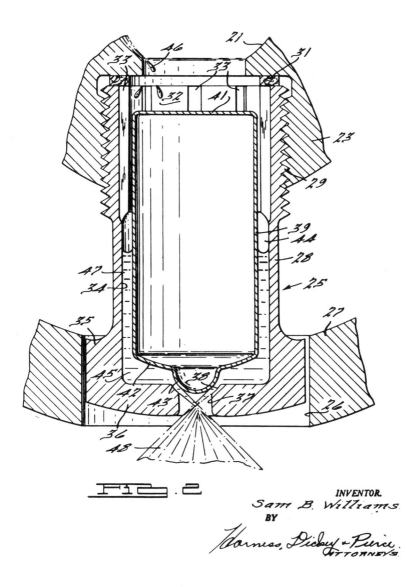

FIG. 2

INVENTOR.

Sam B. Williams

BY

Harness, Dickey & Pierce

ATTORNEYS

Williams fuel slinger and nozzle.

143

the pressure of centrifugal force, and will fill up the entire chamber surrounding the float.

When that is full, fuel will begin to build up in the pockets surrounding the cylinder cavity. The fuel in these pockets will increase the pressure in the outer wide-bore end of the cavity. When the pressure reaches a certain point, it will lift the float cupola off the orifice, and when that occurs, fuel will be sprayed out. Because of the design characteristics of the orifice and the relatively high pressure which exists in the cylinder cavity, the spray will be highly atomized. What's more, good atomization is assured under widely varying flow rates.

The flow will continue until the level of fuel in the pockets has been reduced to such an extent that the pressure in the cavity no longer can sustain the float in its lifted position. The float cupola will then move towards the orifice, and tend to cut off fuel spray by closing it. The degree to which the spray is reduced before the cycle is repeated will depend on the rate of fuel supply to the nozzle unit, the turbine shaft rotational speed, and the relative weights and dimensions of the parts. Experience has proved that the cycle time is rapid enough under all conditions to assure regular combustion.

The control system is basically the same regardless of what type of fuel injection system is used. Most control concepts are based on monitoring of the compressor (gasifier shaft) speed in combination with a turbine inlet temperature sensor. The information is relayed to a control unit which then regulates fuel flow to give the desired gasifier speed for any accelerator position.

On turbine engines with variable geometry on the free turbine nozzle, the nozzle blade angle can be adjusted in accordance with turbine inlet temperature requirement as directed by the control unit. Regulation of (1) fuel flow and (2) nozzle angle is enough to control all engine functions.

The control system must be designed to give optimum fuel economy under all operating conditions and be compatible with transmission requirements. It must be ready to respond instantly to signals from the throttle, and provide engine braking, govern accessory speed at idle, and prevent turbine overspeed in accordance with these signals.

Until quite recently, there was little effort among gas turbine manufacturers to make use of advanced concepts such as integrated circuits or fluidics, although Ford used an electronic control system with electrohydraulic transducers on the 3600 series turbine units, as early as 1970.

Frequency signals from pulse-type electric pickups in the gasifier and power sections, temperature transducers at the turbine, combustor, and compressor inlets, and a nozzle actuator feedback potentiometer provided inputs to the control brain which computed and scheduled the operation of the fuel pump servo cylinder and variable-nozzle actuator valves.

9

The Ignition
System

THE TURBINE ENGINE has a simplified
ignition system, since ignition is required only for starting. The entire electrical system required for the basic turbine engine includes quite simply a
storage battery, starter motor, generator, induction coil and contact breaker
mechanism, and an "igniter."

There are two basic types of igniter. One is a spark igniter, and the other
is a flame igniter. The spark igniter is a large spark plug, with a ceramic
insulator and a heavy center electrode. The electrical energy for firing the
spark igniter is provided by a simple high-capacity coil fed by a heavy-duty
battery. The igniter is automatically turned on in case of flameout during
operation, so that the engine will keep running.

A flame igniter is a small self-contained unit which incorporates a special
low-pressure atomizer and a spark plug. Low-pressure fuel delivery to the
flame igniter is provided by a small booster pump connected to the inlet side
of a main fuel pump, and controlled by a solenoid-operated valve. This
valve is closed during normal operation and when the engine is shut down.
But it is activated at a pre-selected point in the starting cycle. When the
solenoid is energized, fuel flows to the atomizer and is ignited by the spark
plug. The mixture is super-rich and produces a blow-torch type of flame.

The flame igniter is aimed into the primary zone, and the flame is projected into the mixture created by fuel injection into the combustor. The
flame igniter is needed only until the primary zone combustion reaches the
point of being self-sustaining. When the turbine reaches idling speed, the
solenoid is deactivated, and the flame igniter is turned off.

The spark igniter in particular must be located with due regard to its position relative to the fuel spray. The igniter must also extend far enough into

Bendix igniter for industrial gas turbines.

the primary reaction zone to give effective cold starting, but not so deep inside the combustor that it will be damaged by high temperatures.

Service experience with a fleet of Chrysler test cars (using spark igniters) illustrates the hazards imposed on igniter function and life by its environment. George J. Huebner Jr. reported in 1966:

Early igniters showed distress at the thirty-day inspection period required for all of the cars. This distress was indicated both by the appearance of rapid electrical erosion and by severe oxidation of the electrodes, despite the fact that the electrodes are supplied with cooling air discharged as excess from the fuel nozzle air pump.
Since the igniter must be inserted through the combustor sleeve in such a way that it is continuously exposed to some flame impingement and to radiation from the hottest part of the flame, modifications to the hollow electrodes and the means of discharge of the cooling air from them were incorporated. Test mileage on igniters is now in excess of 20,000 miles. Although this may be satisfactory for a piston engine, it is not considered satisfactory for an automotive turbine and redesigned igniters now under test will hopefully more than double this life.

The turbine engine's starting cycle is different from the conventional automobile's. What happens when the ignition switch is turned on depends on the type of igniter used. With a spark igniter, the switch closes a circuit and current flows to the igniter, heating it up until it glows. A red light on the instrument panel stays on until the igniter is hot enough to ensure firing. With a flame igniter, the switch activates the booster pump, and fuel flows to the flame igniter. It is connected to a similar red light, which is turned off as soon as the necessary pressure has been built up.

The starter motor is activated when it gets the start signal (as the red light goes out). It turns the compressor shaft, which assures delivery of compressed air into the combustor. At 4,000–6,000 rpm the fuel supply and igniter are turned on. When the shaft speed reaches 12,400–16,000 rpm, the igniter and starter motor are turned off. In automotive turbines, the warmup/pressure buildup period is about 7–10 seconds, and the period necessary for starter motor and igniter operation is also about 7–10 seconds.

10

Accessory Drive System

THE TURBINE ENGINE needs basically the same essential accessories that a piston engine requires, and the accessory demands in the vehicle itself are unchanged from piston power to turbine power. The turbine's key accessories include a fuel pump, oil pump, generator, tachometer, governor, and regenerator drive.

In a typical passenger car, the engine will also have to drive such accessories as the air conditioner compressor and power steering pump. Some simplification of the engine accessories is possible. For instance, early Chrysler turbines combined the starter motor with the generator, so that when the starter circuit is disengaged, the motor becomes a generator that charges the battery and provides current for local electrical accessories. Field experience with this system soon discouraged Chrysler from this approach to simplification.

The combined function starter-generator caused a severe operational deficiency. Although high-altitude performance testing to 13,000 feet had been carried out in the mountains near Denver, Colorado, it was not initially discovered that a combination of high altitude and low humidity caused rapid and catastrophic destruction of the starter-generator brushes on this otherwise excellent unit. Subsequent investigation indicated that the addition of barium salts to the graphite brush compound would reduce or eliminate the high altitude brush wear, but even with this change a fundamental problem remained.

Under cold starting conditions the brushes were required to carry high current, thus requiring a soft, low electrical resistance, short mileage brush, whereas under generating conditions at commutator rotational speeds up to 20,000 rpm, a hard, long-wearing brush with high resistance, was desirable. These mutually exclusive requirements were finally compromised in a brush

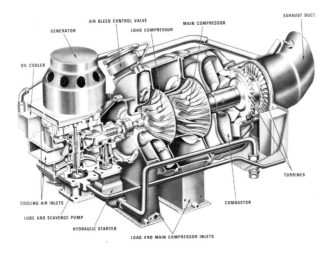

Accessory assembly, with drive from the gasifier shaft, mounted at the front of a Williams Research turbojet engine.

which, under test, showed a life expectancy under 25,000 miles, which was not considered satisfactory. This problem was corrected during the program but convinced Chrysler that automotive turbines should be equipped with separate starters and alternators.

Preceding chapters have shown the simplicity of the fuel injection and ignition systems. Starter motors tend to be larger and more expensive than on piston engines, however, due to the gas turbine's high starting speed and starter drive power requirement. A typical starter motor runs on 24-V direct current. With 16-V applied and at a current draw of 1,000 amperes, the motor runs at 2750 rpm and develops 13.3 horsepower. Its maximum torque is 25.4 pounds-feet. This is enough to drive the compressor shaft to turbine self-starting speed with a suitable gear ratio in the mechanical drive connection to the compressor shaft.

The Prestolite starting motor used on the Ford 3600 series turbine is a new and unique type without a drive end head. The drive end of the motor frame is machined to fit an opening in the turbine housing. The drive end face aligns itself with a reference surface within the turbine, and the motor is held in place by three clamps. A dowel pin inserted between the turbine and the starter insures proper orientation of the single terminal and locks the starter motor securely to the turbine housing.

A positive mechanical connection between the motor and the turbine is assured by the use of shafts with involute splines. The motor output shaft is

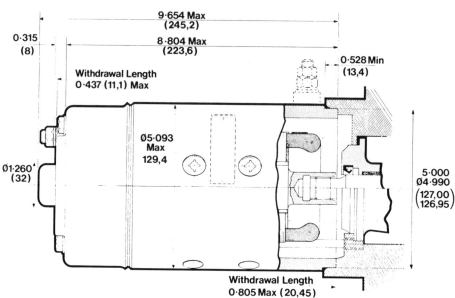

CAV gas turbine starter motor.

recessed in the motor housing and contains an internal spline. Ford's starter drive train has external splines on its input shaft, and this spline coupling supports the drive end of the armature.

It is normal practice to drive the accessories from the compressor shaft. This gives higher inertia in the gasifier section, but it keeps the accessories running when the free turbine is not turning. With a compressor-shaft accessory drive system, the accessories can also be made to consume less power. The reason is simple. Accessories must be given capability to deliver a certain minimum output at idle and low speed. When low speed is 750 rpm, as in a typical V8, the accessories must be designed to deliver this minimum at 750 rpm.

They will therefore be consuming far more power than they need at 5000 rpm, wasting fuel and raising the noise level. In a gas turbine with a low speed of 25,000 rpm and top speed of 60,000 rpm, there is little waste at full speed, as the accessories have been designed to deliver their minimum output at 40 percent of maximum speed.

The free turbine speed ratio in the same turbine is infinite—from 0 to perhaps 55,000 rpm. Nonetheless, there are valid reasons why the accessories—or some of them—should be driven from the free (power) turbine shaft. The power requirements of accessories such as air conditioning throw a heavy load on the accessory drive. With accessory drive from the compressor shaft, there may be a rise in turbine inlet temperature without any change in engine rpm. Any increase in turbine inlet temperature at idle will detract from the acceleration potential. Lowering the turbine inlet temperature at idle will increase the acceleration potential. It has long been acknowledged that inlet temperature at idle can be minimized by coupling the accessory drive to the free turbine shaft.

In the GM Whirlfire turbine installations, all accessories were driven from the gasifier turbine. However, design calculations showed that the accessory loads for the Firebird II installation would overload the gasifier turbine at idle. Therefore, it was deemed advantageous to drive some of the larger accessories from the power turbine.

However, this imposed the problem that, with the vehicle stationary and the turbine output shaft locked to the transmission, there can be no power for the accessory drive. It becomes necessary to provide a clutch or another

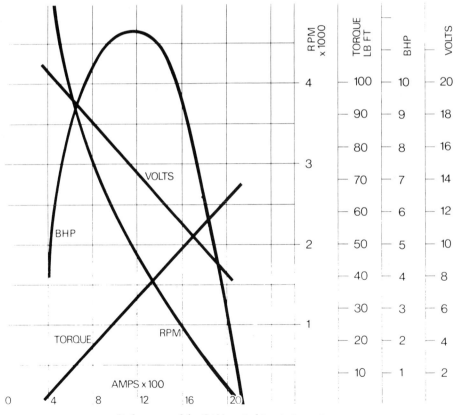

Performance of the CAV gas turbine starter motor.

form of mechanism to disconnect the free turbine shaft from the drive train to the road wheels.

The GM engineers solved it for the Firebird II installation by using a transmission which included a fluid coupling interposed between the propeller shaft and the planetary gear trains. As a result, the power turbine was enabled to turn at all times.

Chrysler had taken the accessory drive from the compressor shaft on the A-831 turbine used in the 50-car series built in 1963–64. But the next (fifth) generation Chrysler turbines took the accessory drive from the free turbine shaft, and the automatic (TorqueFlite) transmission with its hydraulic torque converter provided the necessary slip to allow free turbine rotation at zero rpm transmission output shaft speed.

There is also evidence to support the opinion that it's not necessary to go to such extremes as taking the accessory drive from the free turbine shaft in order to avoid excessive turbine inlet temperature at idle during extensive use of accessory power. Charles Amann of General Motors Research Laboratories has pointed out that variable power turbine nozzles can help in lowering the accessory drive loads on the compressor shaft. Opening the nozzle vanes causes the flow capacity at a given pressure ratio to increase. This will change the pressure ratio split between the first-stage and the second-stage turbines, and shift a larger portion of the total pressure drop to the gasifier turbine. As a result, the pressure ratio across the gasifier turbine will rise, which lowers the turbine inlet temperature requirement for continued operation under the same load.

This is a more attractive solution, for it eliminates the additional cost of the hydraulic torque converter and its hydraulic slippage (power loss).

11

The Lubrication System

THE LUBRICATION requirements of the automotive gas turbine are relatively modest. The principal tasks to be performed by the oil circulating in the gas turbine are the same as in a conventional piston engine: to lubricate and provide internal cooling. These are simpler tasks in a gas turbine because the surfaces to be lubricated in the gas turbine are far smaller than in the piston engine. The turbine is free of large surfaces in sliding contact, and the main lubricating duties are confined to the bearings for the turbine shafts. Since these bearings run at extremely high speeds, the cooling properties of the oil are just as important as the lubricating qualities.

In most gas turbine engines, the main bearings that support the turbine and compressor shafts are either ball bearings or roller bearings. Sleeve bearings are often used in other connections (splines, alignment bearings, etc.).

In a typical gas turbine lubrication system, the oil is circulated through a pressure regulating valve, and then to an oil cooler, which may be mounted separately or attached to the turbine housing. From the oil cooler the flow continues through an oil filter as the last station prior to delivery to the shaft bearings, gears and splines in the engine and gear system.

The oil returns by gravity to the reservoir, which is usually a sump located at the bottom of the turbine housing. Strategically positioned check valves prevent the oil in the system from draining into various collection points or the sump when the engine is shut down. This assures the presence of an adequate oil film immediately when the unit is started up again.

The oil cooler can be air-cooled or liquid-cooled, but most turbines use the air-cooled type since the power unit itself is air-cooled. The air-cooled oil cooler is a simple radiator type of heat exchanger, with the oil circulating in narrow-diameter pipes through a mesh of cooling fins.

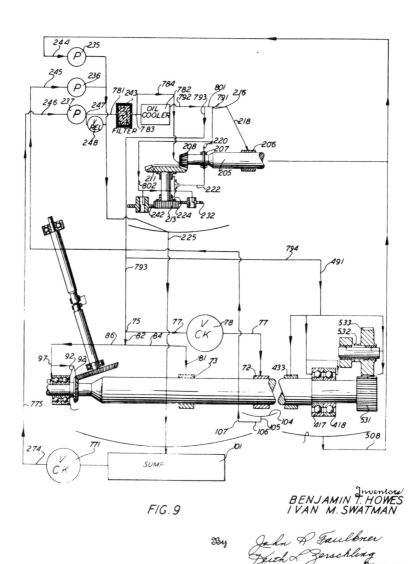

FIG. 9

Inventors
BENJAMIN T. HOWES
IVAN M. SWATMAN

By   John R. Faulkner
      Keith L. Zerschling
                    Attorneys

Lubrication system designed for a Ford automotive gas turbine engine.

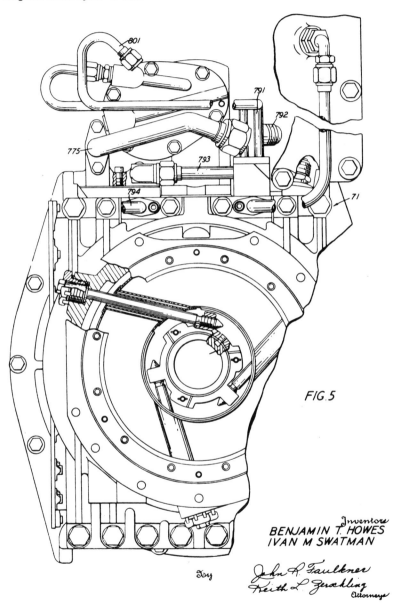

FIG. 5

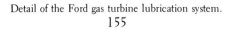

Inventors
BENJAMIN T. HOWES
IVAN M SWATMAN

John R. Faulkner
Keith L. Zerckling
Attorneys

Detail of the Ford gas turbine lubrication system.

155

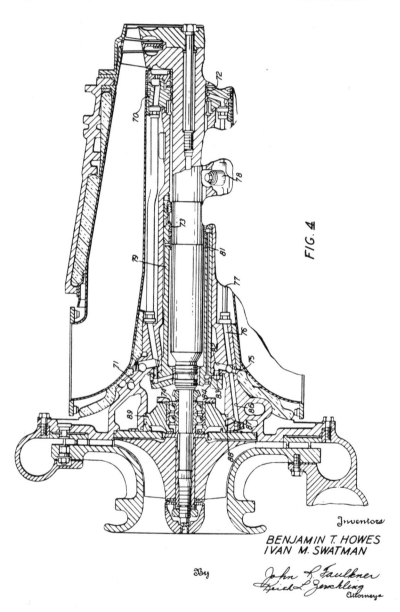

FIG. 4

Inventors

BENJAMIN T. HOWES
IVAN M. SWATMAN

By

John L. Faulkner
Keith L. Zenchling
Attorneys

Detail of the Ford gas turbine lubrication system.

156

Air can be supplied to the oil cooler in several ways. Aircraft turbine oil coolers are cooled by ram air and this principle also works well on cars. With the car in motion, the airflow created by the speed of the car is usually enough to provide the necessary temperature drop in the oil flow. The same will generally be true for highway trucks, but not for off-road vehicles and earth-moving machinery, where the operating conditions are closer to those of industrial-type turbine installations. In such cases a separate cooling fan is added to assure continuous air flow through the oil cooler.

Most oil coolers are made of aluminum. The size depends entirely on the heat rejection rate required for each individual design. On most units, oil flow to the oil cooler is controlled by a thermostat.

Most turbines are built with internal oil passages throughout. For instance, the oil supply to the rear bearings can be fed in through a channel in the power turbine shaft. Oil flow will be assured by the pump and assisted by shaft rotation. This way, the oil does not pass through heated passages, and the second-stage turbine hub gets the benefit of a certain amount of cooling from it.

Conventional motor oil of low viscosity grades (SAE 10) has proved fully useable in automotive gas turbines. Except for exposure to extreme heat, the oil in the gas turbine lubrication system has a relatively easy time. The lubricant is never exposed to the combustion area, and there is no risk of oil contamination from the combustion products (such as blowby gases, for instance).

All gas turbines have very low oil consumption. During the early development period at General Motors, William A. Turunen noted that the greatest loss of oil occurred through the engine breather pipe, and this was cured by improved design and relocation of the breather.

The oil is subjected to very high temperature conditions, even during normal operation. The oil must also be able to withstand the "soaking" it will be exposed to at shutdown. When the engine is shut down, the heat from the hot zones soaks through the shafts and into the bearings. This may cause the oil to coke if the soaking temperatures rise above the oil's danger point. If coking occurs, the coke and carbon particles can cause damage to the bearing.

Synthetic oils are normally used, because they maintain their properties better during long-time service. While some automotive engineers believe a petroleum-based lubricant eventually can be developed to meet the high temperature requirements of turbines, only synthetics are used now—and all test programs on automotive turbines now underway depend upon chemical-based lubricants.

John Hulbert, turbine engineer for Williams Research Corporation, says synthetics are considerably more stable than mineral oils for use in turbines.

"Moving parts are far fewer in a turbine than in a piston-driven engine, but they are also much more compact. The heat buildup is very intense, so we design the engine with 'heat dams'—barriers that permit bearings and other parts to cool. Because a synthetic oil is more stable—it won't break down as quickly in these critical cooling areas—it gives us more design flexibility. Synthetics have played an important role in enabling us to design the more efficient turbines developed to date," says Mr. Hulbert.

Ford points out that with the use of synthetic oils, the need for oil changes between engine overhauls can be assumed to be non-existent.

12

Production Cost

THE BASIC SIMPLICITY of the gas turbine indicates that the turbine engine should be easier and cheaper to build, as well as intrinsically more reliable and hence cheaper to service and maintain than conventional piston powerplants. The multitude of problems associated with the passenger car application will cause certain complications, however, that may increase the cost of a turbine car.

A gas turbine has only about 20 percent as many moving parts as a comparable reciprocating engine. The size is smaller and the weight lighter, as illustrated by the 450-pound weight of the Chrysler 150-hp gas turbine and the 250-pound weight of the Williams Research Corp. 80-hp WR-26 gas turbine.

Truck and industrial regenerative gas turbines, in order to compete with the fuel economy and reliability of the diesel engine, must be produced for $10–20 per horsepower. The passenger turbine engine with low cost and high performance as the main criteria must be produced at $2.00–3.00 per horsepower.

A few years ago, George J. Huebner Jr. stated that the cost of the materials alone amounted to $8.00 per hp in the Chrysler turbine, while the V8 engine at the time did not exceed $2.00 per hp in total production cost.

Because of the large number of variables involved in calculating costs, certain assumptions have to be made in many different areas before we can get down to a discussion in actual dollars and cents. Total engine cost is a function of the cost of raw materials, the manufacturing techniques to be used, and the quantities to be produced per year. The key is in the last item—quantity. And the solution to the cost problem must lie in mass production.

As Noel Penny sums it up: "In order to get the cost reduced, production volume must be high. There's only one way to get truly high volume, and that's to go into passenger cars." To elaborate on the importance of mass production, we have a statement from George J. Huebner Jr.:

To develop a passenger car gas turbine means to concentrate on the application which is the most challenging from the standpoint of engineering skill, but more important than this, it is the most representative application from the standpoint of manufacture and operation.

Through passenger car application, this power plant can enter the transportation life of practically all Americans. Only this way, by using the passenger car engine tooling as a production base, can the unit cost be reduced to a dollar level which will place it in common use.

The most thorough cost analysis that has been made public is a study carried out by Williams Research Corporation under a contract with the EPA in 1972. The basis for the analysis was an enlarged (130 hp vs. 80 hp) version of the WR-26 engine. That is a free-shaft regenerative turbine of proven capability as a passenger car power unit.

The relevant assumptions involve no new technology in either the power unit itself, in materials, or in production equipment and machinery, not even for the target pricing and developed processing. Production volume was set at 1,000,000 units per year, which is a typical figure for a successful car line.

The estimates for the V8 piston engine were calculated by Williams Research Corp. on the basis of known factors. While Williams Research Corp. has no production of piston engines, its engineering staff includes men with backgrounds in the automobile industry and its supplier industries. The figures must be regarded as extremely close to actual 1972 costs.

The total cost picture is not quite that simple, however. Tooling costs must be taken into account, not only for the automobile manufacturer but also for the supplier industry, which will lose its market for piston engine parts while being presented with a new market for gas turbine components. Fringe costs to be charged to a switch to gas turbines will involve the obsolesence of knowhow and the cost of retraining personnel.

With regard to tooling, George J. Huebner Jr. of Chrysler told the press as long ago as 1964:

"Analyses are now being performed beyond the stage of an educated guess, which will eventually allow us to come up with actual figures based on solid realities. Already, there are indications that the tooling cost will be perhaps somewhat lower than it is for piston engines, while the many fewer parts of the gas turbine and the fact that no outstandingly unusual fabrication techniques are involved should permit keeping the cost of manufacturing to a satisfactorily low level."

	V-8 Piston Engine	Automotive Turbine	
		Current Pricing & Processing	Target Pricing & Developed Processing

(Figures in Dollars and Cents)

Base Engine			
Turbine Wheels		36.31	14.19
Turbine Nozzle		9.43	3.25
Regenerators		18.04	7.40
Remaining Parts		91.41	91.41
Total Base Engine	144.00	155.19	116.25
Fuel system	5.85	38.00	30.00
Ignition System			
(including spark plugs)	5.13	2.82	2.82
Air Cleaner & Intake	1.54	3.08	3.08
Cooling System	11.93	—	—
Exhaust System	4.90	9.80	9.80
Starter	4.10	4.10	4.10
Battery	3.89	5.14	5.14
Alternator	5.30	5.30	5.30
Total	$186.64	$223.43	$176.49

Due to its greater simplicity, the gas turbine will require less capital investment for fabricating equipment and machine tools than the piston engine does. When fewer parts per engine are needed, the number and complexity of the machine tools can be reduced. Because fewer parts will have to be processed and stored, inventory costs can be expected to drop.

Many of the complex—shaped parts in a gas turbine engine can be cast from the same stainless steel or other alloys used in a conventional engine at moderate cost. Castings are used for all possible parts in a piston engine because of their low unit cost in mass production, and the automobile industry is justly famous for its precision casting techniques.

With a switch to gas turbine production, engine manufacturers will find that they need to convert production to a completely different type of operation, as well as having to acquire new equipment. But the engine plant and machinery wear out anyway. The average engine production line has an active life of 16–20 years. Sooner or later the equipment must be replaced. From an economical point of view, the auto industry would find it feasible to phase out the piston engine and phase in the gas turbine as the older plant reached the end of its useful life. Some engine lines are approaching the critical age, and more will get there before mass production prototypes can be prepared.

Consequently, one must conclude that the switch from piston engine to gas turbine production could begin with immediate effect, without upsetting existing schedules and budgets for plant reconstruction and re-equipment.

An accelerated conversion pace is possible with minor economic losses, since production equipment is rapidly amortized and engine lines are usually carried with low book values. The factor limiting the pace of conversion would be the financing of new plant and equipment acquisitions.

An excellent case can be argued for almost any markup, since the mass production of a gas turbine is a completely new activity. But on the strength of the above observations, it is also apparent that the markup needed to cover retooling and fringe costs or losses will not necessarily be very high, perhaps only 2–4 percent of the net engine manufacturing cost.

SECTION II

DEVELOPMENT

13

Gas Turbine Pre-History

THE WORD "TURBINE" is derived from the Latin *turbo-turbinis* and was first used in 1824 to describe a fluid-driven vane wheel by Professor Claude Burdin, an instructor at the Ecole des Mines at St. Etienne in Central France. The invention of the gas turbine did not take place in one step. The idea of a vaned wheel mounted on a shaft and made to revolve by impingement of a fluid flow against the vanes dates from ancient times.

About 150 B.C. Hero, a philosopher in Alexandria, Egypt, described a form of steam turbine. It consisted of a spherical base equipped with multiple nozzles. At the center, it was pierced by a shaft running in two bearings. Steam was generated in the base and discharged from the elbow-shaped nozzles, producing a reactive force that caused the sphere to rotate on its shaft. The same principle of action is used in modern steam-driven *reaction turbines*.

In 1629 an Italian scientist, Giovanni Branca, invented a form of steam turbine incorporating a steam generator with a jet nozzle directed against vanes mounted radially on a wheel. His invention constitutes the first steam-driven *impulse turbine*. Credit for the first use of a steam turbine as the prime mover for a wheeled vehicle must go to Ferdinand Verbiest, a Belgian-born religious savant working in a Jesuit mission in China.

The exact year of construction is impossible to ascertain: Verbiest's book "Astronomia Europaea" first described the vehicle and was published in Bavaria in 1687. The text refers to it as being built "three years ago." However, there is evidence that "Astronomia Europaea" had been printed in China between 1668 and 1673—thus placing the date of Verbiest's invention even earlier. No matter what the date of Verbiest's invention, he was definitely ahead of his time. Verbiest's own description of the vehicle is interesting:

While investigating the power of the aeolipile (a spherical steam boiler with a small vent, devised originally by the ancient Greeks in the Second Century B.C.), I made a little chariot, two feet long and on four wheels, in the middle of which I placed a vessel full of coals, and, above that, an aeolipile. On the axle of the front wheel there was a toothed bronze wheel driven by gear wheels by another wheel with four vanes upon which the jet of steam was directed. By means of a tiller and a larger, forward guidewheel connected to the pivoted rear axle, I made the carriage run in a circle.

The early turbines were primitive in the extreme, lacking shrouds for the turbine wheels, and using wheels whose blade profile and angle of incidence were selected more or less at random. Little further progress was made until the early part of the 19th century.

In 1824 Professor Claude Burdin proposed what he called a "free efflux" turbine. It had a vertical axis carrying a turbine wheel with curved blades. Water passed through the gaps between the blades, forcing the wheel to revolve, and issued almost tangentially. Fixed guide vanes, curved in the opposite direction, were mounted in an annular stator placed immediately upstream from the turbine wheel. Burdin's pupil Benoit Fourneyron built a working model of this radial out-flow hydraulic turbine in 1827.

A contemporary French mathematician, Jean Victor Poncelet (1788–1867) proposed a radial in-flow hydraulic turbine in 1826. The machine was built with a vertical shaft, and the curved vane turbine wheel was completely shrouded. In 1849 an American engineer and a pioneer in the science of hydraulics, J. B. Francis improved Poncelet's turbine by adding stationary guide vanes so as to provide for shockless entry to the turbine wheel and minimize the exit velocity from it.

A French scientist named Jonval designed the first axial-flow turbine in 1837. In the latter half of the 19th century, turbine research and development was undertaken on an industrial scale. But most of the efforts were directed at developing a commercial steam turbine, while a few others devoted their attention to the hydraulic turbine.

The gas turbine was an idea whose time had not yet come, and I believe it was ignored because the internal combustion engine was still a theory and not a reality. The case of John Barber tends to support this belief. He was granted a British patent number 1833 for a gas turbine, October 31, 1791, and described the heat cycle correctly, but the machine was never built. Of course, Barber was also faced with the problem of finding materials and tools that would enable him to construct his machine.

The patent claims included a process of heating wood, coal, oil or other hydrocarbons in a receptacle, catching the escaping gases and cooling them. A pump would be used to mix the gases with air in certain proportions and feed the mixture into an "exploder." The mixture would then be ignited and the jet of expanding gases would be used to turn a vaned wheel. Barber also recommended water injection into the "exploder" for the dual purpose of cooling the metal jet and increasing the size of the gas stream. This describes a true gas turbine, and it is interesting that it was proposed before the internal-combustion piston engine was invented.

The first practical steam turbine was invented in 1883 by the Swedish engineer Gustav P. H. de Laval (1845–1913). Of French Huguenot extraction, de Laval was both an engineer and scientist and like Alfred Nobel, he successfully combined the careers of inventor and industrialist.

He received an engineering degree from Stockholm's Royal Institute of Technology in 1866 and six years later took his doctorate in chemistry at Uppsala University. De Laval became one of Sweden's most popular, respected, and prolific inventors with 92 patents to his credit.

An improved steam turbine was demonstrated by Charles A. Parsons in 1884. It consisted of two groups of turbine wheels, having fifteen consecutive wheels in each group and enclosed in a common casing. The steam entered at the middle of the casing and passed through the two groups of turbine wheels in opposite directions. This design distributed the total pressure drop over a number of stages, which enabled the machine to perform the same work at lower rotor speed. Having the fluid enter at the middle of the casing and pass in either direction also cancelled out end-thrust. Turbine wheel diameter was only about 3 inches, and the 10 hp unit ran at 17,000 rpm. In 1891 Parsons added a condenser to exploit the turbine's capacity for utilizing the energy of low-pressure steam down to a near-perfect vacuum. That same year a Parsons steam turbine was harnessed to generate electric power.

In hydro-electric plants, the Pelton water wheel was coming into use. Invented by an American engineer, L. A. Pelton, it was the simplest form of impulse turbine. It consists of a wheel with a series of buckets mounted along its periphery. A nozzle directs a stream of water against the buckets and the velocity of the water causes the wheel to rotate.

From this time on, the development of hydraulic and steam turbines took its own course and had no further influence on gas turbine engineering. In the last two decades of the 19th century, as the internal combustion engine commenced its triumphant march to the revolution in transportation and mobility, a number of inventors began to study the gas turbine.

In 1872 a German scientist, Dr. F. Stolze, took out a patent for a gas turbine comprising an axial-flow compressor and a multi-stage reaction turbine. Stolze did not actually build the engine until 1902–04. When it was tested, the efficiency was so low that Dr. Stolze decided not to put further effort into the project.

About 1880 Emile Hugoniot, a French scientist, was experimenting with a gas turbine. Sir Charles Parsons had mentioned the possibility of a gas turbine in his steam turbine patent from 1884. In Le Mans, France, a mechanic named Amedee Bollee (fils) took out a patent for a gas turbine on December 28, 1894. He gave it up because of excessive fuel consumption and bearing lubrication problems. About 1896 Dr. Aurel Stodola, professor of thermodynamics at the Zurich Technical University in Switzerland, described the operational cycle of the continuous-combustion open-cycle gas turbine.

Charles Lemale and Rene Armengaud formed a company called Societe Anonyme des Turbomoteurs in Paris, and from 1900 to 1906 were very active in gas turbine research and development. They built the first gas turbine of the modern type, with continuous combustion. A centrifugal compressor with 25 impellers was used, and delivered air compressed to 60 psi to the combustor. The compressor had a peak efficiency of 68 percent.

In 1905 Auguste Rateau had designed a new type of centrifugal compressor for Brown, Boveri. After an examination of this design, Lemale and Armengaud decided that was what they wanted. They therefore asked Brown, Boveri to supply a compressor of this type. This machine, which was built and dispatched to Paris in 1906, was one of the largest turbocompressors in the world at that time. It compressed 127,000 cubic feet per hour of air to a final pressure of about 64 psi and ran at a speed of 4500 rpm. Despite Lemale and Armengaud's theoretically correct operating cycle and the use of advanced-design components, the engine failed to produce any useful amount of power.

Dr. Adolf Meyer has pointed out that the main reason for the failure of this turbine was the inability of the turbine blades to withstand temperatures in excess of 1,000° F (538° C) coupled with low component efficiencies. The combustor operated in the 3,300 to 3,600° F (1815–1982° C) range and took in a great volume of compressed air to cool the exhaust gases upstream from the turbine inlet. With an overall efficiency of 53 percent, and turbine inlet temperatures below 1,000° F, the thermal efficiency of the gas turbine cycle was zero! The company was liquidated in 1909 because the prototype turbine never yielded better than 3 percent efficiency.

The next important step of progress came in 1916 when Auguste Rateau (1862–1931) built and tested a gas turbine with a single-stage centrifugal compressor, a turbine inlet temperature of 1472° F (800° C) and a rotor speed of 23,000 rpm. Rateau was born at Royan in the Charente-Maritime Departement on France's Atlantic Coast and was educated at the Ecole Polytechnique in Paris and the Ecole Superieure des Mines. He became a professor at the Ecole des Mines at St. Etienne in 1888. He invented the Belleville washer in 1890, a turbo-fan in 1892 and a steam humidity gauge in 1897. To exploit his inventions, he organized the Societe Rateau at La Courneuve. He patented an anemometer and the Pitot tube in 1898, an airscrew and an ejector-type condenser in 1900. About 1905 he became interested in turbo-supercharging for piston engines, and this line of research led him to study the gas turbine.

Dr. Aurel Stodola gives Hans Holzwarth the credit for having built the first economically practical gas turbine. Hans Holzwarth lived and worked in Mannheim, Germany. Hans Holzwarth designed his first gas turbine in 1905, and the first one was built in the shops of Gebrueder Körting in Hannover between 1906 and 1908. A second unit of Holzwarth's design with 10 combustors was built and tested by Brown, Boveri & Co. in Mannheim between 1909 and 1913. It had a nominal rating of 1,000 hp but actually delivered only 200 hp.

Holzwarth did not envisage continuous combustion but specified a combustible gaseous mixture periodically exploded in separate chambers, with the exhaust gases ducted during their expansion into the actual turbine. The Holzwarth gas turbine had multiple combustors, firing in sequence. Only the moderate precompression required to feed the combustors was used. What was the rationale behind this intermittent-action combustor?

When compared with the theoretically elegant gas turbines of Charles Lemale and Auguste Rateau, the Holzwarth concepts seem somewhat anachronistic, especially in the area of combustion techniques. Holzwarth observed in his patent texts that other gas turbine pioneers tried to make their engines as similar as possible to steam turbines, and that they felt the best working cycle was obtained with an unbroken, uniform current.

Holzwarth argued that such a cycle placed excessive thermal stresses on the key components. He provided for cooling the combustor by scavenging it with cool air, and then refilling it with combustible mixture—perfectly in line with Otto-cycle operation. To obtain this, the combustors needed separate intake valves for air and gas. They were also provided with spark plugs.

The combustion pressure would open a nozzle valve to let the exhaust gas flow to the turbine. A mechanical retarding device would keep this nozzle valve open after the end of the combustion, and let the following blast of cooling air escape the same way. Then fresh gas would be admitted to the combustor, and all valves closed before the moment of ignition. This would result in a series of intermittent firings which Holzwarth claimed had a substantially continuous effect on the turbine.

The nozzle valve had to give an absolutely tight seal during the charging and combustion periods, but Holzwarth fully understood the importance of quick valve opening and high valve lift. He wanted the nozzle valve to open

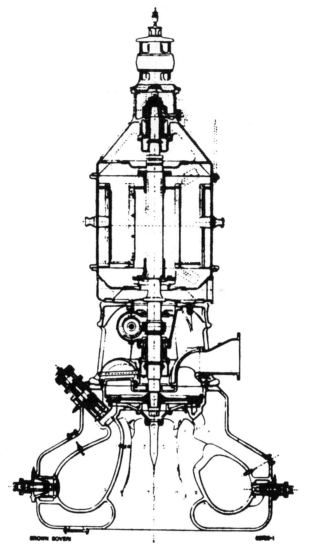

Sectioned view of the second Holzwarth gas turbine.

automatically as soon as the first pressure wave from the explosion reached the valve head, so as to induce turbulence in the combustor and obtain more complete burning. The cooling air from the combustors was also to be fed into the turbine and extend its beneficial cooling effects on the hot-running parts. The cooling air would be mixed with the combustion gases in

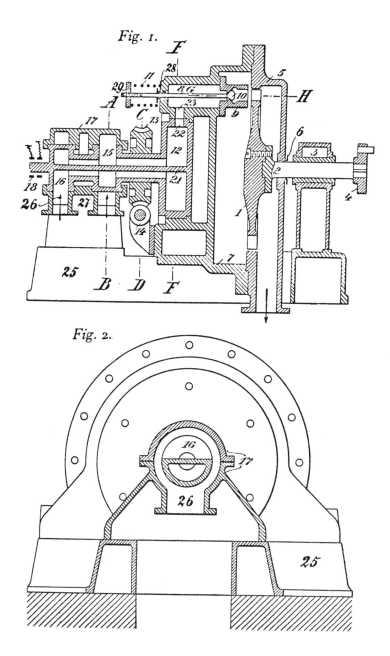

Fig. 1.

Fig. 2.

Sectioned view of Holzwarth's 1905 gas turbine design, showing turbine wheel and nozzle valve.

171

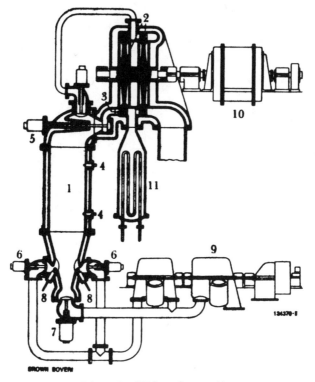

Schematic of Holzwarth gas turbine:

1.	Combustor	7.	Scavenging valve
2.	Turbine wheels	8.	Fuel injection nozzles
3.	Nozzle	9.	Compressor driven by steam turbine
4.	Spark plugs	10.	Generator
5.	Nozzle valve	11.	Heat exchanger
6.	Air valve		

the nozzle stage, he theorized, because the expanding gases traveled at high velocity, while the air head would move at low velocity.

The Holzwarth turbine also required water cooling for the nozzle, impeller, and blades. To recover the heat given up to the water, it had to be evaporated and the steam used to drive a turbine for running the compressor. The steam turbine in turn required a condenser and a cooling water plant. This kind of complexity kept the Holzwarth turbines from gaining large-scale practical success. On the credit side it must be said that Holzwarth's turbine wheels represented an important step forward in the state of the art.

Separate buckets were punched out as one-piece blades, and each bucket

Fig. 1

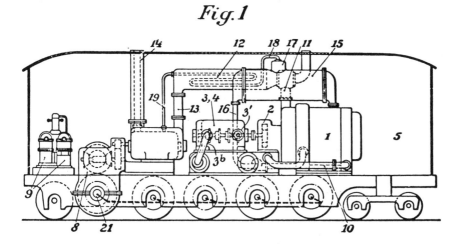

Fig. 2

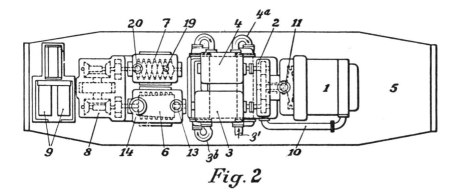

Inventor

Hans Holzwarth.

Holzwarth patent for a gas turbine-driven railway locomotive.

173

Fig. 3

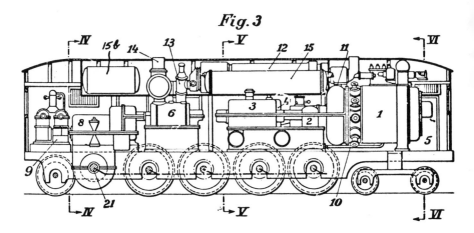

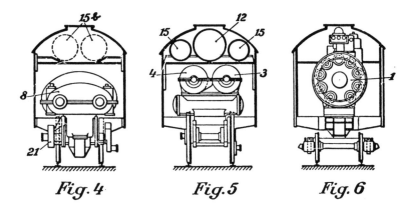

Fig. 4 *Fig. 5* *Fig. 6*

Inventor

Hans Holzwarth

Holzwarth patent for a gas turbine-driven railway locomotive.

174

was provided with a forged-on cap. These caps met, end to end, at the periphery, so as to form a continuous enclosing ring around the turbine wheel. The bucket roots had toothshaped grooves and were locked in place by keys inserted in triangular slots across the root face. The buckets were made of soft electro-iron, which worked satisfactorily more because of the cooling air than because of the material strength.

The fuel originally used in the first turbine was natural gas but Holzwarth soon began to experiment with petroleum gas and coal tar distillates. Experiments with powdered coal were unsuccessful, because only 20 percent of the coal charge would actually ignite. The combustors operated at low explosion pressures, from 70 to 100 psi. The second turbine ran on anthracite gas but this led to problems of fouling in the turbo-blower.

In 1914 Holzwarth incorporated pre-compression into his gas turbine design, which raised the explosion pressures to between 170 and 200 psi. The new design also needed shorter expansion time, which contributed to improving its efficiency (through lower heat losses to the combustor walls and nozzle shrouds). This turbine was built in collaboration with Maschinenfabrik Thyssen & Co. in Mühlheim/Ruhr. Thyssen built a series of Holzwarth turbines from 1914 to 1927, but none was ever placed in continuous operation. By 1920 they had obtained an overall thermal efficiency of 13 percent. In 1928 Brown, Boveri again took up a Holzwarth turbine design and modified it to include a two-chamber two-cycle type of combustor system. This unit was installed in a German steel plant in 1933, running on blast-furnace gas, and was still in operation in 1939.

The work performed by Brown, Boveri in connection with the development of Holzwarth-type gas turbines led to the invention of the Velox boiler. In turn, use of the Velox boiler led Brown, Boveri's technicians to return to the continuous-combustion gas turbine. The Velox boiler is a type of boiler that is fired under pressure from a compressor driven by a gas turbine, which is, in turn, powered by the exhaust gases of the boiler. Most of the pressure was needed to maintain high gas velocities in the heat-transfer sections of the boiiler. What remained of the pressure head was utilized to drive the gas turbine.

Using the gas turbine as an auxiliary made it necessary to use a high-efficiency compressor. Without it, the gas turbine would not develop the power required for driving the compressor, and the need for yet another power source would indicate severe deficiencies in the Velox boiler. The problem was solved by using 4-stage or 5-stage reaction turbines, with a 10-stage or 12-stage axial-flow compressor. Compressor and turbine efficiencies ranged from 70 to 75 percent. Sam Heron has pointed out that the Velox boiler is of academic interest, since it is the only known open-cycle gas turbine in which only the products of combustion pass through the turbine and which can completely employ all the oxygen in the air.

The first commercially successful turboshaft engine was an industrial gas turbine developed by Brown, Boveri of Baden, Switzerland, during the mid 1930s. It was the work of Dr. Adolf Meyer, who had been responsible for turbocharger engineering at Brown, Boveri and had also placed this firm in a leading position in the development of axial-flow compressors. The fact that the gas turbine finally became a practical success was in no small measure due to the high efficiency (up to 85 percent) of Brown, Boveri compressors.

Dr. Meyer calculated that a cycle efficiency of 15–18 percent could be obtained with a turbine inlet temperature of 1000° F (538° C). Raising the temperature to 1200° F (650° C) would raise cycle efficiency to 19–23 percent, and with a turbine inlet temperature of 1500° F (815° C) cycle efficiency could reach 22–26 percent.

Brown, Boveri also judged, on the basis of experience with Velox boilers and exhaust gas turbochargers for diesel engines, that turbine inlet temperatures of 1,000° F were perfectly safe for uncooled turbine blades made of heat-resistant steel.

The type of turbine developed by Dr. Adolf Meyer at Brown, Boveri & Co. in Switzerland was characterized as a "constant-pressure" turbine to distinguish it from Holzwarth's "constant-volume" turbine (in which combustion took place intermittently and therefore produced great pressure variations).

Dr. Meyer himself pointed out that his turbine was better described as the "continuous-combustion" type of turbine, because the pressure in the Brown, Boveri turbines also fluctuated (according to speed and load).

In 1939 the Swiss Federal Railways ordered a gas turbine locomotive with electric drive from Brown, Boveri. The multi-stage axial-flow turbine was rated at 2,200 hp. The locomotive was a 92-ton Type 1A-Bo-A1, and the turbine gave it a top speed of 70 mph. It was placed in service on Swiss and

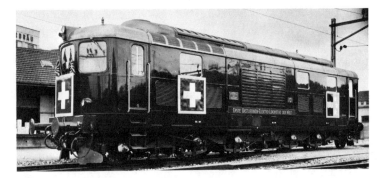

Brown, Boveri & Cie gas turbine locomotive built for the Swiss Federal Railways in 1939.

French lines, and in 11 years racked up a mileage of approximately 175,000 miles. The corresponding running time of the turbine was about 6640 hours and the amount of fuel consumed about 2560 tons. The experience gained in practical operation provided valuable data for improvements in design and further development of details. Even with heavy boiler oil it was possible to obtain combustion free from smoke and smell under all conditions of operation. The problem of noise was considered as satisfactorily solved for practical purposes. The electrical transmission comported itself splendidly.

The train weight varied between 600 and 720 tons. The train ran for 13 or 14 hours a day, covering a distance of about 300 miles. Fuel consumption worked out to about 10,000 pounds per day (or about 17 pounds per train/mile).

This unit had a thermal efficiency of about 18% at full load and ran with a specific fuel consumption of 0.75-pounds per hp-hour. The turbine drove an alternating current generator and idled at a synchronous speed of 3000 rpm.

Also in 1939, Brown, Boveri applied for a patent on an aircraft gas turbine that was part turboprop and part turbojet. An axial-flow compressor pumped air into the combustors, and an axial-flow turbine drove the compressor and airscrew shaft. The exhaust gases were directed to provide some axial thrust.

An interesting sidelight on the pioneering efforts of Brown, Boveri is provided by the fact that Allis-Chalmers Manufacturing Company purchased a license for the Brown, Boveri gas turbine in 1935 and built the first practical industrial gas turbines installed in the United States, beginning in 1938.

14

Modern Gas
Turbine History

THE HISTORY OF the modern gas turbine begins with Frank Whittle and his work. Whittle's first experience with aircraft engines began with three years' study as an RAF apprentice. Later he became a cadet in the RAF college at Cranwell. Here a thesis on a scientific subject was part of each term's work. In 1928 at the age of 21, his fourth term, he wrote a thesis on the future development of aircraft. He was even at that stage thinking in terms of 500 mph cruising speeds and very high altitudes. His considerations went as far as to include rocket propulsion.

He argued that the only way to combine high speed with long range was by flying high. The piston and propeller engine would not be suitable because the thin air affected the power to such an extent that at 40,000 feet the piston engine could not even turn around. Whittle discussed both gas turbines and jet propulsion in his thesis. However, he then thought of the two as separate power systems. It was not until 1929 that he got the idea of combining the gas turbine and the jet propulsion principle.

On graduation from the RAF College, Whittle was sent to an Instructor's Course at the Central Flying School in Witterling. He applied for his basic gas turbine (turbojet) patent on January 14th, 1930 and received British patent Number 347,206. Whittle's decision to patent his ideas was taken on the basis of advice from an instructor at the RAF College, W.E.P. Johnson, who later became the managing director of Power Jets (Research and Development) Ltd.

The patent text defined jet propulsion as a method of propelling a body in one direction by the reaction caused by expelling fluid in the opposite direction. Whittle described the heat cycle of his basic turbojet engine as "consisting of one or more stages of compression, one or more stages of expansion, and a heat addition between the end of compression and the beginning

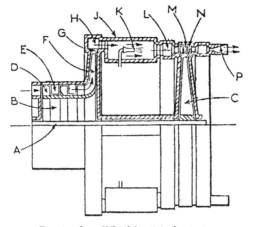

Drawing from Whittle's original patent:

A	Rotor shaft	H	Air collector
B	Compressor	J	Combustor
C	Turbine wheel	K	Fuel injection nozzle
D	Compressor blades	L	Collector
E	Stator blades	M	Nozzle vanes
F	Radial blades	N	Turbine blades
G	Diffuser vanes	P	Exhaust nozzle

of expansion, part of the work done in expansion being employed to do the work of compression, and the remainder to provide the fluid reaction."

Whittle had a clear picture of the implications of his invention, and expressed its advantages over contemporary aircraft engines in no uncertain terms: greater thrust in proportion to weight, higher-altitude capability, higher speed capacity, multi-fuel characteristics, reasonably low fuel consumption, and convenient external form (installation package). Whittle also understood that the low temperature of the upper atmosphere might be of greater importance in its benefits to the thermal efficiency of the turbojet than the possible threat to mass flow posed by low-density high-altitude air.

Whittle's English patent was actually a repeat of a French patent taken out in 1921 by a French physicist, Charles Guillaume, but Whittle had no notion he was duplicating another man's invention. Nor was he aware of the gas turbine proposed in 1928 by Maurice Roy, a French scientist of international repute. Maurice Roy's idea and drawings were published in 1928 in an 118-page paper entitled: *Turbine à Combustion Interne*, published by the Bulletin de L'Association Technique Maritime et Aeronautique.

In 1930 Whittle asked the Air Ministry to allow him to work on developing an engine based on his patent. The answer was a flat "No." When Whittle managed to get an interview with the Air Ministry director of scientific research, the director said, "This is the kind of thing for the City to waste their money with. We don't even know which way 'round the engine will go."

Next, Whittle approached private industry with a view to getting companies to develop his engine, singly or as a group. He went to the steam turbine manufacturers, and he went to the aircraft engine manufacturers. He went to engineering companies in other fields. But, for one excuse or another, no positive decisions were made. Six years went by with the gas turbine in limbo.

In 1934 the RAF assigned Whittle to take Tripos in mechanical sciences at Cambridge and he graduated with top honors. His next step was to form a partnership with two former RAF officers who believed in the gas turbine. They were R. D. Williams and J. C. B. Tinling. Their first attempt to raise money was unsuccessful. Then in October 1935, they succeeded in convincing M. L. Bramson an independent aeronautical consulting engineer, of the gas turbine's potential, and he took an interest in furthering its cause.

Bramson introduced Whittle and his partners to the leaders of a great firm of investment bankers: Sir Maurice Bonham-Carter and Mr. L. L. Whyte, of O. T. Falk and Partners. By the end of 1935, they had agreed to back Whittle's project. One possible snag was that Whittle's turbine had been patented while Whittle was on active duty in the RAF. The rights to the invention belonged in part to the British government.

Whittle requested that the government rescind these rights to him for private exploitation. The Air Ministry declared in writing that it was "unlikely that engine would ever be of military use" and granted commercial and foreign rights to Whittle. A new company, Power Jets Ltd., was formed late in 1935. And Whittle got Air Ministry permission to spend 6 hours a week attending to the affairs of his company!

Whittle's original gas turbine design used a centrifugal compressor to pump air through a diffuser and into a collector ring which distributed the compressed air to a number of separate combustors, where fuel was introduced and ignited. But his first design at Power Jets Ltd. was a turbojet engine which used a single combustor and carried a water-cooling jacket on the turbine casing.

The centrifugal compressor ran at speeds which gave the air supersonic velocity as it left the compressor blade tips, and the compressed air flow was slowed down and redirected in a primary diffuser chamber which fed into a delivery scroll leading to the combustor. The barrel-type combustor was tapered at the intake end so as to form an extended diffuser. The combustor outlet was connected to a volute turbine nozzle extending around the turbine periphery. The combustor carried a fuel injector shielded by a cowl.

The exhaust gases passed into another collector ring with ducts leading into the turbine section. The turbine was a two-stage design with a single stator blade ring separating the two turbine wheels. The exhaust gases from the turbine were ducted to an annular collector formed as a channel between the turbine shroud and the discharge pipe, which contained a number of nozzles directing the gas flow for maximum thrust.

In June of 1936, Power Jets Ltd., which was a design office without a machine shop or testing facilities signed a contract for construction of this gas turbine with the British Thomson-Houston Company. This gave Whittle free access to the Thomson-Houston plant at Derby, and the ability to discuss his engine with their engineers.

Suddenly, in July 1936 Whittle was assigned to postgraduate work at Cambridge. In October 1936 he applied for government funds in the form of a research contract for gas turbines. The backing from Falk and Partners was only £2,000 originally, plus £725 granted in July 1936. These funds soon proved totally inadequate for the ambitious task. But the Air Ministry again rejected the appeal. It was David R. Pye, deputy director of scientific research for the Air Ministry who turned thumbs down on Whittle's request, with the argument that Whittle "was not likely to succeed where so many better equipped had failed".

Shortly afterwards, the British Thomson Houston Company completed the construction of the first experimental Whittle gas turbine. The unit was designed as an aircraft engine, though not intended to fly—it was built strictly as a test laboratory engine. The engine was first tested at Lutterworth in April 1937, and it worked, though its power output was far below expectations.

Whittle had little or no experience in combustion engineering, and was uneasy about the combustor chosen for the prototype engine. When testing began, his fears proved correct. The efficiency was far below the design goal. The disc and blades of Whittle's first engine were made of Firth-Vickers Stayblade steel. Stayblade steel was ultimately superseded by another Firth-Vickers steel, R.ex 78, first made in 1936.

R.ex 78 was a complex alloy steel. At the time of its adoption for the gas turbine project, it marked a very considerable advance in creep-resisting materials.

In any case, the test proved the validity of Whittle's theories, and confirmed the potential of the gas turbine. Whittle again appealed to the Air Ministry for funds. It was August 1937 before he obtained the first Air Ministry promise of financial support. It was May 1938 before the first actual payment was made. And the payment was small, so that Power Jets Ltd. was still largely dependent on private finance for its existence.

Up to mid-1939 Power Jets Ltd. had financed 80 percent of its turbine work without government aid. But the very fact that the Air Ministry was giving its support to the project was enough to place the gas turbine under official rules of military secrecy. That made it even more difficult to raise private capital. Who wants to buy stock in a secret?

Throughout this period of financial woes, the engineering work proceeded apace. A new Whittle turbojet engine was tested in April and May, 1938, and ran 4½ hours. Then the test was broken off due to turbine failure. The engine had destroyed itself on the test bench. The 1938 test engine was called W-U. Air vice marshal Arthur W. Tedder saw it run on a bench test and became a strong supporter of the turbine program.

The British government learned of Brown, Boveri's work on gas turbines in 1936. In 1937, A. A. Griffith was sent to Switzerland to inspect and report on their results. They could not have found a better qualified man. During the period 1920–25 A. A. Griffith of the Royal Aircraft Establishment had developed his theory of axial-flow compressors and gas turbines based on airfoil science. In 1926 Griffith had proposed an axial-flow turbine turboprop engine. The Aeronautical Research Committee had approved "preliminary experiments to verify the theory."

Griffith's first design had a one-stage axial-flow compressor and a one-stage axial-flow turbine with free-vortex blading on a common shaft. Wind tunnel tests for the aerodynamic efficiency of the compressor and turbine were completed in 1927. A complete unit was built and tested in 1929. In 1930 Griffith was reassigned to the Air Ministry laboratories at South Kensington in London, where there were no facilities to continue turbine work. He returned to Farnborough in 1931, but only to find that there was no budget for turbine research any more. Priorities had been reordered in favor of superchargers, fuel injection, and compression-ignition engines.

After Griffith's report the official Air Ministry attitude towards Frank Whittle and Power Jets Ltd. began to change. In the 1938–1940 period, Whittle's work concentrated on the combustion process. But satisfactory results were not obtained until October 1940 when a satisfactory combustor and flame tube designed by I. Lubbock of the Asiatic Petroleum Co. became available.

In July 1939 Power Jets Ltd. got a promise of a contract for the full cost of a complete engine for actual flight. This led to the W-1 design project. The W-1 engine delivered 850 pounds thrust at 16,500 rpm. Installed weight was only 623 pounds! Simultaneously the Gloster Aircraft Company was promised a contract for the air frame (E28/39). It was supposed to be mainly a test bed for the turbo-jet engine, but Gloster built it as a light bomber in the Mosquite class for military reasons.

The W-1 went on test in December 1940 and the Gloster E28/39 jet plane made its first flight on May 15, 1941. Incredibly, there was still opposition in government circles. As late as a week before the first flight, the

Air Ministry wouldn't even send a photographer to record the historic moment. The plane reached 334 mph at 5,000 feet, and 338 mph at 20,000 feet altitude.

Eventually, the war changed everything. Late in 1939 Power Jets received a government promise to pay the development cost of a more ambitious project—a larger and more sophisticated flight engine. This was to be the W-2. The commitment, therefore, was made while W-1 was still on the drawing board. Simultaneously the Gloster Aircraft Company was requested to design a twin-jet interceptor fighter plane. This design was to be designated F9/40, and became the prototype for the fabled Gloster Meteor.

After mid-1940, the Air Ministry began to place direct contracts with a number of firms for the development and manufacture of gas turbines and gas turbine components. As a result of these developments, Power Jets became a research and design center, supplying other firms working on Air Ministry gas turbine contracts with drawings and information.

The Rover Company was signed up for W-2 production early in 1940. The engine remained in the development stage, with a number of parts being modified to facilitate production, until 1943. While Whittle's first designs used straight-through combustors, several subsequent ones including the W-2B were designed with reverse-flow combustors. Rover changed the W-2B specifications to include a new type of straight-through combustor, used in conjunction with a new fuel and control system developed by Joseph Lucas, Ltd. At the end of 1941, the Air Ministry invited Rolls-Royce to participate in development and manufacturing of the Whittle (Power Jets) gas turbine, alongside the Rover Co.

Rolls-Royce, manufacturers of aircraft engines since 1915, began to take an interest in turbojets as early as 1938. The first design projects were made in 1939. Component testing and development started in 1940 and, in June 1941, Rolls-Royce established its own test plant for development work on gas turbine compressors at Derby.

In 1943 the Rover work was handed over to Rolls-Royce as part of a larger contract. The Rover "Shadow" factory at Barnoldswick was taken over by Rolls-Royce in April, 1943. The Rolls-Royce engineering staff scrapped the W-2 design from Rover and went to work on their own version, the WR-1 which became the prototype for the Welland engine—the first production version of a Whittle turbine project, and the engine that was to power the Gloster Meteor.

The W-2B engine also went to the U.S. where it became the basis for the Type I turbojet made by General Electric Company. In September 1941 it was flown to America. U.S. officials would not believe it would work until they tested it. Having completed their tests, it took the American industry only ten months to build its first jet plane.

The W-2B was designed as a single-spool turbojet, with a centrifugal compressor giving a 3.9 pressure ratio. The turbine was a single-stage axial-flow design with 54 blades. The engine had nine straight-through combustors with concentrically mounted colander flame tubes. W-1 weighed 1,100 pounds and was designed to deliver 2,000 pounds thrust. The unit was 54 inches in diameter and 106 inches long.

For flight testing Rolls-Royce converted a Vickers Wellington twin-engined bomber plane into a flying test bed for the W-2B/23 turbojet. The turbojet engine was not mounted in wing pods like the original piston-type engines, but installed in the tail end, in place of the gun turret. The engine used for this series of tests produced a thrust of 1250 pounds, or 37.5 percent short of the objective.

The W-2B/23 went into its test phase on April 1, 1943 under the code name Welland. It had a diameter of 43 inches and was 105 inches long. The final version of the Welland delivered 1700 pounds thrust for an engine weight of 850 pounds. Specific fuel consumption was 1.12 lb per hp-hour.

The first Meteor flew on June 12, 1943. Production began in October, 1943, and deliveries began to the Royal Air Force in May 1914. In the meantime the Rolls-Royce engineers had started design and development work on the Derwent engine. It was based on the Whittle W-2B/26, which had been developed by Rover.

The Gloster Meteor was equipped with new Derwent engines in the winter of 1944, and made its first flight with the new engines in March 1944. The Derwent weighed 920 pounds, and gave a full 2,000 pounds thrust. This was raised to 2,200 pounds in the Derwent II.

Derwent III was an experimental engine which was not developed with a target of increased thrust. Derwent IV was a successor to the series III and gave 2,400 pounds thrust. The last of the line, Derwent V, was rated at 3,500 pounds thrust. A Gloster Meteor powered by two Derwent V engines raised the world air speed record to 608 mph on November 7, 1945. This was raised to 616 mph on September 7, 1946.

Design work on the Rolls-Royce Nene began in March 1944. This was a larger unit than any of the earlier Rolls-Royce designs, with a diameter of 49.5 inches and a weight of 1580 pounds. It gave a thrust of 5,000 pounds and returned a specific fuel consumption of 1.06 pounds per hp-hour.

The Rolls-Royce Trent was the first turboprop engine to fly. Two Trents were installed in a Gloster Meteor plane, which began flight tests in September 1945. Meanwhile, Power Jets Ltd. had been nationalized (it had been a private firm existing solely on government work). Power Jets (Research & Development) Ltd. was formed in June 1944 as a government corporation, to take over the entire assets of Power Jets, Ltd. This in turn led to the turbine section of the Royal Aircraft Establishment becoming affiliated with the new Power Jets (R & D) business.

Power Jets (Research & Development) Ltd. did not survive very long, for on July 1, 1946 its functions were transferred to a new organization entitled the National Gas Turbine Establishment. And the man who had started it all had become Sir Frank Whittle.

THE ROLE OF THE TURBO-SUPERCHARGER

One reason why the American industry was able to get industrial and aircraft gas turbine engines into production without any apparent background in gas turbine research and engineering was that the know-how acquired during 30 years of turbocharger development provided the engine manufacturers with a firm base in metallurgy, high-speed bearing technology, and experience in raising component efficiency in such vital units as compressors and turbines. The turbo-supercharger is usually thought of as an accessory to a piston engine, but it could also be regarded as a gas turbine in which the combustor has been replaced by a piston engine. The exhaust gas from the engine is used to drive a turbine, which, in turn, drives a compressor for boosting the piston engine's air intake. The turbocharger shaft is free-wheeling. The turbocharger was an old invention, and its development history falls in two concurrent parts: its use in diesel engines in Europe, and its use in gasoline-drive aircraft engines in the United States.

The first patent for a turbocharger was taken out in 1905 by a Swiss engineer Alfred J. Buchi, of Winterthur. Buchi joined the famous Belgian pioneer diesel firm of Carels Bros. upon graduating from what is now Zurich University in 1903. While working in Belgium he had the opportunity to see the firm commence work in 1904 on an experimental constant-pressure open-cycle gas turbine according to the basic designs of an Austrian engineer, named A. Vogt. No doubt this experience was the main inspiration behind his invention.

In his patents he proposed the employment of a rotary compressor for super-charging a diesel engine. The drawing supporting these early patents show that a multi-stage axial compressor and multi-stage gas turbine were contemplated together with a charge cooler. In 1908 Dr. Buchi returned to Switzerland, where he took up an appointment with Sulzer Bros. of Winterthur. Here he suggested that his ideas for turbocharging should be tried out, but it was not until 1911 that he persuaded his company to build an experimental turbocharging device.

A noteworthy point about these early experiments is that charge pressure ratios as high as 3.5 to 1 were employed on this experimental rig. Despite the promise shown by the turbocharger tests, Sulzer Bros. did not feel jus-

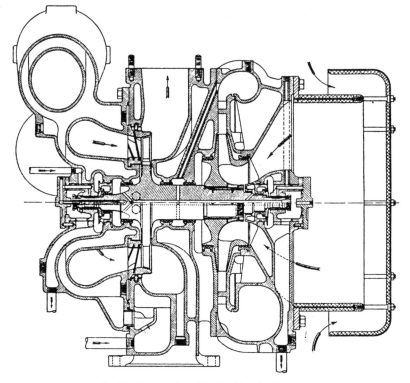

Sectioned view of an Alco-Buchi turbocharger.

tified in continuing these experiments. Dr. Buchi continued his investigations, however, convinced that his ideas were valid. He was no doubt encouraged in this view because no difficulty had been encountered with the bearings, pistons, valves, etc., of the turbocharged engine; nor had the blades or the bearings of the turbine given trouble.

Dr. Buchi proposed a most ambitious next step, namely the designing ad initio of a six-cylinder 2,000 hp engine arranged for high-pressure exhaust turbocharging. This advanced project was turned down by Sulzer Bros. who felt that this project would have run them into difficulties, particularly with regard to the turbine blades and discs, and the pistons, cylinder heads, exhaust valves and possibly the bearings of the engine. Regardless of this lack of support Dr. Buchi persisted in his development of the turbocharging principle.

The first application of the Buchi turbocharger to an actual engine installation did not occur until 1923. The installation was made because W. Laudahn, chief of the design department of the German Navy and a

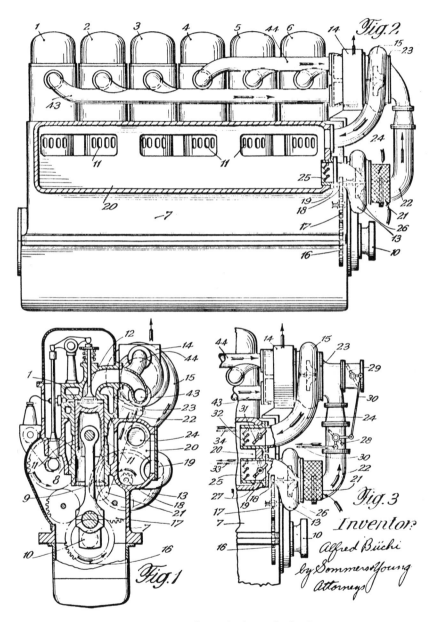

Buchi patent covering modern turbocharger for diesel engines.

187

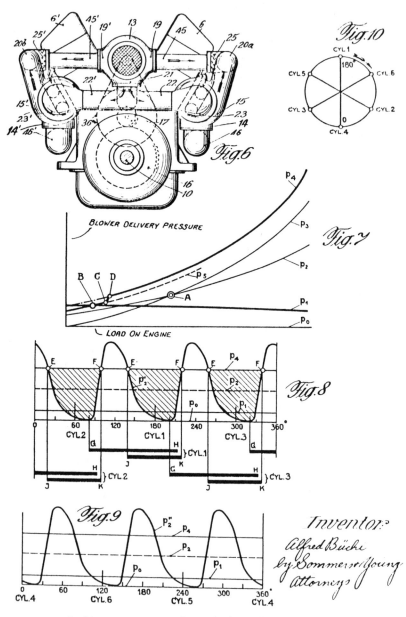

Buchi patent covering modern turbocharger for diesel engines.

188

strong advocate of diesel propulsion for warships of various types, decided to turbocharge the ten-cylinder MAN-type four-stroke engines of the new short sea service motorships Preussen and Hansestadt Danzig. The engines retained their standard valve gear and operated without a large valve timing overlap and the scavenging principle which Dr. Buchi regarded as an essential feature of his invention. Despite this restriction of the turbocharging principle, the output of each engine was raised some 43 percent, from 1,750 to 2,500 hp. These pioneer turbochargers, as well as the engines, were built by Vulkan Werke in Hamburg. Both ships went into service in 1925 and were entirely successful.

In 1926 the Buchi Syndicate was formed with Alfred J. Buchi as the manager, the Swiss Locomotive & Machine Works as the engine-building partner, and Brown, Boveri as the exhaust turbocharger manufacturer. The following year Brown, Boveri furnished a much improved two-inlet turbocharger and this was fitted to a six-cylinder crosshead-type S.L.M. engine.

After 1930, the Buchi turbocharger gained wide acceptance. In 1933 Buchi equipment was installed on Maybach V-12 diesel engines for use on railcars. Each railcar was powered by two engines, rated at 600 hp (at 1400 rpm), and one set a world rail speed record of 134 mph. The German diesel engine industry needed no further persuasion, and Deutz began to offer turbocharged engines in 1934. In Switzerland, Saurer of Arbon followed in 1935.

At this time, American diesel engine builders became interested in the Buchi turbocharger. Cooper-Bessemer was the first to act, and was soon followed by American Locomotive Company and Baldwin. At first they used complete units built by Brown, Boveri, but in 1938 both Alco and Cooper-Bessemer acquired manufacturing licenses.

In 1940 the Elliott Company took out a license and began to produce Buchi turbochargers for other American manufacturers. By that time other types of turbochargers had been developed for aircraft engines running on high-octane gasoline fuel, and were ready for production in time to play a major part in the power systems of World War II U.S. military airplanes.

The story of turbocharging in America started in 1901 when Sanford Moss, as a graduate student at Cornell University in Ithaca, New York, made extensive studies in combustion, heat transfer, and energy conversion, and started work on a gas turbine. He was born in San Francisco in 1872 and had been fascinated with turbines ever since his childhood. His work aroused the interest of the General Electric Company. They engaged Moss to develop a turbine for GE. By 1907 Moss had a running gas turbine on test, but it reached an efficiency level of about 3 percent. GE cancelled the contract in 1907, and experimental work at GE came to an end.

Some years later, General Electric again became interested in turbocharging as a result of studying the patents of Auguste Rateau. He took out French patent Number 524,114 in 1916 covering a turbine-driven supercharger intended for use on high-altitude aircraft engines. General Electric was a Rateau licensee for other inventions connected with steam turbines and multi-stage centrifugal compressors and in 1917 a Rateau turbosupercharger was sent to the United States for testing.

Some GE tests of the turbocharging equipment in 1917 came to the attention of the National Advisory Committee for Aeronautics. This led to GE's being issued a contract for turbocharger research in cooperation with the U.S. Army Air Corps in Dayton, Ohio. It was at that point that Dr. Moss came into the program.

The first full scale test took place in 1918, when his GE turbocharger was installed on a V-12 Liberty Aircraft engine. For a test, it was shipped to Pike's Peak, Colorado, summit of the famous auto racing hill climb, for high-altitude testing. The standard Liberty engine developed 350 hp at sea level. Its power fell to 230 hp at 13,780 feet. With the turbocharger installed, power output was 356 hp at 13,780 feet altitude.

The next step was to use the turbocharger on an engine installed in an airplane. In 1919 Major Schroeder flew a turbocharged Liberty-powered plane to 20,000 feet. Six months later he raised the altitude record to 37,400 feet. The following year Lieutenant McCrady went up over 39,000 feet with the same machine to set a world's altitude record. But there were problems. The engine overheated, fuel pressure sank, carburetors overheated, and the turbine overheated. Air cannot be compressed without its temperature being raised.

The next problems were associated with abnormal combustion at high altitude, as the mixture would ignite prematurely due to the over-heated airfuel mixture. The solution was to install an inter-cooler between the compressor and the engine, carrying the excess heat into the water-cooling system.

Dr. Moss also found it necessary to use a bypass for the exhaust. He installed a bypass valve in the exhaust manifold, shunting part of the gas flow away from the turbine to prevent overcharging the engine. But the biggest problem was turbine inlet temperature. New heat-resistant metals had to be developed to withstand the thermal loads without creep or distortion.

From 1918 to 1922 GE turbochargers used SAE 6150 steel (containing chrome, vanadium and silicon). It had been developed as an exhaust valve metal and proved a good starting point. Dr. Moss began to use Silchrome steel in 1922. It was a chrome-silicon alloy originally developed as an exhaust valve metal capable of withstanding higher temperatures. In 1928

Kayser-Ellison in Great Britain came up with KE-965 steel, and it proved able to withstand a rise in turbine inlet temperatures from 1100° F (593° C) to 1400° F (760° C).

Then, in 1933, chrome-nickel steel became available. With up to 19 percent nickel, turbine life was lengthened to the point where the military began to see the possibility of a practical application. GE development work also went into improving compressor efficiency. Valuable lessons were learned in diffuser design, for instance.

In 1933, Universal Cyclops Steel Corp. introduced its 17W steel (an improvement on KE-965). It contained chrome, nickel, wolfram and molybdenum. Shortly afterwards, turbochargers began to use Stellite, a material that had been developed about 1911 as a cutting tool metal by Dr. Elwood Haynes. In 1936 Hastelloy became available. It was a nickel-molybdenum alloy created by the Haynes Stellite Company. General Electric adopted Hastelloy for its turbochargers in 1937.

The blades were individually forged, with roots for insertion in the turbine wheel hub. This was a slow and costly method of manufacturing turbine wheels, and General Electric began a research effort in casting techniques. Casting complete turbine wheels became possible when the Austenal Co. developed the "lost wax" process in 1939. Until 1936 the turbocharger remained purely experimental in the eyes of the U.S. military experts. Nevertheless, during the whole period from 1919 to 1945 it was the Army that paid the entire cost of continuous development of the turbocharger by an engineering team working under Dr. Sanford Moss at General Electric's Lynn, Mass. works.

The breakthrough came in 1937 when Wright Aeronautical Company (a division of Curtiss-Wright Corporation) started production of the Cyclone R-3350 turbocharged aircraft engine. It was an 18-cylinder radial engine which developed at least 2,800 hp for an installed weight of 3040 pounds. It powered such new military planes such as the Boeing B-17 Flying Fortress and B-24 Liberator. These planes were able to fly at 34,450 feet altitude.

Development of the Cyclone was concentrated in two areas: lighter weight and reduced fuel consumption. It was also modified for better mechanical reliability, with bigger cooling fins on the cylinder heads and cylinders, and the crankshaft was beefed up. GE built around 300,000 turbochargers during WWII, and more than 80 percent of U.S. military aircraft were equipped with them. When GE began to work on the I-series gas turbine, the company had years of experience with metals of high temperature resistance and in turbine wheel manufacture. Due to the turbocharger experience, the GE engineers were able to shave years of development work off the gas turbine time table.

THE LONG ROAD TO JET PROPULSION

The first time jet propulsion was suggested it was not for a flying machine but for a wheeled carriage. And the proposal came from none other than Isaac Newton (1643–1727). About 1663 he evolved an idea for a steam-driven carriage, with a spherical boiler emitting a jet of steam through a conical nozzle directed backwards.

Newton was the first to explain the physical laws of action and reaction, and calculated that the carriage would be driven forward by the reaction of the boiler to the force of the steam jet emanating from the nozzle. Jet propulsion was forgotten for centuries, while inventors, mechanics and engineers strove to harness the force of internal combustion by all manner of machinery that delivered power at a revolving output shaft.

This trend dominated power plant engineering for so long, and so completely, that when a French engineer, Rene Lorin (1878–1933) revived the idea of jet propulsion in 1907, he used a four-cylinder piston engine to provide the thrust! Each cylinder head was equipped with a megaphone-type exhaust nozzle. The engine functioned solely to produce a propulsive jet through the exhaust nozzles, and the crankshaft was used only to keep the pistons in phase and drive the accessories. It failed because the engine could not consume more air than required for combustion, and the mass volume was inadequate to provide the thrust needed for flight.

The next step of progress came in 1917, when O. Morize, a French scientist from Chateaudun proposed an improved type of jet-propulsion engine. Morize used a conventional piston engine to drive a compressor, which delivered air to a plenum chamber preceding a separate combustor, where fuel was injected from a nozzle supplied by an engine-driven fuel pump. Ignition was either electrical or incandescent.

Fuel injection was continuous, sustaining a continuous combustion process. The combustor outlet was shaped like a converging cone. The gas flow through this cone created a low-pressure zone around its mouth, and allowed outside air to be drawn in from radially disposed ports in the housing. This added thrust to the gas jet as it was discharged. Morize also designed an annular combustor, with the annulus tapering off so as to give the nozzle effect needed to draw outside air into the front of the ejector tube.

The Morize jet propulsion engine was never developed to the practical stage, and the engine invented in 1917 by H. S. Harris, an Englishman operating a laboratory at Esher, Surrey, suffered the same fate. The Harris engine used a two-cylinder piston engine to drive a low-pressure compressor which fed air into two tubular combustors discharging into straight ejector tubes. An important refinement to this type of jet-propulsion engine originated in France during World War I and was patented by an inventor named Melot.

His idea was to use several nozzles in sequence as a form of thrust augmentor between the combustor discharge ports and the main ejector tube. The French Air Ministry made several tests of this device, but without results. The only practical use for the device was for civilian use, several years later, when it was applied to the exhaust system of two-cycle engines to aid the gas extraction from the cylinder.

In America, the first turbojet pioneer was R. E. Lasley, who had formerly been working as a steam turbine engineer for Allis Chalmers. Lasley took out a number of patents relating to gas turbine design and operation over a period of years, beginning in 1925. In 1932 he started his own company, Lasley Turbine Motor Company, in Waukegan, Illinois (a suburb of Chicago) to develop and manufacture a turbojet for aircraft.

He lacked the financial backing to conduct a full component development study, and his turbojet gave very low efficiency. His concepts were well thought out, however, and it would seem that if the American industry had supported Lasley in his research work, the history of the gas turbine might well have been different.

The ramjet principle (which uses the forward velocity of the power unit through the atmosphere to increase the air intake volume) was first applied in 1935 by Rene Leduc and his sons, operators of an experimental establishment at Argenteuil outside Paris. A model of the Leduc jet-propelled airplane was displayed at the Salon de l'Aviation in Paris, but a flying example was not built until 1947. For its first test, it was launched from a platform mounted above the wings of a carrier plane (a Languedoc 161) at 10,000 feet altitude above Toulouse. It flew for 12 minutes and reached a speed of 450 mph on half power.

A different type of jet propulsion scheme was advanced by the Italian engineer Secondo Campini, who had been expounding a number of ideas for advanced aircraft engines since 1930. His power unit combined a number of basic principles of gas turbine operation, but was driven by a conventional piston-type radial aircraft engine.

The radial engine was positioned in the front of the fuselage, with its output shaft extending backwards to drive a large-diameter two-stage centrifugal compressor. The compressed air passed through a diffuser ring leading to an annular mixing channel, which discharged the air into a cylindrical combustion space filling up the entire tail end of the fuselage. The discharge nozzle was provided with a conical body carried on a concentric extensible shaft. The position of the cone could be varied to change the nozzle orifice.

This design from 1935 was never built in its original form, but a modified version was built by the Caproni aviation works in 1937, using a 900-hp Isotta-Fraschini engine. This CC-2 (Caproni-Campini, number 2) made a flight from Milano to Rome in 1940, and had a maximum speed of 205 mph at 9800 feet altitude. But the Italian military authorities did not consider this experiment either significant or successful.

The real race to fly the first gas turbine jet-propelled airplane was going to be a contest between Germany and Britain. Germany was first, but the German turbojets were never developed to the point where they were considered of military value by the Nazi leaders. The first German turbojet was created by an airframe manufacturer and not by one of the traditional engine suppliers. This happened because Ernst Heinkel, head of the Heinkel Flugzeugwerke, became interested in the patents of Max Hahn and opened a new department to study gas turbines.

The Hahn gas turbine design consisted of a centrifugal compressor feeding air to a reverse-flow toroidal combustor, whose outlet ports were shaped like an annular duct leading to a radial inflow turbine. The turbine and compressor wheels were mounted back to back on a very short shaft. The exhaust gases escaped from the turbine via a nozzle ring directing the thrust in an axial direction. The Hahn design was a good basis for development, and Heinkel's turbine program accelerated when Pabst von Ohain joined the company in February 1936.

Von Ohain was a student of applied physics and aerodynamics at the University of Göttingen in 1935. His professor, R. W. Pohl, recognized the exceptional ability and dedication of the young man, and recommended him to Ernst Heinkel, who was a personal acquaintance. With von Ohain at the head, Heinkel set up a hush-hush research establishment at Rostock, where the young engineer worked night and day on improvements in the turbojet engine.

The first Heinkel turbine was tested in September 1937, and within a year von Ohain had built a new and more powerful unit. Von Ohain recognized the combustion problem associated with petroleum based fuels and evaded it initially by using hydrogen. It has a very high flame speed, a very wide range of combustibility, and would produce no deposits or corrosive residues.

The second Heinkel turbojet was designated He-S 3B and developed about 1100 pounds thrust at 13,000 rpm. It was installed in a new airplane designed by Siegfried Guenther, a famous engineer who had been with Heinkel since 1931. This airplane was the Heinkel He-178—the first turbojet plane in the world to fly. It took off briefly during taxiing tests on August 24th, 1939, and a full flight test followed three days later.

The test was successful and the performance impressive, but the Nazi government would not award a turbojet engine development contract to Heinkel. Instead, two such contracts were given out in 1939: one to Junkers, another to BMW. Both were intended for development of an engine for a Messerschmitt plane. Heinkel had to go it alone—or drop gas turbine work. Ernst Heinkel opted for a compromise solution by linking his gas turbine research up with Hirth.

The first two Heinkel turbojet engines were made obsolete by the appearance of the new He S-011, which was designed by von Ohain in 1941. It remained in the experimental stage throughout 1944. The He S-011 engine had a 3-stage axial-flow compressor preceded by an axial-flow inducer placed inside the intake duct. Like the previous designs, it used a toroidal combustor. The rotor speed was 10,000 rpm. Installation weight was 2090 pounds, for a thrust of 7500 pounds. The He S-021 was a turboprop version of the He S-011. It was estimated that it delivered 3300 hp at 10,000 rpm.

Junkers did some preliminary work on turbojets in 1936, but the program was a low-priority effort. Junkers did not get serious about turbojets until the Jumo 004 went on the drawing boards under a government contract in late 1939. Two Jumo 004B engines were installed in the twin-engine Me 262 which flew early in 1943. The Jumo 004B delivered a thrust of almost 1900 pounds, and had an installation weight of 1585 pounds.

It had a six-stage axial-flow compressor, a single-stage turbine, and six barrel-type combustors. The Me 262 had a top speed of 543 mph at 19,685 feet altitude and could climb almost 4,000 feet in 60 seconds. Fortunately for the Allied Powers, the Luftwaffe never grasped the potential of this fantastic weapon, and only a relatively small number were built and placed in service. The early BMW turbojet experience is related in the MTU section of the chapter on current programs.

As we have seen, Rolls-Royce built the world's first turboprop engine to fly. But the first patents dealing with turboprop engines were taken out in Sweden in 1936 by two brothers, Fredrik and Birger Ljungström. Their early inventions came to the attention of Gustav de Laval, and he formed an association with them which gave them a laboratory, a manufacturing establishment, and an impressive budget. The Ljungström turboprop was a single-shaft engine with a multi-stage centrifugal compressor, a toroidal combustor, and a five-stage axial-flow turbine. Each successive turbine wheel had a larger diameter than the preceding one. Reduction gearing at the front of the engine turned an output shaft to which was mounted the airscrew.

The first Ljungström turboprop was an 800-hp unit built by Bofors in 1934. It was also the first twin-spool engine. The two turbine stages were attached to separate, concentric shafts. The high-pressure turbine drove a 7-stage compressor, and the low-pressure turbine drove a 4-stage compressor. Overall pressure ratio was placed at a value of 7, and the unit ran with turbine inlet temperatures in the range of 1400–1472° F (760–800° C). Fredrik

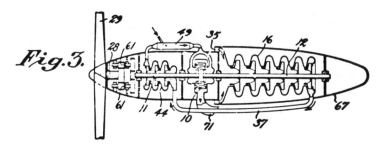

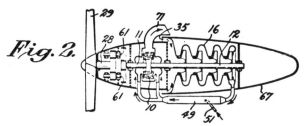

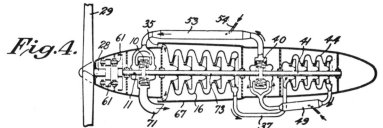

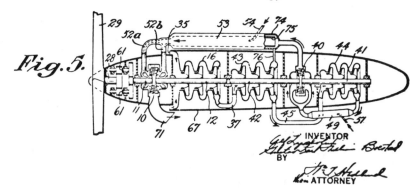

A selection of different turboprop engine layouts proposed by Lysholm in 1936.

196

Ljungstrom is also credited with the invention of the first rotary regenerator.

There was another inventor in Sweden at the same time whose reputation and influence have become household words in the gas turbine, hydraulics, and transmission industries the world over. His name was Alf Lysholm, and he took out a series of patents in connection with both turbojet and turboprop engines. The Lysholm gas turbine designs were taken up by Svenska Flygmotor AB in Trollhättan. This firm later became a division of Volvo and after World War II acquired a license to manufacture Rolls-Royce turbojets.

START OF THE U.S. GAS TURBINE INDUSTRY

The General Electric gas turbine program got underway as a result of an arrangement between the British and American governments. In the summer of 1941, a small group of engineers from Power Jets, Ltd. arrived at West Lynn, Massachusetts with the original W-1X turbine and a full set of drawings for the W-2B.

The General Electric I-A gas turbine was a copy of the Whittle W-2B. The original GE gas turbine design was called I-14, which went into limited production. Two I-14 units were installed in the Bell XP-59A, which became the first American-built jet plane to fly in October 1942. Regular series production started in mid-1943 with the GE I-16, followed in 1944 by the I-40 (a much larger unit of 4,000 pounds thrust). General Electric was also active in turboprop engineering and production, starting with the TG-100A engine, which made its first flight as the power plant for a Consolidated Vultee XP-81 airplane in December, 1945.

Production of the TG-180 turbojet was transferred to Allison in 1945 to let GE concentrate on building the I-40. General Electric's production of industrial gas turbines got under way in 1959. The mainstays of the GE industrial turbine program are the LM100 and the LM1500. The LM100, derived from the T58 helicopter turboshaft engine, is normally rated between 1000 and 1200 horsepower, depending on the type of application and the operating environment. The LM1500, derived from the J79 turbojet engine family, can be rated from 10,000 to 18,000 shaft hp. The only motor vehicle application of the GE gas turbine has been one installation in a 100-ton Lectra-Haul off-road truck.

Westinghouse Electric Corporation got its start in the gas turbine business because of a request from the U.S. Navy Bureau of Aeronautics a few days after the Japanese attack on Pearl Harbor in December, 1941. The first Westinghouse turbojet was designated X-19A and was completed in March, 1943. It was a turbojet with a six-stage axial-flow compressor and a single-stage turbine, carrying eight cellular combustors.

Power output was 1363 pounds thrust at 18,000 rpm at sea level, for an installation weight of 830 pounds. It was followed by an X19B production version. Subsequently Westinghouse built small turbojets down to 260 pounds thrust, but later began to specialize in large turboshaft engines for power generation. No automotive applications have been made with Westinghouse turbines.

Northrop Aircraft Inc. began studies for a turboprop engine without a defense contract shortly after its incorporation by John K. Northrop in 1939. The design came from a Czech-born engineer named Vladimir Pavlecka. After spending about $25,000 on the Turbodyne project, Northrop managed to interest the defense department in its development, and was awarded a joint Army-Navy contract in June, 1941. Northrop made slow progress, however, as the first test engine did not run on the dynamometer until December, 1944, and it was not given an actual flight test until after the end of the war.

Northrop soon dropped its Turbodyne activity entirely, in order to specialize in the activity where its best expertise lay: as an airframe manufacturer of light military aircraft. Vladimir Pavlecka left Northrop, and formed his own business, Turbotron, Inc. As late as 1973 he was acting as a consultant to Lear Motors Corp. of Reno, Nevada, in connection with steam turbine development.

Lockheed Aircraft Corporation started design work on a turbojet even before General Electric, when a large unit called L-1000 went on the drawing board. It was designed by an engineer named Nathan C. Price, who remained as the head of Lockheed's gas turbine engineering staff up to the time of its dissolution in 1945. Price was a steam turbine engineer by profession, who had designed a steam turbine airplane in 1934, and made a number of proposals for different types of gas turbine engines for aircraft between 1935 and 1940, including a hybrid system with a Velox boiler.

The design was ready in 1941 and submitted to the U.S. Army Air Force in 1942. In mid-1943 the Army decided to support its development, but Lockheed's director of engineering, H. P. Hibbard, became aware of the gas turbine work going on at General Electric and at other companies, and in October 1945 the L-1000 program, complete with its staff and chief engineer, was handed over to the Menasco Manufacturing Company.

Menasco built one prototype, and in 1947 sold the project to Curtiss-Wright, whose Wright Aeronautical Corp. division had been completely out of the turbojet picture until then. However, Wright never developed this design to commercial ripeness. Instead, the company signed a license agreement with Metropolitan-Vickers in England for the rights to manufacture the 7,000-pounds thrust Sapphire turbojet.

About 1948 Wright disclosed the existence of a 5,500-hp turboprop engine called Typhoon XT-35. It was a design of incredible complexity, with no less than 36 combustors! But Curtiss-Wright never became a factor in the gas turbine industry, and by the time the first American jetliners (Boeing 707 and Douglas DC-8) went into production in 1958, the aircraft engine field was dominated by General Electric and Pratt & Whitney (a division of United Aircraft, Inc.).

Pratt & Whitney was established in 1925 by a number of former key personnel at Wright Aeronautical Corp. Their first product was the Wasp engine, which soon proved superior to the Army's R-1454 (designed and built at McCook Field). Pratt & Whitney started gas turbine production in 1946 with a turboprop design known as the PT-1. It had been developed during World War II as a company-funded program, at a cost of about $3,300,000. Shortly afterwards, Pratt & Whitney concluded that the major demand was going to be for turbojets, and a new family of engines went on the drawing boards in 1948. The automotive developments associated with Pratt & Whitney turboshaft engines are detailed in the case history covering the ST6 unit built by United Aircraft of Canada, Ltd.

SMALL GAS TURBINES OF UNFULFILLED PROMISE

A number of gas turbine designs were produced in the years following the end of World War II, and some of them seemed to offer a high potential for development as automotive power units. One such engine was the Centrax.

The Centrax gas turbine engine was first unveiled in 1948. Centrax Power Units Ltd. of Acton, Middlesex, was formed in 1946 by three young engineers who had worked with Frank Whittle at Power Jets Ltd. They were Richard Barr, Geoffrey White, and Harry Leach. It was a 160-hp simple-cycle single-shaft design, intended as a prototype for a family of industrial engines.

It weighed 385 pounds without reduction gearing and the rotor shaft turned between 40,000 and 42,000 rpm at full power. Specific fuel consumption was 0.77 pounds per hp-hour. Turbine inlet temperature was 1520° F (827° C)—unusually high for its time. Physical dimensions of the turbine were small—it was 150 mm in diameter. The output shaft was equipped with a 7 : 1 reduction gear.

The Centrax compressor had a high pressure ratio of 5.8 but Richard Barr soon recognized that the single-shaft non-regenerative engine was doomed to poor part load efficiency. The best configuration for the basic Centrax unit followed Rover's approach: radial in-flow turbines with variable nozzle geometry. Centrax Power Units Ltd. was later reorganized as Turbion, Ltd. A 120-hp Turbion prototype was equipped with a rotary regenerator. An initial series of five test engines were made. The company went out of business before production could get under way.

Armstrong-Siddeley had been an automobile manufacturer since 1919,

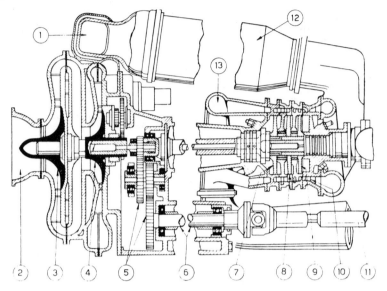

Sectioned view of Armstrong-Siddeley automotive/industrial gas turbine engine:

1. Collector	7. Turbine wheel
2. Air intake	8. Stator member
3. Compressor (first stage)	9. Stator member
4. Compressor (second stage)	10. Turbine nozzle
5. Reduction gear	11. Drive shaft
6. Drive shaft	

and the company's traditions as an aircraft engine constructor go back to the start of World War I when Armstrong-Siddeley built Puma and Tiger water-cooled aircraft engines to the designs of F. R. Smith. The company's first approach to the gas turbine was a contract to develop axial-flow compressors and blade forms for the Royal Aircraft Establishment in 1939, and to manufacture an experimental turbine unit designed for the Royal Aircraft Establishment by Dr. A. A. Griffith.

In 1942 the company suddenly found itself the recipient of a turbojet department, transferred from Metropolitan-Vickers. From 1942 to 1945, Armstrong-Siddeley also designed and developed its own ASX turbojet, which went into production as the Python. Then the company decided to develop a turboprop, which was designated the Mamba and made its first flight test in May, 1948.

Armstrong-Siddeley entered the small turbine field in 1952 with a series of patents, instigated by H. S. Rainbow, for a very compact industrial turbine suitable for installation in cars. The engine consisted of a two-stage centrifugal compressor, a two-stage axial-flow compressor turbine and a single-stage power turbine. From the single combustion chamber, the gas flowed to the rear of the unit and thence forward through the turbines to be exhausted near the center of the engine, close to the reduction gears and accessory drives. This layout was made possible by using a hollow power-turbine shaft, co-axial with the compressor drive-shaft. This unit has never been developed, however.

In 1956 the Standard Motor Co. Ltd. in Coventry announced they had built a 250-hp automotive gas turbine. This was the result of the company's having formed a gas turbine section within its research and development activity in September 1955. The turbine section was headed by S. K. Hambling, who had previously worked on gas turbine projects with other organizations.

The Standard-Triumph gas turbine was designed so as to be adaptable to a number of industrial purposes in addition to the passenger car installation which was its prime target. In the interest of simplicity, the prototype was built without a heat exchanger. It was a single-shaft design with a dry weight of 350 pounds. The 19-vane centrifugal compressor gave a peak pressure ratio of 3, and provided a maximum air flow of 5.2 pounds per second at 24,000 rpm. The turbine was of the radial in-flow type and had 17 blades. Two barrel-type combustors were used.

In 1957 an upgraded version of the same basic engines was built. It was rated at 350–400 hp and aimed at motor truck installation rather than passenger cars. At that time, Standard-Triumph planned to make both units available with recuperators. But the entire program was suddenly canceled when Standard Motor Co. Ltd. went through a retrenchment move in order to stave off a threatened acquisition by the Massey-Ferguson group. The Standard Motor Co. was never revived.

Definitely too big for passenger car installation was a 1,000-hp gas turbine developed by Charles Parsons & Company, Ltd. of Newcastle-on-Tyne in 1954. It was actually designed as a tank engine. Preliminary work on the project began in 1945 under a contract from the Ministry of Supply. The Parsons organization had over half a century's experience with steam turbines, but this was its first acquaintance with the gas turbine.

Designed under the direction of Dr. A. T. Bowden, it was a non-regenerative two-shaft engine. The gasifier section consisted of a single-stage axial-flow turbine, driving a single-stage centrifugal compressor. Maximum gasifier shaft speed was 17,500 rpm, with a pressure ratio of 4. Two straight-through barrel-type combustors delivered their exhaust gases directly to the inlet nozzle of the first-stage turbine. Maximum turbine inlet temperature was 1472° F (800° C). The power turbine was a two-stage axial-flow design, operating at speeds up to 9,850 rpm. The power turbine shaft was coupled to a 3.5 : 1 reduction gear, giving the output shaft a maximum speed of 2800 rpm. Specific fuel consumption was high—0.9 pounds per hp-hour.

The two shafts were concentric and normally running independently of each other. But they were connected via a special synchro-coupling which could be locked up to let the engine operate as a single-shaft unit whenever the driver deemed it desirable. This would prevent overspeeding of the gasifier shaft, and provide engine braking.

The Parsons engineers designed a version of this engine equipped with a rotary regenerator, but it was never built. One prototype tank was tested at the Fighting Vehicles Research and Development Establishment at Chertsey, Surrey, and further development was curtailed.

SECTION III

APPLICATIONS

15

Applications:
A General Review

THE SIGNIFICANCE OF the advantages of the gas turbine over other types of prime movers depends to a large extent on the application. As a corollary, each successful application has a tendency to lead to the development of a more specialized form of gas turbine. The gas turbine design that does the best job in an airplane is perhaps the least suitable for a truck or bus installation. And the unit that proves outstandingly efficient in a stationary generator set may give unacceptable performance in a military amphibious vehicle.

In this book, our attention is focused on the automotive gas turbine but it is impossible to present a complete picture of it while ignoring other applications. Of course, the term "automotive" as understood by the Society of Automotive Engineers, encompasses all varieties of machines that move under their own power, from aerospace equipment to mechanized farm machinery. Our target is not nearly as broad. We shall concentrate on the passenger car, with trucks and buses playing a supporting role.

Even so, it is impossible to get a full understanding of the automotive application in its strictest sense without first reviewing turbine concepts and engineering practice in related fields—aviation, industrial, marine, military and railroad.

AVIATION

It's in the aviation field that the gas turbine has enjoyed its most spectacular success, which has been so complete that the role of the gas turbine amounts to a total takeover as far as military airplanes and airliners are concerned, with piston power being restricted to a certain share in the area of general aviation. The takeover process was a very quick one. Turbine use went from the prototype stage to a virtual monopoly in military and commercial air traffic in about 20 years.

The turbine's advantages in aircraft operation are overwhelming, and have led to the development of highly advanced and very specialized types of machines. The modern aircraft turbine is not only quite unsuitable for other uses, but the advantages that have assured the turbine its prominence in the air disappear when the turbine is transplanted to most other applications.

In its basic form, the gas turbine is a natural for aircraft because it is fundamentally a constant-speed unit. It operates most efficiently at or near maximum speed and full load but very inefficiently at low speed and light loads. Airliners run for hours at steady high speeds and provide near-ideal working conditions for the turbine.

There are two basic types of aircraft gas turbines: (1) the turbojet engine, and (2) the turboprop engine. The turbojet engine propels the airplane by reaction. The exhaust gases are discharged at high pressure. This jet produces a reaction, of equal strength and in the opposite direction. This thrust is applied against the turbine itself, and since the turbine is carried on the airplane, it provides propulsion. The turboprop engine uses the turbines to drive a propeller shaft. The turboprop engine has been supplanted in most applications by the turbojet engine, but some turboprop units are still being made for certain types of special-purpose aircraft.

The basic form of turbojet engine is a marvel of efficiency, and power but only at high speeds and high altitudes. Rarefied air reduces the aerodynamic drag, the skin friction, and the fuel consumption.

Modern turbojet engines offer surprising specific fuel consumption, down to figures lower than that for the diesel engine. They also offer outstanding energy density: hundreds of thousands of kilowatts in a volume a little larger than a car, and a trouble-free life between overhauls which in engines now in service extends beyond 20,000 hours. But the turbojet represents very high capital cost.

Reliability has always enjoyed first priority in aircraft turbine design and development. Fail-safe concepts are part and parcel of every aircraft and its power system, and backup systems that can assure continued operation in the event of failure in one unit are legal requirements for flying. The premium placed on reliability throughout has led to the development of aircraft turbine engines that cost $80 to $100 per horsepower. In contrast, the auto industry has a long history of producing piston engines for between $2 and $3 per horsepower.

A low-altitude flying at low to medium speeds, the turboprop engine is superior to the turbojet (although not quite as efficient as the piston-aircraft engine). The turboprop engine, however, gives lower specific fuel consumption than the piston engine at high altitudes. The turboprop engine has

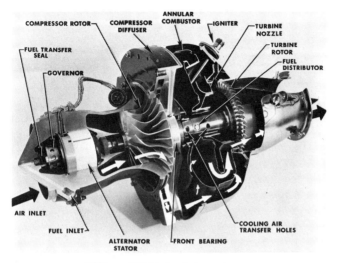

Williams WR-24-6 turbojet engine.

acquired a market in aircraft types that do not require the extreme airspeed possibilities of the turbojet.

Because the turboprop needs less power to lift the same weight, it has an advantage over the turbojet for take-off. It is a cumulative advantage, for the lower power requirement means that less fuel is burned, and consequently the turboprop engine can get along with lower fuel tank loads, which saves weight.

The turboprop cannot reach turbojet speeds, but because of its lower cruising speeds, the airframe construction need not be given the same torsional strength. That saves more weight. For carrying light loads over short distances, the turboprop will give a smaller, lighter and cheaper airplane.

Sam Heron has pointed out that recent turboprop engine installations are partly turbojet engines, since about 10 percent of the effective in-flight thrust is due to turbine exhaust discharge. Conversely, the most advanced form of turbojet has certain elements of the turboprop. This refers, of course, to the fanjet (or turbofan) engine. The turbofan engine carries a large-diameter fan mounted on the basic turbojet engine. It acts the same as an airscrew or propeller—pumping air from one side to the other. The big difference is that the propeller operates in open air, while the wash from the fan is fully ducted.

Of all the air that passes through the fan, only about 15 percent enters the compressor. Most of the air—or about 85 percent—bypasses the gas turbine. It flows through the exterior ducting and is discharged behind the engine. The bypass air from the fan emerges in an annular jet surrounding the hot exhaust jet stream from the hot section. The pressure in the bypass air at its point of discharge is about 1.5 times higher than when it entered the fan blades. It is this bypass air that provides most of the engine's thrust—not the exhaust.

By-pass ratio is the ratio of bypass air to air circulated through the hot section of the engine. It can be as low as 3 in some small fanjets, and between 5 and 7 in giant fanjets. A high by-pass ratio gives the lowest fuel consumption when turbine inlet temperature and gas pressures are sufficiently high.

There are two types of fans: frontfan and aftfan. The frontfan is mounted at the air intake ahead of the compressor, while the aftfan is mounted behind the final turbine stage. With an aftfan, the compressor aspirates atmospheric air with some effect from the fan but without the added pressure. Otherwise the fan action is the same with both types. But the length of the ducting differs a great deal.

The length of the ducting has considerable importance. The frontfan with the longest duct gives the highest pressure rise, but the aftfan with the shortest cowl gives the lowest aerodynamic drag.

Fanjet engines belong in a separate category of gas turbine engines known as the twin spool type. In a twin spool turbojet engine, there are two separate sections, a low-pressure section and a high-pressure section. The low pressure spool carries the final-stage turbine as driving element and the first-stage compressor as the driven element. The high pressure spool carries the first-stage turbine as the driving element and the final-stage compressor as the driven element. The high-pressure section is bracketed by the low-pres-

Williams WR-19 fanjet engine.

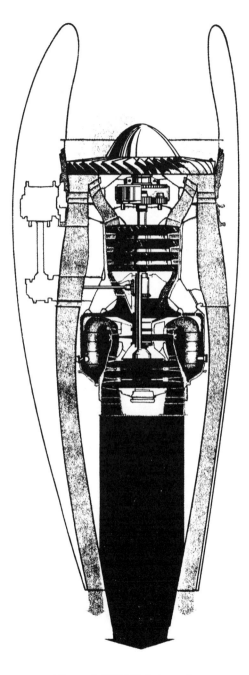

AiResearch TFE 731 fanjet engine.

209

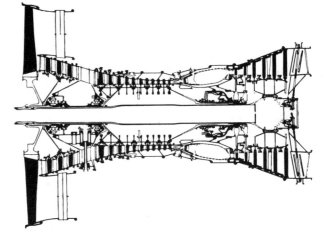

Sectioned view of Pratt & Whitney JT-9D twin-spool front-fan jet engine.

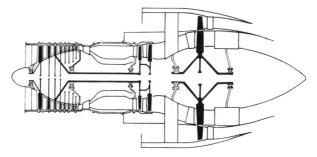

Sectioned view of the General Electric CF-700 twin-spool aft-fan jet engine.

sure section, so that the low-pressure spool shaft has to run through the high-pressure spool. The shafts are coaxial, but free to rotate independently of each other.

This permits optimum speed ratios at varied loads. The high-pressure spool will always run faster than the low-pressure spool, but the difference is greatest at low thrust levels, when the low-pressure spool rpm may be as little as 20–25 percent of high-pressure spool rpm. At high thrust levels, the final-stage turbine will receive far higher input forces, and will speed up the low-pressure spool to about 60–70 percent of high-pressure spool rotational speed. The fan is driven at high speed by the high-pressure turbine(s) and consumes most of its power. The rest is used up in driving the high-pressure spool compressor.

The first twin-spool turbojet was the Pratt & Whitney J-57 of about 1954. About ten years later, Rolls-Royce went to a three-spool design for its

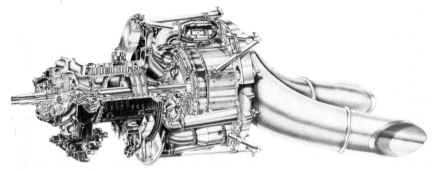

The Bristol Theseus—one of Britain's first successful turboprop engines.

RB 203 Trent turbofan project. The Rolls-Royce three-spool engine separates the fan drive from the high-pressure spool, and uses the first of the high-pressure turbine stages to drive the fan, via a third concentric shaft running inside the two others. This design permits each section of the engine to operate at its own optimum speed according to conditions.

Turbojet and turbofan engines are sometimes fitted with afterburners. The system involves adding fuel to the gases after the final turbine stage and letting the combustion products expand through the exhaust duct. Afterburning delivers an impressive boost in thrust, but can only be used for short periods, as it tends to cause local overheating which can lead to damage of

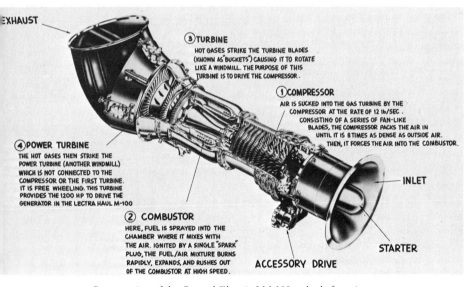

Cutaway view of the General Electric LM-100 turboshaft engine.

Generator set driven by a turboshaft engine.

vital parts. Consequently, afterburners are mainly confined to military aircraft.

Because the aircraft types of gas turbine must operate both on the ground and in the stratosphere, they are subject to exceptional requirements. Aircraft turbines require sophisticated control systems with automatic compensating devices for changes in temperature and altitude.

The aircraft engine may be operating in a 100° F (37.8° C) ambient temperature at one minute and shortly afterwards be called upon to run in a −65° F (−54° C) environment. This means that aircraft fuels also require special volatility characteristics: the more volatile the fuel, the easier it is to achieve good combustion. The overall fuel problems of aircraft are another matter, however, and in this case kerosene may be greatly superior to gasoline.

One key requirement for aviation gas turbines is a fuel having a high calorific value per unit volume, because modern aircraft can more easily lift a little extra weight than accommodate extra bulk. In the engine itself, however, weight is as critical as bulk.

The aircraft industry has found that a one-pound reduction in the weight of the power unit can result in a 5-pound reduction in the overall weight of the aircraft. The most direct approach to lower weight is to increase turbine inlet temperature.

It is estimated that an increment of one degree (centigrade) will provide 100 pounds greater thrust. Current fanjet engines operate with turbine inlet temperatures between 2100 and 2250° F (1150–1235° C). This is possible with metal turbine blades because the turbine blades are provided with a means of cooling.

In summary: in the course of the aircraft turbine engine's evolution, it has become increasingly specialized. Its most advanced features are not applicable to ground vehicles. Only the basic old-type turboshaft aviation unit holds any promise as a multipurpose engine.

INDUSTRIAL USE

Although the origins of the industrial gas turbine owe little or nothing to aviation (as was demonstrated in the historical chapters), the modern industrial turbine engine is usually derived from a successful aircraft engine family. Industrial gas turbines range from single-shaft simple-cycle units to free-shaft regenerative units.

The gas turbine offers a number of important advantages for stationary use. Free-shaft turbines in particular provide smooth power and high torque-rise (torque rise may be defined as the rate at which torque increases as rpm is reduced). Their vibration-free operation allows simplified installation rigs, which usually means lower cost, and greater ease of removal (for maintenance or overhaul). Low noise and vibration are also important factors in limiting operator fatigue.

Its low noise level makes the industrial gas turbine an attractive choice for generator stations, and for many other uses. An unmuffled Pratt & Whitney ST6 generator set will give sound level readings of 90 dBA at 30 feet distance.

Industrial turbines set to run at constant optimum-efficiency speed give very low specific fuel consumption. This is true of simple-cycle units as well as regenerative gas turbines. Low weight and small bulk make the industrial gas turbine more readily portable. Improved portability has brought into existence portable equipment in a power range which lies beyond the limits of feasibility for diesel engines, for instance.

The gas turbine is attractive for certain industrial uses because it has low risk of magnetic interference. Less than half of the parts are magnetic, even with metallic hot-section components.

For field engines running unattended on a programmed, automated schedule, low oil consumption is vital in avoiding forced shutdowns. Pratt & Whitney reports oil consumption figures below 0.1 per hour for such installations.

The same ability to start and function in an extremely wide range of ambient temperatures that proved so great for aircraft turbines also adds an important advantage for the stationary turbine—especially generator sets operating in arctic and desert regions. Good reliability and long life are important points in favor of all turbines, and certainly apply no less to industrial turbines than to those designed for other applications.

The most obvious problem of industrial gas turbine installations is compressor airfoil contamination with oil and grime. This has led to the installa-

Light military tractor powered by a GMT-305 gas turbine engine.

tion of compressor washer systems on industrial turbines. Such a system is made up of a spray ring positioned under the screen for the air intake, with holes arranged to cover the entire compressor annulus. The ring is fed from a pressurized source of washing fluid. The composition of the fluid depends on the exact nature of the contaminants and the ambient temperature. Demineralized water is used for salts and water soluble minerals. Grain alcohol is added in proportions up to 50 percent to depress the freezing points for turbines operating in extremely low ambient temperatures.

Carbon and oil grime deposits can generally be eliminated by spraying in a mixture of water and industrial detergent. For industrial gas turbines in dusty environments it is necessary to equip the machine with erosion control filters to prolong engine life.

For gas turbines used in agriculture or oilfields in sand-rich areas, efficient air intake filters are essential. Ordinary paper filters are out of the question. Oil-bath filters of realistic size lack the capacity for the vast amounts of air consumed by the gas turbine. It takes something more. Pratt & Whitney reports very good results with inertial separator filters of the Farr Dynavane type. This type of filter separates contaminants from the main air stream using the same principle that separates the cream from the milk in an Alfa-Laval milk separator. The contaminants are denser than clean air, and therefore take a wider arc when subjected to centrifugal force. The contaminants are collected in a chamber, and then sucked away by a scavenge pump and dumped.

For the best results, Pratt & Whitney recommends a barrier-type panel filter mounted in series with an inertial filter, but this introduces the need for periodic cleaning or changing of the panel filter. This may be a small point for piston-type stationary engines, which have an extensive maintenance schedule anyway, but it destroys the industrial gas turbine's claim to being virtually maintenance-free.

Industrial gas turbine installations often involve unmanned operating conditions so that the engine is dependent on automatic control systems to assure effective monitoring and guard against exceeding the operating limits in any way. Such systems have been devised, and are most often electronic, with a central control brain which receives signals from a variety of sensors, so that it can automatically order engine shutdown in case of failure to start on time, overtemperature, low oil pressure, excessive oil temperature, turbine overspeed, or chip indication in the oil scavenge system.

Industrial gas turbines come in a wide variety of sizes and shapes for a myriad of different uses. Large numbers of industrial gas turbines are in use all over the world for power generation, pipeline pumping, oilfield repressuring, and chemical processing.

Small gas turbine generator sets have been developed for the military to serve as auxiliary or standby power equipment. Civilian versions of such units are predicted for homes, offices and factories, as sources of energy to provide electric power for lighting, heating and refrigeration.

MARINE USE

Gas turbines have been used in a multitude of marine applications, from small high-speed craft to ocean-going vessels. Naval operation takes advantage of some of the same gas turbine characteristics that airplanes do. Surface vessels of all kinds run for long distances at constant speed, which makes even non-regenerative simple-cycle turbines for boats and ships competitive with the diesel in terms of fuel consumption.

Regenerative gas turbines give superior fuel economy in boats, and also offer torque characteristics highly suited to short-haul operations, such as the work of tugboats, harbor fire-fighting craft, police and coast guard vessels, ferry service, and other applications involving frequent and wide-range load variations.

Because marine turbines cruise at relatively low power levels, the regenerators can be made fairly small and light. More complex cycles with intercooling, regeneration, and reheat have been tried, but have generally been rejected because of additional weight, bulk, cost and complexity.

Gas turbines are far smaller and lighter than diesel engines of similar

Marine installation of the Avco-Lycoming TF-12 1150-hp turboshaft engine.

power. Installation space requirements are reduced, freeing more hull space for cargo, living quarters, or other facilities. Unlike the diesel engine, the marine turbine is not susceptible to changes in attitude. Roll and pitch movements up to 45 degrees have no effect on its operation.

Gas turbines offer tremendous opportunities for improvement in ship operation, especially in terms of reduced down time for overhauls. Drydock time can be reduced by instituting new methods, such as unit replacement of the main power system components while the old units are sent away for off-board overhaul.

Power transmission design poses few problems. Extensive reduction gearing is required for conventional propeller drive, but once the engine is equipped with a two-step reduction gear set, with provision for reversing the drive, there is no further need for a gearbox.

Further advantages of the gas turbine for marine propulsion are found in its freedom from noise and vibration. In the words of Kenneth F. Smith of Ford's industrial engine and turbine operations:

At dockside or under full throttle out in open water, these marine turbines are fantastically quiet. The smooth, continuous operation of a turbine and its rotary motion blend beautifully with the wheel-turning needs of big luxury boats. There's plenty of instantly responsive power, but virtually no vibration—no harmonics problems.

Perhaps most important of all, the gas turbine opens the door for entirely new concepts in ship design. However, due to the marine environment, turbine installations in boats involve specific requirements.

COMPACT SIZE MAKES INSTALLATION EASY.

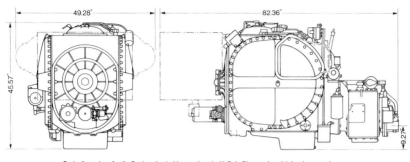

Basic dimensions for the Ford marine turbine, equipped with Twin Disc gearbox. Intake plenum and exhaust connections are indicated by dashed lines. Weight, as equipped, is 2,780 pounds.

FORD TURBINE PERFORMANCE FOR MARINE APPLICATIONS.

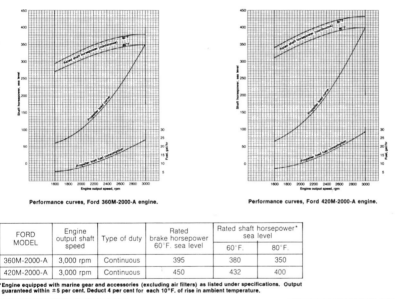

Performance curves, Ford 360M-2000-A engine.   Performance curves, Ford 420M-2000-A engine.

FORD MODEL	Engine output shaft speed	Type of duty	Rated brake horsepower 60°F. sea level	Rated shaft horsepower* sea level	
				60°F.	80°F.
360M-2000-A	3,000 rpm	Continuous	395	380	350
420M-2000-A	3,000 rpm	Continuous	450	432	400

*Engine equipped with marine gear and accessories (excluding air filters) as listed under specifications. Output guaranteed within ±5 per cent. Deduct 4 per cent for each 10°F. of rise in ambient temperature.

Design, materials and/or specifications are subject to change without notice and without liability therefor.

Ford Industrial Engine and Turbine Operations
P. O. Box 1796 • Dearborn, Michigan 48121

Ford Model 710 installation specifications and performance characteristics.

The marine gas turbines require special measures for protection against salt water intrusion, and against corrosion. Salt water ingestion is difficult to eliminate entirely because of the turbine's very high air consumption. But prevention is extremely important because salt water ingestion can cause compressor fouling. The greater the quantity of water ingested, the worse the problem becomes. Sea water droplets in aerosol sizes contain enough salt to cause a deterioration in engine performance after a time. Drawn into the engine and heated during compression, the water turns to vapor and leaves the salt as deposits on the compressor blades. The result of salt deposits buildup on these finely shaped blades is similar to that of ice formation on an aircraft wing: at a critical point of buildup, the airfoil will stall.

To guard against corrosion, marine gas turbines also demand special materials. Magnesium, for instance, will not survive at sea unless treated with protective coatings. It is common for exterior surfaces to be given a coat of epoxy paint. Even inner components must be anodized to prevent corrosion. In addition, the hot-running parts in the marine turbine have a sulfidation problem. To resist the naval environment, higher-grade materials such as titanium alloys must be used, and in the future ceramics may prove to be of enormous value in advancing the use of turbine power at sea.

The first-generation marine turbines were adapted from turboshaft aircraft engines. The second-generation marine engines were based on industrial turbine designs, with low specific fuel consumption, and adapted for the naval environment, with high corrosion resistance, and design consideration given to long life, reliability and maintainability. The regenerative marine gas turbine is usually derived from an industrial-turbine family. Most of them are free-turbine designs. In comparison with the simple-cycle turbine they offer greatly reduced fuel consumption in the low-power cruising range.

Naval combat ships rely heavily on gas turbines derived from turboshaft aircraft engines, which have the highest power density. Regenerative gas turbines are not competitive in this application but can offer improved operating economy in types of vessels in which weight and space considerations are less critical, such as tankers, ore carriers, and naval support ships.

The growth of turbine use for marine installation now has acquired such momentum that the world population of turbine-powered craft totaled 316 vessels at the end of 1972. About two-thirds were small craft with a power output between 100 and 1200 hp. The remaining one-third had larger engines. It was logical for the evolution to start with the small craft, and it was felt for many years that the gas turbine would be restricted to boats under a certain size, due to the preponderance of steam turbines and two-cycle diesels in large sea-going vessels.

In recent years, however, a number of new ships with gas turbine propulsion have been built or ordered. American Export Isbrandtsen Lines operates a large gas-turbine freighter (GTS Admiral William M. Callaghan), and Seatrain Lines will equip four new 32,000-ton container ships with gas turbines. Broken Hill (Pty) Ltd. in Australia is building two cargo ships to be powered by General Electric MS 5212R regenerative gas turbines. An advanced type of the modern small gas turbine propelled vessel is the Vosper Thornycroft semi-amphibious hovercraft for use in car ferry service.

Each craft is equipped with two Lycoming TF 25 engines rated at 2000 shaft hp. A fleet of these are in daily use for crossing the British Channel, cruising at 40 knots, and completing the crossing in about ½ hour.

Hydrofoil applications are increasingly common. For instance, Northwest Hydrofoil lines operates a 37-ton, 40-knot craft "Victoria" which uses twin General Electric LM 100 gas turbines. This unit is derived from the T58 helicopter turboshaft engine and is normally rated at between 1000 and 1200 hp. It weighs 475 pounds and its specific fuel consumption is .71 pounds per hp-hour.

The U.S. Maritime Administration has installed a General Electric LM 1500 turbine for propulsion of a 90-ton 60-knot hydrofoil craft, with an LM 100 unit for maneuvering and docking power. The LM 1500 is derived from the J-79 turbojet engine family and can be rated from 10,000 to 18,000 shaft hp for a weight of only 8250 pounds.

Military Vehicles

Military vehicles can be divided into two broad categories, tactical and administrative. The administrative category is made up of transport vehicles of all sizes. The tactical vehicles are intended for use in front-line operations. Examples are: tanks and armored cars, amphibious assault vehicles, and landing craft. These remarks will be confined to the considerations affecting

Light military tracked vehicle equipped with an Allison GMT-305 gas turbine engine.

tactical vehicles, since the administrative vehicles share the basic requirements with cars and trucks for the civilian market.

Smooth military operations depend on mobility, and mobility depends on
fuel availability. The turbine engine's multi-fuel capability makes it very attractive for a large number of military uses.

The turbine engine's freedom from cold-starting problems, and its ability
to run under load without a warmup period remove any regional restrictions
that climatic conditions might impose. The elimination of anti-freeze for
the cooling system removes an extra source of concern for the logistics of
operations in arctic climates. The gas turbine's ease of operation and maintenance will enable the vehicles to be placed in the hands of relatively
unskilled personnel. The low-speed high-torque characteristics of the free-
shaft turbine make this type of engine especially well suited for tactical
vehicles that must be able to operate at low speeds in all sorts of terrain.

The fuel economy requirements are less stringent in tactical than in administrative vehicles. But unfortunately drive train problems are the same,
and the need for total reliability is a prime consideration in tactical vehicle
engineering. These problems will be fully discussed in the chapter on cars
and trucks.

As for amphibious military vehicles and navy craft, the considerations are
the same as outlined in the chapter on marine use. The conditions regarding military stationary engines correspond to those outlined in the chapter
on industrial gas turbines.

Railroad Locomotives

The railroad industry was not far behind the aviation world in turning its
attention to gas turbines. It soon became clear to railroad men that even the
simple cycle non-regenerative gas turbine would have superior operational
characteristics under a high load factor and for long, uninterrupted hauls.
As a matter of historical fact, turbine locomotives were running before the
turbojet had flown. But the railroad industry has made relatively little
progress with gas turbine propulsion.

The gas turbine is attractive for railroad locomotive installation for a
number of reasons. It offers the possibility of attaining high performance
with a lightweight, self-contained power plant. The performance potential is
important for maintaining speed up-grade, such as when crossing high
mountains.

The only way to improve diesel locomotive performance is to increase
horsepower. That can be done by (1) adding engine displacement, and (2)
turbocharging. Larger displacement means a lot more weight, and a somewhat higher cost. Turbocharging means slightly more weight and greatly
increased cost. The gas turbine offers performance well beyond the possibil-

Jet-propelled locomotive tested by the New York Central Railroad in 1966.

ities of turbocharged diesels, with comparable cost per hp and competitive fuel economy.

The power required to drive a train increases in almost direct proportion to the weight of the train. Since the engine and power transmission form a significant part of the train weight, heavy power units and drive systems contribute to an increase in the power requirement.

Compared with a diesel locomotive engine, a turbine installation gives a weight saving of 2500 pounds for each power plant. In a twin-engined locomotive, that means a saving of 5000 pounds. For long train sets needing four engines, 10,000 pounds can be saved in engine weight alone.

The weight-saving process, initiated with the power unit itself, is contagious in that it can bring to bear some influence on the entire locomotive. A lighter power unit needs less robust structural support. This combined weight saving lightens the forces on the suspension system and load-carrying components. For trains of similar passenger capacity and identical power/weight ratio, the turbine train would weigh only 36 percent of the weight of the diesel-powered train.

Passenger trains have an annoyance factor depending on the obtrusivity and proximity of the engines to the passengers. Diesel locomotives usually carry no passengers (except for diesel-powered railcars as used in local service two- or three-car combinations). The gas turbine is free of vibration and has low noise levels.

This fact is of particular significance when we are not considering a traction engine, but a train set where some of the passenger-carrying cars are equipped with turbines and their drive trains. The normal method is to use powered cars as the lead and "caboose" units in a train set. The entire power train can be accommodated in an underfloor installation. The gas turbine offers the possibility of increasing the useful space by one or two cars per train set. This gain in space will have a big effect in increasing the revenue-producing potential of the train.

As a point of considerable moment to any railroad system contemplating a conversion from diesel engine to either electric or gas turbine power, it is noteworthy that conversion of a railroad's fleet of locomotives to gas turbine propulsion can be accomplished at far lower costs and in less time than electrification of an entire railroad system.

Mainly due to the allure of improved performance, and the ability to cross mountain ranges without any loss of speed, the gas turbine went into service on freight train locomotives in the U.S. long before the railroad companies began to explore its potential for high-speed passenger trains. The freight train locomotives were converted diesel units, and the gas turbine engines were of the turboshaft type.

Union Pacific began to install large General Electric gas turbines in freight-hauling locomotives in 1950. The first of these engines were 4500 hp units, and the second-generation units had 8000 hp. By 1968 power output had been raised to 10,000 hp for one single prime mover. The Union Pacific locomotives used electric drive, which proved extremely reliable. Similar locomotives were produced also by Baldwin-Elliott and Allis Chalmers.

One of the first American attempts to run a turbine-powered passenger train was a turbojet experiment undertaken by the New York Central Railroad in 1965. The project grew out of a proposal by Mr. J. J. Wright, head of the N. Y. Central Railroad technical research center at Cleveland, Ohio.

Two General Electric J-47 aircraft gas turbines were bought as military surplus for less than $35,000 They were installed on a rebuilt standard diesel locomotive which had been in regular commuter and interurban service for years. Reconstruction was undertaken by the Collinwood locomotive shops in Ohio. The two turbojet units were mounted side by side on top of the nose section of the locomotive. The body structure was modified, with a streamlined cowling for the front to reduce its aerodynamic drag, and make high speeds possible. It set a new U.S. speed record in July, 1966, reaching 183.85 mph on a straightaway between Butler, Indiana, and Stryker, Ohio. But this locomotive never went into regular service.

About the same time, the U.S. Department of Commerce decided to sponsor a 3-year 90-million-dollar research program whose objective was to explore brand-new approaches to railroad operations. Two contracts were given out—one to United Aircraft and one to The Budd Company. After the establishment of the Department of Transportation in 1966, the program was handed over from Commerce to the D.o.T.

The United Aircraft TurboTrain was designed in 1965 and scheduled for operation on the routes linking Boston with New York and Montreal with Toronto. From a vehicular engineering point of view, it was an entirely new concept, with lightweight aluminum body construction and low aerodynamic drag so as to give reduced fuel consumption at high speeds. Another revolutionary concept was the single axle design, consisting of a single axle mounted between each pair of cars and supporting one end of two units. A turnbuckle device was used for guidance.

Each locomotive was powered by two or four Pratt & Whitney ST6 turboshaft gas turbine units installed under the floor. A train set could have one or two passenger-carrying locomotives. The ST6 gas turbine used for the TurboTrain weighs only 300 pounds and in its railroad version was rated at 400 to 455 hp., giving the train a top speed in excess of 170 mph. It is a free-shaft non-regenerative unit, 60 inches long and 19 inches in diameter. Two or four of these engines were installed in each locomotive, the number depending on the size of the train and the performance levels required for the route.

Mechanical drive was chosen for a number of reasons. Above all, it offers superior efficiency compared with electric drive, which translates into 10 percent lower power requirement for the same performance characteristics.

In a twin-engine locomotive, the engines were positioned longitudinally in the chassis. The output shaft of each turbine was connected to a right-angle gearbox, whose output went into a collecting gearbox. This collector box had two parallel output shafts, one transmitting power to the nearest axle, and the second one transmitting power to an axle farther back. Each axle was equipped with a double-reduction gearbox, giving two forward speeds (starting and cruising). The reversing function was accomplished in the right-angle gearboxes.

Two three-car TurboTrains went into service on the Boston-New York route on April 8, 1969 (two years behind schedule). By the end of July, 1972 they had carried almost a quarter of a million passengers over the 232-mile course (which was covered in 3 hours 50 minutes with 7 scheduled intermediate stops). The train itself had greater reliability problems than the turbines, however, and the experience cannot be regarded as an unqualified success.

In 1971, one U.S. TurboTrain made a month-long cross-country 12,000-mile tour of 31 states, with no serious problems. On January 29, 1973, the program was turned over to AMTRAK. The Department of Transportation had spent a total of $12,500,000 for the equipment, maintenance, servicing, and modifications during that time.

A four-unit TurboTrain operated by the Canadian National Railways and placed in service on the Montreal-Toronto route collided with a truck at a level crossing on its inaugural run in 1968, and was plagued with service and reliability problems for the rest of its life. The Canadian TurboTrains were forced out of service in 1971. Technically the train remained in the experimental stage, and in a five-year development period, the list of design modifications grew to 13 pages of specifications.

In 1973 a new 9-car version became available. It had a more powerful version of the ST 6 engine rated at 520 shaft hp. The tests ended when a four-unit TurboTrain was destroyed by fire near Montreal after colliding with a freight train on July 25, 1973.

The Budd Turboliner was built from a standard, stainless-steel bodied passenger car. It was equipped with two 535-hp AiResearch turboshaft engines, driving the axles via a Twin-Disc torque converter. The AiResearch model 831-57 gas turbine unit was a simple cycle, single-shaft open-cycle unit with a three-stage axial-flow turbine. The compressor was a two-stage centrifugal design, giving a pressure ratio of seven to one. A single toroidal combustor was used. The whole package including accessory gearbox was 46.5 inches long, 37.6 inches wide, and 23.5 inches high.

The engine weighed 1086 pounds complete with gearbox and accessories. Specific fuel consumption was given by AiResearch as .65 pounds per hp-hour. The chassis was reworked, using pneumatic spring units in place of the steel leaf springs.

The Budd Turboliner was never placed in actual service, but ran for a

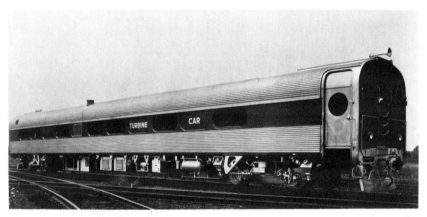

The Budd Turboliner locomotive.

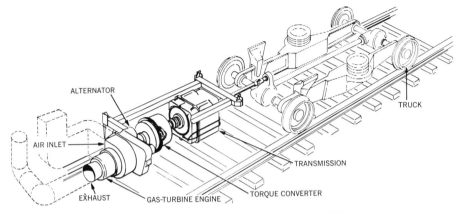

Installation of the AiResearch turboshaft engine in the Budd Turboliner.

long period on different routes as part of a program to evaluate its performance, fuel consumption, safety, reliability, noise levels, vibration, heat characteristics, and exhaust emissions. Primary tests were made on a 20-mile straightaway of the Long Island Rail Road between Bethpage and Ronkonkoma. Tests began in September 1966 and continued for an 8-month period, running six days a week, 16 hours a day. Normal top speed was 75 mph, though the locomotive could reach 100 mph.

While the American industry was making half-hearted attempts like these, the leadership in gas turbine train propulsion was taken over by France. The French National Railways (SCNF) used electric drive in their first-generation gas turbine locomotives, dating back to 1939. Even at that time, most of the French railroad network had been electrified, which must have influenced the decision.

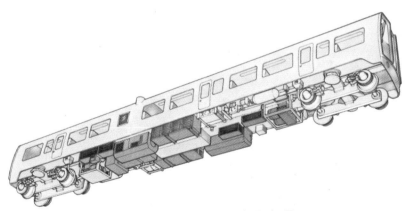

Drive units of Canadian National's Turbo-Train.

Experimental turbotrain TGV with electric drive on test on the Paris-Dijon line.

Electric drive was favored for railroad use because it offers high starting torque. The arguments against it center around the massive weight of the system, and its relatively poor efficiency. In a diesel-electric locomotive, the transmission efficiency is about 85 percent. Some of the losses are friction

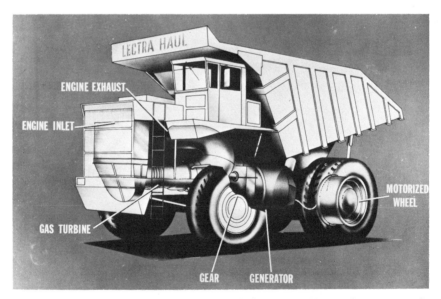

Unit-Rig Lectra-Haul 100-ton truck with a General Electric LM-100 gas turbine engine and electric drive.

APPLICATIONS: A GENERAL REVIEW

losses in gears and bearings, but much of it is due to the control circuitry for the motors and in the cooling losses for both motors and generator.

The control system is complex, bulky, difficult to maintain, and expensive to produce. Modern electronics with solid-state circuitry can alleviate some of the drawbacks, but was not available at the time the SNCF decided to switch to hydromechanical drive. The hydromechanical system provides high starting torque due to its hydraulic torque converter. However, some such units have efficiency no better than that of electric drive. This results from hydraulic slippage, and is directly related to a power loss. The loss is a result of mechanical energy converted to heat, which appears as a rise in the temperature of the transmission fluid.

The current SNCF plan calls for the construction of 16 gas turbine-powered train sets. The first units are already in operation. Each set includes two power cars. The propulsion power unit is a 1400-hp Turbomecca Turmo (free shaft non-regenerative) gas turbine weighing only 500 pounds. It has no accessory drives, since the accessories (lighting, cooling, heating, kitchen) are supplied by an auxiliary power unit—a small 430-hp Turbomecca Astazou gas turbine driving an alternator.

The transmission is direct and simple. The output shaft feeds power to a Voith hydraulic torque converter which drives a series of shafts to axle-mounted gearboxes. The Voith torque converter can reach 90 percent efficiency when only minor torque multiplication is called for.

Germany and Japan are now trying to follow the French lead. MAN (Maschinenfabrik Augsburg-Nürnberg) in Nürnberg has converted six diesel trains to gas turbine power for the Deutsche Bundesbahnen. The KHD (Klöckner-Humboldt-Deutz) gas turbines are called BR-602 and are made under license from Avco-Lycoming. As in the French trains, the drive from the turbine output shaft is passed through a hydraulic torque converter, then via a transfer case to individual gearboxes mounted integrally with the driving axles.

Kawasaki Heavy Industries in Japan has installed a 1200-hp Avco-Lycoming gas turbine in a passenger carrying locomotive that has been evaluated by the Japanese National Railways with good results. Kawasaki is the Lycoming licensee for Japan and the engine was based on the TF-14.

Ishikawajima Harima Heavy Industries, better known as shipbuilders, have also been active in gas turbine train construction. A General Electric LM 100-2 unit developing 1000 hp has recently been installed in a test locomotive.

Cars and Trucks

By the widest possible definition of the term "automotive gas turbine" is meant a gas turbine for installation in passenger cars, trucks and buses, plus

General Electric LM-100 gas turbine and electric generator for installation in the Lectra-Haul.

recreational and utility vehicles for off-road use. Our interest is focused on the passenger car above all other vehicle types. The requirements that passenger car operation imposes on the gas turbine are worlds apart from the needs of industrial, aviation and military uses. Truck and bus use shares some of the passenger car requirements, and imposes others. These differences will be discussed after an examination of the passenger car application.

The particular demands of passenger car gas turbines can be divided into six areas:

1. Small package size.
2. Low part-load fuel consumption.
3. Fast response.
4. Good overall performance.
5. Low noise levels.
6. Low exhaust volume and temperature.

SMALL PACKAGE SIZE

The smaller and lighter the car, the lower its horsepower requirement. That indicates the possibility of very small turbine dimensions. However, most experts feel that the passenger car gas turbine must be equipped with regenerators, which adds considerably to the bulk of the power unit. In the final analysis, it is vehicle size that sets the limits for the installation pack-

Williams WR-26 engine installed in an AMC Hornet.

age. At the present state of the art, the regenerative free-shaft gas turbine is lighter than a piston engine of equal power, but just as bulky.

Low Part-Load Fuel Consumption

The passenger car's normal driving cycle includes long periods of idling and passenger car operation presents extremely wide load variations. Full-load conditions are relatively rare and of short duration. The average passenger car spends most of its running life either speeding up or slowing down. The specific fuel consumption of industrial gas turbines are given at full load, and how much fuel is consumed at idle is of little interest. For the passenger car gas turbine, fuel consumption at idle is of prime importance, and full-load fuel economy is of less concern.

Compared with the piston engine, the gas turbine works under a considerable disadvantage with regard to part-load fuel economy. The compression ratio of the piston engine is independent of engine speed and output, but the pressure ratio in the gas turbine varies with power output. In addition, the geometry of the piston engine's enclosed cylinder is more ideally suited to harnessing energy produced at various pressures and temperatures (due to variations in load) than are the velocity-sensitive contours of turbine nozzles and blades.

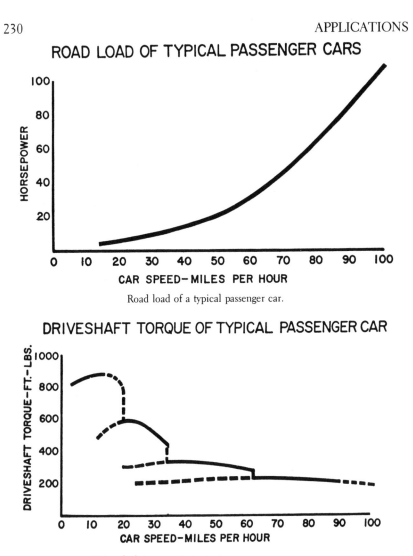

ROAD LOAD OF TYPICAL PASSENGER CARS

Road load of a typical passenger car.

DRIVESHAFT TORQUE OF TYPICAL PASSENGER CAR

Drive shaft torque of a typical passenger car.

In a simple-cycle gas turbine, the drop in pressure ratio that is associated with reduced turbine inlet temperature works in the interest of lower fuel consumption because of reduced frictional losses. But a lot of energy is still wasted. That's where the regenerators come in. And the slower compressor shaft speed that results from operation at light load factors will further add to the benefits of lower turbine inlet temperature and contribute to higher heat exchanger efficiency.

While running the compressor at a low percentage of its rated rpm can as-

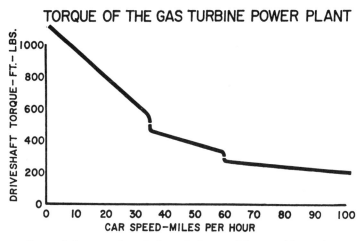

TORQUE OF THE GAS TURBINE POWER PLANT

Output shaft torque of a typical two-shaft automobile gas turbine engine.

FUEL ECONOMY (INSTALLED)

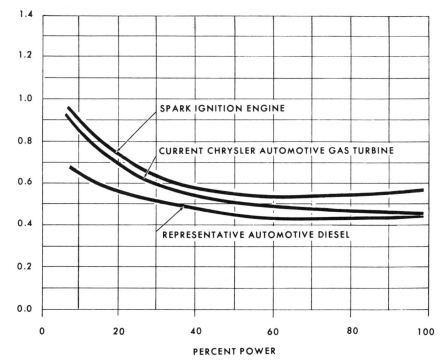

Effects of part-load operation on the specific fuel consumption of automotive power plants.

231

sist materially in improving part-load and idle speed fuel economy, the same low compressor shaft speed may penalize the car's acceleration potential (depending on the turbine nozzle geometry and other design features). There must be a trade off between fuel economy requirements and performance objectives.

Most passenger car gas turbines incorporate a waste gate to lower the compressor speed at idle. The waste gate is operated automatically in accordance with accelerator pedal action. The waste gate will bypass the gases from the first-stage turbine direct to the regenerators, without sending them through the power turbine. This helps conserve the heat in the exhaust gases, and reduces the fuel required for continued combustion. The waste gate is also a valuable instrument in eliminating "creep" when the car is stationary.

Fast Response

The alacrity of gas turbine response to increased power demand as signaled by the accelerator linkage is mostly a factor of gasifier section inertia. This subject was fully discussed in the chapters dealing with the compressor and the turbine.

Good Overall Performance

As in piston-powered cars, the maximum speed, and the speed at which the engine develops a given percentage of peak torque, are determined by the overall gear ratio from the engine output shaft to the driving wheels. The overall gear ratio also has a great deal of influence on the vehicle acceleration rate and fuel consumption characteristics. Ultimately, the selection of overall gear ratios is limited by the torque capacity of the drive train elements and the power turbine wheel maximum stress limits.

The gas turbine transmission involves a speed reduction gear of about 10 to one, because the power turbine shaft spins about ten times faster than the maximum rpm in a piston engine. This is not easily done in one single step. Gear wheels with widely different numbers of teeth cannot easily be matched without giving up proper meshing properties and adequate contact area. Most passenger car turbine transmissions have a simple one-step reduction gear, however.

In a turbine reduction gear, the pinion on the power turbine shaft may go through 10 million cycles in about 3 hours. This indicates a definite threat of fatigue damage.

High-speed turbine gears differ in design and development complexity from gears used in conventional transmissions, because of the high rotational speeds and tremendous torque multiplication involved. The turbine reduction gears must be more accurately processed. They must have greater accuracy in their mounting, and the mounts must have greater rigidity than those needed for lower-speed gear trains. The final drive ratio is selected in accordance with vehicle weight, available torque, maximum output shaft speed, and acceleration and fuel economy requirements.

Theoretically, no additional gearing is needed between the reduction gear on the turbine (with a free-turbine configuration) and the final drive unit. That applies equally to cars, trucks and buses, and off-road vehicles. But in practice, it has been found necessary to include a gearbox with three to five ratios.

With the compressor turbine running at constant speed the power turbine can deliver nearly constant power output over a wide speed range and function as a torque converter. The maximum torque multiplication with the power turbine stalled appears to be about 2½ : 1, but trucks often need ratios of 7 or 8 : 1, and cars go as high as 4 or 5 : 1.

A certain waste of power is associated with use of the free turbine as a torque converter, as even under the most favorable conditions, i.e. full power at rated speed of the free turbine, the free turbine is only developing a maximum of about one-third of the total turbine power. In other words, the compressor turbine is developing twice as much power as the free turbine. Under conditions where the free turbine is inefficient due to torque conversion, the compressor turbine continues to run at its most efficient speed for a given compressor output. This power loss can be reduced by adding other torque-multiplying means (mechanical or hydraulic).

For trucks, a straight mechanical transmission, with a reduction gear, friction clutch and multi-speed gearbox, and a driving axle with either single- or double-reduction final drive can give 92 percent efficiency. Hub reduction can be added at low additional cost in terms of friction losses. The straight mechanical system also has the advantages of light weight, low volume, and low maintenance requirements.

It is also perfectly adaptable to passenger cars, and Rover, for instance, has relied entirely on mechanical drives for all its turbine cars. The American automobile companies, however, prefer automatic transmissions including a hydraulic torque converter. Use of a hydraulic torque converter transmission offers the possibility of driving the accessories from the free shaft, but inevitably causes some power loss through slippage, and adds to the acceleration lag.

Low Noise Levels

The passenger car application imposes stricter noise level limitations on the gas turbine than the truck application. Piston engines have been so well silenced and suspended that the gas turbine will need special attention before it can be made equally unobtrusive. Anybody who has been near an airport knows that gas turbines are not inherently quiet. Federal noise level standards will set limits for trucks and buses, and the pressure of competition in the market place will force the industry to silence the passenger car turbine.

Actually, noise has been greatly reduced by fitting heat exchangers. The jet roar is eliminated from the regenerative gas turbine, but it still has a low-intensity singing noise and a whine. The singing noise is aerodynamic, and the whine emanates from the accessory drive.

Low Exhaust Volume and Temperature

The city-and-suburban environment cannot tolerate turbojet operation of road vehicles, and the exact limit for the gas flow volume it can tolerate has not been set. Common sense tells us the gas flow volume must be kept at levels that will not prove offensive to residents, pedestrians, and other motorists. The obtrusiveness will depend to a great extent on the temperature. A high gas flow volume becomes more tolerable at near ambient temperature than it can be if it radiates high heat to the atmosphere. With modern regenerative gas turbines, the exhaust temperature is quite low and the problem can be regarded as solved (at least until the day specific standards are introduced).

Commercial Vehicle Considerations

Due to the differences in operating conditions, the truck or bus installation avoids several of the problems associated with turbine-powered passenger cars.

The highway tractor-trailer combination runs for long hours under high load and at near-constant speed, so that idle-speed and part-load fuel economy considerations can be given less weight. The same is true of intercity buses.

The acceleration lag is of minor importance in trucks and buses. As far as overall performance is concerned, transmission demands differ greatly but engineering the commercial vehicle drive train is an equally difficult task. The complexity of the heavy road vehicle transmission requirements is due to the truck's extremely wide load factor range, whereas those of the passenger car are due to infinite variations in road and traffic conditions.

The scale effect associated with heavy trucks as compared with passenger cars works in favor of the commercial vehicle. In the 350–400 hp range, the regenerative gas turbine is comparable with the diesel in fuel economy.

With regard to production cost, the truck-type gas turbine is already competitive with the diesel on a dollar-per-horsepower basis for engines in the 300-plus hp range. The key reason for this lies not in the gas turbine but in the diesel engine. The cost of increased power density in truck diesels gets

very high over the 300-hp mark, since it calls for very sophisticated turbocharger systems, and other mechanical features designed to permit reliable operation at a high average cylinder pressure.

Standardization of turbines for truck fleets can offer sizeable savings on
maintenance. Passenger car fleets usually lack the necessary uniformity of
equipment to be able to get this benefit. The excellent cold-starting characteristics will add an extra argument in favor of the gas turbine for emergency
vehicles. In fire apparatus, turbine power can be used also for pumping,
where it gives superior performance compared with piston-engine pumps.

The simple-cycle free-shaft gas turbine could find an excellent market for
emergency vehicles of all types—fire trucks, wreckers, and so on. This type
of vehicle derives great benefits from high power/weight ratios, because agil-
ity, mobility and reliability are more important than fuel economy and first
cost.

In summary, all other road vehicles offer the gas turbine easier working
conditions than the passenger car. Noel Penny outlines the situation and the
significance of the passenger car application very concisely: "Faced with the
parameters of reliability, performance, efficiency, cost and size, by far the
most difficult application is the passenger car. Yet, on the other hand, given
the initial capital investment, this is the one application in which large
quantities would play the biggest part."

16

Case History: Rover

WE BEGIN THIS COLLECTION of case histories with The Rover Company of Solihull, Birmingham, England. To Rover goes the honor of having built the first gas turbine car and setting the first turbine car speed records. Actually, Rover's gas turbine activity dates a long way back, and Rover can justifiably claim to have been "present at the creation" since it was the Rover Company that built the W.2, Frank Whittle's second turbojet engine, in the 1940–43 period. This work was handed over to Rolls-Royce Ltd. in 1943, when Rover was awarded a Ministry of Supply contract for the Meteor V-12 tank engine, and the W.2 became the basis for the Rolls-Royce Derwent and Nene engines.

In 1945 the directors of The Rover Company, two brothers named Maurice and Spencer Wilks, resolved to revive their turbine expertise and explore the potential for small gas turbines, notably for automotive work. The first step was a design study for a free-shaft engine with the designation T.5. The T.5 was designed to deliver 100 hp. The principal design features were a centrifugal compressor driven at 70,000 rpm by a single-stage axial-flow power turbine. A pair of contraflow recuperators were fitted on two sides, and the output shaft was connected to a two-stage, 12 : 1 reduction gear. A turbojet version of the T.5 was tested in 1947. As the results showed problems in balancing, high-speed bearing reliability, and low component efficiency, the T.5 design was shelved.

The T.5 was designed by an Australian-born engineer named F. R. Bell, whom Rover had lured away from Rolls-Royce, where he had been engaged on design and development work on aircraft-type turbojets. He was to remain the top turbine man at Rover until he returned to Australia in 1953 to work on nuclear energy research.

The world's first gas turbine-powered car: Rover JET 1.

JET 1

Rover's next gas turbine project was the T.8—a larger unit intended for an output of 200 hp. The package size was determined by the underhood dimensions of the 1948 Rover, a compact sedan of advanced specifications. The first version of the T.8 used dual barrel-type combustors, but it was redesigned with a single combustor. The first-stage turbine was of the axial-flow type, and the compressor was a centrifugal-flow design of 8.76-inch (222.25 mm).

The plans called for an annular bank of contraflow recuperator elements surrounding the power turbine, but this idea was abandoned as heat exchanger technology was acquired. A T.8 turbine was first tested at full speed in 1949 and reached its target output. The fifth T.8 prototype was installed in a mobile test bed—a special two-seater version of the 111-inch wheelbase production-model Rover 75 passenger car. The license plate appropriately read "Jet 1".

The Rover 75 was a brand-new model for 1949 and was hailed as one of the most noteworthy designs of the first post-war generation of British cars. It had a six-cylinder engine positioned far forward in the chassis, with its center of gravity almost coinciding with the front wheel axis, enabling the engineers to move the front seat, cowl structure and windshield base farther forward. The all-steel body was carried on a sturdy steel frame (unit construction was not yet part of the Rover credo) and featured slab sides and full-width seats. The front suspension had coil springs and two lower control arms giving a wide-angle triangulated linkage, and a narrow upper control arm working under very low fore-and-aft stresses. The rear axle was located by long semi-elliptic leaf springs.

This chassis was chosen for the turbine installation. The body was chopped off at the belt line and the rear doors welded shut. The back seat was removed, and the turbine installed in its place. In other words, it was a *midships* engine installation, not a *rear engined* chassis. Curiously, the rigid rear axle was retained, with a short open propeller shaft, rather than building up an independent rear suspension system. The overall gear ratio, from power turbine to rear wheels, was 22.75 : 1 (with a one-stage 7 : 1 reduction gear on the output shaft and a 3.25 : 1 final drive ratio). The gearbox was a simple forward-and-reverse unit. The compressor ran at 40,000 rpm at full speed and the free turbine reached rotational speeds up to 36,000 rpm.

The fuel system consisted of a Rover gear pump and a simple spill-type injection nozzle, with starting boost pump. The T.8 engine weighed 450 pounds, and Jet 1 had a curb weight of 2688 pounds (1220 kg).

Initially, all the combustion work was carried out by Lucas Gas Turbine Equipment Ltd. at Burnley, and their contribution to Rover's engine designs was of extreme value. Later, in view of Rover's rapid progress with overall engine development, it became necessary to carry out combustion work in more intimate contact with the engine program. Rover therefore took over all aspects of combustion design and development, and this work came to form part of the everyday program.

The turbine unit was first designed *with* a heat exchanger. Later the heat exchanger was removed to increase output, because the engine delivered only half the horsepower it was expected to produce. Fuel consumption averaged between 3 and 4 miles per gallon. The car was first demonstrated to the Royal Automobile Club on March 8, 1950 at Silverstone racing circuit in Northamptonshire. Two more years of continued development on the T.8 resulted in raising power output to 220 hp, and the car was given a few aerodynamic improvements with a view to high-speed testing. That could not be done in England so Rover took the car to Belgium, where a new superhighway from Bruxelles to Ostende was under construction. A long section near Jabbeke ran dead straight for over 8 miles, and had been used for speed-testing by other British companies (Jaguar and Triumph).

The Rover turbine car was officially timed at 152.9 mph (246.02 km/h). It was capable of reaching 100 mph from standstill in 13.2 seconds, and did the 0–60 mph acceleration run in 6.5 seconds. For comparison, the fabulous Jaguar XK-120 in special aerodynamic trim had reached a top speed of 131.6 mph (211.7 km/h) and the standard production model needed 7.2 seconds to accelerate from standstill to 60 mph and 27.2 seconds to reach 100 mph. Rover also installed two T.8 engines in a motor launch named "Torquil", and the Royal Navy bought four units for evaluation testing.

Many valuable lessons were learned with the T.8. One problem was excessively high temperatures in the flame-tube skin. This was solved by letting it be swept by an internal film of air. Another difficulty was an unacceptable temperature traverse, which was overcome by redesigning the air flow to the flame tube, the burner spray pattern, and the size, shape and positions of the dilution holes. The need for urgent development of an efficient heat exchanger became obvious. The Rover engineers were conscious of the theoretical thermodynamic superiority of the regenerator, but decided to use a recuperator in order to keep development costs down. In 1952 there was also a more limited choice of materials available, and regenerator research was then felt to be outside the economic scope of the small team.

In the meantime, two new men had taken over the turbine program at Rover—Noel Penny and Spencer King. Penny had come to Rover in 1950, fresh from the Department of Atomic Energy research station at Risley, where he had been a technical assistant on the development of isotope separation.

His first assignments at Rover were the development of high-speed turbine bearings, turbine sealing, and small turbine design. In 1954 he became senior technical assistant and was placed in charge of combustion and fuel systems. Spencer King is a nephew of former Rover director, Spencer Wilks. He joined the firm in 1945 at the age of 20, and was associated with varied engineering projects for several years. He became chief project engineer in 1954, with responsibility for future production cars as well as for the turbine program.

At this time, Rover did not concentrate on the passenger car turbine to the exclusion of other automotive needs, and even stationary purposes. After evaluation of the T.8 experience, the company decided to produce a single-shaft turbine power unit, for types of service where low specific weight was a prime consideration and fuel economy of secondary importance.

The first unit was called 1S/60 (one shaft, 60 hp). It delivered peak hp at 46,000 rpm, and had a centrifugal 17-vane compressor of 6.5-in. (165.1 mm) diameter driven by a single-stage axial-flow turbine of Nimonic 90. Specific fuel consumption was high—1.45 pounds per hp-hour. However, it was so enthusiastically received by builders of small generator sets, small boats, and light aircraft that Rover formed a subsidiary company, Rover Gas Turbines, Ltd. to handle the manufacture and sales of the single shaft turbines.

In a few years, Rover sold over 500 units of the 1S/60 model. The most noteworthy applications were as auxiliary power units in the Vulcan bomber plane and the Argosy turboprop of the RAF Transport Command.

As a result of continued progress in component efficiency and the availability of improved materials, Rover found it possible to upgrade the single-shaft engine. The new model was rated at 90 hp and designated 1S/90.

The 1S/90 was designed to run with a compressor speed of 46,000 rpm. Unfortunately it had a bad tendency to surge between 38,000 and 42,000 rpm, which was a drawback for its primary target market—the light airplane. Pilots found it necessary to keep the engine under 30,000 rpm for taxiing, and then accelerate the turbine through the surge speed range prior to take-off.

The 1S/90 had a mass flow of 1.75 pounds per second, which is about 30 percent higher than in the 1S/60, but its specific fuel consumption was somewhat lower: 1.38 pounds per hp-hour. In collaboration with Uffa Fox, Rover also installed a 1S/90 power plant in a Brensal day boat. It was found to lack flexibility (due to the torque characteristics inherent in single-shaft turbines) but that drawback was partly overcome by using a variable-pitch propeller.

For the passenger car, the turbine team at Rover decided to stay with the twin-shaft configuration. The T.8 had been abnormally powerful for a passenger car of Rover size, and a scaled-down version was prepared. It was actually a twin-shaft version of the T.6, with the same 6.5-inch (165.1 mm) compressor, designed for a maximum gasifier shaft speed of 52,000 rpm. When it first ran in 1952, the power unit was rated at 100 hp, but early in 1953 it was delivering 120 hp.

T.6 units were installed in Rover sedans for testing. Two versions were built—one with the engine in the trunk, and one with the engine under the hood. These experimental cars proved highly valuable in adding to Rover's bank of knowledge for solving the problems of engine installation, transmission, and exhaust. The test results obtained with the T.6-powered cars showed the need to concentrate on heat exchanger development—the basic power unit was perfectly sound.

THE FOUR WHEEL DRIVE T.3

It was "back to the drawing board" for Spencer King, Noel Penny, and the small but growing number of men on the turbine team. The next design project was known as the 2S/100 (twin shaft, 100 HP). The design followed the same general outline as the T.8 and the T.6, with a 6.5-inch centrifugal compressor driven by an axial-flow turbine. The free turbine was also a single-stage, axial-flow type.

The compressor was made in two parts, both of which were shrunk onto the shaft. The wheel was machined from an aluminum alloy forging and had 17 vanes. Immediately in front of it were rotating inlet guide vanes, made of steel. These vanes were curved on their leading edges to assist the air entry to the compressor wheel eye.

The turbines were Nimonic forgings with the blades integral with the hub. The blades were of free-vortex design, and each turbine wheel was

Four wheel drive Rover T.3 prototype.

fixed to the shaft by a single Nimonic bolt. Annular grooves turned in the turbine volute casings formed a labyrinth pressure seal with the rotating turbine wheel.

Each shaft was carried in two main bearings. A ball bearing on the front end of the compressor shaft worked as an axial thrust-absorbing bearing, and a roller bearing was positioned between the compressor and the first-stage turbine. This roller bearing was flexibly mounted and turned to keep the shaft assembly out of resonance with the natural frequency of the gasifier section. The flexibility was assured by a number of longitudinal arms machined in the extension of the outer race that held it to the casing. The second-stage turbine was mounted on a split angular contact ball bearing, with a roller bearing at the outer end, adjacent to the reduction gearing.

For a heat exchanger, the 2S/100 used a contraflow, secondary-surface stainless steel recuperator. The heat exchanger lay flat on top of the engine, and it showed the least deterioration of all types used by Rover. For starting, the 2S/100 had a 12-V motor driving the gasifier shaft via a 10 : 1 reduction gear, running the shaft up to 15,000 rpm, at which speed the engine is capable of sustaining combustion and accelerating to its 23,500 rpm idle speed. Maximum rated speed was 52,800 rpm.

The accessory drive was located at the front of the engine, driven from the end of the compressor shaft, and arranged to operate the oil pump, fuel pump and governor. The generator was belt-driven from the output (free turbine) shaft to minimize inertia in the gasifier section. The aluminum compressor housing played the role of main structural member, whose base

Sectioned view of the Rover 2S/100—power plant for the T.3 car.

<table>
<tr><td>1.</td><td>Air intake and rear mounting</td><td>11.</td><td>Compressor turbine nozzle</td></tr>
<tr><td>2.</td><td>Compressor housing</td><td>12.</td><td>Compressor rotor</td></tr>
<tr><td>3.</td><td>Compressor rotating guide vanes</td><td>13.</td><td>Power turbine nozzle</td></tr>
<tr><td>4.</td><td>Compressor</td><td>14.</td><td>Power turbine rotor</td></tr>
<tr><td>5.</td><td>Air duct to heat exchanger</td><td>15.</td><td>Support vanes</td></tr>
<tr><td>6.</td><td>Heat exchanger body</td><td>16.</td><td>Turbine exhaust outlet duct</td></tr>
<tr><td>7.</td><td>Combustion air collector duct</td><td>17.</td><td>Turbine exhaust</td></tr>
<tr><td>8.</td><td>Combustion chamber and casing</td><td>18.</td><td>Compressor shaft oil supply and metering nozzle</td></tr>
<tr><td>9.</td><td>Fuel supply</td><td></td><td></td></tr>
<tr><td>10.</td><td>Double-skinned volute casing</td><td>19.</td><td>Power turbine oil supply and metering nozzle</td></tr>
</table>

242

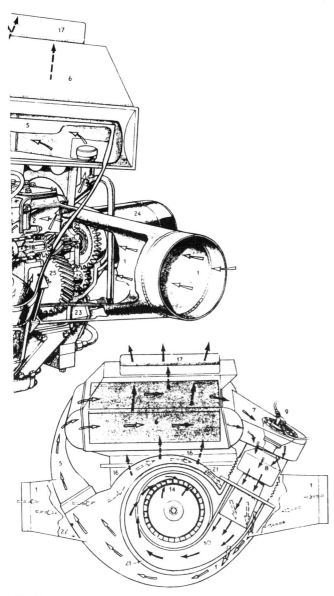

20.	Thermo-couple (one of four)	30.	Differential forward and reverse
21.	Cooling air from compressor	31.	Selector for forward and reverse
22.	Engine main casing	32.	Selector sleeve
23.	Fuel control unit	33.	Crown wheel and pinion
24.	12-volt starter motor	34.	Differential gear
25.	Starter reduction gears	35.	Disc brake
26.	Heater plug	36.	Drive shafts to rear road wheels
27.	Output casing	37.	Freewheel between front and rear wheel drives
28.	Power turbine reduction gear		
29.	Forward and reverse gear train	38.	Output shaft to front wheels

was integral with the oil sump. Light alloy air intakes were bolted to each side of the aluminum casing. The center of the casing had provision for a front main ball bearing for the compressor shaft and the accessory drive.

A sheet metal duct led the compressed air to the combustion chamber, which was a reverse-flow barrel-type with a fuel-atomizing injector nozzle. The combustor was installed tangentially in an involute-curvature plenum chamber. From the heat exchanger, the air entered the combustor at right angles to the barrel axis at the point of intersection with the nozzle axis. This was called an elbow-type of air entry.

The combustor was divided into two sections: the primary zone and the dilution zone. Fuel was sprayed into the primary zone and mixed with a proportion of the incoming air. This mixture was burned completely in the primary zone. The flame was stabilized by a steady toroidal vortex circulating in the combustor, right up to the primary zone. The combustion products flowed to the dilution one where they were mixed with fresh air, and the resulting hot gas was led to the turbines through a Nimonic alloy volute ducting.

The main casings for the turbines were fabricated from stainless steel sheet. The duct was equipped with a shield to prevent heat pickup from the combustion gases. Noel Penny saw this shield as an important factor in controlling the engine's overall thermal efficiency, since any heat added to the air before it enters the compressor would cause a drop in efficiency.

The air flow path from the twin intakes led, first, to the inlet eye of the compressor. After compression, it was ducted through the heat exchanger to the combustor. The gases, after passing the two turbines, still held about 1075° F (580° C), and were ducted through the primary surface of the heat exchanger, to be finally exhausted at close to 400° F (200° C).

Noel Penny observed that oil flow and consumption in a turbine engine are much lower than necessary for the crankshaft bearings in a piston engine, but that the turbine's problems of metering the right amount of oil are more delicate. On the 2S/100 unit, oil was fed through an oil cooler and full-flow filter to metering nozzles which led into the front end of the compressor shaft and the rear end of the free turbine shaft. In each shaft, a drilled channel fed oil under pressure to the bearings through radially drilled holes. A pressurized seal at each bearing was inserted to prevent the oil from reaching the compressor or turbine. A certain amount of air was bled from the compressor diffuser to carry surplus oil back to the sump.

A special car was designed for road-testing the 2S/100 gas turbine. It was a two-door sports sedan with four wheel drive, four wheel disc brakes, and a fiberglass-reinforced plastic body. The car was code-named T.3 (Rover's third turbine car) and the engine was nicknamed "Aurora". The T.3 was displayed at the London Motor Show in Earls Court in October 1956.

It was built on a 94-inch wheelbase and weighed 2016 pounds (914.4 kg). The power plant accounted for 450 pounds, including gearing and heat exchanger (and the recuperator alone weighed 115 pounds). The engine was mounted in the tail, partly above and partly behind the final drive unit and de Dion rear suspension system. The cool (compressor) end was at the rear, with the output shaft pointing forwards. From a two-stage reduction gear, the first stage with a 6.3 ratio and the second with a 1.2 ratio, the drive was taken direct to a rear pinion shaft and from it forward to the front wheel final drive unit, via a freewheel. The final drive ratio, front and rear, was 3.9 : 1. King and Penny regarded the free turbine as capable of providing adequate torque multiplication and cut down the gearbox to a plain forward-and-reverse gear set.

T.3 had a top speed of 115 mph and was able to accelerate from standstill to 60 mph in 10.5 seconds, and to 80 mph in 17.7 seconds. There was a considerable acceleration lag, however, of about 3 seconds.

Fuel consumption was critically high, as T.3 returned only 12.08 miles per U.S. gallon at a steady 60 mph. Strangely, this fell to 11.6 mpg when running slower—at a steady 40 mph. When the car was speeded up to a steady 80 mph, fuel consumption did not rise sharply, however, giving a creditable 10.8 mpg at that speed. T.3 became a valuable research tool, and remained in regular service for many years.

While the heat exchanger fitted to the 2S/100 had brought about a marked improvement in fuel economy, it was evident that its life was not yet satisfactory. Two interesting points emerged:

1. The heat exchanger gas side pressure drop became almost prohibitive in approximately 3000 miles. This was due to fine carbon deposition in the matrix of the heat exchanger on the gas side.

2. Although Rover's industrial experience had indicated that fall-off in power could be quite catastrophic when no air cleaners were used, this was not in evidence from the running carried out in T.3.

During 1962 the 2S/100 engine was rebuilt with a primary surface heat exchanger, and clogging became a less frequent problem.

THE FRONT-WHEEL-DRIVE T.4

While the T.3 with its 2S/100 gas turbine kept racking up test miles, Rover's engineers began designing a new engine. Preliminary design work on the 2S/140 began in 1957. It was based on the 2S/100, enlarged to give 140 hp., and showed the fruits of many lessons learned in terms of component efficiency and weight control. Its total weight, including the 6.82 : 1 reduction gearing and two banks of primary-surface contraflow heat exchangers was only 470 pounds. The pressure ratio was 3.92 at full speed,

and air flow reached 2.15 pounds per second. Early in its development period, the 2S/140 actually put out 150 hp.

The 2S/140 had a specific fuel consumption of .55 pounds per hp-hour at full speed, but 8 pounds per hp-hour at half-flow. The compressor design was carefully coordinated with the geometry of the pre-swirl vanes, the rotating entry guide vanes, and the diffuser. Each section of the compressor affects the others, and a modification to one part involved re-testing of the entire compressor assembly.

The Rover engineers felt that the key to a successful combination lay in finding the most suitable incidence for the rotating guide vanes. The incidence vale was assumed to be in the 5 to 7 degree (positive) range. The blade camber question had to be solved before it could be pinned down, and several designs were evaluated, including parabolical, elliptical and circular arcs. The final choice was a modified circular arc.

The entry angle to the rotating guide vanes was also found to be a vital design point, and the desired flow path was obtained by installing plastic pre-swirl vanes. This made it possible to give the rotating guide vanes a straight profile from the entry to the throat point. The result was a 2–3 percent gain in overall compressor efficiency.

On the 2S/100, there had been fatigue failures in the rotating guide vanes. This was first cured by the installation of a brazed shroud, which had the unfortunate side effect of causing a loss in efficiency. The inlet guide vanes for the 2S/140 were redesigned without a shroud and with extra safeguards against fatigue failure:

1. The blade aerodynamic loading was reduced by enlarging the chord.

2. The natural frequency of the vanes was raised.

3. The blade root was thickened to reduce centrifugal force stresses.

The first point had the added advantage of improving aerodynamic efficiency.

As a result of making the vane roots thicker, the axial velocity was not as constant as had been intended, and the engineers tried splitter vanes and rotating guide vanes. The splitter vanes gave some improvement in the distribution of axial velocity, but no measurable gain in efficiency, and they were therefore discarded.

The next step was to test compressor channel velocity and flow characteristics. Noel Penny has explained that this work was an exploration of unknown territory, since the theory of three-dimensional flow was not fully understood and certainly very complex. The design alterations he made at the time were based on simple and accepted theory. The radial section was changed so that the channel tapered symmetrically about the radial center line, and the tip width was reduced, giving higher radial velocity. In addition, half-vanes were introduced in the radial section of the channel, and the number of full vanes was cut down from 17 to 14. This led to a higher pressure ratio being realized, and even more important, a considerable increase in flow range.

The next area taken under scrutiny was the vaneless space between the

Engine installation in the Rover T.4. The man is Spencer King.

compressor discharge point and the diffuser inlet. The size of this area determines the vibration characteristics of the diffuser vanes. In this space, the
high-velocity compressed air flow must be brought down to subsonic values.
This can be accomplished by free vortex formation, but that leads to inefficient diffusion. Rover's turbine team chose to adopt a convergent wall
shape leading to the diffuser entry, giving log spiral flow paths of 12–14
degrees.

A 9-vane diffuser was chosen because tests showed it gave good overall
performance over a wide range. Noel Penny pointed out that using a higher
number of vanes tends to give slightly higher peak efficiency, but involves
the penalty of increased surge mass flow. The vaned diffuser section was
made with parallel sides for ease of manufacture.

For the first-stage turbine, the 2S/140 was given a radial inflow design.
This decision was made in an attempt to improve efficiency at half-flow (and
to reduce manufacturing cost). It would idle at 40,000 rpm. The power turbine remained the axial-flow type. It was made of Nimonic 90 and had a
hot-life of at least 30,000 hours. The first-stage turbine had a maximum
rated speed of 65,000 rpm and the power turbine's maximum was 50,000
rpm (its proof stress point lay at 56,000 rpm).

The engine housing was a welded-up sheet metal case with a heat exchanger bank on each side. The front cover carried a light alloy assembly
that included the compressor and accessory drive. The barrel-type combustor was supported on one side by the main air casing, and on the other side
by a support platform. The injection nozzle was of the air-assisted atomizing
type. From the combustor, the gases expand into a volute collection duct
and are led through a variable geometry nozzle ring prior to entering the
first-stage turbine inlet.

The 2S/140 unit was designed specifically for a front-wheel drive car, and
had its output shaft and transmission at the rear end. The car was known as
the T.4. While the Jet 1 and even the T.3 had been designed and built as
experimental prototypes without regard for a possible production version, the
T.4 was part of a production design project known as the P-6. The P stands
for passenger car and the 6 is the serial number. P-4 was the code name for
the car that became the 1949-model Rover 75, and the P-5 designation covered the project that culminated in 1957 with the Rover Three-Liter.

The body and chassis for the T.4 turbine car were ramifications of the P-6
prototype project. The P-6 went into production in 1963 as the Rover 2000
and later evolved into the Rover 3500, powered by a V8 engine. The P-6
concept was to create a modern family car in two versions: one with front
wheel drive and the other with rear wheel drive. Eventually, the Rover 2000
went into production with rear wheel drive, while front wheel drive was retained for the T.4 vehicle.

The P-6 had a novel form of unit construction, using a cage-like inner body with the outer panels simply bolted on. The body was developed in conjunction with The Pressed Steel Co. Ltd. (under Budd license) and set new standards for torsional strength in lightweight construction. The T.4 chassis had all-independent suspension, with coil springs on all four wheels. The 2000 had the same front suspension as the T.4 and a de Dion-type rear end. The front suspension had an unusual linkage, as the coil springs were positioned horizontally against the cowl structure, and the suspension geometry gave an uncommonly high roll center (7 inches above ground level).

The power unit was centered on the front wheel axis. From the reduction gearing, the drive was taken to a simple forward-and-reverse gearbox with a direct forward ratio and a 1.8 : 1 down-gearing for reverse. The final drive unit was located below the engine, and had a 3.9 : 1 ratio.

The T.4 steering gear was an Adamant recirculating-ball design giving 3.75 turns of the wheel from lock to lock, with a 38-feet turning diameter. Four wheel disc brakes were used (as on the Rover 2000). The P-6 wheelbase was fixed at 103.5 inches for both versions, and the T.4 vehicle reached a curb weight of 2940 pounds (1333.5 kg). It was a luxuriously equipped four-door sedan.

Despite the heavy weight, its performance was equal to the T.3 in terms of acceleration and top speed. And it returned significantly improved fuel economy, averaging 15–20 miles per gallon. The T.4 made its debut at the New York International Automobile Show in April, 1962, and was demonstrated at the start of the 24 Hours of Le Mans in June, 1962. Subsequently it was driven on a number of different schedules on the road and on proving grounds (Rover's own small test track) and at the Motor Industry Research Association's giant establishment at Lindley.

The secret behind the improvement in fuel economy lay mostly in the new heat exchangers. The performance targets set for the recuperator included a thermal ratio of 80 percent at idle and 75 percent at full load, with a maximum gas pressure drop of 1 psi. The core was asymmetrical with each gas passage 0.559–0.584 mm (0.022–0.023 in.) wide, and each air passage 0.43–0.457 mm (0.017–0.018 in.) wide. The difference was intended to reduce the pressure drop relative to that of the air side. The core had 20 convolutions per inch, with a passage height of 2.54 mm (0.1 inch) and a flow path of 127 mm (5 inches). The thermal ratio was estimated at 76.5 percent. The core was made of titanium-stabilized stainless steel.

Tests showed that the recuperator had a cycle frequency of 56 seconds, which translates into 65 cycles per hour. Pressure in the unit is mainly dependent on temperature. At idle, pressure is 10 psi, and it rises to 45 psi as temperature increases to 1300° F (700° C). But the recuperators had short life, and the T.4 experience led Noel Penny to start a research program on regenerators.

The 2S/140 recuperator's welded edges proved prone to cracking. After

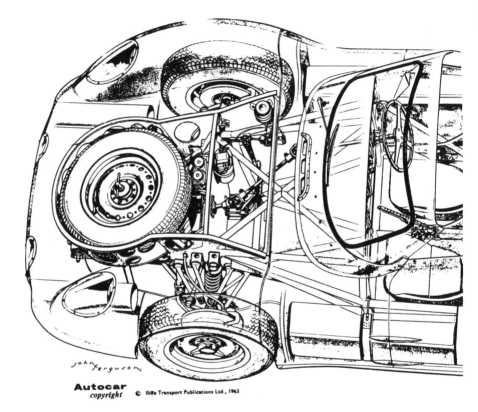

Autocar
copyright © Iliffe Transport Publications Ltd., 1963

Cutaway view of the 1963 version of the Rover-BRM.

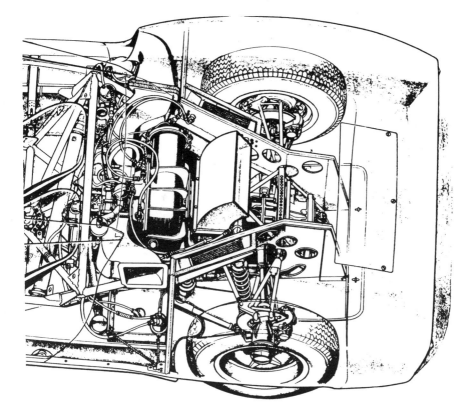

the first 2000 hot cycles, small cracks would appear, causing leakage from the compressor side to the exhaust side. Going from welded edges to simple, folded-over edges increased the life to 3000 cycles. Only when shielding was used did cycle life go to 20,000.

The 1963 Rover-BRM

Following the demonstration of the T.4 turbine car at Le Mans in 1962, Rover decided to enter the 24-hour race with a turbine car the following year. The power unit was to be a development of the 2S/140, upgraded to the designation 2S/150. It had the same radial in-flow first-stage turbine and axial-flow power turbine, and the same centrifugal compressor, but the combustor was an entirely new design.

The barrel-type combustor had been discarded in favor of a new design of the toroidal type. Not a Rover development, it had been designed and manufactured by Lucas. The accelerator pedal was hydraulically connected to the fuel pump. The fuel pump was a Rover three-piston swashplate device with automatic control for both maximum speed and maximum temperature. Minimum speed was controlled by a separate governor.

Fuel was injected via a ring of six flat-sprayed simple atomizers. Ignition was assured by a Lucas dual high-energy system, incorporating a contact breaker, a KLG igniter, and a Park PB 5.4-V coil. The 2S/150 delivered 150 hp at 40,000 rpm of the power turbine with an ambient temperature of 60° F (15.6° C).

At 20,000 rpm, the engine delivered 120 hp. Cutting the speed in half caused a 20 percent drop in power but more than doubled the torque—from 40 pounds-feet to 93 pounds-feet. At 8,200 rpm which corresponds to a road speed just over 25 mph the torque reached a level of 300 pounds-feet. This meant that no gearbox was needed beyond the main reduction gear and the final drive.

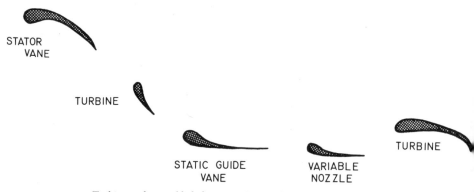

Turbine and stator blade layout in Rover 25/140 gas turbine engine.

At full load, specific fuel consumption ranged from 0.82 to 0.95 pounds per hp-hour. The overall dimensions of the 2S/150 were small: 20 inches high x 24 inches wide x 36 inches long. This very compact engine had separate gasifier and power output sections. For the gasifier section, structural rigidity was provided by both the compressor casing and the accessories casing. For the output section, the outer shell for the turbines provided the necessary structural strength.

The air entered through two intakes, one on each side of the compressor housing. Pre-swirl vanes directed the air flow, free of shock loads, to the rotating guide vanes, which were made of EN 56 D steel. The compressor wheel was made of aluminum alloy.

Narrow tip width compressor blades assured high radial velocity, while the half-vanes in the radial section improved both the pressure ratio and the flow range. The pressure ratio was about 3.9 (or the same as in the 2S/140).

The gasifier section shaft was carried in a deep-groove ball race which took up the end thrust, and a roller bearing whose inner track was ground directly on the shaft, with an outer race flexibly mounted to permit the assembly to run on its own center of rotation. The compressor housing carried an insert spigoted in place to complete the inner contour of the air entry passage. It also served to locate the bearing housing for the roller race adjacent to the compressor wheel and carried an extension for the ball race.

The accessory drive was taken from a high-speed helical pinion on the gasifier shaft and was jet-lubricated. Needle roller bearings were used. With regard to materials, the 2S/150 unit contained no radical elements. The combustor lining and the hot-gas ducting were made from Nimonic 75. The power turbine was machined from a one-piece forging of Nimonic 90A.

Since the engine was designed for high-speed conditions, the variable nozzles for the first-stage turbine were eliminated. Both turbines had fixed nozzles made of Nimocast 242, which is an alloy containing 60 percent nickel, 20 percent chromium, 10 percent cobalt, and 10 percent molybdenum, developed and patented by Rolls-Royce.

The first-stage turbine was made of Inco 713. At full power, the turbine inlet temperature was 1700° F (927° C). The power turbine wheel was mounted on a steel shaft running on one roller bearing and one deep-groove ball race. As in the case of the gasifier shaft, the roller bearing inner track was ground into the shaft, but the outer race was rigidly mounted because it carried the radial load from the reduction gear driving pinion on the outer end of the shaft.

An interstage duct was flexibly connected between the shroud ring for the power turbine nozzle and the rear flange of the main casing. The power turbine shroud ring also carried the bearing housings for the second-stage turbine shaft.

The 2S/150 was made without heat exchangers and weighed only 200 pounds including the reduction gearing. As a result of running without a heat exchanger, the exhaust gas contained a lot of wasted energy, and the maximum exhaust gas temperature was a high 1256° F (680° C).

The oil sump was made as an integral part of the compressor housing, with an Hobourn-Eaton oil pump driven by gears from the compressor shaft. The lubricating oil circulated through internal passages to the ball and roller bearings of both the shafts and to the hollow stub shafts that carried the accessory drive and reduction gearing. The oil from the lower turbine section was returned to the sump by a separate scavenge pump.

The lubricating oil also acted as a high-pressure damper on the roller bearing on the gasifier shaft and minimized any resonant frequencies of the shaft. At 30,000 compressor shaft rpm oil pressure was 15–20 psi. Pressure would rise to 40 psi at 65,000 rpm. The starter was a Lucas 12-V DC unit. An alternator supplied current through a transistorized regulator to a special battery with separate cells.

A mercury, boiler-type temperature control device was provided to shut down the fuel supply in case of overtemperature at the turbine inlet. The engine also had an overspeed trip to cut off fuel supply in case the turbine should exceed its maximum design rpm (due to sudden removal of load, or failure in another section of the turbine).

As for the chassis, the Rover engineers decided against designing and developing their own. They were on a tight schedule, and needed to find the most expedient means—not the most idealistic—of reaching their goals.

By this time, Noel Penny was technical director of the gas turbine program, and Mark Barnard was chief development engineer of the 2S/150 car project. The budget for the Le Mans participation was limited, and Rover approached BRM (the racing car division of the giant Rubery-Owen concern) about taking over a ready-made chassis. It turned out that the 1962 Formula One BRM had adequate installation space for the Rover turbine, and offered full opportunity for adaptation of a sports-car body rather than the original open-wheel single-seater design of the Grand Prix racing car.

The 1962-model Type 57 BRM had a small V8 installed amidships, driving the rear wheels. Wheelbase was stretched to 93 inches (from 89.625 in.) for the Rover turbine. The spare wheel was installed at the nose of the chassis, in place of the radiator that was no longer needed. The chassis had all-independent suspension with coil springs at all wheels. The front suspension was a conventional design with upper and lower control arms and a stabilizer bar. The rear suspension had a linkage whose transverse and longitudinal control arms gave minimal camber changes during wheel deflections.

The Rover turbine was installed with the reduction gearing and output shaft to the rear, and coupled to a gearbox with forward, neutral, and reverse. The output shaft from the gearbox passed below the final drive unit to a set of quick-change spur gears on its rear flange. The top spur gear drove the bevel pinion shaft from behind the ring gear. The reduction gearing had the same 6.82 ratio used in the 2S/140 unit, and the final drive ratio was 3.12, giving an overall gear ratio of 21.3 : 1.

The disc brakes were enlarged to 11-inch diameter in front and 10-inch diameter in the rear to handle the greater weight of the sports car equipment and cope with the lack of engine braking in the turbine.

The frame had to be rebuilt, but remained a tubular steel construction. It was fabricated from Accles & Pollock 5 CM tube of 17-gauge section, and had a weight of 124 pounds (compared with 85 pounds for the Formula One BRM frame).

The body paneling was made up of aluminum sheet. The design was created specifically to conform to the regulations of the Automobile Club de l'Ouest (organizers of the 24-Hours of Le Mans), and was a fully equipped open two-seater with doors. The fuel tanks were carried in the body sides, midway between the front and rear wheels, to minimize the effect on weight distribution and handling of the difference between full and empty tanks. The battery was moved up front, next to the spare wheel. The body carried full lighting equipment, and weighed about 240 pounds complete with trim.

The Rover-BRM was classed with the two-liter sports car category for the purpose of determining the minimum distance to be covered in 24 hours of racing. However, there was no formula governing its rated power, air consumption, weight, or any other criteria, so it was running *hors concours*. The car ran reliably during the entire race and finished at an average speed of 107.83 mph (173.8 km/h) which would have given it eighth place overall in the final classification. The average fuel consumption for the 2592 miles it covered was approximately 6 miles per U.S. gallon.

This test gave Rover the confidence to design a regenerative version of the 2S/150. Noel Penny had been working closely with John G. Lanning and David Wardale of Corning Glass Works on the use of Cercor discs, and they felt highly encouraged by their results. The regenerative 2S/150 weighed 260 pounds and measured 35.75 inches long x 21.25 inches high x 25 inches wide. It was proposed as an industrial/marine power plant and fitted with a single-stage 6.818 reduction gear, giving an output speed range of 0-7330 rpm. Maximum air delivery was 1.4 pounds per second at 29 psi, and the specific fuel consumption was 0.96 pounds per hp-hour.

The heat exchanger covers were bolted to the outside of the main casing. Cast aluminum ducts transferred the air from the compressor to the heat exchangers and were bolted on in front, while the rear part of the regenerator covers formed a flange for the exhaust ducts.

Rover selected a rim drive system, with the disc being supported on carbon bearings which rested on the shoulders of a chrome-plated steel gear driving ring. This ring cradled the disc by means of Nimonic springs sandwiched between the ring and the disc periphery. The springs worked with a sprag action and transferred the drive from the ring to the disc. The ring itself was chain driven from the gasifier shaft. The springs took up the differential expansion between the ring and the disc.

The regenerative 2S/150 unit was installed in a 21-foot Vega launch called Turbinia II with MerCruiser inboard/outboard drive. The original engine had been a Buick V8 engine which had given the best fuel economy at a water speed of 17.5 knots—5 miles per gallon. Fuel consumption with the Buick V8 at the boat's top speed of 26.5 knots was 3.5 miles per gallon.

With the gas turbine, top speed rose to 30 knots, but fuel consumption doubled. At part load, the gas turbine showed even more unfavorable fuel economy. The regenerative 2S/150 was not marketed. Instead, Rover successfully produced an auxiliary power unit for the aircraft industry that was basically identical to the non-regenerative 2S/150 engine as used in the Rover-BRM (with light alloys introduced wherever possible to save weight). It had an installation weight of only 160 pounds and was rated at 145 hp. The first commercial application of this unit was in a fleet of Avro HS.748 aircraft serving in South America.

THE 1965 ROVER-BRM

Despite the disappointing results obtained with the regenerative 2S/150 in Turbinia II, Noel Penny steadfastly continued to develop the rotary ceramic-core heat exchanger. In the winter of 1964/65 the 2S/150R was equipped with a new set of regenerators, 17.5 inches in diameter and 3 inches thick. Each disc comprised 12 segments of a glass-ceramic known as Pyroceram, and was gear-driven from the compressor shaft to rotate at 18 rpm for maximum gasifier speed (64,000 rpm).

Two stainless steel high-pressure bellows-type seals, one on each side of the disc, prevented the escape of compressed air across the disc faces. The seals were shaped like the letter D in outline and were large enough to enclose the 180-degree segments. Tests proved the heat exchanger efficiency to be 90 percent, and specific fuel consumption fell to .57 pounds per hp-hour.

For the 24 Hours of Le Mans in 1965, Rover prepared to enter the Rover-BRM with the 2S/150R gas turbine. The man in charge of this project was 28-year-old Peter Candy, who had joined Rover as an apprentice in 1956 and had returned to Solihull after getting his engineering degree. The chassis was left alone except for a few minor improvements, but Rover's designers built a completely new body with superior aerodynamic efficiency for

The 1965 Rover-BRM.

Rear view of the 1965 Rover-BRM with the rear body panels removed.

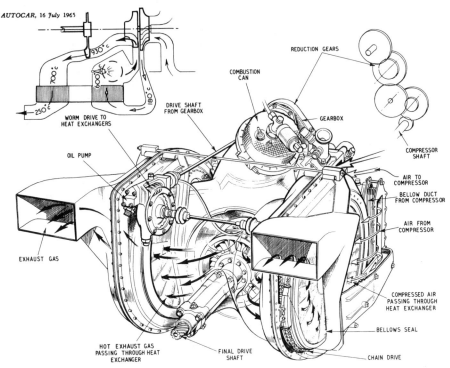

AUTOCAR, 16 July 1965

Gas flow path through the regenerators in the Rover 2S/150 gas turbine engine.

it. This time at Le Mans, the goal was not just to demonstrate speed and reliability, but to prove the car competitive with piston-powered cars in terms of fuel economy.

The Rover-BRM covered 2370.7 miles in 24 hours, which is equivalent to an average speed of 98.87 mph using 207 U.S. gallons of kerosene, which works out to 11.45 miles per gallon. Fuel consumption was almost halved in comparison with the 1963 car, and the average speed had fallen by about 8.3 percent.

This drop in speed was not due to the increased weight of the vehicle, but to an unforseen development in the early stages of the race. On the 29th lap, the car came to the pits for fuel and a change of drivers. It was noticed that the turbine was running with excessive inlet temperature. This had never happened in practice, either in actual road testing, or on the special test dynamometer at the factory (which was programmed to run on a cycle corresponding exactly to driving at Le Mans).

Proper diagnosis could hardly be made during the pit stop, and the engineers guessed it was due to nothing more serious than an air leak in a gasket

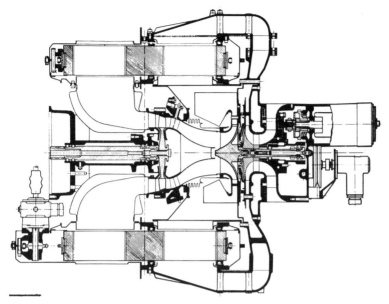

Sectioned view of the Rover 2S/150 gas turbine engine.

or seal. They agreed to continue the race, while holding the turbine inlet temperature down to the allowed maximum, which meant reduced gasifier speed, less power, and lower road speed. The car was running in 10th place when the race ended. The car was freighted back to Solihull, and the engine was torn down for a detailed examination.

The damage was far more extensive than had been optimistically assumed. Some of the compressor vanes had been damaged, probably as a result of foreign matter entering with the unfiltered air. The value of the experience lies in the proof that the turbine can continue to function even after sustaining serious damage. Noel Penny explained that this had been made possible by the flexible bearing support on the compressor shaft, which allows the engine to tolerate abnormally high out-of-balance forces.

The next installation for the Rover 2S/150R gas turbine was in a 22-ton Leyland truck. The Rover Company had been absorbed by British Leyland, and the turbine program was slated for expansion into all kinds of cars and trucks. In 1966 Noel Penny became head of Rover Gas Turbines Ltd. and Mark Barnard was named chief engineer of the turbine car program. Only two years later, Rover Gas Turbines Ltd. became Leyland Gas Turbines Ltd., and was to concentrate exclusively on the development of an advanced low-cost 350–400 hp gas turbine for commercial vehicles.

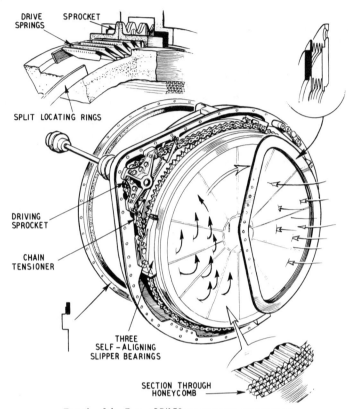

DRIVE SPRINGS
SPROCKET
SPLIT LOCATING RINGS
DRIVING SPROCKET
CHAIN TENSIONER
THREE SELF-ALIGNING SLIPPER BEARINGS
SECTION THROUGH HONEYCOMB

Details of the Rover 2S/150 regenerator arrangement.

THE LEYLAND TURBINE TRUCK

With a small but highly experienced staff, Noel Penny produced a brand new truck turbine in record time. It was first displayed in 1970. The main engineering elements were derived from one or another in the series of Rover gas turbines. There were major differences from the latest Rover engine, as the Leyland turbine had a barrel-type combustor and an axial-flow first-stage turbine. Like the 2S/150R, however, it was a twin-shaft, regenerative design, with a centrifugal compressor and accessory drive from the compressor shaft.

The engine housing was a close-grained cast iron casing which ensured high rigidity and absorbed most of the mechanically generated noise in the power unit. In plain view, the housing generally followed an H-form with the long sides making up the inner supports for the regenerators. The cross member separated the compressed air section from the exhaust section. The

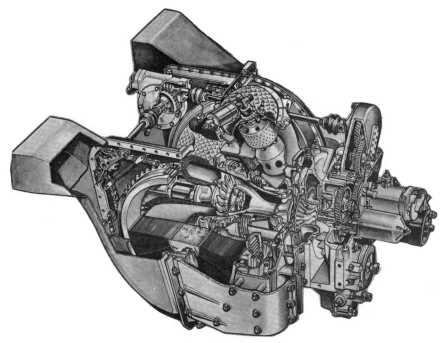

Cutaway view of the Rover 2S/150 gas turbine engine. Drawing by S. E. Porter.

high-pressure section was enclosed by integral walls at the top and bottom, and by the gasifier assembly at the front side. The gasifier assembly was bolted to the front flange on the housing as well as to a flange on the central dividing wall.

Pressure ratio was given as 4 : 1 at an ambient temperature of 80° F (26.7° C) and maximum mass flow was 3.75 pounds per second at full speed (30,000 rpm) under the same conditions. Gasifier idle speed was 19,000 rpm. The power turbine was equipped with variable-geometry nozzles—representing a break with earlier Rover practice and an adoption of theories and methods worked out by Chrysler.

The combustor was a reverse-flow barrel type design mounted on a flange at the top of the high-pressure section shell, between the regenerators. The regenerator discs were geared to run at a maximum speed of 20 rpm. Including the single-stage helical reduction gear, the Leyland turbine weighed 980 pounds (445 kg). The standard rating was 370 hp, but Leyland also revealed a heavy-duty rating of 400 hp. Specific fuel consumption figures were 0.392 pounds per hp-hour at 68° F (20° C) and 0.399 pounds per hp-hour at 80° F (26.7° C).

Standard paper filters fitted into the intake duct gave very good protection

Gas turbine installation on Leyland truck.

against dirt ingress under normal road conditions. A total of six different filter elements were used, and Leyland claimed a replacement interval of 1,000 hours operation. The six filters took up a space of six cubic feet, and formed a complete air silencer assembly. Two 8-inch (203 mm) diameter exhaust ducts were locally increased in size to 13-inch (330 mm) diameter. These extra-width chambers functioned as mufflers and reduced the over-all noise level to passenger car values.

An accessory drive gear train from the gasifier shaft ran the oil pressure and scavenger pumps as well as the fuel pump. The same shaft also carried the regenerator drive worm and a hydraulic pump for operating the gearbox. Oil cooler fan, tachometer drive, generator, power steering pump, and starter motor were all geared to the oil pump shaft.

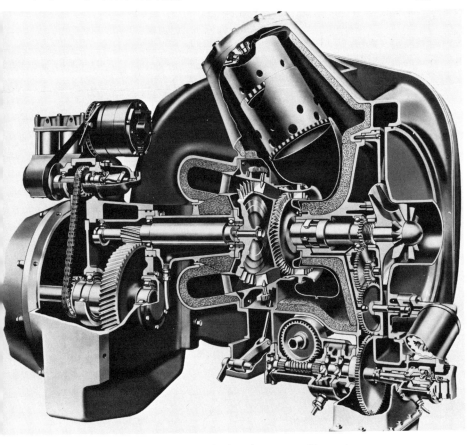

Cutaway view of the Leyland truck-type gas turbine engine.

Some accessories were driven by the power turbine shaft: a two cylinder air compressor for the brake system, and a speed governor for the power turbine. A 60-amp 24-V alternator was belt-driven from the power turbine governor shaft. The engine was completely controlled by the starter switch and accelerator pedal. The starter switch energized the starter motor, the air assist pump, the high-tension spark plug (via a coil and contact breaker), and opened the fuel injector solenoid.

As the gasifier section approached self-sustaining speed, a pressure signal from the compressor would de-energize all starting circuits with the exception of the fuel solenoid. The engine would then idle according to the setting of the governor.

The Leyland gas turbine was installed in a Leyland six-wheel highway tractor designed to operate with a semi-trailer at 38-tons gross train weight at speeds of 70 mph (112 km/h). Coupled to a five-speed planetary transmission, the Leyland turbine would give superior performance compared with any contemporary British diesel-powered truck. Leyland made extremely ambitious claims for engine life expectancy before overhaul, quoting 12,000 hours, which would normally be equivalent to half a million miles.

Noel Penny left Leyland in 1972 to start his own company, Noel Penny Gas Turbine, Ltd. where he is working on other projects, including passenger car gas turbines—an idea that British Leyland has given up on. However, Leyland is continuing the truck turbine research and development program at an intensive pace, and may be the first on the market with a true production-model gas turbine driven truck.

There are no more Rover gas turbines in production, for in the 1968 reorganization, when Leyland Gas Turbines Ltd. was formed, this company took over all the automotive turbine work from Rover. The industrial/marine and aircraft (auxiliary power unit) production was handed over to Alvis in Coventry—another branch of British Leyland. Alvis discontinued car production in 1968 in order to concentrate its activity on piston-type aircraft engines (built under Lycoming license), AiResearch turbochargers, and Rover gas turbines.

Then came December 22, 1972, when British Leyland announced that it had sold its Rover gas turbine business to Lucas Aerospace Ltd. That deal included the work allocated to Alvis only four years previously, and effectively put Rover out of the running as far as gas turbine powered cars are concerned.

17

Case History: Chrysler

The traditions of the Chrysler Laboratories in gas turbine research and development go back even further than the Rover Company's involvement with Frank Whittle and Power Jets Ltd. At the instigation of a leading research engineer, George J. Huebner, Jr., Chrysler Laboratories, which were directed by James C. Zeder from 1933 to 1946, had begun an investigation of the gas turbine in 1938. The annals of Chrysler Corporation describe the investigation as an "exploratory engineering survey" and report its conclusions as showing the gas turbine's strong possibilities of being an ideal automobile engine, but also dwelling on the fact that neither materials nor techniques had then advanced to the point where the cost of intensive research could be warranted.

When Chrysler returned to the gas turbine, it was under different conditions. Turbo-superchargers had become a *sine qua non* of piston-engines for fighter planes, jet planes had flown in Germany and Britain, and several American companies were engaged in aircraft gas turbine engine development. It was 1944 when George J. Huebner, Jr. thought the time was ripe for a renewed evaluation of the gas turbine from an automotive point of view. This led to the start of a new study, involving entirely new concepts for gas turbine power systems.

Huebner's interest in gas turbines was sparked indirectly by an older engineer who worked not in research but in the body engineering department at Chrysler. The men had admiration for each other, and their talks ranged from their daily duties to the philosophy of engineering. The body engineer talked in terms that made Huebner think about his profession with new insight. What kind of engineer was he going to be for the rest of his career—a good, routine engineer who tackles the projects assigned to him with compe-

The first Chrysler gas turbine-powered car.

Instrument panel in Chrysler's first gas turbine-powered car.

tence, or the kind of an engineer who becomes an expert in a new field of activity, and by his skills and enthusiasm can change the course of history? Huebner decided in favor of innovation and against routine.

At the time he made his decision, he had not yet picked the gas turbine as

George J. Huebner, Jr. (right) and William I. Chapman, with Chrysler's first gas turbine-powered car.

the vehicle for making his mark in the engineering world. That selection was due to the influence of people like Dr. Sanford Moss (see chapter entitled "Turbocharging and Its Influence"), and reading about gas turbine developments for various applications. In his 1944 project, Huebner used a piston engine as the gasifier section for a gas turbine, and combined the two so as to get power output from both sections. This work came to the attention of the U.S. Navy, and one day in 1945 Huebner got a call from the Navy's Bureau of Aeronautics, which resulted in Chrysler Corporation's being awarded a research and development contract to create a 1000-hp turboprop engine for a new type of aircraft intended for use in anti-submarine warfare.

The specifications for the Navy engine were unique, calling not only for light weight but for an economy approaching that of reciprocating power plants under cruising conditions. This was a rather startling requirement, because aircraft gas turbines which had been built so far showed their best fuel economy at full power. Yet, the objective of obtaining 1000-hp with a brake specific fuel consumption of 0.52 at 70 percent power was achieved and, in fact, exceeded.

The design for the Chrysler aircraft gas turbine was completed in 1947, and during 1947 and early 1948 its compressor, turbines and heat exchanger were thoroughly tested as individual components. In May of 1948, the complete engine ran in the laboratory for the first time, and almost from the first it proved to be competitive with the reciprocating engine in both weight and fuel consumption. During a brief ensuing period it was improved to the point where it was developing the full power and fuel economy designed into it, and several pre-flight tests were run. At this point, budget restrictions in the armed forces became so extreme that further development by the Navy was dropped.

The Navy gas turbine for aircraft followed very closely in principle the original designs that had been made for automotive use. During the Navy testing and development work it became evident that although the principle used would be highly satisfactory for aircraft, it would fall far short of automobile fuel economy requirements. The aircraft for which the turbine was designed seldom operated at a speed which required less than 70 percent of the engine's maximum power.

Under these conditions, the turbine's fuel economy was quite satisfactory. In an automobile, however, most driving is done at 20 to 25 percent of the full power potential of the engine. The amount of regeneration, or exhaust heat recovery, in the Chrysler aircraft gas turbine engine would have been of little consequence at the low power output of an automobile engine.

The Navy turbine's worst problems were associated with the heat exchangers. The Chrysler turboprop engine was equipped with a recuperator, which was not effective enough. Huebner switched to a regenerator, but he later described the leakage as "awful." Regenerator technology was then in its infancy. "There was a tenth of an inch gap in the seal," Huebner recalls.

Chrysler research scientists and engineers then returned to their original objective—the automotive gas turbine engine. In the early 1950's, experimental gas turbine power plants were operated on dynamometers and in test vehicles. Active component development programs were carried out to improve compressors, regenerators, turbine sections, burner controls, gears, and accessories. In regenerator research, Chrysler collaborated with the National Physical Laboratory in England, which was then the leader in this field, and also with Ljungström Ångturbin in Sweden.

Finally, in October 1949, a project was initiated to determine the potentialities of the gas turbine powerplant for automotive use. A very small group of men were assigned to this work and a number of studies were made. These studies showed that it would be possible to build a gas turbine engine of such size that it could be placed in a production automobile and have fuel economy as good as current reciprocating engines, provided certain requirements could be met.

In 1952—during the Korean conflict—Chrysler started its Missile Branch,

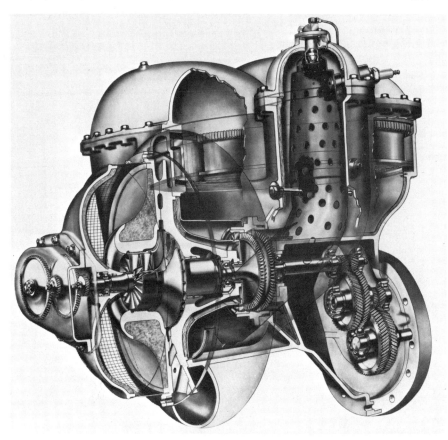

Cutaway view of Chrysler's first-generation gas turbine engine.

and Huebner was named as its executive engineer. Despite the new title, he remained initimately connected with the turbine car project, for he was a car engineer by inclination, education and experience. Born in Detroit on September 8, 1910, he graduated from the University of Michigan in 1932. Even before graduation he had gone to work for Chrysler as a laboratory engineer in the mechanical laboratories.

By 1936 he was named assistant chief engineer of Plymouth (Harry T. Woolson was chief engineer). His three years with Plymouth may have led to a preponderance of gas turbine installations in Plymouth cars later on. In 1939 he moved to Chrysler's Engineering Division as assistant to the director of research (James C. Zeder). As a result, Huebner spent the war years in a position that enabled him to keep abreast of a swarm of technological

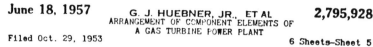

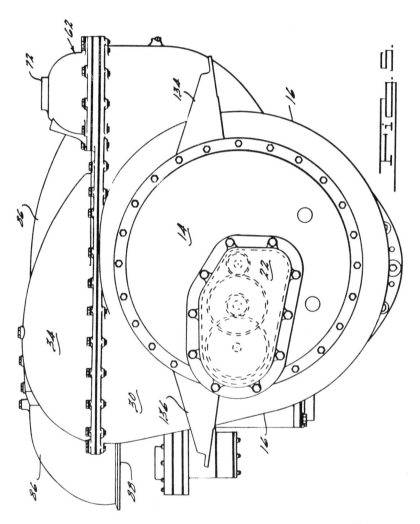

INVENTORS.
George J. Huebner.
Samuel B. Williams.
David N. Borden.

By Harness and Harris

ATTORNEYS.

Housing for the first-generation Chrysler gas turbine engine.

270

INVENTORS
George J. Huebner
Samuel B. Williams.
David M. Borden.

By Harness and Harris

ATTORNEYS

Details of combustor and first-stage turbine in Chrysler's first-generation gas turbine engine.

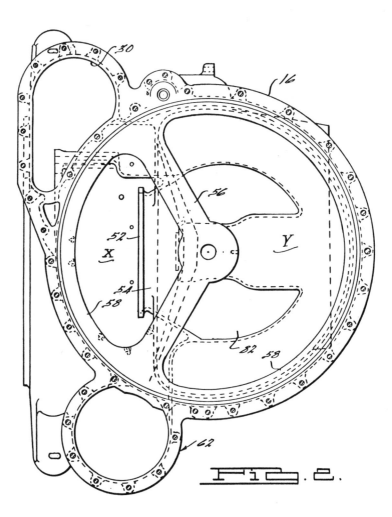

INVENTORS
George J. Huebner,
Samuel B. Williams
David M. Borden

By Harness and Harris
          ATTORNEYS.

Details of regenerator arrangement on Chrysler's first-generation gas turbine engine.

272

developments and study all areas of possible value to the Chrysler Corporation cars of the future. In 1945 he became the Chief Engineer of Research, and he gave the turbine program particular attention.

By mid-1952 Huebner felt that the time was approaching for a turbine installation in a passenger car. The continuing turbine program had resulted in mechanically sound and thermally stable turbine housings, reasonable component efficiency, encouraging engine performance and operating economy, and had provided Chrysler with a group of personnel with experience and unequaled know-how in the area of automotive gas turbines.

For instance, Chrysler-made compressors were used to supercharge a large aircraft engine developed under an Air Force contract during World War II. One of them, an 11-stage axial compressor was among the first aircraft engine axial compressors in the United States and had a very creditable 81 percent maximum efficiency.

Normally, one does not think of the automotive industry as a likely place to find pioneering work in aerodynamic theory, but the design theory for the use of wheel flow in axial compressors did originate in this program and has been used by Chrysler and many others since. Shortly after the war, Chrysler developed (for the Navy) a 17-stage axial-flow compressor which gave an efficiency of 85 percent as initially installed and later obtained 87 percent on multi-stage component tests.

The first Chrysler passenger car gas turbine was designed primarily as a laboratory tool to check the performance of the various components placed together as a power plant and to help determine if a small gas turbine based on the regenerative principle would be practical in an automobile. Design work on a 100-hp car turbine had started in December 1952. The main engine housing was made from nodular iron, and it was decided to use a casting for the first engine to allow instrumentation holes to be located anywhere the engineers might want to take readings. The accessories, consisting of a combined starter-generator, fuel pump, and oil pump, were driven from the front of the compressor shaft through a series of reduction gears.

The compressor efficiency postulated for this first engine was 74.5% at maximum operating speed. Everything then thought possible was done to achieve high component efficiency from the very beginning, with the idea that simplification would come later. For example, a two-stage axial inducer was used to insure that no flow separation would occur before the radial portion of the compressor wheel was reached. The compressor wheel was also completely shrouded, as it was believed this would aid in obtaining high efficiency. Pressure ratio was 4.25.

The compressor wheel itself was an aluminum casting with the vanes fully shrouded. The inducer section—working basically as a set of rotating pre-swirl vanes—was made up of two rows of cast aluminum blades loosely placed in slots in the shaft and retained radially by a steel shroud shrunk to the eye diameter of the compressor wheel shroud. The compressor shaft was rated for a maximum speed of 52,000 rpm. The shaft was made of steel, and was of the built-up type, with a calculated natural frequency of 77,000 rpm. A roller bearing in the front end and a ball bearing at the rear end were jet-lubricated.

The compressed air was redirected through a radial diffuser and fed through a collector which delivered it at low velocity to the engine's top cover. From this area, the air flowed through the regenerator, which rotated on a vertical shaft and filled in the space below the top cover, to a plenum chamber communicating with the area surrounding the combustor sleeve.

The barrel-type combustor consisted of an outer housing and a liner made from aluminized low-carbon steel. After combustion, the gas flow was directed downward through the combustor sleeve and a conductor pipe to a vortex chamber leading to the nozzles for the first-stage turbine.

A twin-shaft design, the Chrysler turbine used two axial-flow turbine wheels fabricated from unit-cast stellite blade rings welded to low-alloy forged discs. After flowing through both turbines, the exhaust gases passed upward through the regenerator and were again redirected downward by the top cover. The key feature in this power plant was the use of a regenerative heat exchanger, which substantially increased fuel economy.

The regenerator also performed another important function. It reduced the exhaust temperature from about 1200° F (650° C) at full engine power to a safe level of less than 500° F (260° C). Even more important, at idle the temperature was reduced to 170° F (77° C). By the time the gases passed through the exhaust ducts to the atmosphere the temperature was reduced even further.

The disc had a diameter of 18 inches. The matrix was fabricated by winding together a flat strip and a corrugated strip .004 inch thick by 3 inches wide of straight chromium stainless steel under controlled tension conditions. The strips were spaced .012 inch apart by the corrugations and the whole unit was copperbrazed together. Approximately 50 pounds of steel strip were used in the unit.

Even with these breakthroughs, a great deal of work and many development problems still remained. On the date of the original turbine disclosure, James C. Zeder stated:

"Whether we ultimately shall see commercial production of gas turbines for passenger cars depends on the long-range solution of many complex metallurgical and manufacturing problems. There is no telling at this time how long it will take to solve these problems."

Since Huebner always thought in terms of mass-producing turbine cars, it was natural for him to choose a standard passenger car as the first mobile test bed for a Chrysler car turbine. This approach contrasts vividly with the General Motors method of building a far-out "dream-car" around the gas turbine engine. This decision on Chrysler's part committed the turbine designers to certain package restrictions, to assure minimum interference with the steering, frame and body. Since this engine was completely exploratory, it was desirable that it should be easy to disassemble for inspection, and allow for easy component modification. To match the turbine to the car's speed and torque requirements, it was provided with a 2-stage 12.5 : 1 reduction gear at the rear end.

The car selected for the first Chrysler turbine installation was a 1954 Plymouth sport coupe. It was first demonstrated to Chrysler executives on March 25, 1954. Then the car went on display from April 7 through 11 at the Waldorf Astoria Hotel in New York City. And, on June 16, 1954, it was demonstrated publicly at the dedication of the Chrysler Engineering Proving Grounds at Chelsea, Michigan. During this event, Huebner explained the low horsepower rating of the gas turbine: "The Chrysler turbine engine is rated at 120-shaft horsepower, but because of its torque characteristics, it delivers essentially the same performance at the rear wheels as a 160-horsepower piston engine with transmission. It is relatively simple to design much more horsepower into the turbine engine whenever it is desired. The real challenge was to design a unit in the horsepower ranges common to most cars used in everyday driving."

The first engine served many useful purposes. It was used to check almost continuous component development work, and was an invaluable laboratory tool in approaching the final integrated gas turbine powerplant that would eventually evolve for automotive use.

A number of minor changes were made in the power plant design as Chrysler's turbine experts gained experience with the car, and a slightly more refined version of the same gas turbine unit was installed in a 1955 Plymouth and used for driving evaluation tests on public streets and roads in the Detroit area. At that point, no long-distance tests had been made, but Huebner knew the turbine car was capable of extremely long distances. He felt that a public demonstration such as a coast-to-coast run would generate favorable publicity for Chrysler Corporation as well as being a boost for the turbine program.

A new turbine of design similar to that of the 1955 version was installed in a standard 1956 Plymouth 4-door sedan. After preliminary testing and preparation at Highland Park, the car was driven to New York, where the official transcontinental run started on March 26, 1956. Four days and 3020 miles later it arrived in Los Angeles, having averaged 13 miles per gallon on white gasoline and diesel fuel. The run was interrupted only twice for minor repairs which did not involve the turbine engine (a faulty bearing in the

1956 Plymouth powered by Chrysler gas turbine engine.

1959 Plymouth powered by Chrysler's second-generation gas turbine. George J. Huebner, Jr. (left) with Paul C. Ackerman.

reduction gear and an intake casting were replaced). The engine itself and its basic components performed very well and without failures of any kind.

THE SECOND GENERATION TURBINE

The design of a second-generation gas turbine was actually started before the test and evaluation program with the first-generation engine had been completed. The second-generation turbine was on the drawing boards as early as August, 1955. Some of the specific design objectives were to eliminate certain drawbacks in the "old" engine.

The first-generation turbine, for instance, had never had a sufficient temperature gradient available for acceleration, and consequently it had never been possible to establish exactly how well a turbine car would fit into the traffic scene at large. As a result, it was decided that the second-generation turbine had to be larger and more powerful. It was to be designed for a rating of 140 shaft hp on a day with 85° F ambient temperature, with component efficiencies of the same order as those which had actually been obtained in the smaller unit.

The long-term goal was 200 hp, because the turbine engineers were on a very steep learning curve, and it seemed possible to get sufficiently sizeable improvements in cycle temperature and component efficiency during the stepped-up development program that was planned in connection with the second-generation turbine.

By the end of 1955, Huebner had relinquished his missile duties and resumed full-time activity as executive engineer for the Chrysler Corporation engineering staff. The missile branch later became one of the constituent sections of Chrysler Aerospace Division. The second-generation turbine followed closely along the design principles of the first one, with barrel-type combustor, centrifugal compressor, axial-flow turbines, and vertical-shaft regenerator located under the top cover. The engine was first operated on July, 1956, and the performance was very close to the projected levels. It was not immediately installed in a car, but instead formed the basis for an in-depth component efficiency development program.

The original compressor had offered very satisfactory performance despite the fact that the turbine team had never been able to design a diffuser that corresponded to the compressor characteristics. However, the compressor was undesirably long from a packaging viewpoint. It was also extremely complex, and had excessive inertia. It was therefore decided to redesign the compressor and to tailor it to the diffuser rather than attempting to make the diffuser correspond to the compressor. Through a development program which consisted of both experimental work and advanced theoretical analysis, the deficiencies of the first compressor were corrected, and improved performance was obtained.

Chrysler's turbine engineers also pioneered regenerator designs and materials. Chrysler invented and patented its own matrix shapes and methods of sealing the high-pressure gas from the low-pressure gas. At the start of this program, the state of the art was not very well defined, and the effects of specific changes in design were not very well mapped. To obtain the necessary bank of basic knowledge, Chrysler tested about 275 different configurations

Instrument panel and controls of the turbine-powered 1959 Plymouth.

and obtained enough test data to establish the relative effects on heat exchanger efficiency of changes in passage shape, passage size, and metal thickness.

Chrysler's work on turbine wheels and nozzles concentrated on studies of the relationships of temperature, pressure and angle conditions, both entering and leaving the blade rows. In conjunction with this basic research, Chrysler also initiated design studies for a reliable type of variable nozzle operating system. A large amount of component development work was also carried out on combustors, passage shapes and control systems.

In December, 1958, a second-generation turbine fitted with variable geometry on the power turbine nozzle, was installed in a standard production-model 1959 Plymouth four-door hardtop. The car was taken on a 576-mile highway trip, from Detroit to Woodbridge, New Jersey, near the Atlantic shore, achieving an average fuel mileage of 19.4 miles per gallon on various types of fuel. Since the 1959 Plymouth had a curb weight of 3545 pounds, this was a highly eloquent demonstration of the gas turbine's fuel economy in normal highway traffic.

The Third Generation Turbine

Early in 1960, Huebner laid down the basic design for the third generation Chrysler turbine. This was the first one with an official designation: CR2A, which means Chrysler Research, Number Two, version A. The pre-

George J. Huebner, Jr. and the 1961 gas turbine-powered Plymouth.

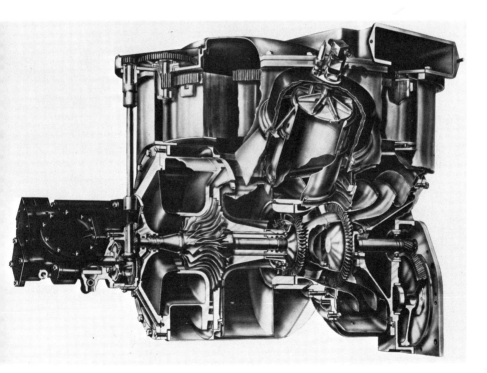

Cutaway view of the Chrysler CR2A gas turbine engine.

ceding gas turbines had been strictly experimental units. The CR2A was developed with an eye on production methods and costs, showing that the turbine was inching closer to reality from a consumer viewpoint.

The CR2A design concept was similar to the second-generation engine, with a vertical-shaft regenerator under the top cover, centrifugal compressor, barrel-type combustor, and axial-flow turbines with variable nozzle vanes for the second-stage turbine. The CR2A weighed 450 pounds complete, was 36 inches long (including accessories), 35 inches wide, and 27 inches high. The basic structure of the engine consisted of a fabricated steel housing which supported the major component assemblies and provided the connected flow passages. The housing was insulated internally and cooled by ambient air, compressor outlet air, and the engine exhaust gas which was maintained at a low temperature by the high regenerator effectiveness. The heat insulation also acted as sound insulation, while the regenerator core served as an effective muffler for the exhaust gases. An intake filter silencer was provided in front of the compressor to prevent dirt accumulation in that component and to reduce the noise generated at the compressor inlet.

The air entered the compressor at a flow rate of 2.2 lbs/sec, at the lowest temperature and pressure in the system, and the compressor operated with 80 percent efficiency at a 4 : 1 pressure ratio. The compressed air was discharged axially from the diffuser into a collector which directed it to the upper surface of the regenerator where it passed down through the front half of the core, picking up heat from the corrugated metal matrix. The regenerator had a maximum speed of 17 rpm and gave 90 percent efficiency, so that exhaust temperature at full power was 500° F (260° C).

The heated air was then passed through the reverse-flow combustor which operated at 95 percent efficiency. The hot gases expanded through both turbine stages and was exhausted up through the rear half of the regenerator core, giving up heat to the matrix. The regenerator core was rotated mechanically at a maximum rate of 17 rpm to transfer the heat recovered from the exhaust gas to the compressor discharge.

Turbine inlet temperature was 1700° F (927° C) at full power. The first-stage turbine ran with 87 percent efficiency, the second-stage turbine with slightly less—84 percent efficiency. Maximum gas generator speed was 44,600 rpm, and the maximum power turbine speed was 45,700 rpm. The drive was taken through a single-stage 8.53 reduction gear to the output shaft. The CR2A delivered 140 hp at 4750 rpm (output shaft speed) and a peak torque of 375 pounds-feet at stall.

The brake specific fuel consumption at rated power was approximately 0.51 lb/hp-hr and increased very slowly as the power was reduced according to the road load requirements of the vehicle. As a result, the over-all fuel economy was very satisfactory for automotive applications and compares favorably with similar reciprocating engines.

COMPRESSOR AERODYNAMIC PROGRESS

Maximum Efficiency Based On 0.93 Slip Factor

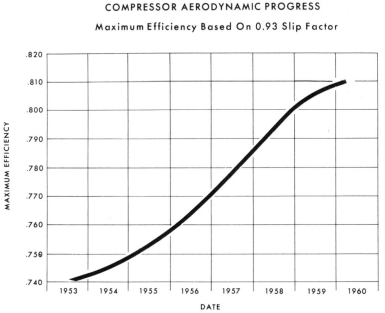

Component efficiency progress as exemplified by the Chrysler compressor.

The accessories were mounted on the front of the gas generator and driven from the rotor by a simple gear train. The fuel system incorporated a gas generator speed governor and a fuel scheduling control for acceleration, integrated with a gear type fuel pump in one housing to minimize plumbing. This assembly, as well as the fuel nozzle air pump and the lubrication pump, were driven from one accessory drive pad.

The starter–generator was geared directly to the gas generator rotor and operated at a maximum of 20,000 rpm. The CR2A was installed and demonstrated in a number of vehicles. The initial showing of the turbine was to newsmen on February 28, 1961. Three vehicles were displayed publicly in Washington, D.C., on March 5–9, 1961, in conjunction with the Turbine Power Conference of the American Society of Mechanical Engineers, cosponsored by the Department of Defense.

The first of these gas turbine vehicles was an experimental model called the "Turboflite". In addition to the engine, other advanced ideas of the car were the retractable headlights, a deceleration air-flap suspended between the two stability struts, and an automatic canopy roof. This "idea" car received wide public interest and was shown at auto shows in New York City, Chicago, London, and Paris. The second car was a production-type 1960 Plymouth sedan, and the third vehicle was a 2½-ton Dodge truck.

The truck completed a 290-mile test run from Detroit to Chicago in the

Dodge Turbo Truck powered by Chrysler CR2A engine.

CR2A-powered Dodge Turbo Dart of 1962.

spring of 1962. In the meantime, late in 1961, several further examples of the CR2A were prepared for passenger car installation. The first was a production-model 1962 Dodge Dart with a few styling modifications to stress the turbine motif. The Turbo Dart was sent on another coast-to-coast expedition, leaving New York City on December 27, 1961, and arrived in Los Angeles on December 31 after traveling 3100 miles through snowstorms, freezing rain, sub-zero temperatures, and 25–40 mph headwinds. This was a combined engineering evaluation run and public demonstration, and it was totally successful. The car never fell behind schedule on any technical account, and when the engine was torn down back at Highland Park, it showed that every part of the turbine power plant was in excellent condition.

Chrysler turbine car of 1963.

A sister car with a Plymouth label—the Turbo Fury—was completed in January 1962, and was sent out on a 440-mile trip with a number of detours from Los Angeles to San Francisco, which it completed without mishap. Afterwards, the "turbo twins" began tours of Chrysler Corporation dealerships around the country to explore consumer reaction. Meanwhile, during the Chicago Automobile show Chrysler Corporation announced on February 14, 1962, that it would build a series of 50 turbine-powered passenger cars for distribution to selected Chrysler product customers beginning in the autumn of 1963.

The Fourth Generation Turbine

Chrysler Corporation announced on May 6, 1963 that about 200 customers would be selected to drive Chrysler turbine cars for periods of up to three months under a no-charge use agreement as part of an unprecedented consumer research program. On May 14, 1963, the fourth-generation Chrysler gas turbine and the car it powered were shown to the press in New York City.

The new gas turbine carried the designation A-831 and had several striking differences from the CR2A. The most obvious change was the removal of the heat exchanger from the top cover and its replacement by twin regenerators—one on each side of the gasifier section.

This arrangement provided much better structural symmetry and improved flow paths to and from the regenerator cores than did the single-disc-type regenerator used on previous Chrysler gas turbines. The single combustor was located between the regenerators at the bottom of the engine for best fitting into the space available in the engine compartment. The accessories were driven from a gearbox mounted in front of the compressor intake, and the single-stage reduction gear provided a vertical offset downwards to meet the desired drive line location.

Despite the switch from one to two regenerators, a considerable weight

George J. Huebner, Jr. at the wheel of one of the 50 Chrysler gas turbine-powered cars built in 1963.

reduction was achieved, from 450 pounds to 410 pounds. Complete with accessories, the A-831 power plant measured 35 inches long, 25.5 inches wide and 27.5 inches high.

After entering through the intake filter and silencer assembly, the air passed through the intake elbow and moved axially into the compressor. This component provided a pressure ratio of 4 : 1 and worked with 80 percent efficiency at a maximum air flow of 2.2 pounds per second. According to George Huebner: "The basic compressor can produce a pressure ratio of 4.5 : 1 and has a maximum efficiency of 84 percent with a specific speed of 72. This compressor has been very successful in its engine applications, but one of the areas of difficulty has been keeping up with the ever-growing demand for more flow range."

The compressor assembly included a cast aluminum compressor wheel, a cast steel inducer, a steel shroud ring, an aluminum spinner, and a steel hub for the compressor wheel. These components were assembled in a sequence of shrink fits, and piloted and clamped to the gasifier shaft.

The cast aluminum compressor wheel had thirty blades with fifteen of them being partial, or splitter blades. It is necessary to have a large blade

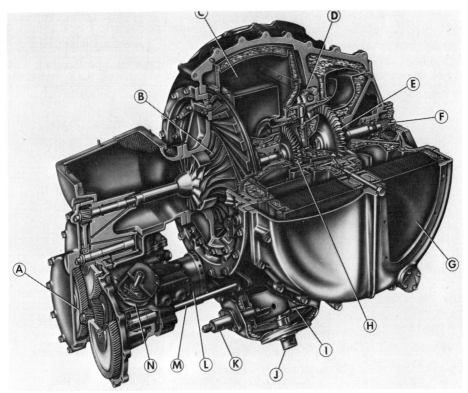

Cutaway view of the Chrysler A-831 gas turbine engine.

area available over which to spread the aerodynamic loading in order to prevent separation. Inlet eye blockage dictated the use of splitter blades so that there were only fifteen blades in the inlet, and aerodynamic stalling in the inducer required that a separate blade row be added ahead of the compressor wheel. This blade row did virtually no turning at the design point; its function was to accept the wide flow angle variation over the engine operating range and thus prevent overloading of the following blade surfaces.

The compressor discharged the air radially into the diffuser. The diffuser channels dumped the compressed air into the space between the engine housing and the chamber surrounding the combustor. The velocity of the air leaving the channels causes it to circulate throughout this space on its way to the regenerator cores.

The diffuser consisted of a short vaneless region followed by a vaned area. The vaneless region was conventionally used to assure subsonic flow at maximum speed so that the vanes could operate without encountering supersonic conditions. It was found that a diffuser with approximately 3° divergence on one pair of walls and 5° on the other was optimum.

There is no unanimous agreement as to the character of the flow in the diffuser area, as can be seen in the variety of configurations in use. A large portion of the compressor losses occur in this area. Chrysler chose a high number of diffuser channels (29) to keep the overall diameter of the compressor as small as practical.

In the A-831 engine, the discharge from the compressor diffuser emptied into the rather irregularly shaped housing on its way to the regenerator. This arrangement gave more trouble than originally expected. The desirability of maintaining uniform static pressure at the compressor discharge was, of course, recognized, but quantitative evaluation was not available until the first housings were received.

Further along the flow path, the air passed through the semi-annulus around the front of the regenerator core and was returned through the front half of the core. The heated air passed inward and down to the combustor, along the outside of the burner tube. The flow was reversed through the annular slots and radial orifices in the tube, setting up a complex vortex flow pattern to stabilize combustion over the operational range.

The combustor sheet metal assembly was clamped between the flanges that formed seal platforms for the regenerator housings. The combustor assembly was sealed to the main housing through use of ceramic fiber packing and gaskets.

The compressor discharge air flowed around the combustor outer skin on its way to the regenerators, washing the entire interior of the front housing section so as to minimize temperature gradients and stresses in the housing itself, and reducing the combustor skin metal temperature to a level that permits the use of low-cost sheet steel for its construction.

The combustor could achieve 95 percent efficiency. The tube was 12 inches in length and approximately 5 inches in diameter, with a volume of 250 cubic inches. A transition section in the burner vortex, located between the burner tube outlet and the turbine nozzle inlet, acted as an extended mixing zone. This extension also served to minimize turbine inlet temperature gradients caused by long flametails burning into or past the dilution slots. Such flametails might arise under conditions of severe burner overload, i.e., cold starting followed by immediate full power requirement with the regenerator not yet at full temperature.

The combustor assembly consisted of three tubular sheet metal sections with the upstream ends flared for aerodynamic cleanliness and for rigidity. The hot gases, mixed to a uniform temperature, were guided by a scross to set up a vortex flow to the first-stage turbine nozzle and wheel. The high ve-

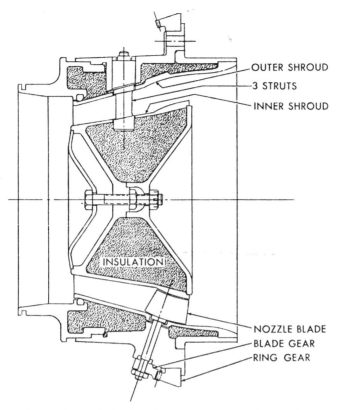

Sectioned view of Chrysler A-831 power turbine nozzle assembly.

locity gas leaving the wheel was diffused and guided to meet the variable nozzle blades directing the flow to the second stage or power turbine wheel.

The power turbine exhaust was diffused and discharged radially, flowing outward through the rear half of the two regenerator cores. The cooled gases were collected by converging ducts and passed to the rear of the car by dual exhaust pipes.

The combustor was equipped with a Delavan air-atomizing nozzle, and the air needed to atomize the fuel was supplied by an engine-driven air pump. This pump was a positive-displacement, double-acting, reciprocating piston unit, with an external by-pass regulator valve.

The first-stage turbine was mounted on the gasifier (compressor) shaft. When assembled, the compressor wheel and turbine wheel were carried on opposite ends of the shaft, outboard of the main bearings. The turbine wheel casting was welded to the shaft. The power turbine assembly was made up of the turbine wheel, the reduction gear assembly, the variable nozzle assembly, and the supporting housing. The turbine wheel was permanently attached to the shaft by a center bolt. The shaft and the wheel were balanced dynamically, and adjustments made on the turbine disc (inside of the blade root area). The wheel was supported by a steel-backed bushing at the front and a ball bearing at the rear. Sealing of the turbine against the hub was assured by a pressurized labyrinth seal. A floating splined shaft connected the power turbine wheel to the reduction gear pinion.

The nozzle blade assembly guided the gas flow from the first-stage turbine to the power turbine. The nozzle had 23 blades carried on the nozzle ring, which was attached to the housing bulkhead. Cooling of the nozzle assembly was assured by a flow of compressed air brought from the compressor outlet at temperatures up to 450° F (232° C) while the temperature through the gas flow passage could be as high as 1400° F (760° C).

The nozzle assembly was designed to minimize the heat loss between the two turbines, to maintain close clearance between the nozzle blades and the turbine wheel tips, and to maintain accurate nozzle operating gear fits regardless of changes in temperature. To obtain these results, it was necessary to adopt a double-wall construction for the nozzle blade assembly.

The shroud that formed the annular flow passage into the nozzle area was very thin, so as to conform to the thermal response time of the turbine blades. The variable-geometry blades pivoted between spherical surfaces formed by the inner and outer shrouds. Each nozzle blade was supported by an integral radial shaft extending from the outer ring, with a spur gear sector fastened on the outer end of each shaft in mesh with a face-type ring gear. Ring gear rotation would then vary the angle of all nozzle blades in unison.

The actuator for the variable nozzle blades was a cam-controlled hydraulic servo unit which received hydraulic power from the lubrication pump. Nozzle blade position was automatically scheduled as a function of accelerator pedal position. At starting or idle, the nozzles were open, with the blades directing the gas flow in an essentially axial direction. With increasing pressure on the accelerator pedal, the blades would move to a higher angle so as to improve part-load efficiency and hold the turbine outlet temperature fairly constant.

On wide-open-throttle, the blades would turn to maximum angle. With abrupt release of the accelerator pedal, the transmission governor would send a pressure signal to the actuator mechanism and swing the nozzle blades to a negative (reverse) angle, directing the gas flow against the rotation of the power turbine—at all speeds above 15 mph. If the car was standing still or moving at a slower pace than 15 mph, the actuator simply returned the blades to their idle setting.

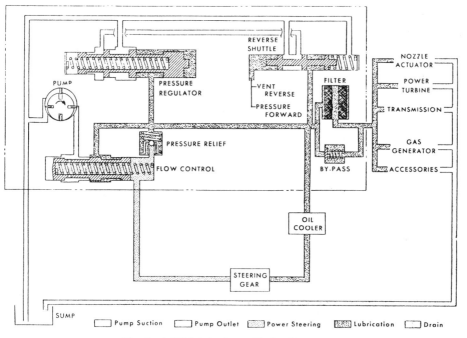

Chrysler A-831 lubrication and hydraulic systems.

The first-stage turbine was rated for a maximum speed of 44,600 rpm, and the power turbine was limited to 45,700 rpm. Idle speed ranged from 18,000 to 22,000 rpm. The first-stage turbine operated with a peak efficiency of 87 percent, while the power turbine did not exceed 84 percent efficiency. Power output was 130 hp at 3,600 rpm output shaft speed (35,155 power turbine rpm), and peak torque reached a value of 425 pounds-feet (at zero power turbine rpm).

The A-831 housing was a two-piece cast iron structure, split vertically along the turbine axis. The two sections were joined to a central bulkhead. The front section acted as a pressure vessel containing the compressor discharge flow to the regenerators. The inner walls of the housing were shaped to carry the pressure loads as a membrane, for minimal stress and deflection.

The housing rear section formed an exhaust chamber for the turbine, guiding the gas flow from the power turbine outlet ports to the rear halves of the regenerator cores. This chamber was insulated to reduce heat loss from the cycle and minimize thermal stresses in the housing structure, with natural convection from the outer shell providing all necessary cooling. The insulation materials were ceramic fibers, in both wool and blanket form, used in accordance with available space and local insulation requirements.

This insulation was retained by thin sheet metal liners that also formed the gas flow passages.

The regenerator cores were 15 inches in diameter. Fabricated from copper-brazed stainless steel honeycomb, they revolved at a maximum speed of 22 rpm. A thin rim and flanges were added to act as a pressure wall and furnish a sealing surface around each core. The hub and rim parts were designed to minimize stresses in the core, allowing it some freedom to distort into a shallow spherical shape according to the cylical temperature gradients during operation. The rim flanges were designed to roll with the core as it distorted so as to maintain a smooth contour on the core assembly face.

The external ring gear that drove the regenerator was mechanically attached to the cooler of the two flanges. The cast iron ring gears were mated with nitrided pinions and proved satisfactory in long-duration tests, even when running unlubricated at temperatures exceeding 400° F (204° C). The seal assemblies divided the core across the matrix into semi-circles, the front half with high pressure air and the rear half with low-pressure gas. The seal grid was made up of flexible metal diaphragms, offering enough clearance to accommodate the thermal expansion and distortion of the core, while permitting a minimal amount of leakage.

Total leakage of high pressure air to the low-pressure gas passage was less than 3 percent of engine air flow. Huebner explained that this leakage percentage stayed nearly constant throughout the operating range. About ¾ of one percent was due to the rotation of the core, and 2.25 percent to actual crossover of air from one section to another. Overall effectiveness of the regenerators was claimed to be 90 percent plus. This was sufficient to ensure a maximum exhaust gas temperature at full power of 525° F (274° C) and a normal exhaust gas temperature at idle of no more than 180° F (82° C).

The regenerators were driven from the compressor shaft, as were the other accessory drives. The main accessory gear case was mounted in front of the gasifier section, with the accessory pinion located at the front end of an extension on the compressor shaft. This extension had resilient joints to provide for torsional isolation, shaft deflection, and alignment tolerances.

The accessory pinion was meshed with an idler gear positioned directly below it. The idler gear drove the starter-generator (at 19,957 rpm maximum) though gearing to the starter-generator shaft. A coaxial pinion on this shaft drove two low-speed gears that turned the shaft for the other accessories at a maximum speed of 2,984 rpm.

The fuel control unit and pump were driven by gear from the second pinion. The regenerator drive was a worm gear arrangement with a four-thread hardened steel worm driving a 32-tooth manganese bronze wheel.

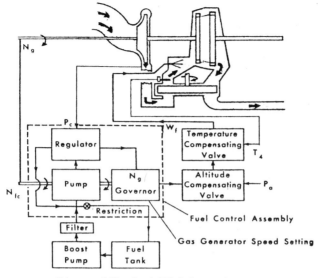

Diagram of Chrysler A-831 fuel control system.

The worm wheel was splined to two cross shafts that drove the two 16-tooth regenerator pinions, which in turn drove the regenerator ring gears.

At the output end of the power turbine shaft, an 18-tooth pinion engaged a 175-tooth gear to provide a 9.72 reduction ratio. The gears were straddle-mounted on ball bearings. Both were of the helical type with 30-degree helix angle having a profile ratio of 1.5 and a helical overlap of 3.0. The normal diametral pitch was 20, and the operating pressure angle 16°38'. Aluminum plates were cemented to the gear web to provide damping and reduce gear noise. The cover for the reduction gear assembly was doweled to the main housing, and centered on four struts on the power turbine nozzle ring assembly, which also formed the shroud for the turbine wheel.

A modified version of the TorqueFlite "8" transmission was used, but minus the torque converter so as to obviate the hydraulic losses. That gave the engine a 3-speed planetary transmission with an automatic control unit, though the control valve body was modified in several ways for specific reasons. First, the flow control valve was replaced with a throttling valve to be compatible with an external oil source. Second, the shift valves were changed to provide automatic upshift in Low range to protect against turbine overspeed. Third, modifications were made for better friction element capacity control, and fourth, the manual shift valve was changed so as to eliminate the neutral position.

The gas turbine, transmission, and power steering gear shared a combined lubrication and hydraulic system. It used a single pump (driven through the accessory drive) drawing oil from the transmission sump. The pump outlet fed the power steering circuit first at pressures up to 1050 psi. The return from this circuit, and the by-pass from the flow control valve, were regulated at a minimum 100 psi with full pump flow available to the lubrication circuit at all times. Drilled passages in the housings supplied oil to the power turbine, regenerator drive, and transmission, with external passages to the gasifier section, accessory drive, and power turbine nozzle actuator mechanism. An oil cooler hooked into the return line from the power steering circuit kept the oil temperature below 300° F (150° C). All sections drained back too the transmission sump.

The fuel system included a Bendix model DE fuel control assembly with an integral fuel pump, a regenerator temperature compensator, altitude compensator, solenoid shut-off valve, and Delavan air-atomizing fuel injection nozzle. In addition, an electric booster pump was used to prevent vapor lock with the wide variety of fuels used. The fuel control assembly contained a fuel pump, governor, pressure regulator, and metering orifice. The accelerator pedal set the spring load on the governor during constant-speed operation, and the governor would then regulate the fuel flow to the injection nozzle to maintain speed as a function of accelerator pedal position.

The system included provision for scheduling fuel flow, using the pressure regulator and orifice as a function of compressor discharge pressure during acceleration of the first-stage (gasifier) turbine, with automatic compensation for altitude and regenerator outlet temperature, so as to hold the turbine inlet temperature essentially constant. During deceleration, the governor throttle valve would close completely, shutting off all fuel supply to the injector nozzle. As the gasifier shaft would slow to conform to the new, lower-speed setting, the governor throttle valve would open and supply enough fuel to maintain the reduced speed.

The generator was designed to do double duty as a 24-V starter motor, which drove the gasifier shaft and accessories until the engine reached low idle speed. This starter-generator was mounted on the rear end of the accessory casing. At idle speed and above, the unit turned into a 12-V generator and supplied electric current to the car's electrical system. The car had two 12-V 59-Amp batteries connected in series, which proved capable of starting the engine in ambient temperatures down to −20° F (−29° C).

The starter was activated with the normal key. Lightoff would occur in 1½ seconds, and a normal start was a matter of six to 6½ seconds. The starter relay dropped out well below idle speed, at 15,000–16,000 rpm due to the reduction in starter current demand, which would energize the generator field.

The ignition unit for the single igniter was triggered by a set of contact

breaker points in conjunction with a standard ignition coil. When the gasifier shaft was rotating, the igniter would fire at the rate of 80 to 200 cycles
per second. This ignition system was set to operate continuously so as to obviate the need for special precautions to automatically restart it in case of
flameout during transient deceleration periods.

The vehicle designed for the A-831 gas turbine was a special model with
standard Chrysler chassis components. It was a luxury-type two-door hardtop
built on a short, 110-inch wheelbase, which in general character resembled
the Ford Thunderbird. It also resembled the Ford Thunderbird in styling,
since the 1961 T-Bird had been designed under the direction of Elwood P.
Engel while he was styling director at Ford, and Engel's first job after he left
Ford to join Chrysler was the Chrysler Turbine Car. The automotive press
was quick to dub it the "Engelbird." It followed normal Chrysler engineering practice, with front engine and drive via a rigid rear axle. The final drive
ratio was 3.23.

In contrast to the typical torsion-bar design used on production-model
Chrysler cars of the time, the Turbine Car used coil-spring independent
front suspension. The rear suspension was fully composed of off-the-shelf
components, however, with asymmetrically mounted leaf springs. The
power steering ratio of 15.7 gave 3.5 turns of the wheel from full left to full
right turn (with an overall ratio of 18.8). Ten-inch diameter brake drums
were used on all wheels, with an electrically driven power-assist compressor
mounted in unit with the master cylinder. The tires were 7.50-14 mounted
on 14-5K wheels.

The car had a front track of 59 inches and a rear track of 56.7 inches.
Turn diameter was 38.8 feet, or just about normal for cars of that size.

The overall length was 201.6 inches; overall width 72.9 inches, and
overall height 53.5 inches. It had a front overhang of 36.2 inches and a rear
overhang of 55.4 inches. Curb weight was 3952 pounds. The time required
to accelerate from 0 to 60 mph was generally around 12 seconds, based on
an outside temperature of 85° F. On cooler days, greater performance could
be achieved.

The turbine engine for the 50 cars was not considered to be a final
production design. Most of the manufacturing techniques used for this limited quantity were necessarily those of the tool room and not the production
plant. In many cases, this required a different approach to the design of the
parts than would be used for engines produced in larger quantity by the
highly automated engine plants of today. But, in its basic concept, Chrysler
felt that the powerplant in the 50 cars appeared to have the potentiality of
becoming an engine which could be manufactured in mass production
volume.

Up to January 28, 1966, Chrysler Turbine Cars were lent, on a rotating basis, to 203 different users in 133 cities in the 48 continental United States and the District of Columbia. Turbines were subjected to all types of terrain and weather conditions. During the evaluation period, the turbine cars were driven a total of more than one million miles.

Of the 203 turbine users, 180 were men and 23 were women. Their ages ranged from 21 to 70 years of age. Sixty percent of the users were owners of Chrysler products.

THE FIFTH GENERATION TURBINE

In 1964, at the height of the 50-car field test and consumer research program, George J. Huebner, Jr. was promoted to Director of Research for the whole of Chrysler Corporation. He immediately took steps to plan for an enlarged experiment, involving 200 cars carrying a Dodge nameplate, using a revised turbine design—the fifth-generation Chrysler turbine. The new turbine unit was developed to overcome the basic deficiencies in the A-831.

At the end of the 50-car evaluation program, the list of deficiencies looked like this:

1. Poor fuel economy at low speeds.
2. Poor initial acceleration due to excessive gas generator rotor lag.
3. Excessive noise at idle.
4. Inadequate engine braking.
5. Incompatibility with air conditioning.
6. Excessive specific weight.

This led to considerable redesign. On the new Chrysler turbine, the accessory drive was shifted from the compressor shaft to the power turbine shaft. That included the air conditioning compressor, the alternator, and the power steering pump.

This allowed better balance of the available pressures between compressor and power turbine, particularly at idle. This change also unloaded the gas generator which, with a 150° F increase in acceleration temperature, reduced the rotor lag from 2.0 seconds to under 1.2 seconds. This made a vast improvement in the driving quality of the car. The engine noise was also decreased because many of the reduction gears were eliminated.

The reduction in the number of accessory gears and bearings, and the reduction in the number of gas generator accessories also greatly improved the cold starting qualities of the engine. Fast reliable starts at −20° F using a 12-volt system were no longer a problem. Modifications to the power turbine flow area and blading, and an increase in allowable temperatures improved the car engine braking to the point where it was equal to or slightly better than that of a piston engine. The increased operating temperatures also increased the specific output and reduced the specific weight of the engine. The fuel economy of this engine, although improved, was still poorer at low car speeds and at idle than that of a piston engine.

Component life had been greatly improved through continual modifications and accelerated endurance testing. Engines were tested on a 24-hour automatic endurance cycle which is very severe. All parts had over 2800 hours, equivalent to more than 75,000 miles of normal car use and many parts have accumulated up to 3800 hours.

As a result of switching the accessory drive to the power turbine shaft, it became necessary to install a hydraulic torque converter in the transmission. Otherwise, the accessory drive would come to a standstill every time the vehicle stopped. The torque converter has a certain amount of hydraulic slippage, which translates into a 2–3 percent loss in fuel economy and performance.

While the reduced gasifier inertia cut the acceleration lag, 0–60 mph acceleration times remained essentially unchanged. The customer found the fifth-generation turbine less objectionable in traffic, however, since it was quicker off the mark, and the overall acceleration rate was comparable with that of a 200 (net) hp V8 installed in a car of similar size and weight.

THE SIXTH GENERATION TURBINE

The 200 Dodge turbine cars were never built. Priorities were reordered by Chrysler Corporation's top management, and the turbine program was put

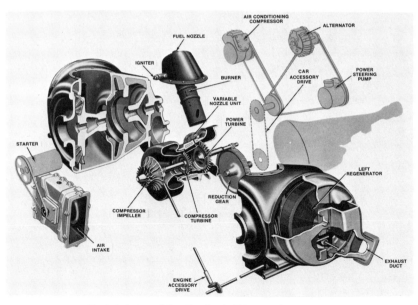

Exploded view of the Chrysler A-128 gas turbine engine.

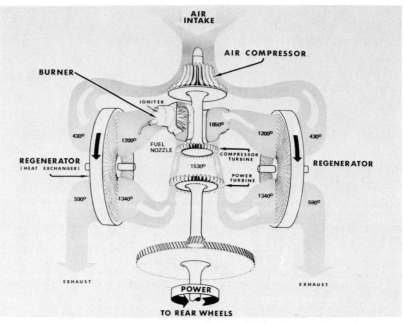

Gas flow path and temperature zones in the Chrysler A-128 gas turbine engine.

on the back burner. But Huebner and his men quietly went ahead and designed the sixth-generation turbine, the A-128.

It was basically the same as the preceding unit, but through gradual improvements in component efficiency, the unit now delivered 150 hp. The second-stage turbine had a maximum speed of 45,500 rpm, and a new 9.69 reduction gear was used to slow down the output shaft. The compressor had a capacity of 2.3 pounds per second and worked with a pressure ratio of 4 : 1. The turbine wheel and shroud materials were capable of withstanding turbine inlet temperatures of 2000° F (1100° C) for brief periods and about 1850° F (1010° C) indefinitely. Regenerator inlet temperature was 1340° F (727° C) and regenerator efficiency 87 percent.

It was installed in a 1966 Dodge Coronet with a curb weight of 4150 pounds, which had sparkling performance: zero-to-sixty mph acceleration in 10.5 seconds, and a top speed of 117 mph. This was better than what the same car was capable of with the 383-cubic-inch (6,279 cc) Chrysler V8 fitted with a four-barrel carburetor, but on a typical driving cycle, the turbine-powered car consumed approximately 15 percent more fuel.

The future of the turbine program did not look bright. Faced with the necessity of building cars to comply with both the Highway Safety Act of 1966 and the Clean Air Act of 1966, Chrysler Corporation broke up the turbine engineering office and reassigned the staff to work on auto safety sys-

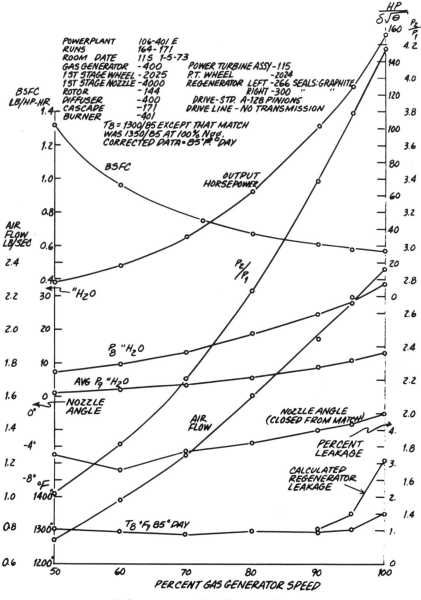

Performance map of the Chrysler A-128 unit.

tems and emission control systems, while also hiring new personnel to assist in these tasks. Many forms of advanced research, including the gas turbine program were summarily shelved.

Then came the Muskie Bill with its stipulation of a 90-percent cut in au-

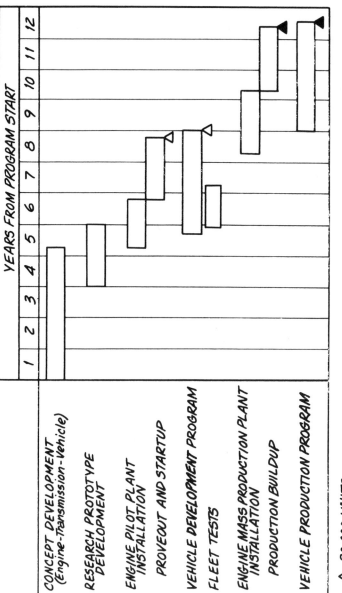

Possible timetable for getting a Chrysler turbine-powered passenger car into production.

George M. Thur displays the working parts of the A-128 unit.

tomotive emissions, enacted as the Clean Air Act of 1970. As Detroit kept shaking its collective head and saying "impossible," the EPA (Environmental Protection Agency, whose job it is to administer and enforce the Clean Air Act) started several programs investigating alternative types of prime movers.

If it was going to be impossible for Detroit to comply with the emissions standards, using the same old internal combustion engine, the EPA was going to steer them towards other types of power units. Miraculously, the turbine was one of those power units. In 1971 the EPA invited bids on a $6.4 million research contract on a passenger car gas turbine. Among the bidders were Williams Research Corporation, Rohr Industries, and Chrysler Corporation. The EPA awarded the contract to Chrysler in November 1972.

Here is a table showing where the turbine ranks in comparison with other alternative power systems tested by the EPA (all numbers in grams per mile):

	HC	CO	NO_x
1975 standards	1.5	15.0	3.1
1976 standards	0.41	3.4	2.0
1977 standards	0.41	3.4	0.4
Chrysler gas turbine	0.32	3.5	1.9
Diesel engine	0.87	1.6	1.8
Mazda Wankel	0.17	2.2	0.93
Steam engine	0.13	0.2	0.26
Stirling	0.01	0.15	0.17

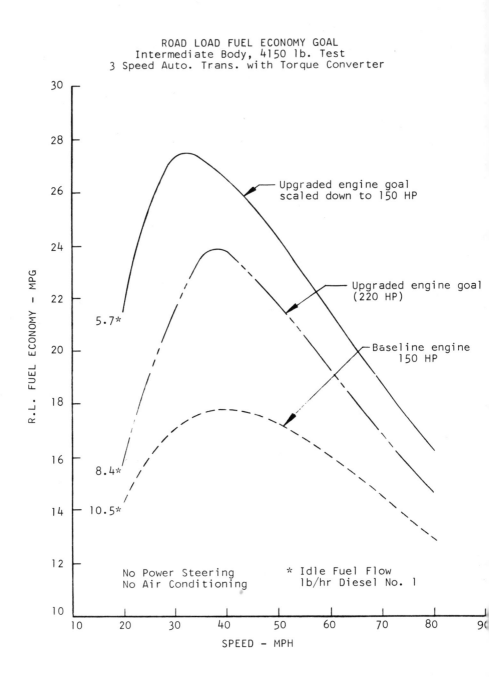

ROAD LOAD FUEL ECONOMY GOAL
Intermediate Body, 4150 lb. Test
3 Speed Auto. Trans. with Torque Converter

Upgraded engine goal
scaled down to 150 HP

Upgraded engine goal
(220 HP)

Baseline engine
150 HP

5.7*

8.4*

10.5*

No Power Steering
No Air Conditioning

* Idle Fuel Flow
lb/hr Diesel No. 1

R.L. FUEL ECONOMY – MPG

SPEED – MPH

E.P.A. program objectives for gas turbine improvement.

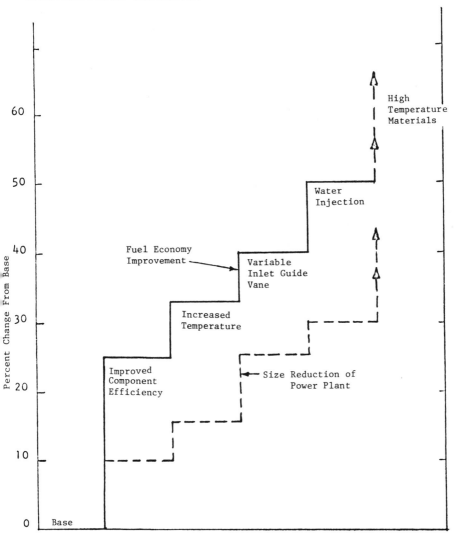

Projected efficiency gains in E.P.A. turbine development program.

Under the terms of the contract, Chrysler was to supply the EPA with three cars powered by sixth-generation gas turbines. The vehicle chosen was the 1974-model Dodge Coronet 5-door sedan. To install the A-128 in the Coronet called for a few minor design changes. The front suspension cross member was redesigned, and the front body structure was altered to accommodate the new cross member. The floor pan was modified to provide

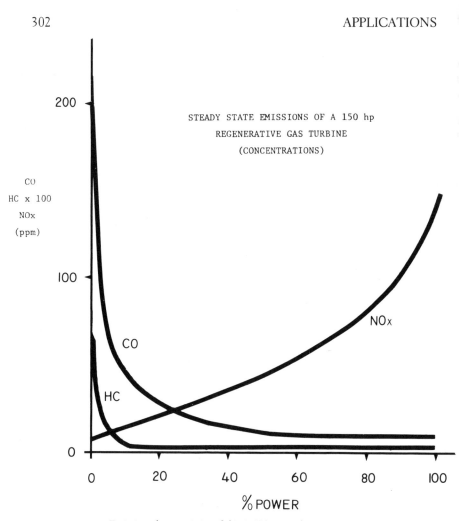

Emission characteristics of the A-128 gas turbine engine.

ground clearance for the exhaust ducts, and the body nose section was changed to incorporate an air intake system.

Following definitive tests on this baseline engine in both dynamometer cells and in vehicles, the design was to be up-graded. This was to be done by incorporating into it proven technical advances developed under the baseline contract and under separate EPA contracts with groups outside the automobile industry. Chrysler would also offer research advances developed since the original definition of the sixth generation, baseline powerplant. Moreover, the contract work also included cost studies and assessment of produceability potential for high volume passenger car manufacture.

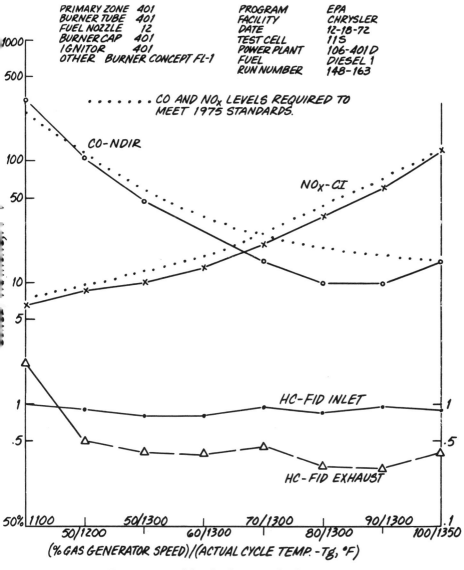

Emissions map of the Chrysler A-128 "baseline" engine.

By the time the EPA held its coordinating meeting with its contractors and other interested parties in Ann Arbor, Michigan on June 7–8, 1973, it was apparent that a fuel shortage was brewing, and the chief of the EPA power systems branch for advanced automotive power systems, George M.

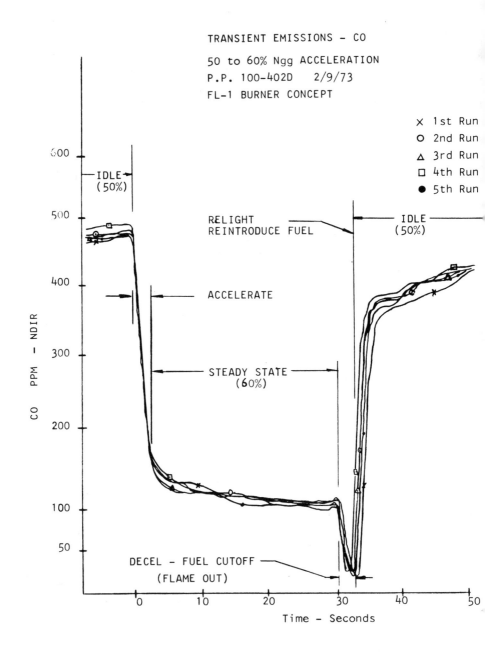

Graph showing carbon monoxide emissions during transient operating conditions.

304

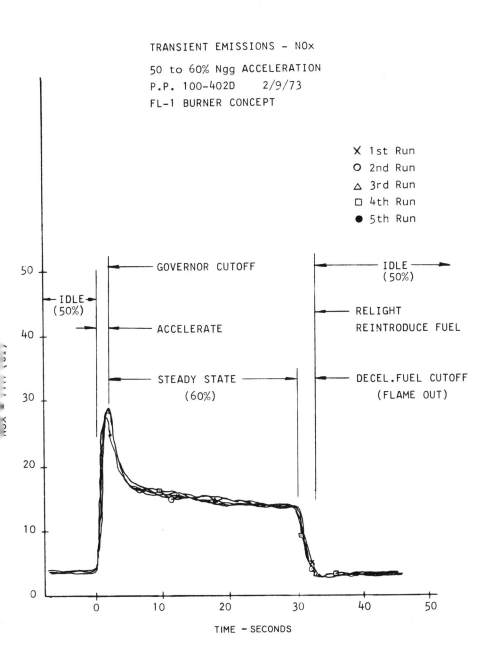

Graph showing oxides of nitrogen emissions during transient operating conditions.

Thur, explained that priorities had to be reestablished so that fuel economy would receive equal attention with emission control.

To explain the aims of the EPA's involvement in research programs on the turbine car, Thur declared: "We are not in the business of building a vehicle. We are in the business of developing a technology. We are advancing technology for private industry to use. We are also trying to make the industry interested in our work, and they are interested."

George M. Thur then presented an 8-point scenario calculated to provide a 50-percent improvement in gas turbine fuel economy.

Improvement Item	Description	Improvement Goal	Miles Per Gallon
1. Water injection	Reduced engine size for same power output	+10% HP	+5%
2. Variable inlet guide vanes	Reduced engine size for same power output	+12% HP	+6–8%
3. Ceramic regenerator	Improved efficiency	+4 points	+6%
4. Higher cycle temperature	Reduced engine size for same power output	+7% HP	+5%
5. Recover and reduce heat loss	Reduced parasitic losses	50%	+6–10%
6. Power turbine	Higher efficiency	+2–4 points	+7%
7. Gasifier turbine	Higher efficiency	+4 points	+8%
8. Compressor	Higher efficiency	+1 point	+2%
		Total	45–51%

1. WATER INJECTION

The EPA proposal calls for a system of water injection (upstream of the compressor). It is calculated that it will give a 10 percent gain in power and a five percent drop in fuel consumption. The principle of water injection has been tested and proved valid in connection with gasoline-fuel and diesel-type piston engines. The first experiments were made in Hungary before 1900 by a mechanic named Benki.

The first scientific attempt to use water injection was carried out in 1913 by Bertram Hopkinson at Trinity College, Cambridge. Water injection became standard equipment on a number of heavy oil engines—as an internal coolant—during the 1920s. In 1938 M. S. Kuhring in Canada demonstrated power gains up to 21 percent by the use of water injection on a supercharged Jaguar aircraft engine, and such systems became common on supercharged World War II fighter planes of both the Axis and Allied powers.

In 1972 Dr. A. E. W. Austen of C. A. V. (a member of the Lucas Group of Companies) showed impressive reductions in NO_x emissions from diesel

CHRYSLER PROTOTYPE COMBUSTOR DESIGN

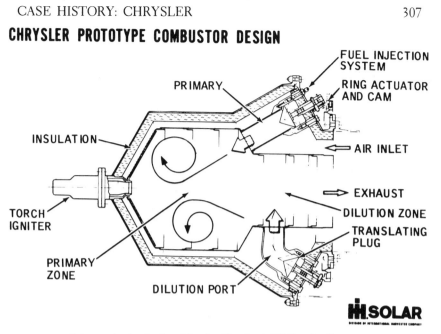

Solar combustor developed for the Chrysler A-128 "baseline" engine.

engines with water injection. At the same time, J. Lyell Ginter, a former diesel engineer who runs an independent research and development company in Glendale California disclosed his invention—the Thermogenerator—which was a device for water or steam injection on gas turbine engines.

The Thermogenerator is a separate combustor mounted on top of the turbine unit. Water injection takes place prior to fuel injection. The presence of water lowers the flame temperature, which will prevent the formation of NO_x. According to Ginter, sufficient burning time is given to the combustion products to minimize the production of unburned hydrocarbons and carbon monoxide that can form as a result of incomplete combustion.

According to engineers of the Garrett Corporation, power augmentation can be obtained by injecting demineralized water at the compressor inlet. Theoretical and experimental work shows that 30–40 percent boost can be obtained by injecting a water-to-air mass ratio of 0.06 on a 100° F day. Lesser amounts of water are required to obtain necessary power augmentation for vehicle acceleration on cooler days, with none required below 60° F. Studies have been conducted which indicate that demineralized water could be made available at service stations for approximately two cents or less per gallon.

Water injection changes the engine's normal operating line, and provides a power boost effect by lowering the inlet temperature and increasing the effective mass airflow of the engine. The evaporating water also gives the effect of a compressor inter-cooler. Power augmentation by water injection, therefore, is one way of reducing initial engine size and cost.

And George Thur claims:

Water injection buys you a lot more than the complexity it causes. It brings the engine size down, for a given output. In a car you have to design an engine too large for the type of transportation you need. This water injection optimizes the size for the whole cycle. As for the power gain and fuel consumption reduction, we are pretty confident of those figures. We tend to be conservative.

Water will reduce NO_x formation, and may just take care of that which cannot be eliminated by other means. Water injection will be most effective in the summer, when ambient temperature is 85° F (30° C) and higher. The presence of water will then serve to restore the power that is lost because of higher inlet air temperature.

2.   VARIABLE INLET GUIDE VANES

Next, the EPA suggests that variable inlet guide vanes be adopted. Most turbines are fitted with vanes at the compressor intake to form a controlled swirl in the air entering the compressor, but they are usually fixed in position. By giving them variable geometry, the EPA claims that a 12 percent power gain is possible, coupled with a six to eight percent reduction in fuel consumption. Variable vanes will cost more, but according to George M. Thur "they pay off in fuel economy." The 12-percent boost in power due to variable inlet guide vanes will slow up in the cycle as an increase in pressure ratio and air flows mass.

3.   CERAMIC REGENERATORS

The third point on the EPA list is a ceramic regenerator. Up to now, Chrysler has been using metallic heat exchangers. Most other turbine developers switched to Cercor several years ago. Owens-Illinois has also been working on a ceramic regenerator. The EPA estimates that the Chrysler turbine would gain four percent in heat exchange efficiency, corresponding to a six percent gain in fuel mileage, by the adoption of ceramic regenerators (two per turbine engine).

The ceramic materials have lower thermal expansion coefficients and are easier to seal, but have other problems (thermal cracking and fatigue cracking). According to George M. Thur:

The key weakness of ceramics is there are no strength properties. Right now the research is concentrating on just how to characterize the material; on building some specifications. Primarily, the material tends to crack. It doesn't last too long, but they are starting to improve that.

4. HIGHER CYCLE TEMPERATURE

Higher cycle temperature, in the EPA estimates, can give seven percent more power and a five percent cut in fuel consumption. These figures seem overly modest. For improvements of that order, all that is needed is a 50° F rise in turbine inlet temperature. And leading turbine experts such as Sam Williams and Noel Penny are talking in terms of raising the turbine inlet temperature several hundred degrees! Aircraft turbines are already operating in the 2100–2200° F (1150–1200° C) range, and Noel Penny, for one, talks of future turbines operating at 2500° F (1370° C).

And George Huebner says: "Gas turbines are unique in that you get both an increase in specific output and a reduction in fuel consumption at the same time. Usually you're at different ends of the same stick."

5. RECOVER AND REDUCE HEAT LOSS

By reducing parasitic losses in the engine, the EPA calculates the turbine of the future can reduce to half of the present level the heat losses in the base line power plant. That would mean a six to 10 percent improvement in fuel economy. The studies in this area have been made by NASA (National Aeronautics and Space Administration). Their work has been centered on the internal aerodynamics of the turbine engine, and in the opinion of George Thur "NASA is a very conservative organization. Nothing comes out of NASA unless it's absolutely right, and NASA is very confident of meeting the improvement goals."

In all, the EPA has contracts worth $1.2 million with NASA's Lewis Research Center in Cleveland, Ohio, for work including low-emission combustor studies, materials development, turbine blade manufacturing techniques, transmission improvement, and controls development.

6. 7. 8. COMPONENT EFFICIENCY

Component efficiency is a controlling factor in overall cycle efficiency. According to Dr. Adolf Meyer of Brown, Boveri, a five percent increase in compressor and turbine efficiency would give a 20-percent improvement in cycle efficiency. The numbers estimated by the EPA are judged to be quite realistic, and can probably be exceeded.

The EPA program estimates that power turbine efficiency can be raised two to four points, for a seven percent gain in fuel economy. The compressor turbine can be developed to be four percent more efficient, giving 8 percent better fuel mileage. As for the compressor, EPA estimates a gain of one point in efficiency would give a two percent improvement in fuel economy.

Says Mr. Thur: "We invested over a million dollars in General Electric advanced turbine studies. Each study shows the turbine can deliver 12–13 mpg over the federal driving cycle (where the baseline turbine gets 7.7 mpg)."

Raising compressor efficiency by just one point will give a two percent improvement in fuel economy. If first-stage turbine efficiency can be raised by four points, that will bring an eight percent improvement in fuel economy. For the power turbine, the immediate aim is to raise efficiency between two and four points, for a fuel saving of seven percent.

Some of the EPA research contracts for studies, components, and methods applicable to the base line gas turbine are worthy of closer examination.

JET-INDUCED CIRCULATION

An EPA research contract for development and testing of a combustor featuring jet-induced circulation was awarded to Solar Division of International Harvester Company, in San Diego, California. Solar has a lot of gas turbine experience (for industrial applications) and approached the matter of NO_x control from two basic observations:

1. The actual quantity of nitric oxides produced is directly proportional to residence time in the primary zone at high temperatures (above 3,000° F—1500° C) prior to cooling by dilution air mixing.

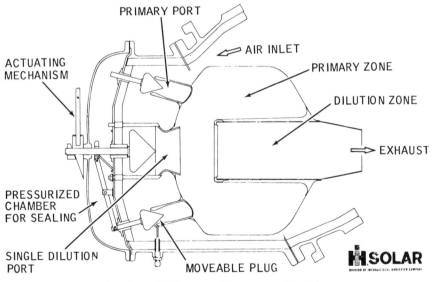

Experimental JIC-type combustor proposed by Solar.

2. The major portion of nitric oxides is produced during the mixing of
   the fuel-rich primary zone exhaust gases with the secondary air.

During earlier research, Solar had obtained very promising results with both
swirl-induced recirculation and jet-induced recirculation. But jet induced
recirculation was preferred, as this type demonstrated better performance
with liquid fuels, and its design generally allowed greater flexibility in terms
of air/fuel ratio control within the combustor.

Solar's first low-NO_x combustor was a lean-mixture design, with pilot
flame stabilization. Fuel for a pilot flame was fed into a conical stabilizer
section, and exhausted into the recirculation zone at the base of the stabilizer. The pilot flame served to ignite portions of the mixture caught in the
recirculating flow, which would then ignite the remaining air/fuel mixture
when mixed back into the mainstream. The pilot flame combustor succeeded in bringing NO_x levels down below target values (0.4 g/mile), but
caused an important rise in CO and HC emissions mainly due to poor mixing characteristics within the combustion zone proper.

Analysis of this experience led Solar to the jet-induced stabilizer. In the
first version, air and fuel were pre-mixed and constrained to pass through a
device resembling an ejector. The air/fuel mixture then passed through a
nozzle to provide a high-velocity jet, which gave extremely high recirculation volume. This combustor was designed JIC-1 and met the EPA's emission targets (under laboratory conditions—not as part of a working turbine
engine). However, the JIC-1 combustor suffered from the same typical defect of all combustors running with a lean primary-zone mixture: Flame stability problems and a high risk of lean blowout. As a result, Solar decided to
explore the rich-mixture primary zone approach and developed the JIC-2
combustor.

Solar felt that pre-mixing could be accomplished within the combustor
proper. JIC-2 did not have true pre-mixing, but gave easy atomization and
rapid vaporization because the angled inlet primary ports also acted as air-
blast atomizers. It proved that increasing the primary zone volume, while
reducing the injection angle and the number of primary ports, led to a
threefold increase in operating range. Through the use of multiple jets with
low pressure drops the JIC-2 combustor could provide the same entrainment
rate for a constant mass flow as a single jet with a high pressure drop. Solar
concluded that multiple jets are preferable for improved stabilization.

While JIC-2 provided superior operational characteristics and could be
predicted to offer improved driveability, it could not match the emission
levels of the JIC-1 combustor. Without abandoning the rich-mixture primary zone approach, Solar decided to try out an alternative form of jet induction, using primary air ports with vortex valves.

Fuel is injected through the primary port wall at the point of maximum air velocity. The vortex valves induced a swirl at each primary port, which assured very high recirculation volume. The vortex flow also provided a high-level tangential air flow which created a low static pressure level on the combustor axis just downstream of the swirl inducer area. This combustor was designed JIC-3. While it failed to meet the goals for NO_x control, it gave superior operational characteristics, and was chosen as the basis for the JIC-B design to be made specifically for the base line turbine engine.

The vortex-induced circulation combustor was designated JIC-3. This design also provided high recirculation volume in the primary zone through the use of a swirl inducer. However, it did not meet the NO_x control goals in its initial form. Some smoke and carbon formation has occurred in combustors using rich-mixture primary zones, but JIC-3 was claimed to give low smoke levels, low flame emissivities, and low exit temperature distribution factors, with low CO and HC emission levels as long as the residence times are made long enough.

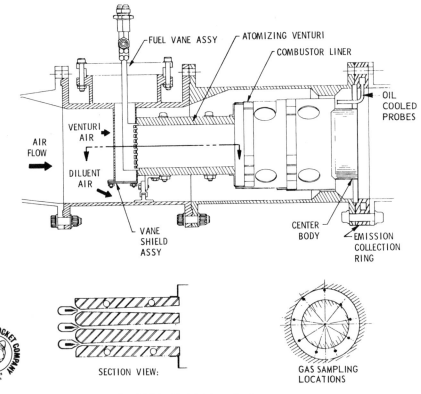

Aerojet Liquid platelet combustor.

Thus, the JIC-B combustor is believed to be the leading candidate. But two more radical types of combustor are still in the running—the platelet combustor and the porous plate combustor.

PLATELET COMBUSTOR

The research contract for a platelet combustor was awarded to the Aerojet Liquid Rocket Company of Sacramento, California. The platelet combustor concept is based on the use of pre-vaporized fuel to eliminate droplet combustion, with pre-mixing of air and fuel to eliminate variations in air/fuel ratio.

This provides control of the temperature, time, and oxygen concentration in the primary zone. The platelet combustor does not have the ordinary type of fuel injection nozzle. Instead, fuel is uniformly injected from multiple orifices in a rail running diametrically across the top of the combustor.

Each orifice injects fuel into a separate atomizing venturi through which the primary zone air is passed. The formation of a finely atomized spray is assured by the combination of high-velocity air and very small injection orifices. The atomized fuel is rapidly vaporized, and the venturi diffuser permits recovery of a large portion of the pressure loss associated with high atomizing velocity. This method of pre-vaporization also allows minimum combustor length and makes for rapid diluent air quenching. The platelet combustor has—under laboratory conditions—given NO_x emission levels below 0.4 grams per mile.

POROUS PLATE COMBUSTOR

The research contract for the porous plate combustor was awarded to the General Electric Co. in Schenectady, N.Y. The combustor shell has an abnormally large diameter to accommodate an inner lining of transpiration modules inside of the porous wall. Each of these modules is a wedge-shaped element, and they are positioned in the same formation as the "boats" in an orange, with their inner points extending to the edge of the core.

The modules are mounted on the porous wall, back to back with vaporizing channels, and separated on both sides from their neighbors by narrow, open spaces. The primary air is ducted inside the combustor outer shell, but its admission to the vaporizing channels is controlled by a butterfly valve and actuator for each channel.

Just below the valve, each channel has an air-atomizing fuel nozzle. The atomized fuel is mixed with the amount of primary air admitted into the vaporizing channel as the air flows to the bottom of the channel, where the flow path is reversed, and the air/fuel mixture is ducted into the bottom of the porous wall which it must penetrate before entering the transpiration modules at various points along the full length of the combustor core. Axial

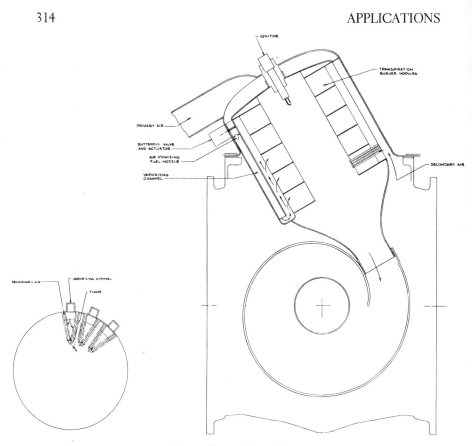

Porous plate combustor design.

tubes for air coolant are embedded in the porous matrix. The igniter is placed at the center of the combustor lid, extending well down into the primary zone. This type of combustor has shown promising results in terms of emission control, but its effect on fuel economy is less encouraging.

Gas Temperature Sensor

The importance of a reliable turbine inlet temperature sensor for reductions in specific fuel consumption cannot be overestimated. The EPA awarded a research contract on a fluidic temperature sensor to Honeywell. The device under development at Honeywell is an acoustic oscillator with an output frequency proportional to the square root of the average gas temperature within the sensor body.

The gas enters through a slot nozzle, impinges on a splitter, which excites the oscillation. The gas flow continues through cavities with resonant length calculated to amplify the oscillation. At the end, the gas is discharged into a region of lower pressure, and flows out of the sensing device through an extension tube and a port in the mounting flange.

The oscillatory pressure signal is sent to a piezoelectric transducer, which converts it to an equivalent voltage. This voltage is then carried through a lead wire to a connector on the mounting flange. Further specifics of the wiring depends on the exact type of control system used.

THE FINAL HURDLE: PRODUCTION

When George J. Huebner, Jr. talks about production plans, the audience gets the idea that Chrysler Corporation wants to bring it about right away. But it won't be tomorrow. "On a crash basis, we could have limited production in about four years," Huebner claims. "That time will be taken up with final design, development and tooling. After 18 months' field experience with those turbine cars, the design can be evaluated. Minor changes can be made. Only at that point can high-volume production equipment be ordered. Delivery time would be about 18 months. In all, you can count four years for small-scale production, evaluation, and high-volume tooling. Expansion to large-scale production would take about two years. So to get into mass production from point zero you would need about 10 years."

Any new product, whether it is a powerplant or a safety pin, must go through three basic stages on its way to the market place. The producer must: 1. Prove a production design, 2. Procure tooling and plants, and 3. Launch production. These steps must be accomplished whether the production volume is high or low, but the techniques used depend heavily on that volume. The first stage of gas turbine production could probably begin at a volume of a few thousand a year using "interim" tooling. There would be a lot of job-shop operations, but many of the basic engine manufacturing problems could be solved. But if gas turbines are to make a significant contribution to clean atmosphere, they must be used in large numbers, so most studies have been made for high volume production. And that is the heart of the problem.

Gas turbines have never been produced in automotive quantities by anyone. To do so will require replacement of current manufacturing methods with equipment and techniques never before used in large-volume manufacturing. It would probably be a mistake to try to jump into mass production the minute an accepted prototype was ready. Why? "If we tooled up for it today," explains Huebner, "the machine tool industry would make such fantastic progress over the next few years that we would soon have to re-tool half the line."

That's only one reason why gas turbine production cost estimates range so widely. The lowest estimate is what you get from the EPA. George Thur told me:

"I can't put a dollar figure on it, but let's say $50 more than a piston engine with the emission controls as originally proposed for 1976 (now on the books for 1977). Cost is a very controversial subject. Investments have to be made. The auto industry gets a triple star for knowing how to make parts in mass production. Our role is to work out the principles of design, then let the auto companies work out the manufacturing."

Nevertheless, the EPA has sponsored production cost studies and studies of low-cost parts and manufacturing methods. Three such programs may play a part in bringing the Chrysler turbine car closer to mass production: Investment casting of turbine wheels, the "Gatorizing" Process, and rubber pattern casting techniques.

INVESTMENT CASTING

A contract for cost studies of investment casting of Inconel 713 turbine wheels was awarded to Williams Research Corporation. Prior to this study, vendor quotations at an annual volume of one million engines were about $43 per wheel. Williams Research Corp. says it can be done for $9.44 per wheel—including a markup for profit:

I.	*Raw Material*			
	A.	Metal per pound		$1.89
	B.	Pattern Mat'l., Refractory		
		& Production Melting (Per Pound)		$0.13
	C.	Raw Material Cost/Wheel		
		$1.89 + $0.13 × 2.7 lbs.		$5.45
II.	*Labor & Overhead*			
	A.	Direct Labor/Wheel		$0.41
	B.	Overhead/Wheel		
		1. Capital & Depreciation	$0.43 *	
		2. Labor, Indirect	$0.56 *	
		3. Misc. Expense	$0.36 *	
		* *Overhead is 345%*		
	C.	Labor Plus Overhead/Wheel		$1.41
III.	*Totals*			
	A.	Raw Material/Wheel		$5.45
	B.	Labor Plus Overhead		$1.41
			Sub Total	$6.86
	C.	Plus G & A (10%) and Profit (25%)		$2.58
	Total Cost Per Wheel			$9.44

Early in the data-gathering stages, several references to European use of investment castings in the automotive sector brought in a mass of data on the GAZ Gorky Automotive Works Investment Casting Foundry in the USSR. An evaluation of these data supported the contention that highly automated investment foundries can produce many types of investment castings at low cost. In addition, there has been substantial progress in the United States on the part of several material suppliers to develop binder materials that will reduce the time required to build investment shell molds.

Williams Research developed a conceptual investment casting process and plant suitable for volume production of automotive turbine wheels. This process includes the physical and cost elements of a production facility, equipment, manpower, raw material, and all other significant manufacturing elements necessary to develop a realistic unit cost for automotive turbine wheels.

The "Gatorizing" Process

Gatorizing is a new forging process developed by Pratt & Whitney Aircraft (Division of United Aircraft Corporation) at the Florida Research and Development Center in West Palm Beach. The Gatorizing forging technique has been applied to the nickel-base alloys, IN100, Astroloy, and Waspaloy; the iron-base alloys, Inco 901, and A-286; and to the titanium-base alloys, Ti-6A1-2Sn-4Zr-6Mo, Ti-8A1-1Mo-1V and Ti-6A1-4V. Both IN100 and Astroloy have been forged starting with a powder product as well as with cast ingots.

This process differs from earlier hot isothermal forging methods in that the temperature and forging rate are controlled to produce and sustain a condition of superplasticity in the alloy being forged. The alloy is placed in a temporary condition of high ductility either during the initial sequence of the actual forging process, or by special billet-processing techniques. As a result, substantially lower pressures are required for forging. After forging, the alloy can be heat-treated to restore its normal high strength and hardness.

Complex contour-shaped parts can be forged to close tolerances due to the superplastic state of the alloy. This will reduce the input weight of raw material and lower the machining cost. It will also permit the use of smaller, less expensive forging equipment that has previously been required for turbine super-alloys. Pratt & Whitney claims it will also reduce the reject rate, as well as eliminating the need for full-scale trial dies.

The Gatorizing process is uniquely scalable. The characteristics of parts forged with subscale dies are precisely reproduced in full-size forgings. Gatorized forgings that are not dimensionally acceptable can be returned to the forging press and reforged several times without degradation of mechanical properties. Gatorized forged alloys also exhibit a uniform metallurgical microstructure providing greater assurance of meeting specific mechanical properties.

Rubber Pattern Casting Techniques

The research that led to the development of rubber pattern casting techniques was started by AiResearch Casting Division (of the Garrett Corporation) well before the EPA entered the picture, and AiResearch has continued the program without a contract with EPA, while it is offering its technology to the industry at large.

Test parts have been produced from Inconel 713, IN100, and air melt 17-4PH with good results and excellent grain control. Cost estimates from AiResearch correlate exceedingly well with the figures budgeted by Williams Research Corporation in the investment-casting study. AiResearch's analyses indicate that suitable turbine wheels can be manufactured for an original-equipment market price of less than $10 apiece at production rates of one million units per year, using the rubber pattern casting techniques.

Conclusions

The EPA contract will bring a great deal of new technology to Chrysler and probably assist Chrysler's turbine engineering section in making a big jump ahead of the competition. At this juncture it should also be pointed out that the EPA activity, being sponsored by the federal government, and its results, are in the public domain. As for Chrysler's attitude about sharing its turbine technology, George J. Huebner, Jr. says:

The results of our work have always been available to everyone on a normal commercial basis. We have a tremendous number of patents on this engine. We have offered all the patents to anyone who wanted a license. This has been done on an extremely reasonable royalty basis. We cannot refuse to open up our expertise in the cause of clean air just because we happen to have what appears to be a monopoly on the turbine engine. We are giving the other people a running start in the business.

18

Case History: General Motors

ALTHOUGH THE FIRST gas turbine powered car did not appear until 1953, the corporation's involvement with gas turbine research had begun many years earlier. Indirectly, it can be said to have started in 1937 when GM's Allison Division in Indianapolis started production of the V-1710-C10 aircraft engine. It was a V-12 piston engine equipped with an exhaust gas-driven turbo-supercharger. The engine went into use in the Curtiss XP-40 in 1938.

Under the leadership of General Manager Edward B. Newill, Allison Division started design and development work on turbojet and turboprop aircraft engines in 1943, and in November 1945 started production of the Model 400-C5 turbojet whose official USAF designation was J-33-A-23. It was followed in September 1946 by a smaller sister version, the Model 450 (USAF designation J-35-A-13). The 400-C5 delivered a maximum thrust of 4600 pounds (2090 kg), while the Model 450 had a maximum thrust of 3750 pounds (1705 kg).

In 1947 Allison discontinued the production of liquid-cooled piston-type aircraft engines to concentrate on gas turbines. Against this background, it was clear that GM in general and Allison Division in particular should be heavily interested in all applications of gas turbine power.

GT-300 AND THE TURBO—CRUISER I

In 1948 Charles L. McCuen, who had succeeded Charles F. "Boss" Kettering as director of the GM Research Laboratories, looked at the Allison turbojets and asked himself: "What are the chances of pulling this principle down from the sky and putting it to work on the ground, turning vehicle wheels?"

As a result, the Research Laboratories got involved in some basic feasibil-

General Motors Firebird I (left), Firebird II (center) and Firebird III (right).

ity studies, and an engineer named William A. Turunen was given the task of bringing what McCuen called "the flying blowtorch" down to earth. His assignment was not to install a turboshaft unit in a car, but to design an entirely new power plant suitable for passenger car propulsion and installation in an advanced-design chassis.

Born in Alston, Michigan, on September 4, 1918, W. A. Turunen (of Finnish extraction) had joined GM in 1939, after graduation from the Michigan Technological University. He was assigned to the Research Laboratories, and was able to complete post-graduate work at General Motors Institute in 1940. He was on active duty with the U.S. Army Corps of Engineers and the U.S. Air Force from 1942 to 1946, and spent a year at Columbia University to get a master's degree in engineering administration before returning to the Research Laboratories.

In the meantime he had married Eleanor McCuen—his boss's daughter. He was named head of the engineering development department in 1948, which was an impressive promotion but also placed the responsibility for the turbine car program on his shoulders. His closest collaborator was John S. Collman, who had come to the GM Research Laboratories in 1941 as a junior engineer in the mechanical engineering department, after graduating from the University of Michigan with a bachelor of science degree in naval architecture and marine engineering. He was transferred to the engineering development department in 1950, and in 1951 was appointed assistant head of the department.

The first gas turbine engine designed by W. A. Turunen and his staff was designated GT-300 internally and given the name "Whirlfire" for the public. The size of the engine was determined by the desire for a rating of 300 shaft hp, and this number was chosen because GM's initial studies had indicated that the automotive gas turbine might best make its initial entry in heavy-duty or commerical vehicle installations.

Turunen also recognized that problems were bound to arise, some anticipated and some unforeseen. To minimize the number of problems and the delays they might cause in the progress of the program, it was decided to emphasize mechanical simplicity and reliability rather than to strive for the ultimate refinements calculated to improve fuel economy.

As in Chrysler's case, GM chose the two-shaft configuration. But the GT-300 was built as a simple-cycle gas turbine, without heat exchangers in any form. The engine was made up of two entirely independent assemblies—the gasifier section and the output section. There was no mechanical connection at all between the two sections. The only link was a flexible duct to transmit the gases from the first-stage turbine to the second-stage turbine.

First, the air entered a splitter-type silencer lined with fiberglass lining material. The compressor casing included a collector chamber and an air inlet flange to which was clamped a flared entrance duct bringing air from the silencer. The compressor casing was completed by a back plate bolted to the main engine housing. In the interest of simplicity, it was decided to use a centrifugal compressor with a pressure ratio of 3.5.

The compressor wheel was pinned to an internally splined sleeve locked to the gasifier shaft by a streamlined nut at the front end of the shaft. The gasifier shaft was supported in the housing by a forward ball bearing and a rear roller bearing. The two-bearing shaft imposed certain limits on rotational speed if adequate bearing life was to be assured. Consequently, the design point gasifier speed was fixed at 24,000 rpm. The commitment to such a low compressor speed set rather large dimensions for the compressor wheel and turbines.

Both turbines were of the single-stage axial-flow type. The blades were individually cast and machined, and fastened to the turbine wheel disc by fir-tree roots. Nozzle vane assemblies for the turbines also had individually cast vanes, which, after machining, were welded to the inner and outer shrouds. The first-stage turbine wheel had 61 blades. For the second-stage turbine, a maximum speed of 12,000 rpm was imposed, in an attempt to benefit from the lower thermal stresses and lower reduction gear ratios such design would entail. This again caused an increase in turbine diameter, which led to higher engine weight and greater package size.

Air discharged from the compressor flowed into a diffuser which was made up of a curved plate design to act as a guide vane for the compressed air. A square-section duct of involute shape led the compressed air to the combustor. The combustor was a barrel-type design, positioned horizontally above the turbines. The combustor had a side entrance, with intake ports

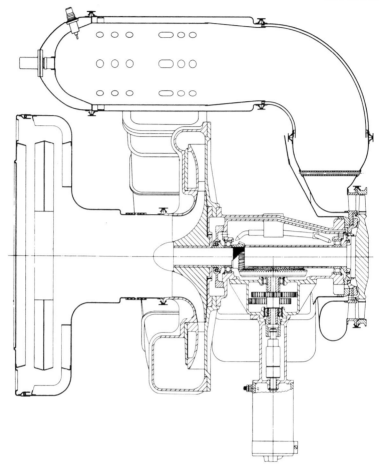

Sectioned view of the gasifier section in the GT-300 unit.

about halfway between the dome and the outlet. An inner shell was provided with ports designed to give the best distribution of primary and secondary air.

A limit of 1500° F (816° C) was imposed on the turbine inlet temperature in order to ensure reasonable turbine blade life. Turbine inlet temperature was measured by a thermocouple mounted in the elbow and projecting through the inner liner.

A duplex fuel nozzle was mounted in the center of the dome. AC Spark Plug Division came up with a special igniter plug for installation in the side of the dome at primary-zone level. The hot combustion products expanded

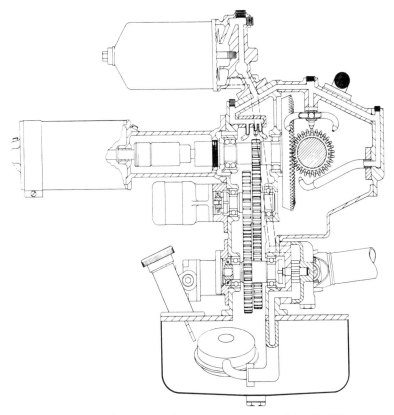

Sectioned view of the power turbine and reduction gear of the GT-300 unit.

through a double-walled elbow duct into the nozzle plenum chamber, and flowed through a nozzle vane unit leading into the first-stage turbine.

The inner liner in the elbow duct was separated from the outer member at the discharge and by sheet metal spacers, and at the upstream end by a flange which extended into the recess formed between the inner liner and the exhaust port on the combustor. The rear end of the combustor liner telescoped into the outer skin of the elbow duct and was provided with an alignment flange to maintain the parts in the same relative locations, while allowing adequate freedom for differential thermal expansion.

The nozzle plenum chamber was welded to a one-piece casting that contained the nozzle vanes. This nozzle vane unit included inner and outer shrouds as well as the vanes, and was precision-cast by the shell-molding process. The power turbine had a similar nozzle unit directing gas flow to the blades at the most advantageous angle.

The exhaust gas flowed from a collector behind the power turbine to the open space contained within an aluminum radiation shield that covered the entire hot part of the engine. Here the exhaust gas was mixed with cooling air drawn in over the faces of both the turbine wheels. The cooled, diluted gases were then expelled around the exhaust collector outlet. This cooling air was drawn in through holes in the reduction gear casing by the action of fan blades on the face of the turbine wheels.

The starter motor was a Delco unit using a conventional engaging mechanism, mounted on the accessory shaft. The accessories included a generator with a tachometer, a fuel pump, a gasifier lubrication pump, an output section lubrication pump, and a power takeoff suitable for driving an electric generator and service air compressor.

The accessory drive was taken from the gasifier shaft via a right-angle spiral bevel gear. The accessory drive shaft ran at right angles to the turbine

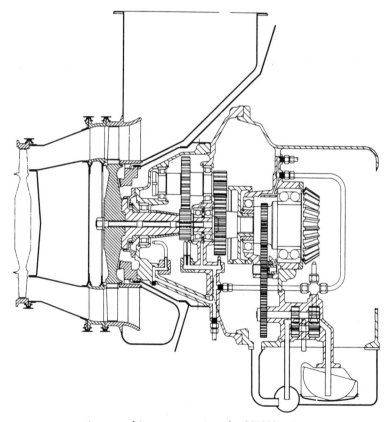

Accessory drive arrangement on the GT-300 unit.

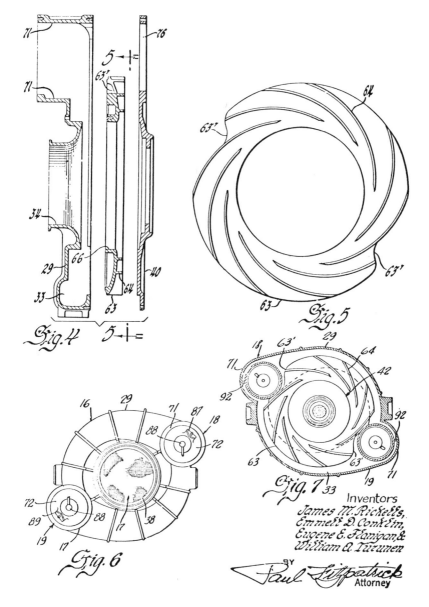

Inventors
James M. Ricketts,
Emmett D. Conklin,
Eugene E. Flanigan &
William A. Turunen

BY
Paul Fitzpatrick
Attorney

Detail of the compressor diffuser design for the GT-300 unit.

325

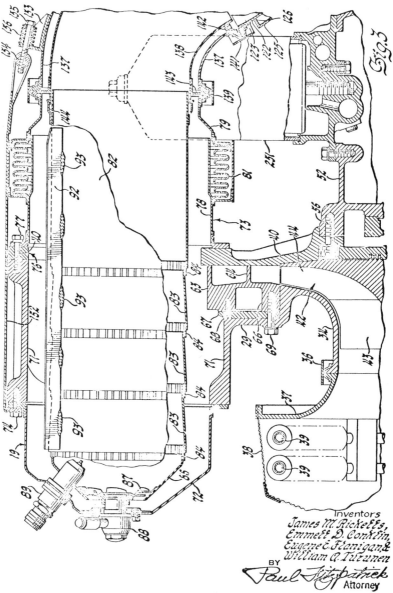

Fig.3

Inventors
James M. Ricketts,
Emmett D. Conklin,
Eugene C. Flanigan,&
William Q. Tilzmen

BY

Paul Fitzpatrick
Attorney

Details of the combustor for the GT-300 unit.

326

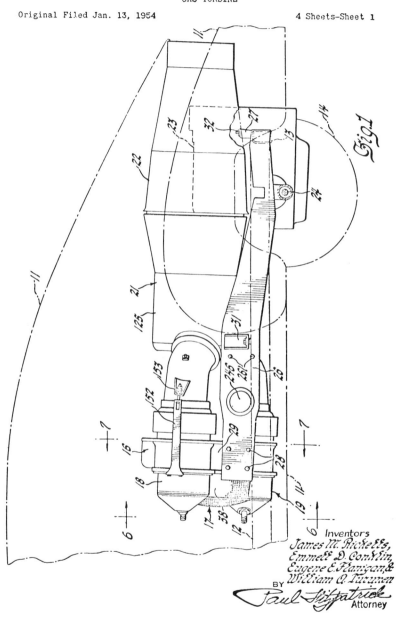

Fig.1

Inventors
James M. Ricketts,
Emmett D. Conklin,
Eugene E. Flanigan,&
William A. Turunen
BY
Paul Fitzpatrick
Attorney

Side view of proposed GT-300 installation in a car.

327

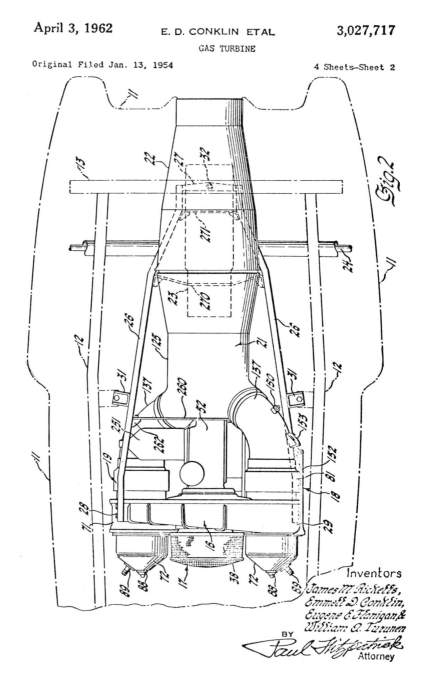

Fig.2

Inventors
James M. Ricketts,
Emmett D. Conklin,
Eugene E. Hanigan,&
William O. Turunen
BY
Paul Fitzpatrick
Attorney

Plan view of proposed GT-300 installation in a car.

GM's first gas turbine powered vehicle—TurboCruiser I.

shaft. Solid jet lubrication of the gasifier shaft bearings and high-speed gears was provided. The oil returned to the sump by gravity.

The power turbine shaft had a splined outer end, carrying the lead pinion in the two-stage reduction gear. Three jackshafts, equally spaced around the power turbine shaft, carried the first-stage gears and second-stage pinions.

The transmission was adapted from the GMC bus transmission. The torque converter was eliminated, since the power turbine itself acted as a torque converter.

In keeping with the heavy-duty theme the design had adhered to, Turunen picked a GMC city bus for the first gas turbine installation. He arrived at this choice through simple logic, based on the facts that the turbine engine must be accommodated inside an existing engine compartment, and the vehicle must offer ample space for installation of special test instruments. Moreover, he wanted a type of vehicle that could be ballasted to represent a wide variety of service conditions.

Outwardly, Turbo-Cruiser I looked almost indistinguishable from the regular bus coming down Woodward Avenue in Detroit. But in the tail, linked to the standard V-drive of the GMC bus, was the GT-300. The silencer and the two engine sections complete with accessories were mounted in a unit cradle. This cradle was matched to an installation frame in the bus chassis, with high-frequency vibration isolators between the frame and the cradle to prevent engine noise from being transferred to the coach body. The Turbo-Cruiser I discharged its exhaust vertically at rooftop level. The bus was used as a rolling laboratory for two years, and racked up a total of 9000 miles, mostly on public highways.

GT 302 and the Firebird I

Before the GT-300 turbine engine could be installed in a car, a new turbine was on the drawing board. This was to be a smaller unit, GT-302, intended for installation in an experimental car, the XP-21 Firebird.

The overall arrangement of the turbine, its installation and transmission, were based on a patent by Emmett D. Conklin, James M. Ricketts, Eugene E. Flanigan and William A. Turunen. The engine was to be placed amidships in the chassis, with drive to the rear wheels. This meant that the same basic engine configuration as the GT-300 could be adhered to. However, the space requirement of the single combustor was not suitable for the low profile of the car, and the GT-302 incorporated a dual combustor arrangement.

The two combustors were located one on each side of the shaft, extending radially in a horizontal plane, with the primary zone in a dome at the outer end. They were kept as close to the shaft center line as possible in an effort to minimize overall package size.

In most other respects, the GT-302 closely resembled the GT-300. The GT-302 was also a simple-cycle turbine without heat exchangers, and the design did not include any provision for engine braking. Turunen pointed out, however, that in special cases, it was possible to obtain engine braking. The driver could shift to reverse when descending a steep hill, which would

Firebird I with canopy open.

GT-300 installed in Firebird I.

reverse the rotation of the power turbine. Braking effect would then be regulated by the accelerator pedal.

The gasifier and output sections were independently mounted on a light box-section frame, with the compressor housing itself functioning as a major load-carrying cross-member. The car was a single-seater with the engine compartment immediately behind the seat.

There are two main reasons why this chassis configuration is advantageous for a sports car: 1. weight distribution, and 2. traction. During acceleration and braking, the center of gravity is not displaced very far from its static position. It is displaced backward under acceleration, which gives improved traction. It is displaced forward under braking. The front wheels do about 2/3 of the braking, and in extreme cases, more. With the midships engine, the center of gravity tends to remain farther back than in any front-engine car. With the engine right next to the transaxle, the drive line is shorter. That means a reduction in power losses through friction in universal joints, splines and other couplings.

More power gets to the rear wheels. With the engine removed from the nose of the chassis, there is less weight on the front wheels. This means that the need for power steering is eliminated. Midships engine location also makes for better weight distribution. It is possible to get the same front/rear weight distribution with a rear-engined car, but there's more to this picture than just front/rear balance. When the engine is overhanging the rear wheels, its mass is farther away from the car's center of gravity. This is important, for it determines the car's polar moment of inertia, which is an indication of its maneuverability and directional stability. The midships engine installation lowers the polar moment of inertia, which tends to give the vehicle faster steering response.

The GT-302 delivered about 400 shaft horsepower. The idle speed of the gasifier shaft was about 8,000 rpm and its maximum speed 26,000 rpm. The GT-302 power turbine wheel was identical with the one used on the GT-300, but all other components in the output section were entirely new.

The power turbine shaft ran on two bearings mounted in a flanged cylindrical housing, and the turbine wheel and bearing assembly was removable as a unit. All the hot-running parts were enclosed in aluminum radiation shielding in the same manner as the GT-300.

Turunen gave a great deal of consideration to the question of gyroscopic effects. He anticipated that the revolving masses in the turbine, and their high rotational speeds, might lead to gyroscopic reactions in the entire vehicle. The designers took steps to minimize this effect by arranging for the power turbine to turn in the opposite direction of the gasifier turbine. That assured low gyroscopic moments, even with the gasifier running at maximum speed and the power turbine stalled. Under the most severe conditions, the gyroscopic moment could not exceed 44 pounds-feet, which would have little or no effect on the control of the vehicle.

Due to the special vehicle application, the GT-302 was equipped with an oil-cooling device that had not been part of the GT-300 design. The screened air inlet incorporated an aluminum-finned oil-to-air heat exchanger protruding into the air stream. The compressor discharged air into two ducts, 180° apart, each leading to one of the two combustors.

The compressor housing formed the center section of the combustor outer shell. At the outer end of the combustor was the domed primary zone with the fuel injector nozzle and igniter. At the inner end, separated by a cylindrical expansion joint, was a double-walled elbow duct.

After passing through the turbine stages, the exhaust was discharged horizontally into a semi-circular arcuate duct located above the transmission assembly. The exhaust outlet size was chosen to minimize back pressure and allow a body shape with reduced form drag. The exhaust collector discharged into the exhaust duct with an ejector effect to carry away ventilating air from the radiation shield and engine compartment.

The GT-302 used a starter-generator, which eliminated the starter motor engagement mechanism and, when the engine was running under its own power, provided energy to recharge the batteries. The accessory drive assembly and housing was also redesigned to make it more compact.

The transmission assembly was designed by the GM Engineering Staff and included the reduction gear. It was a two-speed planetary transmission with a hydraulic control unit, but without a torque converter. The sun gear for both low and high planetary gear sets was formed directly on the power turbine shaft extension. Multiple-disc clutches were used for gear engagement of the forward speeds, and reverse was engaged by a cone clutch. The transmission control lever had four positions: Park, High, Performance, and Reverse. "Performance" was the code-name for the low gear. No neutral was provided, and none was needed, due to the nature of the free-shaft turbine.

The final drive unit was enclosed in the special transaxle housing. No differential was provided. The final drive unit included a pair of quick-change transfer gears in the back cover to facilitate modifications in the overall gearing. The transmission had its own external heat exchanger.

The General Motors approach to a turbine car was a real extravaganza. While Chrysler merely installed gas turbine engines in regular production cars, with the implication that production might not be far off, General Motors emphasized the distant-future possibility of turbine-powered production cars by creating a vehicle of a type you might expect to see in a science-fiction magazine but not in real life.

Aside from the expenditure of creating the advanced engineering and futuristic styling for the turbine car, this approach also involved higher demands on time. It took longer for GM to get its turbine on wheels, and since only one prototype was built, the test program was also severely limited in scope.

The Firebird I was not designed for operation on public roads. And the horizontal exhaust discharge was, of course, incompatible with driving on city streets. It was intended strictly for tests and demonstrations on the GM proving grounds and for static display purposes.

The design was due to body engineer Robert F. McLean, working under the direction of Harley J. Earl, vice president in charge of the styling staff. He conceived the shape to make a car that looked like a jet fighter on four wheels. The excessive emphasis on styling robbed the Firebird I of space for installing test instrumentation and prevented project engineers from riding along. As a test bed, its utility was severely limited.

Firebird I was capable of speeds in excess of 200 mph. It had special experimental suspension and brake systems, but even if these worthy innovations needed testing at the same time that the turbine was being built, it is difficult to understand how GM could expect to get any extra benefits by combining them all into the same prototype.

The Firebird I chassis was designed under the direction of Robert Schilling (1898–1969), a German-born engineer with diplomas from the Breslau Technical Institute and the Munich Technical Institute. He came to

America in 1927 and joined Buick as a staff engineer in Flint. About 1930 he changed over to Oldsmobile and moved to Lansing, where he stayed until 1937. He became well known inside the corporation for his work on independent front suspension systems, a new type of tank suspension, and chassis component fatigue studies.

In 1937 he joined the GM Engineering Staff as a member of the products study division. In 1949 he was transferred to the GM Research Laboratories to work on advanced suspension systems. Out of the studies he made in the years that followed came the basis for the Firebird I chassis design.

The Firebird I was built on a 100-inch wheelbase and had an overall length of 222.7 inches. Overall width was 80 inches, and overall height, to the top of the cockpit bubble was 41 inches. The tail fin extended maximum height to 55 inches. With 6.70–16 tires on all four wheels, the car had a front track of 50 inches and a rear track of 54 inches.

The car was to be used only on smooth runways, so the suspension system was not developed for either ride comfort or handling. The chassis was designed for maximum straight-line stability, not for cornering ability. Steering response was of little concern beyond normal ease of control.

Still, the suspension systems were fairly sophisticated. The independent front wheel suspension used upper and lower A-arms, with ball-joints instead of kingpins, and the lower control arms were linked to torsion bar springs. At the rear end, there was a de Dion axle with longitudinal single-leaf springs.

The lower A-arm was horizontal at normal standing height, with the shorter upper arm inclined so as to provide camber changes of about ½-degree per inch of wheel deflection. This geometry was designed to give faster steering response than was common on GM production cars. The front roll center was 1.9 inches above ground level.

The diagonal torsion bars were inserted into sockets in the lower control arms, and anchored to the frame at their rear ends. A stabilizer bar was linked to the lower control arms via a strut, with its middle section held loosely in brackets on the frame. The de Dion tube connected the rear wheel hubs and kept the wheels permanently at 0° camber angle. This type of suspension gives a high roll center—about the same as is obtained with a beam axle. Rear suspension roll center on Firebird I was located 15.2 inches above ground level.

The driving torque and thrust were taken up by the transaxle casing (from the de Dion tube) so that the leaf springs were fully free of driving duties. The steering gear was located ahead of the front wheel axis. It was moderately geared with an overall ratio of 20, using a recirculating ball type of gear, with a parallelogram linkage.

Due to the Firebird I's high-speed capability and the turbine's lack of engine braking, Schilling placed considerable emphasis on equipping the car with adequate brakes. The brake system included 11-inch drums on all four wheels, with two-leading shoe designs, for maximum self-energizing effect. The drums were finned aluminum castings for high heat rejection.

The brake pedal operated two separate master cylinders—one for the front brakes and another for the rear brakes. No parking brake device was provided but a parking pawl was included in the transmission and actuated by the shift lever. The wheel and brake drum design had originated on GM-built military vehicles. The concept was based on the need for a truly waterproof brake unit. It was adapted for the turbine car because it resulted in excellent air flow over the brake drums and therefore in high heat dissipation. The brakes were not made waterproof, but were ventilated through screened openings in the wheel disc. The six-spoked wheels were aluminum forgings.

In addition, the tail end of the body included an aerodynamic brake system. The brake elements were small wing-like flaps. The brake flaps were supported from the rear cross-member so as to avoid transmitting the aerodynamic braking forces into the body structure. The upper and lower hinge shafts each carried two stub arms, and the flap surfaces were bolted to the stub arms.

The flaps were forced to swing in opposite directions by the gear sectors which coupled them to each other. Extensions of the lower hinges were connected by a short universal-jointed shaft to assure uniform positioning. They were turned by a pair of electric screw-jack actuators. They could open the flaps against the full air drag in three seconds. Operation of the brake flaps was controlled by switches on the steering wheel.

A crude frame of welded box-section members was used. However, the simple structure was light and had high torsional stiffness. At the front end, the frame came to a point, to fit inside the body contour. The side rails were farthest apart at the rear, with a long kickup in the center, so that they blended into the horizontal stub wing surfaces between the body and the rear wheels. Six cross members were used (not counting the compressor housing) with the last one placed behind the rear wheels. It extended beyond the side rails to carry the hinges and operating elements for the split-flap air brakes. The body itself was made of fiberglass-reinforced plastic.

All exterior trim was of anodized aluminum alloy, and all body hardware was of aircraft-type design. A glass-cloth reinforced plastic fuel tank was positioned inside the tapered nose section. It had two venting and overflow lines to assure proper venting even during extreme acceleration and braking.

A single headlamp was carried in the nose section, swinging out like a landing gear nose wheel when in use, and retracting into the body when turned off. The pedals were placed almost on the front wheel axis, with the driver's cockpit extending to a midway point in the wheelbase. The pedals were formed as treadles (similar to those used on buses) with built-in heels. The pedal shaft assembly was made adjustable in the fore-and-aft plane. This was the best way to provide seating adjustments, for the seat and headrest were integral with the cockpit structure.

Cockpit instrumentation was extensive, though some of the items were chosen more for aviation-imagery than for their usefulness in a car, such as an air speed indicator, and a direction-indicator compass. The relevant instruments included two tachometers (gasifier shaft and power turbine shaft), a fuel pressure indicator and fuel injection nozzle pressure indicator, separate oil pressure gauges for engine and transmission, an exhaust temperature gauge, a turbine nozzle chamber temperature gauge, temperature gauges for both engine and transmission oil, a fuel tank gauge, and a brake flap position indicator. The dry weight of the vehicle was only 2440 pounds.

The Firebird I was built in the fall of 1953. Everybody who had been associated with the project turned out to watch its first track test-run on the GM Proving Grounds at Milford, Michigan. The date was October 11, 1953. One of the first to drive it was Charles L. McCuen, in honor of his key role in getting the turbine car program started.

He was running on the high-speed track when he lost control. The car shot over the top of the banking and landed under a fence in the surrounding grassy field. The car was badly damaged, and McCuen suffered serious head injuries. He recovered after a brief period of hospitalization, and resumed his duties, retiring at the age of 66 in 1956.

McCuen came from Stockton, California and studied at the Polytechnic College of Engineering at Oakland. After graduation, he took a special engineering course at the University of California in Berkeley. His first job was as vice president of the Cole California Motor Company, a minor automobile manufacturer whose total output has been estimated at about 50 cars. Next, he worked as a structural engineer at the Panama-Pacific Exposition in 1915. That year he moved to Detroit and joined Packard's engineering staff, but he did not design cars. Instead he was assigned to Packard chairman Henry B. Joy's Isko Ice Machine Co. where he became vice president in 1919, but three years later returned to the automobile industry as experimental engineer for the Rickenbacker Motor Car Co. in Detroit. In 1926 he joined Oldsmobile as an engine designer, and soon began to rise through the ranks.

He served as chief engineer of Oldsmobile from 1929 to 1933, when he was promoted to General Manager of Oldsmobile, an office he held for seven years. In 1940 he became GM vice president in charge of the engineering staff, and in 1947 assumed his post as General Manager of the GM Research Laboratories.

After McCuen's accident, the Firebird I was driven only by one man—

Mauri Rose at speed in the Firebird I.

Mauri Rose, an active racing driver and three-time winner of the Indianapolis 500-miles race.

The Firebird I had very high fuel consumption—about 4 to 5 miles per gallon—but this was expected with the simple cycle type of turbine. What was not expected was a sluggish response to the accelerator pedal below 18,000 gasifier shaft rpm. These were the two major drawbacks in the operation of the GT-302, and two of the key objectives set for the next turbine design, the GT-304, were to obtain substantial improvements in these two areas.

THE GT-304 AND THE FIREBIRD II

Turunen and Collman agreed that the only way to obtain fuel economy more or less in keeping with piston-powered production cars from a gas turbine vehicle was to abandon the simple cycle concept and adopt heat exchangers. Several ways of reducing the acceleration lag were discussed, and the method selected for this purpose was to remove a major part of the accessory drive load from the gasifier shaft and connect a number of accessories to the transmission. Other goals for the GT-304 turbine program were increased durability of components, and a reduction in the amounts of exotic materials needed.

Earlier models of the GM Whirlfire turbine engines operated at 1500° F (815° C) turbine inlet temperature with blades made of GMR-235, an alloy developed by the metallurgy department of the research staff. Experience with these and other test engines indicated that higher turbine inlet temperatures could be used. On this basis, a design-point turbine inlet temperature

Harley Earl with the Firebird II.

of 1650° F (900° C) was chosen for the GT-304 engine. The key components for the GT-304 were developed in several concentrated component-improvement programs. The aim was to raise the efficiency of the individual components, and major test setups were made for the compressor, combustion system, and regenerators.

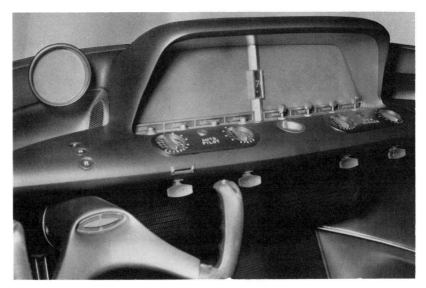

Instrument panel and controls of the Firebird II.

As a result of extensive component testing, the engineers found that a smaller combustor size was preferable for more efficient burning at the design temperatures. This led to a decision to use two small-diameter barrel-type combustors on each side. They were arranged in the same horizontally-opposed pattern used for the large combustors of the GT-302.

Fuel was sprayed into the chambers through nozzles located in the outer ends. The heated gas leaving the combustors was diverted into the turbine inlet annulus by symmetrical transition sections. The hot gas expanded through two mechanically independent turbine stages located in the center of the engine. The combustors were installed on the forward side of the bulkhead, in the space between the regenerator drums.

Different types of compressor and diffuser designs were tested and evaluated, so that the design selected for the GT-304 would be the one that gave the correct air flow characteristics for the turbine requirements.

The engine was made up of three major sub-assemblies: the gasifier section, the output section, and the accessory section. The gasifier section comprised the first-stage turbine, the compressor wheel, the compressor discharge duct, a bearing housing, and the bulkhead and seal assembly. The back cover for the compressor was integral with the bearing housing. Air entered the centrifugal compressor from the front and was delivered to a large-diameter diffuser. After passing through the diffuser, it was diverted 90° and discharged axially into a plenum chamber housing the regenerators, combustion chambers and turbines.

The compressor discharge duct served as a structural component in the engine assembly, linking the compressor housing to the bulkhead and seal assembly. The bulkhead and seal assembly separated the high-pressure section of the air plenum from the low-pressure section.

The plenum enclosure was defined by the side covers, which also served as structural components, tying the compressor housing, bulkhead assembly, and exhaust ducts together. The side panels were covered by aluminum radiation shields.

Besides the power turbine and its shaft, the output section included the exhaust ducts and the reduction gear. The output section was assembled as a separate unit, and then attached to the gasifier and accessory sections by securing the exhaust ducts to the seal bars on the bulkhead.

The first-stage turbine nozzle assembly was attached to the forward side of the bulkhead. It was also piloted on the turbine end of the bearing housing so that differential thermal expansion could be accommodated in the axial plane, with retention of proper radial alignment between the turbine wheel and stator components.

For their first regenerative-cycle turbine design, the GM engineers chose drum-type regenerators. The regenerator drums were supported by a fixed roller shaft located in the exhaust ducting. The drums were gear-driven at the periphery from pinions on a roller shaft on top of the cover. These pinions were driven by a hydraulic motor.

All parts that were exposed to, or contained, the hot gases were confined within the inner diameter of the regenerator drums. The top, bottom, front, and rear surfaces of the engine were exposed to compressor discharge air or exhaust gas cooled by passing through the regenerators. As a result, no thermal shielding or insulation was required for the engine except on the circular regenerator end covers. This reduction of heat loss from the engine minimized engine-compartment ventilation requirements and was undoubtedly reflected in a slight gain in thermal efficiency.

The accessory section included an air inlet duct, the compressor front cover, the oil pump, and drive gear for the basic accessories. These accessories included an automotive type starter motor, fuel pump and governor assembly, a built-in oil supply and scavenge pump, and a hydraulic pump for the regenerator drive motor. The accessory drive was taken from the front (cool) end of the gasifier shaft via spiral bevel gears.

The oil pump assembly was located near the bottom of the housing, inside the oil sump. The pump supplied oil under normal pressure to all essential parts, such as the shaft bearings, reduction gears, and hydraulic pump.

The GT-304 unit weighed 850 pounds. This was uncommonly high, and GM blamed it on the regenerators—each one accounted for 150 pounds. The engine was rated at 200 shaft hp at a gasifier shaft speed of 35,000 rpm. The power turbine was rated for a maximum speed of 28,000 rpm (but had an overspeed allowance up to 35,500 rpm).

The GT-304 was intended for installation in a new experimental car in the Firebird series. However, Firebird II was a very sober creation compared with the first one. The Firebird II was conceived as a prototype study for a possible future high-speed four-passenger luxury car to run for long distances on smooth highways. It was built in 1956 as a practical four-passenger coupe within the size and weight range of GM's 1956-model production cars, with futuristic styling and low-drag aerodynamics.

The passenger compartment was located farther forward relative to the wheels than was common practice on GM production cars of the time. The short distance between the dash and the front wheels was made possible by the use of small tire diameter and the use of a transaxle to drive the rear wheels.

Firebird II was built on a 120-inch wheelbase, with a front track of 60 inches and a rear track of 57 inches, giving a turn diameter of 53.4 feet. Overall length was 235 inches, overall width 70.6 inches, and overall height 52.8 inches. Front overhang was 49 inches, and rear overhang 66 inches.

Minimum road clearance was 5.5 inches. The car had a curb weight of 5300 pounds.

The Firebird II chassis was designed by Joseph B. Bidwell and Robert E. Owen of the GM Research staff. The engine was installed in its conventional place, between the front wheels, and a special driveline with a transaxle (combined transmission and final drive unit) took the power to the rear wheels. Unconventional engineering features included all-independent suspension with pneumatic spring units, disc brakes, and a central hydraulic system. This central hydraulic system provided the necessary power for suspension level control, power brakes, power steering, and windshield wipers.

The pump would go into action whenever the pressure in the system dropped below 850 psi, and by-pass when the pressure reached 1100 psi. The accumulators, one for the front suspension and one for the rear, stored energy to meet peak load demands. The transaxle included provision for driving a number of accessories from the transmission input shaft.

An alternating-current generator was mounted on the left side of the propeller shaft, below and to the left of the rectifier and voltage regulator. On the right side of the propeller shaft was the air conditioning compressor, and directly above it, a hydraulic pump and reservoir for the central hydraulic system.

The reduction gear was a three-stage design with a ratio of 7.27. This was the only gearing at the front end of the drive line. A three-joint propeller shaft transmitted power to the transaxle between the rear wheels. The three-joint propeller shaft was enclosed in a narrow tunnel, which also supported the center joint.

The transmission included a hydraulic coupling of design similar to that of the one used in the standard HydraMatic transmission of that time. Hydraulic slip in this coupling allowed the power turbine to keep running even when the car was at a standstill, so that the accessories were being driven even at idle.

The gearbox was a planetary four-speed unit with electric control. The driver could select one of four drive modes—park, neutral, reverse, and drive—and electric solenoids performed the shifting.

Compared with the Firebird I and Turbo-Cruiser I, the GT-304 produced much lower noise levels. The high noise of the earlier turbines had masked a lot of the gear noise from the reduction gearing. On the GT-304 this gear noise became obvious because the turbine was so much quieter.

The incoming air for the engine flowed through an acoustic silencer mounted on the front side of the engine as an integral part of the body. Engine oil coolers were mounted on the front cross member and cooled by fan-induced air flow. The fans discharged backwards to ventilate the entire engine compartment. Heater and air-conditioning components were mounted on the bulkhead above and behind the engine. The ignition system elements were carried on diagonal frame members. Fuel pump and governor were carried on an extension from the front cover, just above the fan outlets.

The exhaust system was a dual-range design with four tailpipes. Two of the exhaust ducts ran through chassis sill members to vents located just behind the passenger compartment. These were idle speed vents. The main exhaust ducts ran straight back from the engine. They were closed by hydraulically operated shutters when the engine was idling, and opened when the accelerator pedal was depressed. This system was found to be very effective in terms of reducing back pressure thus giving improved performance and fuel economy. The Firebird II had an average fuel mileage of 8–10 miles per gallon, which represents an improvement of more than 100 percent over the Firebird I in view of the far greater weight of the Firebird II.

Fuel tanks were mounted outside of the body proper and positioned under the rear fenders. Batteries, blowers and rectifiers were placed behind the back seat. An air-conditioning system developed by Harrison Radiator Division was used. The axial piston-type compressor was driven from the transmission. An aluminum condenser, cooled by a blower, was used. Both condenser and compressor were placed in the trunk area. The aluminum evaporator core was placed under the dash, near the fresh-air intakes. Heating of the passenger compartment was taken care of by using an oil-to-air heat exchanger.

To provide adequate structural rigidity in the body to support the large transparent canopy roof, it was decided to go to unit body construction. A cage-like primary structure provided a basis for the body panels, which were bonded in place. Two cars were built—one with titanium skin and the other with fiberglass-reinforced plastic body panels.

The flat floor was made up of a thin steel bottom plate used as a base for a number of longitudinal steel tubes of square cross section, spaced out at 3 inches from center to center.

The space between the tubes was filled with foamed plastic and the whole assembly covered with a layer of fiberglass-reinforced plastic. The total floor thickness was one inch. The tubes were used as channels for wiring, fuel lines and hydraulic lines.

The Firebird II had a slight forward bias in weight distribution, with 51 percent of the weight carried by the front wheels. Front and rear static deflection rates were similar to the GM production cars of the time, and calculated to provide satisfactory ride comfort within the limits of the suspension movement allowed. This movement was restricted to 2.75 inches, while about 4 inches was normal in production cars.

The roll stiffness was considerably greater than in GM production cars, while the car had a low center of gravity, so that body roll during cornering was kept to low angles. Front and rear suspension geometry were selected to provide anti-dive effect under hard braking and anti-squat action during acceleration.

The pneumatic spring system was developed by Delco Products. A spring unit was formed as a compressed air cylinder, taking the place of the conventional coil spring. The central hydraulic system eliminated the need for an air pump, as the required power for suspension control was furnished by the hydraulic system. The spring units worked on a simple principle: Each unit contained a fixed air mass which functioned as the springing medium.

The pressure on the air inside the spring unit was transmitted through the oil to the top of a piston which supported the load. The oil passed through internal shock valving to move from the cylinder to the surrounding space. The shock valves effectively prevented aeration in the fluid. Thus, the oil contained in the unit was under pressure. Oil pressure was held to 750 psi for a load of four occupants.

A separate leveling valve which sensed wheel deflections would permit oil to enter or leave the spring unit as required. Leveling action was prevented at speeds above 10 mph to avoid reactions to transient load variations. To accomplish this, the springs were locked out by transmission governor oil pressure, closing off a cutout in the leveling valves.

The front suspension used a parallel A-frame control arm system, with geometry calculated to place the roll center at ground level. The rear suspension system had a roll center height of 11.3 inches. The rear suspension used a swing axle system, with open drive shafts to the wheels.

Each drive shaft had two universal joints—one at the wheel hub and the other at the differential. The inner (differential) joints were of the ball and trunnion type, because of the large changes in angularity, while the outer joints were simple cardan joints.

The wheel hub was supported on box-section diagonal trailing arms, anchored to the frame. Two rear arms crossed each other behind the transaxle. The steering gear for the Firebird II was a ball-nut gear with hydraulic power assist, designed and developed by Saginaw Steering Gear Division.

A moderately quick steering gear ratio of 18 : 1 was used. The steering shaft was articulated, with two universal joints, to obtain the desired steering wheel angle. The disc brake system had metallic linings and ventilated discs. Two wheel cylinders per brake assembly actuated a separate set of metallic pads, clamping them to the rotating disc. The wheels were designed to provide ample cooling air circulation around the discs.

They were magnesium castings with chromium plating. The wheel spokes and the rim acted as a blower for cooling the brake disc. The wheel size was determined by the space required for the brake units. That meant using 16-inch rims. Special low-profile tires were used (8.20–16) with an overall diameter of 27.3 inches.

Turbo-Titan I during a test run.

Later in 1956, a GT-304 unit was installed in a tandem-axle Chevrolet truck called the Turbo-Titan, and matched up with a slightly modified production-model automatic transmission. The Turbo-Titan was driven extensively on public roads as well as on the proving ground test tracks, and was reported as having exceptional hill-climbing ability in comparison with the same type of truck powered by a piston engine of the same 200 hp rating. Due to high fuel consumption and reliability problems, it was decided not to plan turbine truck production until a new gas turbine engine had been developed.

THE GT-305 AND ITS APPLICATIONS

While the GT-304 and the Firebird II were being evaluated, the GT-305 was already on the drawing board. Turunen and Collman remained in overall charge of the turbine program, but two new designers were mainly responsible for the GT-305: Paul T. Vickers and Charles A. Amann.

Paul Vickers had joined GM in 1941 as a GM co-operative student sponsored by Delco-Remy Division in Anderson, Indiana, where he was born on September 27, 1923. When he was discharged from the US Army, he returned to GM in December, 1945, and was placed in the Research Laboratories, where he began to specialize in heat transfer and thermodynamics as applied to gas turbine heat exchangers, automotive cooling systems, brakes, and various other systems. An active inventor, he holds a number of patents.

Charles Amann was the younger of the two—born in Thief River Falls, Minnesota, on April 21, 1926. After getting his master's degree in mechani-

GT-305 gas turbine engine.

cal engineering from the University of Minnesota in 1948, he joined GM as a research engineer and has had growing responsibilities in gas turbines, steam engines, ground-effect machines, diesel engines and free-piston engines. Like Vickers, he is an inventor, and took out his first patent in 1958 (Braking and Reverse Turbine for Gas Turbine Engine). Now he has amassed over a dozen patents.

The goals for the GT-305 turbine design were to achieve a power-to-weight ratio of more than .33 hp per pound, a thermal efficiency approaching that of GM's production-type piston engines, and a cut in nickel or other critical materials to less than 10 pounds per engine.

The entire engine weighed 590 pounds, and it was rated at 225 hp, which gives a power-to-weight ratio of .38 hp per pound—exceeding the objective. The complete engine package was 37 inches long, including accessories, 24 inches high, and 31 inches wide (to the tops of the combustor domes). The GT-305 was designed for a turbine inlet temperature of 1650° F (900° C). The first-stage turbine had a maximum speed of 33,000 rpm. The second-stage turbine developed full power at 24,000 rpm which was reduced to 3500 rpm at the output shaft. A speed-limiting governor was set to allow the output an overspeed margin up to 4500 rpm, taking advantage of the turbine engine's torque characteristics.

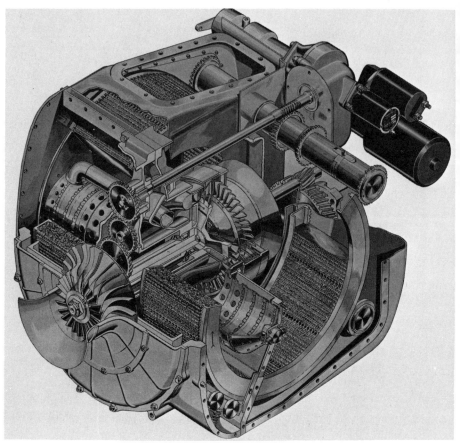

Cutaway view of the GT-305 unit.

Exhaust temperature at full power was 520° F (271° C) and at idle it fell to 275° F (135° C). GT-305 specific fuel consumption was .59 pounds per hp-hour with the original A-type regenerators, and was brought down to .55 pounds per hp-hour with the newer B-type regenerators. The compressor inlet drew air from an absorption-type silencer built into the chassis and worked with 78 percent efficiency at a pressure ratio of 3.5

The GT-305 used a centrifugal compressor with a one-piece compressor wheel which was machined from a solid forging. The diffuser was also machined from a solid plate, to facilitate matching of compressor performance in the light of evaluation of changes in other components. These are experimental-part manufacturing methods, that could never be accepted for

Feb. 12, 1963   J. S. COLLMAN ET AL   3,077,074

REGENERATIVE GAS TURBINE

Filed Sept. 10, 1958   11 Sheets—Sheet 2

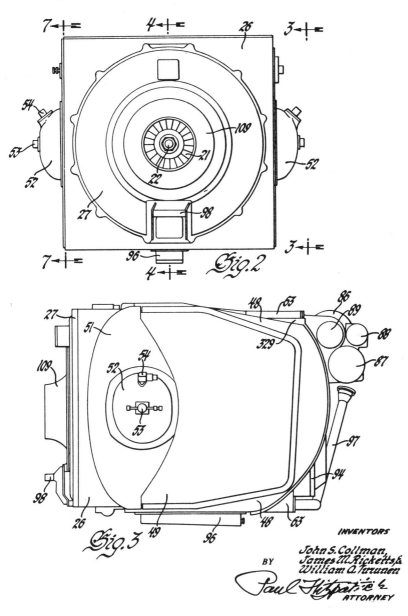

Fig.2

Fig.3

INVENTORS

John S. Collman,
James M. Ricketts &
William A. Turunen

BY

Paul Fitzpatrick
ATTORNEY

Housing design for the GT-305 unit.

347

Main housing structure for the GT-305 unit.

production. GM intended to go to precision casting techniques as soon as the basic development stage had been passed.

The compressor discharged into the high-pressure plenum chamber through an annular passage which was completely surrounded by the dif-

Compressor and diffuser for the GT-305 unit.

fuser. For the GT-305, GM reverted to two large combustors. The two barrel-type combustors were contained horizontally opposed to each other in the open spaces inside the regenerator drums—in the high-pressure section ahead of the bulkhead. The combustors were geared to turn at about 30 rpm maximum.

The air-atomizing fuel nozzle was mounted in the center of the dome, while the igniter plug was inserted at an angle, a little bit below, but still in the domed area. Air for the air-atomizing fuel nozzles was supplied (during starting only) by an electrically driven positive-displacement pump. Primary combustion air was admitted through rows of small holes in the lower dome and on the first two side bands. Secondary air entered through two rows of large holes near the midway point of the combustor barrel. Corrugated bands inserted between the side bands provided a flow of cooling air for the inner liner.

An elbow in the top of the combustor was made to fit a cross-firing tube which connected the two sides of the combustor system. The semi-circular outlet of the transition section discharged the expanding gases directly into the first-stage turbine nozzle vanes.

Operation on No. 2 diesel fuel gave a more luminescent flame than JP-4 or kerosene. Radiation to the dome caused higher metal temperatures, which resulted in buckling of the metal. This was overcome by use of a dome redesigned to provide better skin cooling.

The design of the combustion system provided a very low pressure drop—only 1.75 percent of the component pressure at full load. Measured combustion efficiency was 99 percent.

The basic strength of the GT-305 housing lay in the main members of the cool portion. The cast aluminum front cover served as part of the compressor housing. A conical turbine shaft housing was cantilevered from the stiffened face of the front cover. The first-stage turbine was supported entirely from this turbine shaft housing and was independent of the bulkhead and other housing sections. The bulkhead structure extended into box-section beams on both sides, upper and lower.

A high pressure plenum chamber was formed ahead of the central bulkhead, extending from top to bottom. Behind the bulkhead, the turbine housing formed the outer shell of a low-pressure plenum chamber. The power turbine casing was another aluminum casting, with a shaft housing for the turbine shaft, cantilevered from the end cover.

The power turbine blades were designed for low axial velocity at the trailing edge to minimize exit losses. The alternative would have been to add a diffuser, which would have added to the engine weight and the package size.

The turbine wheels used separate blades fastened to the wheel by the fir-

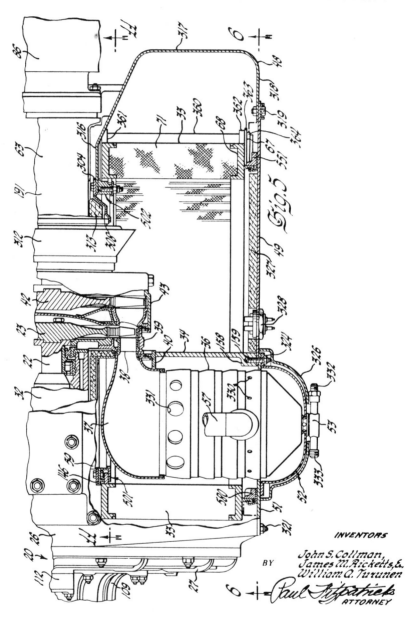

Fig. 5.

INVENTORS

John S. Collman,
BY   James M. Ricketts, &
      William Q. Turunen

Paul Fitzpatrick
                        ATTORNEY

Combustor design and turbine assembly in the GT-305.

350

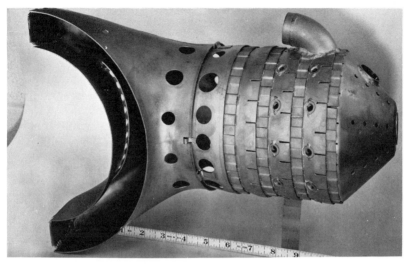

Barrel-type combustor for the GT-305 unit.

First-stage turbine and front cover of the GT-305 unit.

351

tree method. The blades themselves were investment castings. An innovation in blade design for the GT-305 was the root extension between the root and the platform. This small stalk functioned as a heat sink, minimizing heat transfer from the airfoil section to the root. The hub was cooled by a small amount of compressor air.

The blades were made of GMR-235 D alloy, and the turbine wheel discs were fabricated of a hard steel alloy containing 16 percent chrome, 15 percent nickel, and 6 percent molybdenum.

The nozzle vane assembly consisted of four separate castings. Inner and outer shroud bands were cast integrally with the vane sections. Earlier GM turbines had used individually cast vanes welded into machined inner and outer rings. In addition to offering simpler fabrication and lower costs, the casting techniques provided uniform nozzle throat area—which is essential for proper engine operation.

During field testing, GM experienced a number of fatigue failures in the turbine blade roots. Typically, the fir-tree design would crack at the top serration. Analysis of the failures after laboratory testing indicated that they were caused by a resonant vibratory condition at high rotational speeds. Since changing blades in a gas turbine is almost tantamount to a full engine overhaul, the problem was attacked on four fronts:

1. Turbine blade material was changed to Inconel 713.
2. The number of nozzle vanes was reduced, so as to reduce aerodynamic excitation.
3. The turbine wheel hubs were fitted with a thin damping ring.
4. Gas temperatures at the blade root level were lowered by combustor redesign to provide more uniform gas temperature distribution.

Naturally, the turbine experts also realized that it would be necessary to discontinue the use of fir-tree turbine blade roots and explore ways to fabricate one-piece turbine wheels.

Two drum-type regenerators were arranged on either side of the turbine shaft, just behind the compressor casing. This type of regenerator has four significant advantages: (1) it provides a straight line engine airflow path (2) it has a short high-pressure seal perimeter (3) it lends itself to compact engine component arrangements (4) it lends itself to the use of highly efficient heat transfer surfaces. The GT-305 regenerator and seal design was evolved over a period of years and incorporated the latest features in both thermodynamic and mechanical performance. The drum and its seals were treated as a unit in considering the effect of the regenerator on the engine cycle.

The heat exchanger drum was built up of several brazed segments mounted between two steel rims. The brazed segments were made up of thin (.002 inch) corrugated stock interspersed with slightly wider longi-

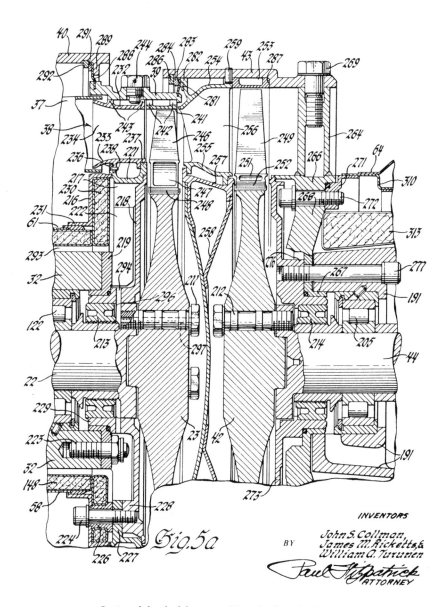

Fig. 5a

INVENTORS

BY   John S. Collman,
James M. Ricketts, &
William O. Turunen

Paul Fitzpatrick
ATTORNEY

Sectioned detail of the two turbine wheels in the GT-305.

353

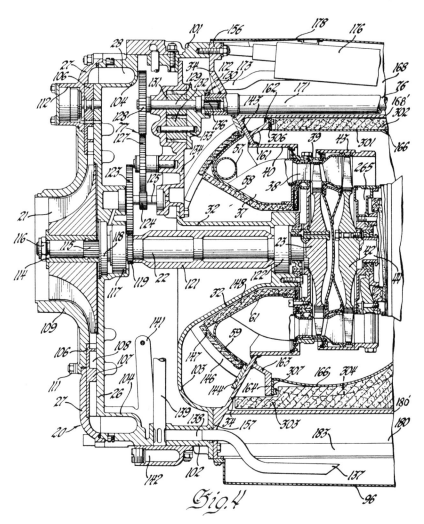

$\mathcal{F}ig.4$

INVENTORS

John S. Collman,
James M. Ricketts, &
William O. Turunen

BY

Paul Fitzpatrick
ATTORNEY

Accessory drive arrangement in the GT-305 unit.

354

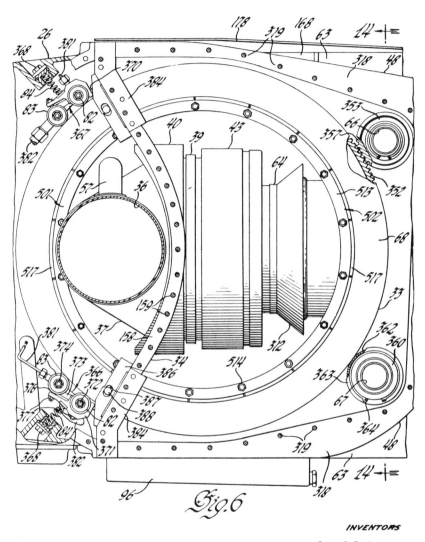

Fig. 6

INVENTORS

John S. Collman,
BY   James M. Ricketts &
William A. Turunen

Paul Fitzpatrick
ATTORNEY

Sectioned view of the GT-305 showing top of combustor, disposition of regenerator, and turbine position.

355

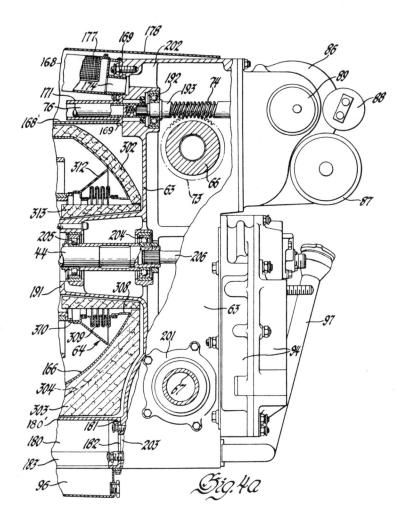

$\mathcal{Fig.}$ 4a

INVENTORS

John S. Collman,
James M. Ricketts, &
William A. Turunen

BY

Paul Fitzpatrick
ATTORNEY

GT-305 regenerator drive system.

356

GT-305 regenerator core.

tudinal strips which cooperated with the primary seals in a labyrinth-like manner. In operation there was a high temperature difference between the inner and outer surfaces of the regenerator. This caused an inward bowing of the drum which had to be accommodated by the primary seals. Stiffening members were spaced out along the periphery to resist the bending effects of the difference in gas pressure at the seals between the high-pressure and low-pressure sections.

Two rollers on each end of the assembly located the seal from the matrix rims to maintain the close clearance required for minimizing leakage. The seals were prevented from moving circumferentially by use of roller trunnions on each end of the seal, which engaged radial slots in the regenerator housing. Some compensation was built into the seal to conform to the changing shape of the matrix as its radial temperature gradient changed. The hot side seal bar expanded when heated, forcing the seal end pieces outward and causing an inward bowing of the cold-side seal bar. Clearance between the seal bars and the labyrinth pack elements was maintained under all operating conditions at only a few thousandths of an inch. Total leakage including matrix carry-over was four percent. Effectiveness at full power was 91 percent and increased slightly as load was reduced.

The exhaust gases raised the core temperature to about 1250° F (675° C) at the inner surface of the drum. The gases gave up so much heat on the way to the outer surface that the surface temperature on the outside periphery was only 400° F (205° C) and the gas had been cooled to about 450° F (232° C). The compressed air entered the regenerator at about 300° F (150° C) and was heated to about 1200° F (650° C) as it passed through the drum. As a result, the inner surface cycled between 1200 and 1300° F, while the outside surface cycled between 350 and 450° F. This meant that the temperature gradient in the circumferential direction was quite small compared with the radial-direction gradient.

The regenerators crossed the bulkhead so that about one-third of the circumference was contained in the high-pressure plenum, and the remaining two thirds in the low pressure section. The regenerator dimensions were selected as a compromise between maximum heat transfer capacity and package size. Each drum was 22 inches in diameter and eight inches wide.

Regenerator support shafts extended from each side cover near top and bottom, borne by roller bearings in the center housing, and carrying rollers to locate the regenerator drums. The regenerator drums were located by rollers on both upper and lower support shafts, so that they were free to rotate about their own axes. The regenerator rims were driven by pinions carried on two generator support shafts, which were turned by a right-angle worm reduction gear.

The main drive reduction gears and the accessory group formed separate sub-assemblies on the end cover. The accessory group included an electric starter motor, fuel pump and governor assembly, a tachometer-generator, and a transmission oil pump.

The accessory drive was taken from the gasifier turbine shaft via a jack-shaft above it, driven by helical reduction gears mounted just behind the compressor. The accessories were mounted at right angles to the shaft for minimum space requirement.

The GT-305 engine was designed for installation in a new experimental car with the code name XP-73. It became better known as the Firebird III. For the body design, GM Styling reverted to the world of science fiction, and the vehicle's engineering specifications had little connection with the actual transportation needs and traffic picture of the time.

Into the Firebird III specification went an exceedingly high number of innovations and experimental systems. Some of the complexity caused by this mass of innovative equipment, in fact, originated in deficiencies in the turbine operation and the refusal of the turbine experts to tackle the problems at the base.

For instance: to free the gasifier shaft from all accessory drive duties, the Firebird III had an on-board auxiliary power unit—just like a modern jet plane. If the engine had been designed with lower inertia in the gasifier section and a different form of accessory drive, the need for an auxiliary power unit to drive the accessories would have been eliminated.

The APU was a two-cylinder 10-hp piston engine running at constant speed. It was connected to a 110-v alternating current generator, a 12-v alternating current generator with rectifier, an air-conditioning compressor, a 3,000-psi hydraulic pump for the suspension system, and a 1,000-psi pump serving all other units requiring hydraulic pressure.

Moreover, if the engine had provided braking on the overrun, there would not have been any need for the special grade retarder. The grade retarder was mounted in back of the final drive unit. It included a series of friction discs, engaged by hydraulic pressure from the transmission, to provide braking torque on the rear wheel drive shafts. On release, the grade retarder was disengaged from the drive line. During actuation, the discs were immersed in oil.

These two systems seem of dubious value except in an application where cost is no object. They cannot be explained as feasiblity studies since there was no unconventional engineering involved with the principles used. The fact that the APU was a high-compression, water-cooled, all-aluminum unit is beside the point.

From the point of view of getting turbine cars into production, these systems were worthless because of their high cost. They could not conceivably form part of a production model, whose detailed specification undergoes the closest nickel-and-dime scrutiny before it is cleared. Since the gas turbine itself involves a cost penalty, it becomes a matter of extra importance to control the cost of the other vehicle systems.

But the Firebird III was not a disciplined experiment with a view towards manufacturing. It was a showcase experiment, intended to astound and to dazzle. Its engineering principles have not found application in GM production cars (while some of the features from the Firebird II— such as the torsion-bar front suspension and the single-leaf rear suspension—have actually been adopted for certain models).

Built in 1958, Firebird III was a two-seater sports car with the engine mounted midships, driving the rear wheels. The engineers responsible for the vehicle and its chassis were Joseph B. Bidwell, Roy S. Cataldo and R. M. Van House. Firebird III was built on a 119-inch wheelbase with a track of 57 inches, front and rear. Overall length was 248.4 inches and overall width (to the tips of the embryonic wings extending from the rear fender panels) was 81 inches.

Height to the top of the canopy was 44.8 inches, and to the top of the ver-

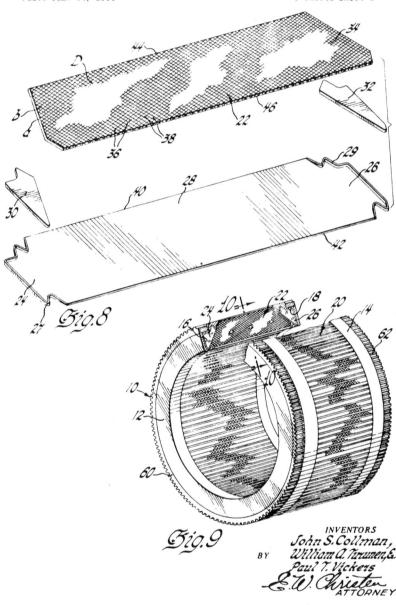

Fig.8

Fig.9

INVENTORS
John S. Collman,
William A. Turunen, &
Paul T. Vickers
BY
E. W. Christen
ATTORNEY

Details of the GT-305 regenerator core structure.

360

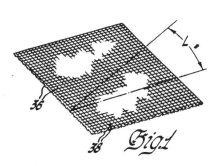

Fig.1

Fig.2

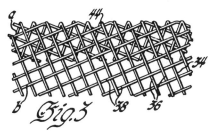

Fig.3

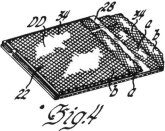

Fig.4

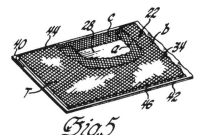

Fig.5

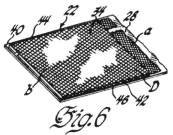

Fig.6

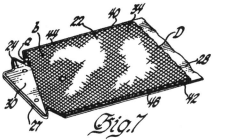

Fig.7

INVENTORS
John S. Collman,
William A. Truman, Jr.
Paul T. Vickers

BY

E. W. Christen
ATTORNEY

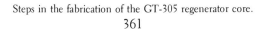

Steps in the fabrication of the GT-305 regenerator core.

361

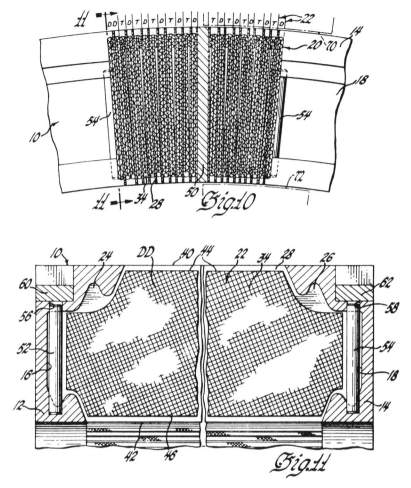

Assembly of the GT-305 regenerator core.

tical tail fin, 57.3 inches. Extremely heavy for its modest dimensions, Firebird III scaled 5275 pounds curb weight, with 46 percent of the load carried by the front wheels and 54 percent by the rear wheels. The rear wheels had larger tires to cope with their extra load-carrying and traction duties—8.50–14 compared with 8.00–14 tires on the front wheels.

The engine was mated to a modified production-type four-speed Hydra-Matic transmission (minus the hydraulic coupling). It was mounted directly to the final drive case of a de Dion type suspension system, forming the Firebird III transaxle. A short open drive shaft with two universal joints was used between each wheel and the final drive unit. A retarder and emergency

Firebird III at the GM Tech. Center in Warren, Michigan.

brake package unit was bolted onto the rear end of this transaxle assembly. Final drive ratio was 3.41, and the unit used a spur gear differential, with the pinion located above and behind the output shaft center.

The transmission was automatically shifted by hydraulic pressure at speeds determined to provide optimum performance with the gas turbine engine.

Ornithologists' nightmare—rear view of the Firebird III.

An interesting feature of the power train mounting arrangement was the provision for an increase in length of about two-tenths of an inch when the engine was hot. The final drive unit was rigidly attached to the frame cross-member at two points. The third mounting point was at the front of the engine, where the compressor housing was attached to a mounting bracket. This 0.125 inch thick plate was flexible, thereby permitting thermal expansion of the engine in the longitudinal plane. The wings of this plate were attached to the frame.

The steel frame and its support members were welded into one unit. A short center spine section served as the principal structural backbone, providing both bending and torsional stiffness under the passenger compartment floor.

The front frame section included two side rails, a cowl, and integral front wheel housings. At the rear, the spine section blended into an engine cradle with integral air intake duct. Frame weight was kept down to 450 pounds by extensive use of light-gauge steel and deep sections.

The fuel tank, frame and suspension components completely filled the body space on one side of the engine. On the other side, the space was taken up by electronics gear and relay panels. Air for cooling the engine compartment was drawn in through louvers in the bottom panel and exhausted through the right lube oil cooler with the aid of electrically driven fans. One fan ran continuously, and the other was thermostatically controlled to go into action whenever the temperature exceeded a certain level

The suspension system is worth a closer look. As in the Firebird II, automatic leveling was provided to keep the car from "bottoming" when loaded. The system used in the Firebird III went one step further, in that a constant level was maintained regardless of load changes such as caused by diminishing fuel load. Hydraulic power was used not only for suspension control, but also for the power steering and power brakes, and the air brake flaps.

In place of the integral air-oil units of the Firebird II, the Firebird III utilized a new type of air-oil spring with a separately mounted air reservoir and displacement cylinder at each wheel. Each air reservoir employed a trapped volume of air as the spring medium. Spring rates and damping characteristics were arrived at following electronic computer studies of car ride motions.

The air and oil media in each reservoir were separated by a rubber diaphragm. Oil entered the unit through a shock valve which worked as a shock absorber. Each spherical reservoir was approximately 4 inches in diameter. Each displacement cylinder was attached to the frame through a rubber shear mounting for noise isolation. The flat end cap of the piston rod extended to the axle where it bore against a similar spherical seat.

When a wheel hit a bump, the piston rod was raised. Movement of the piston forced more oil from the cylinder through a hydraulic connection to the air reservoir. The oil was forced against the rubber separator which expanded against the springiness of the air space. The air contained in the reservoir reacted to bumps with a variable spring rate, the reaction being weaker for small bumps and stronger for larger ones. To level the car, the quantity of oil in the displacement cylinders was regulated by three height control valves which adjusted the height of the pistons in the cylinders and thus the clearance between frame and wheels.

Front and rear spring units were interconnected in such a way as to eliminate pitching motions. Any vertical force acting on the front of the car was also applied simultaneously to the rear (and vice versa) through the interconnected springs. Two air reservoirs and displacement cylinders are used at each rear wheel. The additional units at the rear are used to stabilize the interconnected system and to permit leveling, which would not otherwise be possible with front and rear units connected together.

Bidwell and his assistants chose a beam-type front axle and a de Dion tube at the rear. This unusual combination had been used in the 1955 C6 Cunningham which ran in the 24-Hours of Le Mans that year. A rigid front axle was selected because it kept the wheel permanently perpendicular to the road surface, and offered a high roll center—18.25 inches above ground level in this case, which was very close to center of gravity height, and in combination with a rear suspension system that gave a roll center height of a full 19 inches, the roll axis came so close to coinciding with the center of gravity that roll stiffness was extremely high. The front axle was located by a system of four control arms pivoted from anchorage points on the frame.

A similar control arm system was used to locate the de Dion tube and take up the driving (and braking) torque and thrust loads. The lower arms were parallel and horizontal to provide zero roll steer effect while the upper arms were splayed at 45° to the car center line.

Front wheel alignment specified 0° camber and a 6°38′ steering axis inclination assured center-point steering. This geometry also assured freedom from road shock in the steering linkage. Tie rods from the idle arms were connected directly to the steering arms, and the power assist cylinder was mounted directly on the front axle. There was no mechanical connection between the steering control and the linkage. The inputs to the power steering cylinder and linkage came entirely through electric wires and hydraulic hoses.

Firebird III had no steering wheel, no accelerator and brake pedals. All control functions were combined into a stick with a specially designed free-form handle on the end. When moved forward, it accelerated the car. When pulled back, the brakes went into action. When moved to the left or right, it steered the car accordingly. In each case the response depended upon the amount of stick travel. What the stick actually did was to provide electrical inputs to three analog computers, which determined proper voltages for electrohydraulic servomechanisms located on the front axle, the fuel pump and nozzles, and the brakes.

In a final attempt to design a drum brake system of adequate capacity and fade resistance, regardless of cost, in the face of overwhelming proof that the solution for production cars lay in disc brakes, Bidwell and his assistants created a unique set of brakes. The most valid portion of the brake system was a built-in anti-locking device.

A sensing element automatically detected premature deceleration in a wheel and reduced line pressure to prevent brake lockup. Wheel and brake drum were combined into a single, integral aluminum alloy casting. A series of 36 cooling air passages were located between the drum and wheel sections. Cooling air entered through 18 main inlets at the hub and was forced through the drum and ejected at the wheel rim. The large number of air passages provided a total effective surface cooling area of over 5 square feet compared to about 1 1/2 square feet for a conventional drum brake.

The brake drums had an inner diameter of 11 inches with a friction-area width of 4 inches. Sintered metal linings were used, with a two-trailing shoe arrangement to eliminate self-energizing action. This non-self-energizing design was selected to avoid the erratic conditions sometimes encountered with self-energized brakes. It provided more uniform, non-pulling action. The lack of self-energization was offset by using large diameter wheel cylinders and high hydraulic line pressure.

Supplementing the brakes and grade retarder were three air brake flaps at the rear of the car. These flaps opened automatically when the grade retarder was in use to direct air through its oil coolers, and also when the brakes were applied above 30 mph.

Starting the GT-305 in the Firebird III was accomplished with one button. Pressing the button would start a whole sequence of events, beginning with the closing of a relay to energize the starting motor, fuel nozzle air pump, ignition, and fuel solenoid. When the gasifier shaft reached self-sustaining speed, the starting relay opened, and the engine accelerated to its normal idle speed. The whole sequence took about 10 seconds.

Instrumentation was far simpler than in the Firebird I. Here, the driver had warning lights only for turbine overtemperature, excessive oil temperature, and insufficient oil pressure. Only one instrument gave information about the engine's functions: a gasifier tachometer.

The engine's electrical system drew power from two 12-V batteries placed behind the engine. The generator carried on the auxiliary power unit supplied recharging current to the batteries. Ignition voltage for starting was provided by a high-voltage condenser-type coil. The starter motor was a

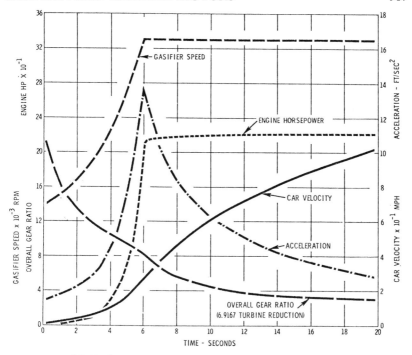

GT-305 horsepower curve and acceleration of the Firebird III.

production-model truck unit. During endurance and fuel-consumption tests, the Firebird III showed a significant advance over the Firebird II, giving averages between 16 and 20 miles per gallon.

In the spring of 1958, Allison Division made a production design study and cost analysis based on the GT-305, and came up with the conclusion that it could be built in production quantities at a price that was no higher than that of an equivalent high-output piston engine. As a result, tooling was released to Allison for the fabrication of a small pilot series of prototype engines. No design changes affecting the operational characteristics were made, but the entire unit was redesigned to facilitate manufacturing. The Allison version of the GT-305 was named GMT-305.

Eleven engines were installed in military vehicles of various types. This program started in December 1959 and the last active engine was installed in July 1960. The first turbine was installed in a light tracked vehicle supplied by the U.S. Army Ordnance Corps. The turbine engine was operated at a reduced rating of 165 hp by placing a speed governor on the compressor shaft. An Allison CD-150 automatic transmission was matched to the turbine output shaft. This was an all-torque shifting transmission with a planetary gear set giving two forward speeds, and a hydraulic torque converter equipped with a lockup clutch.

The vehicle underwent an extensive test program which started at the Cleveland Ordnance Plant of Cadillac Motor Car Division, and was followed by periods at arctic and desert test sites. This vehicle was normally powered by an air-cooled piston engine rated at 162 hp, giving a maximum speed of 28 mph at 3,000 rpm and a wide-open-throttle acceleration capability of reaching top speed from standstill in 16 seconds.

The Allison GMT-305 gave a maximum speed of 33 mph at 3500 output shaft rpm, but was recorded at speeds of up to 40 mph in the arctic test. Zero to 30 mph acceleration was reduced to 15 seconds. In cross-country operation, fuel consumption was higher than for the piston engine, the difference ranging from 4 to 60 percent, according to conditions. However, the turbine engine gave 4–20 percent more miles per gallon at wide-open-throttle.

The second installation was made in a LARC amphibious vehicle made available by the U.S. Army Transportation Corps. The vehicle was basically intended to serve as a lighter, transporting material from ship to shore, with an ability to operate in heavy surf and on sandy beaches. The LARC is normally powered by a 270-hp gasoline-driven piston engine, coupled to a two-speed Borg-Warner automatic transmission with a hydraulic torque converter without a lockup device. The drive train included provision for either four wheel drive or marine propeller drive. The Allison GMT-305 was coupled to the same transmission and drive train. Special ducting was installed to assure air supply during high-surf conditions.

The GMT-305 was rated at 225 hp for this installation running on diesel fuel. The gas turbine gave the same performance as the more powerful piston engine, with fuel economy about 20 percent better. On a test course with dirt tracks and dirt roads cut through forest land, which was partly frozen and partly muddy, the piston-engine powered LARC gave 1.8 mpg. Running at the same speeds, the turbine-powered LARC gave 2.2 mpg.

Climbing a 60 percent gradient was not attempted with the piston engine version, but the turbine-driven LARC negotiated this hill very smoothly, including a restart from standstill on the gradient.

An Allison GMT-305 was also installed in a navy personnel boat furnished by the U.S. Navy Bureau of Ships. It was coupled to reduction and reverse gear systems by Western Gear Corporation (Model N-10S) with standard Morse control for engine and reverse gear. The test program was directed from the base at Annapolis, Maryland and performed in the Chesapeake Bay.

The turbine was more than 1000 pounds lighter than the diesel engine it replaced, which gave the craft higher maximum speed and superior acceleration capability. The regenerative engine used more fuel than the diesel at idle, but the overall fuel consumption was within 2 percent of parity with the diesel even when 10 percent of total operational time was spent idling. The diesel was a 175–200 hp 425 cubic inch Detroit Diesel giving the craft a top speed of 17 knots. The GMT-305 used diesel fuel, delivered 185 hp, and top speed was recorded as 18 knots.

Finally, a Caterpillar DW-15 wheeled tractor was made available by the U.S. Army Corps of Engineers. It was normally powered by a 200-hp diesel engine. The Allison GMT-305 engine was installed in its place and coupled to an Allison CBT-440 all torque shifting 4-speed transmission. The standard transmission was retained, and behind it a two-speed quick-change gearbox was added to give the vehicle a broad range of capabilities, from trailer hauling on the highway to bulldozing and scraper operation. The installation was performed in Indianapolis by Allison, and the test program conducted at Fort Belvoir, Virginia.

The gasifier shaft was restricted to 92 percent of its full speed, which limited power output to about 70 percent of its rated maximum. This was the least successful of the GMT-305 installations.

The overall experience was of great value to the GM Research Laboratories, however, giving much knowledge that would help make the next generation turbine a better automotive engine.

THE GT-309 AND ITS APPLICATIONS

Evaluation and analysis of the entire GT-305 and GMT-305 programs led to a thorough rethinking of the basic design principles. A direct descendant of the GT-305 that was on the drawing board in 1960 was scrapped. GM has never released the specifications for the GT-307. Its replacement, coming five years later, was dramatically different in several ways. The GT-309, first shown in 1965, was a twin-shaft regenerative gas turbine. Instead of the two heat exchangers in the side covers, the GT-309 had a single drum-type regenerator located under the top cover and rotating in the horizontal plane. This can be interpreted as due to influence from Chrysler.

But the GT-309 also introduced a very elegant device that was strictly a GM development—the power transfer system. The power transfer system is discussed in detail at the end of the component description section on turbines. Briefly, it links the gasifier and power turbine shafts by an accessory drive shaft and a multiple-plate slipping clutch. Clutch torque is regulated by a programmer which senses combined clutch and accessory drive torque and gasifier turbine speed. The control system also includes temperature and altitude compensators.

Besides improving part-load fuel economy the power transfer system couples the wheels of the vehicle to the compressor during deceleration, provid-

GT-309 gas turbine engine.

ing two or three times the engine braking power of a comparable piston engine. It also provides engine overspeed protection so it is possible to couple it with either a manual or an automatic transmission. It will hold a rig down to a safe speed going down any hill it can climb. In a further design departure, the GT-309 had a single combustor, standing vertically above the gasifier shaft, and protruding through the regenerator drum center.

This new turbine was built for heavy-duty service in vehicles of all types and sizes, with the emphasis on truck and buses rather than passenger cars. It was powerful enough to haul tractor-trailer gross combined weights from 58,000 to 76,000 pounds.

It was rated at 280 hp at a gasifier shaft speed of 35,700 rpm (with an ambient temperature of 80° F). Maximum power turbine speed was 33,860 rpm. Peak torque reached a value of 875 pounds-feet (at zero output shaft rpm). Package size was impressively compact: 36 inches long x 30 inches wide x 35.5 inches high. The whole unit including accessories weighed 950

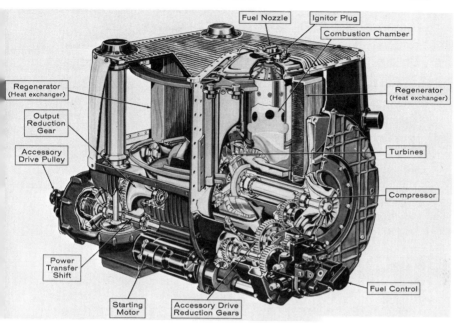

Cutaway view of the GT-309 unit.

pounds, giving a power-to-weight ratio of 0.295 hp per pound. This might seem retrogressive compared with the GT-305, but is only proof of how seriously the designers viewed the stress levels associated with heavy-duty operation. The GT-309 was also intended to be the prototype for a future Allison industrial gas turbine. Specific fuel consumption was a highly creditable 0.45 pounds per hp-hour.

The GT-309 was built up from two major sub-assemblies—the gasifier section and the output section. The gasifier section included the compressor assembly and first-stage turbine, the combustor, the shaft and accessory drive housing, and the central bulkhead. The centrifugal compressor wheel was an aluminum casting with 23 blades. The wheel was shrunk and pinned to a steel hub equipped with spline and pilot provisions for mounting on the shaft. The shroud was designed to run with minimal clearance and finished with an abradable coating to avert catastrophe in case of direct contact with the compressor wheel.

Maximum compressor efficiency exceeded 80 percent, and pressure ratio was 3.9 at full speed with an air flow mass of 4 pounds per second. The GT-309 engine was capable of accelerating the gasifier shaft from a ready-idle speed of 19,300 rpm to a 90-percent level of full speed, or 32,130 rpm in

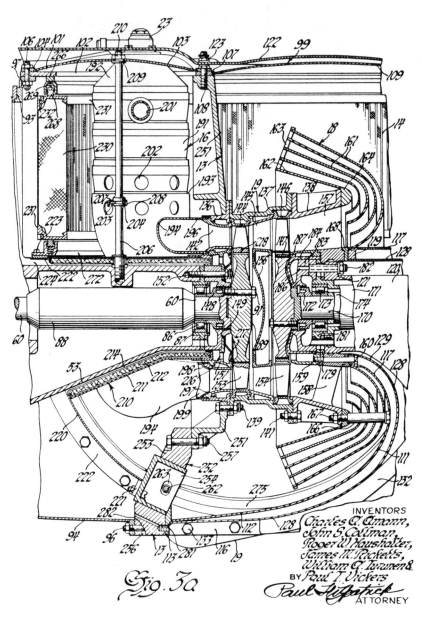

INVENTORS
Charles C. Amann,
John S. Collman,
Roger W. Housholter,
James M. Ricketts,
William C. Turunen &
BY Paul T. Vickers

Paul Fitzpatrick
ATTORNEY

Fig. 3a

Sectioned view of the combustor and turbine arrangement in the GT-309 unit.

372

Compressor and diffuser for the GT-309 unit.

2.7 seconds. The engine control system was set up so as to maintain ready-idle speed as long as the transmission was in gear. Shifting into neutral would automatically lower the speed to its base-idle of 15,000 rpm.

The compressor discharged into a diffuser with 12 passages separated by vanes presenting a wedge-shaped profile to the air flow. The thick end of the vanes was at the outlet, creating a contraction in the passages, and thereby promoting a rise in the air flow velocity. The diffuser blank was an aluminum casting which was finish-machined by tape-milling.

Both turbines were single-stage axial-flow type, made of Inconel 713 C by the investment casting method. The stator nozzles were made of X-40 metal. The first-stage turbine shroud was an extension of the nozzle assembly casting, and several axial slots in the shroud band accommodated differential thermal expansion between the superheated shroud and the center section of the nozzle assembly.

The turbine wheel was attached to the flanged end of the gasifier shaft by three cap-screws, and supported by a roller bearing. At the compressor end, the shaft ran in a ball bearing. The bearings were separated by a spacer sleeve which also helped stiffen the shaft and raise its critical speed above the maximum operating speed. Both bearings were lubricated by oil jets, with the overspray from the ball bearing also serving to lubricate the acces-

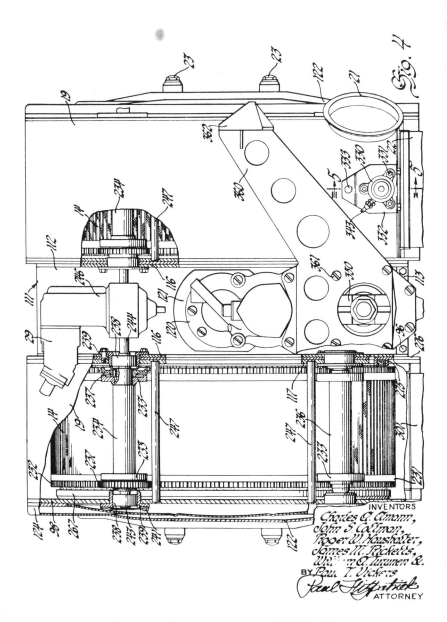

Regenerator drive arrangement in the GT-309 unit.

374

sory drive gears. The accessory drive shaft passed through the front cover and the diffuser, and had a second-stage reduction gear mounted on the front of the compressor discharge duct.

The two turbines, which revolved in opposite directions, were closely spaced axially. The first-stage turbine had a maximum efficiency of 89 percent, with the power turbine having a peak efficiency of 84 percent. The nozzle assembly for the gasifier turbine was completely covered by ceramic insulation. The output section was built up inside a semi-cylindrical cast aluminum housing, with ceramic insulation on its entire inner surface, outside the metallic inner shell. After passing the second-stage turbine, the gas was diverted into a radial path by an annular diffuser, and ducted to the regenerator.

The power turbine shroud ring was supported on the diffuser's outer shell by 8 axial pins engaging corresponding radial slots in the one-piece cast nozzle unit. This design allowed for thermal expansion without affecting the concentricity of the rotating and stator elements. A similar type of construction was used on the nozzle unit.

The regenerator drum received compressed air at about 400° F (205° C) and heated it to about 1100° F (600° C). From the high-pressure plenum chamber, the compressed, heated air is ducted through a receiver into the barrel-type combustor. Fuel was delivered via an air-atomizing nozzle, and the combustor dome contained a single igniter. Maximum turbine inlet temperature was established at 1725° F (940° C). Exhaust discharge temperature did not exceed 500° F (260° C). Vertical support for the regenerator drum was provided by a horizontally mounted roller with bearing surface against the lower rim.

Drum rotation was assured by friction drive against the rim, through one of two vertical shafts at the rear of the housing. These rollers also provided a four-point roller support system for the regenerator. The drum needed no supports at the front end because all the gas pressure forces acted in a rearward direction and held the drum against the rollers as long as the engine was running.

To locate the drum at standstill, a set of spring-loaded rollers went into position and forced the drum against its support rollers. The spring-loaded rollers were activated by a relief in compressor discharge pressure large enough to indicate engine shutdown. The output shaft reduction gear had a ratio of 8.47, which gave a maximum transmission input speed of 4,000 rpm, with maximum power developed at 3550 rpm.

The high-speed pinion on the power turbine shaft was straddle-mounted on roller bearings, and matched with a helical bull gear running on ball bearings. The power transfer system was geared to the bull gear. The lubrication oil pump was mounted on the rear of the power transfer shaft, al-

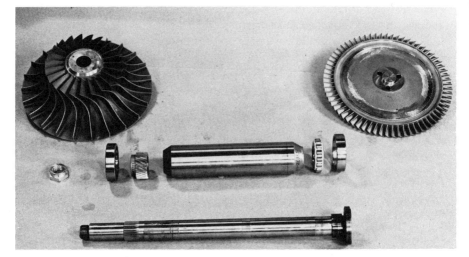

The parts that constitute the gasifier shaft assembly in the GT-309 unit.

Power transfer shaft and clutch (right) used on the GT-309 unit.

though it was driven by the accessory drive shaft, because the engine and transmission shared a common oil sump system.

The GT-309 was installed in a number of commercial vehicle prototypes. The first was Turbo-Cruiser II, a conversion based on a GMC transit coach. The turbine engine was installed longitudinally, in contrast with the standard diesel engine, which was installed transversely. The longitudinal installation enabled the engine to be coupled with a direct transmission instead of the V-drive used with the diesel engine. The transmission was a modified Allison six-speed automatic unit, minus the usual torque converter

Gasifier shaft assembly with jackshaft.

Power transfer clutch disassembled.

TurboCruiser II.

with its hydraulic retarder and oil pumps. The electric batteries were installed on the right side of the engine compartment.

Since the engine was facing to the rear, it was convenient to place the air intake in the left body side of the coach. The exhaust duct included a gas-to-water heat exchanger for supplying the heater core for the conventional heating system. Exhaust gas by-pass controls regulated the amount of heat available for this purpose. The exhaust ducts ended in a louvered vent positioned in place of the rear quarter window on the left side. The Turbo-Cruiser II returned a fuel consumption of between 5 and 6 miles per gallon,

GMC Astro-95 powered by the GT-309 unit.

which compared favorably with the mileage of a diesel-powered GMC bus in similar operation.

Next came a GT-309 installation in a practically standard GMC highway tractor named Astro 95. The gas turbine engine was installed in the front of the tractor, and coupled to an Allison automatic transmission. Chevrolet built a companion model of almost identical specification and called it the Turbo Titan II. These two trucks began test life in 1964, about the same time the Bison went on display at the New York World's Fair.

The Bison was a heavily stylized idea for a future highway truck-tractor combination, designed under the direction of William L. Mitchell. The GT-309 was one of two engines making up the twin-turbine power plant. The other element was a non-regenerative 720-hp unit intended for operation only when its power was needed for acceleration, hill-climbing, or pulling two or more trailers.

The GT-309 alone was to provide the power for all normal highway cruising. Both engines had output shafts connected to a huge electric generator which provided energy to drive electric motors installed in the hubs of all four wheels on the tractor. Both engines were installed in a pod mounted behind the cab. This location was chosen to improve aerodynamic flow between tractor and trailer roofs.

Special engineering features of the Bison included a trailer locking device and a four-option steering arrangement. They provided the stability and safety advantages of a straight bed truck on the highway and also made possible exceptional maneuverability in urban traffic and freight terminals. With

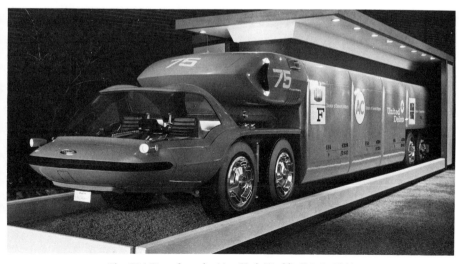

The GM Bison from the New York World's Fair in 1964.

Cockpit of the GM Bison.

an adapter, the Bison could handle present-day semi-trailers, although the trailer concept was tailored for container transport.

The four steering options were (1) single front axle steering for operation as a semi-trailer rig on city streets (2) tandem steering with all four wheels turning parallel and the fifth wheel locked to make the Bison a rigid chassis truck for the highway (3) opposed steering at low speeds, and (4) single rear axle steering for trailer spot-parking in reverse maneuvers.

On July 12, 1965, Chevrolet Motor Division unveiled its own proposal for the "truck of tomorrow." Named Turbo-Titan III, it drove two rear axles via a modified Allison MT-42 transmission, without the usual torque converter, giving six forward speeds. Shifts were manually controlled, with hydraulic activation.

The chassis design was conventional in all respects. The frame was made up of two heat treated channel section side rails with conventional cross members. Front suspension featured a 15,000-lb. capacity I-beam and the rear suspension a 34,000-lb. capacity tandem bogie. The axles were spiral

Turbo Titan III at the GM Proving Grounds near Milford, Michigan.

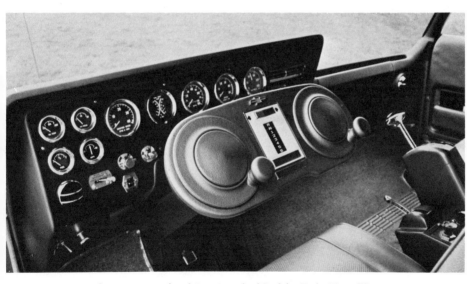

Instrument panel and "steering wheels" of the Turbo-Titan III.

bevel 2-speed units with final drive ratios of 7.17 and 9.77 : 1. Only the 7.17 : 1 ratio was used since it proved the most compatible with the operating speed and power output of the engine.

Rear leaf springs were rated at 17,000 pounds capacity at the ground.

GM Turbo-Cruiser III.

Compressed-air operated brakes were used with self-adjusting units at the rear axles. Super-wide, single 18.00-19.5 tires of 16-ply rating were fitted on the rear wheels while the front tire size was 10.00-20.

The GT-309 was not given to Allison, but to Detroit Diesel Division, as the basis for a future family of industrial gas turbines in the 280-400 hp range. No prerogative was lost to Allison, however, since Allison and Detroit Diesel were merged in September, 1970. Detroit Diesel had been engaged on development of industrial gas turbines since 1964.

In the meantime, the GT-309 had become the power unit for the GMC RTX bus, unveiled in May, 1969. The vehicle was designed by the GMC engineering staff under the direction of chief engineer Harold O. Flynn, in cooperation with the GM Research Laboratories. Flynn was a veteran truck engineer who had started out as a draftsman at Chevrolet in Detroit in 1932, rose through the ranks of the Chevrolet engineering staff, and was named Chief Engineer of GMC in 1961.

The turbine was installed in the tail end of the chassis and drove four rear wheels via a toric transmission providing stepless gear changes. The bus was 40 feet long and designed as a 29-passenger coach (compared with 50 for the standard GMC transit coach of the time). The chassis featured all-independent suspension, oil-cooled disc brakes, and experimental Firestone tires with cantilevered sidewalls. It was intended to cruise at 70 mph with airplane comfort, using an air-oil suspension system derived from the Firebird experiments. At speeds of 65 mph and up, the RTX gave better fuel economy than the diesel-powered GMC transit coach.

General Motors RTX (Rapid Transit Experimental) bus.

The Allison GT-404 Gas Turbine

While the passenger car turbine development program was dormant, GM had ambitious plans for getting into production with a turbine truck. In December 1970, Detroit Diesel Allison Division announced the transfer of the industrial gas turbine activity to Indianapolis.

The Allison engineers were told to design and prepare pilot production of a basic engine suitable for multi-purpose installation, including motor trucks. General Motors president, Edward N. Cole, had no hesitation in saying that when Detroit Diesel Allison had a suitable turbine engine in production, he would expect the truck divisions to use it in their vehicles.

The power plant that resulted from these instructions was the Allison GT-404. It was in no way a scaled-up GT-304, but a new design, with two disc-type stainless-steel-core regenerators arranged on each side, and a one-piece cast iron housing. The gasifier shaft drove the engine accessories, while the remaining accessories were driven from the power turbine shaft. The GT-309's power transfer system was adopted, and the other elements were similar in principle to those of the GT-309, but new designs without exception, and a lot of design influence can be traced to the Allison Model 250 helicopter turbine.

The Allison GT-404 was rated at 325 hp at 37,100 rpm, with a maximum torque of 1410 pounds-feet (stalled output). The centrifugal compressor worked with a maximum pressure ratio of 4.1 and had a rated air flow capacity of 4 pounds per second. The whole package weighed approximately 1700 pounds and filled a package space of just under 30 cubic feet. It was 47 inches long x 28 inches wide x 39 inches high.

Allison GT-404 (right) compared with the Allison 250 helicopter engine.

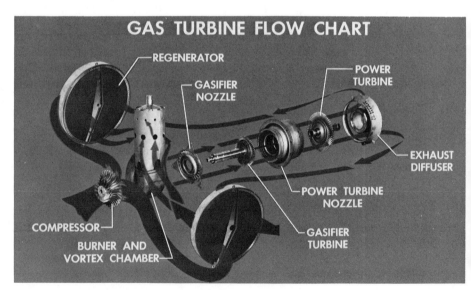

Allison GT-404 gas turbine engine.

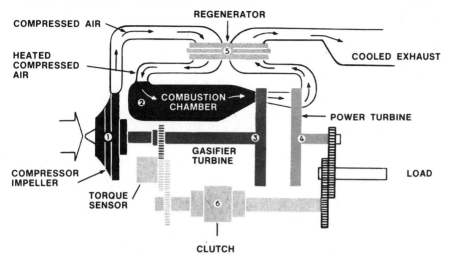

Schematic of the Allison GT-404 layout.

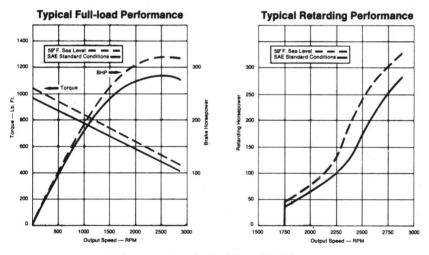

Performance charts for the Allison GT-404 unit.

On March 11, 1970, Martin J. Caserio, general manager of GMC Truck and Coach Division in Pontiac, Michigan, announced that GMC would begin production of turbine-powered trucks and buses on a limited scale in the fall of 1971. On August 26, 1971, Detroit Diesel Allison announced the start of pilot production of the 404 gas turbine scheduled for the following June. That day Emmett B. Lewis, Allison's general sales manager, said:

Allison HT-740-T automatic transmission developed specifically for gas turbine trucks.

Turbine engines will be suitable for a wide variety of uses, including generator sets, marine applications, construction equipment, and highway trucks and buses. The GT-404 will first appear in specialized applications such as generator sets and construction equipment. Truck and bus manufacturers will also receive early prototype turbines. In bus applications, the relatively vibration-free and quiet engine will have important appeal to bus operators as these features add significantly to passenger comfort. Highway trucks, on the other hand, are an extremely demanding application, so further testing and development is anticipated before turbine-powered trucks are in wide-scale use.

On the same date, Donald J. Atwood, manager of the Indianapolis operations, told the press:

The GT-404 is installed with an HT-740T transmission in several trucks. When used with the turbine, the transmission is extremely compact because we do away with the torque converter. The 404 performs the same function, giving us the highest torque at stall. This saves 200 pounds of transmission weight and allows a 2-inch shorter package.

Come June, 1972, neither GMC nor Chevrolet were close to putting turbine trucks into production. As a matter of fact, Detroit Diesel Allison had not been able to start assembly line operation. However, four GT-404 engines were installed in Greyhound coaches in September, 1972, for field testing and evaluation in regular service between Chicago, Indianapolis, Detroit and Philadelphia.

Finally, in November, 1972, Detroit Diesel Allison said it was postponing commerical production of the GT-404 for another year. The basic design was under development for higher output, with a target of 400 to 450 hp. At the same time, Allison disclosed it was working on an enlarged version called the GT-505, with a target output of 550 hp.

Instead of starting production at the end of 1973 or early 1974, Allison continued its far from intensive pilot-line operation, and expected to make no more than 50 industrial engines in 1974. No GM officials even mentioned the prospect of a turbine-powered truck.

White Motor Company, under the leadership of former GM executive Semon E. "Bunky" Knudsen, had been the first outside truck builder to test the Allison GT-404 in highway vehicles. In February 1974 White's Freightliner Division in Portland, Oregon, started in-fleet testing of the Turboliner highway tractor through a truck leasing corporation in Eden, North Carolina. Five more were to be produced for a similar program with Consolidated Freightways.

At the same time, Allison went into a major redesign of the GT-404 involving a complete revision of the material specifications, with cost reductions as the prime objective. The first production version had a list price of $9,000 which was barely adequate to cover production costs, and it is no secret that Allison is trying to get the turbine down to the $4,500 level so as to be more competitive with diesel engines.

Styling director William L. Mitchell and the Astro III.

The GT-225 Gas Turbine

The GM Research Laboratories' turbine team, still headed by Turunen and Collman, with Vickers and Amann in key positions, had almost totally dropped the passenger car turbine. In 1969 they supplied an experimental engine, a scaled-down version of the GT-309, for installation, in the Astro III show car. The turbine program, however, continued with a very low profile until the U.S. Congress passed the Clean Air Act Amendment of 1970. Then passenger car gas turbine research again became a matter of priority because of the turbine's promise as a low-emission power plant.

In one of its rare moves to buy technology from outside sources, General Motors signed a research contract with Williams Research Corporation. This contract was intended to provide the GM Research Laboratories and Engineering Staff with the small gas turbine know-how they had failed to acquire during the few years when all the emphasis had been placed on the truck turbine. The contract was in effect for about 3 years and was greatly beneficial to the state of the art at GM.

In October 1971 GM established a brand new office called the Passenger Car Turbine Development Group at the GM Engineering Staff—in other words, outside of the research activity. The man appointed as director of this

Installation of the GT-225 unit in a 1972 Chevrolet Impala.

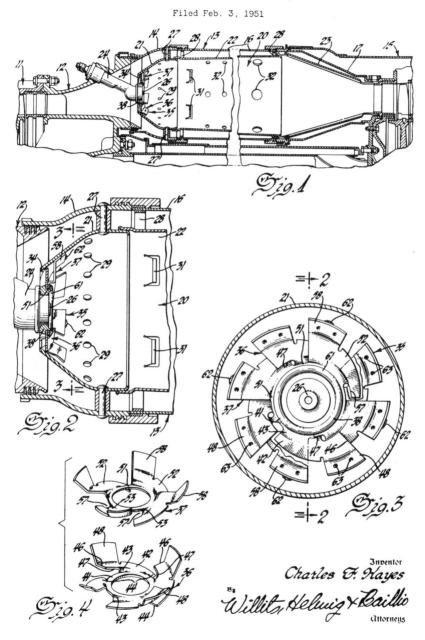

Fig.1

Fig.2

Fig.3

Fig.4

Inventor

Charles F. Hayes

By

Willits, Helmig & Baillio

Attorneys

GM experimental combustor with built-in swirler.

office was Tibor F. Nagey, formerly director of research, gas turbine activity, and transmission engineering at Allison since 1958. He had been in charge of a product quality assurance program at GM Engineering Staff since March 1969.

Hungarian-born (1922), Nagey was a graduate of the Case Institute of Technology and had also attended Northwestern University, Miami (Ohio) University, Cleveland College, and the Western Reserve University prior to joining the National Advisory Committee for Aeronautics in 1944. As a member of the Materials and Thermodynamics Division at the NASA-Lewis laboratory in Cleveland until 1953, Nagey conducted thermodynamic cycle analyses of unconventional prime movers and performed heat transfer experiments associated with nuclear reactor systems. From 1953 to 1958 he was associated with the Martin Company in Baltimore as manager and technical director of its nuclear division.

In his new office, Nagey soon built up a staff of about 40 engineers. Some of the key men were Albert Harvey Bell III (who had been one of the top thermodynamics specialists at Chrysler for many years), Michael E. Naylor (who had considerable experience of gas turbine design at GM), and David L. Dimick, (former manager of a design office at the Engineering Staff).

They worked closely with emission control experts at the Research Laboratories, notably Walter Cornelius and Wallace Wade, who performed some very intricate studies on the combustion characteristics of gas turbines. Nagey's group tested more than 30 candidates for development as low-NO_x combustors. Proposed modifications included all approaches, even opposites, such as rich and lean primary zones, early and delayed quenching, staged fuel delivery, staged air delivery, variable geometry, air-blast fuel injectors, air-assist fuel injectors, and numerous aerodynamic primary zone control devices.

The injection of either steam or water into the burner has proved effective

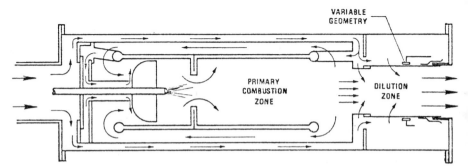

GM experimental combustor with external recirculation.

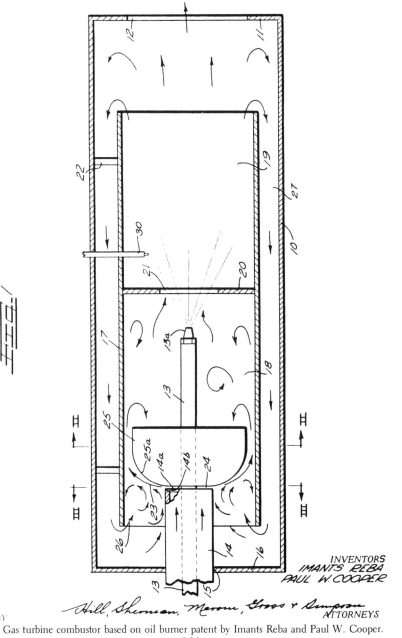

INVENTORS
IMANTS REBA
PAUL W. COOPER

BY   Hill, Sherman, Meroni, Gross & Simpson
ATTORNEYS

Gas turbine combustor based on oil burner patent by Imants Reba and Paul W. Cooper.

391

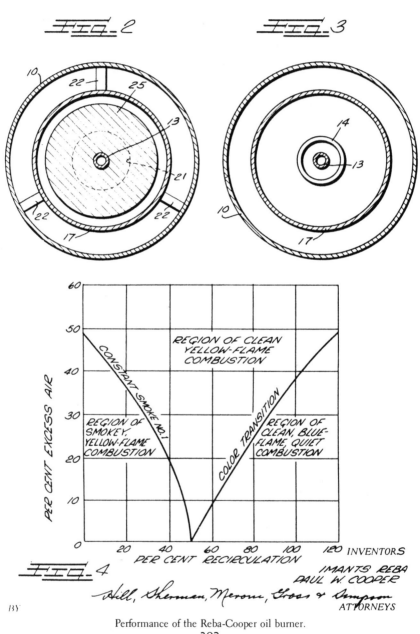

Fig. 2

Fig. 3

Fig. 4

INVENTORS
IMANTS REBA
PAUL W. COOPER

BY Hill, Sherman, Meroni, Gross & Simpson

ATTORNEYS

Performance of the Reba-Cooper oil burner.

392

in NO_x reduction. The fluid acts as a heat sink to reduce the maximum temperature in the primary zone. Charles A. Amann considers that since the water injection rate required for appreciable benefits is of the same order as the engine fuel rate, the attraction of this approach is questionable in an automotive application. With staged combustion, fuel can be introduced at two or more locations in the combustor. Proper scheduling of fuel rates at each location offers the possibility for more precise control of mixture ratio in the combustion zones without necessitating variable geometry.

The basic test engine is the GT-225, which is related to the GT-309 in its overall concept, but readily adaptable to new types of components (combustors, regenerators, etc.).

One of the leading experimental low-NO_x combustors developed at GM is based on a patent taken out in 1967 by I. Reba and P. W. Cooper. The design includes provision for pre-vaporization ahead of the primary reaction zone, pre-mixing of the fuel and primary air before the reaction zone, and convection-cooled combustor walls. Under direction of Al Bell, several other types of combustors were designed. All of them were of considerably larger diameter than earlier types of combustors used at GM.

Al Bell pointed out that it is only after the engine is installed in a car that its emission levels can be accurately measured. So, for the first time, GM converted standard production-model passenger cars to gas turbine power matching the engines to virtually standard automotive transmissions. The GT-225 was first installed in a 1973 Chevrolet Impala, and is now running in a number of full size and intermediate cars.

A step-by-step progress report on the work now being done will not be available for some time. But GM has made no secret of the problems associated with some of the low-emission combustors that have been tested, problems which must be solved before the combustor can be accepted for automotive turbines. These are the main points:

1. Emission performance during ignition and during the initial low combustor inlet temperature warmup period.
2. Emission performance during transient engine operation.
3. Marginal stability limits due to lean blowout.
4. Emission performance "sustainability" during long life (100,000 miles) of operation.
5. Rapid response and exact control of the combustor variable geometry in relation to engine operating conditions.
6. Effect of manufacturing variability on emission performance.

The passenger car turbine development group also conducts, side by side with its emission control studies, programs to improve fuel economy and reduce production costs. New-type turbines can be expected in 1975.

19

Case History:
Ford

WITHOUT ANY TIES to the aircraft industry since the end of Trimotor aeroplane production in 1933, Ford Motor Company lacked the turbine-consciousness that Chrysler and General Motors developed during World War II.

Gas turbine programs and plans for turbine cars at GM and Chrysler were pretty well defined before it dawned on Ford's management that the gas turbine might interact in some way with passenger car production. Ford's gas turbine research began in 1951 at the instigation of Harold T. Youngren, vice president of engineering at Ford from 1947 to 1952. He came to Ford from Borg-Warner, and had previously been chief engineer of Oldsmobile from 1933 to 1944. His aviation experience dated back to the pioneer days of the industry, long before the gas turbine had flown. He had been an engineer with Curtiss Aeroplane Co. during World War I. Later he helped develop the Houdaille shock absorber, designed engines and chassis for Pierce-Arrow in Buffalo, N.Y. and worked for some years as executive engineer in charge of chassis design at Studebaker.

The man he picked to head the turbine program was Connie L. Bouchard who had worked at Allison Division of General Motors from 1939 to 1946. As the top engineer in charge of experimental engine test facilities up to 1944, he was more than familiar with Allison's gas turbine work, and the state of the art. For the next two years at Allison his assignment had been to develop performance calculations for future aircraft and guided missile applications.

A native of Salem, Massachusetts, Connie Bouchard was educated at the Massachusetts Institute of Technology, graduating with a Bachelor's degree in mechanical engineering in 1936, and followed it up with a master's degree in 1937. He became an instructor in aeronautical engineering at M.I.T., and for two years performed laboratory investigations on internal combustion engines at the Sloan Automotive Laboratory.

His first job at Ford in 1946 was to coordinate the planning and construction of the Ford Research and Engineering Center in Dearborn, Michigan. He was assigned to gas turbine studies in 1951, and in 1952 he was named manager of Ford's gas turbine engineering department.

Bouchard started his turbine work with an in-depth study of the fluid dynamics and material problems involved. He recognized that the problems were both numerous and difficult, and determined that substantial progress toward their solution could better be made through step-by-step improvements in component efficiency than by exploration of novel and complex cycle arrangements. Bouchard understood that to obtain components with high efficiency and broad range, high rotational speeds and high air flow mass were essential. Equally apparent was the necessity for high heat release rates and effective regeneration at minimum pressure loss, with all components included in a package of minimum size and weight.

In order to facilitate testing and instrumentation, the components were designed as separate units. The compressors were designed and tested without being combined with the turbines, and vice versa. However, they were designed to be ducted together for operation as a complete power plant.

Considerations of inherent advantages of light weight and clean configuration, however, were deferred in favor of obtaining reliable and flexible test components. The compressor program was the first to produce results. Ford built and tested about 50 different configurations of a centrifugal-flow compressor wheel of 10-inch diameter. This work led to subcontracts in connection with new Westinghouse and Pratt & Whitney turbojet engines.

The direction of this defense-contract work was aviation-oriented, not car-oriented, and Bouchard felt that its benefits to the development of an experimental turbine car were marginal. He steered events in what he felt was the right direction by purchasing two Boeing 502 turboshaft engines in 1954 and installing them in Ford cars—one in a Thunderbird and the other in a Fairlane. Now he could perform road tests with complete vehicles as well as test components in the laboratory. The next step, after analysis and evaluation of the experience with the two Boeing-powered cars, was to build and test a Ford-designed, Ford-built gas turbine.

The individual components that had been so carefully developed over a four-year period were finally combined into a complete engine, the Ford 701 gas turbine, in 1955. It was a twin-shaft regenerative gas turbine with a single-stage centrifugal compressor and two axial-flow turbines. The unit used a single barrel-type combustor and was remarkably up-to-date with a rotary regenerator. After initial dynamometer tests had given satisfactory

Feb. 23, 1965 B. T. HOWES ET AL 3,170,292

LUBRICATING SYSTEM FOR A GAS TURBINE ENGINE

Original Filed April 4, 1960 8 Sheets-Sheet 1

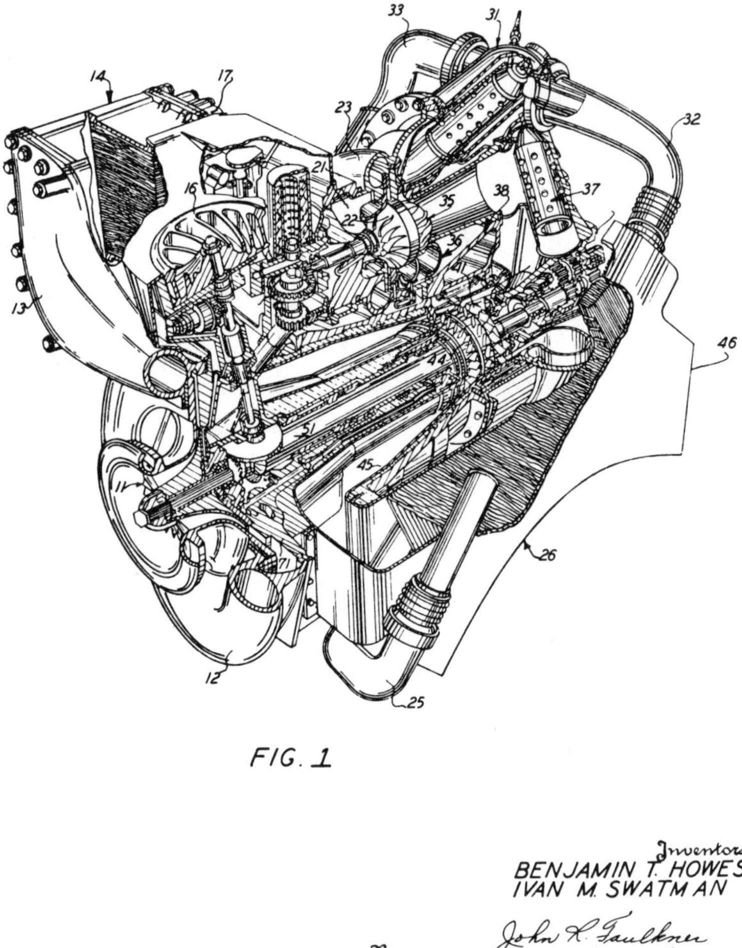

FIG. 1

Inventors
BENJAMIN T. HOWES
IVAN M. SWATMAN

By John R. Faulkner
Keith L. Zerschling
Attorneys

Cutaway view of the Ford Model 704 gas turbine engine.

Ford 704 gas turbine engine installation in a Ford truck.

results, the 701 was installed in a 1954 Ford Fairlane sedan and began its road-test life. It ran reliably, although overall efficiency was very poor.

Its direct successor, the 702, used the same key components. The Ford 702 was installed in a 1956 TC-800 tilt-cab truck (highway tractor). Performance, fuel economy, and overall driveability were disappointing, and led to a full reappraisal of the turbine program at Ford in 1957.

Ford research engineers concluded that a significant advance in the state of the art would be necessary if a gas turbine were ever to be completely competitive. Accordingly, intensive analyses of a series of gas-turbine cycles were undertaken. From these studies, it appeared that an engine of more complex cycle offered the best potential for a gas turbine to compete with the reciprocating piston engine.

A new design, derived from the original concept (the 703) never got beyond the drawing board stage, as work began on a new turbine configuration to achieve low fuel consumption over a wide operating range. This led to the creation of the Ford 704 gas turbine.

THE FORD 704 GAS TURBINE

The 704 operating cycle included supercharging and intercooling, and it remains one of the most complex of all automotive gas turbines ever proposed or built. The cycle may be described simply as a turbocharged gas turbine. The concept was invented by two young turbine engineers working under Bouchard—Benjamin T. Howes and Ivan M. Swatman.

The 704 gas turbine was a twin-spool, three-shaft engine. The high-pressure compressor and first-stage turbine were mounted on a short shaft located high up in the turbine housing. The lower shaft carrying the third-stage turbine also carried a low-pressure compressor. The second-stage turbine ran on its own shaft and was mounted immediately behind the third-stage turbine. This turbine supplied all output power.

Air entered the low-pressure compressor from a silencer and passed through an intercooler on the way to the high-pressure compressor. The compressed air duct led from the high-pressure compressor to a recuperative heat exchanger, which discharged into a plenum chamber surrounding the barrel-type primary combustor.

After passing through the radial in-flow first-stage turbine, the combustion products went into a secondary combustor, and a renewed expansion took place. This final expansion drove the axial-flow second- and third-stage turbines, and the exhaust gases were ducted to the recuperator before being released into the atmosphere.

In the twin recuperators the temperature of the air was raised to 960° F (515° C) at substantially constant pressure. From the recuperators, the air passed through dual conduits to the primary combustor where the temperature was raised to 1700° F (927° C) by the continuous burning of fuel at substantially constant pressure. After the gases from the primary burner passed through the high pressure turbine where the temperature was reduced to 1300° F (705° C) and the pressure reduced to 95 psi, they were reheated in the reheat or secondary combustor to a temperature of 1700° F (927° C) at substantially constant pressure. The heated gas was then supplied to the power turbine where the temperature was reduced to 1400° F (760° C) and the pressure reduced to 40 psi. In the low pressure turbine and the diffuser the gases expanded to a pressure slightly above atmospheric at a temperature of 1070° F (577° C). The gases were then exhausted to the atmosphere through the twin recuperators where the temperature was reduced to approximately 750° F (400° C). The incorporation of a reheat combustor was a means of increasing the total heat added during the cycle, and thus increasing efficiency without raising either turbine inlet temperature.

The two stages of compression gave an overall pressure ratio of 16 : 1, with air-to-air intercooling between compressor stages to reduce the work,

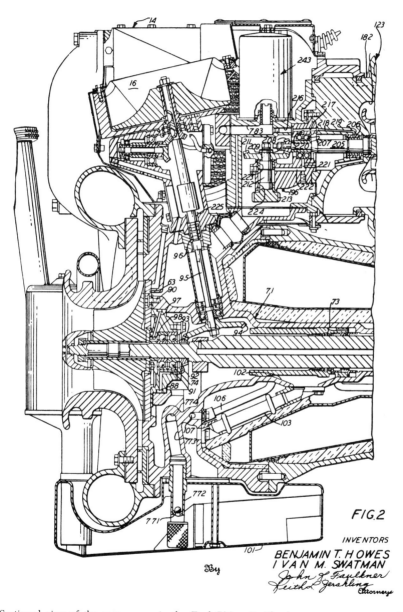

FIG.2

INVENTORS
BENJAMIN T. HOWES
IVAN M. SWATMAN
John Z. Faulkner
Keith L. Gershling
Attorneys

By

Sectioned view of the compressors in the Ford 704 unit. The low-pressure compressor is mounted on the lower shaft; the high-pressure compressor above.

399

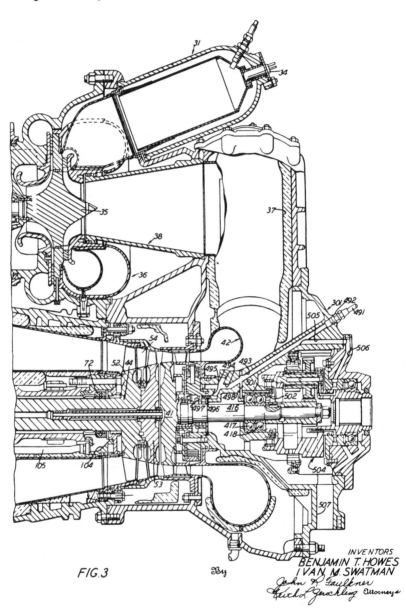

FIG.3

INVENTORS
BENJAMIN T. HOWES
IVAN M. SWATMAN
John R. Faulkner
Keith L. Geschling Attorneys

Combustor, turbine and output section of the Ford 704 unit.

400

size, and top speed of the high-pressure compressor. The high pressure ratio was necessary to fully exploit the potential of the reheat combustor as a means of increasing efficiency. A plate-type recuperator was used between the high-pressure compressor outlet and the primary combustor.

Why the regressive step from the rotary regenerator to the stationary recuperator? Ford's early regenerators suffered from excessive leakage, which could be averted by adopting a stationary type of heat exchanger with far fewer sealing problems.

The matrix had a "Z" flow configuration (cross-counter-flow). The engine used two units, 27 inches long in the no-flow direction and approximately 4½ inches in flow length. The "Z" flow exchanger allowed a portion of the flow to run in a counter-flow direction, resulting in a higher effectiveness for a given volume. Selection of a "Z" flow configuration involved proportioning of the flow area between cross-flow and counter-flow on the cool air side of the matrix. Well aware that the design offering the highest effectiveness for a given volume would have the greatest amount of counter-flow area, Ford made a compromise in order to let the air within the air cell of the matrix be manifolded into the counter-flow corrugations with a minimum pressure drop. The 704 engine recuperator was selected with a 20-70-20 area ratio for the air cell. Distribution of the air within the air cell to prevent thermal buckling and to attain optimum effectiveness was achieved by curving the entrance to the corrugated separator within the air cell. The matrix was fabricated by stacking air cells and gas-side corrugations, and furnace-brazing the assembly. The headers were attached as a second-brazing operation after machining grooves in the matrix to locate the semi-circular manifolds. The matrix material was Type 316 stainless steel.

The recuperator cores were a subject of considerable concern from a mechanical design aspect. At design conditions, the matrix operated with 220 psi pressure within the air cells and a little above atmospheric pressure on the exhaust side at a gas temperature of 1100° F (595° C). Analysis showed that, assuming reasonably good air flow and gas distribution within the core, the stresses were at a sufficiently low level to be of little concern, except in the area where the header manifolds were attached. A high stress concentration existed in the matrix in the area adjacent to the brazing groove due to the temperature gradient between the matrix and the header.

Matrix samples tested on a thermal-shock rig indicated that very little trouble was to be expected from this area, and test of a prototype matrix verified these theories. In initial testing, a matrix was subjected to an over-pressure of 600 psi at an over-temperature of 1300° F (705° C) for 100 hours, equivalent in stress life to approximately 5000 hours of engine operation at design conditions. In addition, the unit did not fail when subjected to 10,000 cycles at temperatures from 600° F (315° C) to 1200° F (650° C) every three seconds, with the air-flow and gas-flow rates varied in accordance with an engine operating schedule. Peak recuperator efficiency was 75%.

A unique feature of the cycle was the location of the power turbine between the high-pressure spool turbine and the super-charging or low-pressure spool turbine. Installation of the power turbine at this point in the cycle provided a very desirable speed relationship between the low-pressure and high-pressure compressors, which resulted in extremely good part-load fuel economy. Near optimum load control was attained by varying the air flow, while turbine inlet temperatures were held almost constant.

The high pressure spool operated near aerodynamic design speed and design inlet temperature through most of the load range. The low pressure spool would accelerate to a speed compatible with the load requirement of the engine. The near constant speed feature of the high pressure spool was largely instrumental in producing good fuel economy over a broad spectrum of loads and speeds, and particularly provided an advantage over simple cycle, low pressure gas turbine engines, that of good part load fuel economy.

The design work lasted over a year—from early in 1957 to well into 1958. Preliminary layouts for an engine with a 300-horsepower rating indicated that a symmetrical arrangement, using two intercoolers, and two recuperators with the compressor spools located in the same vertical plane, was the most compact layout. The design also appeared to offer the greatest advantage from a mechanical and structural standpoint. The final design package achieved the goal of fitting under the hood of a Ford passenger car, although the 704 was essentially designed for truck application.

The main structural loads of the engine were carried by cast iron components, with light sheet-metal ducts used within these castings to guide the gases. The external castings, as well as providing the main structure for the engine, also contained the high-pressure air, which reached 200 psi at design load. The problem of unequal thermal growth of the components was solved by a piston-ring-sealed sliding joint at the high-pressure compressor inlet, which allows differences in axial expansion between the low-pressure and high-pressure compressor assemblies. Growth between the axial center lines of these components is provided by leaving a generous clearance between the diameter of the intercooler connecting duct and the high-pressure compressor inlet, the piston rings providing the air seal.

The high-pressure spool compressor and turbine were constructed in a back-to-back configuration. The radial inflow turbine was an integral part of the compressor wheel, with a labyrinth seal on the nozzle diaphragm between the compressor and turbine halves. An integral turbine-compressor design was necessitated by the combination of stress and temperature in the turbine wheel. Heat transfer to the compressor portion of the wheel allowed

the turbine to operate at a higher tip speed and closer to its optimum velocity ratio. At design speed, the unit rotated at 91,500 rpm. Compressor efficiency was 80 percent, and the radial in-flow turbine reached 83 percent
efficiency.

The turbine wheel and shaft unit on prototype engines was machined
from a one-piece Udimet 500 forging but was later replaced by a one-piece
investment cast wheel of Inconel 713C, with an SAE 4140 shaft flash-butt
welded at the hub of the compressor inducer. Segmented-pinned sleeve
bearings were used for the radial bearings. The thrust bearing, which had to
absorb 300 pounds axial load due to the unequal pressure ratios of the turbine and compressor was a six-segment tilting pad design. The compressor
scroll and front shroud were nodular iron castings, with the diffuser vanes
machined as an integral part of the shroud. The nozzle vanes and diaphragm were a Hastelloy C investment casting; and the turbine scroll and
shroud assembly were fabricated from Hastelloy C stampings.

The high pressure spool ran at a near constant speed over most of the load
range of the engine, from 70% of rated speed at idle to 100% of rated speed
at full power. The high pressure spool thus provided an excellent power
source for the accessories associated with the engine and the vehicle in
which the engine is mounted, such as engine oil pumps, power steering
pumps, fuel control and an electric starter-generator. The power takeoff for
the accessory gears was through a spiral bevel gear which had a pitch-line
velocity of 18,000 ft/min. Gear material was Nitralloy 135 with a flash coating of copper plate.

The low-pressure spool can essentially be regarded as the turbocharger for
the engine. It was an integral unit consisting of a two-stage turbine driving a
single-stage centrifugal compressor at a design speed of 46,500 rpm. The
bearing design was a two-bearing arrangement with a midshaft bumper bearing. The bearing adjacent to the turbine wheel was a full-floating sleeve
bearing and a similar design was used for the bumper bearing. Tandem ball
thrust bearings were used adjacent to the compressor wheel and a spiral
bevel gear drive was provided for the intercooler fan shaft. At an ambient
temperature of 100° F the low-pressure spool compressor pumped in 2.71
pounds of air per second at full speed.

The axial-flow turbines operated with a maximum efficiency of 86 percent, and the low-pressure compressor could reach 80 percent efficiency.

The low-pressure spool assembly included only one sheet-metal component, which was the exhaust diffuser from the turbine wheel. The other
low-pressure spool components were either aluminum or nodular iron castings; or, in the case of the turbine shroud rings, fabricated from stainless-
steel, forged rings. The two turbine wheel stages were precision investment
castings of Inconel 713C alloy. The wheels were one-piece, integral blade-

and-hub castings; and in the second-stage wheel, the hub was flash-butt welded to an SAE 4140 shaft. Bearing areas were induction-hardened, and the C-355, T61 aluminum, cast compressor wheel was spline-coupled to the shaft.

The power turbine and the low pressure spool turbine were positioned in contra-rotating relationship with no nozzles interposed between them. This arrangement was chosen to obtain improved acceleration of the low-pressure spool during transient operation of the engine. Here's how and why: When accelerating from standstill while the power turbine is turning at low speeds, increased energy transfer takes place, and additional torque is applied to the low-pressure spool turbine wheel, thereby improving acceleration of this spool with a resulting increase in the power level of the engine. The effect is aerodynamically similar to that of variable geometry nozzles between the turbines.

Interstage turbine nozzle blades and diaphragm were also a one-piece investment casting of Hastelloy C, with the shroud ring of the nozzle heli-arced through a 0.125 inch diameter hole to the tip of each vane. Provision for radial growth of the turbine wheel shrouds, while maintaining turbine blade tip clearance concentric with the axis of rotation, was provided by six radial slots in the flange of the turbine shroud ring. The ring was located by six square keys bolted to the turbine case-support structure. An adjusting device, which allowed the turbine tip clearance to be adjusted for concentricity at assembly, was incorporated in the key mounting arrangement. Both primary and reheat combustion liners were conventional barrel-type liners fabricated from Inconel X material.

The power turbine was a single-stage unit rotating at 37,500 rpm maximum. The output shaft was reduced in speed to 4600 rpm by a planetary reduction gear. The power turbine wheel rotated in a fully-floating sleeve bearing adjacent to the turbine wheel. Concentricity of the turbine shroud over the wheel was achieved by radially pinning the Hastelloy C nozzle casting to the bearing housing and supporting the shroud from the tip of the nozzle vanes. The turbine wheel was an integral blade-and-wheel casting of Inconel 713C with an SAE 4140 shaft flash-butt welded to the hub.

Gear reduction was achieved through a planetary system using the reaction of the planet pinions against a fixed ring gear to drive the planet carrier and output shaft. The planet carrier was mounted in two bearings which straddled the sun (input) gear on the turbine shaft. A fully-floating, flexible ring gear provided equal loading of the planet pinion gears, allowing for discrepancies in the gear tooth profile and timing. The planet pinion gears, which at design condition rotated at a spindle speed of 20,055 rpm, used pressed-in copper lead bushings running on a nitralloy shaft. Gear material was Nitralloy 135, and the reduction gear housing a nodular iron casting.

Twin scrolls divided the air flow from the low pressure compressor for delivery to a pair of intercoolers. These intercoolers were of the cross-flow air to air type, and were supplied with cooling air by a fan which delivered cooling air outwardly from the center of the power plant through the intercooler structures. From the intercoolers, the air was reunited by means of a pair of ducts and then fed into the inlet chamber of the high pressure spool compressor.

The intercoolers reduced the temperature of the air flowing from the low pressure spool compressor thereby reducing the work of the high pressure spool compressor. The intercoolers lowered the temperature to 220° F (104° C) before it entered the high pressure compressor where the pressure was raised to 224 psi and the temperature was raised to 625° F (330° C). Intercooler efficiency was 65 percent.

A sheet-metal box formed a plenum between the two intercooler matrices, and the intercooler fan discharged into the plenum chamber. The fan was an axial design with a sheet-metal prewhirl vane, turning at 18,200 rpm maximum. The intercooler material was zinc-clad 3002-0 aluminum, furnace-brazed to form the matrix assembly to which the headers were then attached by epoxy resin.

The Ford 704 gas turbine was rated at 300 hp and had a specific fuel consumption of .572 pounds per hp-hour at full power. It showed the lowest specific fuel consumption at 60 percent part load—as low as .480 pounds per hp-hour—and the curve showed a fuel consumption rate of under .5 pounds per hp-hour from 38 to 82 percent load.

The 704 turbine was built and tested in 1959–60, and one unit was installed in a Ford C-1100 tilt cab truck. It was mated with an Allison automatic transmission incorporating a retarder. Actual road testing confirmed the findings from the dynamometer tests—the turbine was reliable and gave remarkable part-load fuel economy. Testing and experimentation with the 704 turbine truck continued, and extended into 1963.

THE FORD 705 GAS TURBINE

In 1960 Ford felt its turbine program had advanced so far that it made a bid for a joint Army-Navy contract for a 600-hp gas turbine. Both Ford and the Military were convinced that this type of powerplant could be competitive with existing diesel engines.

The U.S. Navy Bureau of Ships and the U.S. Army had recognized the need for a gas turbine engine in the 600-horsepower range. The requirements of each of these government agencies were gradually coordinated into preliminary specifications, which were issued to industry for comment in August, 1960, and finally consolidated in a firm specification and request to bid in September 1960.

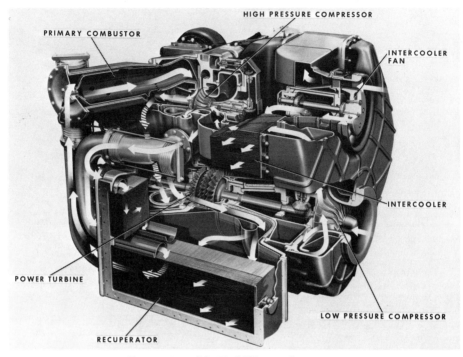

Cutaway view of the Ford 705 gas turbine engine.

The final specification called for an engine with a fuel consumption characteristic equivalent to that of a diesel engine and with comparable overhaul life characteristics. The packaged volume of the powerplant, ready for installation, was to be no more than 60 cubic feet with a weight target of 1250 pounds, with a maximum cost of $12,000 per engine, based on a 1000-engines-per-year production rate. On the strength of the 704 experience, Ford was awarded the contract in February 1961, and the 705 engine was designed as an improved, scaled-up version of the 704.

This new gas turbine was much larger than the 704: 49 inches long as against 38, 44 inches wide as against 29 and 38 inches high as against 28. Contrary to contemporary practice at GM and Chrysler, Ford persisted in using cross-counter-flow recuperators, although the trend was unmistakably toward regenerators. The 705 engine weighed 1475 pounds complete.

There were several minor modifications that seem worthy of note, however. Compared with the Ford 704 engine the 705 differs in that the high-pressure spool compressor and turbine wheels were split in order that sealing could be accomplished at the minimum diameter between the compressor and turbine. In the 704 engine, the pressure differential between the tip of

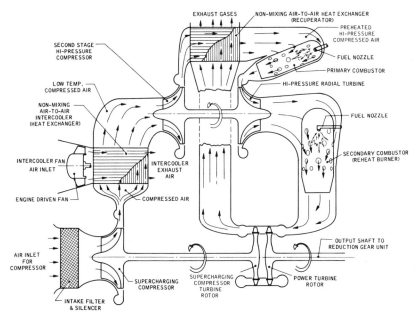

Gas flow path in the Ford 705 unit.

the compressor and the tip of the radial inflow turbine wheel was only 4 psi. Due to the heavier accessory load on the 705 engine, this pressure differential was approximately 30 psi, which, if a rim-type seal had been used, would have resulted in excessive leakage between the compressor and turbine. The 705 engine was also equipped with a new type of secondary combustor.

In the 704 engine, a side entry combustor was used with moderate success. For the 705 engine, however, it was felt that if the side entry concept were retained, a modification to a scroll type entry would be beneficial. In this type of design the velocity of the entering gas could be used to swirl around the outside of the liner for cooling.

Many subtle changes such as modifying clearances and lubrication passages were also made. While the 705 engine operated on the same cycle as the Model 704, there were important differences due to scale effects. The 705 engine consumed 4.4 pounds of air per second, and in the process of compression through the two compressors, the air pressure was raised to approximately 214 psi.

First, the air was compressed in the low-pressure compressor to 4 atmospheres and then ducted through a stainless steel "Z" flow intercooler, after which it entered the inlet to the high-pressure compressor. The intercooler

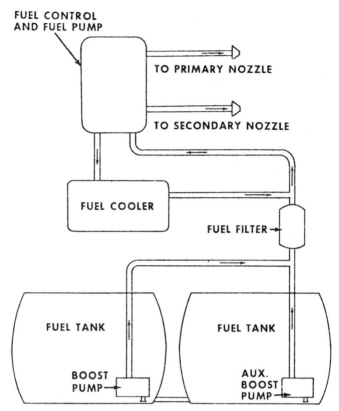

Fuel system for the Ford 705 gas turbine engine.

cooling air was delivered by an axial-flow fan driven by a bevel gear arrangement from the low-pressure spool. The compressed air from the intercooler then entered the second stage compressor, where it was compressed to a final pressure ratio of 16 : 1. From the high-pressure compressor, the air was manifolded to the recuperators. After leaving the recuperators, the air entered the primary combustor where fuel was added to raise the temperature to 1750° F (955° C).

The gas expanded through a radial in-flow turbine, driving the high-pressure compressor and the combined accessory and power take-off gear box. From the high-pressure turbine the combustion products entered the secondary combustor where fuel was added and the temperature again raised to 1750° F (955° C) prior to expanding through the axial-flow power turbine.

This single-stage axial turbine was coupled to a planetary reduction gear, providing an output speed of 3080 rpm. The gas then passed through a two-stage, axial, low-pressure turbine which drove the low-pressure, supercharg-

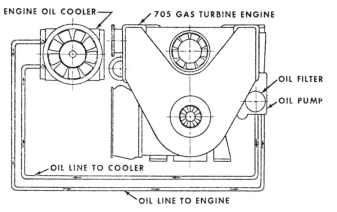

Oil cooling system for the Ford 705 gas turbine engine.

ing compressor and intercooler fan. Exhaust gases were then collected in a diffuser and directed through the gas side of the recuperator before being ducted through the exhaust silencer and out to atmosphere. The temperature of the gases exhausting from the recuperator approximated 660° F (350° C).

Engine design and mechanical development of the components proved more time-consuming than expected, taking up the entire period from 1960 through 1962. Final component testing was completed in the early part of 1963 and testing of the complete power unit began.

Engine test and development progressed with excellent results, and a number of improvements were made to achieve output power and fuel consumption objectives. From the first day of engine operation, late in May, 1963, through October 15, 1964, a total of 400 dynamometer test hours were accumulated on three engines.

The original objective of the joint Army-Navy program had been a minimum fuel specific of .40 pounds per hp-hr by November 1964. Maximum engine output achieved by that date was 510 hp. This power limitation was imposed by the driveshaft coupling the engine to the dynamometer. Best specific fuel consumption obtained was .47 at approximately 200 hp. output. Military participation in the program ceased in August 1963 but Ford Motor Company felt that the original design and development program was sound. Consequently, Ford decided to continue engine-development and component rig operation in order to provide a powerplant for a superhighway transport vehicle program which was already underway in Ford's vehicle concepts department.

This plan led to the use of the 705 engine as the power plant for a gigantic highway freight train combination officially designated the Ford Super

Ford's experimental "super transport" truck.

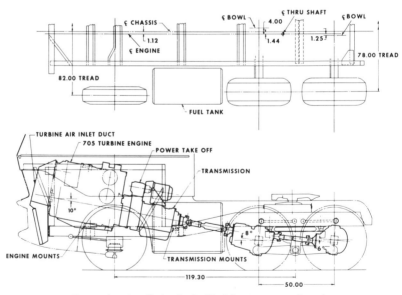

Power plant installation in the Ford "super transport" truck.

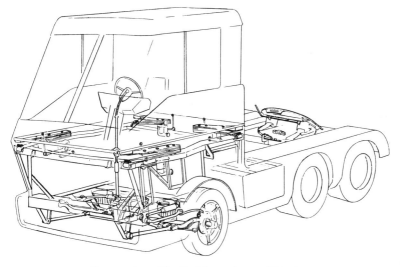

Cutaway view of the Ford "super transport" tractor.

Transport Truck but better known to all associated with the project as "Big Red."

When the installation was undertaken, early in 1964, the 705 engine had been developed to deliver 560 hp at 75,500 rpm of the high-pressure spool and 36,600 rpm of the low-pressure spool and power turbine shaft, which corresponds to an output shaft speed of 3080 rpm. Peak torque (at stall) was an impressive 1660 pounds-feet, tapering off as rotational speed increased to 945 pounds-feet at 3080 rpm. At a useful 1800 rpm, the 705 engine offered 1330 pounds-feet of torque.

The fuel system consisted of two interconnected fuel tanks with a total capacity of 280 gallons, a fuel pump, a fuel electric boost pump, and a fuel control unit. Engine control was maintained by an engine-mounted fuel control unit designed and built by Chandler Evans. The engine lubricating system oil cooler, consisted of an electrically driven fan and an air-to-oil heat exchanger. The fan was thermostatically operated and cycled between oil temperatures of 145° and 165° F (63–74° C). The system was designed for minimum noise level with the motor running. The inlet provided ram air when the vehicle was in motion, minimizing the running time for the fan motor.

The turbine starting cycle was completely automatic. The ignition switch was momentarily depressed, energizing an automatic starting circuit which engaged the starter motor and ignited the primary combustor. When the high pressure spool operation was sustained, the starting system was automatically kicked out. To bring the complete turbine engine into operation, the combuster switch was momentarily depressed, igniting the secondary combustor.

The accessory loads associated with a truck of this type were extremely high. Ford found a way to drive a maximum of accessories from the transmission rather than from the high-pressure spool. The 24-V generator, air conditioning compressor, and air compressor were driven by V-belts and pulleys from a power takeoff on the engine side of the transmission. The generator was driven at 1.68 times engine output shaft speed. The air-conditioning compressor and the air compressor were driven at 1.16 times engine output shaft speed.

Only the power steering pump and a 12-V generator were driven by the accessory drive power takeoff shafts in the engine. The power steering pump consumed an average of 2 hp while the 12-V generator drive took 5 hp. The air system compressor used up an average of 4 hp, while the two air-conditioning compressors needed 8 hp. The heaviest power consumer was the 24-V generator, which took 21 hp.

Various engine inlet duct configurations were designed, built and evaluated for pressure loss and sound attenuation. The selected design consisted of a plenum chamber with a Donasonic silencer section for noise suppression and conventional strainer-type filters for dust protection. This plenum chamber and filter system gave a pressure loss of 4.5 inches of water at the engine inlet at maximum air flow to the engine. The inlet plenum was attached to the engine and had rubber compression seals at the intercooler fan inlet and the low-pressure compressor inlet.

The exhaust system consisted of an engine-attached duct which led from the turbine recuperator to a flexible coupling. The flexible coupling was connected to a body-attached duct which led up the outside right rear wall of the cab to exhaust at the top. Duct work was of sandwich type construction with an inner perforated skin, 5 in. insulation, and an outer skin. Stainless steel was used for the inner and outer skins of the duct, and it was insulated with "Cerafelt".

The flexible coupling between the two ducts was required because of the suspended cab and the relative motion of plus or minus 2.00 inches between the cab duct and the engine duct. The total length of the exhaust system was approximately 15 feet. The cross-sectional area was a relatively large 120 sq. in. which gave low duct velocities resulting in low duct pressure losses.

The 705 powerplant was connected to the biggest Allison automatic transmission available at the time: the Torqmatic HT-70 with 5 forward speeds. The main reduction gear consisted of a compound planetary system with provisions for an accessory drive pad, to be utilized where applications required power-turbine governing, and for a drive for a 2-element lubricating pump for use in cases where the power turbine could be rotated with the engine at rest. The gearing had to be flexible enough to permit a speed range selection from 3,000 to 12,000 rpm and be capable of reversing the output shaft rotation.

This was accomplished by fixing the ring gear and rotating the planet carrier or vice versa to give forward or reverse rotation. The original configuration tested had a counter-clockwise rotation which required a rotating ring gear. The output speed of this box was 6,000 rpm whereas the truck installation required an output speed of 3,080 rpm. Therefore, the sun and planet gears were changed accordingly.

The transmission provided full automatic torque-shifting and incorporated an integral hydraulic retarder and a torque converter with an automatic lock-up clutch. The converter was a single-stage, dual-phase, three-element unit consisting of a pump, turbine, and stator. Maximum torque multiplication ratio in the converter was 2 : 1.

The transmission gear selector was controlled by an electric shift system. With the range selector set on 4, the transmission operated in the 2–5 range. It started in second-converter and automatically shifted through the third-lockup, fourth gear, and then into fifth. The shift was similar for all other selections. For range 3 (2–4), the transmission stopped at fourth gear and could not shift into fifth. The converter lockup clutch engaged automatically when the torque converter was not needed, so as to provide direct engine coupling for maximum efficiency and economy. Transmission ratios were 2.824 : 1, 2.000 : 1, 1.412 : 1, 1.000 : 1, 1,706 : 1 and 4.769 : 1 in reverse. The retarder pedal was mechanically connected to the retarder lever on the transmission. The retarder provided 255 hp of continuous braking and was capable of 600 hp braking for short periods.

The transmission and retarder oil cooling system consisted of an electrically driven fan and an air-to-oil heat exchanger. This system was designed to dissipate 11,600 Btu's per minute continuously in an ambient temperature of 110° F (43.3° C) and was thermostatically controlled to operate between oil temperatures of 200° F (93° C) and 225° F (107° C). The cooling air entered through a grille in the front panel and was ducted to the heat exchanger. Ram air flow due to the motion of the vehicle aided in cooling the oil and reduced the running time of the cooling fan.

This power train was installed in the front end of a three-axle tractor 156 inches high having an overall length of 237 inches, and an overall width of 96 inches built on a 119.3 inch wheelbase with 78 inch rear track and 82 inch front track. The two rear axles were spaced 150 inches apart (hub to hub).

The propeller shafts consisted of a driveshaft from the transmission to the front rear axle and an interaxle shaft between the two rear axles. The rear axles were modified Rockwell Standard SSHD tandem drive axles with a

44,000-lb rating for the tandem. The axles were hypoid, single-reduction, through-drive type, featuring an interaxle differential on the forward unit. This unit divided torque equally between the axles and it could be locked out by an air valve located in the cab to provide equal power to both axles under conditions where maximum traction was required.

This tractor was designed to haul two semi-trailers (one mounted on the tractor's "fifth wheel" and the other towed by a four-wheel dolly with its own "fifth wheel.") The tractor alone weighed 20,000 pounds, and the whole train combination weighed 50,000 pounds unloaded and was rated for a gross train weight of 170,000 pounds. It was 96 feet long and was designed for a cruising speed of 70 mph with a full load. The 705 engine enabled this road train to climb hills of 3 percent gradient at 30 mph and 5 percent at 20 mph with a full load.

The complete vehicle was shipped by rail to Los Angeles so that the public introduction of the gas turbine Superhighway Truck could be made at the national convention of the American Trucking Association on October 26, 1964. After the Los Angeles introduction, the truck was driven on a national tour of approximately 5,500 miles for display to the public, truckers, and government officials in major cities in the United States and Canada.

The fuel economy on the 1200-mile portion from Dallas to Chicago through Oklahoma City, Wichita, and Des Moines was 3.14 mpg. This run represented the best average road conditions encountered on the trip. It contained superhighways, conventional highways, and idle running for display purposes. It was not running with a full load, however, but practically empty, with a gross train weight of 76,000 pounds. After this experience, the 705 gas turbine was quietly shelved. Ford did not need to undertake extensive cost studies to see that the 705 engine would be extremely costly to produce, while its superior part-load economy was of dubious value in a motor truck application.

Connie Bouchard was promoted to executive engineer of engineering planning for the Ford Motor Company in January, 1965 and Ivan Swatman was placed in charge of turbine engineering, research and development. Born in St. Albans, England, in 1924, he had graduated from the Watford Technical College of Engineering in 1940 and got his first job, in the heat of World War II pressure, as an apprentice in general engineering at the T. Mercer Company in St. Albans. In 1943 he joined D. Napier & Son's aircraft engineering division in Acton, London, as a development engineer. Two years later he began to work on experimental gas turbines for Napier. These included the Napier Nomad—a turbo-compound engine—and the Napier Naiad—a turboprop aircraft engine.

Swatman moved to the U.S. in 1947 as a project engineer on 5,000-hp turbine engines for the Flader Company in Buffalo, N.Y. For two years, he was manager of Flader's turbine testing facilities in Toledo, Ohio. From 1950 to 1956 he was a project engineer on industrial turbines under development by the Solar Aircraft Company (now Solar Division of International Harvester Company) in San Diego, California. Then he joined Ford.

He played a major part in the creation of the 704 and 705 turbines, but he was realistic enough to see that simpler mechanical configurations and simpler operating cycles must prevail. He attacked the problem of designing the next-generation Ford gas turbine by hiring one of the top men on Chrysler's turbine team—William I. Chapman.

Chapman had joined Chrysler right after his graduation from Iowa State University in 1941, and had been associated with George J. Huebner, Jr. in the development of the 1,000-hp turboprop engine for the U.S. Navy as well as playing a part in the design of all Chrysler automotive gas turbines from the first-generation engine up to and including the CR2A. Chapman, with his assistants R. G. Cadwell and H. C. Walch, was the chief architect of Ford's next-generation turbine.

THE FORD 707 GAS TURBINE

In overall concept, the Ford 707 gas turbine engine followed the design principles of Chrysler's A-831 unit, complete with variable geometry for the power turbine nozzle vanes. It was a free-shaft engine with two rotary regenerators, one on each side, and a single barrel-type combustor. While the Chrysler A-831 was a passenger car turbine, Ford scaled the 707 for truck application, with a rated power output of 375 hp. It was designed in 1965, tested and developed during 1966, and unveiled in October 1966.

The 707 weighed 1700 pounds and measured 40 inches long x 39 inches high x 33 inches wide. It was intended to power extra-heavy-duty-over-the-road highway tractors pulling 80,000 pounds at speeds up to 70 miles per hour for a normal service life of 500,000 miles. The operating cycle represented a return to normalcy from the 704-705 cycles.

After passing through an intake silencer and filter, air entered the engine through a compressor impeller and was discharged radially through a compressor diffuser. From the diffuser, the air was ducted on either side of the engine to the forward half of the regenerator covers and then through the regenerator cores into the combustor. The combustor discharged the heated air into a plenum which fed a compressor turbine nozzle and wheel. The air then flowed through a variable nozzle to the power turbine wheel, which was connected through a reduction gear to the power output shaft. On leaving the power turbine, the air was diffused through the regenerator and into exhaust pipes located on both sides of the engine.

The compressor in the 707 Ford turbine had a maximum speed of 37,500

The Ford 707 gas turbine engine.

revolutions per minute, the power turbine a maximum of 31,650 rpm and the output shaft 3,000 rpm. Maximum turbine inlet temperature was 1900° F (1040° C) and the exhaust gas temperature did not exceed 525° F (274° C).

The centrifugal compressor impeller was a one-piece aluminum casting with blades spaced radially on a somewhat cone-shaped disc. The inlet section took the form of a series of air scoops, bringing air into the impeller

Ford W-1000 truck powered by the Ford 707 unit.

where it was discharged radially and circumferentially by a combination of pumping action and centrifugal force.

The compressor diffuser was essentially made up of two parallel annular plates separated by wedge-shaped guide vanes. When the high velocity air leaving the impeller moved through the diffuser, the velocity was reduced and the pressure increased, completing the compression process.

The combustor was a relatively large cylinder, pierced by a series of air inlet and cooling holes. The combustor dome contained a fuel nozzle and swirler for atomizing the fuel burned in the engine, with an igniter positioned just below. Both turbines were of the axial-flow type.

The Cercor regenerator was a large disc. This slowly rotating component was mechanically driven by gearing on its rim from the compressor turbine shaft. The compressor air and exhaust gas were separated by means of regenerator seals which rubbed against the faces of the matrix, dividing it into semi-circular segments.

The main housing was a nodular iron casting, as were the bearing housings and front and rear covers. Minimal use of high temperature sheet metal was made in the hot flow path of the unit. Cast aluminum housings covered the ceramic regenerators on either side, forming the exhaust outlets for the engine. Commercially available cast nickel alloys were used for the turbine wheels.

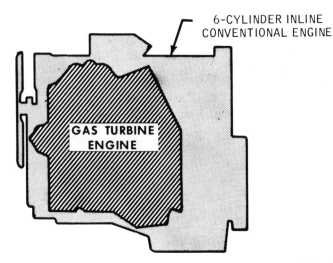

Comparison between the truck installation of the Ford 707 and the same vehicle with a diesel engine of similar power output.

The inlet silencer was a plastic box or plenum containing baffles and sound absorption materials. The inlet filter was a rectangular frame containing a pleated paper filter trapped between large mesh screens.

The Ford 707 gas turbine was installed in a W-1000 tilt-cab truck. The matter of matching the turbine to the vehicle was entrusted to Emmett J. Horton, a reputable engineer who had joined Ford in 1938 as an hourly worker at the River Rouge plant in Dearborn and risen through the ranks to the position of Chief Engineer of Ford's Engine & Foundry Division. In October 1966 he was named General Manager of the turbine operations of the Product Research Office.

A maximum number of accessories were driven from the transmission. That included the air-brake compressor, power steering pump, air-conditioning compressor, and 100-amp alternator. The engine was started by turning on the electric starter motor which was connected by gears to the gasifier shaft. Sequentially, as the compressor began drawing air into the engine, the regenerators began turning, a fuel flow value opened, the fuel pump began operation, the igniter was energized, and the compressor turbine began to develop power to drive the compressor. Once the compressor turbine developed sufficient power to drive the compressor, the starter turned off and the engine went into an idle running condition. The entire sequence was automatic and required only that the operator turn an ignition key to start position.

When the accelerator pedal was depressed to a certain position the engine

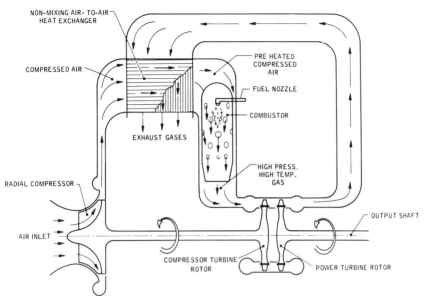

Gas flow path in the Ford 707 gas turbine engine.

ran in steady-state operation, and the fuel control maintained a constant gas generator speed by regulating the fuel flow into the engine. During acceleration the fuel control increased the fuel flow, and the gas generator accelerated at a scheduled maximum turbine inlet temperature up to the new governed setting for the gas generator. When the accelerator pedal was released, the gas generator returned to idle, and the power turbine nozzle switched automatically to the retard position, which assisted in slowing down the gasifier shaft. When the engine ignition key was turned off, the electrically operated fuel valve closed, the engine ran out of fuel, the compressor turbine no longer supplied power to drive the compressor, and the engine stopped.

In 1967 a fleet of 707 turbine-powered Ford W-1000 highway tractors was built and placed in service by Ford's General Parts Division. These trucks began to rack up substantial mileage, hauling parts from Rawsonville, Michigan to Ford plants in Sharonville and Lorain, Ohio, and Owosso, Michigan. Some 707 units ran over 4,000 hours without breakdown or failure, equivalent to between 125,000 and 200,000 miles on the road.

In 1969, Ford made an agreement with Continental Trailways to place a number of 707-turbine-powered buses in long-distance service. Both of these field test programs were highly successful, and Ford began to plan for full-scale production of turbines in its factory in Toledo, Ohio.

Continental Trailways bus powered by Ford's 707 gas turbine engine.

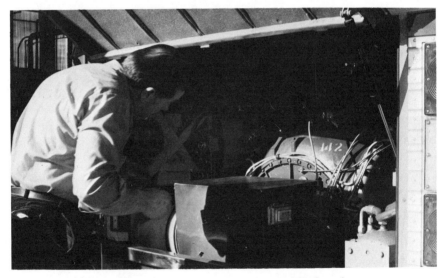

Ford 707 gas turbine installed in a Continental Trailways bus.

The passenger car gas turbine was a very low-priority project at Ford at this time, although a scaled-down version of the 707 (designated Model 706) was developed in 1966–67 and was tested in a number of Galaxie and Thunderbird cars. Cost and durability problems inhibited further development of the 706 unit.

Ford 710 (3600 series) gas turbine engine.

THE FORD 710 GAS TURBINE

With the benefit of improvements in component efficiency obtained in the course of normal development work, the 707 turbine soon reached the stage where Ford felt it could be put in production. The 707 turbine was redesigned with a number of changes made necessary by tooling and assembly considerations. Designated Model 710, it was to be built in three versions: 320 hp, 450 hp and 525 hp. This turbine series was not strictly a truck engine, but designed and developed for a multitude of industrial and marine applications.

Only the 450 hp unit, also designated the Series 3600 engine, has been built in significant numbers. Closely resembling the 707 in size and shape, it weighed 1700 pounds complete, and measured 40 inches long x 42 inches high x 35 inches wide. The main housing was the principal structural

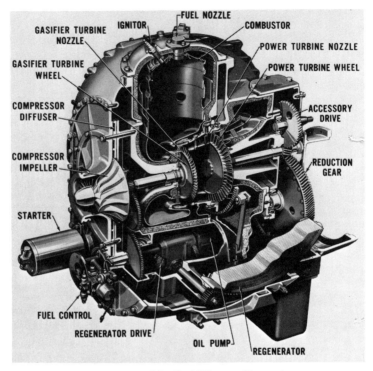

Cutaway view of the Ford 710 gas turbine engine.

member of the engine, to which five major subassemblies are attached. The subassemblies are: the gasifier, a variable power turbine nozzle, power turbine and reduction gear box, combustor and the regenerators.

Each was a self-contained unit. The gasifier rotor, variable nozzle assembly, and power turbine shaft were arranged in a line through the central axis of the main housing. Two regenerators and associated sealing systems were mounted in vertical planes on each side of the main housing and rotated on an axis normal to the main shaft axis. The combustor assembly was mounted vertically through an opening at the top of the housing. Accessories such as air-brake compressor, hydraulic pumps, alternator, and the engine oil cooler fan were belt-driven from the power turbine section.

The compressor had an air flow capacity of 4.7 pounds per second and operated at 79 percent efficiency with a 4.4 pressure ratio. Maximum compressor speed was 37,500 rpm. The blade tips of the cast compressor wheel were machined to match the shroud. The hub was bored for a steel sleeve, permanently installed with an interference fit. This sleeve controlled the fit to a pilot diameter on the turbine shaft, and the rear face seats on a shoul-

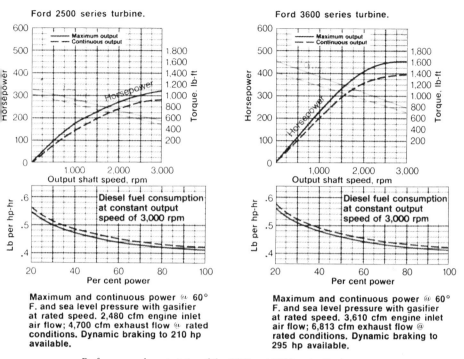

Ford 2500 series turbine.

Ford 3600 series turbine.

Maximum and continuous power @ 60° F. and sea level pressure with gasifier at rated speed. 2,480 cfm engine inlet air flow; 4,700 cfm exhaust flow @ rated conditions. Dynamic braking to 210 hp available.

Maximum and continuous power @ 60° F. and sea level pressure with gasifier at rated speed. 3,610 cfm engine inlet air flow; 6,813 cfm exhaust flow @ rated conditions. Dynamic braking to 295 hp available.

Performance characteristics of the 2500 and 3600 series Ford units.

der. The compressor and sleeve were retained on the shaft by a high axial-clamping load, obtained by stretching the bolt section of the shaft with a nut. This provided sufficient axial load to handle torque and bending loads at the attachment. A sheet metal spinner was attached to the inducer face to provide a suitable aerodynamic contour.

The compressor was balanced in two planes and assembled to the pre-balanced turbine rotor with the accessory drive pinion, and then the complete assembly was balanced. The compressor wheel was indexed in such a manner that it could be removed from the balanced assembly for installation into the gasifier housing and reassembled without changing balance.

The compressor diffuser was composed of two parts, the vaneless space and the vaned section. The function of the vaneless space was to reduce the supersonic Mach number leaving the impeller to a high subsonic value so that efficient entry might be made into the vaned area. The vaneless space had parallel walls with a radius ratio of 1.21 and it reduced the Mach number from a value of 1.091 at the impeller tip to 0.8 at the diffuser vane leading edge. The vaned diffuser had 18 vanes. Each passage had an area ratio of 2.46 and a divergence angle of 9.5 deg. The compressed pre-heated

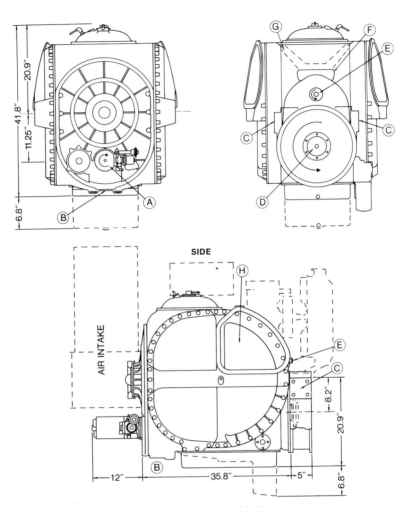

Installation drawings for the Ford 3600 series unit.

air entered the combustor at about 1175° F (635° C). Combustor efficiency was 98 percent, with a 4 percent pressure drop. Maximum fuel flow was 185 pounds per hour.

The combustor assembly consisted of a nodular iron cover, combustor liner, fuel nozzle, and ignitor. This assembly was installed vertically from the top of the engine with the end of the flame tube engaging the turbine

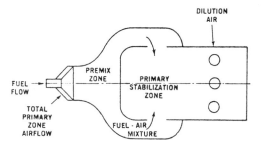

Ford's experimental "clean-air" combustor with external vaporization.

inlet plenum with a slip joint to allow for axial movement. The combustor was fabricated from Hastelloy X sheet metal.

A single air-assist nozzle supplied the fuel. This type of nozzle was selected on the basis of its ability to provide a good spray pattern over a wide range of fuel flows and with all types of fuel. An auxiliary air supply was required for starting. Once the engine has been started, the required amount of air was supplied from the compressor diffuser outlet. Solid state electronics adjusted fuel supply and power turbine nozzle vanes to achieve the speed requested at the load being delivered. Maximum turbine inlet temperature was fixed at 1900° F (1040° C).

The gasifier turbine nozzle was a precision investment casting. The vanes were cast integrally with the inner and outer shrouds. A conical support and mounting flange integral with the inner shroud was bolted to the rear gasifier housing. The conical section provided a mounting, giving accurate control of concentricity between the turbine shroud and the turbine wheel.

The gasifier rotor and shaft assembly and accessory gear train are supported in a two-piece nodular cast iron housing. This material was selected because it meets the requirements of high strength and stability at a temperature of about 500° F (260° C). The housing was split vertically to permit in-

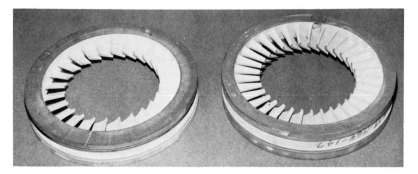

Two experimental nozzle ring assemblies made from ceramic materials.

stallation of the gears. The idler gear rotated on a cantilevered shaft pressed into the front housing. The accessory drive gear and starter drive gear were overhung-mounted on splined shafts, each of which rotated in two bearings pressed into the front housing.

The turbine wheel was a one-piece precision investment casting with integral blades and hub, made of a nickel-base alloy and inertia-friction-welded to the steel shaft. The gasifier shaft was supported radially by two pressure-lubricated sleeve bearings which were floating and pinned to the housing to prevent rotation. The front bearing was located in a separate bearing carrier, which was retained to the gasifier housing with a snap ring. A tapered-land thrust bearing carried the axial load of approximately 750 lb at design speed.

The first-stage turbine operated with a peak efficiency of 90 percent, while the power turbine did not exceed 84 percent efficiency. The power turbine assembly consisted of the power turbine wheel and bearings, reduction gears for the drive train and accessories, the turbine shroud and exhaust duct, an auxiliary lubrication pump, and a split housing to support the above components. The power turbine rotor construction was similar to that of the gasifier turbine wheel.

The power turbine rotor assembly was supported radially by a three-bearing system. At the turbine end was a pressure-loaded floating sleeve bearing of the same design as the turbine-end bearing of the gasifier shaft. The pinion was straddle-mounted between two bushings. The thrust loads on this shaft were small in magnitude because the gear thrust forces opposed the pressure forces on the turbine wheel. A thrust collar was clamped to the pinion by the turbine shaft and transmitted the thrust to tapered-land thrust bearings of the same configuration used in the gasifier section. Two bearings were required as the direction of thrust could change under different operating conditions.

The Ford 710 engines used two Cercor regenerator cores, each measuring 28 inches in diameter and 2.8 inches thick (about 71 by 7.1 centimeters). During operation, regenerator inlet temperatures ranged from ambient to 1,650 degrees F (900° C).

The regenerator cover was made of nodular cast iron, with vertical and horizontal beam sections to control deflection due to pressure loads. The front half of the cover was shaped as a shallow dome to transmit this pressure load into the mounting flange and beam structure. The rear half acted as an exhaust manifold, guiding the cooled gas leaving the regenerator core into the exhaust duct. The regenerator seals consisted of a metal rubbing shoe, coated for low friction and good wear resistance when running against the core surface under prevailing conditions. The shoes were backed by flexible metal diaphragms, pressure-balanced to keep the rubbing shoe in contact with the core at the minimum practical loading. The inner seal assembly was mounted and retained loosely against the seal platform in the engine housing. The outer seal was retained to the regenerator cover. Regenerator effectiveness was 88 percent, although leakage was as high as 6 percent.

The engine accessories were driven from the gasifier shaft. An accessory drive train of four spur gears was located immediately behind the compressor diffuser. This gear train drove the fuel control, front-mounted accessories, engine lubrication pump, and the regenerators. It also provided the starter drive. The starter drive consisted of a cam and roller type one-way clutch built into the starter gear.

The turbine reduction gear was made up of three gears, consisting of a high-speed pinion, a main drive gear, and a rear accessory drive gear. The design requirements for the reduction gears were that they be able to handle engine design horsepower with a power turbine speed of 31,650 rpm and reduce the speed to 3000 rpm. Helical gears were selected for this application because the helical gear offers a more uniform tooth engagement/disengagement, with helical overlap for a greater total contact ratio, and it results in a quieter drive train. In addition, helical gears permitted balancing the power turbine thrust against the pinion thrust.

Ford aimed for a specific fuel consumption of .41 pounds per hp-hour with the 710 engine. It came close but never fully met its objectives, neither for fuel economy nor for power output. Designed to deliver 450 hp, it never got beyond 395 hp in actual use.

It has been tested in a number of marine craft, in earth-moving equipment, in power generating sets, as a fire-engine pump, and in highway trucks. But the program has not been held to the schedule announced on June 23, 1970, which called for a production of 200 turbine engines during 1971. Only 36 had been placed in service by the end of 1972. In August 1973 Ford disclosed that the 710 gas turbine had been brought back from Toledo to Dearborn, where it would undergo a reappraisal and possible total redesign.

FORD'S LOW-NO$_x$ ALL-CERAMIC TURBINES

At the beginning of 1971, Ford began a new program to investigate the emission characteristics of gas turbine combustors. A parallel but independent program called for the development of a passenger car gas turbine engine using ceramic materials for all hot-running parts—combustor, nozzle assemblies, turbine wheels and shrouds. The responsibility for these activities was placed on the shoulders of Arthur F. McLean, manager of Ford's gas turbine research section, and his staff which included Wallace R. Wade, Peter I. Shen, Clifton W. Ounes, John R. Secord, and Nickolas A. Azelborn.

Arthur F. McLean came to Ford in 1961, and worked with Connie

Bouchard until his retirement. When the turbine organization was split up, with Ivan Swatman at the head of the truck turbine program, McLean became head of the turbine research and development section.

McLean was born in Bristol, England in 1929 and educated locally, graduating from the Bristol College of Technology with a degree in mechanical engineering. His first job was as an aircraft engine design engineer with Bristol Aircraft. He then joined Rotol and worked on propeller studies. During his military career, he was an engineering officer in the Royal Air Force, with responsibilities in the area of service and maintenance of turbojet engines. Soon afterwards he emigrated to Canada, where he held an engineering position with Orenda Engines Ltd. for about 18 months. Bendix Aerospace Division provided his next station, and he worked for several years on unconventional power plant systems research, including research on fuel cells and solar energy.

Ford had been experimenting with ceramics for various components since Cercor heat exchanger cores were first adopted for the Model 707. This work was done in collaboration with supplier firms like the Corning Glass Works, Owens-Illinois, and the Norton Company. In mid-1971 this work came to the attention of the Advanced Research Projects Agency—a unit of the U.S. Defense Department—which agreed to finance a five-year program based on Ford's head start in this area.

With ceramic components in all hot-running areas, there was a possibility of raising turbine inlet temperatures to 2500° F (1370° C) and beyond, with attendant benefits in power density, fuel economy, and weight saving. Extensive use of ceramics also promises significant reductions on material and manufacturing costs.

One of the main problems associated with extensive use of ceramic components is the incompatibility of these parts with the metallic shafts, seals, and ducts. Due to the brittle nature of all ceramics, the metal components around them must be able to provide an extra cushion to prevent cracking and deformation. The fact that this must be done without accepting any losses in aerodynamic efficiency aggravates the problem. Cracking, deformation, and fatigue failures of the ceramic parts are typical of design flaws and material mismatching, but are not restricted to the ceramic parts. The metal components are also subject to failure, especially as the cycle temperature is increased.

The initial Ford approach was to create a ceramic turbine wheel and shaft unit from a multi-density silicon nitride (Si_3N_4) combination. The turbine wheel and hub was made from hot-pressed silicon nitride, while the shaft, including bearing journals, was made from reaction-sintered silicon nitride.

During high-temperature spin testing, various failures were experienced. The bonding between the two materials failed at 44,000 rpm in one test, which led to the development of an intermediate-density slip cast ring as a link. It proved to give 50 percent higher strength than the lower-density injection-molded hoop originally used over the bonded area. Current studies and testing include work with silicon carbide parts formed by vapor deposition. This is a highly promising area in which Teledyne has been very active and seems to have taken the lead. Ford is engaged in extremely delicate research and development work here, which could bring extremely valuable results. But Arthur F. McLean leaves no doubt that results are necessarily a long way off. He stands on the threshold of a new branch of gas turbine technology, and while the goals are easy to formulate, the ways and means of achieving them are obscure in the extreme.

In combustor study, Ford's engineers have reported extensive progress, however. The key principles in Ford's approach have been pre-mixing, an advanced form of air-blast fuel nozzle, and flame stabilization by impinging jet.

Progress in turbine efficiency can have an adverse effect on emission control. In the regenerative engine, increased turbine inlet temperature leads to increased combustor inlet temperature, higher NO emissions and lower CO emissions. Ford's proposed low-NO_x combustor consists of a pre-mixing zone, primary reaction zone overlapping with a flame stabilization zone, and a dilution zone. The pre-mixing zone is located upstream from the combustor. All the air that enters the primary reaction zone is pre-mixed with atomized fuel droplets. The pre-mixing zone has enough length to allow time for complete vaporization. The pre-mixed flow is admitted to the primary reaction zone through carefully sized openings to prevent flame flashback.

Stabilizing the combustion process is an essential part of NO_x control. It can be done by various means. The flame can be stabilized by physical boundaries such as bluff bodies, recessed walls, and reverse flow ducts. Stabilization can also be achieved by purely aerodynamic means. Ford tested all possible methods.

All stabilization schemes depend on effective internal separation of the dilution zone air from the primary zone mixture flow. Recirculation must involve only primary zone combustion products, because dilution air entering the stabilizing zone can cause lean blowout. A simple bluff body consists of a fixed device, usually a cone, wedge or cylinder, placed in the air flow to set up vortex formation that provides recirculation within the stabilizing zone. The stability range can be widened by increasing the flow blockage of the flame holder, because that will increase the amount of recirculation. Heating the bluff body can also widen the stability range.

With a single bluff body, a very long combustor core would be required for high combustion efficiency, because the high air flow velocity and flame front velocity in a gas turbine prevent the single bluff body from greatly changing the angle of flame propagation. This might indicate the need for multiple bluff bodies, but the problem with a series of adjacent bluff bodies placed across the combustor is that they would cause a higher pressure drop, which translates into a power loss.

The recessed wall type of stabilizer consists of an enlarged diameter section of the combustor body. That provides an annular ledge which starts vortex formation. The greater the depth of the recess, the greater the amount of recirculation. The recessed wall stabilizer also required a very long combustor core for complete combustion to be attained.

The reverse flow stabilizer consists of ducts blocking the straight-ahead flow path and channeling it from the periphery up through the center of the combustor to the top, where the flow is reversed in a highly turbulent pattern. Studies remain incomplete, and a full evaluation is not yet available.

Aerodynamic stabilization schemes have advantages over the physical types of stabilizer. Mechanical complication is avoided, and their space requirements are smaller. Aerodynamic forms of flame stabilization include opposed jets, impinging jets, and controlled swirl. The opposed jet principle is based on a high-velocity jet opposed to the main air flow. Its momentum decelerates the mainstream and creates a recirculation zone all around the head of the jet. The opposed jet principle has proved to give a wide stabilization range, but unfortunately tends to give lower combustion efficiency.

The principle of swirl stabilization consists of introducing the mainstream tangentially into the primary reaction zone, thereby creating a central low-pressure region. Due to the low pressure, a portion of the air flow is drawn back upstream, and this is what creates a recirculation zone. The volume of the recirculation zone is dependent on the ratio of the angular momentum of the air flow to its axial momentum (swirl number). Tests indicate that swirl stabilization offers full combustion of very lean mixtures, good stability, and high efficiency, within a short combustor core. However, Ford has reported some problems with swirl stabilization. It appears that dilution air can be drawn into the primary zone and cause blowout.

The impinging jet stabilization system consists of air jets injected across the axis of the mainstream, forcing a portion of the flow back upstream to form a recirculation zone at the top of the central core. Combustion stability depends mainly on the amount of air participating in the recirculation. Maximum recirculation occurs, according to Ford, when six penetration holes are spaced out radially around the core. Tests indicate that impinging jet stabilization offers both high efficiency and good stability. With impinging jet stabilization, the risk of dilution air entering the recirculation zone is minimized by the strong mainstream flow.

According to Ford, there is theoretically a temperature of around 3000° F (1650° C) where NO_x as well as HC and CO emissions are below the original 1976 standards set in the Clean Air Act Amendment of 1970. Operation under this condition is largely dependent on raising combustor inlet temperature above the 300° F (150° C) mark while maintaining constant flame temperature.

Ford is also assuring the proper conditions by using special fuel atomization techniques. The basic process of atomization relies on the instability of a liquid jet surface under small disturbances. This instability is increased when the relative velocity between the jet and the air around it is increased. That means the shearing force has become stronger. What keeps the jet surface from breaking up is the surface tension. When surface tension is overcome, the jet will break up into droplets. The required rise in relative velocity can be obtained by a high-velocity air stream on one hand, or by raising the velocity of the liquid jet on the other.

At the outset, three types of atomizers were considered. One was a pressure-atomizing nozzle, using fuel pressure to generate a high-velocity turbulent jet. This same type of nozzle is extensively used in conventional combustors. Its worst drawback is its inability to produce droplets much smaller than 100 microns in diameter. Moreover, the quality of its atomized spray varies with the flow rate. And, of course, no pre-mixing is possible with a pressure atomizer.

The second type was an air-assist atomizing nozzle, also called a pneumatic atomizer or a twin-fluid atomizer. It is capable of producing very small droplets. Using high flow rates, this type of nozzle can deliver spray with an average droplet diameter of 20 microns.

The third type was an air-blast atomizing nozzle. That is a special variety of pneumatic atomizer with a high air-to-liquid volumetric flow ratio. The high air flow is generated by combustor differential pressure. The approximate mean diameter of the droplets produced in an air-blast atomizer is about 50 microns.

Ford finally chose an advanced form of air-blast nozzle. While the air assist or conventional air blast nozzles work with air/fuel ratios of 3–5 : 1, the Ford atomizer works with nozzle air/fuel ratios of 30–40 : 1. In this nozzle, a carefully generated swirling air flow produces a field of high shear rates which assist in breaking up a conical sheet of fuel into fine droplets. It uses low-pressure fuel injection and does not need additional fuel pressure or any form of air assist.

When the latest materials and the most efficient component designs are combined, Ford will build a new prototype passenger car gas turbine engine for installation in the Torino (intermediate size) car. The power plant design and vehicle adaptation will be established by the end of 1974. As far as actual production is concerned, there are no concrete plans. From a technological viewpoint, the earliest possible date for production, according to Arthur F. McLean, is 1982.

20

Case History: Williams Research Corporation

THE WILLIAMS RESEARCH COR-
PORATION is a leading manufacturer of small gas turbines as well as a leading organization in the progress of gas turbine technology. The relatively small company, located at Walled Lake, Michigan, some 21 miles northwest of downtown Detroit, is also a consultant to several automobile manufacturers. Notable clients have included Volkswagen, Toyota, and General Motors. Samuel B. Williams, owner and President of Williams Research Corporation, says his role is to support the auto companies and help them succeed in the gas turbine business. The turbine cars built by Williams Research Corporation have been standard production models converted to gas turbine power as part of contracts from industry or government.

Sam Williams is known as a thorough engineer, an inventive genius, and a tireless developer. He is the son of Dr. Clyde Williams, who for many years was head of Battelle Industries in Columbus, Ohio. Born in Seattle, Washington on May 7, 1921, he grew up in Ohio. He graduated from Purdue University in 1942 with a degree in mechanical engineering, and performed graduate work in thermodynamics and helicopter design. He found a job with the engineering staff of Chrysler Corporation when he left school. Working on a multitude of wartime projects, Chrysler had just initiated work on gas turbines. Sam Williams was assigned to the turbine group, and worked as a project engineer on the T36-D2 recuperative turboprop engine developed for the U.S. Navy by Chrysler.

Later, he was placed in charge of design of Chrysler regenerative automotive gas turbines, reporting to George J. Huebner, Jr., who had sparked the turbine program and later became vice president of research for Chrysler.

Sam Williams demonstrating a model of the toroidal combustion chamber, his forefinger pointing to the fuel ejector orifice in the shaft.

Sam Williams left Chrysler in 1954 to form his own company. His plan was to concentrate on the small gas turbine. He was joined by three of the men who had worked most closely with him at Chrysler: John F. Jones, Jack Benson, and Harold Way. Their first contract came from Outboard Marine Corporation (makers of Evinrude and Johnson engines). Williams and his team persuaded Outboard Marine that a small gas turbine would be ideal for boats, and in 1956 Williams began tests of a small craft equipped with a small gas turbine developed with funds obtained from Outboard Marine Corp. The tests were very successful, but OMC cancelled the contract. The company felt that the gas turbine would also have a great future in passenger cars, and wanted to wait until the automobile industry had developed suitable turbines and started mass production. This way, OMC figured it could obtain well-proven gas turbines at lower cost. Sam Williams, however, forged ahead aided by research contracts from the U.S. Army and from De Havilland Aircraft in Great Britain.

Pioneering in small turbine technology by Williams Research produced the first gas turbine outboard for boats, the first installation of gas turbines in Army jeeps, and the first helicopter rotor tip mounted turbojet.

The Williams automotive gas turbines are descended from a line of small turbojets, starting with the original WR2 of 1956. The prototype WR2 turbojet engine began life with a thrust of only 70 pounds. This design was produced as a company-funded effort, without a contract, on the strength of

Williams WR-19—the world's smallest fanjet engine—weighs 67 pounds and delivers 430 pounds thrust.

Sam Williams' belief that a market would develop if a good small jet engine became available.

It was followed by a 75 hp helicopter engine, the WR-3, the first turboshaft design from Williams. It weighed about 50 pounds. Air flow capacity was 1.4 pounds per second. The WR-3 included the key elements that have become typical of Williams Research turboshaft engines: toroidal combustor, centrifugal compressor, and two axial-flow turbines mounted on concentric but unconnected shafts.

The WR8 automotive turboshaft engine started as an in-house project, without a contract. Wiliams then received a contract for two 75-hp engines for light military vehicles from the U.S. Army Automotive Tank Command. The WR8 was a simple cycle engine, without heat exchangers, and shared many of the key components with the WR-3. Two of these units were installed in Jeeps and became part of a test program that went on for several years.

It was in 1964 that Volkswagen signed an agreement with Williams Research Corporation. This contract is still in force, and the development history will be given in a separate chapter devoted to Volkswagen. The contract with General Motors dated from 1970, and the work was terminated at the end of 1972.

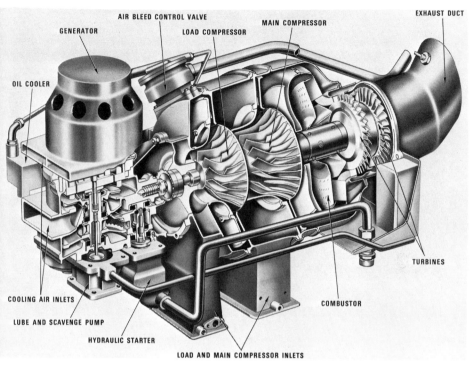

Cutaway view of the Williams WR-27 industrial turboshaft engine. It is commonly used as an aircraft APU (auxiliary power unit).

In 1966 Williams received a design contract for a 500 hp industrial gas turbine from Waukesha Motor Co. The design principles are the same as in the smaller turboshaft Williams engines, but on a larger scale. It is also a regenerative turbine. The T-500-L has an air flow capacity of 6 pounds per second and the compressor works with a pressure ratio of 5.

In 1971 Williams Research Corporation installed its WR26 regenerative gas turbine in an AMC Hornet. Williams Research Corporation did not build this car as part of its regular research and development activity. It was built under a $240,000 contract from the Environmental Protection Administration of the City of New York as part of a five-year study to demonstrate the feasibility of experimental power systems for motor vehicles operating in urban service. It was delivered to New York officials on February 17th, 1972 and was the first gas turbine powered car actually *sold* in the U.S.

The WR26 engine was rated at 80 shaft horsepower (at 4,450 output shaft rpm) and generated 198 pounds-feet of torque at stall. The basic engine

Williams WR-26 gas turbine engine.

Exploded view of the working parts in the WR-26 unit.

weighed 250 pounds, without accessories. It was 24 inches long × 26 inches wide × 16 inches high. It was a two-shaft regenerative gas turbine, with concentric shafts, and with the output shaft extending from the front cover (the cool end).

The compressor had an air flow capacity of 1.25 pounds per second, and worked with a pressure ratio of 4. Air entered the compressor at ambient temperature. The compressor added 350° F (177° C) with its 4 : 1 pressure ratio. The heat exchangers raised the absolute temperature to about 1,000° F (540° C). Combustion temperature could reach 2,100° F (1150° C), but the gases were down to 1,700° F to 1,750° F (927–955° C) by the time they entered the first-stage turbine. Exhaust gases from the second-stage turbine were 1,100° F (590° C) prior to entering the heat exchanger, and the exhaust gas from the tailpipe was under 500° F (260° C) at full power.

The WR-26 used Williams patented toroidal combustor design, with low-pressure fuel injection through the gasifier shaft. Atomization of the fuel was assured by the high air speed around the axis, and this provided excellent uniformity of distribution. Fuel metering was part hydromechanical and

Williams WR-26 heat exchanger assembly (held by the author).

part electro-mechanical. The desired air turbulence was assured by the shape, size and angle of the diffuser orifices that admitted the heated air from the two regenerators—one on each side.

The advantages claimed for the Williams combustion chamber and fuel delivery system are improved mixture uniformity, lower fuel consumption, reduced exhaust gas odors, and more complete combustion. This design also minimizes the effect of temperature variations during operation, which might otherwise cause unevenness in burning or in temperature distribution in the different parts of the chamber. The parts are simple and inexpensive to manufacture, require little or no maintenance, and are consistent with compact construction. The chamber itself was formed of a number of plates of curved or dished shape, combining to form an annulus.

The fuel pump controlled the rate of fuel flow, and the injector nozzles operated by a combination of fluid pressure buildup and centrifugal force. Fuel was fed into a float chamber by centrifugal force. The same centrifugal force also acted on the float and kept the float in a position to block the orifice. When fluid pressure in the float chamber was high enough to overcome the centrifugal force acting on the float, the float was lifted away from the orifice, and fuel sprayed out into the combustor.

A stator member at the exit from the combustion chamber sped up the gas flow while the gases were still expanding, and directed them at a fixed angle towards the blades of the first-stage turbine. The turbine wheels were only 5 inches in diameter. The centrifugal compressor discharged into a diffuser designed for maximum compactness.

The diffuser inner member had a radius at its outer edge, leading to an axially extending section containing a number of spiral-shaped passages created by vanes formed on the outer surface of the inner member. The vanes had gradually increasing cross-sectional area although their outer diameter was constant. The diffuser ports extended radially inward at the forward end of the ducting to the recuperators. This assured a minimal possibility of intereference between the diffuser vanes and the supersonic wake from the compressor vanes.

An exhaust diffuser was attached to the rear edge of the second-stage turbine shroud, and served to conduct the gases into an annular plenum chamber leading to the regenerator ducts. The diffuser contained a number of flared annular members positioned in spaced, nested relation, and held in place by bolts.

The Cercor regenerator discs were 2.75-inch thick and had a diameter of 12.5 inches. They were driven at a maximum speed of 21 rpm by a roller chain with hub drive engagement in the discs. The drive for the two regenerator core shafts was taken via a train of spur gears from the output shaft, with a worm gear connection to the shafts carrying the sprockets for the chain drive to the regenerator core shafts. These chain and sprocket drives are of the same type as used on bicycles, and have relatively large space tolerances between their respective contact areas, so that all parts in the regenerator drive have a generous measure of freedom to expand or distort due to variations in temperature without affecting the reliability of the regenerator core drive.

Williams developed its own bellows-type seals for the heat exchangers. The seals were made of heat-resistant alloy sheet metal, avoiding preformed curvatures in the cross sections of the individual bellows layers, and thereby greatly reducing the production cost of the seals. By means of masking, brazing material was applied to alternate inner and outer edges of the stampings. The assembly of shoes and diaphragms was built up together with shoe guides, spacers and shims. The spacers alternately overlapped the inner and outer diaphragm edges, and were so thick that when the assembly was squeezed together, the diaphragms were distorted. It was the spacers that determined the corrugation height of the finished seal. After brazing, the spacers and shims were removed, and the seal was then finished.

The accessory drive was taken from the compressor shaft. In addition to the engine accessories, the shaft powered a transmission oil pump. Concentric gears were used for the transmission power drive and pump drive, and an overrunning clutch was place between these concentric gears which normally rotate at different speeds (one at gasifier shaft speed, the other at power turbine speed). The clutch was normally inoperative, the normal condition being that the compressor shaft turned at a higher rpm than the power turbine shaft.

Should the power train reach excessive speed, for instance, with the rear wheels spinning on ice, the overrunning clutch would engage, connecting the output shaft to the compressor shaft, and putting a brake on the power turbine. This overrunning clutch was also designed to go into action during coasting, to provide a measure of engine braking.

Starter drive and oil pump were positioned at the other end, with provision for an oil cooler fan. The alternator was located below the heat exchanger drive, driven by belt from a pulley on a gear-driven shaft. The same gear train also served as a drive for the fuel control assembly.

The Hornet 4-door compact sedan had a curb weight of 2,830 pounds and was built on a 108-inch wheelbase with an overall length of 179.3 in. The vehicle design was conventional, with the power unit in front and rear wheel drive. It had independent front suspension with coil springs, and a beam-type rear axle with long-leaf semi-eliptic springs (Hotchkiss drive). The turbine is installed in the place of the standard piston engine in the front end of the chassis. The drive was taken from the front of the engine, with a gear drive to an output shaft running beneath the entire turbine unit to link up with the standard 3-speed Borg-Warner automatic transmission (which included the hydraulic torque converter).

This layout seems puzzling, but there are valid reasons why it was done that way. The WR-26 power plant was based on a prototype designed for a Volkswagen rear-end installation, and when it was decided to make an adaptation for front end mounting, the engine was simply moved forward without turning it around. This installation gave no drawbacks in terms of accessibility to the turbine, but it would have been possible to lower the turbine in the chassis if the unit had been turned around with its power output shaft facing backwards instead of forwards. Since the turbine unit was light and compact, there was no problem retaining the Hornet's low hood line, and the slightly higher engine mounting did not substantially affect the center of gravity height.

For an experimental car, where construction time and expediency are of prime importance, the installation must be judged satisfactory, but it would not be acceptable in a production model. The transmission was readjusted to give shift points more suitable for the turbine's torque characteristics. The reduction gearing at the front of the unit had an 11.5 : 1 ratio, which brought rotational speeds down to the normal level for the hydraulic torque converter and planetary gear system.

On the outside, the car was practically indistinguishable from a standard Hornet, except for the use of special wide-rim light alloy wheels and Michelin X tires. Inside, the standard instrument cluster was supplemented by a

Jim Dunne (left) and the author examine the WR-26 unit installed in the Hornet.

tachometer (recording compressor shaft rpm), an oil pressure gauge, and an oil thermometer. The extra panel also contained a red warning light and a green OK light for use during the starting sequence. The WR-26 had an electrical starting system, wired into the ignition key in the normal fashion. To start the key must be turned to "Start" position and held for 7–10 seconds, until the compressor shaft has reached 40,000 to 45,000 rpm. At that point, the green OK light will come on and the starter and igniter can be disengaged.

The WR-26-powered Hornet had a top speed of 80–85 mph, and was capable of accelerating from standstill to 60 mph in 18 seconds (including an acceleration lag of 1.5 to 1.8 seconds).

The test program planned by the New York City Bureau of Motor Vehicle Pollution Control, was to take place over a 6-month period. The vehicle was to undergo special emissions and performance evaluations, and to go into everyday service in New York City traffic. However, the car was not placed in regular service, but went from one test laboratory to another, shuttling between the EPA establishment in Ann Arbor, Michigan, and the City of New York Department of Air Resources' facility in Greenpoint, Brooklyn. The object of the testing was to determine whether the gas turbine engine was a viable low-pollution alternative to the conventional gasoline engine for urban use. The reports have been inconclusive.

21

Case History: Volkswagen

IT WAS IN 1964 THAT Volkswagenwerk decided to start gas turbine research and development. The program started as an investigation of low-emission power plants for passenger cars. In other words, Volkswagenwerk was attracted to the turbine on the basis of one of its less fully established properties. Volkswagen knew it was starting from scratch, when the other major car companies had a head start in turbines. Therefore VW wanted a connection that would provide instant know-how, and found it at Williams Research Corp. VW and Williams signed a licensing agreement which gave VW access to the Williams patents and technology. In addition, Williams was to design a basic gas turbine engine for Volkswagen. The turbine program was assigned to the research branch directed by Dr. W. H. Hucho, and the top turbine engineer is Dr. Ing. Peter Walzer.

The objective of the turbine program at the outset was to establish the feasibility of turbine power for cars and to gain experience with that type of vehicle. This led to three requirements for the turbine configuration:

1. The gas turbine package must fit into the current VW (1966–72) model range.
2. Performance levels and fuel economy must be comparable with those obtained in current piston engines.
3. The turbine must be adaptable to an existing transmission system.

Volkswagen also thought it would be important to obtain a baseline turbine design that offered particular ease of component modifications, so that individual components could be replaced by other units of different design without causing changes in the rest of the engine system. This was held to be needed in order to obtain a reliable data bank of the effects of specific design changes in terms of part-load fuel consumption, combustion charac-

The VW GT-70 gas turbine engine.

teristics and emission control, manufacturing costs and transmission requirements.

On this basis, Williams Research Corp., in collaboration with VW's technical side, worked out the basic engine configuration. It was to be a twin-shaft gas turbine with two rotary heat exchangers and integral reduction gearing. The first-stage turbine drives the centrifugal compressor, while the second-stage turbine drives the output shaft. The two shafts are concentric, but revolve independently of each other.

Since all VW models at that time used rear-mounted engines, the gas turbine unit was designed for installation in the tail end of the chassis, with reduction gearing and a transmission mounting flange on the forward side. The initial prototype was designed with a toroidal combustor, though provision was included for easy change-over to a barrel-type combustor during the development program. The toroidal combustor has some problems: First, it generates very high heat closer to the shaft and bearings. Secondly, it presents maintenance difficulties, being buried deep inside the housing.

The same basic design has been produced with different types of housings and different types of heat exchangers. It has been built with and without such features as variable nozzle geometry and power transfer. It is essentially a two-shaft design, but it has also been built in a single shaft version. This was easily arranged by locking the two shafts together.

The turbine is built in two separate sections: a gasifier section, and the output section. The gasifier section includes the compressor, combustor, and first-stage turbine. The output section includes the second-stage turbine and the reduction gearing. The housing is a one-piece nodular casting shaped like the intersection of two tunnels. One tunnel runs in the axial plane and houses all the rotating members. The other tunnel connects the two regenerators to the gas flow system.

The centrifugal compressor operates with a 3.7 pressure ratio and 75 percent efficiency. Air flow capacity is 1.3 pounds per second. The compressor wheel is made of aluminum alloy to minimize the inertia. Both turbines are of the axial-flow type, and both are preceded by fixed nozzle guide vanes. The first-stage turbine runs with 81 percent efficiency and the second-stage turbine with 84 percent efficiency.

The toroidal combustor was originally designed without regard for NO_x control, but emission control is now the number one focal point for further development. The primary zone is close to the shaft, since fuel is injected from slinger-type nozzles carried on the shaft by centrifugal force. Combustion starts in this primary zone, where the fuel mixes with up to 15 percent of the air consumed by the turbine engine. A special diffuser controls air flow path and velocity as it enters the combustor so as to assure flame stabilization, and create a dilution zone around the outer area nearest the exhaust ports.

The nozzle assemblies are made of HS 31 cobalt alloy, and the turbine wheels of Inconel 713 LC. The combustor shell is made of Hastelloy X to resist the very high thermal loads it is subjected to. To cool the combustor shell, some of the compressed air is separated from the mainstream and ducted along the combustor skin, and returned to the mainstream in the dilution zone.

Turbine inlet temperature is 1675° F (913° C), and the exhaust gas temperature is restricted to 626° F (330° C) at full power. At idle, exhaust gas temperature is only 300° F (150° C). The gasifier shaft has a maximum speed of 61,400 rpm and the power turbine has a maximum speed of 50,600 rpm. The 10.23 reduction gear ratio assures a maximum output shaft speed of 4550 rpm.

The two concentric shafts are connected in the common reduction gear at the front of the engine with an overrunning clutch. This clutch will be automatically engaged whenever the power turbine speed exceeds the gasifier turbine speed. This connects the power turbine to the compressor and provides engine braking, due to the power absorbed in driving the compressor. Unfortunately there is a lag in the braking action, which is due to the heat exchangers continuing to run hot while not being supplied with adequate amounts of cold air when the accelerator pedal is released.

The accessory drive is taken from the gasifier shaft, and accessory drive power consumption is 4.5 hp at full speed. The Cercor regenerators are driven from the hub through an arrangement consisting of a worm gear on the accessory drive shaft, a train of spur gears, and a final chain-drive stage to the regenerator core shafts. Top speed of the regenerators is 22 rpm. Regenerator effectiveness is 80 percent, with 3 percent leakage losses. The cool side pressure loss is only one percent, while the hot side has a pressure loss of 7.5 percent.

In starting, an electric starter drives the gasifier shaft to 10,000 rpm. When 10,000 rpm is reached, fuel is injected into the combustion chamber and ignition takes place. The gasifier accelerates to its idling speed of 36,900 rpm. At 30,000 rpm the starter is disengaged and the ignitor is cut off.

The GT-70 engine weighs 375 pounds including all accessories and measures 24 inches long x 26 inches wide x 16 inches high. The engine is rated at 75 hp at 4550 rpm output shaft speed, with a peak torque of 86.8 pounds-feet. Specific fuel consumption is .628 pounds per hp-hour. Road-load fuel economy has been extensively tested.

The fuel used during most of the tests was Diesel No. 2, but operation with kerosene, lead free gasoline and methanol was also investigated. The measurements show the fuel economy at typical passenger car operating conditions. Volkswagen adopted an EPA proposal for a 100-mile driving cycle corresponding partly to city traffic, partly steady average suburban traffic and partly fast highway driving. For the 100 miles in this mixed traffic, the experimental gas turbine vehicle consumed 8.7 gallons of Diesel fuel compared with 5.3 gallons of gasoline for the equivalent piston engine vehicle. Test cars included both the Microbus and the Type 3 station wagon (Squareback sedan).

The first test vehicle was running in 1968. It was a VW1600 Squareback (Type 3), with the turbine installed in the rear end of the chassis, in place of the regular VW flat-four piston engine. Later the Microbus was chosen because of its roominess, which enables it to carry more instrumentation and test equipment. In 1971, Volkswagenwerk built two turbine-driven Microbuses. All installations use the Type 3 automatic transmission, manufactured by Fichtel & Sachs.

This 3-speed automatic transmission has a ratio of 2.65 : 1 in first gear, 1.59 : 1 in second gear and 1 : 1 in third gear. The two-shaft gas turbine has an inherent torque factor of approximately 2. Together with the transmission, a torque increase of 5.3 is achieved at the start which is quite sufficient for getting the car in motion. Therefore the hydraulic torque converter normally used in the transmission could be eliminated.

The elimination of hydraulic slip helps shorten the acceleration lag, which is of the order of 1.25 to 1.4 seconds. The turbine-powered Variant

GT-70 unit installation in the VW Microbus.

goes from zero to 60 mph in 14.4 seconds, and the Microbus in about 16 seconds. A comparison with corresponding standard VW vehicles powered by piston engines is illuminating. The initial acceleration of the piston engine car is higher during the first 1.5 seconds. After 6 seconds both vehicles have the same speed and after 14 seconds they have covered the same driving distance.

Analysis of the fuel consumption test results reveals that the higher fuel consumption of the gas turbine is mainly due to excessive idle consumption. Of the 200 minutes driving over the assumed 100 miles, 75 minutes are taken up by engine deceleration and idling. During idle periods, the gas tur-

Shaft assembly for VW GT-70, with compressor at left, turbine wheels at right.

VW Microbus powered by the GT-70 gas turbine engine.

bine consumed 2 gallons of fuel compared with 0.5 gallons for the piston engine.

For a possible solution to this problem, the Volkswagen engineers devised a method to open a bypass in the flow path between the first-stage turbine and the power turbine. This provided an increased enthalpy gradient at the gasifier turbine, which lowered the idling consumption during the driving cycle to 1.4 gallons, while also reducing the power output at idle.

Another cause for higher fuel consumption is the excessive consumption at low speeds. In the mixed load test the vehicles were driven for about 1 hour at average speeds of 30 miles per hour. In this operation the basic gas turbine consumed 0.8 gallons more than the piston engine. Tests with variable nozzle geometry and power transfer prove that significant improvements are possible.

Dr. Walzer believes that the question of whether gas turbine cars will be mass-produced is conditional on three items: First, the future emission standards and the gas turbine's ability to meet them; second, the extent to which

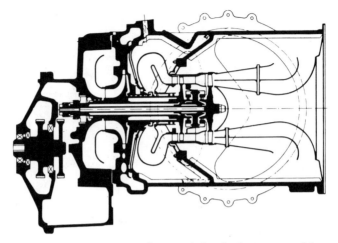

Sectioned view of the VW GT-70 unit, with output shaft and reduction gear at left, regenerators and exhaust ducts at right.

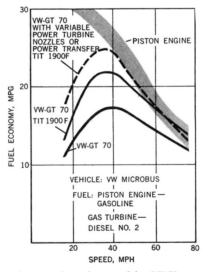

Fuel consumption in the normal speed range of the GT-70-powered VW Microbus.

idle and part-load fuel consumption can be improved without sacrificing performance; and third, whether production costs can be reduced to the level of piston engines. Emission testing is a major part of the turbine program, with encouraging results. The combustion characteristics give extremely low unburned hydrocarbon and carbon monoxide levels. Fuel flow is increased with a rise in gasifier shaft speed. Since combustion improves as

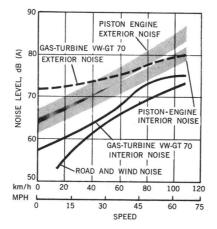

Turbine-powered VW is consistently quieter inside than the standard vehicle.

load is increased, there are practically no HC emissions at high loads. The CO mass emissions rise only slightly. But oxides of nitrogen emission pose a problem. Increasing combustion zone temperatures and rising fuel flow led to a 10-fold increase in NO_x emissions at full load as compared to those at idle.

To evaluate transient state emission performance, the VW-GT 70 was installed in various test vehicles and operated through various driving schedules. The Volkswagen GT-70 gas turbine car already meets the proposed emission standards through 1976. With regard to the proposed standards for 1977, however, the gas turbine's NO_x emissions are still too high.

When asked about the direction further efforts in emission control will take, Dr. Walzer explained:

"Assuming that the devices already mentioned for improving fuel economy will be incorporated it will be seen, that, without modifying the combustion system, this gas turbine would emit only 1.5 grams of NO_x per mile." To get the NO_x emission levels lower, Dr. Walzer indicated that prevaporizing and premixing of the air/fuel mixture before it reached the reaction zone, as well as maintenance of a lean condition in the reaction zone under all conditions would be necessary.

Preliminary cost studies have been undertaken all along. Volkswagenwerk estimated that with a production volume of 400 units a day, the gas turbine would cost 2½ times what it now costs to build a VW production-type piston engine. Dr. Walzer says 50 percent of the cost is accounted for by three items:

1. Precision-cast parts (turbines and compressor wheels).

Emission levels prove gas turbine is "clean air" power						
Driving schedule	Vehicle	Fuel	NOx gm/mile	CO gm/mile	HC gm/mile	Remarks
7-mode California cycle	VW Microbus	JP-4	1.7	3.3	0.7	Continuous analysis
US—22-min., 52-sec. federal driving cycle	VW 1600 Squareback	Leadfree gasoline	2.15	4.5	0.35	Measured at EPA with a CVS system
US—22-min., 52-sec. federal driving cycle	VW Microbus	JP-4	2.6	4.9	0.5	Continuous analysis

Comparison of three turbine-powered VW vehicles in dynamometer emission tests.

2. The control system.
3. The heat exchangers.

If the gas turbine gets the green light, the years 1975–1978 will be spent optimizing the design. Component development and testing would take 4 years (1979–1982). Building a plant and installing the tooling would take 18 months to 2 years, which leaves 1984 as the earliest possible date for mass-production startup of the Volkswagen turbine car. It will not be anything like the Type 2 or Type 3 experimental cars.

Since the VW car line is rapidly evolving from a one-model program to a full range of models from economy cars to compact luxury cars, the turbine concept laid down in 1964 is no longer adequate. A new turbine will go on the drawing board as soon as the period of testing and evaluation with the existing GT-70 unit is ended. The next-generation VW turbine will be rated between 100 and 200 hp. Key design features will be regenerators of reduced diameter, and operation with higher turbine inlet temperature. Ceramic parts are under investigation.

22

Case History: Boeing

THE BOEING COMPANY in Seattle, Washington, was one of the largest airplane builders in the world at the time of the U.S. entry into World War II. As an airframe constructor, however, Boeing had never built its own piston-type aircraft engines. But in 1943 Boeing started its own gas turbine research program as a direct result of the U.S. Army Air Force's having expressed an interest in jet propulsion for large aircraft. Boeing set up a jet-propulsion laboratory in the main plant in Seattle, Washington, and in the initial stage conducted pure research. Later, Boeing designed and built its own gas turbine, and began to test and evaluate each component individually.

Boeing tried both axial-flow and centrifugal compressors, for instance, and experimented with several combustor configurations. At the conclusion of the first component development phase, in 1945, the first experimental gas turbine was assembled. This power unit was designated the Model 500.

Model 500 was a simple-cycle dual-combustor turbojet engine delivering 180 pounds of thrust at 36,000 rmp. It was 29 inches long with 2.2 sq. ft. frontal area, and it had a weight of only 85 pounds. A turboshaft version of the same basic unit was soon developed, with the designation Model 502. It was a two-shaft design without any mechanical connection between the gasifier shaft and the power turbine shaft.

The first turboshaft Model 502 ran in 1947 and delivered 160 hp with a turbine inlet temperature of 1500° F (815° C). In 1950 the U.S. Navy Bureau of Ships placed a production contract for a number of Model 502 turboshaft engines with Boeing. They were to be installed in mine-sweeper vessels, not as part of the propulsion system, but to drive electric generator sets. The Model 502 family of turboshaft engines expanded very rapidly, as

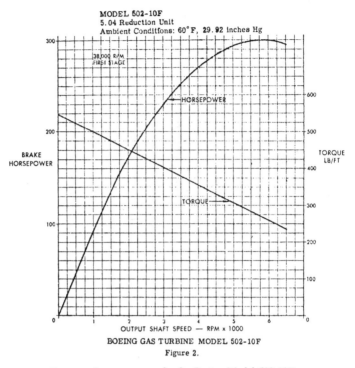

MODEL 502-10F
5.04 Reduction Unit
Ambient Conditions: 60° F, 29.92 inches Hg

BRAKE HORSEPOWER

TORQUE LB/FT

OUTPUT SHAFT SPEED — RPM x 1000

BOEING GAS TURBINE MODEL 502-10F
Figure 2.

Power and torque curves for the Boeing Model 502-10F.

adaptations were made for different applications, and older versions were replaced by new designs as the state of the art progressed.

Model 502-2E and Model 502-8A were developed for use as auxiliary power units or turboprop adaptation, while the Model 502-7B was designed to work strictly as an air compressor. Models 502-2, 502-6 and 502-8A were rated at 175 hp, with a turbine inlet temperature of 1550° F (843° C). As development continued, specific fuel consumption was reduced from 1.4 pounds per hp-hour to 1.35 pounds per hp-hour.

The Model 502-8A was the first to be used for driving a highway vehicle, and a more detailed examination of this particular version is in order. It used a single-stage centrifugal compressor with 22 blades, and compressor airflow capacity was 3.25 pounds per second at 36,000 rpm. The combustors were of the cylindrical straight-through-flow type. They had an outer shell made of stainless steel, while the inner flame tube was fabricated from Inconcel sheet. Each combustor was equipped with a simple fuel nozzle at the front end. The first-stage turbine was rated for a maximum speed of

36,000 rpm while the second stage turbine had a maximum speed of 25,000 rpm.

Both turbine wheels were of the axial-flow type. Each turbine was preceded by a nozzle ring assembly containing 27 nozzle blades. Both turbine wheels had alloy steel disc hubs, with solid nickel alloy blades welded to them. The first-stage turbine had 56 blades, and the second stage turbine 44 blades. Turbine wheel diameter was 7.28 inches. The accessories were driven from the gasifier shaft, and comprised a fuel pump and governor, starter and starter-generator, power turbine governor, and two tachometer-generators (one for each shaft).

The Model 502-8A was adapted for installation in a Kenworth three-axle highway tractor with semi-trailer. The engine weighed 140 pounds and was only 42 inches long. This installation was made in 1950 and over a 12-year period the truck accumulated 60,000 miles. This 10-ton Kenworth truck was a 6-wheel chassis, with both the rear axles driving. The drive line was entirely mechanical, using a 7-speed transmission.

The trailer was loaded to the limit of the Washington state gross vehicle weight regulations, giving a gross road train weight of 72,000 pounds. Tractor weight was 27,500 pounds, payload weight 44,500 pounds (including the semi-trailer). The vehicle was placed in regular freight-hauling service by the West Coast Far Freight Motor Service, and driven by regular truck drivers without any special gas turbine training or background.

By the end of 1951 it had logged 550 hours of service and traveled some 15,000 miles over West Coast highways. Fuel consumption was 1.1 to 1.2

Kurtis-Kraft racing car powered by Boeing Model 502 gas turbine engine. The vehicle is on permanent display in the Indianapolis Speedway Museum.

miles per gallon, while conventionally powered rigs of similar gross vehicle weight averaged 3 to 5 mpg.

Bends in the exhaust stack had caused buildup of back pressure which limited output to 160 hp and contributed to the relatively poor fuel economy. This poor fuel economy in the turbine truck was largely due to the lack of a heat exchanger. On the other hand, its road performance was spectacular.

This Boeing Kenworth truck was raced from a standing start against an equivalent model, equally loaded, but powered by a 200-hp diesel engine. At the end of a half-mile run, the turbine truck was ahead by about 250 feet. But the extra 25 hp in the diesel gave it higher top speed, and after the speed of the turbine truck had leveled off at 55–56 mph the diesel caught and passed it.

Several problems with the Model 502-8A unit appeared early in the test experience. Rubbing contact between the turbine blade tips and the turbine shroud was caused not by expansion of the wheels, but by distortion of the shrouds. This necessitated a change in material specification. Another type of failure resulted from ingress of foreign objects. The damage showed up as blade deformation and cracking. The cause was analyzed as a structural weakness augmented by high-frequency vibration, and the problem was corrected by detail design improvements.

The first-stage turbine blades never failed in the airfoil section, but the power turbine blades did. This was caused by resonant blade vibrations, which led Boeing to make successive steps of stiffening the blades with relatively slight changes in profile and radial section. This raised the natural frequency and reduced the centrifugal stress, and proved to be an effective cure.

The truck was taken out of service by mutual agreement, as it had failed to show competitive fuel economy and maintenance costs, though only after it had demonstrated the gas turbine's potential as a prime mover for highway trucks. The availability of the Boeing Model 502 drew several other companies into gas turbine evaluation programs.

In 1952 the U.S. Army installed a Model 502-9A gas turbine in a 2½-ton 6 x 6 T-55 military ordnance truck. In 1954 a Model 502-2E gas turbine was installed in a Davenport Besler 30-ton switch engine railway locomotive. It was delivered to the U.S. Army Transportation Command for evaluation. Ford Motor Co. bought two Boeing gas turbines for passenger car installation. A Model 502-8C was installed in a Thunderbird in 1955, and a Model 502-10C was installed in a 1956 Ford Fairlane.

A Boeing Model 502-2E gas turbine went into a T-41 tank built by the Detroit Arsenal in 1955. Caterpillar put a Boeing Model 502-10C gas turbine in a DW-15 wheel tractor in 1957, and International Harvestor Co. installed a Boeing Model 502-10C in a track-laying TD 25 tractor in 1958.

Boeing 502 gas turbine installation in the Ford Thunderbird.

Ford Thunderbird powered by Boeing gas turbine engine.

In 1955 a group of engineers working with Strategic Air Command at Offutt Air Force base near Omaha, Nebraska, obtained backing from Firestone Tire & Rubber Company for a project to install a Boeing Model 502 gas turbine in a Kurtis 500 K single-seater racing car of the Indianapolis type. The weight of the Boeing turbine engine was 425 pounds including transmission, compared with 550 pounds for the 4-cylinder Offenhauser engine with

2-speed transmission. The complete Offenhauser-powered car of the time weighed 1700 pounds, while the turbine car weighed only 1375 pounds.

The particular gas turbine version used was a Model 502-10F with a specific fuel consumption of 1.0 pounds per hp-hour at full power. Fuel consumption at idle was 10 gallons per hour. The engine fuel control system was modified to allow extra high speeds, which in turn raised output to 300 hp at an output shaft speed of 5680 rpm.

On paper the turbine car had race-winning potential since the lighter weight indicated longer tire life as well as superior acceleration, while the turbine engine itself promised reduced fuel consumption (with reduced need for pit stops to refuel). Under racing conditions, the gas turbine should consume less since the engines are running continuously under high load, at high speed. The air force engineers calculated that the gas turbine would consume 136 gallons for the 500 miles at racing speed, while the typical 4-cylinder Offenhauser-powered car would consume about 150 gallons. The car was disrespectfully (to General Motors) named the SAC "Fireboid" and proceeded to its initial trials.

The SAC "Fireboid" covered the standing quarter-mile in 13.14 seconds during the 1955 National Drag Meet at Great Bend, Kansas, with a terminal speed of 107 mph. At Offutt Air Base, it convincingly won a quarter-mile drag race against a 300-hp Chrysler V8-powered Allard sports car. The car also made a demonstration run at the Indianapolis Speedway prior to the 1955 500-mile race. But that was the end of its career.

In 1959 the Boeing engineers developed the Model 502-10MA, which was rated at 330 hp, with a turbine inlet temperature of 1775° F (968° C). Its specific fuel consumption was 0.92 pounds per hp hour. A peak torque of 1200 pounds-feet was obtained with the gasifier shaft at full speed and the power turbine shaft stalled.

Model 502-10MA had a centrifugal compressor with an air flow capacity of 3.6 pounds per second. The compressor wheel was a 28-blade design, with 14 full blades and 14 half-blades. The aluminum alloy compressor casing incorporated eight log-spiral diffuser passages and two tangential discharge ports—one for each combustor.

The Model 502-10MA showed notable progress in its material specifications from the original. The turbine wheel had forged hubs of Inconel X with precision-cast and machined blades made of GMR-235 alloy, fastened by fir-tree roots. The first-stage nozzle vanes were made of Inconel 713C with inner and outer rings, shrouds and nozzle box formed and welded from sheets of Hastelloy X alloy. The power turbine nozzle vanes were precision-cast from HS-31 alloy. The combustor sheel was a 356-T6 alloy casting with an inner flame tube rolled from LCN-155 sheet, and a dome machined from an LCN-155 precision casting. The shaft support structures and the main housing remained substantially unchanged.

This engine became well known for its use in three fire trucks on an experimental basis over a period of 4 to 5 years. The fire department of San Francisco, California, was eager to test the gas turbine for use as a pumper. Boeing agreed to supply the engine, and American La France Company, of Elmira, New York, a leading specialist in fire-fighting equipment, installed it in one of their truck models. At the same time, the Seattle fire department became interested in testing a turbine-powered ladder truck. These two vehicles were built in 1960, the pumper being an American La France 900 series with forward cab, and the ladder truck a forward-cab tractor with semi-trailer.

In 1962 the city of Mount Vernon, Virginia, placed an order with American La France for a turbine-powered pumper, and Boeing supplied another Model 502-10MA power plant for installation in a vehicle that turned out to be a fairly close replica of the machine that had been delivered to the San Francisco fire department.

The Boeing gas turbine weighed about 450 pounds complete, compared with about 2100 pounds for the 335 hp Continental piston-type engine normally used. The gas turbine occupied less than half of the installation volume needed by the piston engine. The fire departments that operated these trucks expected to obtain advantages in road performance, improved reliability, and a simplified maintenance schedule. Road performance was measured in two ways—hill-climbing and acceleration.

Hill-climbing tests on San Francisco streets showed that the Boeing-powered fire truck could climb an 8.5-percent grade at 35 mph, whereas a similar truck powered by a 335-hp piston engine could only maintain 22 mph. On steeper hills, the difference diminished, and this is partly explained by the differences in gearing. To maintain 30 mph on a 12.1-percent grade, the turbine truck would have to run in second gear, while the piston engine powered truck could maintain 25 mph in third gear. All these trucks used 5-speed transmissions.

Since fire trucks are emergency vehicles, a great deal of attention was paid to timing the delay from the moment of pushing the starter button to the moment the truck could be driven off. Piston-powered fire engines normally need 5 to 10 seconds "time to roll." With the gas turbine, the delay was 15 to 20 seconds. Boeing began to use starter motors with higher cranking capacity, and that change reduced the "time to roll" by 3–5 seconds. Tests were also made with air-assist starts, which proved to cut starting time to six seconds. But the air-assist starter was never installed on the fire trucks.

Although torque buildup began immediately on depression of the accelerator pedal, it took a full 5 seconds before peak torque was reached. The Boeing-powered fire trucks therefore had a serious acceleration lag and Boeing had no solutions to that. Fuel economy was a minor consideration for these vehicles, where the ultimate criteria were performance and reliability.

A review of the breakdowns experienced with the fire truck engines shows no failures that normal development could not cure. One problem was combustor blowout during deceleration. There were igniter plug failures and transmission shifting difficulties. The engines also suffered cases of failure in the gasifier nozzle assembly, and instances of compressor surge.

The blowout problem was caused by the rapid fluctuations in engine speed and load, since the fire truck's operating cycle is one of constantly alternating acceleration and deceleration. The problem was aggravated by the low idle speed required by a truck with a manual transmission. The combustor design was modified to minimize the risk of flameout, and tests with the new combustor led Boeing to conclude that this problem had been completely eliminated. The igniter plug failures were caused by thermal shock during gasifier shaft acceleration during the initial startup.

Boeing developed a new ceramic material in collaboration with the igniter plug manufacturer, and the new material was able to withstand the high temperatures. The design was changed at the same time, so that in case the ceramic should break, the pieces would be retained within the igniter assembly and not allowed to run through the turbines. Soon, igniter life was 500 hours, and Boeing was confident that figure could be improved.

The ignition unit failures were traced to an error in the wiring diagram. The accessory drive failures were due to the coupling to the brake system of an air compressor with 12 cubic-feet per minute capacity. This load was just too severe, and the air compressor was then relocated to be driven from a power take-off on the transmission.

This did not completely solve the matter, for when the power turbine shaft was turning slowly, the compressor was not working to normal capacity, and the compressed air reservoir could be depleted during repeated brake applications. Boeing concluded that a new accessory drive, from the gasifier shaft, with higher torque capacity, should be developed. This was done and the first engine so equipped was installed in an America La France MB-5 truck built for the U.S. Navy in 1963.

The clutch failures showed up not as excessive wear but in the form of severe heat cracks in the flywheel and intermediate plate. A clutch with higher torque capacity remedied this complaint. Breakdowns became less and less frequent as more experience was gained with these trucks. After this initial development period, nonscheduled maintenance work was practically eliminated. Nevertheless, the maintenance costs were 3 times higher than for piston-engine powered fire trucks. The turbine-powered fire trucks were taken out of service in 1964 and 1965, and no new programs were scheduled.

After evaluation of all the test data and field experience with the Model 502 in its various versions and applications, Boeing designed its next-generation industrial gas turbine. Designated Model 553, it was a free-shaft unit of similar overall configuration to the Model 502, but incorporating all the advances made in the state of the art over a 10-year period. Shortly after it went into production, however, Boeing closed down its gas turbine department and sold its gas turbine designs and other assets to Caterpillar.

23

Case History:
Austin Motor
Company Ltd.

THE AUSTIN MOTOR COMPANY LTD. of Longbridge, Birmingham, was Great Britain's largest automobile producer in 1946. The Austin range of passenger cars went from economy sedans to luxury limousines, and the company produced commercial vehicles from light delivery vans to medium-duty trucks. Austin began to take an interest in automotive gas turbines in 1949, and the turbine program at Austin was assigned to Dr. John H. Weaving and his assistant B. C. Bennie.

John Harold Weaving had been with Austin since his apprenticeship days. Born in Birmingham on September 10th, 1918, he had been educated at Birmingham College of Technology, and Cambridge University. On leaving Cambridge, he returned to Austin as superintendent of research and development, and since 1947 he held the title of chief research engineer.

Austin's first gas turbine design was a 120-hp unit intended to be suitable for passenger car installation, but evaluated with the sole idea of establishing its potential in that application. It was not part of a plan to introduce gas turbine powered vehicles in production, but simply an exploratory effort. The senior research investigators were J. Barton and Dr. C. Rounthwaite.

Dr. Weaving explained the background to the turbine program in a paper presented to the Institute of Mechanical Engineers:

We had a very open mind on whether or not the gas turbine would supersede the conventional piston engine, realizing that there was still plenty of potential development left in the latter type of unit in the direction of increased compression ratios and reduced friction losses. Nevertheless, it was felt that the only way of ascertaining the potentialities and problems of the gas turbine was to build one, to test it in its component parts and as a complete unit on the test bed, and finally to assess a vehicle so powered. It was considered that the most profitable field to investigate would be the larger and more expensive passenger car vehicle, as it was appreciated that gas turbine costs do not come down pro-rata with horsepower.

The 120-hp turbine was designed in 1950 and ready for testing in 1952. It was designed as a two-shaft engine operating on a recuperative cycle. It was a most unusual design, having a two-stage centrifugal compressor driven by a three-stage axial-flow turbine. The reasons why this configuration was chosen are explained by Dr. Weaving's analysis of the duties to be performed by the passenger car gas turbine.

The Austin approach to a passenger car gas turbine was to produce a slow-running unit working at low stress levels, optimized for peak efficiency at part load rather than full load. Dr. Weaving decided that the compressor had to work with a very high pressure ratio in order to obtain the desired combustion temperature with the small heat exchangers that were dictated because of installation space limitations. This reasoning led him to the choice of a two-stage compressor configuration, each stage having a low pres-

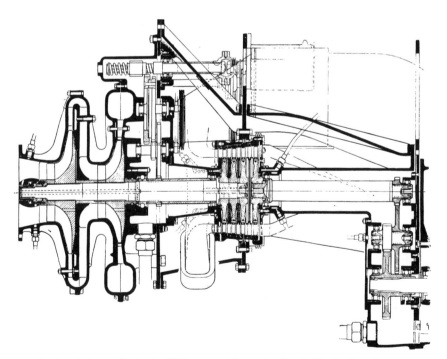

Sectioned view of the Austin 120-hp gas turbine engine installed in the Sheerline car.

sure ratio of 3.5. The low pressure ratio per stage was chosen in order to limit stress loads.

Dr. Weaving was well aware of the fact that while lower pressure ratios give better full-load performance, they also give rise to serious power losses at lower loads. The solution was to combine two low-pressure compressors so as to get an overall pressure ratio of about 6. This doubling-up of compressors reversed the situation with regard to power losses and loads, assuring peak efficiency at part load. The same characteristics might have been obtained by using an axial-flow compressor, but this type of compressor was rejected for cost reasons.

With a two-stage centrifugal compressor, both rotational speeds and centrifugal force stress loads on the turbine wheels were lowered, which in turn was calculated to allow higher cycle temperature than would be possible with a single-stage compressor. Dr. Weaving suspected that some losses must occur in turning the air emanating from the first-stage compressor diffuser at up to Mach 0.5 into the eye of the second-stage compressor, and after a series of tests established that there was about 4 percent loss involved with the use of a centrifugal first-stage compressor in a two-stage setup.

He then tested an Allen 11-stage axial-flow compressor, giving a mass flow up to 4.5 pounds per second and working with a maximum pressure ratio of 5. This gave much higher efficiency, but was mismatched with the turbine characteristics.

The engine included four axial-flow turbine wheels—three stages on the gasifier shaft, and a separate power turbine driving the output shaft via a

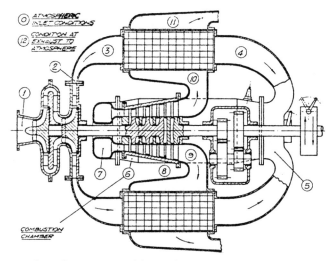

General arrangement of the 120-hp Austin gas turbine engine.

two-stage reduction gear. Dr. Weaving recognized that this was twice as many turbine wheels as strictly necessary in a two-shaft gas turbine engine. He justified his choice by the fact that the design made it possible to use the same blade section throughout.

This gave lower material and machining costs, and did not involve any substantial efficiency loss when compared with free-vortex blading as a result of the small hub/tip ratio in the turbine wheel design. This design also enabled small diameter wheels to be used owing to low gas velocities.

The gasifier turbine was designed to give peak efficiency at about 75 percent of maximum speed in an effort to improve part-load fuel consumption. This meant a peak turbine efficiency of no more than 83.4 percent, while the compressor efficiency at full load was only 75.6 percent. The gasifier turbine had a peak rotational speed of 22,000 rpm. The idle speed was a low 11,000 rpm. Maximum power turbine speed was 23,000 rpm. This is the only automotive gas turbine in which the free-shaft turbine spins faster than the gasifier turbine.

When the engine underwent its first dynamometer test in 1952, it fired right up, but the engineers were too nervous to run the gasifier up to full power, and the first readings showed only about 30 hp.

The turbine blades were machined from forged RR-58 blanks, and the nozzle vanes also used RR-58 nickel-steel alloy. The gasifier turbine wheel hub was forged from Nimonic 90 material, while the power turbine wheels had Nimonic 80A forged disc hubs. The root of each turbine blade was shaped like a tang, drilled in the axial plane for pin insertion. The tang matched a circumferential groove machined in the hub, with the edges also drilled for pin fixing.

The initial design used two combustors—one on each side of the turbine. During a test in August 1952, the first combustor failed to ignite, and raw kerosene was pumped into the first-stage turbine where it was mixed with the hot exhaust gas from the second combustor. This resulted in a fresh combustion inside the turbine shroud, with disastrous results. This experience led Austin to make two important decisions: First, one single combustor was to be used, and second, turbine blades were to be made less expensive (castings instead of forgings).

The combustor was a horizontally positioned barrel-type design, and supported by its own inlet and exhaust ducts. The combustor outer casing was made of aluminized mild steel, while the inner flame tube was fabricated from Nimonic 75 sheet metal. It was equipped with a fuel system supplied by Joseph Lucas, Ltd. An air-atomizing nozzle was combined with a high-energy spark igniter which started the flame very close to the base of the conical fuel spray.

Austin went to an investment casting process for the Nimonic turbine blades. The profiles obtained by this process were highly accurate, and the only machining needed was for the roots. But they did not hold up. In a test in April 1953, some blades in the power turbine flew off at 19,500 rpm. This failure was not due to overstressing the material, but to a weakening of the thin section around the pin fixing due to crystal growth in the area where the blades were slimmest.

After this incident, Austin reverted to using turbine blades fully machined from Nimonic forgings. The blade root was redesigned as a fir-tree type. The blades in the stator vane nozzles were Jessops R-22 precision castings, designed with a constant section and without twist. The gasifier turbine wheel hubs were mounted on the shaft by means of integral dogs, while the power turbine wheel was pegged to the shaft collar. The power turbine shaft bearing was provided with a deep-groove ball race that also took the end thrust.

Provision was made for converting the second-stage turbine to a free-shaft turbine, in case that type of design should be needed for vehicle use in a later stage of development. For this reason, the turbine assembly was overhung from the roller bearings that supported the shaft in the hot section. A combined journal and thrust ball-bearing was used at the compressor end. The whole shaft assembly was held together by one long central bolt.

The engine was built up on a structural framework based on three vertical bulkheads connected by a number of other elements containing the compressor assembly, turbine section, reduction gear and transmission casings. The compressor assembly was attached in front of the forward bulkhead, while the outer shrouds containing the turbines were inserted in the middle of the central bulkhead. The reduction gear and the transmission casing were mounted on the rear bulkhead. The power turbine shaft was supported by a tunnel containing a bearing and registering with the turbine shroud by means of a sliding joint and a bellows seal.

The air entered through an axial intake duct formed as an integral part of the compressor assembly front cover. A silencer was bolted to the upstream end of the intake duct. The compressor casing was built up from three RR-50 light alloy castings, spigoted and bolted together. RR-50 light alloy was also used for the diffuser vanes and the compressed air discharge port.

The compressor casing and the turbine shrouds were not subjected to any structural stresses, and functioned strictly as containers for the air and gas flow masses. The main housing was constructed so that it would be free to expand longitudinally and radially without distortion. The housing was rigidly attached only to the third bulkhead, located at the front end by the shaft bearing supports which incorporated expansion joints.

The reduction gear was made up of a two-stage helical gear train, with the second-stage having a quick-change feature to enable the engine to be easily adapted to different applications. All accessories were driven from the intermediate shaft in the reduction gear. They included a simplified piston-type fuel pump combined with a centrifugal governor, a gear-type oil pump, and an electric starter motor connected via a sprag-type free-wheel device.

Dr. Weaving chose a secondary-surface cross-flow type of recuperator for the 120-hp Austin turbine. It had a modest thermal ratio of 0.65, but gave a 30-percent cut in fuel consumption compared to the same turbine unit in simple-cycle operation. Two separate heat exchangers were placed at right angles to the combustor, mounted on each side of the housing in pannier fashion, and supported by brackets extending from the rear bulkhead.

The cross-flow recuperator matrix was composed of simple sandwiches of thin, corrugated sheet interleaved with plain sheet, these sandwiches being combined so that the respective air and gas flow paths would cross at right angles for each adjacent composite element. The flow area through the gas side corrugations was about double the area on the compressed air side in order to equalize pressure drops and optimize the heat transfer characteristics.

Austin used mild steel for its recuperator. Dr. John Weaving reported that it caused surprise to find out how well mild steel could withstand exhaust gas heat, showing no deterioration up to 1112° F (600° C). Mild steel has the advantages of low cost and being easy to fabricate.

An experimental Ritz regenerative heat exchanger had been demonstrated to the industry by the National Gas Turbine Establishment as early as 1951, but Austin considered that this type lacked the reliability of the recuperator.

The engine was coupled to a planetary reversing gearbox and installed in Austin's largest passenger car—the Sheerline. The Sheerline was normally powered by a six-cylinder 3993 cc (244 cubic inch) engine rated at 120 hp. It was built on a wheelbase of 122 inches and had a dry weight of 4453 pounds.

The car was of conventional design, with front engine and rear wheel drive. The planetary gearbox was designed by Howard F. Hobbs and built by Hobbs Transmission, Ltd. in Leamington Spa. The vehicle installation was made in August, 1954, but the car was not demonstrated publicly until July, 1955, when the Austin Motor Company Ltd. was celebrating 50 years of operation.

From the windshield back, its appearance was indistinguishable from the standard production model apart from the large exhaust tailpipe. The front end was extensively modified. The radiator grille was replaced by a lengthened nose to accommodate the intake air silencer, and to provide vents for excess heat to escape from the engine compartment.

It was estimated that with a turbine inlet temperature of 1545° F (840° C), and a gasifier shaft speed of 22,000 rpm, the engine should have developed enough power to give the Sheerline a top speed in excess of 100 mph. No intensive development work was undertaken, although the research department maintained it as a test vehicle for several years. After the Sheerline experiments, the 120-hp engine was installed in an Austin 10-ton truck, driving the rear axle via a Borg-Warner three-speed automatic transmission.

The car turbine was eventually redesigned with a single-stage gasifier turbine followed by a single-stage power turbine with variable nozzle geometry, and incorporating two Cercor disc-type regenerators. This upgraded version was designed for a turbine inlet temperature of 1742° F (950° C).

By the time the Austin gas turbine program was closed down, Dr. Weaving had concluded that the automotive gas turbine initially had a place only in heavy trucks. Concurrently with the passenger car turbine program, Austin developed a small, 30-hp, two-shaft unit under contract with the Directorate of Industrial Gas Turbines (a branch of the U.K. Government's Ministry of Supply). The contract was granted for the express purpose of encouraging the industry to investigate the possibilities of very small gas turbine units for vehicular use and other light-duty applications.

This 30 hp unit consisted of a single-stage centrifugal compressor driven by a radial in-flow turbine with 5.6-inch diameter. Downstream from this turbine and mounted on a separate shaft, was a two-stage axial-flow turbine with 5-inch diameter. Austin felt that a two-stage power turbine would be necessary in order to minimize the difficulty of diffusing and ducting the gas flow from the relatively small eye of the radial in-flow turbine discharge port to the inlet annulus of the axial-flow turbine.

Dr. Weaving recognized later that the two turbine stages were really quite mismatched, and that this turbine configuration could not be developed to give the desired efficiency. The compressor gave a mass flow of 0.85 pounds per second, and ran with an adiabatic efficiency of 74 percent. Three different types of fuel nozzles were tried out. The first one was a downstream spill-type nozzle, which was very expensive but gave very satisfactory results. The second model was a vaporizer type of nozzle, which proved erratic and unreliable in action and was abandoned. The third model was a low-pressure upstream injection nozzle. It gave good performance, but lacked durability.

The 30-hp Austin turbine ran with a peak turbine inlet temperature of 1472° F (800° C). The combustor had 98 percent efficiency, with a 4-percent pressure drop. This gas turbine engine delivered 30 hp at its design speed of 56,000 rpm. The power turbine shaft drove a 6.95 : 1 reduction gear, giving a maximum output shaft speed of 3600 rpm. During its development period, specific fuel consumption fell from over 1.00 pounds per hp-hour to 0.85 pounds per hp-hour. The Austin cross-flow heat exchanger was found to have a thermal ratio of 65 percent as applied to the small

30-hp unit. This engine did not meet its fuel-consumption target, however, largely because of leakage in the heat exchanger and failure to obtain the necessary efficiency in the turbines.

Austin also developed a 250-hp industrial gas turbine, intended above all for emergency power applications. The industrial engine was designed to be compact and robust, and to have a high power-to-weight ratio. Aluminum castings were used for all parts where temperature posed no threat, such as the compressor assembly and gearbox casing.

It was a single-shaft design with a centrifugal compressor and a two-stage axial-flow turbine. The engine weight was only 900 pounds net, but the installation weight, including heat exchanger and reduction gears came close to 2,000 pounds. The compressor was designed for a pressure ratio of 4 with an air mass flow of 3.5 pounds per second.

The 250-hp industrial engine was originally designed without a heat exchanger, but was later redesigned for use with a contraflow recuperator, which required new ducting and conversion to a double-entry combustor, plus a number of minor modifications. This large-volume recuperator had a thermal ratio of 84 percent.

In 1952 Austin Motor Company Ltd. had merged with the Nuffield Group to form the British Motor Corporation. In the reorganization that followed, far-ranging research was given a very low priority, and the turbine program was canceled. That does not preclude Austin turbine-powered cars and trucks in the long-term future, for the British Motor Corporation merged with Leyland Motors, Ltd., in 1968—and Leyland had absorbed The Rover Company and Rover Gas Turbines in 1966.

24

Case History:
Socema-Gregoire

THE NAME SOCEMA-GREGOIRE has been applied to one single prototype passenger car, which appeared in 1952 and only covered about 20 miles' driving before the program was terminated. It was built at a cost of $400,000 according to its designer Jean-Albert Gregoire. That comes to a cost per mile of $20,000—for this ambitious experiment, which unfortunately led nowhere.

The acronym SOCEMA stands for Société de Constructions et d'Equipements Mecaniques pour l'Aviation, a company that began its gas turbine activity in 1941. This company was a subsidiary of an important electric equipment concern, the Compagnie Electro-Mecanique (C.E.M.).

The first turbine design was designed and developed during World War II under a research contract with the Vichy French government, and in order to deceive the German occupation forces, the contract was channeled through the French Railway Authority rather than through the Air Ministry. The engine was designated TGA which could mean either Turbo-Groupe d'Aviation or Turbo-Groupe d'Autorail. At the end of 1944, the head of the French Air Ministry, Monsieur Tillon, invited the Compagnie Electro-Mecanique to make a study and a recommendation for a turbojet engine of about 2,000 pounds' thrust. The management of C.E.M. then delegated this task to its Socema branch. The head of the turbine project was Monsieur Peru, who led a small staff of about 30 engineers.

The TGA evolved into the TGA-1 bis turboshaft engine, which was still under development in 1947. It was a large unit with a 15-stage axial-flow compressor and a four-stage turbine, weighing 4620 pounds and delivering a continuous output of 3,000 hp. In 1945 the company started a second-generation turbine project, the GTAR-1008 turbojet. This was a large unit intended for a thrust in excess of 4,000 pounds.

The Socema-Gregoire prototype of 1952.

C.E.M. cancelled all aircraft gas turbine work at Socema in 1949, mainly due to Socema's inability to compete with Snecma (formerly Gnome & Rhome) and Turbomeca. In order to exploit its gas turbine experience in the civilian market, C.E.M. decided to sponsor a gas turbine car, a rolling laboratory for the "car of the future". Monsieur Peru and his group were told to design a 100-hp turboshaft engine for passenger car installation.

The gas turbine was designated TGV-1 (Turbine a Gaz pour Voitures) or Passenger Car Turbine Number One. Company literature often refers to it as the Cematurbo. It was a simple-cycle two-shaft gas turbine engine, obviously derived from turbojet origins, with its tight, symmetrical envelope, and a total absence of heat exchange. A single-stage centrifugal compressor was used. It delivered 1.1–1.32 pounds per second of air with a pressure ratio of 4.5.

The engine had three combustors, all discharging into a common duct leading to the nozzle ring for the first-stage turbine. Each combustor had a fuel injector nozzle and an igniter plug, and gave a turbine inlet temperature between 1300° F (700° C) and 1475° F (800° C).

The gasifier shaft had a maximum speed of 42,000 rpm. The power turbine shaft rotated up to 25,000 rpm, and was geared to a simple planetary gear set giving a 5 : 1 reduction. Power turbine inlet temperature was between 935° F (500° C) and 1110° F (600° C). The power turbine was designed as a two-stage unit, and revolved at about half the speed of the gasifier shaft. The power turbine shaft ran in two ball bearings.

The gasifier and power turbine shafts were supported in a robust structure of forged steel, while the main housing was fabricated in aluminum sheet. The gasifier shaft ran in three ball bearings specially designed for high rotational speeds, and lubricated by oil fed in at 30 psi. pressure.

The accessories were driven from three separate jackshafts geared to the cool end of the compressor shaft—one for the starter-generator, the second for the oil pump, and the third for the fuel injection pump. A speed governor was installed at the front end of the accessory drive. The complete engine weighed only 287 pounds.

The engine was first tested in the laboratory at the Scemi (another C.E.M. subsidiary) establishments at Le Bourget in 1951. Then it was tested on the road, installed in a 4½-ton Ford truck. This truck made several test runs over the road between Le Bourget and Senlis, including some under the official supervision of the technical service of the Automobile Club de France. At this point it was decided to build a special car for the turbine.

Monsieur Piaton, who was president of C.E.M., wanted the car to be designed by France's topmost automobile engineer—a title he conferred upon Jean-Albert Gregoire, who was then chief engineer of Automobiles Hotchkiss at Saint-Denis, a northern suburb of Paris. J. A. Gregoire was the creator of the front wheel drive Hotchkiss-Gregoire that had gone into production in 1950, co-inventor with Pierre Fenaille of the Tracta universal joint in 1925, and builder of the front wheel drive Tracta car at Asnieres (a western suburb of Paris) from 1926 through 1934.

He designed the Amilcar Compound front wheel drive car in 1937, and

The power plant for the Socema-Gregoire.

came to Hotchkiss when Amilcar was absorbed by the Hotchkiss company. During World War II he designed and developed a light front-wheel-drive car design, with a two-cylinder air cooled engine, and aluminum frame and body, under contract with Aluminium Français. This design was taken over by Panhard & Levassor, who placed it in production in 1947 as the Dyna Panhard. Parisian by birth, (July 7, 1899) J. A. Gregoire had acquired an engineering diploma from the École Polytechnique plus a doctorate in law before he went into business. This was the man Monsieur Piaton approached for the design of a gas turbine car.

Gregoire, however, was fully occupied with his work for Hotchkiss, and lacked faith in the gas turbine as an automotive prime mover. He did not want the assignment, but he finally did accept. Gregoire designed both the chassis and body, and supervised their construction in the Hotchkiss factory. As the gas turbine was not ready when the car was finished, Gregoire installed a Ford V8 engine for road-testing purposes. The vehicle ran over 6,000 miles with the Ford engine before the gas turbine was installed.

The body was an aerodynamic coupe with high-performance appearance. The body was highly streamlined with a C_x value of 0.19. All body panels were made of aluminum, and the chassis frame was a large aluminum casting. The chassis design was conventional in the sense that the engine was placed in front, and the car had rear wheel drive. But the suspension was anything but conventional, being built under Gregoire's patents for variable-rate coil springs.

The car was built on a 90.55-inch wheelbase with 53.15-inch front track and a narrow 48-inch rear track. With an overall length of 181.1 inches the body was 65 inches wide overall. Overall height was only 53.4 inches. Dry weight of the vehicle was 2811 pounds.

The gas turbine unit was installed in the nose of the chassis, overhanging the front wheel axis, with the planetary reduction gear at the rear end. The output shaft was connected to a short propeller shaft equipped with universal joints at both ends. The rest of the drive line consisted of a series of heavy and bulky elements: first, a small flywheel to provide a driving clutch face for the standard production-type clutch; second, a four-speed Cotal transmission, followed by a Telma electric retarder; and at the end, the final drive unit incorporating a differential.

Why the clutch? It was theoretically unnecessary, but Gregoire believed it might be of value during testing and evaluation. The clutch was a normal Ferodo dry single-plate unit and it was combined with a four-speed Cotal electromagnetic transmission, but it was felt that this arrangement could be greatly simplified for the future. The Socema technicians thought that the clutch could be eliminated altogether, and that a two-speed and reverse gearbox would be adequate.

Underhood view of the Socema-Gregoire gas turbine engine installation.

The gearing was arranged to give a speed of 25.5 mph per 1,000 rpm of the output shaft, giving the car a theoretical top speed of 127.5 mph.

Why the electric brake system? The Socema engineers made no attempt to provide engine braking capability within the turbine engine. Gregoire chose to use a Telma electric transmission brake, as commonly used on trucks and buses operating in Alpine territories. This Telma unit was installed between the Cotal transmission and the final drive unit. The Telma brake control system was connected to the accelerator linkage, so as to provide gradually increasing retardation when the pedal was released.

The brake control system was also connected to the accelerator linkage, so as to provide two additional steps of brake force depending on the pressure on the brake pedal. The car was equipped with rack and pinion steering. Lockheed brakes with drums for all four wheels were used. The light alloy wheels were integral with the brake drums, and the rims that carried the tires were detachable from the rest of the wheel. The car was equipped with Dunlop racing tires of 6.00-16 size.

The instrument panel included all the normal automobile instruments, plus a series of gauges for reading the conditions of gas turbine operation, such as oil pressure, fuel system pressure, turbine inlet temperature, and rotational speed of gasifier shaft and power turbine shaft.

The car project was killed shortly after a few test runs and demonstrations had been made. Apparently, C.E.M. decided that the time for the turbine car had not yet come. The car was displayed at the Salone de l'Automobile in Paris on October 1952, and is now on permanent display in the Musée de l'Automobile at Le Mans.

Also in 1951–2, C.E.M. had made plans for a 10–ton truck to be powered by an enlarged version of the same basic design, with an output of 300 hp. A final study was made for a 50-passenger intercity bus with a gas turbine rated at 150 hp and equipped with heat exchangers. Neither was ever actually built.

25

Case History: Fiat

AT THE END OF World War II, Fiat was not only Italy's principal automobile manufacturer, but also a major factor in Italy's aircraft industry. Fiat had built its first aircraft engine in 1908, and started aeroplane manufacture (under Farman license) in 1915. One would expect that Fiat would become interested in gas turbine cars as a result of experience with aviation turbojets, but the historical facts show that Fiat designed and built its experimental turbine car before the company started production of military turbojets (under General Electric License) and industrial gas turbines (under Westinghouse license).

Fiat started work on a passenger car gas turbine as early as 1948—in other words, as soon as intelligence reports on the work being done by Rover and Centrax in Great Britain reached Italy. Fiat's turbine program was a most slow and deliberate effort. First, 18 months were spent in training technicians in the sector of engineering, and studies of the research experience obtained in other countries.

Design work on the configuration selected for development did not start until September, 1950. Actual construction of the prototype engine components consumed considerable time and called for special tools.

The design of the engine and the special car it was to power was the responsibility of Dante Giacosa, who had been technical director of Fiat since 1945. He was born in Piedmont on January 3, 1905, and got his engineering degree from the Politecnico de Torino in 1927. His first job was in the drawing office of S.P.A., a Fiat subsidiary, where he worked on tractor, military vehicle, and diesel engine design. After a year's time at S.P.A. he was transferred to the aeronautical department of Fiat and became an aircraft engine designer. In 1933 he designed a minicar that was brimming with technical innovations, and became famous as the Topolino. All subsequent Fiat cars up to 1970 were designed under his supervision.

The man entrusted with the actual design work for the turbine car—Project 8001—was Oscar Montabone, who had joined Fiat in 1937 as an aircraft engine designer. He was eight years younger than Giacosa, having been born in Torino in 1913. He studied mechanical and aeronautical engineering at the Politecnico di Torino, and graduated in 1936. Ten years later, Giacosa picked him to take charge of the passenger car engineering office. The body design came from the drawing board of Fabio Luigi Rapi who had been responsible for the styling of the Isotta Fraschini Monterosa in 1947 after a long career of designing special bodies for various Italian coachbuilding companies.

The Fiat gas turbine was unusual in many ways, and borrowed little from the Rover designs that had inspired it. Instead, Fiat independently took a similar approach to Austin's. It was a simple-cycle two-shaft gas turbine rated at 290 hp at full gasifier shaft speed, which was 30,500 rpm, with a turbine inlet temperature of 1472° F (800° C). Fiat's 8001 engine used a two-stage centrifugal compressor, giving an overall pressure ratio of 7 : 1. The compressor was driven by a two-stage axial-flow turbine. The power turbine was carried on its own separate shaft and was rated for a maximum speed of 29,000 rpm.

Three combustors of the straight-flow type, as common on aircraft gas turbines, were used, mounted in a group on top of the main housing. The air inlet ducts extended from the center of the housing, because the air flow

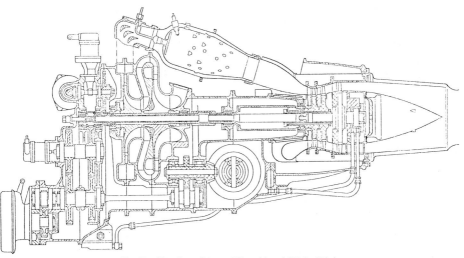

Fig. 17a. Experimental automobile turbine of 290 hp (Fiat).

Sectioned view of the Fiat 8001 gas turbine engine.

path through the compressors was back to front. The second-stage compressor was mounted in front of the first-stage turbine, and diffused the compressed air into three separate ducts, one vertical, and one on each side, to the three combustors.

The accessory drive was taken from the front end of the gasifier shaft, with spur gear drive to a short jackshaft which carried the electric starter motor and provided a bevel gear connection for the fuel injection system. A speed governor was attached to the shaft for one of the intermediate gears in the reduction gear so as to prevent power turbine overspeed.

The gas turbine was assembled in January 1953, and it went on the dynamometer that same month. Another 12 months were spent on bench-testing. Then the engine was installed in the Fiat 8001 vehicle that had been conceived and constructed especially for the turbine engine. The car made its first trial run on the Lingotto test track on April 14th, 1954. That is a small rectangular speedway, built on the rooftop of one of Fiat's main plants.

The car was a two-door, two-seater coupe with futuristic styling—probably in acknowledgement of the lead taken by General Motors with its Firebird I—but far less radical. The Fiat 8001 was intended for use on public roads, and the giant tailpipe outlet merely symbolized turbojet action—it did not add any actual thrust to the vehicle.

The engine was installed in a midships position, behind the seats and in front of the rear wheel axis. The engine included a reduction gear at the front end (the power turbine shaft was concentric with the hollow gasifier shaft and ran inside it). The drive was taken from the front of the engine to the pinion shaft for the final drive unit located below the main housing via a short shaft and a secondary reduction gear.

A three-speed gearbox was added at the front end of the transmission

Fiat 8001 gas turbine-powered car.

Rear view of the Fiat 8001 prototype.

shaft, with a small clutch and flywheel in front of it. The entire transmission and final drive elements were designed as integral parts of the main gas turbine housing, and the entire package weighed about 600 pounds. The car was built on a 94.5-inch wheelbase and had an overall length of 172 inches. Overall width was 63.4 inches and overall height 49.4 inches. Dry weight of the complete vehicle was 3307.5 pounds. The body was designed for low aerodynamic drag, with a C_x number of only .14. The gearing gave it a theoretical top speed of 155.25 mph but no public demonstrations of its performance were ever made.

The chassis engineering was derived from the Fiat 8V Gran Turismo model of 1952. It featured all-independent suspension, with transverse control arms and inboard-mounted coil springs at all four wheels. The coil springs were completely enclosed in aluminum casings and bathed in oil. Piston-type hydraulic shock absorbers provided the necessary damping. Roll centers were only 1.5 inches above ground level, front and rear, and consequently Oscar Montabone added roll stiffness by fitting stabilizer bars both front and rear. Fiat FB-Type drum brakes were used at all four wheels.

A brief test period was enough to show up the problems in the engine. It would have been surprising if an initial design had not given problems. Fiat's engineers learned a lot from the experience, however, in terms of thermal stress distribution in gas turbines, the need for new materials, and the poor part-load fuel economy of simple-cycle gas turbines.

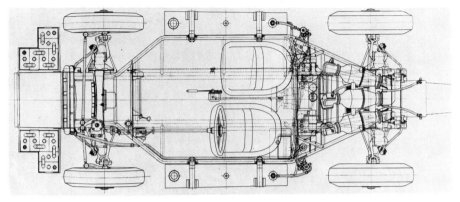

Plan view of the Fiat 8001 prototype chassis.

In 1957 a new 300-hp gas turbine engine was on the drawing board, and this design included regenerators. This engine was never placed in a vehicle, and in 1959 Fiat closed down its automotive gas turbine research. It was revived in a modest way in 1964, this time with the onus on heavy commercial vehicle applications. For four years, study followed study, design proposal followed design proposal, and a considerable amount of component testing was undertaken. Some of the gas turbine engine configurations and variations from this period are interesting.

In 1968 Fiat disclosed a turbine engine with differential compressor drive. It is the invention of Maurizio Wolf. The concept dated from 1954, when the first patents were taken out, and initial studies begun. Design work had started in 1961, and the test engine was built in 1964. The unit was called TDC (for Turbine, Differential, Compressor) 8042. El. It had a single turbine with reduction gearing to the output shaft. The output shaft was connected to the compressor shaft via a planetary gear differential, providing variable compressor speed independently of output shaft rpm.

Pressure ratio was only 2.5 to one. The combustor was a horizontal barrel-type. The turbine was a Holset 4/550, and the compressor was a Holset 4/550 with diffuser. Maximum speed for both turbine and compressor was 65,000 rpm. Compressor inlet temperature was planned for 1472° F (800° C) but it turned out that the unit ran best at 1382° F (750° C). Power output was 80 hp at 40,000 rpm.

Fiat was also working on a hybrid turbine engine designed by Mario Calovolo, using a diesel piston engine for its gasifier section. The diesel engine shaft drove the compressor mechanically. It was a 400-hp unit with an installation weight of 1654 pounds. The diesel engine with accessories weighed 1323 pounds, the compressor section 88.2 pounds, the turbine sec-

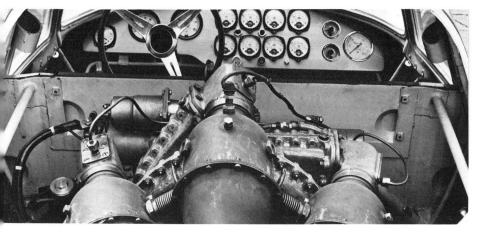

Fiat 8001 gas turbine installation.

tion 88.2 pounds, and the heat exchanger 44.1 pounds. The heat exchanger was interposed between the compressor and the combustor. Mario Calovolo came up with this hybrid in an attempt to obtain lower fuel consumption at part load from a gas turbine engine. But in combining it with a Diesel, the lightness and simplicity of a gas turbine had been lost.

Fiat's gas turbine program had no firm objectives until 1968, when Giovanni Savonuzzi returned from America and was placed in charge of Fiat's research department. Savonuzzi had left Italy in June 1957 to go to work for Chrysler, where he played a considerable part in the development of the CR2A, A-831, and A-128 gas turbines. In 1962 he was named chief engineer of research and appointed a vice-president of Chrysler Corporation. In the gas turbine activity, he was second only to Huebner.

His career as an automobile engineer had started in 1945 (during World War II he operated a textile factory at Racconigi in Northern Italy) when Piero Dusio decided to get motor racing started again, and to provide low-cost single-seater racing cars for the new generation of drivers by building them from standard Fiat production parts. The actual engineering design of the first Cisitalia was done by Giovanni Savonuzzi. When the Cisitalia business was transferred to Argentina, Savonuzzi joined the engineering staff of Fiat.

Under Savonuzzi's direction, Fiat began work on a new family of turbine engines on an intensive scale in 1969. The first new truck turbine was ready for testing in March 1972. Fiat's 400-hp truck turbine can be described as a giant scaled-up version of the Chrysler A-128.

It is a two-shaft design, with a single-stage centrifugal compressor and two axial-flow turbines with variable-geometry nozzle vanes for the second-stage

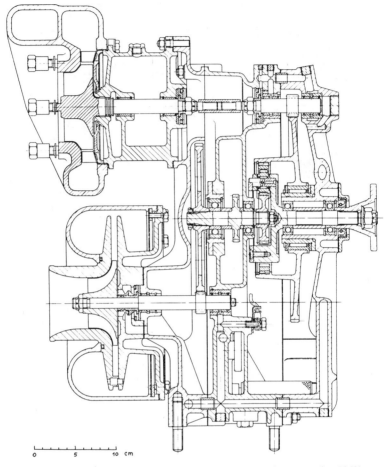

Fiat's experimental differential-drive gas turbine engine (design number 8042).

turbine. Two disc-type regenerators flank the main housing, which is a cast-iron structure with a center bulkhead that provides a mounting base for the front section. The compressor works with a pressure ratio of 4, and air flow capacity is 4.5 pounds per second.

A single barrel-type combustor equipped with an air-atomizing fuel nozzle is used. Fiat is working in close cooperation with Holley and Lucas on new, improved fuel and control systems. Peak power is in the 400–450 hp area at 33,000 gasifier shaft rpm with a turbine inlet temperature of 1700° F (927° C). The package, including accessories, weighs 1,545 pounds, and specific fuel consumption is only .463 pounds per hp-hour.

Experiments comparing Fiat's own metallic regenerators with the Cercor

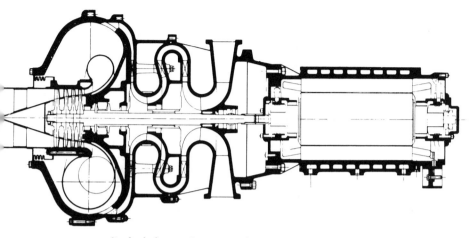

Single-shaft gas turbine engine for Fiat hybrid-electric bus.

Fiat's turbine-electric bus.

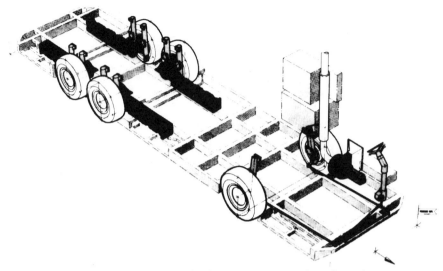

Gas turbine installation (under driver's seat) in Fiat turbine-electric bus.

Transparent view of the Fiat 400 hp gas turbine engine.

discs are still going on. The 28-inch-diameter Cercor discs have several problems—one is fatigue cracking, and the other is conical distortion, which upsets the seal grid. The engine is still undergoing dynamometer tests, but will be installed in a truck this year. The truck will be equipped with an Allison automatic transmission.

Fiat's future turbine program comes in three parts. Part One is the large industrial turbine, which is under study by Fiat Grandi Motori (the division that builds the marine and stationary diesels). Part Two is aircraft turbines—that belongs to Fiat Aviazione. Part Three is ground transportation. This part of the program breaks down into five sub-divisions:

1. railroad
2. marine
3. tractors
4. off-road vehicles
5. road vehicles (truck—bus—passenger car)

The program provides for up- and down-scaling of the same basic turbine to

Front and right side view of Fiat's 400 hp gas turbine engine.

as much as 1,000 hp, and as little as 100 hp. Savonuzzi estimates that the passenger car turbine is 2–3 years behind the truck turbine.

Fiat is testing a bus with a small non-regenerative gas turbine driving an electric alternator at constant speed, charging four sets of electric storage batteries which in turn provide the energy need to drive the motors. This project has been developed jointly by Franco Bertoldi of Fiat's industrial vehicle projects department and Giampiero Brusaglino, who is chief engineer of the electrical section of the research department. The goal was to create a low-emission urban bus, and nine different power systems were investigated. These are:

1. Diesel plus mechanical transmission
2. Diesel plus batteries
3. Regenerative gas turbine plus electrical transmission
4. Regenerative gas turbine plus batteries
5. Non-regenerative gas turbine plus batteries
6. Non-regenerative gas turbine plus flywheels
7. Regenerative gas turbine plus flywheels
8. Rankine engine plus electrical transmission
9. Stirling engine plus electrical transmission

The results showed that the gas turbine with batteries would give the best compromise between fuel economy and emission control. The gas turbine chosen for this bus is a single-shaft design with a two-stage centrifugal compressor and a four-stage axial-flow turbine. For this design, Fiat chose a toroidal combustor. The exact turbine specifications have not been released, but it is estimated it delivers 80 to 100 hp at 75,000 rpm.

26

Case History: Turbomeca

THIS CHAPTER DEALS with the Turbomeca gas turbines and the vehicles they were installed in. One was a special Renault speed record car, and the other was a Laffly truck. Société Turbomeca was established in 1938 by Joseph R. Szydlowski and his partner, M. Planiol, with a small factory in Billancourt—a southwestern suburb of Paris.

Joseph Szydlowski was born in Poland in 1896 and became a naturalized French citizen in 1919. He was an early leader in the field of designing diesel engines for aircraft, and his studies got him involved with turbo-superchargers in the 1920s. The first Turbomeca products were blowers, compressors, and turbines for aeronautical applications. In 1938 Turbomeca turbo-superchargers were tested by Hispano-Suiza and accepted for standardization on the newest range of 12Y45 engines for the new Dewoitine fighter-plane.

In June, 1940, the French government arranged for Turbomeca to move into new premises in the small town of Bordes in the Pyrenees, in order to remove the defense-production facility as far as possible away from the front lines. Despite its location in the Vichy-governed part of France, the factory was pillaged in 1943, and Turbomeca had to make a fresh start after the liberation. The French-German technology transfer was then reversed.

Fritz Nallinger, future technical director of Daimler-Benz, was one of 150 German engineers and scientists who were interned in France at the end of the war and commissioned to undertake studies of aircraft gas turbines. Nallinger became technical director of Turbomeca in 1945 and served in that capacity until his return to Stuttgart in 1948.

With a re-equipped factory, Turbomeca started production of compressors for Hispano-Suiza and Gnome-Rhone piston-type aircraft engines. The company also began developing compressors for aircraft cabin pressurizing systems and air-conditioning systems, as well as making initial studies of a complete gas turbine engine.

A program to develop a production-type gas turbine suitable for use as either a turbojet or a turboshaft engine was started in 1947. The plan was to provide a power plant suitable for light turbojet aircraft as well as an APU (auxiliary power unit) with the same basic components.

Szydlowski invented and patented the toroidal combustor, and made it a feature of the entire range of Turbomeca gas turbines. He pointed out that one of its advantages for use in aircraft was the reduction in front area compared with engines using external or protruding barrel-type combustors. The toroidal combustor was entirely contained with the contour of the compressor envelope.

Szydlowski also patented a low-pressure fuel injection system for the toroidal combustor. Fuel was fed in from the front of the engine through the auxiliary gearbox to a channel in the center of the compressor shaft. At the plane of the combustor, the channel opened up into a fuel chamber inside the shaft. From this chamber, the fuel was driven by centrifugal force through fine radial holes drilled in the shaft and escaped into the combustor. The flame was stabilized in an annular pattern and spread very little in the axial direction.

An injection wheel with radial holes spaced around its periphery was attached to the shaft section containing the fuel chamber. Rotation of the shaft and wheel produced a high centrifugal force, and the fuel was sprayed out of the holes with enough momentum to cause atomization. Normal fuel delivery pressure was only 40–45 psi.

The first Turbomeca turbojet engine was a large unit of 15,000 pounds' thrust, designated Oredon and produced in 1948. Next came the Pimene, which made its first flight in a Mauboussin Cyclone sailplane on July 14th 1949. This engine was rated at 200 pounds thrust at 37,000 rpm, which gave the Mauboussin Cyclone a cruising speed of 185 mph and the ability to climb to 30,000 feet altitude. The engine was 31.5 inches long x 16 inches wide x 15.7 inches high. Its total weight was about 100 pounds. A single-stage centrifugal compressor with a pressure ratio of 3.5 was used.

The Pimene engine was officially designated the TR.011. The turboshaft (APU) version of the same basic design was designated TT.782 and differed from the TR.011 mainly in having a second-stage turbine mounted on a free shaft, and a 7 : 1 reduction gear between the power turbine shaft and the output shaft. The TT.782 weighed 165 pounds including the reduction gear, its own starter and accessories, including a speed governor. Power output was 138 hp at 36,000 rpm with a turbine inlet temperature of 1382° F (750° C).

The first Turbomeca gas turbine used to power a motor vehicle was the Turmo I, installed in 1951 in a 10-ton truck by Establissements Laffly of Billancourt. The Turmo I was a simple-cycle gas turbine engine with a single-stage centrifugal compressor, two combustors and a two-stage axial-flow power turbine. The engine was rated at 180 hp at 30,000 gasifier shaft rpm, with a turbine inlet temperature of 1472° F (800° C). The power turbine had a maximum speed of 24,000 rpm. The output shaft was driven via a 12 : 1 reduction gear. The 2-speed transmission included a low 3 : 1 first gear, and reverse. The rear axle included a double-reduction final drive.

The Laffly truck was a cab-over-engine chassis, with the turbine taking the place of the standard diesel engine. The engine was very compact and fitted well within the frame rails. The truck had a top speed of 70 mph and the turbine's specific fuel consumption averaged 0.89 pounds per hp-hour.

The Laffly engineers provided automatic braking by connecting the compressed-air brake system to the gas turbine control system. When the driver removed his foot from the accelerator pedal, the control system would automatically and progressively apply the brakes.

The Laffly turbine truck was intended only as a basic feasibility study, and no serious development work followed. The Establissements Laffly discontinued production of highway trucks a few years later. For its next attempt to break into the automotive industry, Turbomeca decided not to enter an agreement with a minor manufacturer with a low research and development budget, but to approach the number one company in the French auto industry—Renault.

It was in 1954 that Joseph Szydlowski approached Pierre Lefaucheux, then President of Regie Nationale des Usines Renault, with the proposition

Turbomeca gas turbine engine installed in Laffly truck.

Turbomeca Turmo I gas turbine engine.

that Turbomeca should give Renault a turbine for vehicle installation in order to study the problems of "grounding" the aircraft turbine. Renault had been performing experimental work on gas turbines with a free-piston gas generator for a turbo-diesel railroad locomotive since 1951. The locomotive was permitted to run on the tracks of the SNCF and covered 160,000 miles in 4 years.

Renault's chief of research, Fernand Picard, was favorably disposed towards the idea of gas turbine cars, and recommended that Renault accept Turbomeca's offer. Picard had come to Renault at the end of 1939 as production manager of the engine plant that had been tooled up to produce Goeland 6-cylinder and C-730 V-12 aircraft power units. Born in 1906, he graduated from the Ecole des Arts at Metiers in Paris in 1926 with an engineering diploma and a gold medal. His first job was with Delage, a small manufacturer of high-grade touring and sports cars in Paris as a tool designer. By 1934 he was head of the methods department at Delage. Renault appointed Picard to a seat on the board of directors in 1946, and made him director of research in 1951.

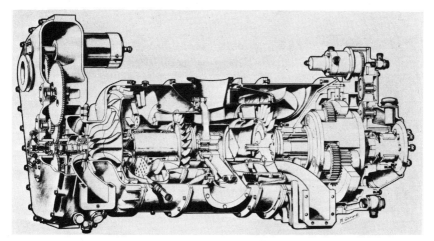

Cutaway view of the Turbomeca Turmo I.

The engine chosen for the Renault experimental turbine car was of the simple-cycle type and designated Turmo 1. It was a two-shaft unit with a free turbine. The gas generator section included one centrifugal compressor, a toroidal combustion chamber, a centrifugal fuel injection system, and an axial-flow turbine attached to the compressor shaft. The output section was composed of an axial-flow power turbine, its shaft, and a reduction gear.

The car was named Etoile Filante (shooting star) and was powered by a Turbomeca Turmo I gas turbine. The Turmo I package weighed only 530 pounds and was very compact: 45.2 inches long x 27.6 inches wide x 21.7 inches high. Power output was 270 hp at 3,500 output shaft rpm (28,000 power turbine shaft rpm). The maximum speed for the gasifier shaft was 33,750 rpm. Specific fuel consumption at full speed was 0.91 pounds per hp-hour.

The technical interest in the Turmo I power unit is focused on the combustor. The compressor fed air into an annular passage which ducted it into a diffuser ring that split up the air flow into three paths, ducted to combustor inlet ports in three separate areas. The air stream forming the primary air arrived at very low velocity into the combustor, and the low velocity was a prime factor in eliminating the risk of flameout.

The primary air ports were all normal to the surface of the rear wall they were part of. As a result, the primary air was aimed at a converging point at the center of the primary reaction zone, to supply air to the heart of the flame at the point of greatest intensity. The primary air flowed in an axial path to the rear of the combustor and into an annular space leading to a loop duct that reversed its direction forward and through a diffuser. The

Jean Hebert at the wheel of the Etoile Filante during a demonstration run.

diffuser aimed the primary air at ports situated near the inner circumference of the combustor shell, and directly into the primary zone.

The stabilizing air was ducted radially inward and through tangential slots in the front wall of the combustor, swirling in opposition to flame swirl, and engaging the combustion products in a highly turbulent flow so as to assure a stable and complete process. The ports in the front combustor shell were preset and radially spaced so as to assure substantially uniform temperature throughout the exhaust gases flowing through the outlet ports.

The center of the combustion zone could be moved radially inward or outward by presetting the tangential intake ports. This arrangement also provided the high turbulence desired for complete combustion. The dilution air entered through 16 ports spaced at regular intervals in a single line adjacent to the periphery of the combustor inner shell. Due to the controlled turbulence inside the combustor, and the proximity of the dilution air entry ports to the exhaust ports, the dilution air was swept through with a minimal residence time.

A double air stream protected the shaft and bearings as well as the combustor outer shell from overheating. The combustor construction used a number of separate sheet metal parts built up to form a toroidal chamber while giving all elements the necessary freedom of displacement to allow thermal expansion and distortion, without disturbing the proper operation of the combustor.

For instance, the pieces defining the rear wall of the combustor were fastened only to a ring which was adapted to slide freely over the labyrinth seal locating the combustor in the housing. The radial expansion and contraction of the wall and the ring were completely independent of those of the other elements. Movements caused by thermal variations in the inner shell of the combustor were also given considerable freedom in both the radial and axial planes because of the shell's tubular connection with the labyrinth seal, which was free to overlap with the outer shell at their junction.

Ignition was provided by a fuel igniter located at the periphery of the combustor. The igniter was mounted in the casing and extended inwardly to a point in front of the tangential ports in the front wall of the combustor so as to ignite and shoot a flame through the ports to ignite the air/fuel mixture inside the combustor. The igniter was connected to a separate fuel feed and carried a sparking device connected to an electrical circuit.

The reduction-gearing was a three-stage system: two stages of cylindrical gears, followed by a single stage of conical gears. The gearing also included a reverse gear, turbine brake, control system, and a dual oil pump. Total reduction brought the 28,000 rpm speed of the output shaft down to 2,500 rpm.

Fernand Picard did not design the Etoile Filante, but engaged a veteran racing-car engineer named Albert Lory for the task. Picard had known Lory at Delage, where Lory had been working since 1921 as a staff engineer on the racing team. He became a racing car designer in 1925 and was responsible for the 1500 cc (91 cubic-inch) straight-eight single seater of 1927. When Delage pulled out of racing in 1936, Lory went to the Société Nationale de Construction de Moteurs. He lived in retirement during World War II but joined the Arsenal de l'Aeronautique in 1946 and designed a new racing car powered by a supercharged four over-head camshaft V8 called the CTA-Arsenal. It never went beyond the prototype stage and was never raced.

Born in the Sarthe in 1895, Albert Lory grew up near Le Mans—a cradle of auto racing. He studied engineering at the Ecole des Arts et Metiers in Paris and got his degree in 1914. He spent the World War I years building aircraft engines, first with Panhard & Levassor at Ivry, and later with Salmson at Billancourt. Picard engaged him to work as a consulting engineer with Renault in 1949, and in 1955 gave him the assignment to produce an ultra-high-speed vehicle to be powered by a gas turbine. Picard's instructions to Lory were no doubt affected by the demonstrations put on by General Motors of the Firebird I. Instead of going the Chrysler route and installing the gas turbine in a production machine, Renault wanted to go GM one better in the direction of speed and spectacle.

The car was designed as a single-seater with an all-enclosing aerodynamic body including extended tail fins for directional stability at high speed. The

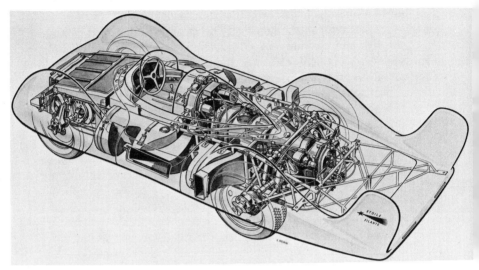

Cutaway view of the Renault Etoile Filante.

Etoile Filante was built on a 94.5-inch wheelbase with 49.5-inch track front and rear, while the tailfins stretched its overall length to 191.0 inches, and the fenders which completely faired-in the wheels gave the body an overall width of 63 inches. The Etoile Filante body was only 39 inches high to the top of the windshield.

The engine was installed in the center of the chassis, with drive to the

Renault's Etoile Filante (minus front body section) at the Bonneville Salt Flats in Utah.

Maintenance work on the Etoile Filante on the Bonneville Salt Flats.

rear wheels. The Etoile Filante frame had an engine suspension system with flexible motor mounts. The transmission had only one forward speed and reverse. The drive from the power turbine was taken through a two-stage reduction gear to the final drive unit.

The frame was a welded-up structure of multiple chrome-molybdenum steel tubes, as commonly used by racing constructors in the 1950s. The complete vehicle weighed only 2090 pounds.

Independent suspension was provided by a dual-trailing arm system based on the same principles used by Aston Martin, Volkswagen and Porsche at the time. Swing-axle rear suspension with semi-trailing arms was used for the rear wheels. The front suspension geometry gave a roll center at ground level, while the low-pivot-point swing-axle rear suspension gave a roll center height of 7.7 inches. Torsion bars with extremely firm hydraulic shock absorbers were used for both front and rear suspension systems. The brakes were Dunlop disc brakes, mounted inboard on the rear drive shafts, and provided with an inboard mounting at front also, with short shafts connecting the discs to the wheel hubs.

The Renault Etoile Filante made its debut at Montlhery autodrome 25 miles south of Paris on June 22, 1956, lapping the banked speedway at an average speed of 117 mph. Two public demonstrations followed, first at the Reims-Gueux-Thillois road circuit, prior to the Grand Prix de l'Automobile Club de France in July, and secondly, before the start of the 24-hour race at Le Mans in August. In September, the Etoile Filante was flown to the U.S. for a series of speed record runs at the Bonneville Salt Flats. A young engineer from Alencon, Jean Hebert drove the car and set three new world's records: 191.2 mph for one kilometer, 191.8 mph for one mile, and 192.5 mph for 5 kilometers.

After this demonstration, the Etoile Filante went into retirement. Renault has not conducted any further research on gas turbine powered cars, and Turbomeca has had no further association with the automobile industry but has become a prime supplier of turboshaft engines for the SNCF turbo-trains.

27

Case History: Bluebird CN-7

AIRCRAFT ENGINES had been utilized to power speed-record cars since the early 1920s, when war-surplus power units combining great power density with high power output became available to constructors of such machinery. When the aircraft industry switched from piston engines to turbojets, it was natural that builders of speed-record vehicles should turn to gas turbines. In the mid-1950s, the world land speed record stood at 394.196 mph and had been set in 1947 by John Cobb, driving a Railton Mobil Special—a four-wheel-drive vehicle powered by two Napier Lion V-12 aircraft engines.

It was only a question of time when this record was going to be broken, and preparations for a challenge to the British hegemony was being mounted in America. The most imminent threats came from Mickey Thompson and his Challenger I powered by four Pontiac V8 engines, and Dr. Nathan Ostich and a turbojet-propelled car called the Flying Caduceus. Faced with this kind of competition, Donald Campbell decided to create a new Bluebird car and raise the world land speed record over the 400 mph mark.

Donald Campbell was the son of Sir Malcolm Campbell, who had built the original Bluebird car, a special vehicle using a 350-hp Sunbeam aircraft engine, in 1924. The milestones in his subsequent career were impressive— he was the first man in the world to exceed a speed of 150 mph on wheels in 1925. He was the first to beat four miles a minute at Daytona Beach in 1931 (249.09 mph) and the first to exceed 250 mph (253.97) at Daytona Beach in 1932. He was the first to travel faster than five miles a minute, averaging 303.13 mph with his new 1935 Bluebird, powered by a Rolls-Royce V-12 aircraft engine for two runs in opposite directions on the Bonneville Salt Flats in Utah. When Sir Malcolm Campbell died in 1948, Donald Campbell was 27 years old. He was then working as a partner in a firm engaged in the manufacture of wood-working machine tools. He had no experience in either motor racing or boat racing.

Donald Campbell had joined the RAF in 1939 to be trained as a pilot, but was discharged in 1940 as a result of strain caused by rheumatic fever which had plagued him since his school days. He was driven into his father's footsteps in 1955 when he heard an announcement that Henry J. Kaiser had built a boat with which he intended to wrest the world water speed record away from England—a record that had been set prior to World War II by Sir Malcolm Campbell at 141.74 mph. This challenge led Donald Campbell to resolve that he would become the fastest man on earth—the unofficial title his father had so greatly treasured.

Donald Campbell took his problem to a well-known firm of engineering consultants, and gave them the task of producing a speed boat that would be capable of raising the record by a substantial margin. The boat was powered by a Metropolitan Vickers turbojet engine.

With this new hydroplane, Donald Campbell regained the water speed record from Kaiser's Miss America on July 23, 1955, with a run at 202.32 mph. Despite a lack of new challengers, he kept improving the craft and its engine, and raised the record to 225.63 mph in 1956, 239.07 in 1957, 248.62 mph in 1958, and finally to 260.35 mph in 1959. In the middle of this campaign the matter of keeping the world land speed record in British hands came up.

Campbell was able to enlist the cooperation of the Ministry of Supply and Bristol Aero Engines Ltd. in his project, and plans for a new Bluebird car to be powered by a Bristol Proteus 705 turboshaft engine resulted. This was a large aircraft engine with a power output equivalent to 3,780 hp. The Proteus delivered up to 1,950 pounds-feet of torque. It was 123 inches long x 40 inches wide x 40 inches high, and weighed 2,580 pounds.

The engine consumed fuel at the rate of 300 gallons per hour at full power. It was a two-shaft engine. The gasifier shaft consisted of a 12-stage axial-flow compressor with a single final centrifugal stage, and a two-stage axial-flow turbine section. The compressor gave a pressure ratio of 7 at 11,800 rpm. The power turbine shaft carried a two-stage axial-flow turbine. The Proteus 705 had eight combustors and no heat exchange.

Campbell's new Bluebird was designed by Lewis H. Norris and Kenneth W. Norris, two of five brothers who ran a design consultant firm at Burgess Hill, Sussex, and had been responsible for the successful Bluebird hydroplanes. They were able to call on support from Professor Squire and his group at the aeronautics department of London University. Reid A. Railton, who had been responsible for the design of John Cobb's Napier-Railton, was also called in as a consultant on some design questions. Other members of the design team were D. N. Stevens, A. W. Wooding, and J. S. Orwovsk-ing.

Design work began in January 1956. The project was known as CN-7 (C for Campbell, N for Norris). The actual construction was carried out in the shops of Motor Panels (Coventry) Ltd. which was a division of the Owen Organization. The entire project was placed under the supervision of Leo Villa, who had been Sir Malcolm Campbell's racing mechanic, and was Donald Campbell's lifelong friend, and J. Phillips, an Owen engineer.

In all, 68 companies in the British motor and aerospace industries collaborated on the CN-7 project. Among them the Owen Organization, the British Petroleum Company, Ltd., Dunlop Rubber Company, Ltd., Joseph Lucas, Ltd., Smiths Industrial Instruments, Ltd., Bristol-Siddeley Engines Ltd., Ferodo, Ltd., and Tube Investments, Ltd. (including the British Aluminium Company and Accles & Pollock, Ltd.).

The Proteus 705 engine was installed in the center of the chassis, with its compressor intake toward the rear. For its normal use in the Bristol Britannia aircraft, the Proteus turboprop had only one output shaft. For use in this four-wheel-drive car, the engine was modified with output shafts (from the power turbine shaft) at both ends. The final drive ratio was 3.643 to one. The final drive units were built by David Brown Gears, Ltd., each weighing 375 pounds!

There was no reduction gearing, which gave the Bluebird a speed of 43 mph per 1,000 rpm of the power turbine shaft. A freewheel was incorporated in the front wheel drive train, so as to eliminate the wind-up effect common in four-wheel-drive vehicles. The Bluebird was built on a 163-inch wheelbase with 66-inch track front and rear. Overall length was 30 feet 4 inches, overall width 96 inches, and overall height a mere 56 inches. The total weight of the vehicle was 9,000 pounds.

Bluebird had all-independent suspension with Girling oleo-pneumatic struts performing the combined duties of load-carrying, deflection, and damping. Girling also delivered the disc brake system. The drive shaft to each wheel carried a disc brake unit on the inboard side. Each disc was 16.375 inches in diameter and had two triple-caliper units, with a combined weight of 53 pounds (33.5 pounds being accounted for by the disc itself). The disc was almost one inch wide and ventilated by radial slots.

The brake pads had an aggregate area of 336 square inches, which gave a total swept area of 880 square inches. Brake actuation was assisted by compressed-air reservoirs. To stop from 500-mph speeds, the car would require aerodynamic brakes as well as road wheel friction brakes. Barn-door type air brakes were built into the body on both sides.

The Dunlop Rubber Company was undertaking special research to produce a tire that would stand up to speeds in excess of 400 mph. The tires

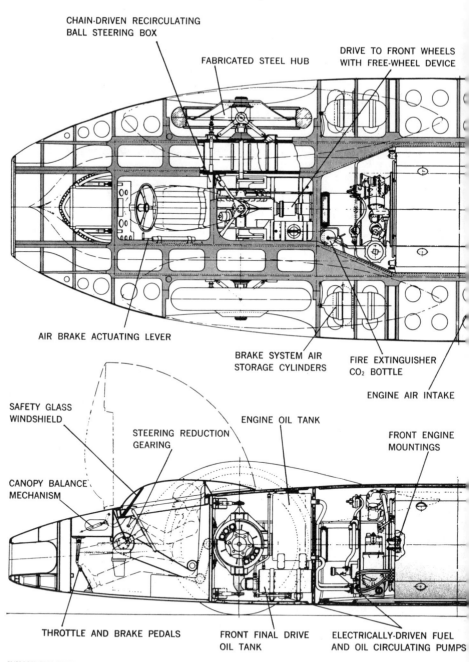

CHAIN-DRIVEN RECIRCULATING
BALL STEERING BOX

FABRICATED STEEL HUB

DRIVE TO FRONT WHEELS
WITH FREE-WHEEL DEVICE

AIR BRAKE ACTUATING LEVER

BRAKE SYSTEM AIR
STORAGE CYLINDERS

FIRE EXTINGUISHER
CO_2 BOTTLE

ENGINE AIR INTAKE

SAFETY GLASS
WINDSHIELD

STEERING REDUCTION
GEARING

ENGINE OIL TANK

FRONT ENGINE
MOUNTINGS

CANOPY BALANCE
MECHANISM

THROTTLE AND BRAKE PEDALS

FRONT FINAL DRIVE
OIL TANK

ELECTRICALLY-DRIVEN FUEL
AND OIL CIRCULATING PUMPS

Plan view and elevation of the Bluebird.

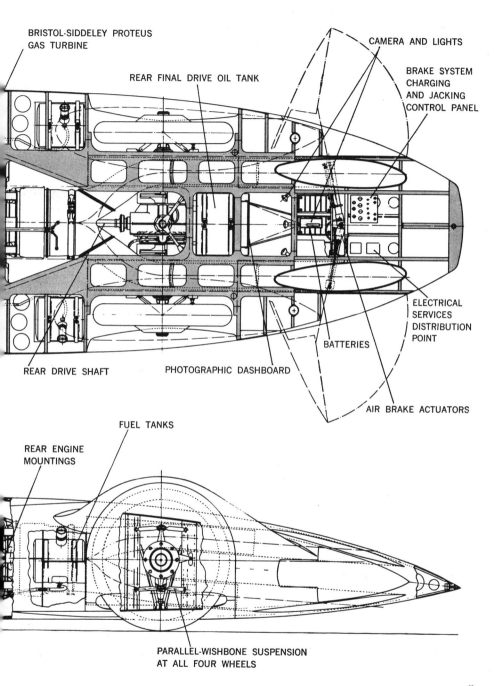

BRISTOL-SIDDELEY PROTEUS
GAS TURBINE

REAR FINAL DRIVE OIL TANK

CAMERA AND LIGHTS

BRAKE SYSTEM
CHARGING
AND JACKING
CONTROL PANEL

ELECTRICAL
SERVICES
DISTRIBUTION
POINT

BATTERIES

REAR DRIVE SHAFT

PHOTOGRAPHIC DASHBOARD

AIR BRAKE ACTUATORS

FUEL TANKS

REAR ENGINE
MOUNTINGS

PARALLEL-WISHBONE SUSPENSION
AT ALL FOUR WHEELS

53

had a rolling radius of 26 inches at all speeds above 100 mph, with a wide section of 7.8 inches when inflated to their design pressure of 180–200 psi.

The Norris brothers designed a box-type frame with four main longerons of "aeroweb" sandwich construction. They were made up of a core of light alloy honeycomb with light alloy skin. Aluminum bulkheads of oval section united the longerons at every possible juncture. The body shape was developed for high directional stability up to 500 mph. A huge tail fin was needed to assure complete stability in yaw. Lift characteristics became a compromise between the conflicting demands of a stable control situation, which demanded zero or negative lift, and tire loading capacity, which could easily be exceeded by adopting a design with strong negative lift.

Three different body shapes were wind-tunnel tested at the Imperial College before the final design was selected. The final shape was claimed to have zero lift with slight negative lift near top speed.

The car made its initial track test under its own power at Goodwood near Chichester in Sussex on July 18th, 1960. It performed to its design levels, and it was taken to the Bonneville Salt Flats for its attempt to break the world land speed record. The car crashed on its fifth test run at the Salt Flats in the early morning of September 16th, 1960. Four preceding runs at speeds up to 300 mph had been satisfactory. On the fifth and faster run, the car veered off course, went broadside into the salt, somersaulted in two 50-yard bounces, kept rolling, and finally came to rest nearly 400 feet from the course. Donald Campbell was hospitalized with severe injuries. The crash had resulted from a combination of three factors. First, the 6–12 mph crosswinds, second, the condition of the course, and third, gyroscopic reaction in the vehicle.

Nothing daunted, as Sir Malcolm would have said, Bluebird was rebuilt to the exact original design. Maurice Britton was named chief engineer for the reconstruction. The rebuilt Bluebird was to be taken to Lake Eyre, South Australia in April 1962, as the Bonneville Salt Flats were expected to be too wet for further use until August. But, the trip to Australia was postponed for a variety of reasons until 1963. The expedition was plagued by bad luck, as it rained for the first time in seven years shortly after Campbell's arrival at Lake Eyre, and the car was almost lost in the resulting floods.

Campbell returned in 1964, and at last moved the world land speed record up to 403.1 mph. To this day, that remains the official record for cars driven through their wheels, although turbojet-propelled cars have since gone much faster.

28

Case History: Pratt & Whitney

PRATT & WHITNEY was a leading division of United Aircraft, and started production of turbojet and turboprop engines in 1948. This led to the development of industrial turbines, and their adaptation to various motor vehicles, from a Canadian snowplow truck to Indianapolis racing cars. The engine used in these automotive applications was the Canadian ST6.

Founded as a sales, service, and overhaul organization, the Canadian Pratt & Whitney Aircraft Company, Ltd. branched out into manufacturing at an early date. Beginning with Wasp engines and Hamilton Standard constant speed propellers, it later developed the capability to manufacture the full line of spare parts of all Pratt & Whitney reciprocating piston engines. In 1958 the company established gas turbine design capability, and provided the preliminary engineering design for the Pratt & Whitney JT12 engines. UACL investment and enterprise then led in 1959 to the design and the development of the PT6 aircraft engine.

Among the PT6 aircraft applications are the Beech King Air, the Twin Otter and Turbo Beaver, the Fairchild Heli-Porter and the Swearingen Merlin II. In the early 1960s a development program was undertaken on the PT6 which led to the ST6 industrial and marine turboshaft gas turbine.

The ST6 was a simple-cycle two-shaft gas turbine engine. Air entered the compressor via an integral, annular plenum between the oil tank and diffuser case. The compressor consisted of three axial-flow stages followed by one centrifugal stage. From the centrifugal stage, the air passed through a radial vaned diffuser, was turned 90°, and entered the combustion chamber through straightening vanes.

Pratt & Whitney chose a toroidal combustor for the ST6. Fuel was injected into the combustion chamber by fourteen nozzles supplied from a

The Pratt & Whitney ST6 gas turbine engine.

common manifold. Two spark plugs provided ignition for starting. The turbines occupied the core space formed by the combustors. The turbine shafts were in-line, extending in opposite directions, with opposite rotations. Single-stage or two-stage planetary gearing, depending on the engine model, provided speed reduction between the power turbine and output shaft. A torque measuring system was incorporated with the reduction gearing. The accessory drive was taken from the compressor shaft.

The ST6 was offered in a number of versions:

Model	Ratings	HP	Specific Fuel Consumption lb/hp/hr	Air Flow Capacity lb/sec	Exhaust Gas Temperature °F
	Maximum	550	0.670	5.4	1075
ST6-60	Intermittent	445	0.714	5.1	1020
	Normal	390	0:743	4.9	990
	Maximum	620	0.640	6.15	980
ST6-70	Intermittent	580	0.650	6.05	955
	Normal	510	0.670	5.85	910

An ideal application for the ST6 engine was presented when the British Columbia Department of Highways had trouble with its diesel snowplows in clearing steep mountain roads. In July 1965 the 2000-pound 250-hp diesel engine was removed from a 40,000 pound 4-wheel-drive snowplow truck and was replaced by an ST6 engine rated at 370 hp. This truck was placed in operation up to 6000 ft altitude above sea level on the 8% grade Kootenay Pass near Nelson, B.C. The truck had been designed by the Department of Highways and was modified by them to a general plan drawn up by United

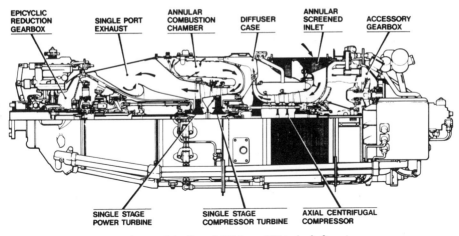

Sectioned view of the Pratt & Whitney ST6 turboshaft engine.

Aircraft of Canada Ltd. The engine was suspended from the chassis by a rigid 3-point mounting system.

The output shaft was geared for a maximum speed of 2100 rpm and connected to the torque converter input shaft of an Allison six-speed Power-Shift transmission. The transmission system included a torque retarder, and the oil for both the engine and the retarder was air-cooled by hydraulically driven fans.

The engine had an independent 24-V starter, and an overspeed trip system was built into the 12-V alternator. The air compressor for the brake system and a hydraulic pump for the power steering and snowplow controls were driven from the transmission input shaft.

The truck was put through a grueling shakedown test before being placed in service. It started easily on Number One diesel fuel (using air assist). Shifting difficulties that had plagued the Boeing-powered fire trucks were eliminated in the snowplow truck by reducing the fuel flow at idle, taking advantage of the operating altitude, so that disengaged power turbine speed could be held to 25 percent of rated maximum. It was possible to engage all gears from neutral, although jolts were felt in first, second, and third. Full power upshifts were smooth, regardless of the gears involved. For downshifts, the power turbine speed was restricted to 65 percent of maximum.

Performance was absolutely outstanding. The truck was able to accelerate uphill on a 3-percent grade, going from zero to 35 mph in 30 seconds, using only 5th and 6th gears. What's more, it could start climbing a 7½-percent grade from standstill with a plow blade packed with snow and accelerate to 25 mph! On that hill, the diesel-powered truck could not maintain 25 mph without snow on the blade.

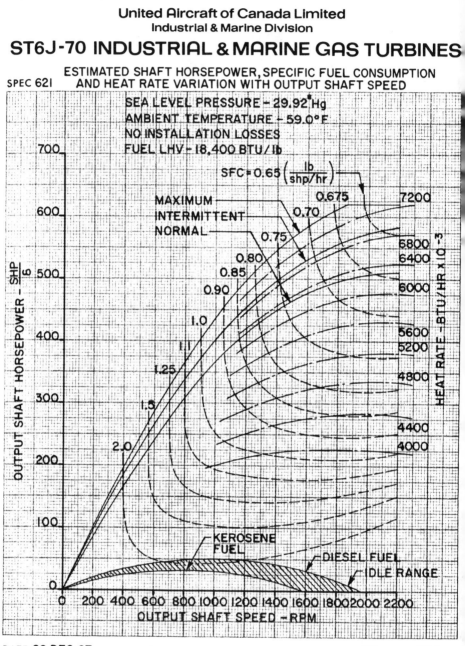

United Aircraft of Canada Limited
Industrial & Marine Division
ST6J-70 INDUSTRIAL & MARINE GAS TURBINES

SPEC 621 ESTIMATED SHAFT HORSEPOWER, SPECIFIC FUEL CONSUMPTION AND HEAT RATE VARIATION WITH OUTPUT SHAFT SPEED

SEA LEVEL PRESSURE – 29.92"Hg
AMBIENT TEMPERATURE – 59.0°F
NO INSTALLATION LOSSES
FUEL LHV – 18,400 BTU/lb

$$SFC = 0.65 \left(\frac{lb}{shp/hr}\right)$$

MAXIMUM
INTERMITTENT
NORMAL

KEROSENE FUEL
DIESEL FUEL
IDLE RANGE

OUTPUT SHAFT HORSEPOWER – SHP

HEAT RATE – BTU/HR × 10⁻³

OUTPUT SHAFT SPEED – RPM

DATE 29 DEC 67
REV I OCT 68

IM CURVE 7001-1

Power output and specific fuel consumption curves for the Pratt & Whitney ST6 turboshaft engine.

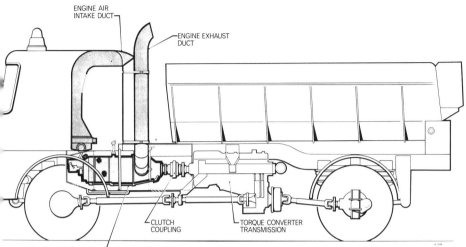

ENGINE AIR
INTAKE DUCT

ENGINE EXHAUST
DUCT

CLUTCH
COUPLING

TORQUE CONVERTER
TRANSMISSION

ST6A TURBINE ENGINE

Canadian snowplow truck powered by the Pratt & Whitney ST6 turboshaft engine.

The gas turbine-powered snowplow truck in action.

505

The turbine consumed more fuel than the diesel, of course, but only about double the quantity. The turbine-powered snowplow averaged 1.65 miles per gallon. Against that it could do twice the amount of work on shallow gradients, and clear roads that were impassable to the diesel truck. In actual operation, the Pratt & Whitney gas turbine lived up fully to the expectations generated during the tests. The truck gave entire satisfaction, and completed its first two winters without any deficiencies—400 hours of flawless operation.

THE 1967 STP TURBOCAR

Perhaps inspired by the Rover turbine car's performance at Le Mans in 1963 more than the actual speed of the Boeing 502-10Z gas turbine-propelled John Zink "Trackburner" Special (which was built for the 1962 500 Miles Memorial Day Race at Indianapolis but failed to qualify), STP president Andy Granatelli decided to abandon further development on the turbocharged Novi V8 racing cars and instead build a gas-turbine powered racing car. Preliminary design started in 1964 in the Paxton Engineering Company's shops in Los Angeles, California. (Both STP and Paxton were subsidiaries of the Studebaker Corporation). The gas turbine chosen for the job was the Pratt & Whitney ST6 B-62, which delivered 550 hp at 6230 output shaft rpm. and gave a peak torque of 890 pounds-feet. Torque level at full power was a healthy 495 pounds-feet, guaranteeing excellent high-speed response.

To handle this kind of power and torque in a single-seater racing car, four wheel drive would be required. There was actually never any doubt that the car would use four wheel drive, for the 1964 STP-sponsored 700-hp V8 Novi had in fact used four wheel drive to great advantage.

The vehicle concept was laid down by Kenneth B. Wallis, an Englishman with an aerospace engineering background who had come to Paxton from McDonnell-Douglas, where he had been a director of experimental systems. He had worked with General Electric in England on nuclear power projects and with Vickers Armstrong in England as a design engineer and test pilot. He came to the U.S. from a position with the Associated Engineering Group of Rugby, England.

He conceived the vehicle as an all-within-the-wheelbase chassis, placing the engine and the driver side by side in the middle, with the engine on the left and the driver on the right. This gave a leftward bias in weight distribution, which is an extra benefit at Indianapolis Speedway with its four left turns. The gas turbine output shaft was connected to a Ferguson transfer case which included a limited-slip differential between front and rear propeller shafts. The shafts from the transfer case to the front and rear final drive units were almost on the center line of the car.

Chassis of the 1967 STP turbocar.

The STP Turbocar was built on a 96.25-inch wheelbase, with 60-inch wide track, front and rear. The vehicle had an overall length of 150 inches, stood 24.5 inches tall, with an overall width of 72 inches. Body width was 56 inches. The complete vehicle weighed only 1750 pounds, with 45/55 front/rear weight distribution and 60/40 left/right weight distribution so that the wheels carried:

Left front	315.0 pounds
Right front	472.5 pounds
Left rear	385.0 pounds
Right rear	577.5 pounds

Ken Wallis designed a frame structure full of aerospace technology using 7178-T6 sheet aluminum for a backbone torsion-box with front and rear sub-structures for suspension system support, cockpit support, and engine mounting. The torsion box carried the gas turbine air intake duct and the fuel tanks. Two rear-mounted Harrison oil radiators cooled the lube oil supply for both the turbine shaft bearings and the transmission system. The car was equipped with Firestone 12. 10-16 tires on all four wheels, which were of the center-lock type, made of magnesium alloy and supplied by Halibrand.

The ST6 gas turbine had no provision for engine braking, so the car was designed with an aerodynamic brake consisting of a stabilizing flap located at the tail end of the body. It was actuated by the brake pedal and designed to go into action after pedal pressure passed a preset detent point. It was very effective at high speeds, providing 0.25-g deceleration by flap action alone between 180 and 130 mph. The four-wheel disc brakes were Airheart compound 12-inch dual-spot caliper type with Raybestos sintered copper friction pads.

It was natural for such a radically novel design to require a longer-than-normal period of development, and the car which had been completed in the summer of 1965, was not race-ready by the time the qualifying trials for the 1966 Indianapolis 500 closed. There was another gas turbine car at Indianapolis that month, however, that was to cause the organizers to revise the regulations governing gas turbines in racing. Though it failed to qualify, it had shown spectacular acceleration, and had been timed at over 200 mph down the pit straight.

This car was called the Jack Adams Aircraft Special and was powered by a 1350-hp General Electric T-58 turboshaft engine. The chassis was an A. J. Watson-built "roadster" with front engine location and rear axle drive. The sponsor, Jack Adams, was the owner of an aircraft sales business in Mississippi. Though it failed to qualify it had shown spectacular acceleration and had been timed at over 200 mph down the pit straight.

The United States Auto Club rules committee hurriedly tried to develop a formula that would limit gas turbines to 500 or 600 hp, and came up with a maximum size of the compressor air intake of 23.999 inches. That rule was in force when Andy Granatelli and the STP turbine car with driver Parnelli Jones came to Indianapolis for tests and qualifying in 1967.

The air intake annulus had been modified to come well within the limit,

The 1967 STP turbocar with the engine cover off.

and was measured as exactly 21.9 square inches. Parnelli Jones qualified sixth fastest in a field of 33 at an average of 166.075 mph for four consecutive laps. When the race started, he took the lead and held it for 171 laps, but then spun out to avoid hitting another car. Two laps later he was back in the lead, but after 197 laps, with three laps to go, a transmission bearing failed and put the car out of the race. He had covered enough ground to be classified sixth with an average speed of 152.35 mph.

Front suspension of the 1967 STP turbocar.

Output shaft and transfer case on the 1967 STP turbocar.

After witnessing this demonstration, USAC lowered the intake annulus area to 15.999 square inches for 1968. At the same time, the side-by-side configuration of engine and driver was outlawed. Andy Granatelli decided to have the 1968 STP cars designed and built in England, and talked over his

Detail of front wheel drive on the 1967 STP turbocar.

Instrument panel of the 1967 STP turbocar.

project with Colin Chapman, head of Lotus Cars in Norwich, and designer of a line of cars that had proved consistent winners in Grand Prix racing since 1961. Colin Chapman assigned the project to one of his leading racing car engineers, Maurice Philippe.

Parnelli Jones at the wheel of the 1967 STP turbocar.

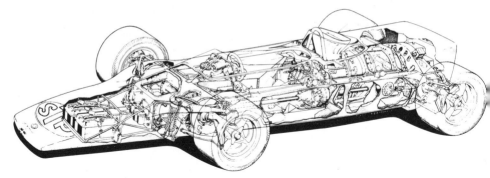

Cutaway view of the 1968 Lotus-STP turbocar.

It was the 56th car project at Lotus, and the car became known as the STP-Lotus 56. It used a different power unit, the newly developed Pratt & Whitney ST6-74N, which had a larger annulus area of 24.5 square inches. To bring it within the air intake size limit, the first two axial-flow compressor stages were removed. The third was small enough. Running with just a two-stage compressor, this unit was rated at 480 horsepower.

The engine was installed on the car's longitudinal center line, with the compressor section at the rear and the power turbine and output shaft in

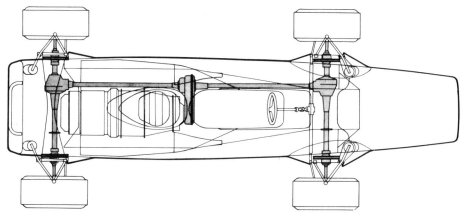

Plan view of the 1968 Lotus-STP turbocar showing the drive train layout.

front. The drive from the engine output shaft was taken to the Ferguson transfer case by Morse chain (instead of the geared coupling used on the 1967 STP-Turbocar). The front and rear propeller shafts and final drive units were offset to the left.

The chassis design was not derived from aerospace technology but from modern Grand Prix car engineering practice. All wheels had independent suspension with transverse control arms and near-vertical coil springs enclosing telescopic shock absorbers. The coil springs were mounted inboard of the upper control arm pivot axis, so that the inboard extension of the upper control arms acted as rocker arms, compressing the springs from the top (against their mounts in brackets extending from the monocoque aluminum alloy sheet chassis structure).

The STP-Lotus 56 was built on a 102-inch wheelbase, with a wider front and rear track of 62.5 inches, and had an overall length of 170 inches. Overall height was 32 inches and overall width, 75 inches. Despite its larger physical dimensions, the new turbocar was considerably lighter: 1360 pounds dry weight.

The driver's seat was pushed forward in the chassis, so that the pedals were mounted well ahead of the front wheel axis. The driver's seat was centrally positioned, with the gas turbine mounted immediately behind. The car had rack and pinion steering, with the transverse rack mounted behind the front suspension at the level of the upper control arms. The brake system used Girling ventilated discs for all four wheels, mounted inboard on the shafts, with underslung twin-spot calipers. The wheels were Lotus magnesium center-lock type with 9.5-inch wide rims.

Three STP-Lotus 56 turbocars qualified on the first day, and the cars

Derek Gardner displays chain drive transfer case for the 1968 Lotus-STP turbocar.

driven by Joe Leonard and Graham Hill both shattered all previous qualifying records with four-lap averages in excess of 171 mph. Art Pollard with the
third car qualified at a 166-mph average. In the race, all three suffered
power failure caused by sustained running at part throttle (due to the yellow
caution light being on for extended periods as a result of accidents on the
track). None of the STP Lotus cars was running at the finish. When USAC
announced the 11.999 square-inch air intake limit soon afterwards, Andy
Granatelli stated that there would be no 1969 STP turbine cars.

There are two interesting postscripts to the STP turbocar story. The first
concerns a new Jack Adams Special powered by an Allison 250 helicopter
engine. The car was built in 1968 but was completed too late in the season
to run at Indianapolis. The Jack Adams Special had four wheel drive also,
but in contrast with the Lotus design, this turbine car had a solid front axle
and de Dion rear suspension. The engine was placed in front of the driver,

and the drive was taken from the output shaft via a torque-dividing intermediate differential to front and rear propeller shafts. Both final drive units included limited-slip differentials. The body was an ultra-streamlined design created by Glenn Bryant who was a professor of aerophysics at Mississippi State University.

The Allison 250 had an inlet annulus area of only 12 square inches. It was a non-regenerative gas turbine with a free shaft. The compressor consisted of six axial stages and one final centrifugal stage. A single barrel-type combustor was mounted at the rear of the engine. The compressor shaft was driven by a two-stage axial-flow turbine, and the power turbine was also a two-stage axial-flow design. The engine was rated at 370 hp and weighed only 158 pounds.

The Jack Adams Special was smaller and lighter than the STP-Lotus cars, and it had an excellent performance potential, but the chassis had not had the benefit of proper development, and the car could not maintain speed in the turns. It appeared at Indianapolis in 1969 as the only turbine-powered entry, but failed to qualify.

The second postscript concerns a revival of the Lotus 56 in 1971, for use by Team Lotus in Grand Prix racing. A new version of the reliable Pratt & Whitney ST6 was used, with the designation STN6/76. The car was essentially unaltered and identified as the Lotus T56B. In its first outing, at the Brands Hatch Easter Meeting, the car was incapable of staying with the piston-engine powered cars on acceleration out of low-speed curves. A second outing at Oulton Park confirmed the findings from Brands Hatch. Its best performance was at Silverstone, a circuit made up from the runways of a World War II military airfield, with slight grades and no slow corners. Still, it was 3–4 seconds per lap slower than the best cars powered by Cosworth-Ford V8s. The project was quietly shelved.

29

Case History: Howmet

TWO ROAD-RACING and speed-record gas turbine cars were built and demonstrated in open competition by a company that is neither an automobile manufacturer nor a producer of gas turbines. The Howmet Corporation is basically a metals company, and a large supplier to the gas turbine industry. Howmet produces compressor rotors, impellers, turbine wheels, turbine supports, turbine nozzles and gas producer assemblies (all investment castings). Howmet Corporation of Muskegon, Michigan, is now controlled by the French Pechiney-Ugine-Kuhlmann combine.

It is perhaps not immediately obvious how the construction and campaigning of a racing car could advance Howmet's business. The Howmet racing cars were built to demonstrate Howmet's technological capabilities in the field of metallurgy. Howmet was willing to undertake the technical complexities of the TX program in the hope that it would add to the industry's understanding of turbine machinery, its development, and its limitations. The Howmet TX was built in 1967 to conform with FIA Group 6 prototype rules.

Group 6 rules called for certain minimum interior dimensions, minimum weight, maximum fuel capacity and other limiting dimensions that result in the configuration of a car which could be used on the road under limited production plans.

The Howmet TX was designed by Ray Heppenstall, who was also an experienced racing driver. Ray Heppenstall, a Howmet project engineer from North Hills, Pa. had worked around cars since the early 40's when he designed and assembled his first electric driven vehicle. He entered his first sports car race in 1954 with a 4-cylinder Nash Metropolitan, and in 1959 he won the Sports Car Club of America National Class H Production Cham-

The Howmet TX-1 at Daytona Speedway.

pionship at the wheel of a Deutsch-Bonnet. Associated with a number of successful cars since then, including a production Cobra and the Essex Wire Team Ford GT 40s, Ray turned his talent to the design of the TX in 1967 and as project engineer was responsible for Howmet's racing program.

The chassis was constructed by Robert S. McKee of McKee Engineering Corporation in Palatine, Illinois. Howmet supplied the aluminum for the all-aluminum body, the turbine blades for the engine, and the machined titanium for the brake assemblies.

The gas turbine used in the Howmet TX was an experimental unit produced by Continental Aviation and Engineering Corporation (a division of Continental Motors Corporation, Detroit, Mich.). This Continental gas turbine was a free-shaft design with heat exchangers. A two stage compressor was used, with an axial-flow first-stage and a centrifugal second-stage. The compressor ran with a maximum pressure ratio of 6.101 and gave an air flow capacity of 3.38 pounds per second.

The compressor shaft was driven by a two-stage axial-flow turbine, and the power turbine was a single-stage axial-flow type. The gasifier shaft was rated for a maximum speed of 57,000 rpm. The Continental turbine used a toroidal combustor. The power turbine shaft drove a reduction gear, with a 7.48 ratio, which reduced the maximum speed of 45,000 rpm to 6017 output shaft rpm. The engine developed 325 hp at 6017 output shaft rpm.

The final drive unit was a limited slip, racing-type differential with quick change spur gears. The final drive ratio was 3.4. The output shaft was coupled to a simple transmission with one forward speed and neutral. It had no reverse gear. To meet the reverse gear requirement of the FIA regulations, the car had an electric reverse device driven by battery power.

Installation of the Continental turboshaft engine in the Howmet TX-1.

Total weight of the power train, including the final drive unit, was just under 250 pounds. The car was built on a 93-inch wheelbase and was 158 inches long overall. Front track was 57 inches and rear track 54.75 inches. It had an overall height of only 37 inches. Dry weight of the complete vehicle was 1420 pounds.

The chassis was of conventional tubular space frame construction. Heppenstall chose rack and pinion steering for simplicity and precision, with two turns from lock-to-lock. Brakes were Kelsey-Hayes disc units with two calipers per wheel. The body was of aluminum quick-detachable panel construction. Goodyear tires were fitted. The rear tires were larger than the front ones—12.35-15 on the rear against 10.40-15 in front.

Top speed was more than 200 mph and, in December 1967, the TX circled the Daytona tri-oval speedway at an average speed of 176.052 mph. The Howmet TX was raced in several of the outstanding 1968 international racing events—Daytona 24 Hours of Endurance at Daytona Beach, Florida on February 3–4; the Sebring 12 Hours of Endurance at Sebring, Florida on March 23; the BOAC International 500 at Brands Hatch, England on April 7; the SCCA National Championship Race at Huntsville, Alabama on June 9; the Marlboro Classic at Marlboro, Maryland on June 16; and the 6 Hour Watkins Glen Classic at Watkins Glen, New York on July 14 where two of the experimental cars were entered. The final appearance of the TX was at

Ray Heppenstall in action with the Howmet TX Mark II.

the rescheduled 24 Hours of Endurance at Le Mans, France on September 28–29, 1968.

Ray Heppenstall was at the wheel in Huntsville and finished the 25 laps on the 2.3 mile circuit at an average speed of 92 mph, establishing the initial record for this new track. This marked the first time a turbine powered car won an officially sanctioned race in the U.S.

The other Howmet TX qualified first and went on to win the 300 miles endurance at Marlboro. This Howmet car set a new lap record of 1 minute and 27 seconds. The previous mark was 1 minute, 27.8 seconds. Elapsed time of the race over the 1.7 mile course was 4 hours and 38 minutes. The winner's average speed was 64.75 mph. On July 14 one Howmet TX finished first in its class and third overall at the 21st running of the Watkins Glen Sports Car Road Race. Running in the Group 6 Prototype category, Howmet won four points toward the World Manufacturers' Championship to put it into a tie with Renault and Chevrolet for fourth place.

Two Howmet vehicles were entered in this annual six hour endurance event. At the end of 2½ hours, one Howmet car was solidly in third place and the other Howmet had a tenuous hold on fourth place. These standings were maintained until half an hour before the end of the race, when the fourth place car was forced to pit by transmission trouble. Working frantically, the pit crew got the car back onto the track shortly before the finish. The first Howmet finished third, and Howmet's repaired car was 12th due to the lengthy pit stop.

The Continental gas turbine was provided with a waste gate connected to the accelerator pedal. When the pedal was released, the waste gate would open and let the exhaust gases escape into the atmosphere without passing through the power turbine.

During the 24-hour race at Daytona, the Howmet's waste gate refused to open when the driver wished to slow down for a curve. As a result, the car continued to accelerate, spun out in the turn, and hit the retaining wall. The impact reduced it to a wreck, but the driver was not seriously injured. The car was repaired. A second vehicle was built and flown to England, where it was to race at Brands Hatch. During the race, the waste gate stuck closed, and the driver was forced to run off the road and into a sand bank. In May 1968 the waste gate linkage problem was eliminated by design changes.

When the two Howmet cars arrived in France, two years without turbine cars had gone by at Le Mans. The Howmet was classified with the 3-liter piston-engine powered cars. Howmet had entered both turbine cars in the 24-hour classic, but neither finished. Lap speeds were disappointing, as they had no gearboxes. But the failures cannot be blamed on the turbines. A rear wheel bearing broke on one car, and the repair took so long that the car was disqualified. The other had an accident.

That put an end to the Howmet racing activity for a while, but in 1970 a new car called the Howmet TX Mark II was built. It was not intended for road racing but for setting speed records. Again, Ray Heppenstall was the *primus motor* of the program, project engineer, and designer of the car.

The Teledyne CAE TS325-1 turboshaft engine, for installation in the Howmet TX Mark II.

THE HOWMET RECORD

Class 2 (car weight—500 to 1000 kg.)

Distance	Previous Record Held by Russia's "Pioneer II"	Houmet TX Mark II
¼ mile	None	11.827 seconds 76.103 mph
½ kilometer	None	13.484 seconds 133.417 km/h (82.947 mph)
1 kilometer	28.68 seconds 134.9 km/h (83.8 mph)	21.185 seconds 169.952 km/h (105.599 mph)
1 mile *	None	30.479 seconds 118.115 mph

Class 3 (car weight—over 1000 kg.)

Distance	Previous Record Held by Britain's "Rover"	Houmet TX Mark II
¼ mile	None	13.868 seconds 64.902 mph
½ kilometer	None	15.737 seconds 114.380 km/h (71.076 mph)
1 kilometer	27.18 seconds 132.6 km/h (82.4 mph)	23.923 seconds 150.285 km/h (93.505 mph)
1 mile *	37.635 seconds 95.7 mph	33.226 seconds 108.365 mph

* No longer a distance recognized by FIA.

The body was built by Gomm Metal Developments Limited of Surrey, England. The chassis was built by McKee Engineering Corporation, Palatine, Illinois. The engine was supplied by Teledyne C A E (formerly Continental Aviation and Engineering) Toledo, Ohio. That company became a part of Teledyne, Inc. In December 1969. On May 1, 1970 the company's name was changed to Teledyne CAE to reflect its new corporate identity. The new name also emphasizes the fact that Teledyne CAE is now devoted to research, development and production of gas turbine engines with a turbine-oriented management and staff.

The engine used in the Howmet TX Mark II was designated Teledyne CAE TS 325-1 and had been designed as a turboshaft industrial gas turbine. It weighed 170 pounds and delivered 330 hp. It was 39 inches long x 20 inches high x 18 inches wide. Maximum gas generator speed was 57,500 rpm and the full power turbine speed of 44,000 rpm was reduced at the output shaft to 6790 rpm. The transaxle, with a specially designed coupling, turned the wheels up to approximately 2,000 rpm.

The chassis was built along the same lines as the original TX. In August, 1971 the Howmet team went to the new NASCAR Talladega Speedway near Talladega, Alabama. At 6:50 A.M. on August 21, the car's designer/driver Ray Heppenstall accelerated the sleek white roadster on its initial run through the timing traps. 35 minutes later, having completed the fourth pass over the newly measured course, the TX Mark II could claim new standing start acceleration records for the ¼ mile, ½ kilometer, and kilometer in two weight categories.

Normally the Howmet car belonged in Class 2 (for cars weighing between 500 and 1000 kilograms). For some runs, 850 pounds of lead ballast were added to increase the car's weight to more than 1000 kilograms so that Class 3 records might also be set.

30

Case History: International Harvester Company

INTERNATIONAL HARVESTER COM-
PANY'S involvement with the automotive gas turbine began with the acquisition of Solar Aircraft Company of San Diego, California, in 1960. At the end of World War II, Solar's main business was the supply of aerospace parts to the military. The rapid march of progress in aviation soon propelled Solar into gas turbine research.

The Solar Mars was an early model produced for industrial and aircraft applications. It was a single-shaft, simple-cycle design with a power output of 50 hp. The single-stage centrifugal compressor had a low pressure ratio of only 2.5 and was claimed to have 75 percent efficiency. It was driven by a single stage radial in-flow turbine which ran to a peak speed of 40,000 rpm. The turbine was 78 percent efficient. Maximum turbine inlet temperature was only 1202° F (650° C). Installation package length was 24.5 in. x 17 in. width x 22 in. height. The unit weighed 98 pounds.

Soon afterwards, Solar was awarded a U.S. Navy contract to design and manufacture an 1,100-hp turbojet engine, the Saturn. It was a success, and Solar president Herbert Kunzel decided to start building industrial gas turbines based on the Saturn components. Two versions were built—one for power generation and one for pipeline pumping. At the time of the IHC takeover, Kunzel and his engineering staff were preparing a new 3,000-hp Centaur industrial turbine.

The giant Chicago-based manufacturer of motor trucks, garden tractors, earth-moving equipment, and a wide variety of agricultural implements was interested in the Solar gas turbine as a basis for turbine applications in any area where competition might make it advisable or necessary. The first In-

Experimental International Harvester farm tractor powered by Solar turboshaft engine and hydrostatic drive.

International Turbostar highway train.

ternational Harvester vehicle to be powered by a Solar gas turbine was not a highway truck, but a light farm tractor. It was first shown at the University of Nebraska's 10th Annual Tractor Day at Lincoln, Nebraska, on July 20, 1962.

The engine used for the experimental HT-340 tractor was adapted from a small unit originally designed for a one-man helicopter or a flying platform, designated T62-T. It had been developed under the direction of Paul A. Pitt, Solar's engineering director. The tractor adaptation was the responsibility of Carl H. Meile, International's Chief of Engineering Research. The T62-T was only 21 inches long and 13 inches in diameter, weighing only 90 pounds including the reduction gearing.

The Solar T62-T was a single-shaft non-regenerative gas turbine engine with a single-stage centrifugal compressor, one barrel-type combustor, and a single radial in-flow turbine. Compressor and turbine wheels were mounted back-to-back on one end of the rotor shaft, which was supported at the opposite end by two bearings—one ball bearing and one roller bearing. This kind of mounting allowed the bearings to be positioned in the cool portion of the engine.

The T62-T was rated at 80 hp and coupled to a hydrostatic transmission system. The engine was designed to run at constant speed, with the output shaft running permanently at about 2,000 rpm. Tractor speed was controlled exclusively through the hydrostatic transmission—the tractor had no accelerator pedal, no brake pedal, and no clutch. Both forward and reverse speeds were infinitely variable. The turbine output shaft drove a Lucas variable-displacement hydraulic pump, and a radial hydraulic motor was installed in each rear wheel hub.

To start, the operator merely pushed a button, and an automatic sequence box would take over. The starter would be connected and the solenoid energized. Fuel injection and ignition would follow. When the turbine shaft reached minimum self-sustaining speed the starter motor and ignition system would be disconnected. After that, the operator has only two controls: the steering wheel and the transmission control.

The tractor became a useful research tool, but no production plans were ever formulated. Instead, Solar was given instructions to develop a gas turbine engine for heavy trucks, and on January 11, 1968, International Harvester Company's motor truck division took the wraps off its turbine truck at a press demonstration at the huge IHC proving grounds near Scottsdale, Arizona.

According to the officials, the experimental gas turbine engine, identified as a Solar "B" series, would replace diesel truck engines, for appropriate applications, in the range above 300 horsepower. No date for production startup was given, nor were prices discussed except to stress the fact that manufacturing considerations had been fully taken into account. For example, development tests to prove casting techniques for such parts as compressor and turbine wheels had shown that earlier estimates of manufacturing difficulty may have been too high. Manufacturing problems may be only slightly more difficult than those encountered with such regular production items as torque converters, IHC claimed.

No specific cost estimate was given for the experimental engine, but the engineers pointed out that it required only a five-speed transmission instead of a ten-speed, as did a comparable diesel. This too, plus the absence of radiator and attendant cooling system, would contribute to lower initial cost of a turbine-driven truck.

The experimental gas turbine was installed in an International CO-4000 chassis, designated Turbostar, a 6x4 tractor designed for line hauling on the Interstate Highway System. At 1,585 pounds, the Solar "B" gas turbine in the Turbostar weighs approximately half as much as a comparable diesel engine. The basic engine is 50 inches long, 41 inches high, and 36 inches wide—smaller than it diesel counterpart and compact enough to fit under short-dimension tilt cabs.

The lighter weight of the turbine-powered truck would enable it to carry a payload some 1,700 pounds heavier than a comparable diesel-powered truck. Turbine speed was 34,000 rpm. The free shaft was geared down via a two-stage reduction gear to a maximum of 4,000 rpm at the output shaft. Despite the enormous difference in physical size, the Turbostar engine borrowed certain design features from the Titan gas turbine.

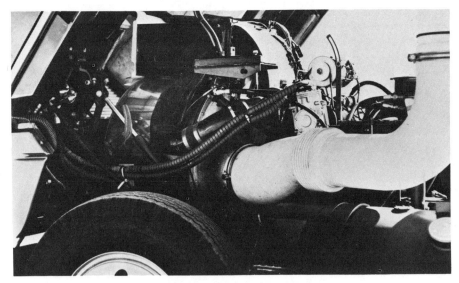

Gas turbine installation in the International Turbostar tractor.

A centrifugal compressor was mounted back-to-back with a radial in-flow turbine, for instance. The power turbine, mounted on a free shaft, was of the axial-flow type. The interstage duct contained a nozzle vane assembly with variable geometry. A toroidal combustor was used, with very small diameter so as to fit inside the inner diameter of the toroidal recuperator.

This stationary heat exchanger captured waste heat from the exhaust to improve fuel economy, especially at a part-load operation. IHC engineers say they selected the stationary recuperator "because it is inherently rugged, has low maintenance and is highly durable." Technology developed by Solar Division in fabricating stainless-steel parts, such as honeycomb structures, solved the problem of obtaining high efficiency in a compact, stationary heat exchanger, they claimed.

The engine operated on the same cycle as other heavy truck turbines of

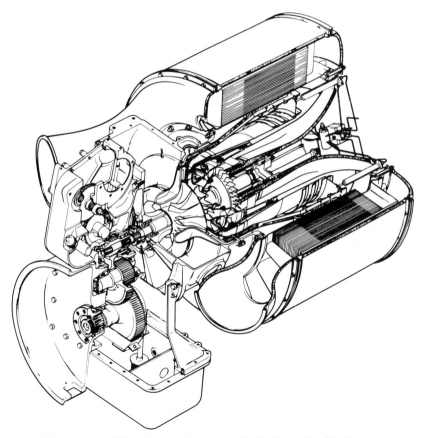

Cutaway view of the Solar gas turbine engine for the International Turbostar.

the same era, such as the GM-309. Air entered the engine inlet plenum and was compressed on its way through the compressor. Leaving the compressor, the air was diverted at right angles from its radial path and discharged into the recuperator. There it was heated through sheet-metal walls by exhaust gases flowing in the opposite direction. The preheated air then entered the combustors, where fuel was injected, and the mixture burned. A single sparkplug in each combustor ignited the mixture during engine starting. The high-pressure, high-temperature gases from the combustor passed through the first-stage turbine driving the compressor and accessories. The gases continued through the power-turbine nozzle vanes and the power-turbine. The gases exhausted from the power turbine were ducted through the recuperator, giving up heat to the compressor discharge air in adjacent passages. The exhaust then left the engine through ports on both sides.

The engine was installed in a "back-to-front" arrangement, with the cool section at the back. This was made possible by making the gasifier shaft hollow, and running the free shaft through it in a twin-spool arrangement. The accessory drive was taken from the rear end of the free shaft, above the reduction gear.

The Turbostar gave high performance and reasonable fuel economy, but the program fell victim to internal reorganization at International Harvester Company and a subsequent reordering of priorities. By 1971, IHC execu-

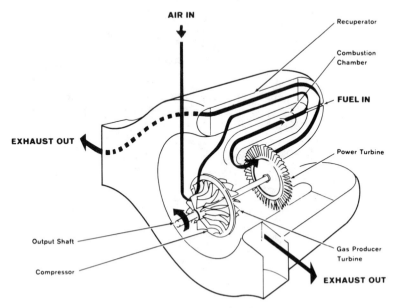

Gas flow path in the Solar truck turbine engine.

tives indicated they expected to buy gas turbine engines from Allison if and when the industry would make a large-scale switch to gas turbines. But before the top management of IHC turned its back on the automotive gas turbine, Solar Division produced a special version of its 1,100-hp Saturn turboshaft engine for use in heavy off-highway trucks.

The single-shaft simple-cycle Saturn engine consisted of an eight-stage axial-flow compressor driven by a three-stage axial-flow turbine. It used a toroidal combustor and ran with a maximum turbine inlet temperature of 1450° F (788° C). Exhaust gas temperature was 860° F (460° C). The Saturn gave a specific fuel consumption of 0.62 pounds per hp-hour. With a weight of 1250 pounds and overall dimensions of 77 inches length x 45 inches width x 44 inches height, the Saturn formed a very attractive package for truck installation.

Several truck installations were made in 1968, and all of them used electric drive. The turbine rotor shaft drove a generator which in turn supplied energy to traction motors built as an integral part of the driving wheels. One was a 100-ton Lectra-Haul (Unit Rig) truck, and a second 100-ton truck was built for Kennecott Copper Company and placed in service on its mining sites in Bingham Canyon, Utah. Two other trucks powered by Solar Saturn

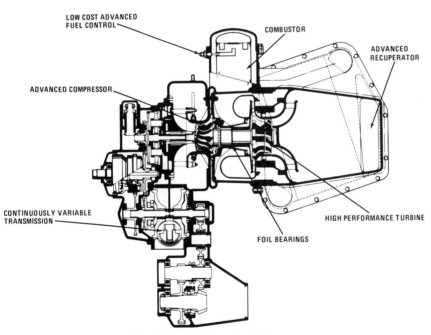

Solar Saturn 1200-hp turboshaft engine.

gas turbines were built by Wabco (Westinghouse Air Brake Company)—one a giant 160-ton unit, and the other a 110-ton machine built for operation in Northern Michigan. They proved fully reliable, and the trucks were capable of climbing hills with a full load at speeds twice as high as those maintained by diesel-powered trucks.

31

Survey of Current Programs

AiResearch Manufacturing Company of Arizona

AiResearch is a division of the Garrett Corporation, and has been a pioneer in the field of small industrial gas turbines. Production of the single-shaft Model 43-44 began in 1946 and featured a radial in-flow turbine, which was to become a trademark of the AiResearch engines for several turbine generations. Most of the early AiResearch gas turbines, such as the Model 70 from 1948 and the Model 85 from 1950, used two-stage compressors. These units became popular as APUs for large aircraft pressurization and air-conditioning systems. Soon the AiResearch engineers, led by Helmut R. Schelp, C. H. Paul, and E. L. Kumm, had produced a range of industrial gas turbines from 30 to 850 hp.

The smallest was the Model 30 from 1959, which delivered 30 hp and weighed only 40 pounds. It was derived from the commercial turbo-supercharger manufactured by AiResearch, using the same main components. They included a single-stage centrifugal compressor and a radial in-flow turbine, with a maximum shaft speed of 52,800 rpm. It ran with turbine inlet temperatures up to 1463° F (795° C).

AiResearch's first free-shaft gas turbine engine was the Model 331 from 1960. It had a two-stage centrifugal compressor giving an overall pressure ratio of about 7.5 driven by a two-stage axial-flow turbine. The free shaft was driven by a single-stage axial-flow power turbine, preceded by a variable-geometry nozzle vane assembly.

The Model 331 was equipped with a heat exchanger. The compressed air was ducted through a cross-flow matrix-type recuperator, making a double pass through the matrix before being admitted to the barrel-type combustor. Specific fuel consumption was 0.6 pounds per hp-hour at full load. This engine led AiResearch to produce a whole family of related engines, such as

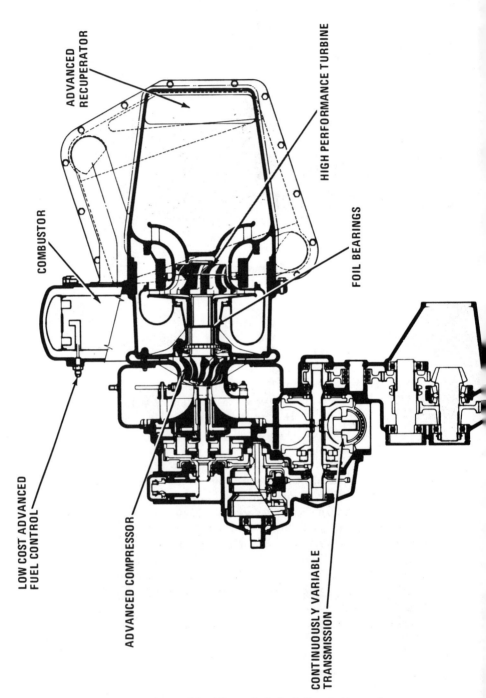

ADVANCED RECUPERATOR

COMBUSTOR

HIGH PERFORMANCE TURBINE

FOIL BEARINGS

LOW COST ADVANCED FUEL CONTROL

ADVANCED COMPRESSOR

CONTINUOUSLY VARIABLE TRANSMISSION

Sectioned view of the AiResearch single-shaft gas turbine engine.

the Model 431, Model 731, and Model 831, installing different components when operational requirements made it advisable. Model 431, for instance, used a radial in-flow first-stage turbine, and an axial-flow power turbine with variable-geometry nozzles. At the small end, AiResearch remained faithful to the single-shaft simple-cycle concept, producing such designs as the Model 105 in 1965 and Model 165 in 1966.

In 1972 AiResearch made a design study under contract with the E.P.A. for a passenger car gas turbine engine and drive train. The study included both single-shaft and two-shaft engines, but AiResearch came out strongly in favor of the single-shaft concept with an advanced recuperator. The design showed highly imaginative thinking and should stimulate further projects along this line.

The objective was an output of 125 hp, and the calculations showed that the unit would weigh no more than 695 pounds including reduction gear and integral transmission system. The installation package measured 39 inches long x 30 inches wide x 27 inches high. The single-stage centrifugal compressor would give a 6.4 pressure ratio, and provide a maximum mass flow of 1.21 pounds per second. A single-stage radial in-flow turbine was proposed.

A single barrel-type combustor would provide a turbine inlet temperature of 1900° F (1038° C). AiResearch calculated with a compressor efficiency of 79 percent, and a turbine efficiency of 88 percent. Combustor efficiency was taken as 99 percent. Special features of the design included continuously variable inlet guide vanes and a water injection system. The water injection nozzles were located upstream from the inlet guide vanes (which preceded the compressor intake duct).

AiResearch single-shaft gas turbine engine with drive train for front wheel drive or real engine installation.

Heat recovery effectiveness was estimated at 85 percent. With these efficiency levels, the engine would reach its target output at a rotor shaft speed of 83,600 rpm, and give a specific fuel consumption of .41 pounds per hp-hour. In order to enable this type of engine to drive a passenger car, it was designed with a unique transmission system, consisting of a two-stage reduction gear followed by an on-off clutch, an infinitely variable toric drive, and a hydraulic torque converter leading to a forward and reverse gearbox.

While pursuing this project, AiResearch has not neglected truck turbine research and development. On December 23, 1968, the Garrett Corporation announced the signing of an agreement with the Cummins Engine Company of Columbus, Indiana for a joint program to explore the feasibility of gas turbine applications to highway trucks and construction equipment.

The plan aimed at getting into production with a line of commercial gas turbine engines at an unspecified future date. Garrett will manufacture and supply the turbine power sections, while Cummins will manufacture the balance of the engines. To follow up this head start in the truck turbine business, Garrett Corporation was parent to a new company formed on August 10, 1973: Industrial Turbines International, Inc. The partners in the venture are Mack Trucks, Inc. of Allentown, Pennsylvania; AB Volvo, of Gothenburg, Sweden; and Kloeckner-Humboldt-Deutz of Cologne, Germany. The background for the new company (which is registered as a subsidiary of the Garrett Corporation) rests on a tentative agreement by the partners to pool their resources in a program to develop a family of advanced gas turbine engines. As its first project, Industrial Turbines International Inc. is designing a 500-hp gas turbine engine for use in trucks and buses. Production is expected to begin about 1980.

Motoren und Turbinen Union

Motoren und Turbinen Union (MTU) was formed in 1968 by two partners—Daimler-Benz AG and MAN (Maschinenfabrik Augsburg-Nürnberg). The origins of MTU date back to 1936 when the Brandenburg Motorenwerke was established as a branch of the Siemens & Halske electrical works in Berlin to manufacture Bramo aircraft engines under license from Pratt & Whitney and Fafnir. Bramo was taken over by the Bayerische Motoren Werke AG (BMW) in 1939.

BMW erected a large factory at Allach outside Munich to produce the famous BMW 801 14-cylinder double-row radial aircraft engine, and as early as 1939 this factory was testing a Type 003 turbojet engine intended for the twin-engine Messerschmitt Me 262. It was designed for a thrust of 1300 pounds. However, the first test engine delivered only 990 pounds thrust.

The first engines were delivered in November, 1941, and the first flight test resulted in dismal failure, as the turbine blades broke during take-off.

The 003 engine was 125 inches long with a diameter of 27 inches. It weighed 1344 pounds. The BMW 003 had a single toroidal combustor with 16 fuel nozzles. It used a 6-stage axial-flow compressor and a single-stage axial-flow turbine. It gave 1760 pounds thrust at 9500 rpm. In its 003C version, with a 7-stage compressor, thrust was up to 1990 pounds. The 003D used an 8-stage axial-flow compressor, and a 2-stage turbine. It gave 2760 pounds thrust.

In 1941 BMW began design work on a much larger turbojet engine, Type 018. The BMW 018 had a 12-stage axial-flow compressor and a three-stage axial-flow turbine. It developed higher thrust at lower speed—up to 7520 pounds thrust, with a maximum rotor speed of 6,000 rpm, and had a diameter of 49.2 inches and a length of 167 inches. It weighed 5080 pounds.

The 018 was designed as a turbojet, but the BMW engineers also proposed a turboprop version which was supposed to give 7000 hp. This design incorporated twin contra-rotating airscrews driven via a reduction gear. Two further BMW gas turbine projects never got farther than the drawing board. The first was a medium-thrust unit identified as Project 3306. It was a direct derivative from the 003A design, with 3760 pounds thrust. The second engine—Project 3307—was not an aircraft engine but a low-cost expendable unit for large-caliber missiles. It weighed 1433 pounds and had a thrust of 1109 pounds.

The Allach plant was converted to a military vehicle overhaul unit by the U.S. occupation forces after 1945. It was handed back to BMW in 1954, and a new subsidiary was started: BMW Triebwerkbau. This was essentially a research organization at first, investigating and evaluating gas turbine technology under the direction of Helmut Sachse. In 1957, BMW Triebwerkbau began production of the Lycoming industrial gas turbine under license from Avco.

Then BMW sold its Triebwerkbau division to MAN in 1965. MAN had acquired licenses to produce turbojet engines from Rolls Royce and General Electric in 1958, and merged the BMW branch with its own gas turbine activity to form MAN Turbo. In 1965, MAN began a truck turbine program by modifying its Model 6022 helicopter gas turbine for truck installation. This was a single-shaft engine rated at 350 hp.

Dr. Hans Hagen was research and development manager for this program. He adapted the single-shaft engine for truck installation, and also produced a two-shaft version using the same components. Two MAN turbine trucks were built and ran for several thousand miles—one with the single-shaft engine, and the second with the two-shaft version. The test showed the single-shaft concept lacked the driving cycle flexibility required for normal highway operation, and it was decided to concentrate further work on the two-shaft unit.

In 1968, MTU was formed as a merger of Maybach Motorenbau and MAN Turbo. The Maybach division of Daimler-Benz AG was building a wide range of diesel engines in its Friedrichshafen works, but had no turbine program. The parent firm, however, had started automotive gas turbine research in 1955 in a small department led by Bruno Eckert. This department was handed over to MTU at the time of its foundation, and moved from Stuttgart to Munich. MTU Munich builds gas turbines, while MTU Friedrichshafen builds diesel engines.

Originally Daimler-Benz AG had begun research work on gas turbines in 1939 and had its first complete turbojet—Type 007—ready for testing in September 1943. It had been designed by Professor Leist. This was a twin-spool engine of considerable complexity, with counter-rotating compressor and ducted fan.

Type 007 had a nine-stage axial-flow compressor on the high-pressure spool and an eight-stage compressor plus a 3-stage fan on the outer spool. The 007 used four barrel-type combustors. The compressor stages delivered a maximum mass flow of 17.6 pounds per second while the fan had a capacity of 35.2 pounds per second. Maximum rotor speed for the high-pressure spool was 12,000 rpm. The 007 weighed 2870 pounds and delivered about 1500 pounds thrust. It was 33.5 inches in diameter and 182 inches long. The German air ministry wanted a simpler engine and killed the project. That was the sum total of Daimler-Benz AG's turbine experience up to the time when Fritz Nallinger (who had served for three years as technical director of Turbomeca in Bordes) decided to begin studies for a truck turbine.

MTU Munich is owned jointly by MAN and Daimler-Benz AG on a 50/50 basis. The partners gave MTU its first contract in 1968. The order was to produce an industrial gas turbine suitable for truck installation. The first test engine ran in November 1971. The MTU truck gas turbine program is headed by Dr. Wolfgang Heilmann.

Heilmann was born in East Germany and educated as an engineer. After getting his diploma, he worked for three years in compressor and turbine research for a company in Dresden. Then he transferred to the DFVLR (German Research and Test Institute for Aeronautics) at Porzwahn near Cologne, where he ramained for 8 years. His next step was to join Daimler-Benz AG in Stuttgart, where he became involved with gas turbine projects for both trucks and aircraft. At the foundation of MTU, Heilmann was transferred to Munich.

The truck turbine is known as Project 7042, and is not yet in production. In its basic engineering principles and layout, Project 7042 is typical of modern design practice for gas turbines of 300-plus hp, such as the Allison

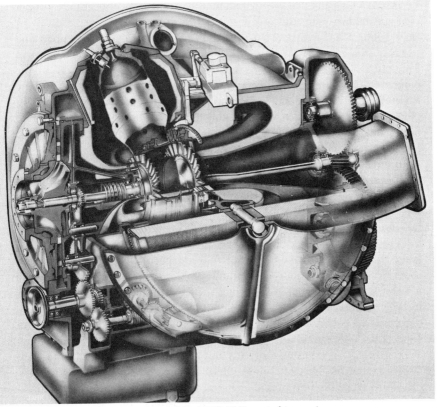

Cutaway view of the MTU 7042 gas turbine engine.

404 and the Ford 710. Project 7042 started with a clean sheet of paper in 1969. The contract with MAN and Daimler-Benz specified a two-shaft regenerative gas turbine engine. Heilmann and his group approached the design by intensive component and whole-engine testing. The MTU 7042 engine weighs about 1325 pounds including accessories, and will deliver 350–400 hp.

It has a two-stage compressor—an axial-flow stage pumping air into a centrifugal stage. The centrifugal compressor has a maximum speed of 54,000 rpm and works with a pressure ratio of 5.4. Both gasifier turbine and power turbine are of the axial-flow type. The power turbine wheel is identical with the gasifier turbine wheel, and the power turbine is provided with a variable-geometry nozzle assembly. Two disc-type regenerators are fitted, one on each side, and gear driven at the periphery. The regenerator discs are the same 28-inch diameter Cercor units used by Ford and Fiat.

The focus of the current gas turbine research effort at MTU is lower production cost. That means a ceaseless search for new materials, plus constant research on advanced technology for component design. MTU is also working in a cooperative arrangement with Pratt & Whitney, Fiat and Alfa Romeo to produce a new generation of low-noise, low-emission turbojets for future jetliners, and is engaged in another cooperative program with Rolls-Royce and Fiat to develop and manufacture the RB-199 turbojet for the Anglo-German-Italian Multi-Role Combat Aircraft (MRCA) project.

NISSAN MOTOR COMPANY LTD.

Nissan Motor Company of Tokyo, Japan, began design work on a truck turbine engine in 1967, and one year later the first engine was completed and went on test. An engine of such high rotational speeds and such a high cycle temperature was beyond all previous experience at Nissan, and many mechanical problems occurred. Several components were redesigned mainly for mechanical reasons, but as the Nissan engineers gained gas turbine know-how, modifications became increasingly associated with improvements in performance as well.

The Nissan gas turbine engine is an open cycle two-shaft regenerative gas turbine with variable power turbine nozzles. At the design condition, the output power is 300 hp, the pressure ratio is 3.8, mass flow capacity is 4.4 pounds per second, the gas generator speed is 40,000 rpm, the power turbine speed is 30,000 rpm and the turbine inlet temperature is 1562° F

Nissan gas turbine engine YTP-12.

(850° C). The single stage centrifugal compressor is driven by a single-stage axial-flow turbine, which is followed by an axial-flow power turbine with variable geometry nozzles. The combustor is a reverse flow barrel-type design and the heat exchanger is a regenerator with two rotary discs.

The fuel injector has a swirl type duplex nozzle. Because air is preheated by a heat exchanger, the air/fuel ratio is generally high. Blow-out does not occur for an air/fuel ratio as low as 120, and the combustion is stable up to an air/fuel ratio of 1,000. Stabilization is assured by a swirler which creates a recirculation zone. Ignition is possible at a gas generator speed as low as about 10% of the gas generator's design speed and consequently the load on the starter motor is relatively light.

An axial-flow compressor was excluded because of its size, cost, and sensitivity to blade contamination. Instead, a centrifugal type was adopted because of its high pressure ratio per stage and a wide operational range compared with an axial type. In order to secure good performance from the centrifugal compressor, the relative Mach number at the inducer tip was kept within the transonic range, and the impeller hub, shroud and blades were designed so that the relative velocity distribution in the blade row was reasonable.

Both the compressor turbine and the power turbine are of the axial flow type. The blade row and blade profiles were designed so that aerodynamic blade loading was kept low. The nozzle ring, with 23 blades, is an X45 cast-

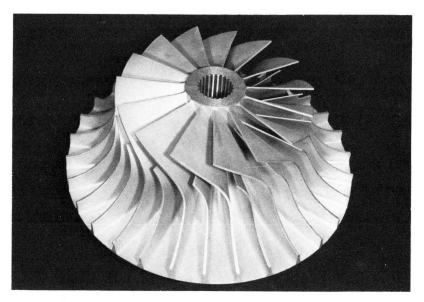

Nissan YTP-12 compressor impeller.

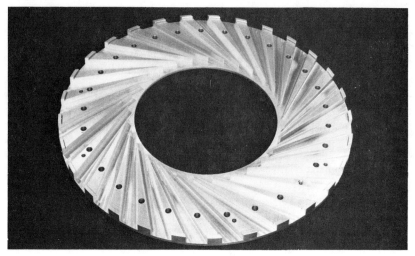

Nissan YTP-12 compressor diffuser.

Nissan YTP-12 first-stage compressor wheel.

ing and the turbine wheel, with 55 blades, is made of Inconel 713C precision cast metal.

For the power turbine, variable nozzles are adopted to improve specific fuel consumption at part load. The power turbine nozzle ring consists of 29 moveable blades which are precision cast of X45 alloy and the turbine

Nissan YTP-12 variable-geometry nozzle assembly.

Nissan YTP-12 power turbine and shaft.

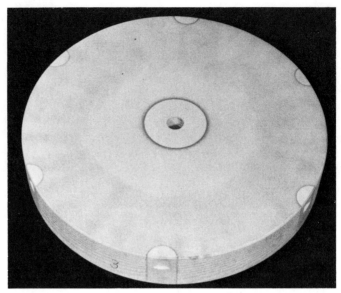

Nissan YTP-12 regenerator disc.

wheel, with 56 blades, is made of Inconel 713C. The power turbine has approximately 50% reaction at the design nozzle angle to secure good performance over a wide range of power turbine speed, from stall to overspeed. The turbine has a large annulus area at the turbine outlet so as to reduce the velocity loss at the discharge ports.

The main components of the heat exchanger are two rotary discs which are located on both sides of the engine, and the center of each core is supported by a center shaft. Each matrix is attached to a circumferential ring gear which is driven by a pinion.

The fuel control system has an electronic controller. The maximum fuel flow corresponding to each compressor speed is pre-set in the controller to avoid surging and flame-out. The actual fuel volume injected is determined by the accelerator pedal, compared with the calculated maximum fuel flow. If the pedal opening is larger than the fuel flow limit, the actual flow is controlled so that the fuel flow is kept within the permitted range.

Engine speed control is assured by a potentiometer attached to the accelerator pedal. The motion of the pedal is indicated as a change of voltage in the signal sent to the electronic unit. The automatic transmission and the power turbine nozzle angle are also connected to the accelerator pedal linkage.

This gas turbine engine was installed in an intercity Nissan bus. In stan-

Nissan gas turbine-powered bus.

dard form, this bus type is diesel-powered and runs in regular service on the Tokyo-Nagoya expressway. It is a 38-seat bus with an overall length of 39.3 feet and a curb weight of 29,000 pounds. The engine is installed in an insulated compartment in the tail end of the chassis. The engine is rated at 300 hp and gives the bus a cruising speed of 62 mph with a full load. The engine remains in the experimental stage, and Nissan has not announced a timetable for getting it into production.

TOYOTA MOTOR COMPANY LTD.

Toyota launched its research program for alternative power sources in 1963, and Kenya Nakamura was named chief designer of the product planning staff. This work included research on steam engines, fuel cells, Wankel engines, electric storage batteries, and gas turbines. The preliminary report was presented to the management in 1967, and concluded that the gas turbine was one of the most promising automotive prime movers. The report recommended that development of a gas turbine for automobiles should be started quickly.

As a starting point, the Toyota engineers copied the Chrysler two-shaft regenerative gas turbine design (A-831). The first Toyota-built version was designed strictly for bench testing, and did not fit under the hood of a Toyota car. When it was deemed ready for road testing, the hood had to be removed, with the turbine's combustor dome extending upwards like a vestigial funnel. The Toyota GT-1 delivered 130 hp at 50,900 rpm. During tests with the GT-1, the Toyota engineers began to introduce design changes. They adopted a radial inflow first-stage turbine and ran the gasifier shaft in plain bearings. Severe problems with oil seals resulted.

After final evaluation of the GT-1 it was decided to spread out further turbine research on three sizes for different applications. Three different truck turbine designs were built and tested—the GT-5, GT-53, and GT-55. The GT-5 was a single-shaft prototype, designed in 1967. It had a single regenerative heat exchanger and used a toroidal combustor. It gave no problems in the areas of combustion control or heat exchange, but the heat exchanger was judged to be too bulky.

The GT-53 was designed in 1958 as an improved version of the GT-5. This unit included a new and unique type of recuperative heat exchanger with remarkably small dimensions. The GT-53 abandoned the toroidal combustor in favor of a barrel-type unit. The GT-55 engine was similar to the GT-53, with barrel-type combustor, but differed in the use of a recuperator.

The intermediate-size Toyota gas turbines were designated GT-11, GT-12, and GT-15 and were intended for light commercial vehicles. The GT-11 was a direct descendant of the GT-1, essentially Chrysler-based, but using a radial inflow first-stage turbine. The gasifier shaft ran in ball and roller bearings, and the regenerator core was made of Cercor material.

The GT-11 was designed and produced in collaboration with the Hino Motor Company (a Toyota subsidiary) and installed in a Hino light bus for testing. The GT-12 engine was the same basic engine equipped with a recuperator, and the GT-15 is a redesign of the GT-11 relying on the same principles but incorporating new components and new materials.

Toyota's passenger car turbines were called GT-14 and GT-16. The GT-14 was a 33-hp twin-shaft recuperative engine, for all intents and purposes a scaled-down GT-11. Toyota indicates its true future may be as an aircraft APU rather than a passenger car engine. With the GT-16, Toyota reverted to an axial-flow first-stage turbine.

Up to 1972, all Toyota turbines used Inconel 713C turbine wheels, but then the company started a vast research program on ceramics centering on aluminum nitride and silicon nitride. This program is still going on.

Bibliography

ARTICLES

ANON.: Advanced 145-bhp twin shaft design. Engine Design and Applications, March, 1966.

ANON.: The Fiat turbine car. The Motor, May 5, 1954.

ANON.: Early history of turbocharging. Gas and Oil Power, May 1955.

ANON.: A Turbine car at Earls Court. The Motor, September 26, 1956.

ANON.: Renault demonstrates their Shooting Star. The Motor, June 27, 1956.

ANON.: Bluebird on trial—first steps at Goodwood. The Motor, July 27, 1960.

ANON.: In his father's footsteps: Donald Campbell's plans for his Bluebird record car. The Autocar, August 8, 1958.

ANON.: Bluebird re-hatched. The Motor, December 6, 1961.

ANON.: "00" A new sound at Le Mans. Autocar, June 14, 1963.

ANON.: The Rover-BRM. Automobile Engineer, July, 1963.

ANON.: Le Mans Rover-BRM. Automobile Engineer, August 1965.

ANON.: Rover 2S/100 gas turbine. Autocar, March 15, 1957.

ANDERSON, WAYNE S. AND ENGEL, GENE: Compactness of ground turbine depends on integral recuperator. Automotive Engineering, August 1971.

ANSDALE, R. F.: Chrysler gas turbine car. Automobile Engineer, November 1963.

BANKS, AIR COMMODORE R. F.: Lessons from Aviation Engines. The Motor, February 28 and March 7, 1951.

BELL, F. R.: The world's record turbine car. The Autocar, July 4, 1952.

BENSON, PROF. ROLAND S.: Die Leistungseigenschaften von duesenlosen Radialturbinen. Motortechnische Zeitschrift, December 1973.

BLAIN, DOUG: If at first . . . The Autocar, October 27, 1961.

BORGESON, GRIFF: Bluebird at Bonneville. The Autocar, September 30, 1960.

BRUNNER, KUNO: Chrysler Turbinenwagen aus der Nähe betrachtet. Automobil Revue, May 23, 1963.

BRYANT, GLENN: Indy's only turbine. Automotive Industries, May 15, 1969.

BÜCHI, DR. ALFRED J.: History of turbo-charging development. Combustion Engine Progress, June, 1957.

BULMER, CHARLES: Towards 500 mph. The Motor, May 25, 1960.

CALLAHAN, JOSEPH M.: Ford's new turbine. Automotive Industries, July 1, 1973.

CALOVOLO, MARIO: Il motore ibrido: un confronto con la turbina a gas rigenerativa. ATA, January 1973.

DE CIZANCOURT, JOEL: La Turbine Renault "Etoile Filante." L'Automobile, July, 1956.

COLLET, PETER J.: A 3-shaft vs. a 2-shaft cycle in automotive gas turbines. SAE Journal, July 1968.

DUNNE, JIM: Will you commute in GM's new turbine-powered bus? Popular Science, September 1969.

DUNNE, JIM, AND NORBYE, JAN P.: We drive the Williams turbine-engine clean-air car. Popular Science, November 1971.

DUNNE, JIM, AND NORBYE, JAN P.: For the gas turbine, it's now or never. Popular Science, September 1973.

ECKERT, DR. ING. BRUNO: Hat die Automobile-Gasturbine eine Chance. Automobiltechnische Zeitschrift, Sept. Oct. Nov. Dec., 1967.

ENGEL, GENE, AND ANDERSON, WAYNE S.: Compactness of ground turbine depends on integral recuperator. Automotive Engineering, August, 1971.

ENSOR, JAMES: Commercial vehicles: Era of the gas turbine. Financial Times, September 21, 1970.

EVES, EDWARD: A fair exchanger. The Autocar, July 16, 1965.

FARINELLI, E. F.: Facciamo il punto sull'auto a turbina. Motor Italia, May–June, 1954.

FLYNN, GREGORY, JR.: Some principles and applications of the free-piston engine. GM Engineering Journal July/August/September 1958.

FLYNN, GREGORY, JR.: Observations on 25,000 hours of free-piston engine operation. SAE transactions, Volume 65, 1957.

FORD, ERIC, B. SC. AND SCHNABEL, W.: Gasturbinen fuer strassenfahrzeuge Motortechnische Zeitung, January 1970.

FREY, DONALD N. WITH KLOTSCH, PAUL, AND EGLI, ADOLPH: The automotive free piston turbine engine. SAE Journal, Volume 65, 1957.

GARNIER, JACQUES: Les moteurs a reaction et l'application des turbines a la propulsion routiere. L'Annee Automobile, edition 1957.

GESCHELIN, JOSEPH: International Harvester's truck gas turbine. Automotive Industries, February 15th, 1968.

GOSTELOW, DR. PAUL: Big-engine aerodynamics. The New Scientist, Jan. 21, 1971.

HAGEMANN, GUNTER, WITH ROTTENKOLBER, PAUL, AND WALZER, DR. ING. PETER: Die Personenwagen-Versuchgasturbine VW-GT 70. Motortechnische Zeitschrift, September 1973.

HARMON, ROBERT A.: Gas turbines—an industry with worldwide impact. Mechanical Engineering, March 1973.

HARRISON, NEIL: Flying a turboprop Auster. Flight, Sept. 9, 1965.

HASTINGS, HAROLD: Power without pistons. The Motor, September 25, 1965.

HAWTHORNE, E. P.: The Automotive Gas Turbine: Some considerations of heat exchanger design. The Oil Engine and Gas Turbine, September and October 1954.

HEMPEL, WOLFGANG: Geräuschuntersuchingen bei Kleingasturbinen. Motortechnische Zeitschrift, April, 1965.

HEMPSON, JOHN: Turbines and tomorrow's engineers. New Scientist, September 3, 1970.

HILL, HENRY C.: Progress of the gas turbine truck tests. SAE Journal, July 1952.

HUBER, ROBERT: Freikolben-Gasgeneratoren fur den Antrieb von Automobilen. Automobil Revue, October 31, 1956.

HUNTINGTON, ROGER: Turbine powered racing cars. Sports Cars Illustrated, March 1960.

JENKINSON, DENIS J.: The Lotus turbine car. Motor Sport, May 1971.

KINCAID, KEN: Shooting Star. Sports Cars Illustrated, September 1956.

KOLBENSCHLAG, MIKE: He thinks small to do big things with gas turbines. Product Engineering, October 6, 1969.

KRONOGAARD, SVEN OLOF: Volvo dual powerplant meets military vehicle needs. SAE Journal, July 1966.

LANNING, JOHN G.: Automobile gas turbine heat exchangers. Gas Turbine International. January–February, 1969.

LAURENT, ANDRÉ: A French gas turbine. The Motor, December 10, 1952.

LOWREY, JOSEPH: Topical Technics. The Motor, June 22, 1960.

LUDVIGSEN, KARL E.: The incredible story of the world's most advanced racing car. Motor Trend, May 1968.

LUDVIGSEN, KARL E.: Those tantalizing turbines. Ward's Auto World, November 1973.

MAROSELLI, JEAN-CLAUDE: Ein Gasturbinen-Versuchswagen von Renault. Automobil Revue, June 27, 1956.

MEYER, ADOLF: The combustion gas turbine. Engineering, March 3, 1939.

MEYER, DR. A.: 2200 h.p. gas turbine locomotive of the Swiss Federal Railways. The Brown Boveri Review, June/July 1946.

MONTABONE, OSCAR: Il futuro degli autoveicoli in rapporto alle difese ecologiche. ATA, May 1972.

MORTIMER, JOHN: I am designing for people, says Italy's gas turbine king. The Engineer, December 7, 1972.

MORTIMER, JOHN: The gas turbine man who came in from the cold. The Engineer, March 29, 1973.

MÜLLER, A. E.: The first gas turbine locomotive for England. The Brown Boveri Review, June/July 1947.

MÜLLER, A. E.: Brown Boveri gas turbine locomotives. The Brown Boveri Review, July/August 1951.

MUNDY, HARRY: Target speed 500! Sports Cars Illustrated, September 1960.

NAKAMURA, KENYA: Toyota's automotive gas turbine. Gas Turbine International, October 1971.

NELSON, J. R., AND PINKEL, BENJAMIN: On turbine engine development policy. Astronautics and Aeronautics, November 1970.

NOBLE, WILLIAM T.: Tiny engines to float you in the air . . . cleaner air. Detroit News Sunday News Magazine, April 18, 1971.

NORBYE, JAN P.: The gas turbine comes of age. Automobile Quarterly, Volume 2, Number 3 (1963).

NORBYE, JAN P.: Gasturbinenauto in New York in Erprobung. Automobil Revue, October 12, 1972.

NORBYE, JAN P., AND DUNNE, JIM: We drive the new Williams turbine-engine clean-air car. Popular Science, November, 1971.

NORBYE, JAN P., AND DUNNE, JIM: For the gas turbine, it's now or never. Popular Science, September 1973.

NOTTS: Power units for large vehicles. Automobile Engineer, January 1970.

VON DER NUELL, DR. ING. WERNER T.: Gasturbinen im Wettstreit mit Kolbenbrennkraftmaschinen. Motortechnische Zeitschrift, May 1968.

PENNY, NOEL: Gas turbines—is there a go-slow? Automotive Design Engineering, June 1963.

PENNY, NOEL: Gas turbines for land transport. Science Journal, April 1970.

PHILIPS, P. A.: Turbocar progress. The Motor, February 27 and March 6, 1957.

PHILIPS, DAVID: Rover-BRM Le Mans Entry. Car and Driver, July 1963.

PINKEL, BENJAMIN, AND NELSON, J. R.: On turbine engine development policy. Astronautics and Aeronautics, November 1970.

PROCHE, CHARLES G.: Hat die Gasturbine als Automobilantrieb eine Chance? Automobil Revue, February 24, 1972.

PROCHE, CHARLES G.: Die Entwicklungsgeschichte der Rennmotoren mit Turbocaufladung. Automobil Revue, June 15, 1972.

REAL, P.: The 300 kw gas turbine locomotive unit. The Brown, Boveri Review, October 1946.

ROTTENKOLBER, PAUL, WITH HAGEMANN, GUNTER, AND WALZER, DR. ING. PETER: Die Personenwagen-Versuchsgasturbine VW-GT 70. Motortechnische Zeitschrift, September, 1973.

RUDD, J. W., AND WEISS, K.: Engine performance improvement—latest developments in water and water alcohol injection. Automobile Engineer, November 1959.

RUTHERFORD, MALCOLM: Motoren und Turbinen Union joining the senior league. The Financial Times, August 3, 1973.

SCHNABEL, DIPL. ING. WOLFGANG, AND FORD, ERIC: Gasturbinen fuer Strassenfahrzeuge. Motortechnische Zeitung, January 1970.

SCHNELL, OBERING. ERWIN: Die Zukunft der Automobilgasturbine im Zivilen Bereich. Automobil Revue, April 20, 1967.

SCHNELL, ERWIN: Flugtriebwerke auf der Deutschen Luftfahrtschau 1968. Motortechnische Zeitschrift, October 1968.

SIMMONS, C. R.: Turbines for the road—the state of the art. The Motor, January 31, 1962.

SNOXELL, FRANK: The Rover gas turbine type 2S/150. Motor Boat & Yachting, February 21, 1965.

SPINKS, J. J.: The Austin turbine motorcar engine. The Oil Engine and Gas turbine, February 1957.

STEVENS, D. N.: An analysis of the circumstances relating to the Bluebird crash on the Bonneville Salt Flats. The Autocar, April 21, 1961.

TAVARD, CHRISTIAN: Les voitures françaises à turbine. L'Automobile, June 1956.

THIRLBY, DAVID: A gas turbine racing formula. The Motor, 1956.

TURNER, PHILIP A.: The sporting side. The Motor, September 21, 1960.

TURNER, PHILIP A.: Obituary—Donald Campbell. The Motor January 14, 1967.

TUTTLE, COL. GEORGE A.: Tankers! There's a turbine in your future. Armor, May–June, 1972.

UNDERWOOD, ARTHUR F.: The GMR 4-4 hyprex engine. SAE Journal, Volume 65, 1957.

WAKEFIELD, RON: STP Paxton turbine racing car. Road & Track September 1967.

WALZER, DR. ING. PETER WITH ROTTENKOLBER, PAUL, AND HAGEMANN, GÜNTER: Die Personenwagen-Versuchsgasturbine VW-GT 70. Motortechnische Zeitschrift, September 1973.

WEISS, K., AND RUDD, J. W.: Engine performance improvement—latest developments in water and water alcohol injection. Automobile Engineer, November 1959.

WILDER, STEPHEN F.: Firebird III—General Motors' Circus on wheels. Sports Car Illustrated, March 1959.

WILKINS, GORDON: Theo Page zeichnet Spitzenfahrzeuge: Der Lotus 56 STP. Automobil Revue, May 23, 1968.

WOLF, MAURIZIO: Un Turbomotore sperimentale Fiat del tipo a differenziale. ATA, July 1968.

YAFFEE, MICHAEL L.: Small aircraft turbofans studied. Aviation Week and Space Technology, February 9, 1970.

TECHNICAL PAPERS

AMANN, CHARLES A.: An introduction to the vehicular gas turbine engine. SAE Paper # 730618, presented in Milwaukee, Wisconsin on March 30, 1973.

AMANN, CHARLES A.: Handling accessory loads on a free turbine engine. SAE paper # 930A, presented in Detroit, Michigan October 21, 1964.

AMANN, CHARLES A. WITH WADE, W. R., AND YU, M. K.: Some factors affecting gas turbine passenger car emissions. SAE paper # 720237, presented in Detroit, Michigan January 10–14, 1972.

AMANN, CHARLES A. WITH LIDDLE, S. G. AND SHERIDAN, D. C.: Acceleration of a passenger car powered by a fixed-geometry single-shaft gas turbine engine. SAE paper # 720758, presented in Milwaukee, Wisconsin September 11–14, 1972.

AMANN, CHARLES A. WITH SHERIDAN, DAVID C., AND NORDENSON, GARY E.: Variable compressor geometry in the single-shaft automotive turbine engine. SAE paper # 740166, presented in Detroit, Michigan, February 27, 1974.

AZELBORN, N. A. WITH WADE, W. R., SECORD, J. R., AND McLEAN, A. F.: Low emissions combustion for the regenerative gas turbine. ASME papers # 73-GT-11 and # 73-GT-12, delivered in Washington, DC on April 9, 1973.

BARBEAU, D. E.: The performance of vehicle gas turbines. SAE paper # 670198, presented in Detroit, Michigan May 18, 1966.

BARR, RICHARD: Gas turbines for road transport. Lecture given at the School of Gas Turbine Technology, Lutterworth, England in June 1948.

BEAUFRERE, A. H.: An exploration of the automotive gas turbine. SAE paper # 437, delivered in Detroit, Michigan January 10–14, 1955.

BECK, ROBERT J.: Evaluation of ceramics for small gas turbine engines. SAE paper # 740239, presented in Detroit, Michigan February 28, 1974.

BIDWELL, JOSEPH B. AND OWEN, ROBERT E.: The experimental chassis for the Firebird II. SAE paper presented in Atlantic City June 5, 1956.

BIDWELL, JOSEPH B., CATALDO, R. S. AND VAN HOUSE, R. M.: Chassis and Control Details of Firebird III. SAE paper presented in Detroit, Michigan January 12–16, 1959.

BLOOMFIELD, WARREN: Grounding the aircraft gas turbine—the design conversion from air to surface use. SAE paper # 700045, presented in Detroit, Michigan January 12–16, 1970.

BOWLIN, R. C. WITH SMALLEY, A. J. AND JONES, H. F.: Transmission for automotive single-shaft gas turbine and turbo-Rankine engines. SAE paper # 730645, delivered in Chicago, Illinois June 18–22, 1973.

BRATTON, R. J. WITH HOLDEN, A. N. AND MUMFORD, S. E.: Testing ceramic stator vanes for industrial gas turbines. SAE paper # 740236, presented in Detroit, Michigan February 28, 1974.

BRETON, R. A. WITH KOBLISH, R. R. AND MARSHALL, R. L.: Design and test limitations on reducing NO_x in gas turbine combustors. SAE paper # 740182, presented in Detroit, Michigan February 27, 1974.

CADWELL, R. G. WITH CHAPMAN, W. I. AND WALCH, H. C.: The Ford turbine—an engine designed to compete with the Diesel. SAE paper # 720168, presented in Detroit, Michigan January 10–14, 1972.

CAMPBELL, J. S. WITH WALLACE, F. J. AND WRIGHT, E. J.: Future development of free piston gasifier turbine combinations for vehicle traction. SAE paper # 660132, delivered in Detroit, Michigan, January 10–14, 1966.

CATALDO, RAY S., VAN HOUSE, R. M., AND BIDWELL, JOSEPH B.: Chassis and control details of Firebird III. SAE paper presented in Detroit, Michigan, January 12–16, 1959.

CHAPMAN, W. I.: Chrysler's gas turbine car. SAE paper # 777B, presented in Detroit, Michigan, January 13–17, 1964.

CHAPMAN, W. I. WITH CADWELL, R. G., AND WALCH, H. C.: The Ford turbine—an engine designed to compete with the diesel. SAE paper # 720168, presented in Detroit, Michigan, January 10–14, 1972.

COE, R. F. WITH LUMBY, R. J., AND LINES, D. J.: The development of silicon nitride to achieve higher inlet temperatures in land-based gas turbines. SAE paper # 720170, presented in Detroit, Michigan, January 10–14, 1972.

COLLMAN, JOHN S., AND TURUNEN, W. A.: The General Motors Research GT-309 gas turbine engine. SAE paper presented in Cleveland, Ohio, October 18–21, 1965.

DAVIS, WARREN W., AND JOHNSON, LLOYD E.: Evolution of a turbine engine for industrial markets. SAE paper # 660035, presented in Detroit, Michigan, January 10–14, 1966.

DAVISON, W. R. WITH WRIGHT, E. S., AND GREENWALD, L. E.: A feasibility analysis of a simple cycle gas turbine engine for automobiles. SAE paper # 720238, presented in Detroit, Michigan, January 10–14, 1972.

DORGAN, ROBERT J. WITH NOLAN, JOHN M. AND RIO, RUSSELL L.: Transmission considerations for gas turbines. SAE paper # 720169, presented in Detroit, Michigan, January 10–14, 1972.

EATOCK, H. C. WITH SAMPATH, P., AND SAINTSBURY, J. A.: Simple automobile gas turbine combustors for low emissions. SAE paper # 730670 delivered in Chicago, Ill. June 18–22, 1973.

ENGDAHL, RICHARD E.: Chemical vapor deposited silicon carbide turbine rotors. SAE paper # 740184, presented in Detroit, Mich. February 27, 1974.

FLAHERTY, ALBERT M.: The Turbo-Chief—San Francisco's gas turbine powered fire apparatus. SAE paper # 650462, delivered in Chicago, Ill. May 17–21, 1965.

FRENCH, RONALD W.: Gas turbines in fire apparatus—the vehicle manufacturer's viewpoint. SAE paper # 650461, delivered in Chicago, Ill. May 17–21, 1965.

GARNER, P. B. AND HULL, W. L.: Gas turbine propulsion system for Budd test railcar. SAE paper # 670967, presented in Pittsburgh, Pa. October 30–November 3, 1967.

GODFREY, D. J.: Silicon nitride ceramics for engineering applications. SAE paper # 740238, presented in Detroit, Michigan February 28, 1974.

GREENWALD, L. E. WITH DAVISON, W. R., AND WRIGHT, E. S.: A feasibility analysis of a simple cycle gas turbine engine for automobiles. SAE paper # 720238, presented in Detroit, Mich. January 10–14, 1972.

GRES, M. E., AND KRAUS, C. E.: A transmission system for single-shaft gas turbine powered trucks. SAE paper # 730644, presented in Chicago, Ill. June 18–22, 1973.

GUERNSEY, R. W.: Field experience with GMT-305 gas turbine in military applications. SAE paper delivered at the 1961 SAE summer meeting.

HARDY, G.: Applications of the ST6 gas turbine engine. SAE paper # 670693 presented in Portland, Oregon, August 14–17, 1967.

HAUPT, C. G.: Exhaust emission by a small gas turbine. SAE paper # 680463, presented in Detroit, Mich. May 20–24, 1968.

HERON, SAM D.: Some elements of gas turbine performance. SAE paper presented in Detroit, Mich. on March 7, 1956.

HOLDEN, A. N. WITH MUMFORD, S. E., AND BRATOON, R. J.: Testing ceramic stator vanes for industrial gas turbines. SAE paper # 740236, presented in Detroit, Mich. February 28, 1974.

HUEBNER, GEORGE J. JR.: The automotive gas turbine, today and tomorrow. SAE paper, presented in Detroit, Michigan October 8, 1956.

HUEBNER, GEORGE J. JR.: The gas turbine engine and its potential. Presentation to the American Petroleum Institute, May 10, 1960.

HUEBNER, GEORGE J. JR.: The Chrysler regenerative turbine powered passenger car. SAE paper # 777A, presented in Detroit, Mich. January 13–17, 1964.

HULL, W. L., AND GARNER, P. B.: Gas turbine propulsion system for Budd test railcar. SAE paper # 670967, presented in Pittsburgh, Pa. October 30–November 3, 1967.

JOHNSON, LLOYD E., AND DAVIS, WARREN W.: Evolution of a turbine engine for industrial markets. SAE paper # 660035, presented in Detroit, Mich. January 10–14, 1966.

JONES, H. F. WITH SMALLEY, A. J., AND BOWLIN, R. C.: Transmission for automotive single-shaft gas turbines and turbo-Rankine engines. SAE paper # 730645, presented in Chicago, Ill. June 18–22, 1973.

KAHLE, GLENN W.: The turbine-powered vehicle—promises or profit. SAE paper # 660171, delivered in Detroit, Michigan, January 10–14, 1966.

KENNEMER, ROBERT E.: The Caterpillar Turbine engine—a complete power package. SAE paper # 660036, presented in Detroit, Mich. January 10–14, 1966.

KINOSHITA, K. AND YAMAZAKI, S.: Development of the Nissan automotive gas turbine. JSME paper presented in Tokyo, Japan, October 4–7, 1971.

KOBLISH, T. R. WITH MARSHALL, R. L. AND BRETON, R. A.: Design and test limitations on reducing NO_x in gas turbine combustors. SAE paper # 740182, presented in Detroit, Michigan, February 27, 1974.

KOEHLER, M.: The influence of flow path geometry and manufacturing tolerances on gas turbine regenerator efficiency. SAE paper # 740183, presented in Detroit, Mich. February 27, 1974.

KOMEYA, KATSUTOSHI, AND NODA, FUMIYOSHI: Aluminum nitride and silicon nitride for high temperature gas turbine engines. SAE paper # 740237, presented in Detroit, Mich. February 28, 1974.

KORTH, M. W., AND ROSE, A. H., JR.: Emissions from a gas turbine automobile. SAE paper # 680402, presented in Detroit, Michigan May 20–24, 1968.

KRAUS, C. E., AND GRES, M. E.: A transmission system for single-shaft gas turbine powered trucks. SAE paper # 730644, presented in Chicago, Ill. June 18–22, 1973.

LANNING, JOHN G., AND WARDALE, D. J. S.: The development of the glass-ceramic axial-flow rotary regenerator. ASME paper # 66-GT-107, delivered in Zurich, Switzerland March 13–17, 1966.

LAPOINTE, CLAYTON W., AND SCHULTZ, WESTON L.: Comparison of emission indexes within a turbine combustor operated on diesel fuel or methanol. SAE paper # 730669, delivered in Chicago, Ill. June 18–22, 1973.

LIDDLE, S. G. WITH SHERIDAN, D. C., AND AMANN, CHARLES A.: Acceleration of a passenger car powered by a fixed-geometry single-shaft gas turbine engine. SAE paper # 720758, presented in Milwaukee, Wis. September 11–14, 1972.

LINES, D. J. WITH LUMBY, R. J., AND COE, R. F.: The development of silicon nitride to achieve higher inlet temperatures in land-based gas turbines. SAE paper # 720170, presented in Detroit, Mich. January 10–14, 1972.

LUMBY R. J. WITH COE, R. F., AND LINES, D. J.: The development of silicon nitride to achieve higher inlet temperatures in land-based gas turbines. SAE paper # 720170, presented in Detroit, Mich. January 10–14, 1972.

MADDOX, CHARLES F., AND McQUAID, JOHN G.: The interstate highway system super transport truck. SAE paper # 991A, presented in Detroit, Mich. January 11–15, 1965.

McLEAN, ARTHUR F. WITH AZELBORN, N. A., SECORD, J. R., AND WADE, W. R.:

Low emissions combustion for the regenerative gas turbine. ASME paper # 73-GT-11 and # 73-GT-12, presented in Washington, DC on April 9, 1973.

MARSHALL, R. L. WITH KOBLISH, T. R., AND BRETON, R. A.: Design and test limitations on reducing NO_x in gas turbine combustors. SAE paper # 740182, presented in Detroit, Michigan, February 27, 1974.

McLELLAN, G. E.: The gas turbine in small craft. SAE paper # 710661, presented in Vancouver, British Columbia, Canada, August 16–19, 1971.

McQUAID, JOHN G., AND MADDOX, CHARLES F.: The interstate highway system super transport truck. SAE paper # 991A, presented in Detroit, Mich. January 11–15, 1965.

MOORE, J., AND PEASE, E.: Lycoming's LTS 101 engine design. SAE paper # 740165, presented in Detroit, Mich. February 27, 1974.

MUMFORD, S. E. WITH HOLDEN, A. N., AND BRATTON, R. J.: Testing ceramic stator vanes for industrial gas turbines. SAE paper # 740236, presented in Detroit, Mich. February 28, 1974.

MYKOLENKO, P. WITH VERKEMP, F. J., NAGEY, T. F., AND NAYLOR, M. E.: The low emission gas turbine passenger car—what does the future hold? ASME paper # 73-GT-49, presented in Washington, DC April 8–12, 1973.

NAGEY, TIBOR F. WITH VERKEMP, F. J., MYKOLENKO, P., AND NAYLOR, M. E.: The low emission gas turbine passenger car—what does the future hold? ASME paper # 73-GT-49, presented in Washington, DC April 8–12, 1973.

NAYLOR, M. E. WITH NAGEY, T. F., VERKEMP, F. J., AND MYKOLENKO, P.: The low emission gas turbine passenger car—what does the future hold? ASME paper # 73-GT-49, presented in Washington, DC April 8–12, 1973.

NODA, FUMIYOSHI, AND KOMEYA, KATSUTOSHI: Aluminum nitride and silicon nitride for high temperature gas turbine engines. SAE paper # 740237, presented in Detroit, Mich. February 28, 1974.

NOLAN, JOHN M. WITH RIO, RUSSELL L., AND DORGAN, ROBERT J.: Transmission considerations for gas turbines. SAE paper # 720169, presented in Detroit, Mich. January 10–14, 1972.

NORDENSON, GARY E. WITH AMANN, CHARLES A., AND SHERIDAN, DAVID C.: Variable compressor geometry in the single shaft automotive turbine engine. SAE paper # 740166, presented in Detroit, Mich. February 27, 1974.

PEASE, E., AND MOORE, J.: Lycoming's LTS 101 engine design. SAE paper # 740165, presented in Detroit, Mich. February 27, 1974.

PEITSCH, GERHARD, AND SWATMAN, IVAN M.: A gas turbine super transport truck power package. SAE paper # 991B, presented in Detroit, Mich. January 11–15, 1965.

PENNY, NOEL: The development of the glass ceramic regenerator for the Rover 2S/150R engine. SAE paper # 660361, delivered in Detroit, Mich. June 6–10, 1966.

PENNY, NOEL: Rover case history of small gas turbines. SAE paper # 634A, delivered in Detroit, Mich. January 14–18, 1963.

PENNY, NOEL, AND SPEAR, PETER: The classification of gas turbine and piston engines for competition purposes. SAE paper # 996B, presented in Detroit, Mich. January 11–15, 1965.

PENNY, NOEL: Technical advances in gas turbine design. Institution of Mechanical Engineers, presentation at Warwick, April 9–11, 1969.

PORTER, K. W., AND WILLIAMS, L. H.: Gas turbines for emergency vehicles. SAE paper # 650460, delivered in Chicago, Ill. May 17–21, 1965.

PROBST, HUBERT B. AND SANDERS, WILLIAM A.: Behavior of ceramics at 1200° C in a simulated gas turbine environment. SAE paper # 740240, presented in Detroit, Mich. February 28, 1974.

RIO, RUSSELL L. WITH DORGAN, ROBERT J., AND NOLAN, JOHN M.: Transmission considerations for gas turbines. SAE paper # 720169, presented in Detroit, Mich. January 10–14, 1972.

ROGO, CASIMIR: Development of a high top speed radial turbine system for a small turbo-alternator. SAE paper # 710552, presented in Montreal, Quebec, Canada, June 7–11, 1971.

ROGO, CASIMIR, AND TRAUTH, RICHARD L.: Design of high heat release slinger combustor with rapid acceleration requirement. SAE paper # 740167, presented in Detroit, Mich. February 27, 1974.

ROSE, A. H., JR., AND KORTH, M. W.: Emissions from a gas turbine automobile. SAE paper # 680402, presented in Detroit, Mich. May 20–24, 1968.

ROSEN, CARL G. A.: Future powerplants to combat air pollution. SAE paper # 710362, delivered at Menlo Park, Calif. September 21–22, 1970.

SAINTSBURY, J. A. WITH SAMPATH, P., AND EATOCK, H. C.: Simple automobile gas turbine combustors for low emissions. SAE paper # 730670, presented in Chicago, Ill. June 18–22, 1973.

SAMPATH, P. WITH SAINTSBURY, J. A., AND EATOCK, H. C.: Simple automobile gas turbine combustors for low emissions. SAE paper # 730670, presented in Chicago, Ill. June 18–22, 1973.

SANDERS, WILLIAM A., AND PROBST, HUBERT B.: Behavior of ceramics at 1200° C in a simulated gas turbine environment. SAE paper # 740240, presented in Detroit, Mich. February 28, 1974.

SCHILLING, ROBERT: A cradle for new power. SAE paper delivered in Atlantic City, New Jersey June 6–11, 1954.

SCHULTZ, WESTON L., AND LaPOINTE, CLAYTON W.: Comparison of emission indexes within a turbine combustor operated on diesel fuel or methanol. SAE paper # 730669, delivered in Chicago, Ill. June 18–22, 1973.

SECORD, J. R. WITH AZELBORN, N. A., WADE, W. R., AND McLEAN, A. F.: Low emissions combustion for the regenerative gas turbine. ASME paper # 73-GT-11 and # 73-GT-12, presented in Washington, DC on April 9, 1973.

SHERIDAN, D. C. WITH AMANN, CHARLES A., AND LIDDLE, S. G.: Acceleration of a passenger car powered by a fixed-geometry single-shaft gas turbine engine. SAE paper # 720758. Presented in Milwaukee, Wis. September 11–14, 1972.

SHERIDAN, DAVID C. WITH AMANN, CHARLES A. AND NORDENSON, GARY E.: Variable compressor geometry in the single shaft automotive turbine engine. SAE paper # 740166, presented in Detroit, Mich. February 27, 1974.

SMALLEY, A. J. WITH BOWLIN, R. C. AND JONES, H. F.: Transmission for automotive single-shaft gas turbine and turbo-Rankine engines. SAE paper # 730645, delivered in Chicago, Ill. June 18–22, 1973.

SPEAR, PETER, AND PENNY, NOEL: The classification of gas turbine and piston engines for competition purposes. SAE paper # 996B, presented in Detroit, Mich. January 11–15, 1965.

STYHR, K. H.: Spin testing of ceramic turbine rotors. SAE paper # 740234, presented in Detroit, Mich. February 28, 1974.

SULLIVAN, ROBERT F.: Development of a high temperature sensor for a gas turbine engine. SAE paper # 720160, presented in Detroit, Mich. January 10–14, 1972.

SUNDBERG, DAVID V.: Ceramic roller bearings for high speed and high temperature applications. SAE paper # 740241, presented in Detroit, Mich. February 28, 1974.

SWATMAN, IVAN M.: Development of the Ford 704 gas turbine. SAE paper # 291A, presented in Detroit, Mich. January 9–13, 1961.

SWATMAN, IVAN M., AND PEITSCH, GERHARD: A gas turbine super transport truck power package. SAE paper # 991B, presented in Detroit, Mich. January 11–15, 1965.

TORTI, M. L.: Ceramics for gas turbines, present and future. SAE paper # 740242, presented in Detroit, Mich. February 28, 1974.

TRAUTH, RICHARD L., AND ROGO, CASIMIR: Design of high heat release slinger combustor with rapid acceleration requirement. SAE paper # 740167, presented in Detroit, Mich. February 27, 1974.

TURUNEN, WILLIAM A.: Pinwheels or pistons? SAE paper delivered in Atlantic City, N.J., June 6–11, 1954.

TURUNEN, WILLIAM A. AND COLLMAN, JOHN S.: The regenerative Whirlfire engine for Firebird II. SAE paper presented in Atlantic City, N.J. June 5, 1956.

TURUNEN, WILLIAM A., AND COLLMAN, JOHN S.: The GT-305 regenerative engine in Firebird III. SAE paper presented in Detroit, Mich. January 12–16, 1959.

TURUNEN, WILLIAM A., AND COLLMAN, JOHN S.: The General Motors research GT-309 gas turbine engine. SAE paper presented in Cleveland, Ohio, October 18–21, 1965.

VAN HOUSE, R. M. WITH BIDWELL, JOSEPH B., AND CATALDO, R. S.: Chassis and control details of Firebird III. SAE paper presented in Detroit, Mich. January 12–16, 1959.

VERKEMP, F. J. WITH NAGEY, T. F., MYKOLENKO, P., AND NAYLOR, M. E.: The low emissions gas turbine passenger car—what does the future hold? ASME paper # 73-GT-49 presented in Washington, DC April 8–12, 1973.

WADE, W. R. WITH AMANN, CHARLES A. AND YU, M. K.: Some factors affecting gas turbine passenger car emissions. SAE paper # 720237, presented in Detroit, Mich. January 10–14, 1972.

WADE, W. R. WITH AZELBORN, N. A., SECORD, J. R., AND MCLEAN, A. F.: Low emissions combustion for the regenerative gas turbine. ASME papers # 73-GT-11 and # 73-GT-12, presented in Washington, DC on April 9, 1973.

WALCH, H. C. WITH CHAPMAN, W. I. AND CADWELL, R. G.: The Ford turbine—an engine designed to compete with the diesel. SAE paper # 720168, presented in Detroit, Mich. January 10–14, 1972.

WALLACE, F. J. WITH WRIGHT, E. J., AND CAMPBELL, J. S.: Future development of free piston gasifier turbine combinations for vehicle traction. SAE paper # 660132, delivered in Detroit, Mich. January 10–14, 1966.

WEAVING, JOHN H.: Small gas turbines. Institution of Mechanical Engineers, presentation in London on December 7, 1961.

WEAVING, JOHN H.: Two-strokes and turbines. The Institution of Mechanical Engineers, presentation in London on October 15, 1968.

WETZLER, JOHN M.: The future of the Allison 250 engine. SAE paper delivered in Detroit, Mich. January 11–15, 1965.

WHEATON, THOMAS R.: Gas turbine engines applied to passenger trains. SAE paper # 670968, presented in Pittsburgh, Pa. October 30–November 3, 1967.

WILLIAMS, L. H., AND PORTER, K. W.: Gas turbines for emergency vehicles. SAE paper # 650460, delivered in Chicago, Ill. May 17–21, 1965.

WOOD, HOMER J.: Gas turbines in future industrial vehicles. SAE paper # 650480, delivered in Detroit, Michigan January 11–15, 1965.

WRIGHT, E. J. WITH WALLACE, F. J., AND CAMPBELL, J. S.: Future development of free piston gasifier turbine combinations for vehicle traction. SAE paper # 660132, delivered in Detroit, Mich. January 10–14, 1966.

WRIGHT, E. S. WITH DAVISON, W. R., AND GREENWALD, L. E.: A feasibility analysis of a simple cycle gas turbine engine for automobiles. SAE paper # 720238, presented in Detroit, Mich. January 10–14, 1972.

YAMAZAKI, S. AND KINOSHITA, K.: Development of the Nissan automotive gas turbine. JSME paper presented in Tokyo, Japan, October 4–7, 1971.

YU, M. K. WITH AMANN, CHARLES A., AND WADE, W. R.: Some factors affecting gas turbine passenger car emissions. SAE paper # 720237, presented in Detroit, Mich. January 10–14, 1972.

BOOKS

ALEXANDER, DR. WILLIAM, AND STREET, DR. ARTHUR: Metals in the service of man. (Penguin Books, Harmondsworth, 1951).

BARJOT, ROBERT: Les Chemins de fer—la locomotion moderne. (Editions S.N.E.P. Illustration, Paris, 1951).

BURSTALL, AUBREY F.: A history of mechanical engineering. (M.I.T. Press, Cambridge, Mass. 1965).

CHAPMAN, D. R., AND UVAROV, E. B.: A dictionary of science. (Penguin Books, Harmondsworth, 1952).

DEMAND, CARLO, AND EMDE, HEINER: Conquerors of the air. (Edita, S.A., Lausanne, 1968).

DUNSHEATH, PERCY: A century of technology. (Hutchinson's London, 1951).

EMDE, HEINER, AND DEMAND, CARLO: Conquerors of the air. (Edita, S.A., Lausanne, 1968).

JONES, W. R.: Minerals in industry. (Penguin Books, Harmondsworth, 1943).

LANOY, HENRI: Les petites turbines a gaz. (Girardot, Paris, 1954).

MILLER, RONALD, AND SAWERS, DAVID: The technical development of modern aviation. (Praeger Publishers, New York, N.Y. 1970).

PFENNINGER, DR. H.: The evolution of the Brown, Boveri gas turbine engine. (Brown, Boveri & Company, Ltd. Baden, Switzerland, 1966).

PLÖTNER, DIPL. ÖK OBERINGENIEUR W.: Verdichter. (VEB Verlag Technik, Berlin, 1966).

ROUGERON, CAMILLE: L'aviation—la locomotion moderne. (Editions S.N.E.P. Illustration, Paris, 1951).

SCHLAIFER, ROBERT: Development of aircraft engines. (Harvard University Graduate School of Business Administration, Division of Research, Boston, Mass., 1950).

SEILIGER, MYRON: Moteurs et turbines a combustion interne. (Editions Dunod, Paris, 1953).

SMITH, G. GEOFFREY: Gas turbines and jet propulsion. (Iliffe & Sons, London, and Aircraft Books, Inc. New York, N.Y., 1951).

STODOLA, AUREL: Steam and gas turbines. (McGraw-Hill Publishing Company, New York, N.Y., 1927).

STREET, DR. ARTHUR, AND ALEXANDER, DR. WILLIAM: Metals in the service of man. (Penguin Books, Harmondsworth, 1951).

SUTTON, OLIVER G.: The science of flight. (Penguin Books, Harmondsworth, 1949).

UVAROV, E. B. AND CHAPMAN, D. R.: A dictionary of science. (Penguin Books, Harmondsworth, 1952).

WITT, PETER: Gasturbinen: Entwicklung, Konstruktion, Anwendung. (Verlag Technik, Berlin, 1962).

Index